REVOLUTION

Edited by

BRUCE MAZLISH

ARTHUR D. KALEDIN

DAVID B. RALSTON

Massachusetts Institute of Technology

The Macmillan Company
New York

REVOLUTION

A READER

Printed in the United States of America

THE MACMILLAN COMPANY
866 THIRD AVENUE, NEW YORK, NEW YORK 10022

COLLIER-MACMILLAN CANADA, LTD., TORONTO, ONTARIO

Library of Congress catalog card number: 76–134517

First Printing

PREFACE

This volume focuses on the varieties of revolution in the twentieth century and endeavors to compare them. After a general consideration of the theory and typology of revolution, it treats of the Russian, Chinese, Cuban, and National Socialist revolutions. In dealing with each, it seeks to understand the nature, the origins, the historical context and development, the consequences, and the meaning of that particular revolution. Then it seeks to compare the various revolutions, one with another, in order better to understand the pecularities of each and to theorize about the nature and meaning of revolution in general. After all, it may well be that the form of social change called revolution is the most important historical phenomenon of our time, and the key to understanding the world that is in the making.

The means by which we, the editors, hope to accomplish our aims are primarily of two kinds: (1) analyses by scholars and (2) reports and reflections on revolutionary experience by revolutionary leaders and other participants. Thus, our volume seeks to combine "objectivity" and "subjectivity" in a meaningful way. The analytic contributions are not only by historians, but by political scientists, sociologists, and other specialists. Thus, the volume draws on many disciplines. To capture the revolutionary experience itself, it uses the speeches and writings of the leaders, the later reflections of participants, the public documents issued at the time, and so forth.

Our hope is that the volume will be useful in a wide range of courses. It was developed and tested, over a five-year period, as an introductory history course at the Massachusetts Institute of Technology. However, it quickly came into increasing demand in all sorts of other courses in history and related disciplines. This demand, plus the success the volume has had at MIT with both students and teachers, has prompted us to make the volume as widely available as possible. We would like to thank the Department of Humanities at MIT, and especially its chairman, Professor Richard M. Douglas, for encouragement and support. A grant from the Carnegie Corporation of New York to the Department of Humanities for educational innovation has assisted the work that culminated in this volume. There can be few tasks more important, as well as intellectually demanding and satisfying, than to seek to understand revolution—perhaps the most significant and powerful historical force sweeping over our world during the twentieth century—and to see it in a comparative perspective.

B. M.
A. D. K.
D. B. R.

CONTENTS

Part I Revolution in the Twentieth Century: General Perspectives 1

Part II The Russian Revolution 93

Part III The Chinese Revolution 225

Part IV The Cuban Revolution 375

Part V The National Socialist Revolution 453

PART I

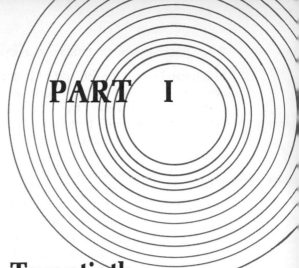

Revolution in the Twentieth Century: General Perspectives

Our historical period is unquestionably a time of revolutions. Two major ones—the Russian and the Chinese—have undoubted canonical status as revolutions, and a host of "minor" ones, such as the Algerian or the Cuban, also crowd the historical stage of the twentieth century. There is a sharp debate as to whether National Socialism was also a "revolutionary" movement.

What, then, is the meaning and significance of this predominating phenomenon of the twentieth century: revolution? No one doubts its omnipresence as a form of social change. But what shape, exactly, has it taken? And why? And to what end? We know that it is closely linked to another great historical phenomenon of our time: war. But is revolution generally the result of war, or the cause of it? Or is the relation so intertwined that simple cause and effect explanations are not useful? Are revolutions progressive steps to greater democracy, or are they preludes to inevitable totalitarianism? Do they lead to enlargements of international interests, or are they primarily vehicles for the expansion of national power?

To ask and answer such questions, and others like them, is to come to grips with the central issues of contemporary history. Such a procedure takes one directly to the heart of our times, and places a stethoscope on its pumping action.

There is, of course, another way of proceeding. One can start at the beginning of the twentieth century, and chronicle its "happenings." In such a procedure, treaties and battles, parliamentary elections and prime ministers, would take the center of the stage. The frame would be the nation state, and domestic crises and internal affairs would be narrated from this perspective.

Much can be said for this sort of history, and its chronological approach can never be discarded in any effort to understand social change over time.

In general, however, the chronologist does not approach history sufficiently as a *problem*, that is, as a problem in how one *does* history and as setting forth a particular historical problem to be *analyzed*. Therefore, the chronologist does not call forth our most acute and thoughtful efforts at understanding, but treats us mainly as a passive receiver of information, a listener to a good story, well told. If, however, we take a more active, intellectual attitude toward twentieth-century history, we shall ourselves be able to enter into the arguments that narrative historians often tend either to be unconscious about or to keep quietly to themselves.

One way to be more self-aware about our history is to treat it in a comparative fashion.[1] By so doing, we are forced, consciously, to ask ourselves about similarities and differences. Did revolution come in one country *because* depressed conditions drove desperate men to revolt? Our faith in this simple explanation is shaken if similar conditions in another country did not produce revolution—what then were the necessary factors? It is further shaken if improved conditions—a revolution of rising expectations—in a similar country formed the prelude to revolution. Or, to take another example, is an intelligentsia of some sort critical to the onset of revolution? Its presence in the Russian, Chinese, and Cuban Revolutions presumably heightens our belief that it is.

Comparative history—in our case, comparative revolution—is not a nostrum for all our historical concerns. It does, however, have the virtue of forcing us to be *analytic*. It allows us to see clearly that a historical event such as the Russian Revolution is a *problem* to be worked over and comprehended in the deepest possible way, and not merely a subject for surface description. Once we approach history analytically, we are forced to ask openly what concepts, theories, and techniques a given historian is using to explain his event. Does he believe his chosen revolution is the work primarily of a great leader? Of a dedicated, revolutionary elite? Of a proletariat? Of a peasantry? And how do all these groups interact? Does content analysis of a leader's words help? Does prosopography, or a Namier-like analysis of the composition of elite groups? Narrative histories, of course, also deal with these questions and use these approaches, but they do not generally deal with them sufficiently in the public light or with enough attention to theory.

This reader, then, on two of the major phenomena of the twentieth century, revolution and totalitarianism, is inspired by a belief in the pedagogic virtue of the comparative, analytic approach to selected large "events," treated as problems both in historiography and in themselves. But, and we underline this most strongly, our approach is still basically *historical*. That is, it allows for—nay, insists upon—the contingent, coincidental, unintended,

[1] The best introduction to the nature and problems of comparative history is still Marc Bloch, "Toward a Comparative History of European Societies," in *Enterprise and Secular Change*, Frederick E. Lane and J. C. Riemersma (eds.), (Homewood, Ill.: Richard D. Irwin, Inc., 1953).

and therefore accidental nature of large-scale social change. The history of revolution does not reduce to a typology of revolution. Instead, each revolution reopens and creatively changes the very views that we have previously had on the subject. It is essential, always, to remember that the *Russian* Revolution grew out of the Russian past, and the *Chinese* Revolution out of the Chinese past; and that both revolutions developed out of the tensions of that past, brought to breaking point by the strains of a "present" moment: 1917, or 1911 (or 1949, if one prefers to date the Chinese Revolution from the time of Communist victory). The "accident" of a particular leader—Tsar Nicholas II, or Lenin; the Empress Dowager, or Sun Yat-sen—or the coincidence of a particular civil or international event can shape the revolution in ways not calculated by static typologies. Thus, it is the *actual* way the revolution occurred, not the class or category into which it can be fitted, that is critical in a comparative history of revolutions. Such actual history, then, must be fully incorporated into our analytic approach, and that is the spirit in which we have set about to construct this book of readings.

Let us add one other avowal. We did not select the articles included in this reader because they deliver final "truths" (though it is to be hoped that they aim at this happy—and utopian—state of affairs). Rather, the articles are intended to stimulate discussion and to further additional probing. History, as we have said before, is a problem, not a "given" to be had for the mere recounting.

II

An initial part of the problem of revolution is to define it. Such a definition should be merely provisional, pointing our way to phenomena that fall under the definition. It should not, however, be a procrustean bed, but rather itself open to stretching and redefining by the phenomenon itself. In a number of our initial selections, the authors wrestle with this problem. Here, we shall not enter into any of the substantive arguments—they are in the articles themselves—but merely point up some of the issues.

A first way of defining revolution is to indicate its origin or etiology, that is, to treat it historically. When was the term first used, and under what circumstances? What was it then thought to mean, and how has that meaning changed over time? One thing is clear, for better or for worse: revolution is a *Western* social invention, a way of change emerging in the period we characterize roughly as modern history. Why? How? These are the questions that need to be answered. In our focus on twentieth-century revolutions, we cannot linger over materials concerning the Puritan Revolution, the American Revolution, the French Revolution, and so forth. A few of our early selections, however (Griewank, for example), at least allow the reader to be aware of the role of these other revolutions as predecessors of *our* revolutions.

Another way of defining revolution, besides the historical approach, is to seek to differentiate it from other forms of social-political change that initially may seem to resemble it (see Eckstein). How is it like and unlike rebellion?

Is it merely a subspecies of something called *internal war*? Does a *coup d'état* qualify as a revolution? And if not, why not? What is the difference in degree of social or political or economic change that is necessary before one feels in the presence of a revolution? And how quickly must such changes take place before one exclaims, along with the Duc de Liancourt, responding to Louis XVI's outcry at news of the fall of the Bastille, "But good God! That is a revolt!", "No, Sire, it is a revolution."?

Definition in itself can be a mere casuistic exercise if carried out in the wrong spirit. Seen as a way, though only one way, of trying to come to grips with complex phenomena, it becomes a means by which significant questions can be posed. As we regard it, then, the effort on the part of a number of our authors to secure a definition of revolution is a heuristic device, and not a way to dispose of the phenomenon by encapsulating it in a tight formula.

III

Cheek by jowl with the effort to define revolution in order further to inquire into the subject, is the effort to construct typologies of revolution. Assuming one achieves a rough understanding of what one means by revolution, what *kinds* of revolution coexist under this rubric? At the very least, one is aware of so-called colonial revolutions, nationalist revolutions, modernizing revolutions, and so forth. Are there other, more systematic ways of ordering the phenomena? James Rosenau, for example, visualizes three major types—ideal types—of "internal war," that is, revolution: what he calls "personal wars," "authority wars," and "structural wars." [2] Chalmers Johnson suggests a sixfold typology: jacquerie, millenarian rebellion, anarchistic rebellion, Jacobin Communist revolution, conspiratorial *coup d'état,* and militarized mass insurrection.[3]

If we are to make useful such typologies as are offered, and criticized, in our initial theoretical articles on the nature and dynamics of revolution, we need to articulate and bring them alive. How does a "colonial revolution" in the name of modernization differ from one animated by a root-and-branch opposition to all things Western? Of which kind, for example, is the Chinese Revolution? Is it, in fact, a "colonial revolution"? What about intentions and consequences? Was the Cuban Revolution intended, originally, by Castro and his followers as a "structural war"? Did it become such a revolution "accidentally"; and if so, then quite specifically, how? What would it mean to consider the Russian Revolution as a "Jacobin Communist revolution," and how does this category set it off from other revolutions? Do any of these ideal types help us decide whether the Nazis led a revolution?

Obviously, history is not simple. No revolution will fit perfectly, by definition, into any ideal type. In historical reality, events are much messier, and each revolution laps over disgracefully into neighboring categories. Yet

[2] James M. Rosenau (ed.), "Internal War as International Event," in *International Aspects of Civil Strife* (Princeton, N.J.: Princeton University Press, 1964).

[3] Chalmers Johnson, *Revolution and the Social System,* The Hoover Institution on War, Revolution, and Peace, Stanford University Press, 1964).

the reader must ask himself whether certain, large structural features do characterize particular revolutions—the Russian, the Chinese, and so forth —and whether the clear perception of these features aids in his understanding of the *meaning* and *significance* of *that* revolution in relation to other, similar but dissimilar, collections of events that he is willing to call revolutions. If any of the typologies, like the efforts at definition of revolution, aid in this effort, then they are worth careful consideration.

IV

For ourselves, the chosen method of approaching revolution is not primarily in terms of definition or typology, but in terms of analysis. Analysis itself, however, must first always be set against the background of what we shall call *phenomenological history;* or, to phrase it more adequately, analysis must be *immersed* in the actual phenomena.

What do we mean by this concept? Most immediately, phenomenological history means the way in which the people actually involved in the events we are seeking to understand themselves understood and felt that which we see only as "history." An example would be the debate over the workers' standard of living during the early Industrial Revolution (this debate is echoed in discussions over the improved conditions of Tsarist Russia before 1917). As E. P. Thompson puts the matter, in his *The Making of the English Working Class* (New York, Vintage Books, 1966), "some of the most bitter conflicts of these years turned on issues which are not encompassed by cost-of-living series. The issues which provoked the most intensity of feeling were very often ones in which such values as traditional customs, 'justice,' 'independence,' security, or family-economy were at stake, rather than straightforward 'bread-and-butter' issues." Thompson continues, "the term 'standard' leads us from data amenable to statistical measurement (wages or articles of consumption) to those satisfactions which are sometimes described by statisticians as 'imponderables.' From food we are led to homes, from homes to health, from health to family life, and thence to leisure, work-discipline, education and play, intensity of labour, etc. From standard-of-living we pass to way-of-life, but the two are not the same. The first is a measurement of quantities: the second a description (and sometimes an evaluation) of qualities." Moreover, according to Thompson, the attempt to measure quantities requires different historiographic means from those involved in the attempt to measure qualities: "Where statistical evidence is appropriate to the first, we must rely largely upon 'literary evidence' as to the second."

Now, some will argue that "literary evidence" itself can be approached statistically, in order to minimize the subjective and chance nature of its existence; and this is undoubtedly so. Yet, the "feel" of a period or an event as it was for at least some of the human beings experiencing it can only be approached through *their* words describing it. A worker, telling us "the way it is" in a nineteenth-century textile mill, an intellectual explaining what it was like to be in Siberian exile in twentieth-century Russia—these are the materials of phenomenological history. And phenomenological history is the bedrock on which analytic history must build itself and to which it must eternally return in order to renew itself.

Closely allied to phenomenological history, examples of which are extremely difficult to get (peasants don't write about their lives), is the more accessible documentary history. The decrees of the National Convention during the French Revolution, the Nazi Nuremberg laws, and the 1927 "Report of an Investigation into the Peasant Movement in Hunan" by Mao Tse-tung are pieces of phenomenological history frozen into seemingly eternal, public forms. In addition, an item such as Mao's "Hunan Report" shades imperceptibly into an *analysis*, by him, of the historical events contemporary to him. One of the most brilliant examples in this genus is Trotsky's *History of the Russian Revolution.*

Where possible, we have introduced into this collection pieces of documentary and what we can call phenomenological-analytic material. We strongly encourage the reader to seek more such materials (they are generally available in other collections or in paperback books). It is only in the context of such materials that analytic history of the kind we are emphasizing here does not become so sterile that it loses contact with the immediacy of human life from which history is drawn.

Analytic history, of course, is for us the presently living, rather than for the contemporary actors of the events under examination. At its best, it allows *us* to see "what was happening" even though the actors at the time neither felt nor perceived it. Analytic history, if successful, gives us an understanding denied to pure phenomenological history. English workers of the nineteenth century may have *felt* their condition worsening; we may be able to see that, in fact, their "objective" standard of living was improving (or vice versa). Both statements can be true, and call for an interpretation that goes beyond each. So, too, Cuban revolutionaries may envision their revolution as a proletarian or a peasant revolution, while an analytic historian explains it as a middle class or an intellectuals' enterprise. The challenge is the same as in the first example.

If analytic history, based on phenomenological history, can be amply justified, we are still left with the problem of how one proceeds. It is hoped that the articles in this reader will show, concretely, how one "does" analytic history. Here, we shall simply highlight a few of the major analytic categories most useful in the attempt to understand revolution and totalitarianism.

A prime concept is ideology (see Lichtheim). Ours has frequently been called an Age of Ideology, and certainly all our modern revolutions have either had an officially proclaimed ideology or have come to terms with the demands by others that they have such an ideology. A major source of revolutionary ideology has been Marxism (though, paradoxically, orthodox Marxism itself claims to be a science that puts into relief the ideological nature of all other social and political schemas). Of those revolutions that consider themselves Marxist, we must ask, for example, about the relations of Marxist ideology and revolutionary actuality. Is the Soviet Union a "classless" state? Is Communist China a postcapitalist society, and if not, how do we reconcile this fact with orthodox Marxism? Even before such questions, however, we must ask a whole series of questions such as these: Why was Marxism the chosen ideology? What changes were made in it to suit particular national and cultural needs? How did it help and how did it hinder the revolution? What effect did it have on the international involvements of the revolution?

We must also allow for the Cuban claim that "action precedes ideology" (see Guevara), and ask what shapes what. We must also evaluate the claim sometimes made by Fascists that they are completely anti-ideological; that their *only* ideology is action. Remembering that the term, and the concept, of ideology, rose out of the experience of the French Revolution, and that therefore the reality and the understanding of it came about at almost the same time, we must be flexible in *our* use of the concept and be prepared to see it change in relation to particular revolutionary and totalitarian situations. Yet, like a beacon, attention to the analysis of ideology can help guide us through the swirling mists of phenomenological history.

Another constant concern of our analysis must be the "Leader." In the more halcyon times of the late nineteenth and early twentieth centuries, the "Great Man in History" thesis fell into disfavor. The quiet summer of parliamentary democracy was undisturbed by charismatic figures; a Giolitti, a Waldeck-Rousseau, was more suitable. Historians reflected the political scene of their time, and focused more on long-range, impersonal forces in history. World War I changed all that. Lenin restored the "Great Man in History" theme with a vengeance. Without him, for most historians, the greatest revolution hitherto in history, the Bolshevik Revolution in Russia, would not have occurred. Then came Mussolini, *Il Duce,* in Italy; Hitler, *Der Führer,* in Germany; and Stalin, *Vodzd,* in Soviet Russia—all claiming to be "the Leader."

How does a given leader lead? Is he necessary, and if so, why? How do power struggles arise—a Mao versus a Chiang Kai-shek, a Stalin versus a Trotsky—what form do they take, and what are the consequences of a particular victory? These are, in a sense, "functional" questions, and there are many more of them. Then, there are a whole series of questions as to the leader's development. What produced him? How can we analyze him from a psychological viewpoint? How did events and experiences shape him? Is he a "charismatic" or an "organizational" man?

Many of these questions, of course, overlap with the functional ones. At this point, too, we shall want to bring the leader into relation with the concept of ideology, and ask how ideology helped shape him, and how he helped shape the ideology. Clearly, we have not exhausted the list of questions about leaders and leadership; but we have indicated the utter necessity of introducing the concept of the leader into our general analysis of revolution and totalitarianism.

Leaders do not lead in isolation. They are surrounded by lesser "leaders" that we shall call elites. Now, elite study is a subject all itself (see Rustow). We hear constantly today of power elites, political elites, social elites, decision-makers, intelligentsia, and so forth. *All* elites become involved, too, with the question of mobility and access to power: Who is allowed in, and at whose expense? Insofar as the most interesting elite in Russia before the Revolution (at least the most interesting thus far to historians) was the "intelligentsia," much attention has been given to their role in revolution. Are "intellectuals" vital to at least preparing a revolution? Would China have had a revolution without the support of a large part of the Mandarin class? A next series of questions revolves around what happens to the intelligentsia after the Revolution. Do they become the ideologists? Are they eliminated, as too "idealistic"?

Intellectuals, however, are only one particularly interesting species of elites. What of military, technical, and political elites? What changes occur in these groups during a revolutionary or totalitarian regime? How are the new elements recruited? Once in power, the new elite, as in Russia, frequently tends to become as closed and co-optative as the one it has replaced. There is then the problem of how a revolutionary society, based on an ideology of total equality, comes to terms with the existence in actuality of an elite. (One need only think of Mao's Cultural Revolution, for one unusual way of dealing with the problem.) Further, elites must adjust to ideology, and vice versa. They must also play a role in relation to the leader: How independent of his power are they? What role can they play in the determination of his successor? Ultimately, we must ask whether new elites, in fact, carry on the Revolution or mark the beginning of its end.

One possible form of an elite is the party (though the latter may also be a "mass" organization). Political parties as such may be said to date from the eighteenth century with, for example, the Whigs and Tories in Great Britain. The emergence of the one-party state is a twentieth-century affair, with the Bolsheviks leading the way, and then quickly followed by the Fascists and the Nazis. Although revolutions seem not to be made solely by one party, they do seem to eventuate in one-party rule. In any case, it is apparent that analysis of party—its composition and function—is one critical part of the analysis of revolution and totalitarianism.

Often, the party can be viewed as a mass organization, or as an elite organization, which, to use a favorite term of the political scientists, is "politicizing the masses." What are the "masses," a term that comes into existence only in the nineteenth century? Are they a result of high population increase—the demographic revolution—and to be found only in large countries? Is "mass" a pejorative term for the working classes? A portmanteau term, which allows one to talk rather indiscriminately of "mass psychology" and "mass markets"?

Class analysis may be more useful in understanding revolution and totalitarianism. Such analysis breaks up the mass into proletarians and peasants, or at least separates a working class from a middle, and perhaps an upper, class. Class, like mass, is an early nineteenth-century classification, replacing the earlier division of society into ranks and estates. It is, basically, an economic stratification, one which takes rent, profit, and wages —the divisions of capital introduced by classical economic science (for example, Adam Smith)—and translates them into upper, middle, and lower classes. (In the process, it replaces the former division into clerical, aristocratic and "third" estate.)

Karl Marx sought to reduce the tripartite class structure to a struggle between only two classes: capitalists and proletarians. The student of revolution and totalitarianism must ask himself how much this is part of ideology, with perhaps a self-fulfilling prophecy aspect, and how much it is a useful device for analyzing existing social phenomena. In any case, it is clear that a revolution such as the Chinese, if not the Russian Revolution itself, cannot be understood without centering attention on the peasantry. Is it useful, and real, to think of peasants as proletariat? Or does the existence of large numbers of peasants suggest that a country has not yet gone through the capitalist development, predicted by Marx, and thus has ahead of it (if it so chooses) an industrial as well as political-social revolution? What we can then call a "modernizing" revolution?

Leader, elites, party, masses, classes, peasants, and proletarians, these are analytic categories that it will be useful to investigate for all our examples of revolution and totalitarianism. To these categories, however, we must add other constant factors to be examined. Of overwhelming importance seems to be the role of war. The Russian Revolution occurred during the course of World War I; the Italian Fascists and German Nazis were heavily composed of veterans of that war; and the Chinese Communists came to victory, according to at least one commentator, Chalmers Johnson, as a result of their position during the Japanese war against China (see "Peasant Nationalism in China"). Does major war foster the conditions propitious to revolution? How and why? Or is it revolution that leads to major war? For example, if the Nazi seizure of power was a revolution, did it lead to World War II?

War itself, in its relation to revolution, must be considered under at least two guises: total and guerrilla. World Wars I and II point in the direction of "total" war, mobilizing, in theory, all the resources of the countries involved, and being global in scope. Is it this, in part, that leads to "totalitarianism," or at least serves as its model? Guerrilla warfare, at first blush, seems the opposite of total war. It is waged by small groups, against what often seems like a "total" state. Yet, it, too, draws no distinction between military and civilian forces, and is therefore a "total" campaign. Moreover, as viewed by many commentators, it inevitably becomes part of an "international civil war," because it is generally ideological as well as no respecter of national boundaries.

If revolutionary war today is waged largely in terms of guerrilla activity, does this tell us that it must take place mainly in a peasant society? Or an "underdeveloped nation"? Then what of the Cuban Revolution? How about the possibility of urban guerrilla warfare? Does the atomic bomb rule out any future "total" war (unless as the last "total" war)? How, then, can big power intervention take place? (Clearly, in analyzing the relation of war to revolution, we must always introduce, as well, a consideration of the international setting in which these phenomena have their being.)

Mention of the bomb reminds us that science and technology must also be introduced as a category in our analysis. What is the effect of technology in bringing about revolution? (As Lenin remarked, Communism is Soviet power plus electrification.) How does it afford new means of communication for the leader (for example Hitler's use of the airplane, Goebbels' of the radio)? New means of party control and indoctrination of the masses? Does technology produce the proletariat, which then brings about the revolution? And then the totalitarianism, which reduces the proletariat to the dictated rather than the dictating class? How does technology affect war, both total and guerrilla? To ask such questions is to indicate the myriad of relationships that must be constantly studied.

Above all else, however, we must not let our analytic categories—elites and masses, wars and technologies—become procrustean beds into which we cram the phenomena of revolution and totalitarianism. Our eye must always be on what we can call "unintended consequences," the "man proposes, God disposes" aspect of history. Such an aspect seems difficult if not impossible to put into analytic compartments. For example, though Lenin may have wished for a "dictatorship of the proletariat," civil war, a poor harvest, peasant recalcitrance, unexpected power struggles among individuals and elites, the personality traits of Trotsky and Stalin, may have brought about a dictatorship *over* the proletariat unintended by the Bolshevik leader. We must struggle to understand these seeming accidental phenomena in any way we can, but we must allow for the fact that they may escape the sieves of our analytic categories. In so doing, they return our attention to what, earlier, we referred to as phenomenological history.

In short, analytic history helps us to understand such large-scale phenomena as revolution and totalitarianism. It does not become a "cookie cutter," which allows us to discard the rest of the dough of which history is composed. Nor does it relieve us of the necessity of making what we shall call "judgments" about the phenomena of revolution and totalitarianism, and especially of specific examples thereof. On the simplest level, for example, we must try to decide the question of whether the Nazi seizure of power was a revolution. And was the Cuban Revolution a peasant revolution? On a more complicated level, we must then render judgment on such questions as whether modern revolutions inevitably "degenerate" into totalitarian regimes, and whether the latter tend strongly to war, or perhaps against war (depending on the ideology). These are judgments that analysis can help us make, but cannot make for us.

Other, larger, questions call for valuation, that is, judgments as to the desirability or worth of the phenomena. Is modern revolution a "progressive" phenomenon? And, as one scholar, Denis W. Brogan, put it, is "the Price of

Revolution" worth it? [4] Perhaps such large questions are best put aside, and more specific valuations attempted. Was the Russian Revolution "progressive," and was it "worth it"? Was it, perhaps, "inevitable"? (Or is this what we called a "judgment"?) And, inevitable or not, is it a model for the way in which social change should be accomplished elsewhere? Is Chinese, or Cuban, revolutionary society a model? Ultimately, in our effort to comprehend revolution and totalitarianism as human phenomena, we must ask their "meaning" and "value" both for those who partook in them and for us who come after the actual events.

Our ultimate approach, then, to two of the predominating phenomena of the twentieth century—revolution and totalitarianism—is analytic, phenomenological, and human. We do not believe that the effort to understand our history, rationally, relieves us of the effort to value, meaningfully, that experience. For us, history is the crucial determinant of the "human condition"—and to say that is also to remind ourselves that history is "human, all too human."

[4] *The Price of Revolution* (London: Hamish Hamilton, 1951).

The concept of revolution as forcible and fundamental political innovation was unknown to antiquity and the middle ages. Professor Griewank, who at the time of his death in 1953 was Dean of the Philosophical Faculty in the University of Jena (German Democratic Republic—East Germany), here traces the emergence of the modern concept of revolution in the sixteenth and seventeenth centuries.

Emergence of the Concept of Revolution

KARL GRIEWANK

The word *revolution* entered the domain of political thought proper by way of natural philosophy [science]. The growing importance of the word for astronomy, and for science generally, coupled with an inclination to fit each change of the heavenly bodies into an astrological or scientific scheme, helped to make the word *revolution* an ever more popular term and paved the way for its introduction into the language of politics. Sixteenth- and seventeenth-century theorizers were very prone to link both the name and the course of every kind of cosmically-determined upheaval with that regular circulation of the firmaments to which Nicholas Copernicus had devoted his principal work, *De Revolutionibus Orbium Celestium* [*On the Revolutions of the Heavenly Bodies*]. People were taking it for granted that the world they lived in was full of change. They could detect change most readily in political affairs, but there was no mistaking it in religion, mores, institutions and inventions as well: after all, a change in religion was often the evident cause of political change. Scientists, political theorists, and statesmen alike came to occupy themselves with the question of how these changes, the decisive and sweeping political changes especially, were related to the motions of the heavens. So sober a thinker as Bodin did not disdain such endeavors [nor did the brilliant Johannes Kepler]. Kepler had, through observation and mathematics, discovered the laws of planetary motion, the foundation of celestial mechanics, which had hitherto been inaccessible to the purely speculative Aristotelian conceptions that had prevailed. Yet this same Kepler, for all that he fought against the superstitious pseudo-prophecies of the astrologers, constantly tried to puzzle out in what way the fluctuations in the affairs of men were connected with the motions of stars and constellations, believing as he did that the creator had instilled the same geometry and harmony into all things, creatures possessed of a soul and heavenly bodies alike. This pioneer of the new physico-mathematical science sought gratification for his intellectual longings in a speculative system deriving from Platonic and Neo-Platonic ideas, a system in which earthly creatures and heavenly bodies were embraced in a single universal harmony and were also jointly subject to disturbances. He associated the appearance of

From Karl Griewank, *Der Neuzeitliche Revolutionsbegriff* (Weimar: 1955), pp. 171–182. Translated by Heinz Lubasz with permission of the publishers, Hermann Böhlaus Nachfolger. With one exception, the footnotes have been omitted.

comets with the genesis of "protracted evil doings" (*langwirige böse Händel*) which [according to him] were not to be attributed solely to the "departure of a potentate and the changes in government ensuing thereon" (*Abgang eines Potentatens ond darauff erfolgende Newerung im Regiment*). To be sure, Kepler himself was on his guard against the attempts of the "great crowd of astrologers" (*grossen Haufen der Astrologen* [*vulgus astrologorum*]) to conclude from the "revolution" of an astronomical year to a *Revolutio Mundana* [earthly revolution], to a lawlike regularity [*Gesetzmässigkeit*] in earthly affairs during the same time-span. But the belief in a very precise correlation between celestial motions and worldly changes nevertheless took root far and wide. It found expression, for example, in a dictum attributed to Kepler's Italian contemporary, Galileo Galilei: "The revolutions of the globe we inhabit give rise to the mishaps and accidents of human existence."

This new picture of a universe of stars rotating in regular motion, and of the earth moving within it, gave many people something to hold onto in their attempts to understand life and the world at a time when they no longer found security in the medieval-Christian doctrine of a harmonious world order. The astronomical conception of *revolution* suggested that it was possible to fit worldly changes into an orderly scheme; and this thought provided one important impetus, though not the only one, for the introduction of this conception into the language of politics. This despite the fact that the traditional desire prevailed for a time to conceive of change as circular, as a return to the good old ways, and so to think of *revolution*—akin to the ancient idea of *reformation*—as a turning away from abuses, lapses, and aberrations. Bodin, for example, sought to interpret the "conversion" to monarchy of insecure democratic and aristocratic regimes as the *re*-establishment of a stable and felicitous state of affairs. When Henry IV (Bodin's ideal king) disarmed his enemies, the League, by converting to Catholicism, and they all one by one went over to his side, it was widely said, "This is a revolution"—meaning that a reversion to a state of affairs similar or equivalent to an earlier one had taken place as irresistibly as a star rotates, so that resistance to it had become pointless. The contemporary *Histoire des dernières troubles de France* of 1599 observed that the king had accomplished a salutary change in the state (*changement en l'Estat*) at a moment when sun and moon were propitiously placed.

The great English Revolution of the seventeenth century (a term which may be used to designate the whole course of development from the outbreak of the Great Rebellion in 1640 to the Glorious Revolution of 1688) has often been made the basis of a cyclical conception of revolutions, following Polybius' old cyclical theory of constitutions: from the collapse of monarchy and aristocracy through a more and more democratic republic to military dictatorship and eventually back to monarchy. A cycle of this sort did indeed recur in the great French Revolution, and one can find it adumbrated in classical antiquity, in the Greek city-states and in the Roman Republic. But this must not be allowed to obscure the fact that modern revolutions [do not simply return to their starting points; they] always have further effects which shape and direct the subsequent development of the nation, and of those nations connected with it. We must understand the English Revolution in terms of the same preconditions as the Dutch struggles for independence from Spain which began in the sixteenth century (and which, in their turn, strike us as so much more modern than the Swiss struggles of the fifteenth). The thrust of political revolution took several directions, which stemmed from a spectrum extending all the way from conservative Calvinism to the anti-ecclesiastical, chiliastic sectarian movements of religious Puritanism. These revolutionary assaults were directed against the royal, episcopal, established church; against the monarchy itself; against compulsory religious institutions; and, finally, against every sort of political discrimination against the less powerful. The common objective of these endeavors was to secure the personal rights of individuals—rights which were derived from the birthright of free Englishmen (a right supposedly dating from Saxon times, but not extended to Papists or unbelievers); from the divinely-ordained right to freedom of conscience; and from the natural right to life, liberty, and property—three kinds of right that largely merged into one another. Chiliastic movements—which, incidentally, were increasingly coming to accept the principle of private property—were defeated by socially more conservative movements like Cromwell's which aimed only to change the social and political situation of certain segments of society without altering the structure of society as a whole. Parliament, which was evolving from an assembly of estates into the acknowledged organ of popular representation, gained the ascendant over king and church. At the same time it accepted as the fundamental principle of the constitution, if not the explicitly democratic ideas of the Rebellion, then at least the inherent individual rights of all Christian Englishmen (Catholics excepted). These changes acted as powerful forces making for the integration of the English nation and of that growing number of nations in the old world and the new which followed its example.

It has been shown elsewhere, in conjunction with some striking texts,[1] that it was not the—to us—revolutionary events of the years 1640 to 1660, but rather the return to tranquil conditions and to the old order, which some people at the close of the "Great Rebellion" connected with the motions of the firmaments and welcomed as a *revolution*. In the House of Commons Clarendon introduced the restoration of the monarchy with the following words: "The good genius of this kingdom is become superior and hath mastered that malignity, and our good old stars govern us again." And Hobbes, the sworn enemy of all insurrection against a political authority [which he conceived of as having been] created by a contract of all the citizens—Hobbes writes at the close of his *Behemoth* concerning the acts of the Long Parliament, on the occasion of Charles II's return: "I have seen in this revolution a circular motion of the sovereign power through two usurpers, father and son, from the late king to his son." In fact, he was overjoyed to see that now, at the close of the upheaval, Parliament was definitively conceding to the king a right which hitherto he had only been able to derive unilaterally from his sovereign title. This it was that Hobbes regarded as the positive outcome of the whole matter. The republican Commonwealth of 1649 had, for its own part, sought to legitimate itself with the claim that it represented the restoration of ancient liberties. In that way it had made allowance for the still deep-seated desire for a return to the olden ways; the legend inscribed on the Great Seal of 1651

[1] E. Rosenstock, "Revolution als politischer Begriff in der Neuzeit," *Festgabe der rechts- und staatswissenschaftlichen Fakultät in Breslau für Paul Heilborn,* Abhandlungen der Schlesischen Gesellschaft für väterländische Cultur, Geisteswissenschaftliche Reihe, 5. Heft (Breslau: 1931), pp. 83–124.

read: "In the third year of freedom by God's blessing restored." In just the same way Charles VIII of France, upon the overthrow of the Medici in 1494, had had himself fêted as the restorer and protector of the freedom of Florence (*restitutor et protector libertatis fiorentinae*). In all these instances the concept of the cycle was employed for the purpose of justifying a new state of affairs which, following upon an upheaval, was looked upon as final.

But the concept of revolution which astronomy had made familiar did not remain restricted to such conservative usage in the quest for tranquility and permanence and, thus, in a restorative sense. It would in fact be completely wrong to ascribe the introduction of the concept of revolution into politics and statecraft to astrological speculations and astronomical parallels exclusively, or even to regard these as having played a decisive and enduring role in the transmission of the concept. At a time when political thinking was becoming more flexible, the keen political mind could see a variety of possible applications for the simple notions of revolving, rotating [*Umwälzung, Umdrehung*]. In the seventeenth century the word *revolution* was already linked with that objective, non-evaluative conception of *transformation* introduced by Machiavelli on the basis of classical models, and subsequently extended to the social realm—albeit, once again in a more limited and conservative sense—by certain French statesmen. A new, dynamic conception of political change underlies the words which the Duke de Rohan used in dedicating his *Interest des Princes et Etats de la Chrestienté* to Richelieu in 1634, a conception of change that is no longer bounded by fixed conditions and that flies in the face of every known piece of political wisdom, ancient or medieval: "Whatever it is that causes the cyclical revolutions of the things of this world, also causes the basic principles of good government to change." Revolution here becomes synonymous with reversal and alteration in things political, and with alteration in the world generally. The word *revolution* replaces the old terms *mutazione, commutatio, conversion,* and *changement* to denote alterations that have taken or are taking place on the objective plane; and though it does not denote subjective manifestations such as insurrections and conspiracies, still it carries with it that overtone of restlessness and movement which attaches to it from earlier and vulgar usage. Therewith the word *revolution* becomes the standard term for the doctrine of political and worldly change whose emergence we have been able to trace from the sixteenth century on.

The most important step in the history of the term was the event which permanently introduced the word *revolution* into historical writing and political theory—the Glorious Revolution of 1688. In contrast to the period of the civil war (1640–1660), which had been introduced into historiography by its first historian, Clarendon, as "the Great Rebellion," the later event, which brought about lasting political changes with far less internal turmoil, was unequivocally labeled a *revolution*. Historically, that was in keeping with current usage. A history of *England's Revolutions from the Death of the Protector Oliver to the Restoration of the King* (Charles II) appeared in Paris in 1689. It was a very superficial chronicle, most deferential to monarchy in general and to the French monarchy in particular. The author takes it for granted that his readers will take transformations of the kind he describes to be *revolutions,* not in the modern sense, as being manifestations of insurrection and disintegration, but simply as being turbulent changes in the body politic. The undertaking which had led to yet one more revolution of this kind was termed *glorious* because of its successful outcome: writers of biographical and political apologias for William of Orange thought it important to call his domestic and foreign policy illustrious because it was successful. By calling it "the Glorious Revolution" they meant that it was really just one more change of sovereigns, albeit one that had taken place in circumstances reflecting glory on the king and on the nation represented in Parliament. An apologetic tract in Latin, published in London, correctly translated the phrase into the ancient wording: "*insignis nostra rerum commutatio*" or "*rerum conversio.*" "*La dernière Révolution d'Angleterre*" [England's latest revolution]—with this phrase one more change was added to a long line of changes.

For all that, the Glorious Revolution constituted a new point of departure for the political significance of the concept of revolution. The application of the word *revolution* to this event may be regarded as a counterblow to the restorationist concept of revolution held by Clarendon and Hobbes: a victorious Parliament was snatching from the hands of a king who had jeopardized the laws of the land, from the hands of a king in flight, the very concept of revolution that had been used in behalf of his predecessor! In the same way the concept of restoration, which had first been used by rebels, in Florence and then in London, to signify a "restoration of liberty," had subsequently been turned against them and used in behalf of the restored monarch.

The Settlement of 1688–89 was not an act of reversal. It was the confirmation of a constitutional state of affairs which Parliament considered it essential to legitimize in accord with all extant principles of English law, historical and natural. It was, therefore, a revolution only in the sense that it was a return to stable conditions after a period of fluctuation. It was a "liberation" of the Church of England and of the English nation from the arbitrary will of the monarch, a revolution without rebels or rebellions. But it was at the same time an event of the kind hitherto known as a *mutation:* a transition to a new dynasty upon new conditions which, with whatever foundation in law, had been laid down by Parliament. As an historical event the Revolution of 1688 itself soon came to be looked upon as something final and unrepeatable and, thus, as something not to be drawn into precedent ["*etwas theoretisch nicht weiter Verwertbares*"]. At the end of the eighteenth century Hume and Burke were still speaking of *revolution* as a unique historical event—and what they had in mind was the event of 1688. The naming of the "Glorious Revolution" was the beginning of the successful career of the modern meaning of *revolution* as a non-evaluative term for great transformative events, first and foremost in the political realm, but also for natural cataclysms and intellectual changes.

The American Revolution, which created another new nation by severing the ties of external dependence, was later to build upon the intellectual arsenal of the English Revolution. But with the Declaration of Independence and the founding of the United States that arsenal was once again enlarged in characteristic fashion. The equality of all men, their inherent and inalienable rights, and the sovereign right of peoples to institute their own governments were now no longer derived from historical or divinely ordained rights but exclusively from the rational right of nature which had been elaborated in west European thought. The French Revolution, however, being a process of purely internal transformation, was to have a truly incalculable impact upon the moulding of old and new nations in Europe and throughout the world. Its impact proceeded from a number of enduring fundamental principles. These principles were not drawn from the peculiar right of a particular people, as they had been in England; they were formulated in comprehensible terms of universal validity.

Professor Harry Eckstein of Princeton University has worked extensively on internal war studies. He has also been studying the factors correlative with democratic institutions, using the smaller countries of Europe for this purpose.

On the Etiology of Internal Wars

HARRY ECKSTEIN

THE CONCEPT "INTERNAL WAR"

The term "internal war" denotes any resort to violence within a political order to change its constitution, rulers, or policies.[1] It is not a new concept; distinctions between external and internal war (*guerre extérieure* and *guerre intérieure*) were made already in the nineteenth century by writers on political violence.[2] Nor does it mean quite the same thing as certain more commonly used terms, such as revolution, civil war, revolt, rebellion, uprising, guerrilla warfare, mutiny, *jacquerie, coup d'état,* terrorism, or insurrection. It stands for the genus of which the others are species.

Using the generic concept alongside, or even in place of, the more specific terms is justifiable on several grounds.

[1] Elsewhere I have used more cumbersome specifications for the term, holding that internal war is "a kind of social force that is exerted in the process of political competition, deviating from previously shared social norms, 'warlike' in character (that is, conducted practically without mutually observed normative rules), and involving the serious disruption of settled institutional patterns." *Internal War: Problems and Approaches* (New York, 1964), 12. The differences between the two formulations are due to the fact that here I am defining a term, while in the other essay I was delimiting a theoretical subject. (For what I mean by delimiting a theoretical subject, see *ibid.,* 8–11.)—I am grateful to the Center of International Studies at Princeton University for supporting the work that went into this study as part of a wide-ranging set of inquiries into internal war. The Center's internal war studies, in turn, have been supported by grants from the Carnegie Foundation. Another, very different, version of the paper was published in a report prepared by the Research Group in Psychology and the Social Sciences, Smithsonian Institution, Washington, D.C., *Social Science Research and National Security* (government circulation only).

[2] For example, in Pierre Kropotkin, *Paroles d'un révolté,* ed. by Elisée Reclus (Paris, not dated, but circa 1885). The term was used by Count Fersen as early as 1790 and occurs also in the writings of Sismondi and the Federalist Papers.

Most obviously, all cases of internal war do have common features, however much they differ in detail. All involve the use of violence to achieve purposes which can also be achieved without violence. All indicate a breakdown of some dimension in legitimate political order as well as the existence of collective frustration and aggression in a population. All presuppose certain capabilities for violence by those who make the internal war and a certain incapacity for preventing violence among those on whom it is made. All tend to scar societies deeply and to prevent the formation of consensus indefinitely. There is, consequently, at least a possibility that general theories about internal war may be discovered—general theories which may also help to solve problems posed by specific instances.

Another justification for grouping internal wars in a single universe is that actual instances of internal war often combine different types of violence, in space and time. Guerrilla warfare in one area may be combined with terrorism in another; it may be preceded by insurrections and develop into full-scale civil war, or culminate in a mere *coup d'état*. Indeed the large-scale and prolonged instances of internal war that we generally call revolutions are notable chiefly for the fact that they combine, in strikingly similar sequences, many different types of violence.[3] To focus analysis from the outset on particular species of internal war therefore makes it necessary to abstract from actual internal wars occurrences which may not in fact be strictly separable. This may be fine for working out abstract theories, but will not do for developing theories closely relevant to historical (i.e., concrete) cases in all their complexity.

A third justification for studying internal wars generically is furnished by the very limited results so far obtained in comparative historical studies of revolutions, particularly the pre-war studies of L. P. Edwards, Crane Brinton, and George S. Pettee, and the more recent study of Hannah Arendt.[4] These studies deal only with the so-called Great Revolutions of history—conspicuous and much-studied disturbances that occurred in relatively advanced, mildly autocratic, western societies, between 1640 and 1917. Consequently, they seem to say little that is reliable about, or even relevant to, much of the political violence of our more far-flung and variegated world, or of pre-modern times, or, for that matter, of the period they cover. They draw mammoth inferences from very few cases; and they ignore not only the vast spectrum of *coups*, *Putsches*, uprisings, riots, and so forth, but also Mr. Hobsbawm's hero, the "primitive rebel", once so important, and again come to the center of affairs.[5] Thus, they are neither very "scientific" nor very historical. A more extensive view of the subject should yield not only knowledge more relevant to many particular cases but generalizations more trustworthy, by sheer weight of numbers, for the cases covered in the classic

[3] "The [French] Revolution is a series of shocks, each shock displacing power from Right to Left, from larger groups, to smaller and more determined groups, each shock taking on more and more the aspect of a *coup d'état,* less and less that of a widespread, spontaneous outbreak of the people, until finally, in a commonplace *coup d'état* hardly worthy of a good operetta, power comes to rest in the hands of the dictator Bonaparte." Crane Brinton, *A Decade of Revolution, 1789–1799* (New York, 1934), 1. This inspired characterization of the French Revolution might well serve as a rudimentary developmental model for any internal war that begins in large-scale, mainly spontaneous, popular violence.

[4] L. P. Edwards, *The Natural History of Revolutions* (Chicago, 1927); Crane Brinton, *The Anatomy of Revolution* (New York, 1958—first published 1938); George S. Pettee, *The Process of Revolution* (New York, 1938); Hannah Arendt, *On Revolution* (New York, 1963).

[5] E. J. Hobsbawm, *Primitive Rebels* (London, 1960).

comparative histories. Pettee does say that by studying the more egregious cases he intends to illuminate all the rest —but he never does, and one doubts that he can.

Finally, the terminologies presently used to distinguish types of internal war vary greatly, are generally ambiguous, often define overlapping phenomena or phenomena difficult to distinguish in practice, and are rarely based on clearly discernible analytical needs. For few phenomena do social science, history, and conventional language offer so various and vague a vocabulary. Consider a few examples—a mere small sample of what there is to consider. Lasswell and Kaplan divide internal wars into palace revolutions, political revolutions, and social revolutions. Palace revolutions, as they define the term, are changes in rulers contrary to the "political formulas" of governments (that is, their formal constitutions), are usually effected by members of the ruling group themselves, and rarely lead to important changes in policy; political revolutions are changes in "authority structures" (formal power structures), and social revolutions changes in the overall "control structures" (effective power structures) of society, usually effected by men not already in ruling positions. A conventional distinction often made is that between revolutions and rebellions, the former being something broader in purpose and more tightly organized, as well as longer in duration and more violent, than the latter. Gabriel Bonnet, perhaps the most illustrious exponent of the French military doctrine of "revolutionary warfare", distinguishes between civil wars of liberation, and revolutionary wars, with civil wars further divided into riots, insurrections, pronunciamentos, and revolutions —terms which perhaps speak sufficiently for themselves.[6] Huntington talks about revolutionary wars and *coups d'état*, the key distinctions between them being their duration (*coups* are decided quickly, revolutions not) and the extent to which the insurgents already participate in the existing system of power (they do in *coups*, but not in revolutionary wars); *coups* are then further distinguished into governmental *coups*, which lead to no significant changes in social or political institutions; revolutionary *coups*, which do attempt to achieve such changes; and reform *coups*, which fall somewhere between the other two.[7] George Blanksten speaks of "real" revolutions, "near" revolutions, and mere non-constitutional changes of government in Latin America,[8] and Stokes uses a still more complicated typology to characterize Latin American political violence: *machetismo*, *cuartelazo*, *golpe de estado*, and *revolución*.[9]

One can derive from these and similar classificatory schemes a sort of composite typology, distinguishing between relatively unorganized and spontaneous *riots* by crowds with low capabilities for violence and modest aims, *coups d'état* by members of an elite against other members of the elite, full-scale *political revolutions* to achieve important constitutional changes, *social revolutions* to achieve large-scale socio-economic as well as constitutional changes, and *wars of independence* to achieve sovereignty in a previously dependent territory. But this typology is not necessarily better than the others. It does relate the various typologies by including most of the terms of the complicated schemes and

[6] Gabriel Bonnet, *Les guerres insurrectionelles et révolutionnaires* (Paris, 1958), 34 ff.

[7] S. P. Huntington, ed., *Changing Patterns of Military Politics* (New York, 1962), 22 ff.

[8] George I. Blanksten, "Revolutions", in Harold Eugene Davis, *Government and Politics in Latin America* (New York, 1958), Chapter 5.

[9] W. S. Stokes, "Violence as a Power Factor in Latin American Politics", *Western Political Quarterly*, Summer 1952, 445–68.

adding more terms to the simple ones; but this alone does not make it more precise, easier to apply or more suited to the substantive tasks of study.

For all of these reasons it can do no harm and might do much good to consider internal wars as all of a piece at the beginning of inquiry and to introduce distinctions only as they become necessary or advisable. In this way, the possibilities of developing general theories are increased, as is the likelihood that the distinctions made will be important and precise. In any event, that is how I shall proceed here, showing at the end how a general theory about the genus "internal war" can be adapted to give an account of special cases.

The Problem of Etiology

The theoretical issues raised by internal wars can be classified according to the phases through which such wars pass. They include problems about their preconditions, the way they can be effectively waged, the courses they tend to take, the outcomes they tend to have, and their long-run effects on society.

Curiously enough, the later the phase, the less there is to read about the issues involved. Despite the protracted normative argument between pro-revolutionaries and anti-revolutionaries, initiated by Paine and Burke, almost nothing careful and systematic has been written about the long-run social effects of internal wars, least of all perhaps about some of the most poignant and practical problems they raise: how political legitimacy and social harmony may be restored after violent disruption, what makes internal wars acute or chronic, and what the comparative costs (and probabilities) are of revolutionary and evolutionary transformations. Little more is available on the determinants of success or failure in internal wars. A fair amount has been written about the dynamic processes of revolutions, above all in the comparative historical studies already mentioned and in a very few more recent books, like Crozier's *The Rebels.*[10] But in regard to etiology, to "causes", we are absolutely inundated with print.

This abundance of etiological studies is not, however, an unmixed blessing. If studying other aspects of internal wars poses the basic problem of thinking of theoretical possibilities, studying their etiology poses a difficulty equally great: how to choose among a rare abundance of hypotheses which cannot all be equally valid nor all be readily combined. This problem exists because most propositions about the causes of internal wars have been developed in historical studies of particular cases (or very limited numbers of cases) rather than in broadly comparative, let alone genuinely social-scientific, studies. In historical case-studies one is likely to attach significance to any aspect of prerevolutionary society that one intuits to be significant, and so long as one does not conjure up data out of nothing one's hypotheses cannot be invalidated on the basis of the case in question.

That most studied of all internal wars, the French Revolution, provides a case in point—as well as examples in abundance of the many social, personal, and environmental forces to which the occurrence of internal wars might be attributed. Scarcely anything in the French *ancien régime* has not been blamed, by one writer or another, for the revolution, and all of their interpretations, however contradictory, are based on solid facts.

Some interpreters have blamed the outbreak of the French Revolution on

[10] Brian Crozier, *The Rebels: A Study of Post-War Insurrections* (London, 1960), Parts III–V and Postlude.

intellectual causes, that is to say, on the ideas, techniques, and great public influence of the *philosophes* (who were indeed very influential). This is the standard theory of post-revolutionary conservative theorists, from Chateaubriand to Taine, men who felt, in essence, that in pre-revolutionary France a sound society was corrupted by a seductive and corrosive philosophy.

Other writers have blamed the revolution mainly on economic conditions, although it is difficult to find very many who single out as crucial the same conditions. The revolution has been attributed to sheer grinding poverty among the lower classes (who were certainly poor); to financial profligacy and mismanagement on the part of the government (of which it was in fact guilty); to the extortionate taxation inflicted on the peasants (and peasant taxation verged upon brutality); to short-term setbacks (which actually occurred and caused great hardship) like the bad harvest of 1788, the hard winter of 1788–89, and the still winds of 1789 which prevented flour from being milled and made worse an already acute shortage of bread; to the over-abundant wine harvests of the 1780's (one of the first historic instances of the harmful effects of overproduction); to the increased wealth and power of the bourgeoisie in a society still dominated to a significant extent by aristocrats, the growth of the Parisian proletariat and its supposedly increasing political consciousness, and the threatened abrogation of the financial privileges of the aristocracy, particularly their exemption from taxation —all unquestionable facts producing manifest problems.

Still another set of writers locates the crucial cause of the revolution in aspects of social structure. Much has been made, and with sufficient reason, of the fact that in the last years of the *ancien régime* there occurred a hardening in the lines of upward mobility in French society—for example, a decline in grants of patents of nobility to commoners and the imposition of stringent social requirements for certain judicial and administrative positions and the purchase of officerships in the army. This, many have argued (following Mosca's and Pareto's famous theory of the circulation of elites), engendered that fatal yearning for an aristocracy of wealth and talent to which the *philosophes* gave expression. Much has also been made, with equal reason, of popular dissatisfaction with the parasitic life of the higher nobility, with its large pensions and puny duties, its life of hunting, love-making, watch-making, and interminable conversation. And much has been attributed to the vulnerability of the privileged classes to the very propagandists who wanted to alter the system that supported them ("How," asked Taine, "could people who talked so much resist people who talked so well?"), reflected in the Anglomania which swept through the higher aristocracy toward the end of the *ancien régime* and in the rush of many aristocrats to the cause of the Americans in their war of independence.

There are also certain well-founded "political" explanations of the French Revolution: that the revolution was really caused by the violation of the tacit "contract" on which the powers of the monarchy rested (a contract by which the aristocracy surrendered its powers to the monarchy in return for receiving certain inviolable privileges), or that the revolution was simply a successful political conspiracy by the Jacobins, based on efficient political organization. Personalities, needless to say, get their due as well: the revolution has been blamed, for example, on the character, or lack of character, of Louis XVI (who was in fact weak, vacillating and inconsistent), the supposed immorality of the Queen (who indeed was the subject, justly or not, of many scandals), the effect on the public of the dismissal of Necker, and, of course, on the "genius", good or evil, of unquestionable geniuses like Mirabeau, Danton, Marat, and Robespierre.

We could take other internal wars and arrive at the same result–similarly large lists of explanations, most of them factual, yet inconclusive. The more remote in time and the more intensively analyzed the internal war, the longer the list of hypotheses. Yet even so recent a case as the Chinese Communist Revolution has given rise to a fearful number of plausible hypotheses, many directly contradictory.

The Chinese Revolution has been blamed on plain conspiracy: a plot by a small number of Kremlin agents or power-hungry Chinese intellectuals. It has been blamed on social forces, like the rise of an urban working class or a "new" urban middle class, large-scale mobility from countryside to cities and the attendant weakening of traditional social patterns (the growth of a "mass" society),[11] or the effects of a "population explosion". Its genesis has been located in political culture, structure and decisions: in hyper-nationalism and the hatred it engendered of those cooperating with "imperialist" powers; in the corruption of the incumbent regime; in that regime's supposedly selfish and reactionary policies, ignoring the interests of land-hungry peasants, urban workers, and the new urban middle class; in administrative incompetence; in exorbitantly harsh policies toward all actual and potential opposition. Economic explanations are available too; the revolution, it has been argued, was caused by general poverty, by the exploitation particularly of the peasants, by the breakdown of the peasant crafts due to Western imports, by intellectual unemployment, and by various natural disasters. Finally, there are the usual theories about great and puny men and, not least, the interpretation perhaps most familiar to us of all: that the revolution was caused by insufficient and untimely external support for the incumbents compared to the external support available to the insurgents.[12]

How can this embarrassment of interpretative riches (one hesitates to say theoretical riches) be reduced? If the examination of any single case allows one to determine only whether an interpretation of it is based on facts, then broad comparative studies in space and/or time are needed to establish the significance of the facts on which the interpretations are based. Was a blockage in the channels of social mobility a significant precondition of the French Revolution? We can be reasonably confident that it was only if it can be shown that elite circulation and political stability are generally related. Was the Chinese population explosion really an important cause of the Chinese revolution? Surely this is unlikely if demographic pressures do not generally affect the viability of regimes.

This is the simplest conceivable methodology, and easy to indicate abstractly. But actually to find the broad general relationships on the basis of which particular interpretations can be assessed is not so easy. For this purpose we need a tremendous amount of historical work that comparative historiographers of in-

[11] For an explanation of this term and its use in the explanation of large, illegitimate political movements, see W. Kornhauser, *The Politics of Mass Society* (New York, 1959).

[12] I am indebted to my colleague Davis B. Bobrow for this list; his, I should mention, was in fact much larger. For a similar, still more extensive, treatment of the literature on the American Civil War, which is also very instructive on the general problems of causation of historical events, see Lee Benson and Cushing Strout, "Causation and the American Civil War. Two Appraisals", *History and Theory*, I, 2 (1961), 163–185. See also Thomas J. Pressly, *Americans Interpret their Civil War* (Princeton, 1954).

ternal wars have hardly even begun to do. There are so many possibilities to be tested against so many cases. A general etiology of internal wars, at this stage, can only be a remote end of inquiry, and neither limited comparative studies nor interpretations of particular instances of internal war should pretend otherwise.

But even prior to undertaking that work, theoretical reflection can introduce some order into the chaos that internal war studies present. Most important, it can produce useful judgments as to the more economic lines to pursue in empirical inquiry. We can in a small way approach an etiology of internal wars by classifying the theoretical possibilities available, indicating the analytical choices they require and do not require to be made, and attempting to determine what lines of analysis are most likely to prove rewarding. Where the theoretical possibilities are as varied and chaotic as in the case of internal war, such reflection, to organize and restrict inquiry, is a necessary preliminary to the more definitive work of rigorously testing well-formulated propositions.

"Preconditions" or "Precipitants"?

Perhaps the first thing that becomes apparent when one tries to classify causal explanations of the sort sketched above is that many of the explanations do not really require a choice to be made by the analyst. The propositions do not always contradict one another; often, in fact, they are complementary, differing only because they refer to different points in the time-sequence leading to revolution, or because they refer to different kinds of causality, or because they single out one factor among many of equal significance.

The most important distinction to make in this connection is between preconditions and precipitants of internal wars. A "precipitant" of internal war is an event which actually starts the war ("occasions" it), much as turning the flintwheel of a cigarette lighter ignites a flame. "Preconditions" of internal war, on the other hand, are those circumstances which make it possible for the precipitants to bring about political violence, as the general structure of a lighter makes it possible to produce a flame by turning the flintwheel. Some of the causal explanations of the French Revolution already mentioned clearly fall into the first category, while others fall equally clearly into the second; and between explanations singling out precipitants and explanations emphasizing preconditions of internal war there obviously is no genuine contradiction. The distinction between precipitants and preconditions can therefore prevent much pointless argument between those who stress short-run setbacks and those who emphasize long-term trends in the etiology of civil strife. Clearly no internal war can occur without precipitant events to set it off; and clearly no precipitants can set off internal war unless the condition of society makes it possible for them to do so.

The greatest service that the distinction between precipitants and preconditions of internal war can render, however, is to shift attention from aspects of internal war which defy analysis to those which are amenable to systematic inquiry. Phenomena which precipitate internal war are almost always unique and ephemeral in character. A bad harvest, a stupid or careless ruler, moral indiscretion in high places, an ill-advised policy: how could such data be incorporated into general theories? They are results of the vagaries of personality, of forces external to the determinate interrelations of society, of all those unique and fortuitous aspects of concrete life which are the despair of social scientists and the meat and drink of narrative historians.

Closely related, the distinction between precipitants and preconditions of internal wars will also help one to avoid what is perhaps the most misleading theory about their causes: an unqualified conspiracy theory of internal war. To be sure, conspiracy seems to play an essential role in certain types of internal war, particularly those previously referred to as *coups* and palace revolutions. As well, one undoubtedly finds conspiratorial organizations in every internal war of any consequence—in one case Jacobins, in others fascists, in still others communists. This is precisely what tempts so many to attribute internal wars solely or mainly to conspirators, and thus to regard them, in the manner of Malaparte, essentially as matters of technique—plotting on one hand and intelligence and suppression on the other. In many cases, however, the conspirators seem to do little more than turn the flintwheel in volatile situations, or indeed not even as much as that; sometimes they merely turn the revolutionary conflagration to their own purposes. Internal wars do not always have a clear aim, a tight organization, a distinct shape and tendency from the outset. Many seem to be characterized in their early stages by nothing so much as amorphousness. They are formless matter waiting to be shaped, and if there is an art of revolution, it involves, largely at least, not making or subduing it, but capitalizing on the unallocated political resources it provides.

This reference to techniques of revolution leads to another point. If one leaves precipitants aside and focuses solely on data the social scientist can handle, one does not even leave out of consideration anything that matters from a practical standpoint. Preconditions are the crucial concern of men of affairs, revolutionaries or anti-revolutionaries, no less than of social scientists. After all, they have an interest in the etiology of internal wars in order to anticipate such wars in good time, prevent them when they are preventable, further their actual occurrence, or otherwise prepare for them. But unique and ephemeral phenomena cannot, by their very nature, be anticipated; they simply happen. The vital knowledge to have concerns those conditions under which almost any setback or vagary, any misguided policy or indiscretion, can set society aflame.

Certain kinds of precipitants of internal war have a special importance of their own, however, in what one might call "practical etiology"—the anticipation of internal wars for policy purposes. A precipitant may be found so frequently on the eve of internal wars that its existence can be treated as a particularly urgent danger signal, particularly if its effects are delayed sufficiently to allow some adaptation to the danger. As far as we know, both of these conditions are satisfied by economic precipitants of internal war. The point deserves some elaboration, particularly in view of the persistent emphasis on economic conditions in writings on internal war.

It now seems generally agreed that persistent poverty in a society rarely leads to political violence. Quite the contrary. As Edwards points out, following an argument already developed by de Tocqueville, economic oppression, indeed all kinds of oppression, seems to wane rather than increase in pre-revolutionary periods.[13] Brinton makes the same point. While not underestimating the amount of poverty in the societies he analyzes in *The Anatomy of Revolution*, he does point out that all

[13] Edwards, *The Natural History of Revolutions*, 33.

of these societies were economically progressive rather than retrograde. He points out also that revolutionary literature, at any rate in the pre-Marxist period, hardly ever dwelt on economic misery and exploitation—one hears about economic grievances, to be sure, but not the sort of grievances which arise out of "immiseration".[14] Even some Marxists seem to share this view. Trotsky, for example, once remarked that if poverty and oppression were a precipitant of revolution the lower classes would always be in revolt, and obviously he had a point.

It is equally difficult to establish a close link between economic improvement and internal war. Pre-revolutionary periods may often be economically progressive, but economic progress is not always (or even often) connected with internal war. From this, however, one need not conclude that economic tendencies are simply irrelevant to the occurrence of political violence. Only the long-term tendencies seem, in fact, to be irrelevant. The moment one focuses on short-term tendencies, a fairly frequently repeated pattern emerges—and one which tells us why it is that some writers adhere stubbornly to the immiseration theory of internal war and others, with just as much conviction, to the economic progress theory. It so happens that before many internal wars, one finds both economic improvement and immiseration; more precisely, many internal wars are preceded by long-term improvements followed by serious short-term setbacks. [15] The bad harvests and unfavorable weather conditions in pre-revolutionary France, the American recession of 1774–1775, the bad Russian winter of 1916–1917 (not to mention the economic impact of the war on Russia) and the marked rise of unemployment in Egypt before Naguib's *coup* are cases in point. All dealt serious short-term blows to economic life and all followed long periods of economic progress, especially for those previously "repressed".

It is this dual pattern which really seems to be lethal, and it is not difficult to see why. In times of prolonged and marked economic progress, people become accustomed to new economic standards and form new economic expectations, which previously they could scarcely imagine. Confidently expecting continuous progress, they also tend to take risks (like accumulating debts) which they might not take otherwise. All this greatly exaggerates the impact of serious temporary setbacks; both psychologically and economically the costs of such setbacks are bound to be greater than if they occurred after long periods of stagnation or very gradual progress.

Occasionally, perhaps, the study of precipitants of internal war may play a minor role in "theoretical" as well as "practical etiology". It could conceivably shed some light on the preconditions themselves in that there might be a connection between revolutionary conditions and how internal wars are actually brought about. For example, someone may blame internal war on dissatisfactions in the rural population of a society; but if we find peasants playing no role in the fomenting of violence, then we have good reason to doubt the interpretation. Precipitants may not directly tell us what the preconditions of internal war are, but they can sometimes indicate what they are not—be useful for falsifying hypotheses, or at least shedding doubt on them. But this does not alter the basic point: that the

[14] Brinton, *The Anatomy of Revolution,* 29–37.

[15] See James C. Davis, "Toward a Theory of Revolution", *American Sociological Review,* 27 (1962), 5–19. This paper traces the pattern in Dorr's Rebellion, the Russian Revolution, and the Egyptian Revolution.

task of an etiology of internal wars is to discover their preconditions.

Common Hypotheses About the Preconditions of Internal War

We can profitably relegate to a secondary role most of those greatly varying, unique, and largely fortuitous events which occasion the outbreak of internal wars. But even if we do, a great variety of hypotheses remains—great enough if we confine ourselves to general treatments of internal war, and greater still if we deal with hypotheses formulated to deal with particular cases. In this connection, it might be useful to supplement the explanations of particular revolutions listed above with a sample of propositions frequently found in the more general literature on internal war. These include: [16]

a) *Hypotheses emphasizing "intellectual" factors:*
   1. Internal wars result from the failure of a regime to perform adequately the function of political socialization.
   2. Internal wars are due to the coexistence in a society of conflicting social "myths".
   3. Internal wars result from the existence in a society of unrealizable values or corrosive social philosophies.
   4. Internal wars are caused by the alienation (desertion, transfer of allegiance) of the intellectuals.

b) *Hypotheses emphasizing economic factors:*
   1. Internal wars are generated by growing poverty.
   2. Internal wars result from rapid economic progress.
   3. Internal wars are due to severe imbalances between the production and distribution of goods.
   4. Internal wars are caused by a combination of long-term economic improvement and short-term setbacks.

c) *Hypotheses emphasizing aspects of social structure:*
   1. Internal wars are due to the inadequate circulation of elites (that is, inadequate recruitment into the elite of the able and powerful members of the non-elite).
   2. Internal wars result from too much recruitment of members of the non-elite into the elite, breaking down the internal cohesion of the elite.
   3. Internal war is a reflection of *anomie* resulting from great social mobility.
   4. Internal war is a reflection of frustration arising from little general social mobility—from general social stagnation.
   5. Internal wars result from the appearance in societies of new social classes.

d) *Hypotheses emphasizing political factors:*
   1. Internal wars are due to the estrangement of rulers from the societies they rule.
   2. Internal war is simply a response to bad government (government

[16] The hypotheses come from a large variety of sources, including: Lasswell and Kaplan, *Power and Society* (New Haven, 1950); the works by Edwards, Pettee, and Brinton cited above; Rudé, *The Crowd in the French Revolution* (Oxford, 1959); Trotsky, *The History of the Russian Revolution* (Ann Arbor, Michigan, 1957); De Grazia, *The Political Community* (Chicago, 1948); Gaetano Mosca, *The Ruling Class* (New York, 1939); and Vilfredo Pareto, *The Mind and Society* (New York, 1935).

which performs inadequately the function of goal-attainment).

3. Internal wars are due, not to the attacks of the governed on those who govern, but to divisions among the governing classes.
4. Internal wars are responses to oppressive government.
5. Internal wars are due to excessive toleration of alienated groups.

e) *Hypotheses emphasizing no particular aspects of societies, but general characteristics of social process:*

1. Political violence is generated by rapid social change.
2. Political violence results from erratic and/or uneven rates of social change, whether rapid or not.
3. Internal war occurs when a state is somehow "out of adjustment" to society.

From this sample of propositions, all of them at least plausible, we can get some idea of the overwhelming ambiguities that general studies of the preconditions of internal war have created to supplement those originating in case studies. These ambiguities arise most obviously from the fact that many of the propositions are manifestly contradictory; less obviously, from the sheer variety and disparity of factors included, not all of which, surely, can be equally significant, or necessary, in the etiology of internal wars. For this reason, even when precipitants are subtracted, a considerable range of choices between theories remains to be made.

Insurgents or Incumbents?

One crucial choice that needs to be made is whether to put emphasis upon characteristics of the insurgents or incumbents, upon the side that rebels or the side that is rebelled against. Not surprisingly, the existing literature concentrates very largely on the rebels, treating internal war as due mainly to changes in the non-elite strata of society to which no adequate adjustment is made by the elite. This would seem to be only natural; after all, it is the rebels who rebel. At least some writings suggest, however, that characteristics of the incumbents and the classes that are usually their props must be considered jointly with characteristics of the insurgents, indeed perhaps even emphasized more strongly. Pareto, for example, while attributing revolution partly to blockages in a society's social mobility patterns, considered it equally necessary that certain internal changes should occur in an elite if revolution was to be possible; in essence, he felt that no elite which had preserved its capacity for timely and effective violence, or for effective manipulation, could be successfully assailed, or perhaps assailed at all. One must, according to this view, seek the origins of internal war not only in a gain of strength by the non-elite, but also in the loss of it on the part of the elite. Brinton makes the same point: revolutions, in his view, follow the loss of common values, of internal cohesion, of a sure sense of destiny and superiority and, not least, of political efficiency in elites, and thus must be considered results as much as causes of their disintegration. And in Edwards's and Pettee's studies as well, revolutions emerge as affairs of the elites (if not always directly of the actual rulers): the crucial roles in them are played by intellectuals, by men rich and powerful but "cramped" by their lack of status or other perquisites, and by the gross inefficiency of the ruling apparatus.

Significantly enough, this view is stated perhaps more often in the writings of actual revolutionaries than in those of students of revolution. Trotsky, for example, believed that revolution requires three elements: the political consciousness of a revolutionary class, the discontent of the "intermediate layers" of society, and, just as important, a ruling class which has "lost faith in itself", which is torn by the conflicts of groups and cliques, which has lost its capacity for practical action and rests its hopes in "miracles or miracle workers".[17]

The joint consideration of insurgent and incumbent patterns thus would seem to be the logical way to proceed in the early stages of inquiry into the causes of revolution. But one should not overlook the possibility that sufficient explanations of the occurrence of many internal wars might be found in elite characteristics alone. A ruling elite may decay, may become torn by severe conflict, may be reluctant to use power, may come to lack vital political skills—and thus make it perfectly possible for a relatively weak, even disorganized, opposition of a sort that may exist in any political system to rise against it and destroy it. Indeed, there are theories which maintain that internal wars are always caused solely or primarily by changes in elite characteristics, and that one can practically ignore the insurgents in attempting to account for the occurrence of internal wars.

One such theory is propounded in Mosca's *The Ruling Class.* If the elementary needs of human life are satisfied, argued Mosca, one thing above all will cause men to rebel against their rulers, and that is their feeling that the rulers live in a totally different environment, that they are "separated" from their subjects in some profound sense. In other words, the estrangement of the elite from the non-elite is inseparable from the alienation of the latter; only the elite itself, consequently, can undermine its political position. In this regard Mosca made much of the feudal societies of Poland, Ireland, England, and Russia. The Polish nobles of the Middle Ages, for example, practiced extreme economic extortion, taking in levies almost all the peasant produced; they were ruthless and violent; they scrupulously extracted the *droit du seigneur;* and despite all that, and more, the peasants never rebelled—as long as the nobles "lived among them, spoke their language, swore the same oaths, ate the same kind of food, wore the same style of clothes, exhibited the same manners or lack of them, had the same rustic superstitions".[18] But a drastic change occurred when the nobility acquired French manners and tastes, "gave luxurious balls after the manner of Versailles and tried to dance the minuet". Despite more humane treatment, vicious and frequent revolts attended the estrangement of the nobles from their people.

This interpretation certainly makes sense in light of French experience: the French Revolution was far more an attack upon the refined and parasitic court nobility than upon the coarse, and little less parasitic, provincial nobility. It makes sense also in the case of Britain, for the British nobility (in the main) always preserved close ties to the soil and to the manner and morals of its tenantry; Squire Western is the embodiment of that fact. That is why it was for so long the butt of jokes among the more sophisticated, and shorter-lived, continental aristocracies.

Perhaps the most prolonged period of civil unrest in American history, the late nineteenth century, can be, and has been, interpreted in much the same manner—not only by political sociologists like De Grazia, but also by acute literary observers like Mark Twain and

[17] Trotsky, *The Russian Revolution*, 311.
[18] De Grazia, *The Political Community*, 74–75.

historians like Miriam Beard.[19] One of the more conspicuous features of that period was the compulsive attempt of the American plutocracy to imitate European "society". At no other time in American history was the elite so profoundly estranged from American life. Mark Twain gave this period a name which fits it exactly and has stuck to it ever since. It was the Gilded Age, the age of English clothes and accents, Roman orgies, continental travel, title-mongering, art-collecting, butlers and footmen, conspicuous consumption of every sort—the age which invented those now much more Americanized institutions, the debutante and the society page. Not until the American plutocracy had returned to its old habits of thrift and earthiness, of being plain Americans, was there a return to relative civil calm in the United States.[20]

More examples of the instability that ensues from the estrangement of elites are furnished in profusion by the westernized elites of many currently underdeveloped areas. The elites referred to in this case are not those who learn Western skills but remain identified with their native context; rather it is the westernized in lifeways, the visitors to the Riviera and the riders in Cadillacs, who try to lead a life totally different from that of their people. For such estranged elites, living abroad may indeed be a course preferable to the imitation of alien ways at home; at any rate, they are in that case rather less conspicuous.

It is worth noting that in the postwar period internal wars have been relatively rare in two kinds of societies: either thoroughly modernized countries or very underdeveloped countries whose elites have remained tied closely to the traditional ways and structures of life.[21] Of course, a generalization of this kind is becoming increasingly harder to test, since the number of societies without a gulf between highly modernized elites and much less modernized masses seems to be rapidly shrinking. Nevertheless the notion is given credibility by the fact that, while transitional societies seem to suffer more from internal wars than either traditional or modern societies—as one would expect upon many hypotheses—a very few seem to have strikingly low rates of violence compared to the rest. Egypt is one example, and Pakistan another. These societies seem to differ from the rest in one main respect. They have had "secondary" revolutions, so to speak, in which men of rather humble origins and popular ways (colonels' regimes) have unseated previously victorious transitional elites.

All this is not meant to validate the idea that elite estrangement is the main cause of internal war but only to show why it should be taken very seriously. The possible consequences of elite estrangement are not, however, the only reason for emphasizing studies of the incumbents at least as much as studies of insurgents in the etiology of internal wars. Another is the fact that internal wars are almost invariably preceded by important functional failures on the part of elites. Above all is this true of difficulties in financial administration—perhaps because finance impinges on the ability of governments to perform all their functions.[22] And finally, insur-

[19] De Grazia, *The Political Community*, esp. 117 ff. and Miriam Beard, *A History of the Business Man* (New York, 1938).

[20] For evidence of acute unrest in the United States in this period, see De Grazia, *The Political Community*.

[21] Cases in point are the stable, highly developed democracies on the one hand, and countries like Ethiopia and Somalia on the other.

[22] One of the most common conditions found before large-scale political violence is the financial bankruptcy of government, due to profligacy, over-ambitious policies, or the failure of a traditional tax structure in an inflationary situation, followed by an attack upon the financial

gent groups seem rarely to come even to the point of fighting without some support from alienated members of incumbent elites. On this point, agreement in the literature on internal war is practically unanimous.

Structural or Behavioral Hypotheses?

A second strategic choice to be made in constructing an etiology of internal wars is between structural and behavioral hypotheses. A structural hypothesis singles out, so to speak, "objective" social conditions as crucial for the occurrence of internal war: aspects of a society's "setting", such as economic conditions, social stratification and mobility, or geographic and demographic factors. A behavioral hypothesis, on the other hand, emphasizes attitudes and their formation—not setting, but "orientations" (such as degrees of strain and *anomie* in societies, the processes by which tension and aggression are generated, and the processes by which human beings are "socialized" into their communities). The great majority of propositions regarding the causes of internal war are, on the basis of these definitions, structural in character. But, in concentrating upon structural explanations have writers on internal war taken the more promising tack?

At first glance, there would seem to be little to choose between structural and behavioral approaches. Since most human action is motivated, not reflexive, one always wants to know, if one can, about attitudes underlying men's actions. At the same time, there can be little doubt that attitudes are always formed somehow in response to external conditions. The difference between structural and behavioral theories would therefore seem to be, at best, one of emphasis or point of view. Yet emphasis can make a difference. Certain research results do seem to be associated with one point of view or the other. Behavioral approaches, for instance, may lead to theories stressing "intellectual" and voluntaristic factors in the etiology of political violence, or to theories attributing internal war mainly to efficient revolutionary indoctrination or inadequate value-formation by the incumbents. Structural explanations may lead to theories of mechanical imbalance in society, or to theories attributing internal war mainly to specific situational conditions, attitudes being treated as mechanical responses to such conditions.

Which approach is preferable? Despite the fact that there is a danger that the behavioral approach might lead to naive conspiracy theory (the belief that internal wars are always the results of insidious indoctrination by subversive elements, and could therefore always occur or always be avoided) the arguments against a primary emphasis on structural theories are very strong.

One such argument derives from the general experience of modern social science. Purely structural theories have generally been found difficult to sustain wherever they have been applied, and one fundamental reason for this is that patterns of attitudes, while responsive to the settings in which men are placed, seem also to be, to an extent, autonomous of objective conditions, able to survive changes in these conditions or to change without clearly corresponding objective changes. This is one of the basic insights underlying the sociological theory of action, which, to be sure,

privileges of strata which were previously the main props of the regime. R. B. Merriman, in *Six Contemporaneous Revolutions, 1640–1660* (Oxford, 1938) points out that the seventeenth-century revolutions in England, France, the Netherlands, Spain, Portugal, and Naples all had this point in common.

assigns an important role to the situations in which human action occurs, but treats "culture" largely as a separate variable and attaches particularly great significance to agencies of socialization and acculturation. It underlies as well the relatively successful use of mediational models, rather than simple S-R models, in behavioral psychology.

No doubt this point should be much elaborated.[23] But one can make a cogent case for stressing behavioral theories of the causes of internal wars without going lengthily into the general nature and past experiences of social science.

The most obvious case for behavioral theories of internal war derives from the very fact that so many different objective social conditions seem capable of generating it. We may have available many interpretative accounts of internal wars simply because an enormous variety of objective conditions can create internal-war potential. Certain internal wars do seem to have followed economic improvement, others seem to have followed closely the Marxist model of internal wars; however, many more have followed some combination of the two. Some internal wars have in fact been preceded by great, others by little social mobility; some regimes have been more oppressive and others more liberal in the immediate pre-revolutionary period, some both and some neither. Is it not reasonable to conclude that one should not seek explanations of the occurrence of internal wars in specific social conditions, but rather in the ways in which social conditions may be perceived? Instead of looking for direct connections between social conditions and internal war, should one not look rather for the ways in which an existing cognitive and value system may change, so that conditions perceived as tolerable at one point are perceived as intolerable at another; or, concomitantly, look for the ways in which old systems of orientation are in some cases maintained rather than adapted in the face of social change, so that changes which one society absorbs without trouble create profound difficulties in another?

The point is not that objective conditions are unrelated to internal war. Rather it is that orientations mediate between social setting and political behavior, and—because they are not simply mirrors of environment—so that different objective conditions may lead to similar political activities, or similar conditions to different activities in different contexts; that in a single context a considerable change in political activity may occur without significant changes in objective conditions or changes in objective conditions without changes in activity. What should be avoided is linking aspects of social setting *directly* to internal war or *mechanically* to orientations. Internal wars are best conceived as responses to political disorientation (such as "cognitive dissonance", *anomie,* and strains in the definition of political roles), particularly in regard to a society's norms of legitimacy; and political disorientation may follow from a considerable variety of conditions, due to the variable nature of the orientations themselves and of the agencies that implant them in different societies.

One conspicuous point of agreement in comparative studies of revolution gives further credence to this argument. This is that revolutions are invariably preceded by the "transfer of allegiance" of a society's intellectuals and the development by them of a new political "myth". If intellectuals have any obvi-

[23] Useful summaries of action and behavior theories can be found in Roland Young, ed., *Approaches to the Study of Politics* (Evanston, Illinois, 1958), 217–243 and 285–301. [Eds. fn.: S-R means Stimulus-Response.]

ous social "functions", in the sense social scientists understand the term function, they are surely these: to socialize the members of a society outside of the domestic context, in schools and adult learning situations; to reinforce and rationalize attitudes acquired in all social contexts; and to provide meaning to life and guidelines to behavior by means of conscious doctrines where events have robbed men of their less conscious bearings. Intellectuals are particularly important in the education of adolescents and young people, and it has been shown quite definitely that political socialization occurs (or fails) mainly in the years between early childhood and full maturity.[24] It could also be shown that among revolutionaries the young tend to predominate, sometimes quite remarkably. Together these points go far to explain why the alienation of intellectuals is, in Edwards's language, a "master-symptom" of revolution: a condition that makes revolutionary momentum irreversible.

Another point that speaks for behavioral propositions is that internal wars can, and often do, become chronic. In some societies, the most manifest cause of internal war seems to be internal war itself, one instance following another, often without a recurrence of the conditions that led to the original event. This means that political disorientation may be followed by the formation of a new set of orientations, establishing a predisposition toward violence that is inculcated by the experience of violence itself. In such cases, internal wars result not from specifiable objective conditions, and not even from the loss of legitimacy by a particular regime, but from a general lack of receptivity to legitimacy of any kind. Violence becomes a political style that is self-perpetuating, unless itself "disoriented".

The very fact that elite estrangement so often precedes acute political unrest itself fits the case for behavioral propositions. It fits in part because the Establishment of any society includes its intellectuals, but also for a more important, rather technical, reason. Orientations, particularly as treated in action theory, are not purely internal and self-sufficient, as it were, but involve expectations from others ("alters")—mutualities or complementarities in behavior. Hence men are likely to become disoriented and alienated when those with whom they interact become aliens to them, even if the alien ways involve, from abstract moral standpoints, a change for the better. The Polish peasant probably did not positively like to be beaten, but he *expected* to be, and he himself undoubtedly committed a good deal of institutionalized mayhem on anyone subordinated to his authority. A liberal aristocrat would appear to him not only to act strangely but arbitrarily, and, in a way, as a constant personal reproach.

To give still more support to the argument for behavioral theories there is the object lesson provided by the sad history of Marxist theory. Marxism singles out certain objective social conditions as underlying internal wars. It also singles out certain social groups as indispensable to the making of internal war. But Marxist revolutions themselves have been made neither under the social conditions nor by the groups emphasized in the theory. What is more, these revolutions have been made in a large variety of conditions, with a large variety of means, by organizations constituted in a large variety of ways. This is true even if one can show that the appeal of Marxism is greatest in transitional societies, for the term transition, in its very nature, denotes not a particular social state but a great many dif-

[24] For evidence, see Herbert H. Hyman, *Political Socialization* (Glencoe, Illinois, 1959).

ferent points on whatever continuum social development may involve.

Particular Conditions or General Processes?

This argument has a close bearing upon a third strategic choice to be made in analyzing the causes of internal war. Even if one emphasizes behavioral characteristics in theories of internal wars, one must, as I have said, always relate these characteristics to the social setting. The question is how to do this. Should one, in the manner of most of the hypotheses listed above, develop propositions emphasizing particular social conditions or, in the manner of a few of them, select propositions about general characteristics of social process? In the first case, one would relate internal war to particular socio-economic changes, in the second to characteristics of the general phenomenon of social change itself, such as rapid change or erratic change in any sectors of society, or conditions that may result from any social change whatever, such as imbalances between social segments (e.g., between elites of wealth and elites of status) or incongruities among the authority patterns of a society.

The proper choice between these alternatives is already implied in the arguments of the previous section. If many particular social conditions may be connected with internal wars, then clearly one should stress broad propositions about social processes and balances that can comprehend a variety of such conditions. The same position results if disorientation is conceived, in large part, as a breakdown in mutualities and complementarities of behavior. Not least, there is overwhelming evidence to show that "*anomie*", the feeling that one lacks guidelines to behavior, is increased by rapidity of change in any direction (for example, by rapid economic betterment no less than rapid economic deterioration) and that "strain," the feeling that one's roles make inconsistent demands, is aggravated by uneven or incongruent changes in different social sectors (for example, when the economic sector of society becomes significantly modern while the political remains largely traditional).

What has been said about economic conditions preceding internal wars fits the argument particularly well. It is not just that cases can be found to support both immiseration and improvement theories of revolution, hence the view that internal wars are related to economic changes as such, not to change in any particular direction; more suggestive still is the fact that internal wars most frequently follow an irregular—an anomalous—course of economic change, long-term trends being interrupted by abrupt and short-lived reversals. Such a course exhibits at least two of the general characteristics of social processes that would, upon earlier arguments, seem to be related to the occurrence of internal wars: rapidity of change and eccentricity of change.

From this standpoint it would be most interesting to investigate whether *any* rapid and eccentric course of economic development tends to be related to internal war, perhaps even one involving long-term stagnation or deterioration followed by abrupt short-term improvement. This idea is not as farfetched as may seem; after all has not Durkheim fully documented the argument that "*fortunate crises,* the effect of which is abruptly to enhance a country's prosperity, affect suicide like *economic disasters*"? [25]

Undoubtedly there is a danger that broad formulations concerning general social processes will turn into empty

[25] Emile Durkheim, *Suicide* (London, 1952), 243 (my italics).

and untestable generalizations, trivialities like the much-repeated proposition that political violence tends to accompany social or economic change. But this danger is avoidable; one can, after all, be specific and informative about general social processes as well as about their substantive content.

Obstacles to Internal War

So far I have tried to make two related points. The first is that one is most likely to gain understanding of the forces impelling societies toward internal war if one avoids preoccupation with the more visible precipitants of internal wars, including conspiracies, and directs one's efforts to the analysis of their preconditions, stressing disorientative general social processes and particularly taking into account elite behavior, performance, and cohesion. The second point is in a sense the converse of this: that existing etiologies of internal wars are chaotic and inadequate precisely because studies have so far concentrated on precipitants rather than preconditions, insurgents rather than incumbents, and particular aspects of social structure rather than the effects on orientations of general social processes.

An important point must now be added. Even if we had better knowledge of the forces which push societies toward political violence, a crucial problem relating to the etiology of internal wars would remain, one that is generally ignored in the studies available to us. This problem concerns forces that might countervail those previously discussed: "obstacles" to internal war, as against forces which propel societies toward violence.

In the real world of phenomena, events occur not only because forces leading toward them are strong, but also because forces tending to inhibit, or obstruct, them are weak or absent. An automobile may generate a great deal of force, but if driven up a steep incline is unlikely to go very fast. A government may have the desire and technical capacity for rapid industrialization, but if faced by the rapid growth of an already too great population may simply find it impossible to channel sufficient resources into capital goods to achieve a certain rate of development. So also internal wars may fail to occur solely or mainly because of certain hindrances to their occurrence.

Some of these hindrances may be absolute in character, in that wherever they exist internal war fails to materialize; hence their obverse may be considered "requisites" of internal war (necessary, but not sufficient, conditions). In the main, however, obstacles to internal war, like forces making for internal war, are better conceived as factors making such wars more or less likely, rather than either inevitable or impossible—their actual significance depending, at least in part, on the strength of forces pulling in a contrary direction. It certainly seems unlikely that we shall ever find a condition that makes internal war quite inevitable under any circumstances, and equally unlikely that we could discover conditions that always rule it out (except perhaps purely definitional ones: e.g., the absence of any perceived frustrations). In real life, internal war, like other concrete events, results from the interplay of forces and counterforces, from a balance of probabilities pulling toward internal war and internal peace.

Repression. The most obvious obstacle to internal war is, of course, the incumbent regime. It goes almost without saying that by using repression the established authorities can lessen the chances of violent attack upon themselves, or even reduce them to nil. Internal wars, after all, are not made by impersonal forces working in impersonal ways, but by men acting under the stress of external forces. This much at least there is in the conspiracy theory of revolution: wholly spontaneous riots by wholly unstructured and undirected mobs may occur, but hardly very frequently or with much effect. Actual cases of internal war generally contain some element of subversion, some structure for forming political will and acting upon decisions, however primitive and changeable. On this point, if no other, the great enemies of revolution (Burke, Chateaubriand, Taine) are at one with the great revolutionaries (Lenin, Trotsky); it is also this point, rather than some more subtle idea, which underlies Pareto's and Brinton's argument that revolutions are due to elites as much as non-elites. And anything with a structure can of course be detected and repressed, though not always very easily.

The matter, however, is not quite so simple. Repression can be a two-edged sword. Unless it is based upon extremely good intelligence, and unless its application is sensible, ruthless, and continuous, its effects may be quite opposite to those intended. Incompetent repression leads to a combination of disaffection and contempt for the elite. Also, repression may only make the enemies of a regime more competent in the arts of conspiracy; certainly it tends to make them more experienced in the skills of clandestine organization and *sub rosa* communication. No wonder that botched and bungled repression is often a characteristic of pre-revolutionary societies. The French *ancien régime,* for example, had a political censorship, but it only managed to make French writers into masters of the hidden meaning, and whet the appetite of the public for their subversive books. "In our country", a French aristocrat said, "authors compete with one another for the honors of the bonfire"; even the Queen seems to have spent many delicious evenings reading the forbidden Encyclopedia with her ladies.[26] Russia, under the later Czars, was practically a model of repressive bumbledom; her policy of exile, for example, created close-knit communities of revolutionaries more than it destroyed their cohesion.

The worst situation of all seems to arise when a regime, having driven its opponents underground, inflamed their enmity, heightened their contempt, and cemented their organization, suddenly relaxes its repression and attempts a liberal policy. The relaxation of authority is a part of the pre-revolutionary syndrome, no less than other forms of social amelioration; in that sense, repression in societies with high internal war potential is little more than a narcotic, intensifying the conditions it seeks to check and requiring ever larger doses to keep affairs in balance—if other things are equal. We can see this dynamic at work in the development of totalitarian rule, particularly if we remember that blood-letting, while certainly the ultimate in repression, is only one form that coercion can take.

From this standpoint, repression may be both an obstacle to and precipitant of internal war. Repression is of course least likely to prevent internal war in societies which, unlike totalitarian regimes, have a low capacity for coercion. In such societies, adjustive and diversionary mechanisms seem to check revolutionary potential far better. Indeed, they may in any society.[27]

DIVERSIONS AND CONCESSIONS. Diver-

[26] For much information relevant to this point, see Hippolyte Taine, *Origines de la France contemporaine,* rev. ed., 12 vols. (Paris, 1899–1914), vol. 1.

[27] "Power", says Merriam, "is not strongest where it uses violence, but weakest. It is strongest where it employs the instruments of substitution and counter-attraction, of allurement, of participation . . ." C. E. Merriam, *Political Power* (New York, 1934), 179–80.

sionary mechanisms are all those social patterns and practices which channel psychic energies away from revolutionary objectives—which provide other outlets for aggressions or otherwise absorb emotional tensions. If Elie Halévy's theory is correct, then English nonconformist evangelicalism, especially the Methodist movement, furnishes an excellent case in point.[28] Halévy, being French, was deeply puzzled by the fact that England did not have any serious revolution in the early nineteenth century, despite conditions which, on their face, seem to have contained very great revolutionary potential—conditions resulting from the industrial revolution and from the fact of endemic revolution throughout the Western world. His solution was that English evangelicalism, more than anything else, performed a series of functions which greatly lowered the revolutionary level of British politics. Among these functions were the provision of outlets for emotional expression and the inculcation of a philosophy which reconciled the lower classes to their condition, made that condition seem inevitable, and made patient submission to it a sacred obligation. In England, at least at the time in question, religion seems indeed to have been the opiate of the people, as Marx and Engels, no less than later and different-minded historians, seem to have realized.

England may have been spared major political violence since the seventeenth century for other reasons too: for example, because at least twice in English history, just when she seemed to be on the very brink of civil war, external war opportunely occurred, unifying the country as external wars will: at the time of the Napoleonic wars, and again in 1914 after the mutiny in the Curragh threatened to develop into something much more serious. Indeed, diverting popular attention from domestic troubles by starting foreign wars is one of the most venerable dodges of statecraft. This too, however, is a weapon that cuts two ways. Military adventures are excellent diversions, and military successes can marvellously cement disjoined societies, but military failure, on the evidence, can hardly fail to hasten revolution in such cases. Russia may well have entered the first World War to distract domestic unrest, but, if so, the outcome was revolution rather than the contrary.

Orgiastic excitements—festivals and dances, parades and circuses, *Reichsparteitäge* and mass gymnastics—also provide diversionary outlets for popular discontent. "If the late czardom," says Edwards, "instead of abolishing vodka, had made it more plentiful and very cheap—if, in addition, they had stimulated to the utmost those forms of religious frenzy and excitement to which the Russian populace appear to be so susceptible—then it is at least possible that the people would have been so exhausted mentally, emotionally, and financially by their alcoholic and religious orgies that they would not have had sufficient energy left to carry out a successful revolution." [29]

Totalitarian regimes seem to be shrewder about such matters, as well as being more coercive. The massive sports programs which are a feature of every totalitarian regime (German, Russian, or Chinese) may have a variety of purposes—physical fitness as preparation for war, or the inculcation of discipline—but one of them assuredly is to absorb the energies of the young and the interest of the not-so-young. No less than eschatological ideology, sport is the opiate of the masses in totalitarian countries, and not in these alone.

[28] Elie Halévy, *A History of the English People,* 6 vols. (London, 1960), vol. 1.
[29] Edwards, *The Natural History of Revolution,* 49.

Adjustive mechanisms reduce, or manage, tensions, rather than providing for them surrogate outlets. Concessions are perhaps the most obvious of such mechanisms. It is banal, but probably true, to say that timely concessions have been the most effective weapons in the arsenal of the British ruling class, and one of Halévy's more cogent points about the pacific effects of evangelicalism on nineteenth-century England is that it made the elite extraordinarily willing to ameliorate the lot of the masses. It enjoined upon them philanthropy as a sacred duty and educated them in the trusteeship theory of wealth —remember Wesley's counsel "gain all you can, save all you can, give all you can"—at the same time as it made the masses extraordinarily willing to suffer their burdens in peace. (For this reason, we can of course regard all functioning institutions for adjusting conflict as barriers to internal war.) But concessions too may work in two directions, no less than repression and certain diversionary tactics. They may only lead to further and greater demands, further and greater expectations of success, and must therefore, like repression, be continuous, and continuously greater, to succeed. "There is no better way [than a conciliatory policy]" according to Clemenceau, "of making the opposite party ask for more and more. Every man or every power whose action consists solely in surrender can only finish by self-annihilation. Everything that lives resists . . ." [30]

FACILITIES FOR VIOLENCE. A final set of obstacles to internal war are conditions that affect the capacities of alienated groups to use violence at all, or, more often in real life, to use it with fair prospects of success. These conditions do not always prevent violence. But they can prevent its success. For this very reason, they help determine the likelihood of decisions to use violence at all. What are some of these conditions?

Perhaps the first to come to mind is terrain. While practically all kinds of terrain can be used, in different ways, for purposes of rebellion, not all can be used to equal advantage. The ideal, from the viewpoint of the insurgents, seems to be an area which is relatively isolated, mountainous, overgrown, crisscrossed by natural obstacles (hedges, ditches, etc.), and near the sea or other sources of external supply—terrain which affords secure bases to the insurgents in their own territory, gives them the advantage of familiarity with local conditions, and allows ready access to them of external supporters.[31]

The communications facilities of a society are another relevant condition. Marx, among many others, seems to have realized this when he argued that urbanization increases the likelihood of revolution, if only in that it makes men accessible to one another and thus makes revolutionary organization easier to achieve. "Since the collective revolutionary mentality is formed by conversation and propaganda," writes the French historian Lefebvre, "all means that bring men together favor it." [32] In this one case, a condition which may heighten the chances of successful internal war (bad communications) may also discourage its outbreak. There may

[30] Quoted in G. Sorel, *Reflections on Violence* (New York, 1915), 71.

[31] For examples of how such terrain benefits insurgents, see Peter Paret, *Internal War and Pacification: The Vendée, 1793–1796* (Princeton, 1961); W. E. D. Allen, *Guerrilla War in Abyssinia* (London, 1951), 19; Chalmers Johnson, "Civilian Loyalties and Guerrilla Conflict", *World Politics,* July 1962; and Ernesto Guevara, *Che Guevara on Guerrilla War* (New York, 1961)—among many others.

[32] G. Lefebvre, "Foules Révolutionnaires", *Annales Historiques de la Révolution Française,* 1934, 23.

be nothing more mysterious to the celebrated peaceability of peasants, as compared to city-dwellers, than the physical difficulty in rural life, especially if fairly primitive, to form a "collective revolutionary mentality".

Terrain and communications are physical obstacles to (or facilities for) internal war. There are human obstacles as well. For example, internal wars seem rarely to occur, even if other conditions favor them, if a regime's instruments of violence remain loyal. This applies above all to the armed forces. Trotsky for one, and Lenin for another, considered the attitude of the army absolutely decisive for any revolution;[33] so also did Le Bon.[34] Pettee, on the other hand, dissents, but for a rather subtle reason: not because he considers the attitude of the armed forces insignificant, but because he feels that armies never fail to join revolutions when all other causes of revolution are present, and that they never fail to oppose them when this is not the case.[35] We could enlarge this point to read that internal wars are unlikely wherever the cohesion of an elite is intact, for the simple reason that insurgent formations require leadership and other skills, and are unlikely to obtain them on a large scale without some significant break in the ranks of an elite. Even if elites do not always "cause" their own downfall by becoming rigid or foreign to their people, they can certainly hasten their own demise by being internally at odds. From this standpoint, if not from that of Mosca's theory, elite cohesion is a factor which should be classified among the obstacles to internal war, as well as among its causes.

A final human obstacle to internal war—perhaps the greatest of all—is lack of wide popular support for rebellion. It seems generally accepted among modern writers on internal war, indeed it is the chief dogma of modern revolutionaries, that without great popular support the insurgents in an internal war can hardly hope to win (and with it are hardly likely to lose)—unless by means of a *coup d'état*. So vital is this factor that some writers think that the distinctive characteristic of internal war is the combination of violent techniques with psychological warfare, the latter designed, of course, to win the active support of the non-combatants; this is asserted in the much repeated pseudoformula of the French theorists of *guerre révolutionnaire:* revolutionary warfare = partisan war + psychological warfare.[36] To be sure, psychological warfare occurs nowadays also in international wars. Its role in these, however, is not nearly so crucial as in internal war; it is incidental in one case but seems to be decisive in the other.

One reason for this is that in internal wars, unlike international wars, there is generally a great disparity in capacity for military effort between the incumbents and insurgents. The former tend to be in a much stronger position—not always, of course, for this is where the loyalties of the established instrumentalities of violence enter the picture, but more often than not. The insurgents are therefore forced, in the normal case, to supplement their capabilities by taking what advantage they can of terrain and the cooperation of the non-combatant population. Like terrain itself, a well-disposed population affords a secure base of operations to rebels, as well as providing them with indispensable logistical support. Rebels who can count

[33] Trotsky, *The Russian Revolution,* 116.

[34] Gustave Le Bon, *The Psychology of Revolution* (New York, 1913), 29.

[35] G. S. Pettee, *The Process of Revolution,* 105.

[36] G. Bonnet, *Les guerres insurrectionelles* (Paris, 1958), 60. The point that in guerrilla warfare almost everything turns on popular support is argued in many sources, most strongly perhaps in C. A. Johnson, "Civilian Loyalties and Guerrilla Conflict", *World Politics,* July 1962.

on popular support can lose themselves in the population (according to Mao "the populace is for revolutionaries what water is for fish"), count on the population for secrecy (in wars in which intelligence is practically the whole art of defense), and reconstitute their forces by easy recruitment; if they can do all of these things, they can be practically certain of victory, short of a resort to genocide by the incumbents.

Great popular support is necessary also because internal wars, precisely because the common disparity of forces rules out quick victory by the insurgents (except by *coup*), tend to be long drawn out wars of attrition—perhaps better, either very prolonged or very quickly settled. In such wars, when victory always seems remote, when, at times, impasse is the best that can be hoped for, when the disruption of normal life is greater even than in external war, the morale of the revolutionaries, their ultimate trump card against their opponents, can hardly be sustained if they feel themselves isolated from their own people.

For all of these reasons, calculations about popular loyalties normally play a role in the decision to resort to political violence. The calculations may be mistaken but they are almost always made, sometimes, as in the case of the Algerian nationalist struggle, in ways approaching the survey research of social science.[37]

Toward an Etiology of Internal Wars

Needless to say, these arguments do not amount to anything like a finished etiology of internal wars. My concern here has been with preliminary, but fundamental and neglected, questions of strategy in theory-building, no more. Nevertheless, taking it all in all, this study does imply something more than that certain lines of inquiry are more promising than others in internal-war studies. When its arguments are added up, there emerges at least a considerable clue to the *form* that an adequate etiology of internal wars should take, even if little of a very specific nature can as yet be said about content. We have arrived at a paradigm, if not a fully-fledged theory.

Two points can serve as summary, as well as to spell out the nature of the paradigm I have in mind. One is that internal-war potential (the likelihood that internal war in some form will be precipitated)[38] should be conceived formally as a ratio between positive forces making for internal war and negative forces working against it—with the *possibility* that internal war of some kind may be fomented existing no matter what the overall potential, and the *probability* of its occurrence increasing as internal-war potential rises. This is certainly elementary, but it is in fact far more usual, in both general theories and specific interpretations of internal war, to speak of revolutionary or pacifying forces alone, and to depict rebelliousness as either absolutely present or absolutely lacking in societies. The other, and more important point, is that the forces involved should be conceived in both cases as functions of four factors. The positive forces are produced by the *inefficacy of elites* (lack of cohesion and of expected performance), *disorienting social processes* (delegitimization), *sub-*

[37] Interview with M. Chanderli, F. L. N. Observer at the United Nations, December, 1961.

[38] I stress internal-war *potential* because this is all one can assess if the actual occurrence of internal wars depends on precipitants beyond the scope of systematic analysis or even the predictive capacities engendered by practical wisdom. Needless to say, however, the actual occurrence of internal wars gives the best assurance that the societies concerned indeed had great internal-war potential.

version (attempts deliberately to activate disorientation, to form new political orientations and to impede the efficacy of elites), and the *facilities* available to potential insurgents. Countervailing these factors are four others: the *facilities* of incumbents, *effective repression* (not any kind of repression), *adjustive concessions* and *diversionary mechanisms*—the first referring to the incumbents' perceived capacity to fight if internal war occurs, the others to preventative actions.

This summation provides at least the minimum that one expects from paradigms: a formal approach to study and a checklist of factors that should be particularly considered whether one is interpreting specific cases or constructing general theory. But a minimum is not much. It is necessary to go further, particularly in the direction of determining the relative values of the factors and their relations to one another. After being stated, the variables must be ordered. Consequently, to conclude, I should like to add some suggestions that indicate how one might proceed from the mere cataloguing of promising variables toward their systematization.

In the first place, it seems, from what has been said about possible obstacles to internal war, that the negative forces vary within a much smaller range than the positive ones, so that beyond a point, internal-war potential can be reduced only with geometrically decreasing effectiveness, if at all. Take, for example, adjustive concessions. These cannot be indefinitely increased, for, in the end, they would be tantamount to surrender, and long before that point, would only serve to increase the insurgents' capabilities (not to mention the probable effects on the insurgents' demands and the incumbents' cohesion). Repression is intrinsically limited as well, among other reasons because it requires repressors and because its use will tend to intensify alienation; as in the case of concessions there may be an optimum of repression, but a maximum of it is as bad as none at all. And one can doubt the efficacy of diversions where disorientation is very widespread and goes very deep; besides, intrinsic limitations operate in the case of this factor too, for a society that lives on diversions to the extent of, say, the Roman Empire is for that very reason in decay. The factors that make for internal-war potential clearly are less inherently circumscribed. More clearly still, certain of them, like the crucial facility of popular support, belong to the realm of zero-sums, so that an increase of forces on the positive side implies a concomitant decrease on the other. In this sense, the variables involved in internal-war potential have a certain hierarchical order (an order of "potency"): one set is more significant than the other.

Such an order seems to exist within each set as well. For example, no one rebels simply because he has appropriate facilities—otherwise, the military and police would be everywhere and constantly in rebellion. At the very least, internal war presupposes some degree of subversion as well as brute capabilities. Subversion in turn, however, presupposes something that can be subverted—disorientations to activate and to reshape toward new legitimizations. And much evidence suggests that, whatever forces may be at work in a society, in whatever fashion, disorientation and subversion are both unlikely where the elite performs well, is highly cohesive, and is deeply enough attuned to the general spirit of social life to provide the mutualities and complementarities that settled social orientations require—granted that certain social processes make this extremely improbable. Per contra, elite inefficacy in itself always invites challenge, from within or without, no matter what other forces may be at work in the non-elite; in one form (incohesion), it implies the likelihood of internecine elite conflict, in others the probability of alienation of the non-elite. If disorientation arising from other sources is added, the brew obviously becomes more lethal (and its explosion tends to take a different form), with or without much concerted subversion. The latter, and insurgent facilities, are essentially extra additives, the more so since insurgents can hardly lack facilities on some scale where elite inefficacy and political disorientation are great; these factors may intensify internal-war potential, but do not create it.

The factors that reduce internal-war potential can be arranged (with rather more ambiguity, to be sure) in a similar order of potency. The essential criterion that establishes their weight is the extent to which they are intrinsically limited, either because they can become self-defeating or because they are zero-sums that do not allow increases on the positive side to be balanced by increases on the other. Diversions, while certainly not unlimited, are probably the most potent of the factors, for they can apparently be carried very far before they thoroughly devitalize societies. Repression and concessions seem to have a much lower optimum point. It is difficult at present to say which of them is the less potent; in all probability, however, it is repression—if only because concessions may increase the legitimation of authority among potential dissidents (that is, serve as surrogates for other kinds of elite "performance") while acts of repression, as well as being inherently self-denials of legitimacy, are well-tailored to cope only with the less potent factor of subversion. Incumbent facilities, finally, while being by all odds the most ambiguous factor, seem to belong somewhere between diversions on one hand and concessions on the other. The reasons for this are three: First, since the most vital of them are zero-sums, they can be, in a sense, either very weak or very potent, a decrease in them implying a corresponding increase in insurgent facilities and the reverse holding as well (a sort of inherent limitation different from that operating in the case of the other factors). Secondly, it seems, on the evidence, more difficult for incumbents to regain lost facilities (especially lost loyalties) than for insurgents to multiply their stock of them, even if "logical" reasons for this are not readily apparent. And thirdly, while an increase in incumbent facilities most clearly reduces one of the positive factors, that factor happens to be least potent of the four.

The catalogue of forces making for internal-war potentials thus takes on a certain preliminary order—even if this order is as yet far from precise.

A further element of order can be introduced into the list of variables by noting that, to an extent, they can be paired with one another, specific negative and positive forces being particularly closely related. This is manifest in the case of insurgent and incumbent facilities—clearest of all where the facilities in question are zero-sums. All else being equal, it is obviously not the absolute value of facilities on either side that matters, but the ratio of the facilities concerned. Just as obviously, as already stated, there is a special relation between subversion and repression. Disorientation or elite inefficacy can hardly be repressed; only subversion can.[39] Less manifestly, but pretty clearly still, adjustive concessions bear a particular relation to certain elite failures, particularly in performance, and diversions can, to an extent, provide gratifications that alleviate the psychic stresses of disorientation; but neither is likely to counteract anything else.

[39] To avoid misunderstanding, it should be clearly understood that repression here refers not to putting down rebels in internal wars but preventative actions by the incumbents.

One final point that bears more indirectly upon the ordering of the variables listed above requires consideration. It is an appropriate theme on which to conclude, for it is the point with which we started. Throughout the discussion, no distinction has been made between types of internal war, and this not without reasons.[40] The fact remains, however, that internal wars, although in some ways similar, are in most respects greatly various. An adequate etiology of internal wars should therefore be able to tell one more than whether internal war in some form will occur in a society. It should also enable one to account for the specific forms internal wars take in different circumstances.

Any discussion of this matter is at present greatly handicapped by the lack of a settled, well-constructed typology of internal wars—and constructing such a typology is a task great enough to require another, and rather extensive, study. This much can be said, however, without settling on specific typological categories: Approaching the etiological study of internal wars in the manner suggested here makes it possible to deal with the many different phenomena covered by the term internal war within a single theoretical framework, yet in a way that yields quite different accounts of clearly disparate events. And this is surely desirable where phenomena that differ in many respects have also much in common.

The point is that two things can be done with the paradigm I have sketched. By weighing the general balance of positive and negative forces, one can arrive at an assessment of the overall degree of internal-war potential in a society. By considering the *particular* forces, combinations of forces, and ratios of forces that are strong or weak—the forces that are especially instrumental in determining the overall result—one can arrive at definite ideas of what kinds of internal war are likely to occur (quite apart from the possibility that the general degree of internal-war potential may itself set limits to the varieties that internal war can take). For example, where elite inefficacy, especially incohesion, greatly predominates among the positive forces, something like what many have called palace revolution is a very likely result. Where disorientation is very great but other positive factors are negligible, one might expect relatively unorganized, sporadic rioting as the normal response. Where subversion looms large relative to other factors, *coups*, *Putsches* or terrorism are more likely. Where incumbent and insurgent facilities are rather equally matched and elite cohesion is particularly tenuous, the stage is probably set for full-scale civil war. One could, in fact, contrive a useful, although very complex, typology of internal wars by working out probable results for the various possible constellations of factors included in the paradigm; and one could similarly take any typology otherwise worked out and produce for it a set of appropriately corresponding combinations of the factors.

The signal advantage of this procedure is that it avoids what defaces the whole corpus of historical studies of internal war available to us, the *ad hoc* piling up of unrelated theories, and prevents also the most conspicuous flaw of unhistorical, abstract models of revolutionary processes, the disregarding of special forces in particular cases. As well, the procedure I suggest can deal coherently with another eminently historical and theoretical matter, the transformation of many internal wars in the course of their development—the revolutionary "process". It can do so simply by applying typological theories dynamically. For the constellations of forces

[40] See above [pp. 18–21].

that provide initial impetus to internal wars are likely to undergo constant transformation in their course, much as such constellations may vary in the pre-revolutionary period. Subversion may become more intense, more purposeful; the balance of facilities may shift; incumbent elites may become more cohesive or disunited under fire; mild disorientation may become severe as authority is challenged and society disrupted by violence; the insurgents may win power, but at the cost of their own cohesion and without being able to provide effective new legitimations—and thus internal wars may proceed from stage to stage, from type to type, in unique or characteristic, continuous or spasmodic, dynamic patterns.

Lawrence Stone, Professor of History at Princeton University, is an English scholar who has written especially on the crisis of the aristocracy in seventeenth-century England.

Theories of Revolution

LAWRENCE STONE *

In attacking the problem of revolution, as most others of major significance in history, we historians should think twice before we spurn the help offered by our colleagues in the social sciences, who have, as it happens, been particularly active in the last few years in theorizing about the typology, causes, and evolutionary patterns of this particular phenomenon. The purpose of this article is not to advance any new hypothesis, but to provide a summary view and critical examination of the work that has been going on.

The first necessity in any inquiry is a careful definition of terms: what is, and what is not, a revolution? According to one view, it is change, effected by the use of violence, in government, and/or regime, and/or society.[1] By *society* is meant the consciousness and the mechanics of communal solidarity, which may be tribal, peasant, kinship, national, and so on; by *regime* is meant the constitutional structure—democracy, oligarchy, monarchy; and by *government* is meant specific political and administrative institutions. Violence, it should be noted, is not the same as force; it is force used with unnecessary

From *World Politics,* Vol. XVIII, No. 2 (January, 1966), pp. 159–76.

* I am grateful to Professors Cyril E. Black, Arno J. Mayer, and John W. Shy for some very helpful criticisms of this article.

[1] Chalmers Johnson, *Revolution and the Social System,* Hoover Institution Studies 3 (Stanford 1964).

intensity, unpredictably, and usually destructively.[2] This definition of revolution is a very broad one, and two historians of the French Revolution, Crane Brinton and Louis Gottschalk, would prefer to restrict the use of the word to the major political and social upheavals with which they are familiar, the "Great Revolutions" as George S. Pettee calls them.[3]

Even the wider definition allows the historian to distinguish between the seizure of power that leads to a major restructuring of government or society and the replacement of the former elite by a new one, and the coup d'état involving no more than a change of ruling personnel by violence or threat of violence. This latter is the norm in Latin America, where it occurred thirty-one times in the ten years 1945–1955. Merle Kling has arrived at a suggestive explanation of this Latin American phenomenon of chronic political instability, limited but frequent use of violence, and almost complete lack of social or institutional change. He argues that ownership of the principal economic resources, both agricultural and mineral, is concentrated in the hands of a tiny, very stable, elite of enormously wealthy monoculture landlords and mining capitalists. This elite is all-powerful and cannot be attacked by opposition groups within the country; externally, however, it is dependent on foreign interests for its markets and its capital. In this colonial situation of a foreign-supported closed plutocracy, the main avenue of rapid upward social mobility for nonmembers of the elite leads, via the army, to the capture of the government machine, which is the only accessible source of wealth and power. This political instability is permitted by the elite on the condition that its own interests are undisturbed. Instability, limited violence, and the absence of social or institutional change are therefore all the product of the contradiction between the realities of a colonial economy run by a plutocracy and the facade of political sovereignty—between the real, stable power of the economic elite and the nominal, unstable control of politicians and generals.[4]

The looser definition of revolution thus suits both historians of major social change and historians of the palace coup. It does, however, raise certain difficulties. Firstly, there is a wide range of changes of government by violence which are neither a mere substitution of personalities in positions of power nor a prelude to the restructuring of society; secondly, conservative counterrevolutions become almost impossible to fit into the model; and lastly, it remains hard to distinguish between colonial wars, civil wars, and social revolution.

To avoid these difficulties, an alternative formulation has recently been put forward by a group of social scientists working mainly at Princeton. They have dropped the word "revolution" altogether and put "internal war" in its place.[5] This is defined as any attempt to alter state policy, rulers, or institutions by the use of violence, in societies where violent competition is not the norm and where well-defined institu-

[2] Sheldon S. Wolin, "Violence and the Western Political Tradition," *American Journal of Orthopsychiatry,* XXXIII (January 1963), 15–28.

[3] Brinton, *The Anatomy of Revolution* (New York 1938); Gottschalk, "Causes of Revolution," *American Journal of Sociology,* L (July 1944), 1–8; Pettee, *The Process of Revolution* (New York 1938).

[4] "Toward a Theory of Power and Political Instability in Latin America," *Western Political Quarterly,* IX (1956).

[5] Harry Eckstein, ed., *Internal War* (New York 1964), and "On the Etiology of Internal War," *History and Theory,* IV, No. 2 (1965), 133–63. I am grateful to Mr. Eckstein for allowing me to read this article before publication.

tional patterns exist.[6] This concept seems to be a logical consequence of the pre-occupation of sociologists in recent years with a model of society in a stable, self-regulating state of perpetual equipoise. In this utopian world of universal harmony, all forms of violent conflict are anomalies, to be treated alike as pathological disorders of a similar species. This is a model which, although it has its uses for analytical purposes, bears little relation to the reality familiar to the historian. It looks to a society without change, with universal consensus on values, with complete social harmony, and isolated from external threats; no approximation to such a society has ever been seen. An alternative model, which postulates that all societies are in a condition of multiple and perpetual tension held in check by social norms, ideological beliefs, and state sanctions, accords better with historical fact, as some sociologists are now beginning to realize.[7]

The first objection to the all-embracing formula of internal war is that, by covering all forms of physical conflict from strikes and terrorism to civil war, it isolates the use of violence from the normal processes of societal adjustment. Though some of the users of the term express their awareness that the use of violence for political ends is a fairly common occurrence, the definition they have established in fact excludes all times and places where it *is* common. It thus cuts out most societies the world has ever known, including Western Europe in the Middle Ages and Latin America today. Secondly, it isolates one particular means, physical violence, from the political ends that it is designed to serve. Clausewitz's famous definition of external war is equally applicable to internal war, civil war, or revolution: "War is not only a political act, but a real political instrument; a continuation of political transactions, an accomplishment of them by different means. That which remains peculiar to war relates only to the peculiar nature of its means." [8]

It is perfectly true that any means by which society exercises pressure or control, whether it is administrative organization, constitutional law, economic interest, or physical force, can be a fruitful field of study in its own right, so long as its students remain aware that they are looking at only one part of a larger whole. It is also true that there is something peculiar about violence, if only because of man's highly ambivalent attitude towards the killing of his own species. Somehow, he regards physical force as different in kind from, say, economic exploitation or psychological manipulation as a means of exercising power over others. But this distinction is not one of much concern to the historian of revolution, in which violence is a normal and natural occurrence. The concept of internal war is too broad in its comprehension of all types of violence from civil wars to strikes, too narrow in its restriction to normally non-violent societies, too limited in its concern with one of many means, too arbitrary in its separation of this means from the ends in view, and too little concerned with the complex roots of social

[6] The formula has been used by a historian, Peter Paret, in *Internal War and Pacification: The Vendée, 1793–96* (Princeton 1961).

[7] Barrington Moore, "The Strategy of the Social Sciences," in his *Political Power and Social Theory* (Cambridge, Mass., 1958); Ralph Dahrendorf, "Out of Utopia: Toward a Reorientation of Sociological Analysis," *American Journal of Sociology,* LXIV (September 1958), 115–27; C. Wright Mills, *The Sociological Imagination* (New York 1959); Wilbert E. Moore, *Social Change* (Englewood Cliffs 1963). It should be noted that both the equilibrium and the conflict views of society have very respectable ancestries. The equilibrium model goes back to Rousseau—or perhaps Aquinas; the conflict model to Hobbes, Hegel, and Marx.

[8] Quoted in Edward Mead Earle, ed., *Makers of Modern Strategy* (Princeton 1943), 104–5.

unrest to be of much practical value to him.

The most fruitful typology of revolution is that of Chalmers Johnson, set out in a pamphlet that deserves to be widely read.[9] He sees six types, identified by the targets selected for attack, whether the government personnel, the political regime, or the community as a social unit; by the nature of the carriers of revolution, whether a mass or an elite; and particularly by the goals and the ideologies, whether reformist, eschatological, nostalgic, nation-forming, elitist, or nationalist. The first type, the *Jacquerie,* is a spontaneous mass peasant rising, usually carried out in the name of the traditional authorities, Church and King, and with the limited aims of purging the local or national elites. Examples are the Peasant Revolt of 1381, Ket's Rebellion of 1549, and the Pugachev rebellion in Russia in 1773–1775. The second type, the *Millenarian Rebellion,* is similar to the first but with the added feature of a utopian dream, inspired by a living messiah. This type can be found at all times, in all parts of the world, from the Florentine revolution led by Savonarola in 1494, to the Anabaptist Rebellion in Münster led by John Mathijs and John Beukels in 1533–1535, to the Sioux Ghost-Dance Rebellion inspired by the Paiute prophet Wovoka in 1890. It has attracted a good deal of attention from historians in recent years, partly because the career of Hitler offered overwhelming proof of the enormous historical significance of a charismatic leader, and partly because of a growing interest in the ideas of Max Weber.[10] The third type is the *Anarchistic Rebellion,* the nostalgic reaction to progressive change, involving a romantic idealization of the old order: the Pilgrimage of Grace and the Vendée are examples.

The fourth is that very rare phenomenon, the *Jacobin Communist Revolution.* This has been defined as "a sweeping fundamental change in political organization, social structure, economic property control and the predominant myth of a social order, thus indicating a major break in the continuity of development." [11] This type of revolution can occur only in a highly centralized state with good communications and a large capital city, and its target is government, regime, and society—the lot. The result is likely to be the creation of a new national consciousness under centralized, military authority, and the erection of a more rational, and hence more efficient, social and bureaucratic order on the ruins of the old ramshackle structure of privilege, nepotism, and corruption.

The fifth type is the *Conspiratorial Coup d'État,* the planned work of a tiny elite fired by an oligarchic, sectarian ideology. This qualifies as a revolutionary type only if it in fact anticipates mass movement and inaugurates social change—for example the Nasser revolution in Egypt or the Castro revolution in Cuba; it is thus clearly distinguished from the palace revolt, assassination, dynastic succession-conflict, strike, banditry, and other forms of violence, which are all subsumed under the "internal war" rubric.

Finally, there is the *Militarized Mass Insurrection,* a new phenomenon of the twentieth century in that it is a deliberately planned mass revolutionary war,

[9] *Revolution and the Social System.*

[10] N. R. C. Cohn, *Pursuit of the Millennium* (New York 1961); Eric J. Hobsbawm, *Primitive Rebels* (Manchester 1959); S. L. Thrupp, *Millennial Dreams in Action,* Supplement II, Comparative Studies in Society and History (The Hague 1962); A. J. F. Köbben, "Prophetic Movements as an Expression of Social Protest," *Internationales Archiv für Ethnographie,* XLIX, No. 1 (1960), 117–64.

[11] Sigmund Neumann, quoted in Chalmers, 2.

guided by a dedicated elite. The outcome of guerrilla warfare is determined by political attitudes, not military strategy or matériel, for the rebels are wholly dependent on broad popular support. In all cases on record, the ideology that attracts the mass following has been a combination of xenophobic nationalism and Marxism, with by far the greater stress on the former. This type of struggle has occurred in Yugoslavia, China, Algeria, and Vietnam.

Although, like any schematization of the historical process, this sixfold typology is concerned with ideal types, although in practice individual revolutions may sometimes display characteristics of several different types, the fact remains that this is much the most satisfactory classification we have so far; it is one that working historians can recognize and use with profit. The one obvious criticism is semantic, an objection to the use of the phrase "Jacobin Communist Revolution." Some of Johnson's examples are Communist, such as the Russian or Chinese Revolutions; others are Jacobin but not Communist, such as the French Revolution or the Turkish Revolution of 1908–1922. It would be better to revert to Pettee's category of "Great Revolutions," and treat Communist revolutions as a subcategory, one type, but not the only type, of modernizing revolutionary process.

Given this classification and definition of revolution, what are its root causes? Here everyone is agreed in making a sharp distinction between long-run, underlying causes—the preconditions, which create a potentially explosive situation and can be analyzed on a comparative basis—and immediate, incidental factors—the precipitants, which trigger the outbreak and which may be nonrecurrent, personal, and fortuitous. This effectively disposes of the objections of those historians whose antipathy to conceptual schematization takes the naïve form of asserting the uniqueness of each historical event.

One of the first in the field of model-building was Crane Brinton who, as long ago as 1938, put forward a series of uniformities common to the four great Western revolutions: English, French, American, and Russian. These included an economically advancing society, growing class and status antagonisms, an alienated intelligentsia, a psychologically insecure and politically inept ruling class, and a governmental financial crisis.[12]

The subjectivity, ambiguity, and partial self-contradiction of this and other analyses of the causes of specific revolutions—for example the French Revolution—have been cruelly shown up by Harry Eckstein.[13] He has pointed out that commonly adduced hypotheses run the spectrum of particular conditions, moving from the intellectual (inadequate political socialization, conflicting social myths, a corrosive social philosophy, alienation of the intellectuals) to the economic (increasing poverty, rapid growth, imbalance between production and distribution, long-term growth plus short-term recession) to the social (resentment due to restricted elite circulation, confusion due to excessive elite recruitment, anomie due to excessive social mobility, conflict due to the rise of new social classes) to the political (bad government, divided government, weak government, oppressive government). Finally there are explanations on the level of general process, such as rapid social change, erratic social change, or a lack of harmony between the state structure and society, the rulers and the ruled. None of these explanations are invalid in themselves, but

[12] *Anatomy of Revolution.*

[13] "On the Etiology of Internal War."

they are often difficult or impossible to reconcile one with the other, and are so diverse in their range and variety as to be virtually impossible to fit into an ordered analytical framework. What, then, is to be done?

Fundamental to all analyses, whether by historians like Brinton and Gottschalk or by political scientists like Johnson and Eckstein, is the recognition of a lack of harmony between the social system on the one hand and the political system on the other. This situation Johnson calls *dysfunction,* a word derived from the structural-functional equilibrium model of the sociologists. This dysfunction may have many causes, some of which are merely cyclical, such as may develop because of personal weaknesses in hereditary kingships or single-party regimes. In these cases, the revolution will not take on serious proportions, and will limit itself to attacks on the governing institutions, leaving regime and society intact. In most cases, however, including all those of real importance, the dysfunction is the result of some new and developing process, as a result of which certain social subsystems find themselves in a condition of relative deprivation. Rapid economic growth, imperial conquest, new metaphysical beliefs, and important technological changes are the four commonest factors involved, in that order. If the process of change is sufficiently slow and sufficiently moderate, the dysfunction may not rise to dangerous levels. Alternatively, the elite may adjust to the new situation with sufficient rapidity and skill to ride out the storm and retain popular confidence. But if the change is both rapid and profound, it may cause the sense of deprivation, alienation, anomie to spread into many sectors of society at once, causing what Johnson calls multiple dysfunction, which may be all but incurable within the existing political system.

In either case the second vital element in creating a revolutionary situation is the condition and attitude of the entrenched elite, a factor on which Eckstein rightly lays great stress. The elite may lose its manipulative skill, or its military superiority, or its self-confidence, or its cohesion; it may become estranged from the nonelite, or overwhelmed by a financial crisis; it may be incompetent, or weak, or brutal. Any combination of two or more of these features will be dangerous. What is ultimately fatal, however, is the compounding of its errors by intransigence. If it fails to anticipate the need for reform, if it blocks all peaceful, constitutional means of social adjustment, then it unites the various deprived elements in single-minded opposition to it, and drives them down the narrow road to violence. It is this process of polarization into two coherent groups or alliances of what are naturally and normally a series of fractional and shifting tensions and conflicts within a society that both Peter Amman and Wilbert Moore see as the essential preliminary to the outbreak of a Jacobin Revolution.[14] To conclude, therefore, revolution becomes *possible* when a condition of multiple dysfunction meets an intransigent elite: just such a conjunction occurred in the decades immediately before the English, the French, and the Russian Revolutions.

Revolution only becomes *probable* (Johnson might say "certain"), however, if certain special factors intervene: the "precipitants" or "accelerators." Of these, the three most common are the emergence of an inspired leader or prophet; the formation of a secret, military, revolutionary organization; and the crushing defeat of the armed forces in foreign war. This last is of critical

[14] Amman, "Revolution: A Redefinition," *Political Science Quarterly,* LXXVII (1962).

importance since it not only shatters the prestige of the ruling elite, but also undermines the morale and discipline of the soldiers and thus opens the way to the violent overthrow of the existing government.

The first defect of Johnson's model is that it concentrates too much on objective structural conditions, and attempts to relate conditions directly to action. In fact, however, as Eckstein points out, there is no such direct relationship; historians can point to similar activity arising from different conditions, and different activity arising from similar conditions. Standing between objective reality and action are subjective human attitudes. A behaviorist approach such as Brinton's, which lays equal stress on such things as anomie, alienation of the intellectuals, frustrated popular aspirations, elite estrangement, and loss of elite self-confidence, is more likely to produce a satisfactory historical explanation than is one that sticks to the objective social reality. Secondly, Johnson leaves too little play for the operation of the unique and the personal. He seems to regard his accelerators as automatic triggers, ignoring the area of unpredictable personal choice that is always left to the ruling elite and to the revolutionary leaders, even in a situation of multiple dysfunction exacerbated by an accelerator. Revolution is never inevitable—or rather the only evidence of its inevitability is that it actually happens. Consequently the only way to prove this point is to indulge in just the kind of hypothetical argument that historians prudently try to avoid. But it is still just possible that modernization may take place in Morocco and India without revolution. The modernization and industrialization of Germany and Britain took place without revolution in the nineteenth century (though it can be argued that in the latter case the process was slow by twentieth-century standards, and that, as is now becoming all too apparent, the modernization was far from complete). Some think that a potentially revolutionary situation in the United States in the 1930's was avoided by political action.

Lastly it is difficult to fit into the Johnson model the fact that political actions taken to remedy dysfunction often themselves precipitate change. This produces the paradoxical hypothesis that measures designed to restore equilibrium in fact upset equilibrium. Because he begins with his structural-functional equilibrium model, Johnson is a victim of the fallacy of intended consequences. As often as not in history it is the *unintended* consequences that really matter: to mention but one example, it was Louis XVI's belated and half-hearted attempts at reform that provoked the aristocratic reaction, which in turn opened the way to the bourgeois, the peasant, and the sansculotte revolutions. Finally the dysfunction concept is not altogether easy to handle in a concrete historical case. If societies are regarded as being in a constant state of multiple tension, then some degree of dysfunction is always present. Some group is always in a state of relative deprivation due to the inevitable process of social change.

Recognition of this fact leads Eckstein to point out the importance of forces working *against* revolution. Historians, particularly those formed in the Western liberal tradition, are reluctant to admit that ruthless, efficient repression—as opposed to bumbling, half-hearted repression—involving the physical destruction of leading revolutionaries and effective control of the media of communication, can crush incipient revolutionary movements. Repression is particularly effective when governments know what to look for, when they have before their eyes the unfortunate example of other governments overthrown by revolutionaries elsewhere. Reaction, in fact, is just as infectious as revolution. Moreover diversion of energy and attention to successful—as opposed to unsuccessful—foreign war can ward off serious internal trouble. Quietist—as opposed to activist—religious movements may serve as the opiate of the people, as Halévy suggested about Methodism in England. Bread and circuses may distract popular attention. Timely—as opposed to untimely—political concessions may win over moderate opinion and isolate the extremists.

Basing himself on this suggestive analysis, Eckstein produces a paradigm for universal application. He sees four positive variables—elite inefficiency, disorienting social process, subversion, and available rebel facilities—and four negative variables—diversionary mechanisms, available incumbent facilities, adjustive mechanisms, and effective repression. Each type of internal war, and each step of each type, can, he suggests, be explained in terms of these eight variables. While this may be true, it is fair to point out that some of the variables are themselves the product of more deep-seated factors, others mere questions of executive action that may be determined by the accidents of personality. Disruptive social process is a profound cause; elite inefficiency a behavior pattern; effective repression a function of will; facilities the by-product of geography. One objection to the Eckstein paradigm is therefore that it embraces different levels of explanation and fails to maintain the fundamental distinction between preconditions and precipitants. Secondly, it concentrates on the factors working for or against the successful manipulation of violence rather than on the underlying factors working to produce a revolutionary potential. This is because the paradigm is intended to apply to all forms of internal war rather than to revolution proper, and because all that the various forms of internal war have in common is the use of violence. It is impossible to tell how serious these criticisms are until the paradigm has been applied to a particular historical revolution. Only then will its value become apparent.

If we take the behaviorist approach, then a primary cause of revolutions is the emergence of an obsessive revolutionary mentality. But how closely does this relate to the objective material circumstances themselves? In every revolutionary situation one finds a group of men—fanatics, extremists, zealots—so convinced of their own righteousness and of the urgent need to create a new Jerusalem on earth (whether formally religious or secular in inspiration is irrelevant) that they are prepared to smash through the normal restraints of habit, custom, and convention. Such men were the seventeenth-century English Puritans, the eighteenth-century French Jacobins, the twentieth-century Russian Bolsheviks. But what makes such men is far from certain. What generates such ruthlessness in curbing evil, such passion for discipline and order? Rapid social mobility, both horizontal and vertical, and particularly urbanization, certainly produces a sense of rootlessness and anxiety. In highly stratified societies, even some of the newly-risen elements may find themselves under stress.[15] While some of the *arrivistes* are happily absorbed in their new strata, others remain uneasy and resentful. If they are snubbed and rebuffed by the older members of the status group to which they aspire by reason of their new wealth and position, they are likely to become acutely conscious of their social inferiority, and may be driven either to adopt a pose *plus royaliste que le Roi* or to dream of destroying the whole social order. In

[15] Emile Durkheim, *Suicide* (Glencoe 1951), 246–54; A. B. Hollingshead, R. Ellis, and E. Kirby, "Social Mobility and Mental Illness," *American Sociological Review*, XIX (1954).

the latter case they may try to allay their sense of insecurity by imposing their norms and values by force upon society at large. This is especially the case if there is available a moralistic ideology like Puritanism or Marxism to which they can attach themselves, and which provides them with unshakable confidence in their own rectitude.

But why does the individual react in this particular way rather than another? Some would argue that the character of the revolutionary is formed by sudden ideological conversion in adolescence or early adult life (to Puritanism, Jacobinism, or Bolshevism) as a refuge from this anxiety state.[16] What is not acceptable is the fashionable conservative cliché that the revolutionary and the reformer are merely the chance product of unfortunate psychological difficulties in childhood. It is possible that this is the mechanism by which such feelings are generated, though there is increasing evidence of the continued plasticity of human character until at any rate post-adolescence. The main objection to this theory is that it fails to explain why these particular attitudes become common only in certain classes and age groups at certain times and in certain places. This failure strongly suggests that the cause of this state of mind lies not in the personal maladjustment of the individuals or their parents, but in the social conditions that created that maladjustment. Talcott Parsons treats disaffection or "alienation" as a generalized phenomenon that may manifest itself in crime, alcoholism, drug addiction, daytime fantasies, religious enthusiasm, or serious political agitation. To use Robert Merton's formulation, Ritualism and Retreatism are two possible psychological escape-routes; Innovation and Rebellion two others.[17]

Even if we accept this behaviorist approach (which I do), the fact remains that many of the underlying causes both of the alienation of the revolutionaries and of the weakness of the incumbent elite are economic in origin; and it is in this area that some interesting work has centered. In particular a fresh look has been taken at the contradictory models of Marx and de Tocqueville, the one claiming that popular revolution is a product of increasing misery, the other that it is a product of increasing prosperity.

Two economists, Sir Arthur Lewis and Mancur Olson, have pointed out that because of their basic social stability, both preindustrial and highly industrialized societies are relatively free from revolutionary disturbance.[18] In the former societies, people accept with little question the accepted rights and obligations of family, class, and caste. Misery, oppression, and social injustice are passively endured as inevitable features of life on earth. It is in societies experiencing rapid economic growth that the trouble usually occurs. Lewis, who is thinking mostly about the newly emerging countries, primarily of Africa, regards the sense of frustration that leads to revolution as a consequence of the dislocation of the old status patterns by the emergence of four new classes—the proletariat, the capitalist employers, the urban commercial and professional middle class, and the professional politicians—and of the disturbance of the

[16] Michael L. Walzer, "Puritanism as a Revolutionary Ideology," *History and Theory*, III, No. 1 (1963), 59–90.

[17] Parsons, *The Social System* (Glencoe 1951); Merton, *Social Theory and Social Structure* (Glencoe 1957), chap. 4.

[18] W. Arthur Lewis, "Commonwealth Address," in *Conference Across a Continent* (Toronto 1963), 46–60; Olson, "Rapid Growth as a Destabilizing Force," *Journal of Economic History*, XXIII (December 1963), 529–52. I am grateful to Mr. Olson for drawing my attention to Sir Arthur Lewis's article, and for some helpful suggestions.

old income patterns by the sporadic and patchy impact of economic growth, which creates new wealth and new poverty in close and conspicuous juxtaposition. Both phenomena he regards as merely transitional, since in a country fully developed economically there are strong tendencies toward the elimination of inequalities of opportunity, income, and status.

This model matches fairly well the only detailed analysis of a historical revolution in which a conscious effort has been made to apply modern sociological methods. In his recent study of the Vendée, Charles Tilly argues that a counterrevolutionary situation was the consequence of special tensions created by the immediate juxtaposition of, on one hand, parish clergy closely identified with the local communities, great absentee landlords, and old-fashioned subsistence farming, and, on the other, a large-scale textile industry on the putting-out system and increasing bourgeois competition.[19] Though the book is flawed by a tendency to take a ponderous sociological hammer to crack a simple little historical nut, it is nonetheless a suggestive example of the application of new hypotheses and techniques to historical material.

Olson has independently developed a more elaborate version of the Lewis theory. He argues that revolutionaries are déclassé and freed from the social bonds of family, profession, village or manor; and that these individuals are the product of rapid economic growth, which creates both *nouveaux riches* and *nouveaux pauvres*. The former, usually middle-class and urban artisans, are better off economically, but are disoriented, rootless, and restless; the latter may be workers whose wages have failed to keep pace with inflation, workers in technologically outdated and therefore declining industries, or the unemployed in a society in which the old cushions of the extended family and the village have gone, and in which the new cushion of social security has not yet been created. The initial growth phase may well cause a decline in the standard of living of the majority because of the need for relatively enormous forced savings for reinvestment. The result is a revolution caused by the widening gap between expectations—social and political for the new rich, economic for the new poor—and the realities of everyday life.

A sociologist, James C. Davis, agrees with Olson that the fundamental impetus toward a revolutionary situation is generated by rapid economic growth but he associates such growth with a generally rising rather than a generally falling standard of living, and argues that the moment of potential revolution is reached only when the long-term phase of growth is followed by a short-term phase of economic stagnation or decline.[20] The result of this "J-curve," as he calls it, is that steadily soaring expectations, newly created by the period of growth, shoot further and further ahead of actual satisfaction of needs. Successful revolution is the work neither of the destitute nor of the well-satisfied, but of those whose actual situation is improving less rapidly than they expect.

These economic models have much in common, and their differences can be explained by the fact that Lewis and Olson are primarily concerned with the long-term economic forces creating instability, and Davis with the short-term economic factors that may precipitate a crisis. Moreover their analyses apply to different kinds of economic growth, of

[19] *The Vendée* (Cambridge, Mass., 1964).

[20] "Toward a Theory of Revolution," *American Sociological Review*, XXVII (February 1962), 1–19, esp. the graph on p. 6.

which three have recently been identified by W. W. Rostow and Barry Supple: there is the expansion of production in a pre-industrial society, which may not cause any important technological, ideological, social, or political change; there is the phase of rapid growth, involving major changes of every kind; and there is the sustained trend toward technological maturity.[21] Historians have been quick to see that these models, particularly that of Rostow, can be applied only to a limited number of historical cases. The trouble is not so much that in any specific case the phases—particularly the last two—tend to merge into one another, but that changes in the various sectors occur at irregular and unexpected places on the time-scale in different societies. Insofar as there is any validity in the division of the stages of growth into these three basic types, the revolutionary model of Olson and Lewis is confined to the second; that of Davis is applicable to all three.

The Davis model fits the history of Western Europe quite well, for it looks as if in conditions of extreme institutional and ideological rigidity the first type of economic growth may produce frustrations of a very serious kind. Revolutions broke out all over Europe in the 1640's, twenty years after a secular growth phase had come to an end.[22] C. E. Labrousse has demonstrated the existence of a similar economic recession in France from 1778,[23] and from 1914 the Russian economy was dislocated by the war effort after many years of rapid growth. Whatever its limitations in any particular situation, the J-curve of actual satisfaction of needs is an analytical tool that historians can usefully bear in mind as they probe the violent social upheavals of the past.

As de Tocqueville pointed out, this formula of advance followed by retreat is equally applicable to other sectors. Trouble arises if a phase of liberal governmental concessions is followed by a phase of political repression; a phase of fairly open recruitment channels into the elite followed by a phase of aristocratic reaction and a closing of ranks; a phase of weakening status barriers by a phase of reassertion of privilege. The J-curve is applicable to other than purely economic satisfactions, and the apex of the curve is the point at which underlying causes, the preconditions, merge with immediate factors, the precipitants. The recipe for revolution is thus the creation of new expectations by economic improvement and some social and political reforms, followed by economic recession, governmental reaction, and aristocratic resurgence, which widen the gap between expectations and reality.

All these attempts to relate dysfunction to relative changes in economic prosperity and aspirations are hampered by two things, of which the first is the extreme difficulty in ascertaining the facts. It is never easy to discover precisely what is happening to the distribution of wealth in a given society. Even now, even in highly developed Western societies with massive bureaucratic controls and quantities of statistical data, there is no agreement about the facts. Some years ago it was confidently believed that in both Britain and the United States incomes were being levelled, and that extremes of both wealth and poverty were being steadily eliminated. Today, no one quite knows

[21] Rostow, *The Stages of Economic Growth* (Cambridge, Mass., 1960); Supple, *The Experience of Economic Growth* (New York 1963), 11–12.

[22] Hobsbawm, "The Crisis of the Seventeenth Century," in T. H. Aston, ed., *Crisis in Europe, 1560–1660* (London 1965), 5–58.

[23] *La Crise de l'Économie française à la fin de l'Ancien Régime et au début de la Révolution* (Paris 1944).

what is happening in either country.[24] And if this is true now, still more is it true of societies in the past about which the information is fragmentary and unreliable.

Secondly, even if they can be clearly demonstrated, economic trends are only one part of the problem. Historians are increasingly realizing that the psychological responses to changes in wealth and power are not only not precisely related to, but are politically more significant than, the material changes themselves. As Marx himself realized at one stage, dissatisfaction with the status quo is not determined by absolute realities but by relative expectations. "Our desires and pleasures spring from society; we measure them, therefore, by society, and not by the objects which serve for their satisfaction. Because they are of a social nature, they are of a relative nature." [25] Frustration may possibly result from a rise and subsequent relapse in real income. But it is perhaps more likely to be caused by a rise in aspirations that outstrips the rise in real income; or by a rise in the *relative* economic position in society of the group in question, followed by a period in which its real income continues to grow, but less fast than that of other groups around it. Alternatively it may represent a rise and then decline of status, largely unrelated to real income; or if status and real income are related, it may be inversely. For example, social scientists seeking to explain the rise of the radical right in the United States in the early 1950's and again in the early 1960's attribute it to a combination of great economic prosperity and an aggravated sense of insecurity of status.[26] Whether or not this is a general formula for right-wing rather than left-wing revolutionary movements is not yet clear.

Moreover the problem is further complicated by an extension of the reference-group theory.[27] Human satisfaction is related not to existing conditions but to the condition of a social group against which the individual measures his situation. In an age of mass communications and the wide distribution of cheap radio receivers even among the impoverished illiterate of the world, knowledge of high consumption standards elsewhere spreads rapidly, and as a result the reference group may be in another, more highly developed, country or even continent. Under these circumstances, revolutionary conditions may be created before industrialization has got properly under way.

The last area in which some new theoretical work has been done is in the formulation of hypotheses about the social stages of a "Great Revolution." One of the best attacks on this problem was made by Crane Brinton, who was thinking primarily about the French Revolution, but who extended his comparisons to the three other major Western revolutionary movements. He saw the first phase as dominated by moderate bourgeois elements; their supersession by the radicals; a reign of terror; a Thermidorian reaction; and the establishment of strong central authority under military rule to consolidate the limited gains of the revolution. In terms of mass psychology he compared revolution with a fever that rises in intensity, affecting nearly all parts of the body politic, and then dies away.

A much cruder and more elementary model has been advanced by an historian of the revolutions of 1848, Peter

[24] Gabriel Kolko, *Wealth and Power in America* (New York 1962); Richard M. Titmuss, *Income Distribution and Social Change* (London 1962).

[25] Davis, 5, quoting Marx, *Selected Works in Two Volumes* (Moscow 1955), I, 947.

[26] Daniel Bell, ed., *The Radical Right* (Garden City 1963).

[27] Merton, chap. 9.

Amman.[28] He sees the modern state as an institution holding a monopoly of physical force, administration, and justice over a wide area, a monopoly dependent more on habits of obedience than on powers of coercion. Revolution may therefore be defined as a breakdown of the monopoly due to a failure of these habits of obedience. It begins with the emergence of two or more foci of power, and ends with the elimination of all but one. Amman includes the possibility of "suspended revolution," with the existence of two or more foci not yet in violent conflict.

This model admittedly avoids some of the difficulties raised by more elaborate classifications of revolution: how to distinguish a coup d'état from a revolution; how to define the degrees of social change; how to accommodate the conservative counterrevolution, and so on. It certainly offers some explanation of the progress of revolution from stage to stage as the various power blocs that emerge on the overthrow of the incumbent regime are progressively eliminated; and it explains why the greater the public participation in the revolution, the wider the break with the habits of obedience, and therefore the slower the restoration of order and centralized authority. But it throws the baby out with the bathwater. It is impossible to fit any decentralized traditional society, or any modern federal society, into the model. Moreover, even where it might be applicable, it offers no framework for analyzing the roots of revolution, no pointers for identifying the foci of power, no means of distinguishing between the various revolutionary types, and its notion of "suspended revolution" is little more than verbal evasion.

Though it is set out in a somewhat confused, overelaborate, and unnecessarily abstract form, the most convincing description of the social stages of revolution is that outlined by Rex D. Hopper.[29] He sees four stages. The first is characterized by indiscriminate, uncoordinated mass unrest and dissatisfaction, the result of dim recognition that traditional values no longer satisfy current aspirations. The next stage sees this vague unease beginning to coalesce into organized opposition with defined goals, an important characteristic being a shift of allegiance by the intellectuals from the incumbents to the dissidents, the advancement of an "evil men" theory, and its abandonment in favor of an "evil institutions" theory. At this stage there emerge two types of leaders: the prophet, who sketches the shape of the new utopia upon which men's hopes can focus, and the reformer, working methodically toward specific goals. The third, the formal stage, sees the beginning of the revolution proper. Motives and objectives are clarified, organization is built up, a statesman leader emerges. Then conflicts between the left and the right of the revolutionary movement become acute, and the radicals take over from the moderates. The fourth and last stage sees the legalization of the revolution. It is a product of psychological exhaustion as the reforming drive burns itself out, moral enthusiasm wanes, and economic distress increases. The administrators take over, strong central government is established, and society is reconstructed on lines that embody substantial elements of the old system. The result falls far short of the utopian aspirations of the early leaders, but it succeeds in meshing aspirations with values by partly modifying both, and so allows the reconstruction of a firm social order.

Some of the writings of contemporary social scientists are ingenious feats of

[28] "Revolution: A Redefinition."

[29] "The Revolutionary Process," *Social Forces*, XXVIII (March 1950), 270–79.

verbal juggling in an esoteric language, performed around the totem pole of an abstract model, surrounded as far as the eye can see by the arid wastes of terminological definitions and mathematical formulae. Small wonder the historian finds it hard to digest the gritty diet of this neo-scholasticism, as it has been aptly called. The more historically-minded of the social scientists, however, have a great deal to offer. The history of history, as well as of science, shows that advances depend partly on the accumulation of factual information, but rather more on the formulation of hypotheses that reveal the hidden relationships and common properties of apparently distinct phenomena. Social scientists can supply a corrective to the antiquarian fact-grubbing to which historians are so prone; they can direct attention to problems of general relevance, and away from the sterile triviality of so much historical research. They can ask new questions and suggest new ways of looking at old ones. They can supply new categories, and as a result may suggest new ideas.[30]

[30] See Werner J. Cahnman and Alvin Boskoff, eds., *Sociology and History: Theory and Research* (New York 1964); H. Stuart Hughes, "The Historian and the Social Scientist," *American Historical Review*, LXVI, No. 1 (1960), 20–46; A. Cobban, "History and Sociology," *Historical Studies*, III (1961), 1–8; M. G. Smith, "History and Social Anthropology," *Journal of the Royal Anthropological Institute*, XCII (1962); K. V. Thomas, "History and Anthropology," *Past and Present*, No. 24 (April 1963), 3–18.

George Lichtheim has been a visiting scholar at a number of outstanding universities, and is a frequent contributor to various journals on a wide range of subjects. His books on Marxism and on socialism are now standard works.

The Concept of Ideology

GEORGE LICHTHEIM

Few concepts play a larger part in present-day discussions of historical and political topics than does that of ideology, and yet it is not always clear what meaning is applied to the term by those who employ it. Even if one confines one's attention to the utterances of sociologists and historians, leaving out of account the terminological misuse seemingly inseparable from ordinary political discourse, it is apparent that different and conflicting meanings are intended by writers who casually refer to the "ideology" of this or that political movement.

From the vulgar misunderstanding inherent in the familiar phrase "we need a better ideology to fight the enemy", to the refinements of academic dispute over "the ideology of science", one encounters a terminological vagueness which appears to reflect some deeper uncertainty about the status of ideas in the genesis of historical movements.

It is here intended to clarify the theme by examining the different significations attached to the term "ideology", and the shifting status of the phenomenon itself, granted that a propensity so widespread as the duplication and distortion of reality in thought lends itself to the historical approach. If this initial assumption is allowed to pass as a working hypothesis, it is hoped that the term "ideology" will be shown to possess both a definite meaning and a particular historical status: the history of the concept serving as a guide to the actual interplay of "real" and "ideal" factors whose dialectic is obscurely intended in the formulation of the concept itself. The subject has recently been dealt with by, among others, Mr. Ben Halpern (" 'Myth' and 'Ideology' in Modern Usage", *History and Theory,* I, 2, 1961, 129–149). In what follows it is not proposed to take issue with his analysis, but to pursue a line of thought suggested by the present author's concern with the manner in which the ideology concept relates to what is usually known as the "philosophy of history", notably in its Hegelian form.

The Revolutionary Heritage

Historically, the term "ideology" made its first appearance at the time of the French Revolution, its author, Antoine Destutt de Tracy, being one of the group of *savants* whom the Convention in 1795 entrusted with the management of the newly founded *Institut de France.*[1] During the brief period of its predominance—until Napoleon in 1801 made his peace with the Church, and concurrently turned against the liberal intellectuals who had helped him into the saddle—the *Institut* became associated in the public mind with an outlook which indeed pre-dated the Revolution, but was now made official and brought into relation with the practice of the new regime. In 1794, at the height of the Terror, the guiding ideas of the faith had been given their final expression, under the most dramatic circumstances possible, by Condorcet in his *Tableau historique des progrès de l'esprit humain;* but it was under the Directory, with moderate liberalism briefly in the saddle, that the *"idéologues"* of the *Institut* placed the official seal on his doctrine.[2] Their prestige flattered the vanity of Bonaparte, who in 1797 became an honorary member of the Institute. How much the distinction meant to him appears from the fact that during the Egyptian campaign of 1798–9 he signed his proclamations to the Army as "Général en chef, Membre de l'Institut". It was a justified appreciation of their influence over the educated middle class that in 1799, at the time of the *coup d'état de Brumaire,* induced him to seek the support of the *"idéologues"*, who in turn helped to promote his accession to power.[3] It was likewise fear of their hold over public

[1] Georges Lefebvre, *La révolution française* (Paris, 1957), 443. The creation of the Institute was part of an attempt to provide France with a nation-wide system of higher learning committed to the philosophy of the Enlightenment.

[2] Lefebvre, 578: "Destutt de Tracy se proposait de déterminer par l'observation comment se forment les idées: de là le nom de l'école."

[3] Lefebvre, 534: "Arrivé à Paris . . . il montrait une discrétion toute républicaine et fréquentait l'Institut, où il fraternisait avec les idéologues." Cf. A. Aulard, *Histoire politique de la révolution française* (Paris, 1926), 694, for the illusions of the liberal intellectuals, who firmly expected Bonaparte to inaugurate the enlightened commonwealth of their dreams.

opinion which in January 1803 led him to cap his growing personal despotism (and his Concordat with Rome) by the virtual destruction of the Institute's core, the *classe des sciences morales et politiques*, from which liberal and republican ideas radiated throughout the educational "establishment". The story of Bonaparte's degeneration can be written in terms of his relations with the *"idéologues"*: down to the day in December 1812 when—returned to Paris from the disaster in Russia—he blamed them, in address to the *Conseil d'Etat*, for the catastrophe into which his own despotism had plunged the country.[4]

The "ideologists" of the Institute were liberals who regarded freedom of thought and expression as the principal conquest of the Revolution. Their attitude was "ideological" in the twofold sense of being concerned with ideas, and of placing the satisfaction of *"ideal"* aims (their own) ahead of the "material" interests on which the post-revolutionary society rested. They could put up, at least temporarily, with an enlightened dictatorship which safeguarded the major gains of the Revolution, but not with a regime which visibly steered back towards an absolutism supported by established religion. Napoleon ignored them, though he defended the social foundations of the new order and in 1815, after his return from Elba, made a last attempt to win their support. Under the Bourbon Restauration they headed the liberal opposition. In 1830 the July Revolution, by introducing parliamentary government, at long last realized one of their chief aims, though in a somewhat prosaic form. Marx, from a different standpoint, shared Napoleon's disdain for them. In 1845, remarking upon the manner in which the bourgeois character of the Revolution had gradually disclosed itself, he commented ironically upon their illusions, having previously noted that "Robespierre, Saint Just and their party fell because they confused the realistic democratic commonwealth of antiquity, which rested on the basis of real slavery, with the modern spiritualist-democratic representative state based on the emancipated slavery of bourgeois society." [5] Yet the ideologists, whatever their political fancies, had another and tougher side to them: they were the forerunners of positivism. The *Institut* under their direction became a centre of experimental studies. While Destutt de Tracy turned his attention to the history of ideas, Cabanis pioneered experimental psychology, Pinel placed the treatment of mental illness on a new foundation, Dupuis (in his *Origine de tous les cultes*) treated the natural history of religion in an empirical manner; others extended the new viewpoint to the history of literature and art. This intellectual ex-

[4] "C'est à l'idéologie, à cette ténébreuse métaphysique qui, en cherchant avec subtilité les causes premières, veut sur ces bases fonder la législation des peuples, au lieu d'approprier les lois à la connaissance du cœur humain et aux leçons de l'histoire, qu'il faut attribuer toutes les malheurs de notre belle France." Cited in Hans Barth, *Wahrheit und Ideologie* (Zürich, 1945), 30; cf. Taine, *Origines de la France contemporaine* (Paris, 1898), II, 219–220. On other occasions he put it more briefly, e.g., "Cannon killed feudalism. Ink will kill modern society." (Napoléon: *Pensées;* Paris, 1913; 43).

[5] *Die Heilige Familie* (1845 [reprinted Berlin, 1953]), 191; cf. *The Holy Family* (London, 1957), 164. "It was not the revolutionary movement as such that became Napoleon's prey on the 18th Brumaire . . . it was the *liberal bourgeoisie* . . . Napoleon was the last stand of revolutionary terrorism against the bourgeois society which had likewise been proclaimed by the Revolution . . . If he despotically suppressed the liberalism of bourgeois society—the political idealism of its daily practice—he showed no more concern for its essential material interests . . . whenever they conflicted with his political interests. His contempt for the industrial *hommes d'affaires* was the counterpart of his scorn for the ideologues." (*Ibid.*, tr. from 1953 German edition, 193–194.)

plosion was the counterpart of the better known and perhaps even more brilliant achievements of Lagrange, Laplace, Monge, Berthollet, Cuvier, Saint-Hilaire, and Lamarck in the natural sciences, which between 1790 and 1830 raised France's contribution in this field to a pinnacle of achievement never equalled before or since. When Comte around 1830 synthesized the new world-view (in the light of what he had learned from the far more original Saint-Simon), he was drawing upon the work of a generation of scholars who had already transformed the inherited eighteenth-century view by introducing the historical approach. If the ideologists continued the rationalist tradition, they also began the process of modifying it, though—unlike the German Romantics—they did not abandon its basic principles.[6]

The twofold character of the liberal "ideology", as a system of normative ideas and as an incipient critique of the very notion of absolute norms, makes its appearance already in the work of Destutt de Tracy from which the school derived its name. His *Eléments d'Idéologie* (1801–15) presents a "Science des idées" for which he cites the authority of Locke and Condillac.[7] They are praised for having inaugurated the "natural history of ideas"—that is, the scientific description of the human mind —though Condillac had qualified his naturalism by retaining the traditional religious emphasis upon the substantive reality of man's soul and the uniqueness of man compared with the animal creation.[8] For Destutt, who superimposed the materialism of Cabanis upon the Lockean sensationalism of Condillac, the study of "ideology" is part of zoology. What he means is that human psychology should be analyzed in biological terms; that is, without paying attention to religion. Moral problems are relegated to metaphysics, described as a realm of illusory fancies "destinés à nous satisfaire et non à nous instruire".[9] The true foundation of the sciences is rather to be found in a "Science des idées" which will describe the natural history of the mind, that is, the manner in which our thoughts are formed. There is no supersensible reality behind the individuals and their several "ideas" (sensations and notions).

> Il est seulement à remarquer qu'il n'existe réellement que des individus et que nos idées ne sont point des êtres réels existant hors de nous, mais de pures créations de notre esprit, des manières de classer nos idées des individus.[10]

But this "materialist" theme is crossed by a normative purpose: the "Science des idées" is to yield true knowledge of human nature, and therewith the means of defining the general laws of sociability. The reduction of individual "ideas" to generally held notions is intended to lay bare the common ground of human needs and aspirations, thus providing the lawgiver with the means of furthering the common good. What is "natural" is also "social". Once human nature is properly understood, society will at last be able to arrange itself in a harmonious fashion. Reason is the guarantor of order and liberty.[11] As with

[6] Lefebvre (*op. cit.*, 578) includes Madame de Staël's *La littérature considérée dans ses rapports avec les institutions sociales* (1800) among the notable productions of the school.

[7] A. Destutt de Tracy, *Eléments d'Idéologie* (2nd. ed., Brussels, 1826), I, 3; cf. Barth, *Wahrheit und Ideologie,* 16 f.

[8] Condillac, *Oeuvres complètes* (Paris, 1798), III, 592.

[9] *Eléments,* I, XIV.

[10] *Eléments,* I, 301.

[11] "Le perfectionnement des lois, des institutions publiques, suites des progrès des sciences, n'a-t-il point pour effet d'approcher, d'identifier l'intérêt commun de chaque homme avec l'intérêt commun de tous?" Condorcet, *Tableau historique* (Paris, 1822), 292.

Condorcet, Destutt's aim is pedagogical: it is to lay bare the guiding principles of republican citizenship. His theorizing has a practical, normative, purpose. The freeing of the human mind from ignorance and superstition is not undertaken for its own sake, but because only a mind delivered from error can perceive those universal laws which make it plain "que la nature lie par une chaîne indissoluble la vérité, le bonheur et la vertue".[12] The pathos of the Enlightenment is retained in the "Science des idées", for all its incipient naturalism. Reason progressively discloses a true picture of humanity which constitutes the foundation of civic virtue. Morality is anchored in nature. The best social order is that which corresponds to the permanent needs of man.

The antecedents of this faith are Baconian and Cartesian. To Condillac, who preceded the ideologues and the Revolution, it had already seemed plain that Bacon's criticism of the "idols" must be the starting point of that reformation of consciousness which was the principal aim of the Enlightenment.[13] Bacon's *idolum* becomes Condillac's *préjugé,* a key term also in the writings of Holbach and Helvétius. The idols are "prejudices" contrary to "reason". To remove them by the relentless application of critical reasoning is to restore the "unprejudiced" understanding of nature. Holbach maintains that

> l'homme n'est malheureux que parce qu'il méconnait la Nature . . . La raison guidée par l'expérience doit enfin attaquer dans leur source des préjugés dont le genre humain fût si longtemps le victime . . . La vérité est une; elle est nécessaire à l'homme . . . C'est à l'erreur que sont dues les chaînes accablantes que les Tyrans et les Prêtres forgent partout aux nations.[14]

Helvétius (a favourite of both Marx and Nietzsche) develops this notion in the direction of a rudimentary sociology of knowledge: "Our ideas are the necessary consequence of the societies in which we live."[15] Scepticism is held in check by the rationalist faith inherited from Descartes: reason has the power of correcting its own errors.[16]

For Helvétius, the idols (*préjugés*) are the necessary fruit of social constraint and selfish interest, but he is convinced that they can be discredited by reason and removed by education. "L'éducation peut tout."[17] The cure for popular superstition is pedagogy on a national scale. This is the point where Marx later introduced his criticism of the Enlightenment.[18] Helvétius in fact never succeeded in clarifying the rela-

[12] Condorcet, *ibid.,* 10.

[13] "Personne n'a mieux connu que Bacon la cause de nos erreurs, car il a vu que les idées, qui sont l'ouvrage de l'esprit, avaient été mal faites, et que par conséquent pour avancer dans la recherche de la vérité il fallait les refaire." Condillac, *Essai sur l'origine des connaissances humaines* (Oeuvres, I, 507); cf. the article on Bacon in the *Encyclopédie,* III, and d'Alembert's "Discours préliminaire".

[14] Holbach, *Système de la Nature* (Paris, 1770), preface.

[15] *De L'Esprit* (1758), 114; cited by Barth, *op. cit.,* 62. For Rousseau's share in the elaboration of this attitude cf. Irving Fetscher, *Rousseaus politische Philosophie* (Neuwied, 1960), *passim.*

[16] "ce qu'on nomme le bons sens ou la raison, est naturellement égale en tous les hommes . . . la diversité de nos opinions ne vient pas de ce que les uns sont plus raisonnables que les autres, mais seulement de ce que nous conduisons nos pensées par diverses voies" (Descartes, *Discours de la méthode,* cf. *Oeuvres,* ed. Pléiade, 1952, 126).

[17] Helvétius, *De l'Homme* (1773), II, 332.

[18] Cf. *Theses on Feuerbach:* "The materialist doctrine that men are products of circumstances and upbringing . . . forgets that it is men who change circumstances and that the educator himself needs to be educated. Hence this doctrine necessarily divides society into two parts, of which one is superior to the other . . ."

tionship of "interest" to "education". Wandering off into cynicism, he anticipated Nietzsche by arguing that the sole motor of human action is self-love and the will to power.

> Chacun veut commander parce que chacun veut accroître sa félicité . . . L'amour du pouvoir fondé sur celui du bonheur est donc l'objet commun de tous nos désirs . . . toutes les passions factices ne sont-elles en nous que l'amour du pouvoir déguisé sous ces noms différents: [19]

A suggestion which greatly pleased Nietzsche when he came across it.[20]

The confusion in which Helvétius landed himself was inherent in a "materialism" which treated the mind as the passive receptacle of sense impressions. At the same time he retained enough of the rationalist faith to remain confident that "prejudices" could be shown up as such, and that interest psychology could be subordinated to an objective understanding of the real needs of society. The "justesse de l'esprit" displays itself in the discovery of general laws whose truth is demonstrable. Their application to social life is a political problem, that is, a problem of power. Philosophy and politics have their common ground in education, whereby inherited prejudices (mainly religious) are overcome and replaced by insight into the true nature of man and his environment. The place of religion is taken by a secular morality, inherently social because man is a social being.

By and large—and allowing for disputes between deists, materialists, and agnostics—this was the faith which the "ideologues" of the Institute inherited from their pre-revolutionary ancestors and which eventually became the official doctrine of French democracy and indeed of the French Republic. The point here is that, for all the inherent scepticism with respect to shared beliefs, the power of rational thought was not seriously called in question. Almost a century later, Comte's positivism, notwithstanding its authoritarian features, was still rooted in the same confidence. His complacent certainty that the "philosophie positive" represented the "véritable état définitif de l'intelligence humaine" [21] may today strike one as humorous, bearing in mind the paucity of discoveries attributable to the new method; but there is no mistaking the rationalist pathos which rings through his pseudo-religious rigmarole. Compared with the older generation, the change lies in the hierarchical strait-jacket imposed upon the social order by a theorist in whom the generous optimism of the Enlightenment had congealed into a worried concern with social stability.[22] For Comte the "development of the human mind" issues in the recognition that all historical phenomena are subject to "invariable natural laws",[23] but this chilling thought somehow sustains reason's faith in itself. To anticipate Engels's later formulation (itself an amalgam of Comtean and Hegelian determinism), freedom is anchored in the recognition of necessity. *Science* enables us to bind these extremes together. The dogmatism of Comte does not subvert the conviction that the study of society yields the discovery of universal rational principles.

The Hegelian Tradition

Although Comte on some points anticipates Marx (or at any rate the ver-

[19] *De l'Homme,* I, 238–239.
[20] Cf. Barth, 316.
[21] *Cours de philosophie positive,* ed. Ch. Le Verrier (Paris, Garnier), I, 23.
[22] For this aspect of Comte cf. Herbert Marcuse, *Reason and Revolution* (London, 1955), 342 ff.
[23] Comte, *op. cit.,* 26.

sion of Marxism subsequently canonized by Engels and his successors), his critique of the "ideologists" cannot be regarded as the forerunner of Marx's onslaught on the "German ideology", which latter had evolved quite independently of the French variant. The two lines of development must not be confused just because Marx affected to believe that Feuerbach and the young Hegelians were the legitimate heirs of the *idéologues* (whence the title of his bulky tract which was not published in full until 1932).[24] The officially sanctioned "German ideology" of the 1840's had come into being as a reaction against the theory and practice of the French Revolution. Its true originator was Hegel, who from his youthful Jacobinism [25] had gradually moved to an almost Burkean worship of continuity, without ever quite renouncing his faith in universal reason and the rule of law.[26] His radical critics retained the historical approach he had introduced, and at the same time restored the moral iconoclasm he had abandoned. Their target was the conservative "Christian-German" ideology then invested with a quasi-official function by the pre-1848 regime. In assailing it, Feuerbach, Bruno Bauer, and the left-wing Hegelians in general, inevitably went back to the ultimate source of their own faith: the French Enlightenment and its naturalist critique of theology and metaphysics.[27] A few years later Marx was to claim that their criticism of the official ideology was itself ideological. The precise significance he gave to this charge needs to be understood in the light of the philosophical situation then prevailing.

The belief that general concepts, though held by particular individuals, are of universal application, is common to all thinkers who can be described as rationalists. It was retained by Hegel, notwithstanding his disillusionment with the outcome of the French Revolution, in which he had originally seen the practical working of Reason. Kantian philosophy had already synthesized Cartesian rationalism and Lockean empiricism in a procedure which restored the primacy of mind over matter: general concepts, though rooted in experience, were held to be independent of experience, inasmuch as they organized the sense data into intelligible wholes. The imposition of order upon the chaos of sense impressions was the work of the mind, which was in possession of the true and universal forms of understanding, the categories. The dependence of the individual mind upon the material presented by the senses—that hobbyhorse of empiricism, from Locke to Hume—was not disputed, but treated as a state of affairs which occupies merely the foreground of reasoning. The "given" experience present to the individual is not an assemblage of brute "facts", but an ordered whole. In extending this Kantian approach from the

[24] For the following cf., *Die deutsche Ideologie: Kritik der neuesten deutschen Philosophie in ihren Repräsentanten, Feuerbach, B. Bauer und Stirner, und des deutschen Sozialismus in seinen verschiedenen Propheten, MEGA*, V (1932); and the various translations.

[25] Cf. *Briefe von und an Hegel* (Leipzig, 1887); *Hegels theologische Jugendschriften* (Tübingen, 1907), *passim*.

[26] Cf. *Philosophy of Right* (1821): "It is part of education, of thinking as the consciousness of the single in the form of universality, that the ego comes to be apprehended as a universal person in which all are identical. A man counts as a man in virtue of his manhood alone, not because he is a Jew, Catholic, Protestant, German, Italian etc. This is an assertion which thinking ratifies, and to be conscious of it is of infinite importance" (Tr. T. M. Knox, Oxford, 1942, para. 209; 134).

[27] Cf. Bruno Bauer, *Das entdeckte Christentum. Eine Erinnerung an das achtzehnte Jahrhundert und ein Beitrag zur Kritik des neunzehnten* (1843). For the influence of Holbach, Helvétius, and the *Science des idées*, on Feuerbach, Bauer and Marx, cf. Barth, *op. cit.*, 73 ff.

realm of nature to history, Hegel affirmed the governing principle of the idealist faith: matter is organized by mind. Experience—the shibboleth of the British school—ceased to be a final datum. The way to the attainment of universality lay in grasping the principles which held the sensible world together.

Seen from Hegel's standpoint, Kant had remained in a half-way position between empiricism and true universalism. The latter required the assumption that the mind recognizes a world independent of the subject, whereas the Kantian categories were merely the necessary forms of any singular subject's possible experience. They constituted a phenomenal world, one and the same for all experients, yet Kant never took the decisive step of acknowledging that the world can be common to all experients only if all finite minds are differentiations of a universal mind: he did not, that is, conceive Mind as a "concrete universal". Reason for him is not indeed passive, but the individual consciousness is not seen as transcending itself, and its activity is not viewed as the immanence of a universal reason working through finite minds. If Kant in consequence has "no philosophy of Nature, only a philosophy of natural science",[28] Hegel on the contrary has a philosophy of History precisely because for him Reason is at once general and particular: a concrete universal which differentiates itself into particular thinking minds. On this view, the problem for the individual thinker is to apprehend the movement of Reason, of which his own thinking is a reflex. What manifests itself to philosophic thought is the history of Mind—veiled by its embodiment in Matter, but still plainly discernible as the motive force of the universal process. When "stood on its feet" by materialism, this philosophy yields the conviction that the logic of history is decipherable through an understanding of Man's capacity to "produce" his own world. Beyond the recorded facts there lies the totality of history which men have made, and are therefore able to understand. It is worth stressing this continuity, so often obscured by emphasis upon the naturalist inversion effected by Feuerbach and Marx. Feuerbach indeed "saw through" Hegel's terminology to the theology of Spirit lying behind it, but his return to the naturalism of the French Enlightenment did not imply acceptance of the empiricist mode of reasoning. Nature is a universal for Feuerbach, as history is for Marx. This is not to say that either of them was uncritical of Hegel's manner of treating logical concepts. (It was left for Marx's less intelligent followers to personify History into an independent entity: a misunderstanding against which he had protested in advance.) [29]

We are here concerned with the concept of ideology, not with the truth of Hegel's philosophy. What needs to be retained is that on Hegel's assumption the problem of overcoming the particularity of thinking is not insoluble; nor does it follow that because philosophers —or for that matter ordinary men—are born and raised under particular circumstances, they cannot rise above them. Man is essentially a thinking being, and as such able to apprehend the concrete universality which is history. Our historical concepts possess true generality because they relate to a universal agent that unfolds through the histories of particular peoples and civilizations. This agent for Hegel is Mind, for Marx it is human activity, *praxis:* the practice of men struggling to subdue nature and to

[28] G. R. G. Mure, *An Introduction to Hegel* (Oxford, 1940), 105.

[29] "History, like truth, becomes a person apart, a metaphysical subject, of which the real individuals are merely the bearers." *Die Heilige Familie* (Berlin, 1953), 116.

develop their own latent powers. The determinant in each case is conscious activity, though Marx protests that for Hegel the historical process tends to become an independent entity superior to the individuals who compose it.[30]

The problem of ideology (in the sense of "false consciousness" or "imperfect consciousness") arises for Hegel because in his view individuals, and even entire nations, are instruments of history, executors of a process whose meaning is concealed from them, and which becomes selfconscious only *post festum* in the philosopher who sums up the essence of the epoch.[31] Hegel was aware that history is set in motion by men's interests and passions. He did not question its rationality just because men commonly behaved in an irrational manner: the process had its own logic, which was not that of the individuals. The "cunning of reason" [32] could be observed in the manner in which the Idea (the rationality of the whole) triumphed at the expense of its own agents. The individual's fate was swallowed up in the dialectic of the process. The youthful Marx rebelled against this world-view, which struck him as theological; he lived to see it reinstated (with his own silent acquiescence) by Engels, though it was only gradually that the wheel came full circle, with the determinist emphasis upon "general laws" governing the course of history: laws apparently general enough to conform to Hegel's "cunning of reason", and scientific enough to be acceptable to a generation raised on positivism.[33]

For Hegel the problem had been to justify the ways of God to man. He did not doubt that these ways could be understood, at any rate retrospectively. This understanding is the work of philosophy, which in every age makes its appearance when a particular phase of Spirit has come to a close. Philosophy does not change the world: it interprets it and thus reconciles the world to itself. Yet Hegel's own philosophy was to change the world—if only because, even on its most conservative interpretation, it was subversive of revealed religion.[34] On the other hand, his system—more particularly his teachings on Right and the State—appeared to his radical critics as the "ideology" of the political status quo: its intellectual projection and justification. From here it was only a step to the notion that speculative philosophy as such barred the way to that re-

[30] "Hegel's conception of history presupposes an abstract or absolute spirit which develops in such a way that humanity is nothing but a mass which more or less consciously bears it along. Within the framework of empirical exoteric history, Hegel introduces the operation of a speculative esoteric history. The history of humanity becomes the history of the abstract spirit of humanity, a spirit beyond the real man. Concurrently with this Hegelian doctrine, there developed in France the theory of the doctrinaires, who proclaimed the sovereignty of reason in opposition to the sovereignty of the people . . ." *Die Heilige Familie* (1953), 57; cf. *MEGA*, 1/3, 257; *The Holy Family* (London, 1957), 115.

[31] *Vorlesungen über die Geschichte der Philosophie*, ed. Lasson (Leipzig, 1930), I, 9 ff. 25 ff. 78 ff.; cf. *The Philosophy of History*, ed. C. J. Friedrich (New York, 1956), *Introduction* and *passim;* Marcuse, *Reason and Revolution*, 224 ff.

[32] *Vorlesungen*, I, 83; cf. *The Philosophy of History*, 33.

[33] Engels, *Ludwig Feuerbach and the Close of Classical German Philosophy, passim.* Cf. Engels to Mehring, July 14, 1893 (in Marx-Engels *Selected Correspondence*, Moscow, 1954, 541): "Ideology is a process accomplished by the so-called thinker consciously, it is true, but with a false consciousness. The real motive forces impelling him remain unknown to him; else it simply would not be an ideological process."

[34] Barth, 78 f. To Hegel's followers the matter presented itself in a somewhat different light: since his philosophy was the fulfilment of speculative thinking in general, its appearance plainly marked the end of European history; cf. K. Löwith, *Von Hegel zu Nietzsche* (Stuttgart, 1950), 44 ff. This may well have been Hegel's own view.

construction of the world which was required to realize the aims of philosophy: liberty and rationality. This step was taken by Marx, with the help of Feuerbach who had taught him to regard speculative thinking as the ultimate barrier to the understanding of man's role in the world.

The Marxian concept of ideology thus fuses two different principles: Hegel's insight into the transitory character of the successive manifestations of Spirit, and Feuerbach's materialist inversion of Hegel, with its stress on the this-worldly character of natural existence. Separated from each other these concepts remained speculative; joined together they yielded an explosive mixture. The explosion, however, did not depend for its effect on the kind of scepticism which follows from the alleged discovery that abstract thinking does not yield access to universal truths. The despairing conclusions drawn by Kierkegaard from this conviction do not form part of the intellectual revolution underlying the new philosophy of history: they belong—with Nietzsche's kindred writings—to the attack on rationalism which in our own age has given rise to the existentialist analysis of the lonely individual. Nietzsche and Kierkegaard—just because they are concerned with the individual's role in a world whose functioning is indifferently taken for granted—have nothing to say about the manner in which history operates. Their revolt against rationalist metaphysics issues in subjectivism. Among the first universals to be cast overboard by these influential critics of rationalism was the concept of humanity.[35]

From Hegel to Marx

What Marx meant by "ideology" appears plainly enough from the *Theses on Feuerbach*, where the latter is blamed for not having carried through to the end his inversion of Hegel's system. He says, for example:

> Feuerbach sets out from the fact of religious self-alienation, the duplication of the world into a religious and a secular one. His work consists in resolving the religious world into its secular basis. But the fact that the secular basis deserts its own sphere and establishes an independent realm in the clouds, can only be explained by the cleavage and self-contradiction within the secular basis.[36]

This radicalization of Feuerbach's naturalist starting-point (itself a continuation of a tradition rooted in antiquity) left intact the rationalist principle which Marx shared with Hegel: namely, the belief that cognition gives access to universal truths not present in immediate

[35] Kierkegaard still tried to find logical flaws in Hegel's system. With Schopenhauer's disciple Nietzsche, subjectivism and aestheticism have already reached the point where logic is consciously discarded. One cannot take seriously Nietzsche's so-called critique of traditional thought. When he says (*Jenseits von Gut und Böse,* in *Werke,* ed. K. Schlechta, Munich, 1960, II, 571) "It has gradually emerged that every great philosophy has hitherto been the confession of its author and a kind of unintended and unnoticed *mémoires*", he is being trivial in the Voltairean manner, which is caricatured throughout this overrated essay; cf., his similar observations (in *Werke,* I, 448) on the "hereditary fault of philosophy": "All philosophers share the fault of proceeding from the currently existing man (*vom gegenwärtigen Menschen*) and expecting to reach the goal through analyzing him. Insensibly they have an image of "Man" as an *aeterna veritas* . . . as a sure measure of all things. Yet everything said by the philosopher about Man at bottom only applies to the men of a very limited period. Lack of historical sense is the hereditary fault of all philosophers . . ." That this kind of thing should have been taken seriously *after Hegel* testifies to a state of affairs perhaps best described as the collapse of responsible thinking.

[36] *Karl Marx: Selected Writings in Sociology and Social Philosophy,* ed. Bottomore and Rubel (London, 1956), 68.

experience. The Marxian conception of world history as a process of human self-alienation draws on Feuerbach's impassioned protest against the sacrifice of nature and of real, living, human beings, whose activities and whose sufferings Hegel had obscured. But Marx retains the Hegelian conviction that in the final analysis "history makes sense". The historical process vindicates Reason because it can be understood. To this extent Marx always remained a Hegelian, for all the emphasis upon "the real history of real people" which occupies so prominent a place in his polemics against his former associates.[37]

Marx's conception of ideology as "false consciousness" leads back to the problem of establishing the true consciousness which will enable men to understand their role. There is only one truth about history, and only one criterion for judging the discrepancy between what men are and what they might become: this criterion is supplied by philosophy, specifically by its understanding of man as a rational being. Thus philosophy, as the norm of reality, entails an implicit critique of this reality. Yet Marx also held that the philosophy of every age is the "ideological reflex" of determinate social conditions. How then could it function as the source of normative judgments pointing beyond the existing state of affairs? The problem did not arise if human self-alienation was conceived in the manner of Fichte and Hegel, as a mere misfortune which could be rectified by opposing a true consciousness to a false one. This had been Marx's standpoint in 1843, when he was already a revolutionary, but not yet a materialist.[38]

It might seem that on the materialist assumptions Marx accepted as part of his conversion to socialism in 1844–5, he was bound to arrive at a radical historicism and relativism. But although in many places the language of the *Holy Family* and the *German Ideology* (not to mention the *Communist Manifesto*) seems to support this conclusion, he did not in fact do so. He took over from his French predecessors the critical demolition of traditional metaphysics, yet he also went on ascribing a rational content to history. The rationality was a hidden one and had to be discerned in the logic of the "material" process itself, not in the "ideological" reflex it left in the minds of the participants. Like Hegel, he distinguished between Reality and Appearance. The reality of the historical process for Hegel was alienated Mind coming to terms with itself; for Marx it was alienated human labor reflecting itself in an ideological cloud-cuckooland. What he was later (in *Das Kapital*) to describe as the "fetishism of commodities", appears in his early writings as human self-alienation, whereby man's creations acquire a status independent of their creator.

The Marxian concept of ideology takes shape in this context, and from the start has a meaning different from that which it had for his eighteenth-century predecessors. Interest psychology is replaced by a metaphysic of human nature whose outline Hegel had developed in the *Phenomenology of Mind.* Alienated social activity is to

[37] *Deutsche Ideologie,* 28 ff. and *passim.* In 1844–5 Marx (then resident in Paris) had partly excerpted Destutt de Tracy's *Eléments d'Idéologie,* and his use of the term "ideology" reflects a clear awareness of the devaluation it had meanwhile undergone.

[38] Cf. *Ein Briefwechsel von 1843,* in *Der historische Materialismus,* ed. S. Landshut and J. P. Mayer (Leipzig, 1932), 226. "The reform of consciousness consists only in this, that one enables the world to become aware of its own consciousness, that one awakens it from its dream, that one *explains* its own actions to it. Our entire purpose, as with Feuerbach's critique of religion, can only consist in transforming the religious and political questions into the self-conscious human form . . . It will then appear that the world has long possessed the dream of something of which it need only possess the consciousness in order to have it in reality."

Marx what alienated mental activity is to Hegel. For both, the distinction between Reality and Appearance is involved in the manner in which *real* processes are transformed into *apparently* fixed and stable characters. Reality is process, appearance has the form of isolated objects. The task of critical thinking is to grasp the relations which constitute these apparent objects.

This approach still left unsolved the problem of relating the social content of ideology to the rational meaning of the process, as it differentiates itself through its various concrete manifestations. The historical character of the Marxian dialectic, and with it the problem of ideology in the modern sense, is a consequence of the discovery that there is not—as Feuerbach had thought—a single universal human standpoint from which to judge the alienations imposed by history; there are only particular human standpoints, corresponding to forms of society which arise from the interplay of material conditions and (more or less) conscious attempts to organize the "productive forces". The dialectic of being and consciousness is worked out in history; not, as Hegel had implied, as a shadow-play reflecting a metaphysical process, but as the "real" play. The "actors" are individuals and groups whose changing circumstances are mirrored in varying modes of thought. These modes are "ideological" in that the participants fail to comprehend the situation in which they are involved. But even the most thorough clarification of their actual historical role cannot, it would seem, enable them to transcend the particularity of their standpoint, since this is bound up with the concrete needs of their time and place. The only difference between "objective" and "ideological" thinking appears to lie in the capacity of the critical intellect to comprehend the particular determinations which condition each successive phase of human activity.

The principle that "social being . . . determines consciousness" [39] appears to imply that every social order (however defined) has forms of consciousness peculiar to it. Yet Marx also asserts that "mankind always sets itself only such tasks as it can solve",[40] thus placing a statement about the whole process within the framework of a doctrine intended to supersede the "pre-scientific" viewpoint. To invoke "mankind" is to make an assertion about the totality of history, however empirical and nonmetaphysical the writer's intention. There is not in Marx a clear distinction between sociological statements relative to particular situations, and philosophical generalizations pertaining to history as a whole. How is the dilemma to be met?

The principle that social being determines consciousness must be understood as itself an historical one: it refers to a state of affairs which has characterized history from the very beginning, but which is due to disappear when a rational order has been created. For the attainment of such an order implies the conscious direction of social life, hence the emancipation of consciousness from blind, uncomprehended, necessity. Consciousness is ideological because it is powerless. When it becomes the determining factor, it sheds its blinkers along with its dependence on material circumstances. *A rational order is one in which thinking determines being.* Men will be free when they are able to *produce* their own circumstances. Historical material-

[39] Marx, *A Contribution to the Critique of Political Economy,* preface. Cf. *Selected Works* (Moscow, 1958), I, 363.

[40] *Ibid.*

ism is valid only until it has brought about its own dialectical negation. When this stage has been reached, it will no longer be possible to speak of historical "laws", for history is subject to "laws" only in so far as it is unconscious, that is, in so far as it is *not,* properly speaking, human history at all. The mature consciousness which in retrospect comprehends the necessity of this lengthy process of "pre-history" will not be an ideological one: it will be shared by all men, and will mark mankind's understanding of its own past.

Marx preserved the original motive of his thinking (together with the conception of history he had inherited from Hegel) by refusing to recognize the dilemma inherent in the principle that modes of thought are to be understood as "expressions" of changing social circumstances. He took it for granted that, though consciousness is conditioned by existence, it can also rise above existence and become a means of transcending the alienation which sets the historical process in motion. The *truth* about man is one and the same for all stages of history, even though every stage produces its own *illusions.* This truth is likewise the criterion for the practical activity which seeks to overcome man's alienation from his "true" being. The concept of ideology illumines the historical circumstance that men are not in possession of the true consciousness which—if they had it—would enable them to understand the totality of the world and their own place in it. Marx regarded his theory as a step towards the attainment of such a consciousness. The unity of mankind, and the universality of truth, were as real to him as they were to Hegel, and it was left to his disciples to destroy the coherence of this thought by abandoning its unspoken assumptions and transforming his doctrine into a variant of positivism.

. . . .

The Problem of Consciousness

The problem of history is the problem of consciousness. It was Hegel who first pointed this out, and his successors—including Marx, who inverted his logic but did not replace it by a radically different manner of thought—continued to pose the question he had raised: how could the rationality of history be perceived by the intellect, given the fact that men are both inside and outside the historical process? The subsidiary problem of "false consciousness" arose from the awareness that the various possible standpoints were inadequate as well as incompatible. Meantime the analysis of cognition had led to the search for the "identical subject-object" of history: a universal whose activity was synonymous with the disclosure of history's peculiar logic. The pursuit of this aim over the past two centuries is not simply to be understood as a dispassionate search for objective truth, though belief in a *ratio* common to all men was inherent in the attempt to discern an historical logic. The intellectual effort was itself a factor in that theoretical and practical unification of the world which is now proceeding under our eyes. The mounting concern over the phenomenon of "false consciousness" was an index to the awareness that the future of civilization—if not the existence of mankind—may come to depend on the attainment of a "true consciousness" in which individuals and groups belonging to the most varied societies and cultures can share. From the standpoint here chosen it may thus be suggested that the attempt to discern a logic of history was more than an idle play with concepts: it responded to a practical purpose which in our own age has become more urgent as the globe shrinks, and historically divergent and disparate cultures press against one another. Because these pressures are experienced as ideological conflicts among people holding different and incompatible aims in view, it remains the task of the critical intellect to evolve modes of thought which will enable men to recognize the common purpose underlying their divergencies.

In this perspective, the transformation undergone by the concept of ideology appears as an index to the tension between the actual historical process and a critical consciousness nourished by the traditions of classical rationalism. In its original eighteenth-century form, the concept represented an implicit critique of society from the standpoint of early liberalism: a standpoint which was itself "historical" in that it took for granted (and therefore treated as "natural") the social relations proper to a particular phase of European history.[41] This naive certainty disappeared during and after the French Revolution. The latter marked a turning-point in that the critique of existing (traditional but decaying, hence plainly irrational) institutions could no longer be delivered in the name of apparently self-evident principles. For the new institutions, which claimed to be in accordance with reason, turned out to be rational only in terms of the particular historical purpose they served: the emancipation of the "third estate" could not forever be equated with the attainment of a natural order conceived as the embodiment of absolute reason. Hence the fleeting balance attained around 1800 gave way to a deepening scepticism about the very "ideology" whose original proponents had set out to trace the natural history of ideas. In Hegel's philosophy, which arose directly from the urge to comprehend the meaning of the Revolution, there already appears in germ the notion that forms of consciousness are relative to changing historical situations. The universality of the whole has to be reconstructed, as it were, from the entire sequence of historical fossils—the latter comprising *inter alia* the conscious (subjective) aims of the individuals who occupy the foreground. These aims now appear as unconscious means of realizing a hidden purpose; they have become "ideological" in a sense not intended by the original *idéologues*.

This is the concept of ideology which Marx inherited from Hegel. It served him as a means of discrediting the universal claims of the liberal ideology he encountered in his passage from philosophy to politics. At the same time he retained the rationalist faith in an objective logic of the historical process—now understood as the process of man's self-creation. To Marx, as to any Hegelian, the actual world of empirical perception was only an imperfect realization—at times indeed a caricature—of the real or rational world, in which man's essential nature (his rationality) will have overcome the reified existence he leads while the surrounding object-world is not perceived as the product of his own creativity. The attainment of this liberated state is the work of history, whose dialectic is not disclosed by empirical perception, but by critical (philosophical) reflection upon the totality of the process. An understanding fixed upon isolated aspects of this totality necessarily falls short of the goal of philosophical reason. It is *ideological* at a second remove, in that it mistakes the reified structures of immediate experience for permanent constituents of real-

[41] Jürgen Habermas, *Theorie und Praxis: Sozialphilosophische Studien* (Neuwied, 1963), *passim.* For a recent defence of the positivist standpoint cf. Arnold Gehlen, *Studien zur Anthropologie und Soziologie* (Neuwied, 1963), *passim.* For a critique of positivism from a neo-Hegelian viewpoint cf. H. Marcuse, *One-Dimensional Man* (Boston, 1964), *passim.* For a critical view of the neo-Marxist position cf. Morris Watnick, "Relativism and Class Consciousness: Georg Lukács", in *Revisionism: Essays on the History of Marxist Ideas* (London and New York, 1962), 142 ff. [Editors' note: Footnote 76 in the original.]

ity. It treats, for example, war, poverty, class distinctions, and so on, as permanent features of history, instead of viewing them as temporary objectivations of mankind's gradual and painfully slow emergence from the realm of nature. So understood the concept of ideology recovers its ancient pathos: it is now employed to demonstrate the transitoriness of those arrangements which—irrational in themselves—nonetheless serve the rationality of the whole.

It is only with the loss of this dimension that "ideology" ceases to denote *false consciousness*. It now becomes synonymous with any kind of consciousness that can relate itself to the ongoing activity of a class or group effective enough to make some sort of practical difference. This is the ideology concept of contemporary positivism. Its limited practical relevance ought not to veil its incompatibility with the intellectual tradition (ultimately rooted in classical metaphysics) that is intended when one speaks of the philosophy of history. This philosophy arose from a complex of theoretical and practical problems, of which the original *idéologues*, and their eighteenth-century forerunners, took note in sketching a rudimentary model of world history. Essentially what concerned them was the growth of rationality and the imposition of conscious control upon "natural" chaos. The pragmatic character of this enterprise was never wholly obscured by its theoretical language. It was from the first an attempt to impose an ideal order upon the world, by making an appeal to man's "nature". Its success or failure was and is bound up with the power of Reason to see through the veil of ideology to the enduring realities of human existence. An understanding of what is involved in the concept of ideology is thus at the same time an exercise in that historical imagination which enables us to see our predecessors as men engaged in an enterprise whose outcome still concerns us. In Hegelian language we may say that—the final category retaining and preserving within itself the content of all the previous ones—the unification and pacification of the world (if it can be achieved) will demonstrate that history is indeed a concrete universal. For it is only at this level that what is called world history becomes synonymous with mankind's collective emergence from the state of nature. Whatever their residual differences, this is a perspective which liberalism and Marxism have in common.

Professor Dankwart A. Rustow of the School of International Studies at Columbia University is a student not only of elites, as in the article that follows, but of "great men" as well. His work on Kemal Atatürk is outstanding, placing the leader in fascinating juxtaposition to the elite surrounding him.

The Study of Elites: Who's Who, When, and How

DANKWART A. RUSTOW *

T. B. Bottomore, *Elites and Society*, New York, Basic Books, 1965, 154 pp. $4.50.
Frederick W. Frey, *The Turkish Political Elite*, Cambridge, M.I.T. Press, 1965, xxvi, 483 pp. $12.50.
Harold D. Lasswell and Daniel Lerner, editors, *World Revolutionary Elites: Studies in Coercive Ideological Movements*, Cambridge, M.I.T. Press, 1965, xi, 478 pp. $15.00.
Dwaine Marvick, editor, *Political Decision-Makers*, International Yearbook of Political Behavior Research, Vol. 2, New York, The Free Press of Glencoe, 1961, 347 pp. $7.95.
James H. Meisel, editor, *Pareto and Mosca, Makers of Modern Social Science*, Englewood Cliffs, Prentice-Hall, 1965, 184 pp. $2.45 (paper).
Marshall R. Singer, *The Emerging Elite: A Study of Political Leadership in Ceylon*, Cambridge, M.I.T. Press, 1964, xix, 203 pp. $7.50.

I

The study of politics is the study of influence and the influential. . . . The influential are those who get the most of what there is to get. . . . Those who get the most are *elite;* the rest are *mass*.[1] Thus, three decades ago, Harold Lasswell tersely presented the reader with some cardinal tenets of his credo as a social scientist. More recently Lasswell in two separate essays (Marvick, 264–87; Lasswell and Lerner, 3–96) has surveyed the progress of a branch of research that he has done so much to foster. "Contemporary studies of elite phenomena in politics," he finds, "are enormously diversified in conception and procedure. The field has abounding vigor, despite, or because of, its conspicuous lack of elegant intellectual unity" (Marvick, 264). Despite or because? Lasswell takes little time to consider the problems of method encountered in past research. Instead, with characteristic verve, he launches into an exploration of the political and scholarly future.

Four of the books here reviewed illustrate the variety of concept and theme in recent elite research; by implication they raise some of the broader

From *World Politics*, Vol. XVIII, No. 4 (July 1966), pp. 690–717.

* I am grateful to Annette Baker Fox and William T. R. Fox of Columbia University and to Joseph Goldsen of The RAND Corporation for critical comments on an earlier draft.

[1] Harold D. Lasswell, *Politics: Who Gets What, When, How* (New York 1936), 13.

questions of method that confront the comparative study of politics. Marvick includes four accounts of leadership recruitment and political careers in Western Europe and the United States. Lasswell and Lerner present investigations of Soviet Russian, Fascist Italian, Nazi German, and Kuomintang and Communist Chinese leaders.[2] An essay by Edward Shils (Marvick, 29–56) deals with the political role of Indian intellectuals; and Frey and Singer pursue the research into two other Asian countries, Turkey and Ceylon, where parliamentary institutions have grown somewhat painfully amid rapid cultural and social change. Marvick concludes with two reviews, one by a political scientist (Lucian W. Pye) and one by a psychoanalyst (Daryl DeBell), of Erikson's *Young Man Luther,* with its suggestive hypothesis about the parallel crises of identity in founders of new creeds and in their mass following.[3]

The remaining volumes place the study of elites in its context of social philosophy. Meisel's selection of critical writings on Pareto and Mosca, together with a thoughtful introduction (pp. 1–44), takes us back to a time when elite theory still did have its theoretical unity—and its empirical innocence. (In passing one notes that, whereas the other editors freshly assembled their materials, Meisel's anthology of previously published writings achieves a greater degree of coherence than does either of the other collective volumes.) Bottomore combines a critical examination of earlier elite theories with the sketch of a social theory into which the contemporary study of elites might be fitted.

II

Readers of the volume *World Revotionary Elites* will encounter Lasswell in all his familiar and endearing poses. There is Lasswell in pontifical robes giving his most casual opinions the resonance of true authority: "By this time the recognition is widespread. . . . By this time most scientific observers realize . . ." (p. 4). There is Lasswell the superrevolutionary, ready to patronize Marx himself (pp. 71, 73), yet more likely in the end to *épater le bourgeois* than to expropriate him. There is Lasswell the visceral activist whose "verbalization may be broken off at any time and discharged into action," who "slams into action with glandular accelerators" as he "swings toward commitment" (pp. 90f.). Seizing next the wand of science fiction, Lasswell takes us to "the threshold of the era of astropolitics," warns that the " 'paralysis bomb' and its derivatives can make large-scale coercion truly obsolete," and promises not to "overlook the abolition of death by the technique of detecting worn-out molecules and making suitable replacements" (p. 95). And, ready to bow for his exit, here is Lasswell in the costume of a humanitarian Mephistopheles reassuring us that the "policy sciences" of the future will "aid in forestalling" worse, indeed altogether "unspeakable contingencies" (p. 96).

In his bibliographical footnotes in the

[2] The Italian study appeared in the *American Political Science Review* in 1936; the Russian, German, and Chinese ones are Nos. 2, 3, and 8 of the Hoover Institution Studies, Series B: Elite Studies (Stanford 1951–1955). Lasswell's essay "The World Revolution of Our Time" (pp. 29–96) is an adaptation of No. 1 in the parallel Series A: General Studies (1951). Series B, No. 1, Harold D. Lasswell, Daniel Lerner, and C. Easton Rothwell, *The Comparative Study of Elites* (1951), No. 4, Maxwell E. Knight, *The German Executive: 1890–1933* (1952), and No. 5, Ithiel de Sola Pool and others, *Satellite Generals* (1955), are not reprinted in the present Lasswell and Lerner volume.

[3] Erik H. Erikson, *Young Man Luther: A Study in Psychoanalysis and History* (New York 1958).

same volume and in his contribution to the Marvick volume, Lasswell compounds the impression of variety. As in 1936 he still equates the study of elites with the study of politics and still defines the elite as the "influential." But he adds that "any single definition for such a key term . . . is inadequate" (p. 4); and his greater liberality of concept now enables him to claim as students of elites authors across the continents and through the centuries—from Ibn Khaldun to Karl Wittfogel, from Milovan Djilas to C. Wright Mills, and from James Burnham to Robert Redfield.

Behind the versatility of phrase and the copious notes, the reader discerns Lasswell's lifelong desire to formulate the basic concepts of an empirical social science that can serve as a reliable instrument of control. Among some of the contributors to Marvick's *Political Decision-Makers* and Lasswell and Lerner's *World Revolutionary Elites* this aspiration leads to a search for the social atom, for the irreducible unit upon which a mechanistic, quantitative, and predictive science of politics can be built. It is this same impulse that has launched the phrases "decision-making" and "decision-maker" as fashionable synonyms for politics and the politician. If only all political decisions could be identified, tallied, and fed into a computer—then at long last political scientists might rival the physicists in precision, efficacy, and prestige! The goal is exhilarating enough that the difficulties are often ignored. A critic addicted to plain common sense might object that statesmen must not only make but also delay or bypass decisions.[4] (While pacifists demand to know whether we would rather be red or dead, responsible diplomats have done their best to avoid the need for such a choice.) He might insist that knowledge of such decisions as *are* made must depend on information about the motives of rulers and the alternatives before them, and that such knowledge comes at the end rather than the beginning of laborious research. He might even point out that the politician has no monopoly on decisions, that the private citizen, too, must decide what trade to learn, whom to take for a wife, which suit to wear in the morning, and where to drive the car on a weekend.

Lasswell, unlike many a lesser scholar, is aware of the difficulties inherent in the behaviorist vision—but his remedies are not always persuasive. The last objection, for instance, he removes by a simple act of definition. "Decision-makers" form a "power elite" (p. 12) because "decisions" (as distinct from mere "choices") create situations where "severe coercive measures are actually employed or expected to be employed with success against the challengers of the result" (p. 10). Here we come upon a hard, Hobbesian strand in Lasswell's thought. Lasswell's dedication to humane and democratic values combines with an avid sensitivity to the dangers of manipulation and coercion in modern society—and it is of course in a world of universal selfishness, cunning, and coercion that the notion of a deterministic social science becomes most nearly plausible. Lasswell's man, like Hobbes', is out to "get" things, indeed to "get the most of what there is to get" ("a perpetuall and restlesse desire of Power after power, that ceaseth onely in Death") and, together with his fellows, he must be kept in check by "severe coercive measures" (a "power able to overawe them all"). The chief difference is that what was once the state of nature now is represented as a condition of civil society. Where Hobbes was con-

[4] For a further critique of "the illusion of decision-making," see Renzo Sereno, *The Rulers* (New York 1962), 82–88.

fident that a properly constituted authority would redirect men's restless desire toward peaceful arts and industry, Lasswell grimly sees the war of each against all continuing beneath a thin veneer of civilization. And whereas life in Hobbes' state of nature, mercifully, was "poore, nasty, brutish, and *short,*" Lasswell, by abolishing death, undertakes to prolong the misery.[5]

The political scientist familiar with the Lasswellian, or behaviorist, rationale for elite study will do well to glance briefly at the work of historians who have employed a similar technique—the social group profile composed of individual careers—though with different preconceptions. There is, for example, Sir Lewis Namier, who shares Pareto's and Lasswell's misanthropy, though not their passion for bold hypothesis, as he contemplates British members of parliament who are to him like so many ants.[6] There is Nikolaus von Preradovich, whose feat of sheer "data gathering" on the Austrian and Prussian elites in the nineteenth century is unmatched among behavioral scientists.[7] And there is Sir Ronald Syme, whose work is the more instructive for being sustained by a clear sense of purpose. In his major work *The Roman Revolution,* Syme adopts the "prosopographic" method: he painstakingly assembles available information (and disciplined inference) on the family connections, training, public careers, and private fortunes of office-holders in the time of transition from Roman Republic to Roman Empire. "The period," he explains, "witnessed a violent transference of power and property; and the Principate of Augustus should be regarded as the consolidation of the revolutionary process. Emphasis is laid, however, not upon the personality and acts of Augustus, but upon his adherents and partisans. The composition of the oligarchy of government therefore emerges as the dominant theme of political history, as the binding link between the Republic and the Empire: it is something real and tangible, whatever may be the name or theory of the constitution." [8] More recently, Syme has in a series of lectures extended his Roman perspective to the political leadership of the Spanish and British colonial empires in America—without abandoning his skepticism. "In all ages of history," he insists, "it is desirable to get away from generalizations and study individuals and families." [9]

Syme's warning reveals his purpose only by indirection—much as did Ranke's famous (and essentially hollow) injunction to study history *wie es eigentlich gewesen ist*. Their attitude is characteristic of periods of scholarly transition. Both are wary of the misleading

[5] Hobbes, *Leviathan,* chaps. 11, 13.

[6] "Here is an ant-heap, with the human ants hurrying in long files along their various paths; their joint achievement does not concern us, nor the changes which supervene in their community, only the pathetically intent, seemingly self-conscious running of individuals along beaten tracks" (*The Structure of Politics at the Accession of George III,* preface to the first edition, quoted here from the second [London 1961], xi).

[7] *Die Führungsschichten in Österreich und Preussen (1804–1918)* (Wiesbaden 1955). The book presents, in only 189 pages, detailed information for nine key years during the period 1804–1918 on the regional and social origins of all ambassadors, provincial governors, members of parliament, ministers of interior, foreign affairs, and war, as well as holders of the highest decorations. One of the author's conclusions: "Austria did not lose the Prusso-Austrian War of 1866 but the German-French War of 1870; for, after the founding of the Empire by Bismarck, naturally far fewer Reich Germans went to Austria, since they now enjoyed, to a more tangible extent, the advantages of a large state in their country of origin" (p. 66, my translation).

[8] *The Roman Revolution* (Oxford 1939), vii.

[9] *Colonial Elites: Rome, Spain, and the Americas* (London 1958), 52.

and dogmatic abstractions of a previous generation of historians: while abjuring generalities, both are eager to explore new, and equally general, concepts. As Ranke replaced a Hegelian, metaphysical world history with a series of parallel national histories, so Syme's work makes the transition from history conceived as the deeds of leaders or as the principles of constitutions to history conceived as the rise and fall of social classes. And like Ranke and any other good historian, Syme does formulate generalizations of his own—the one underlying his conspectus of *Colonial Elites* being that "the strength and vitality of an empire is frequently due to the new aristocracy from the periphery." [10]

Neither elite studies nor any other method is likely to bring us closer to the deceptive ideal of behaviorism, of politics as a branch of mechanics. But individuals, families, and social groups *are* "real and tangible." They can offer a concrete island of refuge to a scholar who has seen old abstractions founder and who needs time and fresh materials to build a more seaworthy set of abstractions. In the field of comparative politics today, and particularly in research on the totalitarian and the so-called "developing" countries, elite studies hold great promise for a number of reasons. First and foremost, scholars in comparative politics have been turning away from the institutional-legal approach of a previous generation without having developed any new concept of equal scope or validity. Second, all the totalitarian and most of the "developing" countries are indeed oligarchies, being typically ruled by cohesive elites drawn from a party or a military establishment (cf. Bottomore, 63–84). In both types of country, there is an evident discrepancy between this reality of oligarchy and the liberal and democratic tenor of the constitutions; hence the institutional approach is even less fruitful when transferred from Western to non-Western countries. Finally, politics throughout Asia, Africa, and Latin America is in rapid flux; hence, while constitutions and other formal arrangements would project a false image of stability, individuals and groups can be seen as a "binding link" from regime to regime.

The leading claim today to the heritage of the institutional-legal approach, of course, is that advanced on behalf of functionalism—whether based on the notion of "decision-making" or on one of the sets of functions proposed by scholars like Talcott Parsons or Gabriel Almond. But I doubt whether the functionalist claim can be sustained. This is not because of the vagueness or banality that is said to be inherent in the search for universal social functions,[11] nor because of the static or conservative bias said to be implicit in the related notion of equilibrium, nor yet because of the danger of confusing correlation and causation.[12] All these difficulties, I think, can be remedied or avoided within a functional scheme. But there are two other difficulties that are more commonplace—and hence all the more serious. First, scholars of varying semantic tastes will not readily agree on the functions that a political system is thought to perform; there tend to be as many functional vocabularies as there are functionalists—and cumulative scholarship becomes impossible. Second, the researchers will find it difficult to fit empirical data into the analytic cate-

[10] *Ibid.*, 4.

[11] Barrington Moore, Jr., *Political Power and Social Theory* (Cambridge, Mass., 1958), 101f., 131.

[12] For these lines of criticism see, *ibid.*, 136–38; W. G. Runciman, *Social Science and Political Theory* (Cambridge 1963), 113ff., 120ff.; and Reinhard Bendix, *Nation-Building and Citizenship* (New York 1964), 301 and *passim*.

gories, however these may have been labelled and defined. Many decisions, for example, are made by Asian and African rulers—but the scholar is rarely privy to them. Similarly, articulation and aggregation may perhaps be accepted as basic political functions—but where does articulation of diverse interests stop and aggregation into a common policy begin? Once this line is drawn, how is articulation to be recorded or measured—by column inches of newsprint and volume of circulation? by attendance at outdoor rallies? or by its effect on the rulers? In short, it is difficult to agree what functions to look for and even more difficult to recognize a function when we see it. Hence, instead of fostering exact comparative studies, a functional scheme will at best permit broad intuitive characterizations of political systems.[13]

In contrast to the precision and uniformity that are the elusive aim of the functional schemes, the very flexibility and looseness of the technique of elite study is one of its chief recommendations in the present state of our knowledge (or rather, ignorance) about Asian, African, and Latin American politics. A concept that appeals to men as different as Gaetano Mosca and Lewis Namier, as Ronald Syme and Harold Lasswell, shows promise of permitting cumulative efforts by scholars working in many different locales among the eighty or more "developing" countries. Hence it is *because* of its diversity that the field may be expected to display "abounding vigor." Of course, the field of elite studies, too, has its scholarly requirements—and these are at once simple but far from easy. The student may start out by just immersing himself in the empirical data—but there must be enough information to permit such immersion, and the information must be accurate. Having done this, he must then construct some seaworthy hypotheses that will keep him from drowning. Only after his return to terra firma ought he to confront his readers.

III

The empirical studies presented in four of the six volumes here reviewed follow a consistent pattern. Each of them draws a quantitative group portrait of members of parliament, of cabinet ministers, or of party officials. The number of political leaders considered varies widely. In Lasswell and Lerner's *World Revolutionary Elites,* George K. Schueller concentrates on the 27 men who sat in the Soviet Politburo from 1917 to 1949; Robert C. North (with Ithiel de Sola Pool) compares 287 Kuomintang Central Executive Committee members (1924–1945) with 86 members of the Chinese Communist Politburo or Central Committee (1921–1945); Lerner (with Pool and Schueller) examines 538 out of some 1600 biographies in the Nazi *Führerlexikon* of 1934; and Lasswell (with Renzo Sereno) tabulates data on 539 Fascist officials of about the same time. Similarly, Singer in his book deals with 537 Ceylonese legislators (1924–1960). By contrast, Frey reports on 2210 Turkish deputies (1920–1957)—a larger group than is considered by the other five studies taken together—and Mattei Dogan (Marvick, 57–90) deals with as many as 2786 deputies of the French Third Republic (including 427 ministers) and 1112 deputies of the Fourth.

Judging by this sample, there seems to be a positive correlation between an author's assiduity and his methodolog-

[13] For one such set of characterizations see Gabriel A. Almond and James S. Coleman, eds., *The Politics of the Developing Areas* (Princeton 1960), which includes a chapter by the present writer on the Near East.

ical sophistication. The contributors to the Lasswell-Lerner volume illustrate some of the pitfalls. Schueller wisely goes little beyond reporting some elementary data on his twenty-seven Politburo members—though it is hard to tell what he adds to the knowledge that can be obtained from standard histories—whereas North repeatedly yields to the temptation to calculate percentages to the first decimal when his entire "population" is only forty-two or forty-four. Lasswell's Italian study includes data on "skills," some of which are rather whimsically defined. "Skill in ceremony," for instance, "includes persons who are masters of etiquette, e.g., aristocrats or retired army officers and high officials . . ." (p. 182). The circularity here is evident: persons are said to have moved into certain posts because of their skills, but these skills in turn are inferred from their careers. On the strength of what data the Fascist officials have been grouped into "proletariat," "lesser bourgeoisie," and "plutocracy" the reader is never told (pp. 181f.). Lerner's study of the Nazi elite digests more information than the companion studies and employs a greater variety of statistical techniques—yet his results are hardly more convincing. There are some minor inconsistencies: the total sample is said to include 577 persons, of whom 39 turn out to be double listings (pp. 195, 303). Wavering between two definitions of "propagandist," he now includes 128 of them and now 100 (which of course reduces the total further); and although he emphasizes that the differences between these two groups are "*in all cases* small and in the same direction" (p. 302), he does not say how small or in what direction.

More significant is the manner in which Lerner sets out to prove his central thesis that the Nazis were "marginal men." As a hypothesis the statement is plausible enough.[14] One recalls that Hitler was born on the Austrian side of the border, that Alfred Rosenberg was from the Baltic, that Goebbels had a clubfoot—and in view of their performance one is more than ready to believe that the Nazis were borderline humans in a variety of ways. And indeed Lerner finds that of his random sample from the *Führerlexikon* 56.5 percent are "marginal men," and of the sample of Nazi administrators (or "core Nazis," as he also calls them) no fewer than 82.1 percent (p. 288). But a closer look shows that Lerner used a list of no fewer than twenty-six characteristics of marginality (under thirteen headings) and was prepared to convict his suspects on any *one* of the counts (pp. 304f.). His statistics thus prove no more than that one-half to four-fifths of various Nazi groups were *either* Catholics, *or* did not complete their higher education, *or* married before twenty-one or after thirty-five, *or* were sons of peasants or artisans, *or* served as enlisted men before 1918—to name just a few of the categories. If the reader wonders what proportion of German adult males in 1934 satisfied one or another of Lerner's generous criteria, he will have to do his own supplementary research. It will not take him long, however, to deduce that (by virtue of their religion alone) an even half of today's West German population are definitely "marginal"—and that the percentage of "marginal" Christian Democratic members in the Bundestag today probably exceeds that of Lerner's Nazis.

Lerner, aside from his German investigation, has undertaken to sum up the empirical studies of the various authoritarian or totalitarian groups. ". . . Our

[14] Lerner fails to mention that the hypothesis was formulated a decade earlier by Sigmund Neumann who suggested that "the modern dictator is a *marginal man* of a marginal group" (*Permanent Revolution,* 2nd ed. [New York 1965], 62). Neumann's study first appeared in 1942, Lerner's in 1951.

elite studies," he finds, "[have] shown the mythologies created by the revolutionary elites to be seriously misleading in important respects. The Bolshevik elite was not proletarian; nor was the Nazi elite composed of sturdy German peasants." And, "Again, the impression created by propaganda—that the Kuomintang was led by a landlord clique, while the Chinese Communist Party was a movement of the masses—turned out to be inaccurate and misleading. Our data showed that 'a major portion of the elite of both movements came from quite similar high social strata and responded to similar Western and native influences during their years of growth and education'" (pp. 463, 465). These conclusions are sound enough, though perhaps not as startling as Lerner suggests. For even the Bolsheviks did not claim that Marx and Lenin were factory workers, nor the Nazis that Hitler, Himmler, and Goebbels were blond peasants; rather their claims were that the party was the *vanguard* of the proletariat or that it would restore *future* German generations to Aryan strength in *Blut und Boden.* The findings of the Lasswell-Lerner volume, therefore, show rather clearly that a study of social backgrounds can furnish clues for a study of political performance, but that the first cannot substitute for the second.

The two other M.I.T. studies carry the research into "developing" countries. Singer's book supplies some information on legislators and cabinet ministers in Ceylon during the late colonial and postcolonial periods. He shows that since independence (1948), and especially since S.W.R.D. Bandaranaike's dramatic election victory in 1956, the level of education and the average wealth of political leaders have somewhat declined, and the proportion of lawyers and (small and middling) landowners has gone up. Ceylon, like most "developing" countries, has few biographical handbooks and Singer's naively inquisitive questionnaire (Was the legislator ever "detained or imprisoned?" "Where does he stand with regard to ayurvedic medicine?" "List in order of preference the three things about Ceylon of which he is most proud"—pp. 151–54) elicited few responses. He therefore resorted to the expedient of relying on a single, anonymous informant, said to be "thoroughly knowledgeable about Ceylonese elites," and of having him fill in questionnaires for "more than five hundred" Ceylonese politicians (pp. 51–52). Apparently neither Singer nor his informant could obtain precise information on age; nor does the study correlate socioeconomic characteristics with party membership. The conclusion "that the emerging elite in Ceylon is a synthesis of the traditional thesis and the Western antithesis" (p. 144) is neither very original nor closely derived from his empirical data, nor yet does it do justice to the intense ethnic, political, and cultural struggle that has been fought in Ceylon over the last decade. The combination of haphazard research and trivial conclusion is perhaps not entirely accidental.

Frey was luckier than Singer. He was able to use official directories covering most Turkish parliaments and containing information on each deputy's place of birth, education, knowledge of foreign languages, occupation, and family status. (The Turkish government, with its methodical habits of record keeping, has required deputies since the early Atatürk period to supply this information so as to facilitate rational committee assignments.) But Frey has several further assets that Singer and other students of elites might well envy: in a decade of research on Turkey he has acquired an intimate knowledge of the language, social structure, history, and literature of the country; his use of statistical technique shows great versatility and perception; and he writes in a lucid style equally free from jargon and false flamboyance. Even more important, Frey formulates his hypotheses unequivocally and, in welcome contrast to Lerner, shows consistent regard for the canons of evidence. Some recent books on the politics of Asia, Africa, or Latin America are praised by area experts as solid contributions but shrugged off by the generalist as shallow and descriptive; others are admired for their theoretical brilliance and condemned for their inaccuracy. Frey's is one of the rare works that will satisfy both groups of critics.

Frey's analysis appropriately begins with a chapter called "Education: The Hallmark of the Elite" (pp. 29–72). He finds that "the basic bifurcation in Turkish society between the educated elite and uneducated masses . . . provided Mustafa Kemal with a rather convenient 'halfway house' in the reshaping of the country. He could, to a large extent, forget about the submerged masses and concentrate on solidifying his hold over the dominant intellectual group. . . . Put another way, . . . he *exploited* the educational bifurcation in the society instead of deploring it, as other leaders have often done" (p. 41). During the single-party period, the leaders tended to name candidates who had (in this order of preference) achieved a high level of education, served in high government posts, or held positions of local power in their home provinces (p. 156). As a result, "in a society in which about three fifths of the male population . . . could *not read and write*, at least three fifths of the [members of parliament], on the other hand, were *university*-educated" (p. 43). Party competition since the late 1940's, however, set in motion certain "capillary" processes (p. 282). As a result, the "lawyer and the merchant" have replaced "the soldier and the bureaucrat" in parliament and cabinet, and "the deputies have changed from being primarily a national elite group, oriented toward the tutelary development of the country, to being primarily an assemblage of local politicians, oriented toward more immediate local and political advantages" (pp. 195f.). Although the level of education has not much declined, the old bifurcation is under vigorous attack. But Frey reminds us that the Turkish crises of 1960–61 occurred at a level of political development that most other modernizing countries have not yet reached (p. 4).

IV

The student of political elites typically seeks to establish a correlation between political power and social status. He therefore must do three things: identify each of the two correlates and demonstrate a connection between them. Moreover, to make his results meaningful, he will do well to compare them with parallel findings for other times and places.

1. If he selects his politicians according to their formal office, he is back to some of the problems of the institutional-legal approach. Should he compare British cabinet members to the Soviet Council of Ministers or the Politburo—or to some other, more elusive, group? Are the parliamentarians of the French Third and Fourth Republics comparable to those of the Fifth? Or (to take an example from one of the studies here reviewed) did the Central Executive Committee of the Kuomintang, which grew from 24 members in 1924 to 223 in 1945, really remain the same body? Hence does it make sense to make summary calculations for the entire period, assigning the same weight to each member (Lasswell and Lerner, 385, 403, 414)? And were any of these successive

Kuomintang committees comparable to the six- or seven-man Politburo or the forty-four-man Central Committee of their Communist rivals?

If instead the student searches for some functional criterion by which to identify the "real" power holders, he is likely to open "a veritable Pandora's box of arbitrary decisions" (Singer, 52). There is also the danger of circularity: to study politics beneath the facade he wants to examine the real leaders, but to do so he must already know enough about the real process to identify them.[15]

In practice, most researchers take the safer, institutional course. Frey, moreover, is careful to demonstrate, and not just to assume, the power of his group —and for the period before 1960 this argument is fairly convincing (pp. 6–15). Beyond this, he uses consolidated ratings by nine experts to establish the relative power of officials within the assembly.[16] Lerner comes closest to a functional selection, made in this case by the compilers of the *Führerlexikon*—an elegant solution wherever a source of that type is available.

2. The social characteristics to be examined are usually limited by available information. It is easier to ascertain a politician's age, birthplace, and previous occupation than his wealth or the occupation of his father. Any figures given for the legislators should always be compared with the corresponding figures for the country as a whole—a rule that Frey consistently observes in his Turkish study and Lerner conspicuously disregards in his calculus of Nazi "marginality." To insure comparability with other countries, the researcher should abstract from peculiarities of the local culture and follow, wherever possible, the classifications of earlier elite studies. For example, Dogan may be justified in lumping together French officers and priests (Marvick, 67)—two groups that rarely sit in parliament, that often derive from the same social stratum, and that sometimes hold the same opinions—yet for the sake of comparison with Turkey, Ceylon, or even Germany one wishes he had not. Similarly, Frey, who is more interested in a politician's training than in his class origin, does not distinguish between factory workers and industrialists, or bank clerks and bank directors; for the sake of comparison with most other studies, one wishes he had.

3. Frey rightly warns that "to leap from some knowledge of the social backgrounds of national politicians to inferences about the power structure of the society is quite dangerous. Even to proceed from such knowledge to judgments about the political behavior of these same politicians can be treacherous . . ." (p. 157). And Bendix and Lipset, in an earlier review of elite studies, criticized those who overlooked the dangers. "To know who the power wielding individuals are is thought to be sufficient; it is a secondary matter to inquire into how they use their power. That they will do so in their own interest is [considered] self-evident, and the nature of that interest is inferred from the status which they occupy." Such a set of assumptions, they rightly conclude, can easily

[15] Cf. C. Wright Mills, *The Power Elite* (New York 1956), 366f.

[16] Frey describes fully the ingenious calculations by which he converted these ratings into numerical indices of power for each deputy (pp. 225–46, 443–47). He then tabulates such traits as age, education, and regional origin separately for "top leaders," "middle leaders," and "backbenchers" (pp. 264–68). It turns out that the first two groups deviate from the assembly as a whole in the same direction as (though slightly less than) cabinet members (see diagrams, pp. 279f.)—who of course could be much more easily identified. One wonders, therefore, whether the enormous additional effort that went into these calculations really paid off in additional knowledge obtained.

"explain away the very facts of political life." [17]

A striking demonstration that neither social background nor training determines political action is provided by the career of the late S.W.R.D. Bandaranaike, which is only briefly touched upon in Singer's book. Son of a wealthy planter family of the coast, brought up as a Christian and in the English language, he completed his studies at Oxford where he was chairman of the English-Speaking Union. Learning Sinhalese on his return to Ceylon and converting to Buddhism, he won his spectacular election victory of 1956 on the slogan of "Sinhala Only" (that is, the promise to make Sinhalese the sole official language in preference to English and Tamil). His chief supporters were Buddhist small farmers of the hill country; his bitterest enemies the Anglicized planter families. Nor is his case unique: the spokesmen of the Third Estate in 1789 included the Abbé Sieyès and the Marquis de Condorcet; most early Socialist leaders were of middle-class origin; border nationals have often been the most vocal nationalists; Lloyd George did not rule Britain in the interest of Welshmen, nor Churchill of Anglo-Americans—the examples could be multiplied *ad libitum*. Before we can hope to generalize about the influence of social background on the motives and actions of individual leaders, we need many more psychological studies on the model of Erikson's *Young Man Luther*.

Meanwhile, there are a number of ways in which the correlation between politicians and their social background can be made meaningful. First, one can try to salvage the postulate of class interest by applying it not to individuals but to large numbers. A Sieyès or a Condorcet, it may be argued, will perhaps join the bourgeoisie and make quite a stir when he does, but an entire parliament of marquises and abbots is likely to make short shrift of bourgeois interests. The statement in this form certainly is more plausible; yet it is a presumption at best, and the Bendix-Lipset injunction still stands—that the facts of politics must be studied in their own right and not just inferred from the politicians' social background.

Second, it is well to remember that the connection between politics and society is a two-way street. The social composition of parliament may affect the decisions of that body, but even more surely political decisions affect the social composition of a parliament. Dogan found in his study of France that the "Republic of the Dukes" of the 1870's, after half a century of universal suffrage, made way for the "reign of the lower middle class" (Marvick, 73). And Frey contrasts the effect of the "semi-co-optative" process of recruitment during the Kemalist period with the effects of party competition in the 1950's. But here again one must beware of simplistic assumptions. Donald R. Mathews found that in stratified societies such as Britain there is indeed "a tendency to look to one's own class for political leadership" but that in a more mobile society such as the United States voters do not hesitate to choose representatives from a higher class.[18] In Turkey, during the competition between the nationalist movement of Kemal in Anatolia and the Sultan's imperial government in Istanbul (1919–1922), each side tended to give a maximum number of high government posts to those groups from which it received *least* support—the nationalists to civil

[17] Reinhard Bendix and Seymour Martin Lipset, "Political Sociology," *Current Sociology,* VI, No. 3 (1957), 85, as cited in Marvick, 14.

[18] *United States Senators and Their World* (Chapel Hill 1960), 45, n. 39. Cf. Matthews' earlier study *The Social Background of Political Decision-Makers* (Garden City 1954).

servants, and the Sultan to military officers—the motive being both camouflage and courtship.[19]

Third, it is possible to shift the emphasis from the social or class origins of politicians to their education, training, and other formative experiences. This, by and large, is the approach favored by Frey, although he pleads for further studies of the process of "political socialization in the broadest sense," and meanwhile expresses himself with commendable caution: "While unacceptable as direct evidence, speculations about the distribution of power based on inferences from social background analysis may nevertheless be useful if viewed as hypotheses or suggestions demanding more explicit confirmation" (p. 157).

Fourth, comparisons over time and among countries can greatly help in the formulation of such suggestions and hypotheses. This may be illustrated by the accompanying table, which I have compiled mostly from the works here reviewed. (I have added some Scandinavian data from two older studies that deserve to be more widely known.) It shows graphically that whereas a majority of Kuomintang and Chinese Communist leaders have been professional, lifelong party organizers, or else military men, elective parliaments in Europe and Asia are drawn from a wide range of professions. The effects of party competition that Frey observed in Turkey after 1950 recur in Ceylon after 1956: merchants and landowners replace government officials. (Singer reports no data that might show whether local influence also has increased.) In both countries the changes in social composition that have occurred are more pronounced in the cabinet than in the parliament. Yet Turkey also has had a marked influx of physicians and engineers—a group less numerous in the Ceylonese parliament and entirely unrepresented in recent cabinets.[20] It would be interesting to trace the effects of this difference on each country's economic policy.

Finally, a comparative study can establish what traits are common to the parliamentary profession as such, and for what reasons. Frey, noting a prevalence of lawyers in recent Turkish parliaments comparable to that in the United States, France, and several Commonwealth countries surmises "that a Western, multi-party parliamentary democracy gives special sway to persons adept in verbal presentation, superior in their comprehension of the formal and legal intricacies of government, facile at interpersonal relations, . . . and with the stamina and ability to attend to a plethora of organizational and administrative details and duties" (p. 396). The hypothesis is plausible enough; yet the Swedish data suggest a different explanation. In Swedish politics, lawyers are extremely rare. On the other hand, all public officials and employees—from the permanent undersecretary to the municipal street-car conductor, and including teachers in schools and universities—are eligible to run for public office; if elected they are entitled to leaves of absence during the legislative sessions without loss of seniority or pension rights. It is obvious that only a nation with a meticulous sense of role separation can operate such regulations without politicizing its civil service. But since these rules are deeply entrenched

[19] See Rustow, "The Army and the Founding of the Turkish Republic," *World Politics,* XI (July 1959), 527ff.

[20] In fact, the Ceylonese figures in my consolidated table refer only to physicians, since Singer did not list engineers. It is not clear whether he found no engineers at all in Ceylonese cabinets and parliaments, or whether he included them in other categories such as "public service" or "business" (p. 171).

Occupations of Political Elites (in %)

	Turkey				Ceylon				China			Germany	France			Sweden			
	Parliament		Cabinet		Parliament		Cabinet		KMT C.E.C.		C.P. Cen. Comm.	Nazi Leaders	Cabinet	Parliament		Parliament		Cabinet	
Occupation *	*1920*	*1954*	*1920–23*	*1954–57*	*1924*	*1964*	*1924–31*	*1964–65*	*1924*	*1945*	*1945*	*1934*	*1898–1940*	*1898–1940*	*1940–58*	*1867*	*1933*	*1809–44*	*1920–34*
Government, Party	23	9	20	18	37	14	52	14	61	51	46	34			7	15	12	64	49
Education, Journalism	7	12	9	9	6	18	9	14	8	9	4		38	31	21	11	16	2	13
Medicine, Engineering	5	17	9	24	1	9	4	–	..	..	..	35			11	1	–	–	0
Law	13	27	17	33	35	26	22	27	..	..	..		37	25	13	–	0	–	1
Business	13	19	3	12	8	12	4	9	..	..	..	19	14	31	16	16	9	2	8
Agriculture	6	10	6	3	6	26	4	32	..	..	..	5			12	52	40	2	8
Labor	..	..	..	..	..	..	..	..	..	..	11	1	3	9	12	–	20	–	2
Military	15	4	29	–	–	–	–	–	26	38	39	3	8	4	2	2	1	30	17
Religion	17	1	9	–	3	–	4	–	..	..	..	–	..	..		3	2	–	–
Other	2	1	–	–	1	5	–	1	4	2	–	4	–	–	7	–	–	–	–
N =	361	537	35	33	86	110	23	22	23	220	44	159	427	2786	112	190	230	44	287

* Occupational groupings have been standardized and simplified. – means none; .. means none or included in another category; 0 means less than ½%. Percentages have been rounded and therefore may not add to 100. Figures for the Kuomintang have been recalculated to eliminate unknowns. In bicameral systems, "Parliament" refers to the lower chambers.

Sources: Frey, 181, 283; Singer, 171; Lasswell and Lerner, 384f. (China), and 200 (Germany); Marvick, 67, 73 (France); [Uppsala, Universitetet, Seminariet för Statskunskap], *Studier över den Svenska Riksdagens Sociala Sammansättning* (Uppsala 1936), 221; [*idem*], *De Nordiska Ländernas Statsråd* (Uppsala 1935), 22f. (The last two works are vols. 7 and 4 respectively in the series "Skrifter Utgivna av Statsvetenskapliga Föreningen i Uppsala.")

in Sweden, and since, next to Australia and New Zealand, Sweden has the highest ratio of government employment in the non-Communist world,[21] political parties can draw on nominees from a vast reservoir of civil servants, university professors, school teachers, and the like. In countries where public employees are barred from active politics, lawyers fill the vacuum—not perhaps because they are adept at law-making, but rather because a law practice that can be dropped or resumed almost at will offers a refuge from the uncertainties of periodic election.

Whatever the particular correlations he wishes to establish, the student of elites will do well to classify his politicians into common-sense groupings—men in their thirties, university graduates, natives of Kwangtung, up-country Sinhalese, journalists, West Pointers, noblemen, and the like. He should use categories, in other words, that (a) correspond to some group consciousness among the subjects themselves or that (b) he himself can precisely define. Above all, he should beware of giving to his officeholders a spurious unity by applying to them some vague and ill-defined label. The difficulty of Lerner's fuzzy concept of "marginal men" has already been noted. Somewhat similarly, Edward Shils has asserted that "the intellectuals of underdeveloped countries have created the political life of their countries; they have been its instigators, its leaders, and its executants" (Marvick, 30). And Lasswell finds, even more sweepingly, that the world is in the midst of a "permanent revolution of modernizing intellectuals" (Lasswell and Lerner, 80). Soberly examined, these propositions turn out to be a pretentious way of saying that to enter politics these days, especially in underdeveloped countries, it is most helpful to have received a higher education. For if the intellectuals are defined in some strict sense (e.g., "journalists, lawyers, and educators"—Shils in Marvick, 31), then a great many underdeveloped countries are *not* ruled by intellectuals; and if the term is broadened to include all college graduates, then the statement will remain true whether power is seized by army officers, by civil servants, or by professional party organizers.[22] And in that case, of course, the intellectuals will be found to dominate not just politics but nearly all urban careers, at least in the more developed societies. In New York these days even department stores prefer salesgirls with college degrees.

Although it is difficult to conceive of "the intellectuals" as rulers in Asia or as leaders of a revolution throughout the world, such statements as Shils' or Lasswell's derive a certain plausibility from the echoes they convey of the theories of Marx, Pareto, and others. It is time that we turned to a brief examination of these elite theories which preceded by several generations the more empirical elite studies.

V

It is not really surprising that European sociologists should have started talking of the ruling class, of the po-

[21] Bruce M. Russett and others, *World Handbook of Political and Social Indicators* (New Haven 1964), 70f.

[22] Bottomore finds that Western intellectuals today do not fully qualify as a ruling elite "because they lack any distinctive group organization or ideology" (p. 71); yet the same may be said of the intellectuals of developing countries, particularly in Asia and Latin America. Political competition still is largely confined to the urban educated groups, but that competition is sharp; and ideological tenets like nationalism, social justice, and economic progress are invoked by everyone. Lasswell himself concedes that "intellectuals . . . are not fully conscious of a distinct identity" (Lasswell and Lerner, 87) but does not seem to realize how precarious that makes his construct of the intellectuals as a revolutionary elite.

litical elite, and of perennial oligarchy in the second half of the nineteenth century when the phenomenon of a closed, hereditary oligarchy was disappearing from the European scene. Where oligarchy remained unshaken—in eighteenth-century Britain, or Venice, or Switzerland—no ingenious theory or laborious research was required to find out from what class the rulers were drawn. The revolutions of 1789 and 1848, and the conservative response to them, changed the picture thoroughly. The proclamation of popular sovereignty now sharply posed the question of who among the people really did the ruling. During the slow and painful European transition to democracy between the French Revolution and the First World War, Marx, Pareto, and others elevated to the status of universal principle what were valid enough observations of their immediate surroundings. England before 1832, where landed magnates freely trafficked in parliamentary seats and where the Hobbeses and the Burkes were in the pay of the Devonshires and the Rockinghams, lent support to Marx's notions of the economic base of power and of philosophy as part of the intellectual superstructure. Southern Italy in Mosca's youth was a setting designed to "display parliamentary institutions to their maximum discredit" (H. Stuart Hughes in Meisel, 150). And German Social Democracy under Bebel and Kautsky—a party that relied on the "powerful authority of the middle-class State" to protect it "from the consequences of its own 'revolutionary' speeches" [23]—amply illustrated Michels' view of the "oligarchical tendencies of modern democracy."

Elite theory thus grew as the lengthening shadow of democracy. Theorists, from Marx and Pareto to Michels and C. Wright Mills, measured existing political and social reality against the democratic ideal and found a vast disparity. They differed more in their therapy than in their diagnoses (cf. Bottomore, 30): Marx contended that the disparity could and should be remedied, Michels that it should but could not, Pareto that it neither could nor should. The fourth position—that it could be remedied but should not—of course, had been that of the original defenders of the *ancien régime*. From 1789 onward, indeed, these doctrines evolved in logical sequence.[24] French aristocratic exiles cried in anguish that the majority (or rather *la canaille*) had seized power and that this would be the end of religion and culture. Later conservatives like Taine and Burckhardt took courage: the majority had seized power but did not know how to use it—here was the minority's chance to preserve the cultural tradition. Marx outflanked the heirs of the bourgeois revolution on the Left and accused them of having restored minority rule in more brutal and less hypocritical form; but the proletarian revolution, he promised, would do away with minorities and indeed with rule itself. To Pareto, Mosca, and Michels this seemed so much nonsense: minorities have always ruled, they protested (in tones of satisfaction, regret, or dismay), and always will.

A crucial turn along this road separates Marx from later elite theorists. Bottomore reminds us that Pareto and Mosca were arguing not only against the egalitarian pretensions of existing regimes but also against the Marxian promise of future equality. (Max Weber, it has been observed, "became a sociologist in a long and intense dialogue

[23] This is the judgment of Arthur Rosenberg, *A History of Bolshevism* (London 1934), 66.

[24] On the importance of Taine and Tocqueville as precursors of elite theory see Sereno's subtle and urbane study *The Rulers,* 8–17.

with the ghost of Karl Marx."[25] The same is true of his contemporaries, such as Pareto, Mosca, Durkheim, Veblen, and Toennies.) Marx had stated the correlation between "political decision-makers" and their "social background" with precision: The owners are the rulers, the workers are the subjects. When technology makes one means of production obsolete, the owners of the more up-to-date means of production will overthrow the old ruling class. This process will continue, with politics limping one step behind economics, until technology enables the workers to assume collective ownership and thereby to abolish the distinction between owner and worker, between ruler and subject. The ruling class changes, but it always has a clear, economically defined identity: landowners under one system, capitalists under the next, and proletarians in the transition to the final stage. To Marx's clear-cut theory there corresponded a clear-cut moral attitude. The bourgeois are condemned as exploiters, and scorned as obsolescent exploiters. The proletarians are hailed as the wave of the future which will wash away exploitation once and for all.

Into this simple, forceful doctrine, Pareto, Mosca, and Michels introduced two significant changes. They applied the theory to all societies, past and future, and they admitted a number of other bases of power in addition (or in preference) to the economic base. Bottomore rightly considers that this attempt to avoid Marx's empirical errors deprived the doctrine of much of its clarity and suggestiveness (pp. 26, 32).[26] The theory did not become more accurate—only harder to disprove. The ambiguities are fully apparent in a paragraph in which Mosca states his central thesis:

> Among the constant facts and tendencies that are to be found in all political organisms, one is so obvious that it is apparent to the most casual eye. In all societies—from societies that are very meagerly developed and have barely attained the dawnings of civilization down to the most advanced and powerful societies—two classes of people appear—a class that rules and a class that is ruled. The first class, always the less numerous, performs all political functions, monopolizes power and enjoys the advantages that power brings, whereas the second, the more numerous class, is directed and controlled by the first, in a manner that is now more or less legal, now more or less arbitrary and violent, and supplies the first . . . with material means of subsistence and with the instrumentalities that are essential to the vitality of the political organism.[27]

It is this doctrine which Michels was to call the "iron law of oligarchy"—with evident allusion to Lassalle's "iron law of wages"—and which Lasswell, paraphrasing James Bryce, was to restate succinctly: "Government is always government by the few, whether in the name of the few, the one, or the many."[28]

[25] In the words of Albert Salomon, "German Sociology," in Georges Gurvitch and Wilbert E. Moore, eds., *Twentieth Century Sociology* (New York 1945), 596.

[26] The above account follows, in part, both Bottomore and the similar critique in Runciman, 64–86.

[27] Gaetano Mosca, *The Ruling Class,* ed. Arthur Livingston (New York 1939), 50.

[28] Lasswell, Lerner, and Rothwell, 7. For similar formulations see Lasswell, *Politics: Who Gets What, When, How,* 168, and *Power and Personality* (New York 1948), 109. Bryce had written that "in all . . . organized bodies of men . . . direction and decisions rest in the hands of a small percentage, less and less in proportion to the larger size of the body, till in a great population it becomes an infinitesimally small proportion of the whole number. This is and always has been true of all forms of government, though in different degrees" (quoted *ibid.* from *Modern Democracies* [New York 1921], chap. 75).

Generalizations intended to apply to all societies at all times, it has been suggested, are likely to be either trivial or false.[29] Mosca in the span of just two sentences covers both possibilities. He starts with the distinction between rulers and ruled, which the observer may of course draw in a number of ways. And indeed it is not difficult to think of a definition by which the rulers will always turn out to be the less numerous group. On this score, incidentally, the rulers find themselves in good company with the performers of other specialized functions. There are in most societies fewer bakers than eaters of bread, fewer teachers than students, and fewer clergymen than communicants. But this is not to say that rulers and ruled each constitute a *class* in the usual sense of that word. And just as in most societies the bakers do not eat all the bread nor the parsons maintain a monopoly on piety, so it does not follow that the rulers have a monopoly of power nor that they perform all political functions. These propositions, as Lasswell has rightly observed, are likeliest to hold true in "regimes that are ascendant by the overt use of force" (Marvick, 265) —that is, in freshly conquered societies.

A meaningful elite theory must show that the rulers have some group identity derived from sources other than their political function—from prior group consciousness, from descent, from schooling, from appointment by previous rulers, from economic interest, or the like. But too often an author assumes what he ought to prove, and ends up with a tautology instead of a theory. As Lasswell and Kaplan have said of Pareto's central tenet: "Every people is governed by an elite, by a chosen element in the population; what is said, in effect, is that every people is ruled by—rulers." [30] Another danger is a simple ambiguity of definition—leaving it open whether the rulers themselves are a class (or elite) or whether they are merely the spokesmen or instruments of such a class [31]—and this in turn opens the door to what Robert Dahl has called "an infinite regress of explanations." "If the overt leaders . . . do not . . . constitute a ruling elite, then the theory can be saved by arguing that behind the overt leaders there is a set of covert leaders who do. If subsequent evidence shows that this covert group does not make a ruling elite, then the theory can be saved by arguing that behind the first covert group there is another, and so on." [32]

A far subtler line of reasoning is adopted by Robert Michels, whose major work amounts to a brilliantly fallacious argument *a fortiori*. Whereas Pareto had inconclusively piled up evidence of aristocracy from here, there, and everywhere, Michels concentrates on the hierarchic, self-perpetuating tendencies among the leaders of European Socialist parties. If even the Socialists, the avowed champions of equality, are hopelessly addicted to oligarchic prac-

[29] Barrington Moore, vii, 101f.

[30] Harold D. Lasswell and Abraham Kaplan, *Power and Society* (New Haven 1950), 202. The quotation is from Vilfredo Pareto, *Mind and Society* (New York 1935), 246. Cf. Bottomore, 26: "When we ask, who has power in a particular society, the reply is, those who have power"; and the comment by Carl J. Friedrich in Meisel, 177.

[31] Lasswell, for example, defines the elite alternatively (1) as those who wield influence or make decisions (see the quotation at the opening of this review) and (2) "as the collectivity from which active decision makers are drawn . . ." (Lasswell and Lerner, 12). The other empirical studies, by implication, accept the first definition. The second echoes the *Communist Manifesto* in which contemporary rulers are called a "committee for managing the common affairs of the whole bourgeoisie." Cf. Friedrich in Meisel, 177.

[32] "A Critique of the Ruling Elite Model," *American Political Science Review*, LII (June 1958), 463.

tices—so Michels' argument runs in essence—what may one expect of bourgeois or conservative parties that do not even pretend to be egalitarian? Michels might have discovered his error if he had pursued his own insight that "organization is the weapon of the weak in their struggle with the strong." [33] This formula would have helped him understand why the conservative and aristocratic defenders of the old European order generally organized much later and much more loosely than the challengers on the Left. A few years before Michels' book first appeared, a Swedish conservative leader took a visitor on a tour of the country homes of his parliamentary friends. "Now you see—here they all live in their estates and mansions like so many princes," he exclaimed with an audible sigh; "it's no use trying to keep discipline in a party such as this." [34] Michels, that is to say, could have supplemented his evidence of the "oligarchical tendencies of democracy" with converse evidence of the egalitarian tendencies of aristocracy—and upon that double paradox built a more accurate and more comprehensive conception of politics.

Subtle or crude, the fallacies of the elite theorist serve to protect a moral position that is ambivalent and hence inherently vulnerable. Mosca, for example, is rightly outraged at the coercion and crude exploitation that he depicts. But, supposing such to be characteristic of all societies, he retreats from indignation to cynicism. The same attitudes, in varying mixtures, have often been noted in other writers. One of Pareto's critics speaks of his "psychology of the disappointed lover" and finds him, in his later years, "brimful with contempt for the human race" (Werner Stark, in Meisel, 47, 48). Robert Dahl, in his critique of Mills, observes that the ruling elite model "is simple, compelling, dramatic, 'realistic.' It gives one standing as an inside-dopester. For individuals with a strong strain of frustrated idealism, it has just the right touch of hard-boiled cynicism." [35] Lasswell's characteristic combination of hardheaded realism in assessing the effects of manipulation and coercion in modern society with an almost utopian faith in the possibilities of its rational reconstruction may perhaps be regarded as a special form of the elite theorist's ambivalence. Lasswell has shrewdly exposed some of the fallacies of his precursors; but it is surely significant that he no longer commits himself to any one definition of the elite concept (Lasswell and Lerner, 4) and that he has not, in three decades, found time to relate his propositions about elites very closely to any empirical research. Surprisingly, for example, one of the three Hoover Institution Elite Studies of 1951–1955 that is *not* reprinted in the current volume by Lasswell and Lerner is the one that was intended to introduce the hypotheses and justify the research design of the earlier series.[36]

James Meisel has aptly characterized Mosca's and Pareto's original impulse. "The counterrevolutionary radical will often be a revolutionist *manqué*. . . . Counterrevolution knows the sadness of the morning after" (p. 4). Or as Lasswell himself has said (of historians like Spengler and Toynbee), "Holding himself responsible for every discrepancy between fact and aspiration, man turns against himself as the author of his own betrayal" (Lasswell and Lerner, 30).

[33] *Political Parties: A Sociological Study of the Oligarchical Tendencies of Modern Democracy* (New York, n.d.), 21. This edition by Dover Publications is a reprint of the English translation of 1915 based on the first German edition of 1911.

[34] Patrik Reuterswärd, quoted in Rustow, *The Politics of Compromise* (Princeton 1955), 167.

[35] P. 463.

[36] Lasswell, Lerner, and Rothwell (cited, n. 2).

The elite theorist typically starts out as an egalitarian of more than usual sensitivity and perception and he turns into a relentless critic of democracy because he takes its ideals more seriously and sees its defects more sharply. For this reason no purely logical critique of the elite model is fully adequate: the fallacies and the cynicism stem from a true sense of indignation, from a genuine moral sentiment. Equality is the most widely proclaimed political ideal of the modern age; yet it is the one most imperfectly achieved. Modern organization, in particular, is an ambiguous instrument that is likely to erect new structures of unequal power as it dismantles old ones.[37] Americans, who have espoused the egalitarian creed more ardently and developed organization more highly than have most other societies, are the more readily conscious of that tension. Hence the wide appeal among them of recent books on *The Taste Makers, The Hidden Persuaders,* or *The Power Elite.*

The basic fallacy of this recent genre of writing has been laid bare by H. Stuart Hughes who, in 1954, explained why Mosca's concept of the "political class" no longer applies to "a country like the United States, with a standard of living unparalleled in history and the majority of the population assimilated in habits and attitudes to a vast middle class. . . . It is too rigid to embrace realities of our current society. In a situation in which the locus of political influence is almost impossible to establish, in which authority is diffused among a wide variety of mutually interacting pressure and 'veto' groups, it is idle to speak of a clearly defined political class. In practice the rule of minorities still obtains; but their influence is exerted in so shifting and amorphous a fashion that it cannot be described any longer in terms of a specific ruling group" (Meisel, 160). Two years later, Mills published his *Power Elite,* whose recurrent stridency contrasts with Hughes's sober evaluation.[38]

VI

Bottomore finds Marx's ruling class theorem empirically inadequate in the light both of subsequent and of contemporary evidence; but, as we noted, he prefers it to later, vaguer formulations because of its "greater fertility and suggestiveness and . . . its value in the construction of theories." To separate fruitful theory from empirical error he is ready to surrender "the Marxist view of the concept" of the ruling class "as a description of a real phenomenon which is to be observed in all societies in the same general form, and to regard it instead as an 'ideal type,' in the sense which Max Weber gave to this term" (p. 32). Although he considers the possibility that universal suffrage would move society away from the Marxian model, he doubts that in Europe outside of Scandinavia this has occurred to any great extent. His chief evidence is data on income distribution in Britain, although surprisingly he does not consider whether the continuing inequalities are hereditary or whether there has been circulation among the wealthy (pp. 34f.). Elsewhere he criticizes the definition of democracy as competition among a plurality of elites, which in one form or another has been proposed by Mannheim, Schumpeter, Aron, and (he might

[37] The relationship of modernization to equality is considered further in my forthcoming study of political modernization.

[38] By implication, however, Mills concedes from the start that his quarrel is with the power of organization rather than with a specific ruling minority (p. 11).

have added) Lasswell,[39] and which is probably espoused by the majority of Western intellectuals today. Bottomore's objection is that their attempt at reconciling elite theory with democracy yields too much democratic ground to the elitist. His conclusion on this point deserves to be quoted more fully: "The preservation, and especially the development and improvement, of a democratic system of government does not depend primarily upon fostering the competition between small elite groups whose activities are carried on in realms far removed from the observation or control of ordinary citizens, but upon creating and establishing the conditions in which a large majority of citizens, if not all citizens, can take part in deciding those social issues which vitally affect their individual lives—at work, in the local community, and in the nation—and in which the distinction between elites and masses is reduced to the smallest possible degree" (pp. 119f.). Here a student of Asian or Latin American politics might object that Bottomore underrates the importance of political competition in bringing about other democratic developments. I should judge, for example, that Turkey, Ceylon, and India (to consider only three countries mentioned earlier in these pages) have on balance made more progress toward popular education, social equality, and informed civic participation during periods of elite competition than under the tutelary regimes of Atatürk or of the British Raj. But these, of course, are matters for empirical investigation; and in planning further research on the development of democracy, both in the West and in the late-modernizing countries, it will be well to bear in mind Bottomore's basic assumption. ". . . In the conception of democracy as government *by* the people which prevailed during most of the nineteenth century," he reminds us, "democracy was conceived as a continuing process in which political rights, the power to influence decisions on social policy, were progressively extended to groups in the population which had formerly been deprived of them. . . . It was regarded as a movement towards an ideal condition of society in which men would be fully self-governing, which might never be completely achieved, but which democrats ought to strive for" (p. 110).

From Marx to Michels, three generations of social scientists formulated comprehensive statements about ruling classes, oligarchies, and political elites. These theories were suffused with strong sentiments of moral indignation and social protest but were sustained by inadequate evidence or were cast in ambiguous formulations. More recently, C. Wright Mills has resumed the earlier critique with renewed fervor. Meanwhile, Harold Lasswell's pleas for the accumulation of precise empirical data presaged a new departure.

Such data over the past thirty years have been assembled in great profusion—mostly on legislators and cabinet members in elective systems, but also on party officials in dictatorships of the Communist or Fascist type. Today, research on the social background of political elites holds particular promise in the study of Asian, African, and

[39] Following his statement of the iron law of oligarchy (see above, p. [87] and n. 28), Lasswell continues: "But this fact does not settle the question of the degree of democracy. . . . The key question turns on accountability." At the conclusion of his essay in the Marvick volume he asks "how elite studies will affect elites, recognizing this as a special case of how science, and especially social science, affects society"; and emphasizes his own answer: "*To the extent that procedures and results are public and competitive, democratic tendencies are favored, since they foster simultaneous improvement of insight and understanding*" (p. 281).

Latin American politics, where the institutional approach tends to mislead and the functionalist approach to confuse. The scarcity of biographical data would seem to be the only serious limitation on the possibilities of such research. Most recent students of elites, however, have lacked the intellectual breadth and sophistication of Michels or Lasswell, let alone of Marx. Theories with little factual support therefore have been replaced by masses of facts with little theoretical structure. It is by now obvious that elites are a vast subject; that quantification of social data about them is a technique of potential precision and versatility; but that neither subject nor technique will add to our knowledge except as we ask significant questions of one and manage to answer them by the other. Among recent works, Frey's analysis of two generations of Turkish legislators shows a unique awareness of these methodological problems and opportunities—of the variety of data that may be assembled about elites, of the many statistical relations that may be calculated, and of the cautious inferences that may be drawn from such material. His book thus may well serve as a model for future elite studies in democracies or dictatorships, in Western or non-Western countries.

Careful empirical research alone, nonetheless, cannot answer the fundamental questions that provided the original impulse for the early theories about elites and the later research into their social composition. Bottomore's work has the merit of shifting the argument back to a philosophic plane where questions of epistemology, of ethics, and of empirical fact may fruitfully be considered together. At such a level, the fallacies can be resolved, the cynical poses can be relinquished, and the emotional ardor can be harnessed to programs of reliable research and of effective political action. Bottomore also reminds us that the study of the rulers' social background is only a supplement, not a substitute, for the study of their performance in office—and (we may add) of the effect of that performance on the recruitment of future rulers. If this context of interaction between social and political forces is kept in mind, research on elites can contribute to a future comparative theory of political and social change. Bottomore, in sum, has identified more clearly than has any other recent writer the problems that students of elites must resolve before they can combine the theoretical sweep of a Marx or a Pareto with the conceptual clarity and empirical accuracy that sound scholarship demands.

PART II

The Russian Revolution

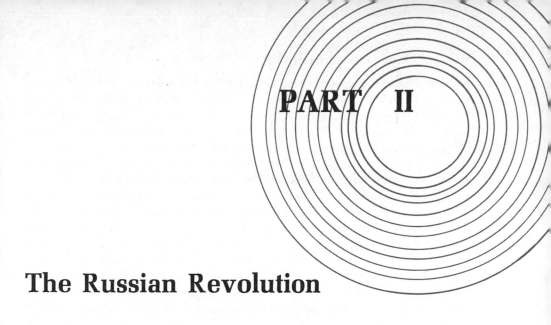

Now more than half a century behind us, the Russian Revolution looms more than ever as one of the great events of human history. Few events of our time—perhaps only the brutal experience of Nazism, or the advent of the nuclear age at Hiroshima—have had so profound an impact on the course of history, or have so deeply affected men's minds. The year 1917 in effect inaugurated our modern revolutionary era; all subsequent revolutions of our time are linked to the Russian Revolution; and though that revolution has been followed by others of at least equal intensity and sweep, it remains the "classic" version against which others are compared. The French Revolution provided men with a model and a political lexicon for nearly a century and a quarter; the Russian Revolution now dominates men's language and imagination in much the same way 1789 once did. "Bolshevik" and "Menshevik" have replaced "Jacobin" and "Girondist"; and "Leninism" and "Stalinism" have become too easily and loosely used designations for certain general political views and styles.

Despite all of this, disillusionment with the Russian Revolution is now widespread. The trauma of the Stalinist era has not healed. The Revolution has not led to freedom and equality but has culminated in an autocratic police state more efficiently repressive than Tsarist Russia ever was. Young revolutionaries, increasingly anarchistic and anti-ideological, find the stodgy, bureaucratic, "bourgeois" and obviously class-ridden character of contemporary Soviet society distasteful. The Soviet Union's claim to leadership of the "world revolutionary movement" has for many been challenged successfully by younger revolutions still in their heroic phase. It is Mao and Che, and not Kosygin and Brezhnev, who have the allegiance of young rebels today. But the Russian Revolution nonetheless remains in many ways a compelling reality for many men. Its undeniable material—and to some degree social—achievements make it a still relevant model for underdeveloped societies seeking freedom and power through technological and industrial progress; for others, it retains the fascination of a great and noble experiment gone awry. The Russian Revolution is still, whatever transformations it has gone through, a political reality of enormous importance in the contemporary world. The "ten days that shook the world" continue to do so, no matter how middle-aged the Revolution has become.

Of all the paradoxes associated with the Russian Revolution, none is more obvious than the fact that though it was made in the name of Marx, it simply did not follow the Marxian paradigm. It was a "proletarian" revolution made in an overwhelmingly agrarian society in which capitalism had not even come close to that overripeness that was to be the condition for its socialist transfiguration. (Indeed, the "Marxist" revolutions of our era have not at all occurred where, when, and how Marx had predicted they would.) It is true that, late in his life, after long having excoriated Imperial Russia as a "bulwark of reaction," Marx had, at the request of some of his early Russian disciples, begun to reconsider some of his predictions. He began to think seriously about the possibility that agrarian Russia, given its increasingly ardent and determined revolutionary intelligentsia and the communal or semisocialist structure of rural Russian society, might be able to leap beyond the capitalist phase of development directly into socialism. But his reflections in this direction were incomplete. Moreover, he suggested finally that this would become a possibility only if capitalism was simultaneously overthrown by proletarian revolutions in the advanced capitalist nations of the West. His own final uncertainties lived on as confusions among Russian Social Democrats—especially among the Mensheviks—most of whom continued to believe that historical and economic circumstances were not yet ripe for a socialist or proletarian revolution, that therefore it would be premature for Russian socialists to seize power and that capitalism (and bourgeois democracy) had to develop fully before such seizure would be possible. Lenin was less inhibited by such thoughts than were his opponents on the left.

But if the Revolution did not occur "according to Marx," the fundamental causes of the development of a powerful revolutionary movement in the nineteenth- and early twentieth-century Russia, and of the growing instability of the Tsarist autocracy, are perfectly clear. The last decades of Romanov rule constituted a period of unparalleled reform and "progress" in Imperial Russia. In response to intensifying internal and external pressures for change, Russia's autocratic rulers, without relinquishing ultimate power and without surrendering the principle of autocracy, launched reforms that produced fatal instabilities in Russian society. Serfdom was abolished, modest and restricted experiments in democratic governance (the zemstvos) were inaugurated, the legal system was made considerably more independent of royal power, educational institutions made more accessible, industrial growth encouraged, economic regulatory legislation introduced, and so on. In Russia, an era of reform preceded—even launched—the revolutionary movement; and the example of Russia verifies the by now familiar observation that revolutions occur generally not in static and depressed societies but in societies in which change has raised hopes, introduced the idea of alternative structures and social arrangements, and made the vision of a better future seem plausible.

The consequences of reform in Russia were dramatic. Tsarist reforms led to an intellectual ferment, to a social mobility, to an increasingly widespread politicization, and to a deepening desire for freedom that could not be contained within the autocratic system, the framework of which remained unyielding. The reforms that were granted were always compromised or emasculated when it became clear how much they were in conflict with either conservative social and economic interests or with the power of the autocracy. The Russian serfs were legally freed but remained in many ways unfree, burdened with an impossible indebtedness. They ominously continued to expect that a second emancipation—the "real" emancipation—was on its way. The zemstvo law (1864) introduced the idea of local democracy. It too was emasculated by conservative forces; but it had irrevocably given life to the idea of democracy, so that in the autocratic political system a contradictory—a dysfunctional—principle of political organization had been introduced. Such examples could be multiplied. What this halfhearted and hesitant era of reform accomplished was to produce in Russia a vast restlessness and an even more intense desire for change that led ultimately to the upheavals of 1905 and 1917. The reform "program" of the autocracy in effect pushed the society into revolutionary disequilibrium, with all its classical symptoms: the multiplication of ideologies, the loss of the authority of traditional institutions and forms, an intensification of criticism, and a rising resort to force, repression, and violence.

The social system thus was changing, but in an uncoordinated, confused, and hesitant fashion. And it was in the context of change and retreat, of alternatives glimpsed and reforms aborted, that a revolutionary elite developed. Late Imperial Russia provides us with a vivid illustration of the way in which an intellectual elite is radicalized. Social change and reform (e.g., the opening of the universities to larger numbers of young Russians) greatly increased the size of the intelligentsia; yet the structural and institutional complexity of Russia did not change rapidly enough to accommodate a large number of "free" and autonomous individuals. Appalled by the backwardness—the "cursed darkness"—of their country, increasingly alienated from the traditional values and institutions of Russia, isolated from the great mass of as yet unenlightened Russians, offered little opportunity to gain experience in practical politics, frustrated in their ambitions for meaningful careers, holding no hope that reform under the autocracy would be anything but marginal, and increasingly repressed for their criticism, educated young Russians turned more and more to revolution as the only feasible means of changing their society.

Though clearly driven in some degree by psychological compulsion and social frustration, these remarkable people cannot be explained by sociopsychological analysis alone, as if they were simply seeking political solutions for their emotional torments. They were also powerfully animated by ideals of liberty and equality, ideals to which they generously and heroically devoted their lives. Their efforts to change Russia, ranging from the gentlest kind of populism to revolutionary terrorism and accompanied by a proliferation of revolutionary ideologies, created a complex heritage of revolutionary thought and action from which the next generation of Russian revolutionaries—Lenin's generation—learned their lessons.

Two increasingly dominant features of the nineteenth-century Russian revolutionary movement—its voluntarism (i.e., the assumption that by an act of will, by sheer determination and desire, even a tiny minority of men can deflect the course of history and transform a society), and the example of total personal commitment to revolution—found culmination in the extraordinary Lenin. The Russian Revolution—indeed one might argue the twentieth century—is dominated by the towering figure of Lenin. His *What Is to Be Done?*, repeating the question perpetually on the lips of Russian revolutionists, grew, as it were, out of the whole Russian revolutionary experience. It crystallized a new revolutionary ideology and strategy, and it is of central importance in understanding the Russian Revolution. It is perhaps the major revolutionary document of our era, not simply because it sketches the theoretical basis for the development of the "revolutionary party"—the conspiratorial organization of professional revolutionists totally committed to the task of seizing political power and transforming society—but also because of its striking and confident assertion that men make history and that they need not wait for historical circumstances to be perfectly "ripe" before acting. Lenin's major elaboration of orthodox Marxism—one could even say total departure from Marxism—is here forcefully stated. If Marx was the theorist of historical change, Lenin was the theorist of revolutionary tactics and strategy, of the means of seizing power—of the "politics of power." *What Is to Be Done?* is built on his deep conviction that the revolution *might not occur,* that one could not wait for, or even expect, the people (the proletariat) to make the revolution, that they must be shown the way, led, even coerced, to socialism. However humane and democratic a man Lenin himself may have been, we see at work in *What Is to Be Done?* all those assumptions and convictions the implications of which have now been fully worked out in the totalitarianism of contemporary Russia. *What Is to Be Done?* is the classic statement (along with *State and Revolution*) of the doctrine of Revolution from Above, of the "made" or the "engineered" revolution. It is also a foreshadowing of the authoritarianism in which the Leninist Revolution was to culminate.

We tend to be so fascinated by Lenin and by the idea of a revolution brought off by force of will, that we easily forget that no revolutionary elite, however wilful and clever, has been able to accomplish anything without (1) the widespread support of the masses or even a more or less simultaneous popular upheaval, and (2) the failure of more moderate reformers either to seize power or to maintain it should it fall into their hands. Trotsky made a superb effort to write a Marxist or "scientific" history of the Russian

Revolution, in which he sought to demonstrate that October 1917 was the result of ineluctable social processes the most important of which was the mass revolution. But even he wavered when he had to evaluate the role of Lenin. Denying that Lenin was the "demiurge of the revolutionary process," he nevertheless stated that the Bolsheviks without Lenin "might have let slip the revolutionary opportunity for many years" and that Lenin was "a great link" in the chain of "objective historic forces." With Lenin is raised, in the sharpest possible way, the question of the role of the individual in history.

But the question of the role of the masses in revolution is also of the deepest importance for the student of revolution, and 1917 saw not only a political revolution engineered as it were by Lenin and his Bolshevik colleagues, but also a massive social upheaval that tore asunder the thin fabric of war-weary Tsarist society and that in effect finally destroyed all existing arrangements of power in Russia. Without the social revolution that swirled through rural and urban Russia alike, it is inconceivable that Lenin would ever have been able to seize power.

What were the causes of this popular upheaval, and what were its aims? What was the relationship of the peasant "revolt" to the Bolshevik Revolution? It is not so easy to generalize about the aims of "mass" participants in revolutionary movements as it is about those of the articulate leaders of such movements; an intellectual elite can formulate and analyze its purposes perhaps too well, but the dreams and ideas of the inarticulate often remain inaccessible even to the most imaginative of historians and social analysts. Still, the actions of the Russian peasants and workers in 1905 and in 1917, and the two great revolutionary slogans of the latter year—"Bread, Peace and Land" and "All Power to the Soviets"—make clear enough the chief goals of the social revolution. They were, for the peasantry, ownership of the land; for the proletariat, democracy (worker's control and economic justice); and for all, an end to the suffering caused by the war. Briefly, in 1917 the aims of the two revolutions coincided; indeed, Lenin's strength stemmed from the fact that his purposes at that moment could best be served by the most extreme manifestations of the social revolution, that is, by the most extensive and violent disruption of existing social and political processes. (The same was not true for the Menshevik or even the Socialist Revolutionary Parties, and certainly not for the Kadets.) The tragedy of the Russian Revolution is that subsequently the Bolshevik conception of a centrally organized and controlled socialist (or communist) transformation of Russian society went far beyond the purposes of the social revolution and was *not* supported by the Russian peasantry or proletariat, which had to be repressed (as for example, at Kronstadt in 1921) or coercively collectivized (as in the famous collectivization program of 1929–1932).

This is not to say, of course, that the Russian Revolution in its Bolshevik culmination was devoid of libertarian, equalitarian, and democratic aspirations. To the contrary, in the midst of the Revolution in 1917 Lenin took time in *State and Revolution* to give shape to his vision of the completely free and equalitarian society to which the Revolution would ultimately lead.

But immense tasks were faced by those who would "modernize" Russia. The country was huge, its state of economic development rudimentary, the Russian people weary, and the masses "backward" in their *petit bourgeois* aspirations. And Lenin's Party, which lived on after his death as the embodiment of his doctrine of elitist revolutionary leadership, was powerfully dominant. All in all, the totalitarian denouement of the Revolution seems in retrospect, as Alec Nove remarks, to have been far more fated by the unfortunate character of postrevolutionary circumstances than by the ferocious character of Joseph Stalin.

The accomplishments of the Revolution have nonetheless been extraordinary. The Soviet Union is now indeed the technological powerhouse Lenin dreamed it could become, and her people are vastly better off in terms of social and educational opportunity than before the Revolution. Still, one by one, the great ideals of the revolution were, as one of the chief architects of 1917, the arch-revolutionary Leon Trotsky himself put it, "betrayed." More than fifty years after the revolution, neither a classless nor a democratic society is a reality in the Soviet Union. And however much more relaxed the Soviet system has become since Stalin's death, the struggle for freedom of Russia's most articulate spirits—her artists, writers and scientists—reminds us that the achievements of the revolution have been bought at a very high price.

The following essays on the Russian Revolution should provide the reader with an opportunity to amplify or correct the above observations, and should provide some basis for the exploration of the following questions about the revolution: Was the revolution the only route to successful modernization for Russia? Was the system created by half a century of Tsarist reform viable? Why did political forces and parties more moderate than the Bolsheviks fail, and what accounts for the triumph of the Bolsheviks? What was the role of the "masses" (the peasantry and the proletariat) in the revolution? Why did the revolution culminate in totalitarianism? Was the Stalinist route to economic modernization necessary? In what ways did the history, culture and social structure of prerevolutionary Russia shape the course of the revolution and its consequences? What similarities can we detect between pre- and post-revolutionary Russia, and are these similarities—or continuities—significant?

Cyril Black is Director of the Center of International Studies and Professor of History at Princeton. He has edited (with T. P. Thornton) *Communism and Revolution*, and is the author of *The Dynamics of Modernization*.

The Nature of Imperial Russian Society

CYRIL BLACK

I

How does one go about describing briefly a large and complex society in the process of rapid change? The problems involved are not only of space but also of conceptualization. To be comprehensive yet succinct one must fall back on generalizations, which always run the danger of concealing the very nuances that make up the richness and diversity of a culture. Moreover, the nature and direction of change in modern societies is a matter of continuing controversy, and a common basis of theory and terminology cannot be taken for granted. No society in modern times has been more subject to conflicting assumptions and interpretations than that of Russia. Under these circumstances, perhaps the best solution is to adopt an approach sufficiently general to do justice to the complexities involved and at the same time definite enough in its point of view to offer a consistent interpretation—as well as a reasonably clear basis for controversy.

The interpretation suggested here is one which sees the world as composed of well over one hundred politically organized societies, each with its own deep-seated traditional institutions, undergoing at different stages a process of change which has certain universally common features. This process of change, which can be traced to the revolutionary expansion of knowledge originating in Western Europe in the Middle Ages, tends to affect in one degree or another all aspects of human activity. It seems likely to result eventually in a world of modern societies which will be essentially similar in function but which will retain for the foreseeable future significant features of their diverse traditional structures of institutions and values. There is no set pattern which guides the interaction of the modern and the traditional, and indeed in any society there are innumerable ways in which traditional institutions can be adapted to modern functions. The course of change therefore depends to a considerable degree on the nature of leadership, and in practice an important element in the history of a society consists of arguments, conflicts, rivalries, and struggles among individual leaders and groups of leaders representing a wide variety of points of view and interests. Chance, in the form of the presence or absence of far-sighted and effective leaders at critical moments, has an important share in this process.

Russia is one of these societies, differing from others in her traditional culture as others differ from each other, but also undergoing like them the charac-

From *Slavic Review*, Vol. 20, No. 4 (December 1961), pp. 565–82. Reprinted by permission of *Slavic Review* and Cyril E. Black.

teristic interaction of the traditional and the modern. It is not possible in brief scope—if it is possible at all—to describe the intricacies of this subtle and many-faceted process of change. What will be attempted here is something much more limited: a brief description of certain distinctive features of traditional Russian society as it existed in the eighteenth and early nineteenth centuries, an indication of the principal ways in which that society was changing under the impact of modern ideas and institutions, and finally some suggestions as to the significance of this interaction of the traditional and the modern. It is scarcely feasible to document these observations in any detail, for there is an enormous body of literature which deals with this period, but a few references will be made when they seem to be called for in regard to specific matters of interpretation.

II

A brief statement of the features that distinguished Russian imperial society must of necessity be highly selective and impressionistic, and it is proposed here to touch on only five characteristics: the physical setting, the autocratic state, the system of social stratification, the agrarian economy, and the multinational structure.[1]

The most significant features of the physical setting of imperial Russia were its size, its location, and its poverty. The conquest of Siberia in the sixteenth and seventeenth centuries resulted in a vast increase in the territory under the rule of Moscow. This large territory inherited by Peter nevertheless lacked either well-defined frontiers or suitable maritime outlets for commerce, and at the same time was subject to many pressures on the long frontier with Europe and Western Asia. In the course of the many wars of the eighteenth and nineteenth centuries the frontiers of the empire were further extended, and indeed throughout this period Russia was by all odds the largest country in the world in terms of territory. At the same time the number of inhabitants grew from 14 to 170 million, with the result that Russia was by 1917 inferior in population only to China and India. As significant as its size was its location, bordering as it did on Europe and on the broad sweep of Asia stretching from the Bosporus to the Kuril Islands. In earlier centuries Byzantine influences, and to a much lesser extent Mongol and Ottoman, had played a vital role in the culture of Muscovite Russia. To this extent Russia, like Byzantium itself, could be said to have cultural roots in both Europe and Asia. In the period of the empire, which was one of almost exclusively European influences, the principal significance of geographical location lay in the realm of foreign policy. In an age in which Europe was embracing the world, a country of Russia's size and position could not well avoid being drawn into the affairs of the many countries on its borders and beyond.[2]

Economic poverty was also an im-

[1] Boris Brutzkus, "Die historischen Eigentümlichkeiten der wirtschaftlichen and sozialen Entwicklung Russlands," *Jahrbücher für Kultur und Geschichte der Slaven,* X (1934), 62–99, and Rushton Coulborn, "Der europäisch-russische Gegensatz," *Die politische Meinung,* II (February, 1957), 13–26, offer suggestive interpretations of imperial Russian society.

[2] George Vernadsky, "The Expansion of Russia," *Transactions of the Connecticut Academy of Arts and Sciences,* XXXI (July, 1933), 391–425, provides a succinct account. The very extensive development of the lands beyond the Urals after 1861 is described in Donald W. Treadgold, *The Great Siberian Migration: Government and Peasant in Resettlement from Emancipation to the First World War* (Princeton, 1957).

portant element in the Russian setting. The vast size of the country was to a considerable degree illusory, since only a small part of it was suitable for agriculture, and much of that had a poor soil or climate. It is now known to be rich in natural resources, but before the First World War only its petroleum and a few other minerals had been adequately developed. In per capita terms Russia was very poor by the standards of the European countries which were her principal competitors. Perhaps the best way of expressing the problem confronting the statesmen of the empire was that they had to find a means of converting her rather meager and scattered resources into effective national power. This is no doubt a rather abstract formulation, yet Peter the Great must have looked at things somewhat in this fashion when he undertook to strengthen the administrative apparatus of a state which already had a claim to autocratic power well established in theory if not in practice.

It would probably not be going too far to say that in no other major society in the eighteenth and nineteenth centuries did the sovereign and the state play as great a role as they did in Russia. Prussia in the eighteenth century and China and Turkey in earlier times are among the first examples that come to mind of centralized political systems which had a comparable role in the life of the country. In the nineteenth century, at any rate, the Russian empire stood alone as a society in which a great many aspects of human activity were to a large extent administered or at least regulated by the state. The Russian government was formally an autocracy in the sense that all political authority was vested in the autocrat. The theory of autocracy came from Byzantine political thought and, modified by adaptations from Tatar and Ottoman administrative practices, it became a reality in the course of the fifteenth and sixteenth centuries as the princes of Moscow succeeded in consolidating the political power which had been shared since the thirteenth century by the various principalities of northeastern Russia and their Tatar overlords. What was in theory an autocracy was often for all practical purposes an oligarchy, however, for the princes of Moscow had great difficulty in establishing effective and orderly control over the ruling families whose lands they successively incorporated into the new state. The reigns of the principal architects of the Muscovite political system—Vasilii II the Blind, Ivan III the Great, and Ivan IV the Terrible—were marked by continual internecine strife culminating in the Time of Troubles. After the establishment of the Romanov dynasty in 1613 it was half a century or more before the central administrative system was sufficiently effective to permit the sovereign to free himself from the assembly of notables which had established the dynasty and guided its early fortunes. It was this system which Peter the Great reshaped and rationalized on the basis of Swedish and other European models to form the "regulated state" which, with significant changes to be sure, lasted until 1917.[3]

Under the system established by Peter the emperor was more of an autocrat than the tsars had ever been, yet the oligarchy composed of high civilian and military officials and leading families of noble landowners continued to play an independent role throughout the eighteenth century during the reigns of eight rulers who were relatively weak for reasons of youth, sex, or mental dis-

[3] Б. И. Сыромятников, *«Регулярное» государство Петра Первого и его идеология* (Moscow, 1943) offers what is probably the most perceptive discussion of Peter's reforms.

ability. Paul, the last of these rulers, is generally portrayed as mad—but there was a method in his madness. He took the first measures in the direction of reaffirming the authority of the autocrat, and this authority was further consolidated by his successors.[4] Despite the many political changes which occurred during the last century of the empire, the sovereign remained an autocrat in theory and to a considerable extent in practice, although only in the reign of Nicholas I did he in fact approximate the theoretical model.[5]

A more fundamental question than the relationship of the autocrat to the oligarchy is that of the role of the state in society. No less than two-fifths of the forty million peasants in European Russia were directly administered by the state before emancipation, as were many economic enterprises as well. Through its administration of the Holy Synod, the Academy of Sciences, all higher education, and most primary and secondary education, and through the censorship, the state had a direct and permeating influence on the intellectual life of the country. The rapid economic and social changes which occurred after the emancipation of the serfs did not have the effect of reducing the role of the state. On the contrary, the state played a leading role in this process. There were few phases of Russian life in which it was not directly interested, and over many of the most important it had a virtual monopoly through direct administration and a decisive influence in policy-making.

One of the most significant consequences of the "omnicompetence" of the Russian state, to borrow Sumner's felicitous term,[6] was its influence on the position of social strata. It was as though the autocrat could imagine no other way to assure the state of the support of its leading citizens and a regular income from the rather backward agrarian economy than by binding all individuals to its service. In a purely formal sense, all citizens of the empire were divided into three general categories: natives, nonnatives, and Finns (who were a separate category by virtue of inhabiting an autonomous Grand Duchy). The native citizens in turn were divided by statute into four estates or strata—nobility, clergy, townsmen, and peasants—but these categories were not very meaningful. There were important differences between hereditary and personal nobles; townsmen were separated into four quite distinct categories—notable citizens, merchants, tradesmen, and artisans; the clergy were an occupational group rather than a social stratum, for both those who left the clergy and children of clergymen in general were legally regarded as townsmen of the rank of notable citizens; moreover a nobleman could also be a member of the clergy. Perhaps only the peasants were a legally homogeneous class, although there were significant differences between state peasants and serfs as well as those imposed by the widely varying customs of the diverse regions of Russia.[7]

More fundamental than these formal

[4] М. В. Клочков, *Очерки правительственной деятельности времени императора Павла I* (Petrograd, 1916) develops this theme.

[5] Nicholas V. Riasanovsky, *Nicholas I and Official Nationality in Russia, 1825–1855* (Berkeley, 1959), and Sidney Monas, *The Third Section: Police and Society in Russia under Nicholas I* (Cambridge, Mass., 1961) present in graphic detail the theory and practice of autocracy in the reign of Nicholas I, and offer a valuable guide to the large literature on this subject.

[6] Benedict H. Sumner, *A Short History of Russia* (New York, 1943), pp. 84–85.

[7] Н. М. Коркунов, *Русское государственное право* (2 vols; St. Petersburg, 1913), I, 274-368, provides the best analysis of the formal system of stratification; the historical background is discussed in В. О. Ключевский, *История сословий в России* (3rd ed.; Petrograd, 1918).

distinctions was that which prevailed substantially until the revolution of 1905 between the privileged and the unprivileged. The privileged were not subject to direct taxes or corporal punishment and could travel freely within the country. Only the nobles and townsmen of the rank of notable citizens, totaling between 1 and 2 per cent of the population, enjoyed these privileges. The nobles also had the privilege until 1861 of owning serfs. Moreover, the privileged had access to political power, if they did not actually share it, while the unprivileged bore the burden of supporting the privileged as well as the heavy superstructure of the state. The unprivileged were subjected to severe restrictions as to movement, along with other forms of personal and social discipline, and had virtually no access to the ranks of the privileged before the middle of the nineteenth century. Indeed the gap between the two groups tended to widen during much of this period, as the privileged gained in education and influence while the position of the peasants in particular became more depressed. These hardships weighed even more heavily on the nonnatives—the Jews, the Moslems, and the various indigenous peoples of Siberia. The grosser inequities were relaxed in the latter part of the nineteenth century and were largely removed after 1905, but the government yielded reluctantly and only under great pressure. The growth of civil liberties in the last decades of the empire thus released accumulated tensions which could be contained only by a political system whose authority was not weakened by economic distress or foreign defeats.[8]

The system of social stratification also had the effect of inhibiting the development of a sense of political responsibility. This was in part the result of the corporative organization of the social strata, which tended to isolate them from each other. Thus the hereditary nobles, three categories of townsmen (the merchants, the tradesmen, and the artisans), and the peasants were organized in corporative associations by province, town, or village. These associations were collectively responsible for the conduct of their members, and in the case of the townsmen and the peasants had important fiscal and disciplinary functions. This form of social organization encouraged these groups, which formed the bulk of the population, to negotiate directly with the government rather than to seek common cause against it. This attitude was further encouraged by contradictory prevailing trends of political thought which maintained either that the autocratic state was good, or that it must be eliminated, or that it should be ignored as a necessary evil. It was not until the end of the nineteenth century that the possibility of effective political action against the state within the framework of the empire was widely accepted.[9]

The system under which the peasants were bound to the soil and to the noble landowner is known as serfdom, and it existed in its most rigorous form between 1649 and 1861. Russian serfdom must be distinguished from feudalism as it existed in Western Europe. Feudalism

[8] The structure and functioning of the stratification system are discussed in К. Кочаровский, *Социальный строй России* (Prague, 1926); Г. Б. Сліозбергъ, *Дореволюціонный строй Россіи* (Paris, 1933), pp. 78-108, 258-79; Robert A. Feldmesser. "Social Classes and Political Structure," *The Transformation of Russian Society: Aspects of Social Change Since 1861*, ed. Cyril E. Black (Cambridge, Mass., 1960), pp. 235–52 (hereafter cited as *Transformation of Russian Society*); and Robert C. Tucker, "The Image of Dual Russia," *Transformation of Russian Society*, pp. 587–605.

[9] Leopold H. Haimson, "The Parties and the State: The Evolution of Political Attitudes," *Transformation of Russian Society*, pp. 110–45.

was a political system characterized by a contractual relationship between lord and vassal, whereas in serfdom the relationship was primarily economic and was based not on contract but on the edict of the sovereign. There had been elements of the lord-vassal relationship earlier in Russian history, but these had disappeared with the rise of serfdom.[10] The state created serfdom as a means of assuring itself of a reliable source of revenue in a situation in which land was plentiful but labor was scarce, and agriculture was the principal source of income. The conditions of peasant life were so hard in Russia in the fifteenth and sixteenth centuries, because of the endemic civil strife and the increasing need of the state for revenue to meet the requirements of national defense, that the peasants tended constantly to escape to the south or east to avoid oppression. Various efforts were made to restrict the freedom of movement of the peasants, and these finally culminated in the middle of the seventeenth century in the imposition of a form of serfdom noted for its oppressiveness.[11]

There were numerous and large-scale peasant revolts both before and after the imposition of serfdom, but in every case they were repressed. In the course of the two centuries during which serfdom was in force, the machinery of government underwent a fundamental transformation, the noble landowners won a substantial relaxation of their obligations to the state, and modest beginnings were made in the development of an industrial system. There was no comparable improvement in the status of the peasants, whether under the state, the crown, or the landlords, however, and in the case of the latter it tended to become more oppressive. This is not to say that the nobles benefited by the system either, for most of them were persons of limited means and they were increasingly going into debt during the first half of the nineteenth century.

Serfdom had been established principally for the benefit of the state, and no doubt it provided the basis for a type of stable administrative and fiscal control over the peoples and the resources of the country which could not readily be achieved by other means. Stability was achieved at the price of stagnation, however, for there was no Russian counterpart of the rapid economic and social change which the societies of Western and Central Europe experienced during the period in which serfdom prevailed in Russia. Serfdom tended to discourage initiative on the part of peasant and noble landowner alike, and in a variety of ways inhibited the growth of industry. It may be argued that the real obstacle to social and economic change in Russia was in the minds of its leaders, and that much could have been done even within the framework of serfdom to stimulate technological improvements in agriculture and to encourage industry. In any event, as the conception of a modern society began to gain adherents among Russian leaders, a process in which the defeat in

[10] For a discussion of this important question see Marc Szeftel, "Aspects of Feudalism in Russian History," *Feudalism in History,* ed. Rushton Coulborn (Princeton, 1956), pp. 167–82; and Rushton Coulborn, "Russia and Byzantium," *ibid.*, pp. 344–63. The extensive controversy in Russian historiography on this issue is reviewed by Marc Szeftel in *ibid.*, pp. 413–19. A similar conclusion is reached in George Vernadsky, "Feudalism in Russia," *Speculum,* XIV (July, 1939), 300–323.

[11] Jerome Blum, *Lord and Peasant in Russia from the Ninth to the Nineteenth Century* (Princeton, 1961), provides a comprehensive account of the origins and development of serfdom.

the Crimea appears to have had a large influence, serfdom was the first institution which they undertook to reform.[12]

The attempt to present a brief characterization of a complex society runs a particular danger in the case of Russia, since only 43.3 per cent of the population was Great Russian at the end of the nineteenth century, and the many minority peoples enjoyed a wide diversity of traditional institutions. What has been said about the decisively centralizing character of the administration must be modified to the extent that the Ukraine, the Baltic provinces, and Congress Poland all enjoyed a degree of autonomy during parts of the period under consideration, and the Grand Duchy of Finland had substantial privileges except for the short period between 1903 and 1905. Similarly as regards social stratification and the agrarian system, there were many differences in the position of the various minority peoples. Indeed, it was long the practice of the imperial government to respect the diverse institutions of the peoples annexed in the course of the expansion of the empire, and it was only toward the end of the nineteenth century that a rigorous policy of administrative and cultural Russification was attempted.[13]

The multinational character of imperial Russian society also had grave consequences in the realm of foreign policy. The chief concern of Russia in annexing these peoples, located almost entirely on her borders with Europe and Western and Central Asia, was for her own security. The territories they inhabited either blocked Russian access to the Baltic and Black seas; or, as was the case with Poland and Central Asia, might have come under the rule of other great powers to the detriment of Russia's interests; or again, as was the case with the Ukraine and Georgia, actually sought Russian protection against neighbors they feared more. It would doubtless be going too far to say that Russia had no imperialist ambitions, for numerous proposals for annexing noncontiguous territories can be found in her diplomatic records. The ambitions of Russia's statesmen were nevertheless limited, by the standards of the time, and were concerned principally with adjacent territories of strategic significance for commerce or defense. In this sense Russian statesmen favored a continental policy, resembling perhaps that of China in earlier times and of the United States in the nineteenth century, and did not undertake to create an extensive overseas empire such as those carved out by the seafaring societies of Western Europe.

III

It has already been noted that the institutions of imperial Russian society underwent many changes in the course of two centuries, and indeed the history of this period is punctuated with numerous reforms, revolts, assassinations, wars, territorial issues, and social conflicts reflecting the continuing readjustments in the structure of Russian society as well as the idiosyncrasies of its leaders. At the same time it was undergoing a more fundamental transformation, which was stimulated primarily by the example of the societies of Western and Central Europe. These societies were in

[12] G. Pavlovsky, *Agricultural Russia on the Eve of the Revolution* (London, 1930), and Geroid T. Robinson, *Rural Russia Under the Old Regime* (New York, 1932).

[13] These developments are reviewed in L. I. Strakhovsky, "Constitutional Aspects of the Imperial Russian Government's Policy Toward National Minorities," *Journal of Modern History*, XIII (December, 1941), 467–92.

the forefront of a revolutionary process, intellectual in its origins and political in its initial impact, accompanied by economic growth and social change of unprecedented proportions. The levels of achievement attained in the course of this revolutionary transformation, which may be referred to in general terms as "modern" or at least "modernizing," were the prototypes of those which were eventually to become the goal of virtually all societies.

The initial reaction of Russia's political leaders to this momentous development was to adopt, or at least adapt, those modern institutions which seemed best suited to preserving the traditional Russian society from the increasingly threatening competition of its neighbors. This reaction is represented typically by the reforms of Peter the Great, which rationalized the civil and military structure of the central government and tightened the control of the state over the noble landowners and the townsmen, and of the landowners over the peasants. No attempt was made, however, to adapt to Russian society the economic and social institutions which were being developed in the more modern societies. Peter's reforms were explicitly defensive in their motivation and implications, and they were successful in preserving the traditional social structure of the country with relatively few changes for a century and a half. In the course of time the gap between a relatively static Russia and an increasingly dynamic West grew to a point where it could not fail to cause concern to Russian leaders, and during the reigns of Alexander I and Nicholas I many plans and proposals for reform were considered and some actually undertaken. Nevertheless, human nature being what it is, they preferred the certainty of problems which they understood and felt confident in handling to the uncertainties of a thoroughgoing social transformation. It took the defeat in the Crimea to shift the balance of official opinion in favor of reform, and it has become customary to regard the emancipation of the serfs in 1861 as the turning point between the passive and the active phases of the attitude of Russia's political leaders toward modern ideas and institutions. It will of course be recognized that 1861 is in most respects simply a symbolic date, since some segments of Russian society felt the breath of reform a generation or more earlier, while others were relatively unaffected until a good deal later. Indeed, it was not until the end of the nineteenth century that Russian society as a whole was gripped by thoroughgoing change.

It has already been noted that the modern revolution was intellectual in its origins, resting as it did on the phenomenal expansion of knowledge which had its roots in the Middle Ages, and its initial impact on Russia was similarly intellectual. This impact may be traced back to the movements favoring the revision of religious texts and doctrine in the fifteenth and sixteenth centuries, and to the appearance in the seventeenth century of isolated nobles with a Western outlook.[14] It was nevertheless not until the eighteenth century that there was a general turning to the West on the part of the state and the nobility, and only in the nineteenth century did the problem of "Russia and Europe" come to absorb the full attention of Russian intellectuals. The diversity and brilliance of Russian political and literary thought concerning the relationship

[14] Dmitrij Čiževskij, *History of Russian Literature from the Eleventh Century to the End of the Baroque* (The Hague, 1960), chaps. vi and vii, provides a valuable discussion of early European influences.

of traditional to modern values and institutions is probably matched only by that of China and Japan among non-European peoples. It produced a wide spectrum of interpretations, ranging from the strongest reaffirmation of the rightness and sanctity of the Russian way of doing things to the view that the imperial state was a form of "oriental despotism" which must be destroyed to make way for the socialist society toward which mankind was alleged to be moving ineluctably.

This rich body of thought moved in two currents, which were continually intermingling but which remained reasonably distinct. The first was represented by the political leaders and high officials, starting with Peter the Great and ending with Witte and Stolypin, who sought to adapt imperial Russian society in one degree or another to the requirements of the modern world. Their views were set forth in speeches, reports, memoranda, and statutes, and perhaps in deeds more than in words. The second source of intellectual activity was that represented by the intelligentsia, who almost by definition were disassociated and not infrequently alienated from the governing circles. The intelligentsia left a fascinating heritage of speculation and interpretation which reflected a broad understanding of European society and a deep concern for the destiny of the Russian people. They had a profound influence on the development of Russian society during the period of the empire, since their works were read and discussed by all educated people. They nevertheless remained until the end alienated from official Russia, which bore the burden of responsibility and deserves much of the credit for the extent to which Russian society was transformed by the time of the First World War. The intelligentsia as a group did not gain access to political power until the fall of the empire, and this access was terminated for all but a few when the Bolsheviks began to suppress deviations from orthodoxy in the early 1920's. In the realm of scholarship Russia joined the world of modern knowledge in the course of the eighteenth and nineteenth centuries and made distinguished original contributions.

The history of Russian thought in the nineteenth century as a general phenomenon has yet to be written. Much able work has been done on individual writers and on the leading intellectual movements, such as the Decembrists, the Slavophiles, the Populists, and the Marxists. The thought of the reforming officials has not, however, received comparable attention. Neither the prerevolutionary intelligentsia nor the writers of the Soviet Union have been attracted to this subject, for reasons which are not hard to find, and Western scholars are only now beginning to explore it. Interest in intellectual history seems to have been concerned principally with a desire to study the background of the political revolution of 1917, and this has resulted in a serious neglect of the fundamental process of political, economic, and social change as a central issue in Russian thought.[15]

In the political sphere the adoption of modern institutions in Russia can be seen in the many reforms which had the purpose of rationalizing the system of law and administration, integrating the various territories and social strata, and establishing a closer rapport between

[15] The literature on this subject is virtually inexhaustible. Among recent American contributions, Theodore H. Von Laue, "The Industrialization of Russia in the Writings of Sergej Witte," *American Slavic and East European Review,* X (October, 1951), 177–90, and Marc Raeff, *Michael Speransky: Statesman of Imperial Russia, 1772–1839* (The Hague, 1957), are examples of a renewed interest in the thought of reforming bureaucrats.

state and society to the end that political decisions could be effectively formulated, communicated, and implemented. The reforms of the eighteenth century had performed a similar function for the state itself, and it was now a question of extending this process to the entire society. The codification of the laws by Speransky was the first significant step in this second phase, and it was followed in the 1860's by an extensive reform of the judiciary and local government and of the administrative system of the central government. As late as 1905, however, the state had relatively few direct administrative contacts with the peasants except for a rather scanty police force and the land captains established in 1889. Peasant affairs were handled largely by the peasants themselves. The administration of the Stolypin land settlement required the government for the first time in its history to establish organs for administering directly at the local level policies ultimately affecting a large proportion of the population and involving the co-ordination of several ministries.[16] This was a very late development, however, and the weakness of the imperial bureaucracy was soon revealed in the harsh test of war.

The effort to transform the political system of imperial Russia along the lines pioneered by the societies of Western Europe provoked a struggle among several trends of thought. One was that of the supporters of the traditional system as it had been consolidated in the eighteenth and early nineteenth centuries. This was the view of the imperial family and its immediate entourage, and it had strong support in the army and bureaucracy and in the cabinet, even when that body was headed by a reforming minister. The reforms of the 1860's had indeed been launched by the emperor himself, but more in the Petrine spirit of trying to achieve a new conservative stability than with a view to a thoroughgoing social reconstruction. This approach continued to have strong official support until the end, and one may well attribute the catastrophic character of the fall of the empire to the stubbornness with which one group of its leaders resisted change.

Another main trend was the very large one represented by those both in the government and among the intelligentsia who favored fundamental change by evolutionary means and looked to models ranging from England and France to Prussia and Japan. The diversities of their various programs make it difficult to contain these many groups in a single category, but the Fundamental Laws of 1906 provided them with a more or less acceptable basis for action and there was a significant degree of continuity from the four successive Dumas to the Provisional Government. Included also in this category were the leaders of the national minorities who demanded a degree of self-government. Only the Poles insisted unconditionally on independence. This issue has been beclouded by war, revolution, and civil war, but it appears that under "normal" circumstances the leaders of the other minority peoples would in all likelihood have been satisfied on the eve of the First World War with some form of federalism.

A third trend was composed of those who had no faith in evolutionary changes within the framework of the empire. This was the view of the Bolsheviks and many Socialist Revolutionaries, who saw their political role principally as a destructive one so long as the empire survived. The final arbiter

[16] This subject has been studied recently in George L. Yaney, "The Imperial Russian Government and the Stolypin Land Reform," unpubl. Ph.D. diss. (Princeton, 1961).

among these various approaches, as it turned out, was the First World War. The strains of the conflict eroded the political structure of the empire, and in so doing undermined the prospects for evolutionary change within its framework. The collapse of the empire opened the way for a revolutionary approach, and the revolutionaries were much more at home than the liberals in the ensuing chaos.[17]

Among the changes which occurred during the last half-century of the empire, those in the intellectual and political realm have attracted the most attention, but the remarkable economic growth in its later decades deserves equal emphasis. Agricultural production, which had not been able to keep up with the growth of the population during the first half of the century, increased much more rapidly, especially after the 1880's. Not only did agricultural production surpass the rate at which the population was growing, but it was also significantly diversified to include industrial crops and potatoes. The expansion of industrial production was of course much more rapid, with an annual average rate of growth of somewhat over 5 per cent for the period 1885–1913. The rate for the 1890's, the period of most rapid growth, was surpassed only by that of Japan, the United States, and Sweden. Underlying the increased rates of growth in agriculture and industry was the construction of an extensive railroad network, which grew from 1,000 miles in 1860 to 40,000 miles at the time of the First World War. In terms of national income, the Russian rate of growth for the period as a whole was higher than that of the United Kingdom, France, and Italy, somewhat below that of Germany, and considerably below that of the United States and Japan. On a per capita basis Russia's position was of course less favorable, owing to the rapid growth of her population. By the time of the First World War real income per capita was about the same as that of Italy, which means that it was still a great deal lower than that of the advanced industrial societies.[18]

Although Russia had thus in no sense attained a leading position as an industrial society at the time of the First World War, what is significant is that by the 1880's it was launched on a pattern of economic growth comparable in rate and dimensions to that of the more advanced societies. It should also be noted that this was very largely the achievement of the imperial government, which took the initiative and bore the main burden of building railroads and supplying capital to industry, and also provided the principal market for the output of heavy industry. No doubt the sovereign and the conservative-minded courtiers and ministers, like Peter the Great in his day, still thought of industrialization principally as a means of bolstering the autocratic system. The leading cabinet members and high officials, however, had a vision of a Russia transformed into a modern industrial society. Their goal may be said to have been of a West European character, but their methods were quite different. Little attention was devoted

[17] The adaptation of Marxism to the Russian environment is a matter of particular interest. See especially Adam Ulam, "The Historical Role of Marxism and the Soviet System," *World Politics*, VIII (October, 1955), 371–401; and Karl A. Wittfogel, "The Marxist View of Russian Society and Revolution," *World Politics*, XII (July, 1960), 487–508.

[18] Alexander Gerschenkron, "The Rate of Industrial Growth of Russia Since 1885," *Journal of Economic History*, VII, Supplement (1947), 144–74; and Raymond W. Goldsmith, "The Economic Growth of Tsarist Russia, 1860–1913," *Economic Development and Cultural Change*, IX (April, 1961), 441–75.

to agriculture, and such income as it normally provided was channeled into industry. Railroads and heavy industry were favored as against consumer goods. Modern technology was imported from the West to make up for deficiencies in skilled labor, and economies were made in management and supervision by concentrating production in large plants. A not inconsiderable role in this growth was played by private entrepreneurs and small businessmen, but the pace was set by the government and by the large enterprises which it controlled or patronized. Indeed, it was the role of the government as planner, investor, entrepreneur, and consumer which distinguished economic growth in Russia from that in the societies which started earlier.[19]

This economic growth was accomplished by fundamental social changes. The urban population grew from 7 to 20 million during the last fifty years of the empire, the rigid system of social stratification disintegrated rapidly, and the foundations were laid for a new stratum of professional people, businessmen, and officials. This "middle class" was drawn from all of the traditional strata. The nobles, clergy, and townsmen were naturally the principal sources of recruitment for this new stratum at the start, but the peasantry and workers were gradually drawn into it and represented in the long run its principal reserve of manpower. The nobles lost much of their distinctive position in the last decades of the empire and, with the exception of the relatively few families of great wealth, did not gain much advantage from their remaining formal privileges in the evolving industrial society. At the same time the industrial working class grew apace, and numbered some 3.5 million at the end of this period. In 1913, according to the official classification, 70.2 per cent of the population were farmers, 16.7 per cent were wage and salary workers, 7.2 per cent were craftsmen, 3.6 per cent were self-employed townsmen, and 2.3 per cent were military and others.[20]

The institutions of higher education were the chief training ground for this new class, and their enrollment in proportion to the population increased more than nine times between 1885 and 1914. The increase in secondary-school enrollment was even greater, and by the time of the First World War Russia had made substantial progress toward a system of universal elementary education. The social mobility accompanying the growth in higher education is reflected in the fact that the proportion of children of peasants, craftsmen, and workers enrolled in the universities grew from 15.7 per cent in 1880 to 38.8 per cent in 1914, and in the higher technical institutes was 54 per cent in the latter year.[21] The officer corps was no doubt the most conservative branch of the bureaucracy, but it appears that by

[19] See Alexander Gerschenkron, "Problems and Patterns of Russian Economic Development," *Transformation of Russian Society*, esp. pp. 42–61, for a discussion of the underlying economic policies of the imperial government.

[20] Warren W. Eason, "Population Changes," *Transformation of Russian Society*, pp. 72–90, summarizes and interprets Russian statistical materials; Valentine T. Bill, *The Forgotten Class: The Russian Bourgeoisie from Its Earliest Beginnings to 1900* (New York, 1959) has performed a useful service in calling attention to the role of the entrepreneur; Gaston V. Rimlinger, "Autocracy and the Factory Order in Early Russian Industrialization," *Journal of Economic History*, XX (March, 1960), 67–92, discusses the status of the workers in the last decades of the empire.

[21] Nicholas Hans, *History of Russian Educational Policy (1701–1917)* (London, 1931), pp. 229–42, provides a convenient summary of educational statistics.

the end of the empire a majority of the new officers came from non-noble families as did some of the leading generals in the First World War.[22] In recording these changes it should be noted that this rapid growth in educational opportunities and social mobility was not achieved without a momentous struggle. In the central government the reformers waged a constant battle with the traditionalists, and were strongly aided by the increasingly effective support which they received from the local government institutions, the municipalities, and the Duma. At the time of the First World War, Russia was still a country where 78 per cent of the population was agricultural and rural illiteracy was high. The changes of the last half century had been so rapid, however, that contemporary reforming statesmen could look forward with confidence to the day when the empire would attain the level of achievement of Western societies.

Something should also be said about the personality changes which may have accompanied this general process. National character in the sense that it is used by the social psychologists is a controversial concept which is still in an early stage of formulation, and one hesitates to venture into a territory so ridden with pitfalls. Yet it is clear that the personality of the individual reflects the character of his upbringing in the family setting, which in turn depends on the larger social context. When the latter undergoes the drastic changes represented by urbanization, one would expect the family and its individual members to be vitally affected. In the case of the Great Russian people, for example, it has been maintained that the characteristically patriarchal peasant family tended to produce a personality which was markedly ambivalent. This is to say that the Great Russian personality contained simultaneously elements of great vitality and serious depression, which may be explained as resulting from a family setting in which an awesome father was both feared and resisted. As a peasant society with these characteristics is urbanized, with the mother as an urban worker gaining a position of authority more nearly equal to that of the father, an altered family setting is produced in which the children are exposed to somewhat different influences and will develop correspondingly different personalities. This example suggests what is meant by the effects of social change on personality, and it also reveals the difficulties which confront one in trying to deal with Russia in these terms. Russia was a vastly complex empire with many traditional cultures, of which the Great Russian was only one. Moreover, the available studies deal principally with the Soviet period, and there is little factual data from earlier decades to draw on. One may argue that Chekhov, Gorky, and their literary colleagues did a pretty good job of reporting social change at the family level without benefit of professional training in the behavioral sciences, but it is difficult for a historian to generalize on the basis of their findings. It is also clear that the impact of social change on personality was at its very earliest stages in the last decades of the empire, and that one would not expect to find general manifestations of a transformation of national character in Russia until well into the twentieth century. Under the circumstances the best one can do is to call attention to this important aspect of

[22] Raymond L. Garthoff, "The Military as a Social Force," *Transformation of Russian Society*, pp. 326–27, reviews the available evidence on the changing social status of the officer corps.

social history and to regret that one cannot do it justice.[23]

IV

The interaction of traditional and modern institutions and values in imperial Russian society should be considered in terms both of its general implications and of its particular significance for the crisis provoked by the collapse of the empire in the First World War.

The prevailing Western approach between the two world wars to Russian developments was to assume that the institutions characteristic of the more advanced societies of the West represented the model which other societies were destined to follow. There was therefore a tendency to judge the empire as well as its successors by the extent to which they adopted the Western pattern in such matters as civil liberties, representative government, education, and the role of the state in economic growth. By this standard the empire was reactionary, the Provisional Government had liberal aspirations, and the Soviet Union represented a bewildering combination of modern and traditional elements. In the course of the past quarter of a century many other societies have entered and some have completed the experimental phase of adapting the traditional to the modern, and the process of transformation can now be seen as a much more complex matter than one of simply duplicating Western institutions. It seems clear that there are certain functions which all modern societies must perform—political decision-making effective for the entire population, sufficient savings to permit a reasonable rate of economic growth, education, social mobility, and so on—and perhaps most important of all, a value system compatible with the necessary institutional changes. It is also clear, however, that there is a wide degree of variety in the extent to which the diverse traditional institutional systems are adaptable to the functions of modern societies. No society can avoid very profound changes as it modernizes, but some traditional institutions are much more adaptable than others.

What is significant in the case of Russia is that its traditional institutional system was different from those of the societies of Western Europe, as indeed it was from those of non-European societies as well. In Western Europe modern political institutions, for example, evolved from those of feudalism into a characteristic form of liberal government in which political power was shared by elected representatives and a permanent civil service. In Russia, by contrast, the starting point was not a feudal system but an autocratic state which had characteristically exercised very extensive political functions. It was not difficult for this state, in the generation after the defeat in the Crimea, to initiate a very fundamental reorientation of national life. Between 1861 and 1917 the autocracy in Russia put into effect a series of reforms which resemble in many respects those achieved by very different methods in France between 1789 and 1848—if one may risk an historical analogy.[24] To extend the analogy

[23] A valuable introduction to this subject will be found in Clyde Kluckhohn, "Recent Studies of the National Character of Great Russians," *Human Development Bulletin* (February 5, 1955), pp. 39–60; Henry V. Dicks, "Some Notes on the Russian National Character," *Transformation of Russian Society*, pp. 636–52; and Alex Inkeles and Daniel J. Levinson, "National Character: The Study of Modal Personality and Socio-cultural Systems," *Handbook of Social Psychology*, ed. Gardner Lindzey (2 vols.; Cambridge, Mass., 1954), II, 977–1020.

[24] Theodore H. Von Laue, "Die Revolution von aussen als erste Phase der russischen

a step further, one may suggest that the autocratic state in Russia played a role similar not only to that of the middle class and the Napoleonic empire in France but also to that of the samurai in Japan, the Young Turks in the Ottoman Empire, the army officers in Egypt, and the European-educated politicians in Africa today. Modernizing political leadership may take many forms, and the alternatives available to political leaders cannot fail to be profoundly affected by the traditional political institutions which a society has inherited from earlier centuries. This is not to assert an institutional or a cultural determinism. It is rather to suggest that, however similar the ultimate functional goals, political leaders in different societies are likely to proceed by different routes.

It would be outside the limits set for this paper to venture beyond the fall of the empire in February/March, 1917, but it is relevant to discuss the bearing on subsequent developments of the changes which the empire was undergoing in its final decades. It is well enough to attribute the fall of the empire to the strains of the First World War, for the connection between the two is clear, but it is also necessary to note that the crisis was not so great that a more effective government might not have been able to cope with it. The vital struggle in the last decades of the empire was that which was going on within the government between those who supported the traditional autocracy to the bitter end, and those who favored the transformation of Russia into a modern bureaucratic and constitutional state. The Wittes and Stolypins were still separated by a wide gap from the liberals, but the gap was perhaps no wider than that which separated them from the emperor. The lines dividing the various conservative and liberal conceptions of an evolutionary constitutionalism were becoming increasingly blurred in the last years of the empire, and much would have depended on the leadership which might have emerged.

The war came at a time when these conflicts between the emperor and his critics within the government were still unresolved, and in fact it only served to make them more bitter. The fragmentation of Russian politics at this stage was such that the collapse of the autocracy in 1917 resulted in a situation in which no alternative had any wide support. There was of course a significant group of leaders favoring parliamentary democracy who had gained political experience in the Duma and in local government, but the political methods which they favored were not generally understood or accepted. Where parliamentary democracy has been successful it has in fact been a value system widely supported by many elements of a society rather than one reflecting the interests of a particular social stratum. The vast majority of Russians—whether peasants, workers, bureaucrats, officers, or professional people—were not generally familiar with the values and techniques of parliamentary democracy. To this extent the task of leaders favoring parliamentary methods in 1917 was infinitely more difficult than that of those prepared to rely on force. This does not necessarily mean that the empire might not under other circumstances have developed into a political democracy of the type familiar in the West, or even that something resembling such a system may not yet develop in Russia

Revolution 1917," *Jahrbücher für Geschichte Osteurepas,* IV (1956), 138–58, stresses the differences between the Russian and French revolutions, in contrast to Isaac Deutscher, "The French Revolution and the Russian Revolution: Some Suggestive Analogies," *World Politics,* IV (April, 1952), 469–81.

at some future time. It means only that, at the time the empire collapsed, the balance of domestic political experience weighed heavily in favor of those leaders who were prepared to employ authoritarian methods.

Martin Malia teaches Russian history at Berkeley and is the author of *Alexander Herzen and The Birth of Russian Socialism.*

What Is the Intelligentsia?

MARTIN MALIA

To blasé Westerners one of the most engaging qualities of the Russian intellectuals of the old regime is the moral passion with which they attacked the great questions of the human condition, and their pursuit to a ruthlessly logical conclusion—in life no less than in thought—of the heady answers such exalted inquiry invariably brings. It is this quality which the two giants of the tradition, Tolstoy and Dostoevsky, in spite of so much that separates them, have in common and which gives Russian literature of the last century its unique character and power. In lesser figures this same moral quest is often expressed just as intensely but with a naïve, utilitarian bluntness that is conveyed by such classic titles of their works as *Who Is To Blame?*, *What Is To Be Done?*, *Who Are The Friends of The People?* Like Marx, whom some of them eventually followed to a shattering outcome of their searchings, they wished "not just to understand the world, but to change it."

Still, they had first to understand, and their moral utilitarianism was ultimately founded on an exacerbated faculty of introspection. Their initial question was always, "Who are we?"—as individuals, as Russians, as thinking men in a barbarous society. A more pragmatic way of putting the same question was, "What is the intelligentsia?" The number of works so entitled is legion, with almost as many different, ardent answers. The subject of this essay, then, is one of the classic questions of modern Russian life, yet about which it is always possible to say something new, since it is as rich as that life itself.

The term intelligentsia was introduced into the Russian language in the 1860's by a minor novelist named Boborykin, and became current almost immediately. This fact is of more than anecdotal significance, for it suggests that the group so designated did not acquire full awareness of its identity until that time. Yet almost all authorities would agree that the origins of the group itself went back to the "circles"

Reprinted by permission from *Daedalus*, Journal of the American Academy of Arts and Sciences, Boston, Mass., Vol. 89, No. 3 (Summer 1960).

of the 1830's and 1840's, which introduced into Russia the ideological turn of mind in the form of German philosophical idealism. Still, the fact that there was a term for the group under Alexander II, whereas there was none under Nicholas I, indicates a watershed in its development that coincides with the beginning of the Great Reforms after 1855.

It was Turgenev who, in his greatest novel, gave the classical terminology to describe these two stages: the aristocratic "fathers" and the plebeian "sons." Very roughly, the intellectual difference between the two was the difference between idealists and materialists; nevertheless, both were what Napoleon once contemptuously dubbed "ideologues." A third stage came after the assassination of Alexander II in 1881 with the advent of a more heterogeneous body sometimes baptized the "grandsons," or the various Populist, Marxist, and even neo-Kantian groups of the end of the old regime, who revived in different ways the legacy of their predecessors, but who remained just as thoroughly ideological.

It is this primacy of the ideological that is fundamental to the group as a whole; the intelligentsia, therefore, should not be taken to mean just the revolutionary opposition. Indeed, the word ever since it came into being has had two overlapping meanings: either all men who think independently—of whom Pisarev's "critically thinking realists," or "nihilists," were only the most extreme and famous manifestation; or, more narrowly, the intellectuals of the opposition, whether revolutionary or not. "Fathers," "sons," and "grandsons," therefore, are all unmistakably intelligentsia, and might for convenience's sake be designated "classical intelligentsia."

There are two other groups, however, which are candidates for inclusion under the same rubric. Some writers on the subject would consider as intelligentsia all oppositional figures since the end of the eighteenth century, including Radishchev and Novikov under Catherine II and the Decembrists under Alexander I. Yet here we find nothing approaching a consensus, and this in itself indicates that although these figures had certain characteristics in common with their successors, they were not yet the real thing. Because of this equivocal status, therefore, they are best considered as no more than a "proto-intelligentsia," and though some account must be taken of them here, they will not be central to the story.

Finally, it is clear that after 1917 the term intelligentsia suffered a drastic change. Although Marxism makes no provision for such a class, the Soviet regime has officially proclaimed what it calls the intelligentsia as one of the three pillars of the socialist order, together with the proletariat and the toiling peasantry. The term, however, no longer has any connotations of "critical" thought, because all questions have now been answered; still less does it have the "classical" and "proto-"intelligentsias. In addition, it should be simply all those who "toil" with their minds instead of with their hands, that is, the technological, liberal-professional, managerial, administrative, or merely white-collar personnel of the state. Only the Party presents a partial exception to this definition, for, as we shall see, it has preserved something of the intelligentsia's spirit, if not of its personnel. Otherwise, the Soviet intelligentsia is so different from its predecessor as to deserve a separate name—such as Trotsky's "bureaucracy" or Djilas' "new class"—and just as certainly, a different mode of analysis.

This discussion, therefore, will be limited to what has been called the "classical" and "proto-"intelligentsias.

In addition, it should be said that, since the subject is complex, much simplification is inevitable. In the remarks that follow, the emphasis will be on the more radical and revolutionary elements of the intelligentsia, who, if they were by no means the whole of the movement in the nineteenth century, are a likely choice for special consideration in a general survey for the practical reason that they eventually had the greatest impact on history.

The word intelligentsia itself most probably is no more than the Latin *intelligentia*—discernment, understanding, intelligence—pronounced with a Russian accent. Yet such bold use of a term for an abstract mental faculty to designate a specific group of people obviously implies a very exalted notion of that group's importance, and its members—*intelligenty*, "the intelligent or intellectual ones"—are clearly more than intellectuals in the ordinary sense. Whether merely "critically thinking" or actively oppositional, their name indicates that they thought of themselves as the embodied "intelligence," "understanding," or "consciousness" of the nation. In other words, they clearly felt an exceptional sense of apartness from the society in which they lived. To use an old qualificative of German idealism which the intelligentsia in its more lucid moments understood only too well, and which in a diluted sociological meaning now enjoys a great vogue in America, they were clearly "alienated" intellectuals of some sort.

Alienated intellectuals, of course, exist everywhere, even in such sound societies as Britain and the United States. In Britain they fulminate in anger against the injustice that keeps them "outsiders." In America, where they seem to have more money, they formerly emigrated to Paris and its Left Bank and got "lost"; at present, and somewhat more democratically, they hitch-hike to California and become "beat." In each of these cases, however, the most that results is picturesque behavior and a few novels, which in college classrooms inspire the next generation's quest for identity and its consequent revolt against parents, authority, and convention. Still the peace of society is never fundamentally disturbed, even when in times of exceptional stress matters go to the point of voting for Henry Wallace or forming a small Communist party.

The alienation of the Russian intellectual was far deeper, however, and its social impact infinitely more devastating. In any society, individuals who take thought seriously experience an alienation which arises from a tension between the ideal and the real, or between what the individual wishes to become and what society permits him to be. In Russia this phenomenon was pushed to its ultimate development. It led to the formation of what can only be termed a separate social category, indeed, a "class." Lest this term seem too strong, it should be pointed out that not only did the intelligentsia assume a distinctive name, but other, more indubitably "real" classes accepted this name and the apartness it connoted as justified. To be sure, the other classes and the government did not concede the intelligentsia's pretention to be the incarnate consciousness of Russia, but they took account of its existence as a fact and, with time, as a force.

Indeed, so real was this force that for decades the intelligentsia was able to exert a political pressure on the autocracy greater than that exercised by more palpable classes such as the gentry or the bourgeoisie. Moreover, when the collapse of the old order came, one faction of the intelligentsia was able to exploit the furies of peasant and worker anarchy to the extent of assuming absolute power over all classes more "real" than it, before being dissolved in the conditions created by its own success. No class in Russian history has had a more momentous impact on the destinies of that nation or indeed of the modern world. In defining it, therefore, we would do well to bend our categories to its characteristics, rather than to attempt to reduce it to the familiar and the known with minor adjustments for "alienation."

This does not mean that the Russian intelligentsia is absolutely *sui generis* in modern history. Both in its headily ideological temper and in its impact on the world it is in many ways comparable to the French *philosophes* of the Enlightenment and to the German romantic thinkers of the years between 1770 and 1840. Indeed, it borrowed most of its fundamental ideas from one or another offshoot of these traditions. Nevertheless, the Russian intelligentsia is sufficiently different from all similar groups of intellectuals to be treated as a distinct social category, and thus to make necessary a thorough-going revision of our usual notions of class in attempting to account for it.

It is precisely the failure to make this revision that explains much of the confusion in discussions of the intelligentsia. No recognized system of social analysis, either those known to the intelligentsia itself or those elaborated since by modern sociology, makes provision for a "class" held together only by the bond of "consciousness," "critical thought," or moral passion. Most writers on the problem, therefore, have concluded that the intelligentsia must be founded on something other than ideology alone. One suggestion, made at the end of the last century by the Populist, Mikhailovsky, is that the *intelligenty* were "conscience-stricken noblemen," but since large numbers of the intelligentsia were clearly not noble, this does not get us very far. Another school of thought, represented most melodramatically by Berdiaev, holds that the *intelligenty* were largely sons of priests and that their cult of absolute reason was a demonic perversion of the absolute faith of Orthodoxy; in fact, however, only a minority of the intelligentsia came from the clergy.

A more sophisticated version of these two approaches consists of an attempt to give the intelligentsia a separate rather than a derivative position in the old-regime system of legal "estates" which existed in Russia down to 1917. In this view (the most widespread among the intelligentsia itself under Alexander II) the intelligentsia were the *raznochintsy*, that is, "people of diverse rank," or "people of no estate in particular." Concretely, this meant those stray individuals who were left over after Peter the Great, who gave the Russian estate system its final form, had exhausted all the more obvious social, economic, or bureaucratic categories. In other words, the notion of *raznochintsy* was, by definition, not very meaningful in the Russian estate system, particularly by the nineteenth century, when the system was beginning to disintegrate. Moreover, the intelligentsia also clearly came from all the other recognized and more meaningful estates: the gentry, the clergy, the merchantry, and even eventually the peasantry. Therefore, it was made up of *raznochintsy* only in the loose sense that it was from all estates in general and from no one estate in particular, and that as its members moved away from their estate of origin they became *déclassé*. One of the primary characteristics of the *intelligenty*, then, was that they could no longer fit into the official estate system.

The Marxist intellectuals were hardly more successful when their turn came to explain "who they were," for where does the intelligentsia belong in the economic definition of class that divides society into feudal aristocracy, bourgeoisie, proletariat, etc.? Still, the problem had to be faced, and since the intelligentsia was more or less a "middle class" between the gentry and the people, Lenin made a valiant stab at defining it as a "bourgeois intelligentsia," although in some way that was not explained he nonetheless considered that his type of intelligentsia really represented the proletariat. It is hard to see how he could have done much better, since in this system of classification the intelligentsia cannot be anything but "middle class," and yet they fit no meaningful economic notion of a "capitalistic bourgeoisie." At the most, they could be only a "petty bourgeoisie," but this class, in Marxist theory, is not the vanguard of the assault against "feudal" autocracy that the intelligentsia clearly represented.

Nor can the intelligentsia be accounted for by refining the socio-economic approach to say that a class is determined by the way its members make their living, and that intellectual work creates a different mentality than is created by manual labor or business. Such a classification can establish the identity of a professional class as opposed to a business or working class. But by no means all members of the Russian professional class were *révolté;* quite a number of them were successful and "integrated" professors, doctors, or lawyers. Yet if this is so, why should other "intellectual workers" of very similar background set themselves apart as an intelligentsia?

It is this confused catalogue of class definitions which is the legacy of the question of the intelligentsia, and it must be faced before it is possible to move in new directions. The intelligentsia's agonies of introspection, however, have not been entirely in vain; there is much that is partially true in their speculations. The intelligentsia came, in fact, from all estates in general and from no one estate in particular, in the loose meaning of *raznochintsy.* It did begin in the gentry, owed much to the clergy, and with time came increasingly to be dominated by commoners of more and more indeterminate origin. Herzen and Bakunin were unmistakably gentry; Chernyshevsky and Dobroliubov came just as clearly from the clergy; Zheliabov or Tkachev, Lenin, Trotsky, or Stalin, Martov or Chernov, are harder to place in a meaningful spectrum of estates. At the same time, if the intelligentsia was not very "bourgeois" economically, it clearly occupied the middle social position, between the gentry establishment and the masses, of a bourgeoisie that did not exist, or that at least was inarticulate. Finally, there was something about it of a petty-bourgeois class of "intellectual workers" gravitating around the editorial offices of the "thick journals" in which they labored.

Even the sum of these partial truths does not give the whole truth, however, and we are still faced with the dilemma with which we started. Since efforts to define the intelligentsia as a discrete phenomenon in and for itself inevitably seem to fail, the only remaining solution is to approach it in terms of the "dynamics" of its position in Russian society as a whole. The classical approach to the problem has been through analytical abstraction; let us now examine the concrete historical conditions under which this "class" emerged.

The historian Kliuchevsky has aptly emphasized the extreme simplicity of Russian historical processes as compared to those of Western European countries, a fact which derives largely from the rudimentary nature of the Russian class structure under the old regime. Until well into the nineteenth century there were in effect only two classes in Russia, or at least only two that counted. There was the aristocracy or gentry (*dvorianstvo*), which in spite of its small numbers possessed almost all the wealth, monopolized all privilege, and alone participated in the higher life of the nation. Then there was the peasantry, which was important, not because of any active role in the national life, but because it was so dangerous, at least potentially, since it was both so oppressed and so huge—roughly ninety percent of the population. To be sure, other estates existed as well—the merchants and the clergy—but they were insignificant numerically and counted for even less socially. Under such circumstances the Russian government could be only a very simple and brutal affair: a military autocracy ruling through an irresponsible bureaucracy, officered of course by the gentry, and whose principal function was to maintain order internally and wage war externally.

This system worked admirably throughout the eighteenth century, defeating Swedes, Poles, and Turks and suppressing Pugachev and his peasant hordes. Its success, however, rested on a precarious equilibrium and concealed an acute intrinsic instability. As Pugachev said on his capture in 1774: "I am not the raven but the fledgling, and the real raven is still hovering in the heavens." There was yet another menace to this structure: "critical thought." With great prescience, Joseph de Maistre remarked at the beginning of the nineteenth century, when the fermentation of ideas had barely begun in Russia, that the real danger to order in the country was not the peasants as such but an eventual "*Pougatchev d'université*." It was from the conjunction of these two intuitions that the radical intelligentsia would soon be born: men reared on the general theories of the universities would reach out to greet the hovering democratic storm of a new *Pugachevshchina*. They would have to wait a long time, almost a century, but eventually their dream would come true, if not exactly in the form that all of them had dreamed it.

Nevertheless, de Maistre was more nearly right than Pugachev: the new democratic storm began to gather at the top, rather than at the bottom, of Russian society. The first rumblings were heard in the last years of Catherine II and under Alexander I among the most privileged order, the gentry. Contrary to what is often asserted, the cause of this was not primarily Western "influence"—the gallicization of the gentry, the reading of the *philosophes*, and conversion to the rights of man. The trouble began because under Catherine the gentry for the first time acquired those rights in fact.

Until 1762 the gentry had been bound to serve the state in the same way the peasants were bound to serve their masters: they were in a sense the serfs, although highly privileged serfs, of the autocrat. Since in reality, however, they held all the levers of command in the army and the bureaucracy, they were in time able to extort from the monarchy the grant of unconditional personal liberty. After 1762 they were free to "serve" the state or not to serve, as they chose; they could dispose of themselves and their property entirely as they deemed fit. In consequence, they developed the attitudes of free men, a sense of personal dignity, of pride, even a touchy independence —in a word, all those endowments modern humanism claims for man. It is for this reason that they became Westernized, and took over such ready-made ideological justifications of their new individuality as Montesquieu's "honor," Voltaire's "natural reason," or, in more extreme cases, Rousseau's democratic "rights of man."

Nonetheless, the monarchy remained autocratic, and the gentry's new-found "humanity" was a product of tolerance rather than of imprescriptible right; they lived constantly at the mercy of a capricious return to integral autocracy, such as in fact occurred under Paul. Still worse, if they had any sense of the logic that natural reason commanded, they could not but be disturbed by the contrast between their liberty and the servitude of the majority. With each new generation, raised by French tutors, amidst general principles and ideas, and remote from "life," the sense of moral scandal at the spectacle of autocracy and serfdom grew more acute. How, they asked, can some be free unless all are free, and unless the very principle of servitude that menaces everyone—autocracy—is eradicated? With each generation of freedom, the younger, better educated, more humane members of the gentry generalized from a sense of their own dignity as individuals to the ideal of human dignity for all. Such, by 1790, was the meaning of the protests of Novikov and Radishchev.

This is not to say that a majority of the gentry felt this way. Most of them, particularly after they had inherited the family estate, had the "good sense" to realize that the best way to insure their own independence was to maintain "order," and to keep the peasants in their place, for which it was necessary to preserve the paternal police force of autocracy. There was, however, in each generation a minority of the young and sensitive who put principle before privilege and demanded an end to the existing barbarous state of affairs. It is this primacy of general ideals over immediate interests, and the consequent alienation of the young gentry from their official class, that made of them, by the reign of Alexander I, a prefiguration of the intelligentsia. Held together by no other bonds of cohesion than youth, idealism, and a humane sensitivity, this gentry opposition, goaded to desperation by Alexander's reluctance to reform, at last in 1825 embarked on a military assault against autocracy and serfdom. The Decembrists, as they came to be called, failed, but the shock of their action precipitated the full development of the intelligentsia they had adumbrated.

Perhaps the principal reason for refusing to call the Decembrists *intelligenty* is that, although in their supreme moment they placed ideals before interests, ideas were by no means the whole of their lives. The Decembrists were primarily army officers, men of the world and of action; moreover, in spite of their opinions, they continued to serve the state. Even their revolt was strictly an affair among gentlemen, with no participation by the people, and was designed to take over the existing state from within rather than to destroy it from without. The real intelligentsia came into being only under Nicholas I, when the next generation of young gentry idealists became totally alienated from the state and were left with ideas alone as their whole world.

After the close call for Russia's precariously balanced order that attended his accession, Nicholas, together with the majority of the gentry, was obsessed by the possibility of further betrayal by the educated elite, as well as by the permanent anarchic menace of the masses. Thus, he excluded the now unreliable gentry as much as possible from participation in government, and instead relied on more docile bureaucratic servants. Iron discipline was enforced in the army and the country at large, and captious individualism and "freethinking" were put down wherever the Emperor's Third Section detected their presence. Matters only grew worse as "red" disorder erupted again, in the Polish lands of the Empire in 1830, and then all over Europe in 1848. The Russian military autocracy quite rightly felt mortally menaced by such developments and defended its existence with all the vigor it could command.

Under such circumstances the more sensitive younger members of the gentry obviously would have no more to do with the state than it would with them. Whereas in 1812 the highest form of idealism had been to serve in the army, after 1825 to serve in Nicholas' national and international "gendarmerie" was a betrayal of all idealism and humanity. The result of this was an exodus of the young gentry from "service" to the universities. Whereas in the generation of Pushkin and the Decembrists, almost all the significant figures of Russian culture had been either army officers or men close to the aristocratic and court circles of the capital—in other words, highly integrated into official society—under Nicholas, and forever after, almost all such figures, the nonpopolitical writers no less than the revolutionaries, received their decisive formation in and around the universities and, in varying degrees, were at odds with official society.

The impact of the universities was to transform their noble charges from gentry intellectuals into intellectuals from the gentry, or from dilettante "ideologues" into professional writers, critics, and professors. Just as important, the universities changed them from idealists in the everyday sense into idealists in the metaphysical sense. Following Schelling and Hegel, they came to believe that the essence of the universe was idea, and that the whole of nature and history culminated, indeed acquired meaning and reality, only in the "consciousness" of man, and that they, therefore, were the bearers of the Absolute Idea. Thus, their chief activity and their only sphere of free endeavor was exalted to the level of the first principle of life. In short, the universities made the more serious younger gentry morally *déclassé,* a rootless "internal emigration" with no home but its ideal visions.

At the same time the universities brought together these noblemen with other young men from the lower orders, the clergy, the minor professional and bureaucratic classes, or the famous *raznochintsy,* if that term is taken not in its legal meaning but in the loose sense of all those who came to the university and the higher life of the mind from estates below the gentry. These men had risen only painfully from poverty and social obscurity, making their way precariously by tutoring, translations, or petty journalism, to attain to the dignity of knowledge and that "consciousness" which is liberty. Even more literally than the gentry *intelligenty,* they had no other life than ideas. If worse came to worst, a Bakunin or a Herzen could make it up with father and find refuge on the family estate; a Belinsky, a Chernyshevsky, or a Dobroliubov, if they wished to exist as "human beings," indeed if they wished to exist at all, had no choice but to labor at the tasks of *intelligentia.* This faculty alone conferred on them at the same time dignity, "personality," and the freedom of a livelihood which permitted them to escape from the oppression of their origins yet which did not make them dependent on the state.

These new men came from Belinsky's "cursed Russian reality" and from Dobroliubov's "kingdom of darkness," from provincial, clerical and petty-bourgeois squalor, patriarchal tyranny, and superstition (the epithets must be accumulated in the manner of the day), in a word, from all the human degradation of sub-gentry Russia. It is Dostoevsky who has given perhaps the most unforgettable, if highly caricatured, portraits of this type in his various Raskolnikovs, Verkhovenskys, and Kirillovs. From this "underground" world, "the humiliated and the offended" emerged to the light of the Idea, "consciousness," "humanity," "individuality," and "critical thought." Thereby they took their place beside the only "human beings" who hitherto had existed in Russia—those sons of the gentry who had already cast off the class privileges which had made them free men—and the two groups together embraced the Universal Rational Idea of Man. By the end of the reign of Nicholas the relatively mild frustration of the Decembrists had been generalized into the most sweeping, abstract, and intransigent denial of the real in the name of the ideal.

It is all these things taken together that by the 1840's created what was unmistakably an intelligentsia, at last purged of any other principle of cohesion than intellection and endowed with an exalted sense of difference from and superiority to the barbarous world around it. It is first of all in this abstract but nonetheless real ideological and psychological sense that the intelligentsia constituted a distinct "class" in Russian society.

There were, nonetheless, significant class differences of a more ordinary sort within this fundamental moral unity. Although in the 1840's the intelligentsia included men from all classes, it was in fact dominated by those who came from the gentry. By the 1860's the center of gravity had shifted to the *raznochintsy*. This change, by submerging the group's only privileged element, the gentry, broke the last moorings to official society, and thereby put an end to any possible ambiguity about its separate existence. It is this development which precipitated the group's full awareness of its own identity and thus led, by the 1860's, to the adoption of the distinctive name of intelligentsia. This change, moreover, gave rise to the famous dichotomy of the "fathers" and the "sons."

To rehearse the conventional catalogue of contrasts, the fathers were philosophical idealists and romantics, while the sons were materialists and devotees of empirical science. The fathers were esthetes who believed in art for its own sake as the highest self-realization of the individual; the sons were utilitarians who accepted only a civic, pedagogical art useful for the reform of society. The fathers introduced into Russia the great ideals of humanity, reason, liberty, and democracy; the sons attempted to translate these ideals into reality. Finally, the sons were more bitter and irascible than their better-bred fathers.

The filiation between the two generations, however, was equally unmistakable, for both wished to make "cursed Russian reality" conform to the universal Ideas of Man and Reason, even though the fathers wished to accomplish this primarily by "enlightenment" or education, and the sons preferred direct action. The filiation extends even further, for both believed in the primacy of principles and the ideal vision of Justice over the intractability of everyday life, or what the vulgar call reality. This was true whether they were idealists or materialists, for, as any good empiricist or positivist could tell them, both idealism and materialism are metaphysics. A world in which ideas derive rigorously from matter is no less of an ideal construct, unverifiable by scientific examination of sensory data, than a world determined by *a priori* principles. Both views are passionate ideological visions, founded on acts of faith and will, that are all the more "irresponsible" for entertaining the illusion of being founded on scientific rationality. Both fathers and sons, idealists and materialists, were men of ruthlessly logical ideology, and this bond was far stronger than the social and philosophical differences between them.

There was, however, a more concrete common denominator among the intelligentsia as well: the Russian educational system and what it led to. Roughly, down to 1825 all that counted in the country's educational life was the "cadet schools," or the various military and technical academies maintained by the state to train future officers from the gentry. Until 1825 almost everyone who counted—for instance, most of the Decembrists—came from these schools; after 1825 almost no one did.

As of the same date, civilian education was only a very recent phenomenon in Russia. To be sure, there was an Academy of Sciences that went back to 1725, and one university, that of Moscow, had been founded in 1755. But until the nineteenth century neither institution, especially the university, was impressive, and neither, in spite of Lomonosov's exceptional achievements, counted for much in national life. In effect, education as a disinterested venture in Russia began under Alexander I.

After 1803 the Imperial government for the first time set up a network of civilian educational establishments: five new universities were created; high schools (gymnasia) were established in almost all provincial capitals; something was even done for elementary education; finally, diocesan seminaries, which went back to Peter, were reformed and modernized. The government did this in part because Alexander and his advisors (his young friends on the "Official Committee" and Speransky) shared the "humanism" which would later drive the Decembrists to revolt: they sincerely believed that "enlightenment" was necessary to prepare Russia for freedom. The government did this also because it increasingly needed competent nonmilitary personnel to staff an ever more complex bureaucracy. By the 1830's and the 1840's this system was for the first time in full operation. Even Nicholas, though he hardly believed in enlightenment, could not afford to abolish it as a practical matter. Indeed, to meet the demands of his perfected bureaucracy, he was forced to improve it.

It was on the rungs of this ladder—seminary, gymnasium, university—that the *raznochintsy* climbed to the light of day; without it they could never have existed. It was the universities, moreover, that brought the *raznochintsy* together with the young gentry into the "circle," or discussion group, of the 1830's and 1840's, and the "student commune," or cooperative living group, of the 1860's and 1870's. The most down-to-earth definition one can give of the intelligentsia is to say that they were the "student youth" trained in the various establishments of the "Ministry of National Enlightenment." Indeed, for the unlettered mass of the population, an *intelligent* was anyone with a gymnasium or a university training.

The alienation of the intelligentsia may be put in equally concrete terms. In a society that throughout the nineteenth century was over ninety percent illiterate, a gymnasium or a university education was in fact an extraordinary thing, which set its recipients apart in an exalted but also an extremely isolated position. In the 1840's, in any one year there were only 3,000 university students in an empire of some 50 million inhabitants; in the 1860's there were only 4,500, and in the 1870's, just a little over 5,000, out of a population of some 60 million. Quite literally then, the intelligentsia was the embodied "intelligence" of Russia. In the Hegelian language of the 1840's, they personified the penetration of the "darkness" of Russian life by the accumulation of mankind's "consciousness."

In addition to the schools, the only other "institution" which gave cohesion to the intelligentsia was the periodical press. Those intellectuals who took their mission most seriously continued after graduation—or expulsion—to live the life of ideas on the pages of the "thick journals," which served as vehicles for almost all creative culture under the old regime. Before the emergence of political conspiracy in the 1870's, these journals were the intelligentsia's sole means for making the ideal impinge on the real.

Both the schools and the "thick journals," however, were very unsatisfactory institutions for the accomplishment of the intelligentsia's high mission. The schools were subject to continual harassment by a suspicious government, and this often led to isolated protests or general disturbances, from which expulsions inevitably followed. Indeed, it is striking how large a number of *intelligenty,* from Belinsky and Herzen to Lenin, Trotsky, and Stalin, were expelled or arrested students. Then, after expulsion or return from exile, there was the further discouragement of censorship, the suppression of periodicals, and perhaps another arrest if one put too much in print. Again it is noteworthy how many leaders of the intelligentsia, from Chaadaev to Chernyshevsky and Pisarev, experienced a violent end to their journalistic careers. And once the "thick journals" were closed to them, the last recourse of the *intelligenty* was to turn from "critical thought" to revolutionary action. "Socially" or occupationally the intelligentsia was as simple as its own ruthless logic: it was a "class" of expelled students and censored journalists, who in desperation were driven to conspiratorial extremes.

Put less crudely, the dilemma of the intelligentsia was one of an unsatisfactory "circulation of elites." This does not, however, mean that there was a quantitative "overproduction" of intellectuals in Russia; on the contrary, the tiny contingent of the *intelligenty* could easily have been absorbed by the constantly expanding bureaucratic apparatus of the state or the growing range of the liberal professions. Rather there was a qualitative overproduction of "humanism" for the possibilities of mature, individual initiative offered by government service or such professions as law and teaching, both of which were largely under the tutelage of the autocracy. Education meant the development of talent, of ambition, of pride and imagination—in a word, of "individuality." But the state could accommodate only technical competence, not "individuality."

In effect, the experience of the state with its would-be intellectual servants repeated in different form the earlier experience with its military servants, the gentry. By raising each group to an exceptional position in society, the autocracy inadvertently created free men in an order based on unreflecting obedience at the top and servitude at the bottom. Since by its very nature this structure was incapable of accommodating any significant degree of individual initiative, alienation and revolt resulted.

The alienation and revolt of the "student youth," however, was much deeper than that of all save a minority of the gentry. The *raznochintsy* had no concrete privileges to give substance to their "humanity." Moreover, they were cramped in the development of their "personality," not just by the autocracy, but also by the unbending privilege of the majority of the gentry, who steadfastly refused to admit them into the establishment. Indeed, the alienation of the intelligentsia arose much less from their sense of difference from the masses than from their hostility to the majority of the gentry, whom they considered to be poorly educated in their military schools, uninterested in ideas as such, brutal, boorish, and overbearing. Therefore, the *intelligenty,* rebuffed in their efforts at social betterment, fell back on their Human and Rational essence, and ideology became their sole means of mastery over a hostile world.

Since, however, such self-realization was somewhat abstract for creatures of flesh and blood, many of the intelligentsia eventually turned their gaze from the top to the bottom of society. Aroused by what they considered to be the incomplete and niggardly emancipation of the peasants by Alexander II, they "went to the people" to learn the great human truth of a humiliation far deeper than theirs, a truth beside which their own "rationality" paled into insignificance. Their final ambition was to become the authentic spokesmen of this truth. The quest of the intelligentsia for its own "humanity" ended in the ultimate democratic pathos of "merging with the people," *narodnichestvo,* or Populism.

But how was this handful of turbulent students and ideological journalists able to play so extraordinary a role in Russian life? The answer to this question lies in the idea of Kliuchevsky with which these considerations on the historical development of the intelligentsia began, namely, the extreme simplicity of the Russian social structure under the old regime. In Western Europe, no matter how authoritarian and undemocratic society might have been, there always existed some solid interest groups which could give substance and practical meaning to the generalized protest of the intellectuals. In nineteenth-century Russia the almost total absence of such groups left a great vacuum. It was into this vacuum that the intelligentsia stepped, unfettered in their extremism by the concrete interests of anyone with a potential stake in the existing order. Thus the intelligentsia could speak with absolute purity for man in general, since they had no one to speak for in particular but themselves.

Man in general, however, could also be the people, the great anarchic base and the simplest element of all in Russian society. In spite of the Emancipation of the serfs in 1861 and of the other Great Reforms which followed, Russian society remained essentially an old regime, founded on sharp class inequalities and a lack of significant social mobility. The peasants in particular remained as poorly integrated into the structure as before. Indeed, their first taste of freedom in 1861 simply whetted their appetite for definitive elevation to the status of full "human beings." Thus, it was the ever-present possibility of exploiting the elemental destructiveness of the desperate masses that gave the Russian intelligentsia a leverage against official society which alienated intellectuals elsewhere almost always lacked.

Paradoxically, it was the disintegration of the social system which had brought the intelligentsia into being that at last gave it a chance to act. So long as Russian society remained simple, the intelligentsia failed to make contact with the masses because the very brutality of social relationships made it easy for the autocracy to keep the peasants in hand. In the 1890's, however, under the impact of rapid industrialization, Russian society began to develop the diversity of modern social classes common to the West; business, professional, and other activities in no way dependent on the state became increasingly prevalent. From 1906 on there was even a parliament, and politics became legal for the first time in modern Russian history. Thus, the sole path to self-fulfillment for a free man was no longer pure reason or revolutionary action. It became possible for the less alienated intellectuals to adapt to the real world. Under the impact of these changes the intelligentsia began to have doubts about their self-righteousness and the necessity of their apartness. By 1909, with the self-critique of *Vekhi,* this crisis of identity was thrust into the open. By 1914 bands of die-hard intelligentsia exiles, such as that grouped around Lenin, were becoming increasingly anachronistic.

At the same time this diversification of society created an unprecedented crisis for the government, for it set the masses in motion in ways unpredictable to bureaucrats trained under the old order. The still vital remnants of the radical intelligentsia, however, who for decades had been reflecting on how to foment disorder, were better prepared to cope with the new events. Indeed, this preoccupation with tactics was among the principal contributions of the "grandsons" who emerged on the scene in the 1890's at the outset of industrialization. They added little to the general principles and mentality elaborated by the "fathers" and the "sons," but they were infinitely shrewder, with the wisdom of accumulated experience, about practical revolutionary politics. Then in 1917, when the fortunes of the intelligentsia seemed at their lowest ebb, war knocked apart Russia's expiring old regime. The radical intelligentsia at last got its new *Pugachevshchina,* on which the most hardheaded, tactics-conscious "intelligent ones" rode to power.

With this triumph the extraordinary fortunes of the intelligentsia as a group came to an end, for in the new society which it created the conditions that had called it into being no longer existed. Nonetheless, even though the body of the intelligentsia died, much remained of the spirit. It has often been noted that the ordinary logic of revolutions has not obtained in Soviet Russia and that for over forty years, in spite of temporary retreats, no real Thermidor has come to put an end to the original ideological impetus. This remarkable staying-power has not been founded, however, on the continuity of the nucleus of *intelligenty* who established the regime, since most of them eventually perished at its hands. Nor is this continuity wholly supplied by the equally unconventional yet real "new class" which has come into being with the Party bureaucracy. Rather, the cohesion of the Soviet regime is most clearly founded on the primacy, for all "classes" who have held power in it, of abstract principles over life, and on a ruthless will in bending reality to the tenets of what it claims is a scientific materialism, but which, to the profane, appears as a passionate ideological vision.

How and why all this should be, however, is a problem as vast and as difficult to encompass as that of the intelligentsia itself, and one that can properly be the subject only of a separate study. Nevertheless, there is one remarkable element of continuity between the old "class" of the intelligentsia and the "new class" of the Party which must be emphasized here. The brutal utilitarian use of the ideological by the Soviets is no more than a sectarian version of the spirit of the pre-Revolutionary *intelligenty* carried to a *nec plus ultra* by the experience of power. In spite of its demise as a group, the more radical intelligentsia is with us still as a force. Its ideal vision, whatever one may think of it, has become, in a debased but potent form, the very fabric of Russian reality.

A Note on the Derivation of the Word "Intelligentsia"

No one has any documentable idea of where the word "intelligentsia" came from, but the derivation suggested here seems a plausible one. As has already been indicated, the word *intelligentsia* emerged in the 1860's, just when the lower-class *raznochintsy* came to dominate the movement. Whereas the first foreign language of the gentry was French, the principal foreign language of the *raznochintsy,* trained as they were in the seminaries and gymnasia, was Latin, the language of clerical learning (even in Greek Orthodox Russia) and of classical humanism. Indeed, Latin was usually their principal language of higher culture—they were obliged to speak it in the seminaries—and their knowledge of modern Western languages was usually poor. For example, in *Fathers and Sons*—and Turgenev was an excellent social reporter—when the young *intelligent* Bazarov, who is of humble, lower-gentry origin, wishes to make an impression by using a foreign phrase, he does so in Latin, whereas the affluent and elegant upper-gentry family, the Kirsanovs, make their *mots* in French. Thus, Latin was something of a symbol for the cultural identity of the *raznochintsy.* Consequently, it is logical to suppose that they took a term from their school jargon to designate the value of intellection that set them apart.

This supposition is reinforced by the word *intelligent.* Nouns ending in "-ent" are extremely rare in Russian, and all are of foreign origin. Since *intelligent* is not an invention of the gentry, it cannot come from the seemingly likely French adjective of the same spelling. Besides, the use of this adjective as a substantive is impossible in French, and the gentry knew that language well. On the other hand, since *intelligent* is unmistakably a product of the plebeian 1860's, it most probably comes from the Latin adjectival substantive, [*vir*] *intelligens—intelligentis* in the genitive—and hence is logically related to the quality of *intelligentia.*

Sir Isaiah Berlin, a leading historian of ideas, is President of Wolfson College, Oxford. He is the author of *Karl Marx* and *The Hedgehog and the Fox* among other works.

The Russian Populists

ISAIAH BERLIN

. . . Russian Populism is the name not of a single political party, nor of a coherent body of doctrine, but of a widespread radical movement in Russia in the middle of the nineteenth century. It was born during the great social and intellectual ferment which followed the death of Tsar Nicholas I and the defeat and humiliation of the Crimean War, grew to fame and influence during the 'sixties and 'seventies, and reached its culmination with the assassination of

Tsar Alexander II, after which it swiftly declined. Its leaders were men of very dissimilar origins, outlooks and capacities; it was not at any stage more than a loose congeries of small independent groups of conspirators or their sympathizers, who sometimes united for common action, and at other times operated in isolation. These groups tended to differ both about ends and about means. Nevertheless they held certain fundamental beliefs in common, and possessed sufficient moral and political solidarity to entitle them to be called a single movement. Like their predecessors, the Decembrist conspirators in the 'twenties, and the circles that gathered round Herzen and Belinsky in the 'thirties and 'forties, they looked on the government and the social structure of their country as a moral and political monstrosity—obsolete, barbarous, stupid and odious—and dedicated their lives to its total destruction. Their general ideas were not original. They shared the democratic ideals of the European radicals of their day, and in addition believed that the struggle between social and economic classes was the determining factor in politics; they held this theory not in its Marxist form (which did not effectively reach Russia until the 'seventies) but in the form in which it was taught by Proudhon and Herzen, and before them by Saint-Simon, Fourier and other French socialists and radicals whose writings had entered Russia, legally and illegally, in a thin but steady stream, for several decades.

The theory of social history as dominated by the class war—the heart of which is the notion of the coercion of the 'have-nots' by the 'haves'—was born in the course of the Industrial Revolution in the West; and its most characteristic concepts belong to the capitalist phase of economic development. Economic classes, capitalism, cut-throat competition, proletarians and their exploiters, the evil power of unproductive finance, the inevitability of increasing centralization and standardization of all human activities, the transformation of men into commodities and the consequent 'alienation' of individuals and groups and degradation of human lives—these notions are fully intelligible only in the context of expanding industrialism. Russia, even as late as the 'fifties, was one of the least industrialized states in Europe. Nevertheless, exploitation and misery had long been amongst the most familiar and universally recognized characteristics of its social life, the principal victims of the system being the peasants, both serfs and free, who formed over nine-tenths of its population. An industrial proletariat had indeed come into being, but by mid-century did not exceed 2 or 3 per cent of the population of the Empire. Hence the cause of the oppressed was still at that date overwhelmingly that of the agricultural workers who formed the lowest stratum of the population, the vast majority being serfs in state or private possession. The Populists looked upon them as martyrs whose grievances they were determined to avenge and remedy, and as embodiments of simple uncorrupted virtue, whose social organization (which they largely idealized) was the natural foundation on which the future of Russian society must be rebuilt. The central Populist goals were social justice and social equality. Most of them were convinced, following Herzen, whose revolutionary propaganda in the 'fifties influenced them more than any other single set of ideas, that the essence of a just and equal society existed already in the Russian peasant commune—the *obshchina*, organized in the form of a collective unit called the *mir*. The *mir* was a free association of peasants which periodically redistributed the agricultural land to be tilled; its decisions bound all its members, and constituted the corner-stone on which, so the Populists maintained, a federation of socialized, self-governing units, conceived along lines popularized by the French socialist Proudhon, could be erected. The Populist leaders believed that this form of cooperation offered the possibility of a free and democratic social system in Russia, originating as it did in the deepest moral instincts and traditional values of Russian, and indeed all human, society, and they believed that the workers (by which they meant all productive human beings), whether in town or country, could bring this system into being with a far smaller degree of violence or coercion than had occurred in the industrial West. This system, since it alone sprang naturally from fundamental human needs and a sense of the right and the good that existed in all men, would ensure justice, equality and the widest opportunity for the full development of human faculties. As a corollary of this, the Populists believed that the development of large-scale centralized industry was not 'natural', and therefore led inexorably to the degradation and dehumanization of all those who were caught in its tentacles: capitalism was an appalling evil, destructive of body and soul; but it was not inescapable. They denied that social or economic progress was necessarily bound up with the Industrial Revolution. They maintained that the application of scientific truths and methods to social and individual problems (in which they passionately believed), although it might, and often did, lead to the growth of capitalism, could be realized without this fatal sacrifice. They believed that it was possible to improve life by scientific techniques without necessarily destroying the 'natural' life of the peasant village, or creating a vast, pauperized, faceless city proletariat. Capitalism seemed irresistible only because it had not been sufficiently resisted. However it might be in the West, in Russia 'the curse of bigness' could still be successfully fought, and federation of small self-governing units of producers, as Fourier and Proudhon had advocated, could be fostered, and indeed created, by deliberate action. Like their French masters, the Russian disciples held the institution of the state in particular hatred, since to them it was at once the symbol, the result, and the main source of injustice and inequality—a weapon wielded by the governing class to defend its own privileges—and one that, in the face of increasing resistance from its victims, grew progressively more brutal and blindly destructive. The defeat of liberal and radical movements in the West in 1848–9 confirmed them in their conviction that salvation did not lie in politics or political parties: it seemed clear to them that liberal parties and their leaders had neither understood nor made a serious effort to forward the fundamental interests of the oppressed populations of their countries. What the vast majority of peasants in Russia (or workers in Europe) needed was to be fed and clothed, to be given physical security, to be rescued from disease, ignorance, poverty and humiliating inequalities. As for political rights, votes, parliaments, republican forms, these were meaningless and useless to ignorant, barbarous, half-naked and starving men; such programmes merely mocked their misery. The Populists shared with the nationalistic Russian Slavophils (with whose political ideas they had otherwise little in common) a loathing of the rigidly class-conscious social pyramid of the West that was complacently accepted, or fervently believed in, by the conformist bourgeoisie and the bureaucracy to whom this bourgeoisie looked up.

The satirist Saltykov, in his famous dialogue between a German and a

Russian boy, immortalized this attitude when he declared his faith in the Russian boy, hungry and in rags, stumbling in the mud and squalor of the accursed, slave-owning Tsarist régime, because he had not, like the neat, docile, smug, well-fed, well-dressed German boy, bartered away his soul for the sixpence that the Prussian official had offered him, and was consequently still capable, if only he was allowed to do so (as the German boy no longer was), of rising one day to his full human height. Russia was in darkness and in chains, but her spirit was not captive; her past was black, but her future promised more than the death in life of the civilized middle classes in Germany or France or England, who had long ago sold themselves for material security and had become so apathetic in their shameful, self-imposed servitude that they no longer knew how to want to be free.

The Populists, unlike the Slavophils, did not believe in the unique character or destiny of the Russian people. They were not mystical nationalists. They believed only that Russia was a backward nation which had not reached the stage of social and economic development at which the Western nations (whether or not they could have avoided this) had entered upon the path of unrestrained industrialism. They were not, for the most part, historical determinists; consequently they believed that it was possible for a nation in such a predicament to avoid this fate by the exercise of intelligence and will. They saw no reason why Russia could not benefit by Western science and Western technology without paying the appalling price paid by the West. They argued that it was possible to avoid the despotism of a centralized economy or a centralized government by adopting a loose, federal structure composed of self-governing, socialized units both of producers and of consumers. They held that it was desirable to organize, but not to lose sight of other values in the pursuit of organization as an end in itself; to be governed primarily by ethical and humanitarian and not solely by economic and technological—'ant-hill'—considerations. They declared that to protect human individuals against exploitation by turning them into an industrial army of collectivized robots was self-stultifying and suicidal. Ideas of the Populists were often unclear, and there were sharp differences among them, but there was an area of agreement wide enough to constitute a genuine movement. Thus they accepted, in broad outline, the educational and moral lessons, but not the state worship, of Rousseau. Some of them—indeed perhaps the majority—shared Rousseau's belief in the goodness of simple men, his conviction that the cause of corruption is the crippling effect of bad institutions, his acute distrust of all forms of cleverness, of intellectuals and specialists, of all self-isolating *côteries* and factions. They accepted the anti-political ideas, but not the technocratic centralism, of Saint-Simon. They shared the belief in conspiracy and violent action preached by Babeuf and his disciple Buonarroti, but not their Jacobin authoritarianism. They stood with Sismondi and Proudhon and Lamennais and the other originators of the notion of the welfare state, against, on the one hand, *laissez faire*, and, on the other, central authority, whether nationalist or socialist, whether temporary or permanent, whether preached by List, or Mazzini, or Lassalle, or Marx. They came close at times to the positions of Western Christian socialists, without, however, any religious faith, since like the French Encyclopaedists of the previous century, they believed in 'natural' morality and scientific truth. These were some of the beliefs that held them together. But they were divided by differences no less profound.

The first and greatest of their problems was their attitude towards the peasants in whose name all that they did was done. Who was to show the peasants the true path to justice and equality? Individual liberty is not, indeed, condemned by the Populists, but it tends to be regarded as a liberal catchword, liable to distract attention from immediate social and economic tasks. Should one train experts to teach the ignorant younger brothers—the tillers of the soil, and, if need be, stimulate them to resist authority, to revolt and destroy the old order before the rebels had themselves fully grasped the need or meaning of such acts? That is the view of such dissimilar figures as Bakunin and Speshnev in the 'forties; it was preached by Chernyshevsky in the 'fifties, and was passionately advocated by Zaichnevsky and the Jacobins of 'Young Russia' in the 'sixties; it was preached by Lavrov in the 'seventies and 'eighties, and equally by his rivals and opponents—the believers in disciplined professional terrorism—Nechaev and Tkachev, and their followers who include—for this purpose alone—not only the Socialist-Revolutionaries but also some of the most fanatical Russian Marxists, in particular Lenin and Trotsky.

Some among them asked whether this training of revolutionary groups might not create an arrogant *élite* of seekers of power and autocracy, men who would, at best, believe it their duty to give the peasants not what the peasants asked for but what they, their self-appointed mentors, thought good for them, namely, that which the masses ought to ask for, whether they in fact did so or not. They pushed the question further, and asked whether this would not, in due course, breed fanatical men who would pay too little heed to the actual wants of the vast majority of the Russian population, intent on forcing upon them only what they—the dedicated order of professional revolutionaries, cut off from the life of the masses by their own special training and conspiratorial lives—had chosen for them, ignoring the hopes and protests of the people itself. Was there not a terrible danger here of the substitution of a new yoke for the old, of a despotic oligarchy of intellectuals in the place of the nobility and the bureaucracy and the Tsar? What reason was there for thinking that the new masters would prove less oppressive than the old? This was argued by some among the terrorists of the 'sixties—Ishutin and Karakozov, for example—and even more forcibly by the majority of the idealistic young men, who 'went among the people' in the 'seventies and later, with the aim not so much of teaching others as of themselves learning how to live, in a state of mind inspired by Rousseau (and perhaps by Nekrasov or Tolstoy) at least as much as by more tough-minded social theorists. These young men, the so called 'repentant gentry', believed themselves to have been corrupted not merely by an evil social system but by the very process of liberal education which makes for deep inequalities and inevitably lifts scientists, writers, professors, experts, civilized men in general, too high above the heads of the masses, and so itself becomes the richest breeding-ground of injustice and class oppression; everything that obstructs understanding between individuals or groups or nations, that creates and keeps in being obstacles to human solidarity and fraternity, is *eo ipso* evil; specialization and university education build walls between men, prevent individuals and groups from 'connecting', kill love and friendship, and are among the major causes responsible for what, after Hegel and his followers, came to be called the 'alienation' of entire orders or classes or cultures. Some among the Populists contrived to ignore or evade this problem. Bakunin, for example, who, if he was not a Populist himself, influenced Populism profoundly, denounced faith in intellectuals and experts as liable to lead to the most ignoble of tyrannies—the rule of scientists and pedants—but would not face the problem of whether the revolutionaries had come to teach or to learn. It was left unanswered by the terrorists of the 'People's Will' and their sympathizers. More sensitive and morally scrupulous thinkers—Chernyshevsky and Kropotkin, for example, felt the oppressive weight of the question, and did not attempt to conceal it from themselves; yet whenever they asked themselves by what right they proposed to impose this or that system of social organization on the mass of peasants who had grown up in a wholly different way of life, that might embody far profounder values of its own, they gave no clear reply. The question became even more acute when it was asked (as it increasingly came to be in the 'sixties) what was to be done if the peasants actually resisted the revolutionaries' plans for their liberation? Must the masses be deceived, or, worse still, coerced? No one denied that in the end it was the people, and not the revolutionary *élite*, that must govern, but in the meanwhile how far was one allowed to go in ignoring the majority's wishes, or in forcing them into courses which they plainly loathed? This was by no means a merely academic problem. The first enthusiastic adherents of radical Populism—the missionaries who went 'to the people' in the famous summer of 1874—were met by mounting indifference, suspicion, resentment and sometimes active hatred and resistance, on the part of their would-be beneficiaries who, as often as not, handed them over to the police. The Populists were thus forced to define their attitude explicitly, since they believed passionately in the need to justify their activities by rational argument. Their answers, when they came, were far from unanimous. The activists, men like Tkachev, Nechaev, and in a less political sense, Pisarev, whose admirers came to be known as Nihilists, anticipated Lenin in their contempt for democratic methods. Since the days of Plato, it had been argued that the spirit was superior to the flesh, and those who know must govern those who do not. The educated cannot listen to the uneducated and ignorant masses. The masses must be rescued by whatever means were available, if necessary against their own foolish wishes, by guile, or fraud, or violence if need be. But it was only a minority in the movement who accepted this division and the authoritarianism that it entailed: the majority were horrified by the open advocacy of such Machiavellian tactics, and thought that no end, however good, could fail to be destroyed by the adoption of monstrous means.

A similar conflict broke out over the attitude to the state. All Russian Populists were agreed that the state was the embodiment of a system of coercion and inequality, and therefore intrinsically evil; neither justice nor happiness were possible until it was eliminated. But in the meanwhile what was to be the immediate aim of the revolution? Tkachev is quite clear that until the capitalist enemy had been finally destroyed, the weapon of coercion—the pistol torn from his hand by the revolutionaries—must on no account be thrown away, but must itself be turned against him. In other words the machinery of the state must not be destroyed, but must be used against the inevitable counter-revolution; it cannot be dispensed with until the last enemy has been—in Proudhon's immortal phrase—

successfully liquidated, and mankind consequently has no further need of any instrument of coercion. In this doctrine he was followed by Lenin more faithfully than mere adherence to the ambivalent Marxist formula about the dictatorship of the proletariat seemed to require. Lavrov, who represents the central stream of Populism, and reflects all its vacillations and confusions, characteristically advocated not indeed the immediate or total elimination of the state but its systematic reduction to something vaguely described as the 'minimum'. Chernyshevsky, who is the least anarchistic of the Populists, conceives of the state as the organizer and protector of the free associations of peasants or workers, and contrives to see it at once as centralized and decentralized, a guarantee of order and efficiency, and of equality and individual liberty too.

All these thinkers share one vast apocalyptic assumption: that once the reign of evil—autocracy, exploitation, inequality—is consumed in the fire of the revolution, there will arise naturally and spontaneously out of its ashes a natural, harmonious, just order, needing only the gentle guidance of the enlightened revolutionaries to attain to its proper perfection. This great Utopian dream, based on simple faith in regenerated human nature, was a vision which the Populists shared with Godwin and Bakunin, Marx and Lenin. Its heart is the pattern of sin and fall and resurrection—of the road to the earthly paradise the gates of which will only open if men find the one true way and follow it. Its roots lie deep in the religious imagination of mankind, and there is therefore nothing surprising in the fact that this secular version of it had strong affinities with the faith of the Russian Old Believers—the dissenting sects—for whom, since the great religious schism of the seventeenth century, the Russian state and its rulers, particularly Peter the Great, represented the rule of Satan upon earth; this persecuted religious underground provided a good many potential allies whom the Populists made efforts to mobilize.[1] There were deep divisions among the Populists; they differed about the future rôle of the intellectuals, as compared with that of the peasants; they differed about the historical importance of the rising class of capitalists, gradualism versus conspiracy, education and propaganda versus terrorism and preparation for immediate risings. All these questions were interrelated and they demanded immediate solutions. But the deepest rift among the Populists arose over the urgent question of whether a truly democratic revolution could possibly occur before a sufficient number of the oppressed had become fully conscious—that is, capable of understanding and analysing the causes of their intolerable condition. The moderates argued that no revolution could justly be called democratic unless it sprang from the rule of the revolutionary majority. But in that event, there was perhaps no alternative to waiting until education and propaganda had created this majority—a course that was being advocated by almost all Western socialists—Marxist and non-Marxist alike—in the second half of the nineteenth century. Against this the Russian Jacobins argued that to wait, and in the meanwhile to condemn all forms of revolt organized by resolute minorities as irresponsible terrorism or, worse still, as

[1] Professor Venturi is exceptionally illuminating on the rôle played by some of these sectarians—Martyanov, Kelsiev, Shchapov, for example, as well as such odd figures as Khudyakov and Tolstoy's friend, Bochkarev. His pages on their part in the revolutionary movement, and particularly on their influence on the peasants to whom they spoke in the familiar religious language that was natural to them, contain rare and valuable information.

the replacement of one despotism by another, would lead to catastrophic results: while the revolutionaries procrastinated, capitalism would develop rapidly; the breathing space would enable the ruling class to develop a social and economic base incomparably stronger than that which it possessed at present; the growth of a prosperous and energetic capitalism would create opportunities of employment for the radical intellectuals themselves: doctors, engineers, educators, economists, technicians, and experts of all types would be assigned profitable tasks and positions, nor would their new bourgeois masters (unlike the existing régime) seek to force them into any kind of political conformity; the intelligentsia would obtain special privileges, status and wide opportunities for self-expression—harmless radicalism would be tolerated, a good deal of personal liberty permitted—and in this way the revolutionary cause would lose its most valuable recruits. Once those whom insecurity and discontent had driven into making common cause with the oppressed had been partially satisfied, the incentive to revolutionary activity would be weakened, and the prospects of a radical transformation of society would become exceedingly dim. The radical wing of the revolutionaries argued with great force that the advance of capitalism, whatever Marx might say, was not inevitable; it might be so in Western Europe, but in Rusisa it could still be arrested by a revolutionary *coup*, destroyed in the root before it had had time to grow too strong. If recognition of the need to awaken the 'political consciousness' of the majority of the workers and peasants (which by this time, and partly as a result of the failure of the intellectuals in 1848, had been pronounced absolutely indispensable to the revolution both by Marxists and by the majority of the Populist leaders) was tantamount to the adoption of a gradualist programme, the moment for action would surely be missed; in place of the Populist or socialist revolution would there not arise a vigorous, imaginative, predatory, successful capitalist régime which would succeed Russian semi-feudalism as surely as it had replaced the feudal order in Western Europe? And then who could tell how many decades or centuries might elapse before the arrival, at long last, of the revolution? And when it did arrive, who could tell what kind of order it would, by that time, install—resting upon what social basis?

All Populists were agreed that the village commune was the ideal embryo of those socialist groups on which the future society was to be based. But would the development of capitalism not automatically destroy the commune? And if it was maintained (although perhaps this was not explicitly asserted before the 'eighties) that capitalism was already destroying the *mir*, that the class struggle, as analysed by Marx, was dividing the villages as surely as the cities, then the plan of action was clear: rather than sit with folded hands and watch this disintegration fatalistically, resolute men could and must arrest this process, and save the village commune. Socialism, so the Jacobins argued, could be introduced by the capture of power to which all the energies of the revolutionaries must be bent, even at the price of postponing the task of educating the peasants in moral, social and political realities; indeed, such education could surely be promoted more rapidly and efficiently after the revolution had broken the resistance of the old régime. This line of thought, which bears an extraordinary resemblance, if not to the actual words, then to the policies pursued by Lenin in 1917, was basically very different from the older Marxist determinism. Its perpetual refrain was that there was no time to lose. Kulaks were devouring the poorer peasants in the country, capitalists were breeding fast in the towns. If the government possessed even a spark of intelligence, it would make concessions and promote reforms, and by this means divert educated men whose will and brain were needed for the revolution into the peaceful paths of the service of the reactionary state; propped up by such liberal measures, the unjust order would continue and be strengthened. The activists argued that there was nothing inevitable about revolutions: they were the fruit of human will and human reason. If there were not enough of these, the revolution might never take place at all. It was only the insecure who craved social solidarity and communal life; individualism was always a luxury, the ideal of the socially established. The new class of technical specialists—the modern, enlightened, energetic men celebrated by liberals like Kavelin and Turgenev, and at times, even by the radical individualist Pisarev—were for the Jacobin Tkachev 'worse than cholera or typhus', for by applying scientific methods to social life they were playing into the hands of the new, rising capitalist oligarchs and thereby obstructing the path to freedom. Palliatives were fatal when only an operation could save the patient: it merely prolonged his disease and weakened him so much that in the end not even an operation could save him. One must strike before these new, potentially conformist, intellectuals had grown too numerous and too comfortable and had obtained too much power, for otherwise it would be too late: a Saint-Simonian *élite* of highly paid managers would preside over a new feudal order—an economically efficient but socially immoral society, inasmuch as it was based on permanent inequality.

The greatest of all evils was inequality. Whenever any other ideal came into conflict with equality, the Russian Jacobins always called for its sacrifice or modification; the first principle upon which all justice rested was that of equality; no society was equitable in which there was not a maximum degree of equality between men. If the revolution was to succeed, three major fallacies had to be fought and rooted out. The first was that men of culture alone created progress. This was not true, and had the bad consequence of inducing faith in *élites*. The second was the opposite illusion—that everything must be learnt from the common people. This was equally false. Rousseau's Arcadian peasants were so many idyllic figments. The masses were ignorant, brutal, reactionary and did not understand their own needs or good. If the revolution depended upon their maturity, or capacity for political judgment or organization, it would certainly fail. The last fallacy was that only a proletarian majority could successfully make a revolution. No doubt a proletarian majority might do that, but if Russia was to wait until it possessed one, the opportunity of destroying a corrupt and detested government would pass, and capitalism would be found to be too firmly in the saddle. What then must be done? Men must be trained to make the revolution and destroy the present system and all obstacles to social equality and democratic self-government. When this was achieved, a democratic assembly was to be convened, and if those who made the revolution took care to explain the reasons for it, and the social and economic situation that made it necessary, then the masses, benighted though they might be today, would assuredly, in the view of the Jacobins, grasp their condition sufficiently to allow themselves to be—indeed to welcome the opportunity of being—organized into the new free federation of productive associations. But supposing they were still, on the morrow of a successful *coup d'état,* not mature enough to see this? Herzen did indeed ask the awkward question again and again in his writings in the late 'sixties. The majority of the Populists were deeply troubled by it. But the activist wing had no doubt of the answer: strike the chains from the captive hero, and he will stretch himself to his full height and live in freedom and happiness for ever after. The views of these men were astonishingly simple. They believed in terrorism and more terrorism to achieve complete, anarchist, liberty. The purpose of the revolution, for them, was to establish absolute equality, not only economic and social, but 'physical and physiological': they saw no discrepancy between this bed of Procrustes and absolute individual freedom. This order would be imposed in the beginning by the power and authority of the state, after which, the state, having fulfilled its purpose, would swiftly 'liquidate' itself. Against this, the spokesmen of the main body of the Populists argued that Jacobin means tended to bring about Jacobin consequences: if the purpose of the revolution was to liberate, it must not use the weapons of despotism that were bound to enslave those whom they were designed to liberate: the remedy must not prove more destructive than the disease. To use the state to break the power of the exploiters and to impose a specific form of life upon a people, the majority of whom had not been educated to understand the need for it, was to exchange the Tsarist yoke for a new, not necessarily less crushing one—that of the revolutionary minority. The majority of the Populists were deeply democratic; they believed that all power tended to corrupt, that all concentration of authority tended to perpetuate itself, that all centralization was coercive and evil, and, therefore, that the sole hope of a just and free society lay in the peaceful conversion of men by rational argument to the truths of social and economic justice and democratic freedom. In order to obtain the opportunity of converting men to this vision, it might indeed be necessary to break the existing obstacles to free and rational intercourse—the police state, the power of capitalists or of landowners—and to use force in the process, whether mass mutiny or individual terrorism. But this concept of temporary measures presented itself to them as something wholly different from leaving absolute power in the hands of any party or group, however virtuous, once the power of the enemy had been broken. Their case is the classical case, during the last two centuries, of every libertarian and federalist against Jacobins and centralizers: it is Voltaire's case against both Helvétius and Rousseau; that of the left wing of the Gironde against the Mountain; Herzen used these arguments against the doctrinaire communists of the immediately preceding period—Cabet and the disciples of Babeuf; Bakunin denounced the Marxist demand for the dictatorship of the proletariat as something that would merely transfer power from one set of oppressors to another; the Populists of the 'eighties and 'nineties urged this against all those whom they suspected of conspiring (whether they realized this or not) to destroy individual spontaneity and freedom, whether they were *laissez faire* liberals who allowed factory owners to enslave the masses, or radical collectivists who were ready to do so themselves; whether they were promoters of capitalist combines or Marxist advocates of centralized authority; indeed they looked upon the entrepreneurs (as Mikhailovsky wrote to Dostoevsky in his celebrated criticism of his novel *The Possessed*) as the more dangerous—as brutal, amoral 'social Darwinists', profoundly hostile to variety and individual freedom and character. This, again, was the main political issue which, at the turn of the century, divided the Russian Socialist-Revolutionaries from the Social-Democrats; and over which, a few years later, both Plekhanov and Martov broke with Lenin: indeed the great quarrel between the Bolsheviks and the Mensheviks (whatever its ostensible cause) turned upon it. In due course Lenin himself, two or three years after the October revolution, while he never abandoned the central Marxist doctrine, expressed his bitter disappointment with those very consequences of it which his opponents had predicted—bureaucracy and the arbitrary despotism of the party officials; and Trotsky accused Stalin of this same crime. The dilemma of means and ends is the deepest and most agonizing problem that torments the revolutionary movements of our own day in all the continents of the world, not least in Asia and Africa. That this debate took so clear and articulate a form within the Populist movement makes its development exceptionally relevant to our own predicament.

All these differences occurred within the framework of a common revolutionary outlook, for, whatever their disagreements, all Populists were united by an unshakable faith in the revolution. This faith derived from many sources. It sprang from the needs and outlook of a society still overwhelmingly pre-industrial, which gave the craving for simplicity and fraternity, and the agrarian idealism which derives ultimately from Rousseau—a reality which can still be seen in India and Africa today, and which necessarily looks Utopian to the eyes of social historians born in the industrialized West. It was a consequence of the disillusionment with parliamentary democracy, liberal convictions and the good faith of bourgeois intellectuals that resulted from the fiasco of the European revolutions of 1848–9, and from the particular conclusion drawn by Herzen that Russia, which had not suffered this revolution, might find her salvation in the undestroyed, natural socialism of the peasant *mir*. It was deeply influenced by Bakunin's violent diatribes against all forms of central authority, and in particular the state; and by his vision of men as being by nature peaceful and productive, and rendered violent only when they are perverted from their proper ends, and forced to be either gaolers or convicts. But it was also fed by the streams that flowed in a contrary direction: by Tkachev's faith in a Jacobin *élite* of professional revolutionaries as the only force capable of destroying the advance of capitalism helped on its fatal path by innocent reformists and humanitarians and careerist intellectuals, and concealed behind the repulsive sham of parliamentary democracy; even more by the passionate utilitarianism of Pisarev, and his brilliant polemics against all forms of idealism and amateurishness, and in particular the sentimental idealization of the simplicity and beauty of peasants in general, and of Russian peasants in particular, as beings touched by groups remote from the corrupting influences of the decaying West. It was supported by the appeal which these 'critical realists' made to their compatriots to save themselves by self-help and hard-headed energy—a kind of neo-Encyclopaedist campaign in favour of natural science, skill and professionalism, directed against the humanities, classical learning, history and other forms of 'sybaritic' self-indulgence. Above all it contrasted 'realism' with the literary culture which had lulled the best men in Russia into a condition where corrupt bureaucrats, stupid and brutal landowners and an obscurantist Church could exploit them or let them rot, while aesthetes and liberals looked the other way.

But the deepest strain of all, the very centre of the Populist outlook, was the individualism and rationalism of Lavrov and Mikhailovsky. With Herzen they believed that history followed no predetermined pattern, that it possessed 'no libretto', that neither the violent conflicts between cultures, nations, classes (which for Hegelians constituted the essence of human progress) nor the struggles for power by one class over another (represented by Marxists as being the motive force of history) were inevitable. Faith in human freedom was the cornerstone of Populist humanism; the Populists never tired of repeating that ends were chosen by men, not imposed upon them, and that men's wills alone could construct a happy and honourable life—a life in which the interests of intellectuals, peasants, manual workers and the liberal professions could be reconciled; not indeed made wholly to coincide, for that was an unattainable ideal; but adjusted in an unstable equilibrium, which human reason and constant human care could adjust to the largely unpredictable consequences of the interaction of men with each other and with nature. It may be that the tradition of the Orthodox Church with its conciliar and communal principles and deep antagonism both to the authoritarian hierarchy of the Roman Church, and the individualism of the Protestants, also exercised its share of influence. These doctrines and these prophets and their Western masters—French radicals before and after the French revolution, as well as Fichte and Buonarroti, Fourier and Hegel, Mill and Proudhon, Owen and Marx, played their part. But the largest figure in the Populist movement, the man whose temperament, ideas and activities dominated it from beginning to end, is undoubtedly that of Nikolai Gavrilovich Chernyshevsky and his immediate allies and followers. The influence of his life and teachings, despite a multitude of monographs, still await its interpreter.

Nicholas Chernyshevsky was not a man of original ideas. He did not possess the depth, the imagination or the brilliant intellect and literary talent of Herzen, nor the eloquence, the boldness, the temperament or the reasoning power of Bakunin, nor the moral genius and unique social insight of Belinsky. But he was a man of unswerving integrity, immense industry and a capacity rare among Russians for concentration upon concrete detail. His deep, steady, lifelong hatred of slavery, injustice and irrationality did not express itself in large theoretical generalizations, or the creation of a sociological or metaphysical system, or violent action against authority. It took the form of slow, uninspired, patient accumulation of facts and ideas—a crude, dull but powerful intellectual structure on which one might found a detailed policy of practical action appropriate to the specific Russian environment which he desired to alter. Chernyshevsky was in greater sympathy with the concrete, carefully elaborated socialist plans, however mistaken they might be, of the Petrashevsky group (to which Dostoevsky had belonged in his youth, crushed by the government in 1849), than to the great imaginative constructions of Herzen, Bakunin and their followers.

A new generation had grown up during the dead years after 1849. These young men had witnessed vacillation and outright betrayals on the part of liberals which had led to the victories of the reactionary parties in 1849. Twelve years later they saw the same phenomenon in their own country, when the manner in which the peasants had been emancipated in Russia seemed to them to be a cynical travesty of all their plans and hopes. Such men as these found the plodding genius of Chernyshevsky, his attempts to work out specific solutions to specific problems in terms of concrete statistical data; his constant appeals to facts; his patient efforts to indicate attainable, practical, immediate ends rather than desirable states of affairs to which there was no visible road; his flat, dry, pedestrian style, his very dullness and lack of inspiration, more serious and, ultimately, more inspiring than the noble flights of the romantic idealists of the 'forties. His relatively low social origin (he was the son of a parish priest) gave him a natural affinity with the humble folk whose condition he was seeking to analyse, and an abiding distrust, later to turn into fanatical hatred, of all liberal theorists, whether in Russia or the West. These qualities made Chernyshevsky a natural leader of a disenchanted generation of socially mingled origins, no longer dominated by good birth, embittered by the failure of their own early ideals, by government repression, by the humiliation of Russia in the Crimean War, by the weakness, heartlessness, hypocrisy and chaotic incompetence of the ruling class. To these tough-minded, socially insecure, angry, suspicious young radicals contemptuous of the slightest trace of eloquence or "literature", Chernyshevsky was a father and confessor, as neither the aristocratic and ironical Herzen nor the wayward and ultimately frivolous Bakunin could ever become.

Like all Populists, Chernyshevsky believed in the need to preserve the peasant commune and to spread its principles to industrial production. He believed that Russia could profit directly by learning from the scientific advances of the West, without going through the agonies of an industrial revolution. 'Human development is a form of chronological unfairness', Herzen had once characteristically observed, 'since late-comers are able to profit by the labours of their predecessors without paying the same price'; 'History is fond of her grandchildren', Chernyshevsky repeated after him, 'for it offers them the marrow of the bones, which the previous generation had hurt its hands in breaking.' For Chernyshevsky history moved along a spiral, in Hegelian triads, since every generation tends to repeat the experience not of its parents, but of its grandparents, and repeats it at a 'higher level'. But it is not this historicist element in his doctrine that bound its spell upon the Populists. They were most of all influenced by his acute distrust of reforms from above, by his belief that the essence of history was a struggle between the classes, above all by his conviction (which derives nothing, so far as we know, from Marx, but draws upon socialist sources common to both) that the state is always the instrument of the dominant class, and cannot, whether it consciously desires this or not, embark on those necessary reforms the success of which would end its own domination. No order can be persuaded to undertake its own dissolution. Hence all attempts to influence the Tsar, all attempts to evade the horrors of revolution, must (he concluded in the early 'sixties) remain necessarily vain. There was a moment in the late 'fifties when, like Herzen, he had hoped for reforms from above. The final form of the Emancipation, and the concessions which the government had made to the landowners, cured him of this illusion. He pointed out with a good deal of historical justification that the liberals, who hoped to influence the government by Fabian tactics, thus far merely succeeded in betraying both the peasants and themselves: first they compromised themselves with the peasants by their relations with their masters; after that, the governing class found little difficulty, whenever this suited their convenience, in representing them as false friends to the peasants and turning the latter against them. This had occurred in both France and Germany in 1849. Even if the moderates withdrew in time, and advocated violent measures, their ignorance of conditions and blindness to the peasants' and workers' actual needs usually led them to advocate utopian schemes which in the end cost their followers a terrible price.

Chernyshevsky had evolved a simple form of historical materialism, according to which social factors determined political ones, and not *vice versa*. Consequently he held with Fourier and Proudhon that liberal and parliamentary ideals merely evaded the central issues: the peasants and the workers needed food, shelter, boots; as for the right to vote, or to be governed by liberal constitutions, or to obtain guarantees of personal liberty, these meant little to hungry and half-naked men. The social revolution must come first: appropriate political reforms would follow of themselves. For Chernyshevsky the principal lesson of 1848 was that the Western liberals, the brave no less than the cowardly, had demonstrated their political and moral bankruptcy, and with it that of their Russian disciples —Herzen, Kavelin, Granovsky, and the rest. Russia must pursue her own path. Unlike the Slavophils, and like the Russian Marxists of the next generation, he maintained with a wealth of economic evidence that the historical development of Russia, and in particular the peasant *mir*, were in no sense unique, but followed the social and economic laws that governed all human societies. Like the Marxists (and the Comtian positivists), he believed that such laws could be discovered and stated; but unlike the Marxists, he was convinced that by adopting Western techniques, and educating a body of men of trained and resolute wills and rational outlook, Russia could 'leap over' the capitalist stage of social development, and transform her village communes and free cooperative groups of craftsmen into agricultural and industrial associations of producers who would constitute the embryo of the new socialist society. Technological progress did not, in his view, automatically break up the peasant commune: 'savages can be taught to use Latin script and safety matches'; factories can be grafted on to workers' *artels* without destroying them; large-scale organization could eliminate exploitation, and yet preserve the predominantly agricultural nature of the Russian economy.[2]

Chernyshevsky believed in the decisive historical rôle of the application of science to life, but unlike Pisarev, did not regard individual enterprise, still less capitalism as indispensable to this process. He retained enough of the Fourierism of his youth to look upon the free associations of peasant communes and craftsmen's *artels* as the basis of all freedom and progress. But at the same time, like the Saint-Simonians, he was convinced that little would be achieved without collective action—state socialism on a vast scale. These incompatible beliefs were never reconciled; Cherny-

[2] Professor Venturi very aptly quotes Populist statistics (which seem plausible enough) according to which the number of peasants to that of landowners in the 'sixties was of the order of 234:1, while the land owned by them stood to that of their masters in the ratio of 1:11½, and their incomes were 97·5:2·5; as for industry, the proportion of city workers to peasants was 1:100. Given these figures it is perhaps not surprising that Marx should have declared that his prognosis applied to the Western economies, and not necessarily to that of the Russians, even though his Russian disciples ignored this concession, and insisted that capitalism was making enormous strides in Russia, and would soon obliterate the differences that divided it from the West. Plekhanov (who stoutly denied that Chernyshevsky had ever been a Populist) elaborated this theory, and Lenin acted upon it, with results that mankind will not easily forget.

shevsky's writings contain statements both in favour of and against the desirability of large-scale industry. He is similarly ambivalent about the part to be played (and the part to be avoided) by the state as the stimulator and controller of industry, about the function of managers of large collective industrial enterprises, about the relations of the public and private sectors of the economy, and about the political sovereignty of the democratically elected parliament and its relation to the state as the source of centralized economic planning and control.

The outlines of Chernyshevsky's social programme remained vague or inconsistent, and often both. It is the concrete detail which, founded as it was on real experience, spoke directly to the representatives of the great popular masses, who had at last found a spokesman and interpreter of their own needs and feelings. His deepest aspirations and emotions were poured into *What is to be done?*, a social utopia which, grotesque as a work of art, had a literally epoch-making effect on Russian opinion. This didactic novel described the 'new men' of the free, morally pure, cooperative socialist commonwealth of the future; its touching sincerity and moral passion bound their spell upon the imaginations of the idealistic and guilt-stricken sons of prosperous parents, and provided them with an ideal model in the light of which an entire generation of revolutionaries educated and hardened itself to the defiance of existing laws and conventions, and acceptance of exile and death with sublime unconcern. Chernyshevsky preached a naïve utilitarianism. Like James Mill, and perhaps Bentham, he held that basic human nature was a fixed, physiologically analysable, pattern of natural processes and faculties, and that the maximization of human happiness could therefore be scientifically planned and realized. Having decided that imaginative writing and criticism were the only available media in Russia for propagating radical ideas, he filled the *Contemporary*, a review which he edited together with the poet Nekrasov, with as high a proportion of direct socialist doctrine as could be smuggled in under the guise of literature. In this work he was helped by the violent young critic Dobrolyubov, a genuinely gifted man of letters (which Chernyshevsky was not) who, at times, went even further in his passionate desire to preach and educate. The aesthetic views of the two zealots were severely practical. Chernyshevsky laid it down that the function of art was to help men to satisfy their wants more rationally, to disseminate knowledge, to combat ignorance, prejudice and the anti-social passions, to improve life in the most literal and narrow sense of these words. Driven to absurd consequences, he embraced them gladly. Thus he explained that the chief value of marine paintings was that they showed the sea to those who, like, for instance, the inhabitants of central Russia, lived too far away from it ever to see it for themselves; and he maintained that his friend and patron Nekrasov, because by his verse he moved men to greater sympathy with the oppressed than other poets had done, was for that reason the greatest Russian poet, living or dead. His earlier collaborators, civilized and fastidious men of letters like Turgenev and Botkin found this grim fanaticism increasingly difficult to bear. Turgenev could not long live with this art hating and dogmatic schoolmaster. Tolstoy despised his dreary provincialism, his total lack of aesthetic sense, his intolerance, his wooden rationalism, his maddening self-assurance. But these very qualities, or, rather, the outlook of which they were characteristic, helped to make him the natural leader of the 'hard' young men who had succeeded the idealists of the 'forties. Chernyshevsky's harsh, flat, dull, humourless, grating sentences, his preoccupation with concrete economic detail, his self-discipline, his passionate dedication to the material and moral good of his fellow men, the grey, self-effacing personality, the tireless, devoted, minute industry, the hatred of style or of any concessions to the graces, the unquestionable sincerity, the combination of brutal directness, utter self-forgetfulness, indifference to the claims of private life, innocence, personal kindness, pedantry, moral charm, capacity for self-sacrifice, created the image that later became the prototype of the Russian revolutionary hero and martyr. More than any other publicist he was responsible for drawing the final line between 'us' and 'them'. All his life he preached that there must be no compromise with 'them', that the war must be fought to the death and on every front; there were no neutrals, that, so long as this war was being fought, no work could be too trivial, too repulsive or too tedious for a revolutionary to perform. His personality and outlook set its seal upon two generations of Russian revolutionaries; not least upon Lenin, who admired him devotedly.

In spite of his emphasis on economic or sociological arguments, the basic approach, the tone and outlook of Chernyshevsky and of the Populists generally, is moral, and at times indeed, religious. These men believed in socialism not because it was inevitable, nor because it was effective, not even because it alone was rational, but because it was just. Concentrations of political power, capitalism, the centralized state, trampled upon the rights of men and crippled them morally and spiritually. The Populists were stern atheists, but socialism and orthodox Christian values coalesced in their minds. They shrank from the prospect of industrialism in Russia because of its brutal cost, and they disliked the West because it had paid this price too heartlessly. Their disciples, the Populist economists of the 'eighties and 'nineties, Danielson and Vorontsov,[3] for example, for all their strictly economic arguments against the possibility of capitalism in Russia (some of which seem a good deal sounder than their Marxist opponents have represented them as being), were in the last analysis moved by moral revulsion from the sheer mass of suffering that capitalism was destined to bring, that is to say, by a refusal to pay so appalling a price, no matter how valuable the results. Their successors in the twentieth century, the Socialist-Revolutionaries, sounded the note which runs through the whole of the Populist tradition in Russia: that the purpose of social action is not the power of the state, but the welfare of the people; that to enrich the state and provide it with military and industrial power, while undermining the health, the education, the morality, the general cultural level of its citizens, was feasible but wicked. They compared the progress of the United States, where, they maintained, the welfare of the individual was paramount, with that of Prussia, where it was not. They committed themselves to the view (which goes back at least to Sismondi) that the spiritual and physical condition of the individual citizen matters more than the power of the state, so that if, as often happened, the two stood in inverse ratio to one another, the rights and welfare of the individual must come first. They rejected as historically false the proposition that only powerful states could breed good or happy citizens, and as morally unacceptable the proposition

[3] Who wrote under the pseudonyms of Nikolay ———on and V.V. respectively.

that to lose oneself in the life and welfare of his society is the highest form of self-fulfilment for the individual. Belief in the primacy of human rights over other claims is the first principle that separates pluralist from centralized societies, and welfare states, mixed economies, 'New Deal' policies, from one-party governments, 'closed' societies, 'five-year plans', and, in general, forms of life built to serve a single goal that transcends the varied goals of differing groups or individuals. Chernyshevsky was more fanatical than his followers in the 'seventies and 'eighties, and believed far more strongly in organization, but even he neither stopped his ears to the cries for immediate help which he heard upon all sides, nor believed in the need to suppress the wants of individuals who were making desperate efforts to escape destruction, in the interests of even the most sacred and overmastering purpose. There were times when he was a narrow and unimaginative pedant, but at his worst he was never impatient nor arrogant, nor inhumane, and was perpetually reminding his readers and himself that in their zeal to help, the educators must not end by bullying their would-be beneficiaries, that what 'we'—the rational intellectuals—think good for the peasants may be not what they themselves want, and that to ram 'our' remedies down 'their' throats is not permitted. Neither he nor Lavrov, nor even the most ruthlessly Jacobin among the proponents of terror and violence, ever took cover behind the inevitable direction of history as a justification of what would otherwise have been patently unjust or brutal. If violence was the only means to a given end, then there might be circumstances in which it was right to employ it; but this must be justified in each case by the intrinsic moral claim of the end—an increase in happiness, or solidarity, or justice, or peace, or some other universal human value that outweighs the evil of the means, never by the view that it was rational and necessary to march in step with history, ignoring one's scruples and dismissing one's own 'subjective' moral principles because they were necessarily provisional, on the ground that history herself transformed all moral systems and retrospectively justified only those principles which survived and succeeded.

The mood of the Populists, particularly in the 'seventies, can fairly be described as religious. This group of conspirators or propagandists saw itself, and was seen by others, as constituting a dedicated order. The first condition of membership was the sacrifice of one's entire life to the movement, both to the particular group and party, and to the cause of the revolution in general. But the notion of the dictatorship of the party or of its leaders over individual lives—in particular over the beliefs of individual revolutionaries—is no part of this doctrine, and is indeed contrary to its entire spirit. The only censor over the individual's acts is his individual conscience. If one has promised obedience to the leaders of the party, such an oath is sacred, but it extends only to the specific revolutionary objectives of the party and not beyond them, and ends with the completion of whatever specific goals the party exists to promote—in the last resort, the revolution. Once the revolution has been made, each individual is free to act as he thinks right, since discipline is a temporary means and not an end. The Populists did indeed virtually invent the conception of the party as a group of professional conspirators with no private lives, obeying a total discipline—the core of the 'hard' professionals, as against mere sympathizers and fellow-travellers; but this sprang from the specific situation that obtained in Tsarist Russia, and the necessity, and conditions for effective conspiracy, and not from belief in hierarchy as a form of life desirable or even tolerable in itself. Nor did the conspirators justify their acts by appealing to a cosmic process which sanctified their every act, since they believed in freedom of human choice and not in determinism. The later Leninist conception of the revolutionary party and its dictatorship, although historically it owed much to these trained martyrs of an earlier day, sprang from a different outlook. The young men who poured into the villages during the celebrated summer of 1874, only to meet with noncomprehension, suspicion and often outright hostility on the part of the peasants, would have been profoundly astonished and indignant if they had been told that they were to look upon themselves as the sacred instruments of history, and that their acts were therefore to be judged by a moral code different from that common to other men.

The Populist movement was a failure. 'Socialism bounced off people like peas from a wall', wrote the celebrated terrorist Stepnyak Kravchinsky to his fellow revolutionary Vera Zasulich in 1876, two years after the original wave of enthusiasm had died down. 'They listen to our people as they do to the priest' —respectfully, without understanding, without any effect upon their actions. 'There is noise in the capitals/The prophets thunder/A furious war of words is waged/But in the depths, in the heart of Russia,/There all is still, there is ancient peace.' These lines by Nekrasov convey the mood of frustration which followed the failure of the sporadic efforts made by the revolutionary idealists in the late 'sixties and early 'seventies, peaceful propagandists and isolated terrorists alike—of whom Dostoevsky painted so violent a picture in *The Possessed*. The government caught these men, exiled them, imprisoned them, and by its obstinate unwillingness to promote any measures to alleviate the consequences of an inadequate land reform drove liberal opinion towards sympathy with the revolutionaries. They felt that public opinion was on their side, and finally resorted to organized terrorism. Yet their ends always remained moderate enough. The open letter which they addressed to the new Emperor in 1881 is mild and liberal in tone. 'Terror', said the celebrated revolutionary Vera Figner many years later, 'was intended to create opportunities for developing the faculties of men for service to society.' The society for which violence was to blast the way was to be peaceful, tolerant, decentralized and humane. The principal enemy was still the state.

The wave of terrorism reached its climax with the assassination of Alexander II in 1881. The hoped-for revolution did not break out. The revolutionary organizations were crushed, and the new Tsar decided upon a policy of extreme repression. In this he was, on the whole, supported by public opinion, which recoiled before the assassination of an Emperor who had, after all, emancipated the peasants, and who was said to have been meditating other liberal measures. The most prominent leaders of the movement were executed or exiled; lesser figures escaped abroad, and the most gifted of those who were still free—Plekhanov and Akselrod —gradually moved towards Marxism. They felt embarrassed by Marx's own concession that Russia could in principle avoid passing through a capitalist stage even without the aid of a communist world revolution—a thesis which Engels conceded far more grudgingly and with qualifications—and maintained that Russia had in fact already entered the capitalist stage. They declared that, since the development of capitalism in Russia was no more avoidable than it had been in its day in the West, nothing was to be gained by averting one's face from the 'iron' logic of history, and that for these reasons, so far from resisting industrialization, socialists should encourage it, indeed profit by the fact that it, and it alone, could breed the army of revolutionaries which would be sufficient to overthrow the capitalist enemy—an army to be formed out of the growing city proletariat, organized and disciplined by the very conditions of its labour.

The vast forward leap in industrial development made by Russia in the 'nineties seemed to support the Marxist thesis. It proved attractive to revolutionary intellectuals for many reasons: because it claimed to be founded on a scientific analysis of the laws of history which no society could hope to evade; because it claimed to be able to 'prove' that, although much violence, misery and injustice—exploitation, pauperization, conflicts between classes, nations, interests—were bound to occur as the pattern of history inexorably unfolded itself, yet the story would have a happy ending. Hence the conscience of those who felt guilty because they acquiesced in the miseries of the workers, or at any rate did not take active—that is, violent—steps to alleviate or prevent them, as Populist policy had demanded, felt assuaged by the 'scientific' guarantee that the road, covered though it might be with the corpses of the innocent, led inevitably to the gates of an earthly paradise. According to this view the expropriators would find themselves expropriated by the sheer logic of human development, although the course of history might be shortened, and the birth pangs made easier, by conscious organization, and above all an increase in knowledge (that is, education) on the part of the workers and their leaders. This was particularly welcome to those who, understandably reluctant to continue with useless terrorism which merely led to Siberia or the scaffold, now found doctrinal justification for peaceful study and the life of ideas, which the intellectuals among them found far more congenial than bomb-throwing.

The heroism, the disinterestedness, the personal nobility of the Populists, was often admitted by their Marxist opponents. They were regarded as worthy forerunners of a truly rational revolutionary party, and Chernyshevsky was sometimes accorded an even higher status and was credited with insights of genius—an empirical and unscientific, but instinctively correct, approach to truths of which only Marx and Engels could provide the demonstration, armed as they were with the instrument of an exact science to which neither Chernyshevsky, nor any other Russian thinker of his day, had yet attained. Marx and Engels grew to be particularly indulgent to the Russians: they were praised for having done wonders for amateurs, remote from the West and using home-made tools; they alone in Europe had, by 1880, created a truly revolutionary situation in their country; but it was made clear, particularly by Kautsky, that this was no substitute for professional methods and the use of the new machinery provided by scientific socialism. Populism was written down as an amalgam of unorganized moral indignation and utopian ideas in the muddled heads of self-taught peasants, well-meaning university intellectuals [4] and other social casualties of the confused interim between the end of an obsoles-

[4] Professor Venturi's account both of peasant risings and, still more, of the student movements out of which Populism, properly so called—the *Narodnik* groups of 1876–8—wholly sprang, are among the most original and valuable contributions to our knowledge of what the author likes to regard as a kind of Russian Carbonarism.

cent feudalism and the beginning of the new capitalist phase in a backward country. Marxist historians still tend to describe it as a movement compounded of systematic misinterpretation of economic facts and social realities, noble but useless individual terrorism, and spontaneous or ill-directed peasant risings—the necessary but pathetic beginnings of real revolutionary activity, the prelude to the real play, a scene of naïve ideas and frustrated practice destined to be swept away by the new revolutionary, dialectical science heralded by Plekhanov and Lenin.

What were the ends of Populism? Violent disputes took place about means and methods, about timing, but not about ultimate purposes. Anarchism, equality, a full life for all, these were universally accepted. It is as if the entire movement—the motley variety of revolutionary types which Professor Venturi describes so well and so lovingly—Jacobins and moderates, terrorists and educators, Lavrists and Bakuninists, 'troglodytes', 'recalcitrants' and 'country folk', members of 'Land and Liberty' and of 'The People's Will', were all dominated by a single myth: that once the monster was slain, the sleeping princess—the Russian peasantry—would awaken and without further ado live happily for ever after.

This is the movement of which Professor Venturi has written the history, the fullest, clearest, best written and most impartial account of a particular stage of the Russian revolutionary movement in any language. Yet if the movement was a failure, if it was founded on false premises and was so easily extinguished by the Tsarist police, has it a more than historical interest—that of a narrative of the life and death of a party, of its acts and its ideas? On this Professor Venturi discreetly, as behoves an objective historian, offers no direct opinion. He tells the story in chronological sequence; he explains what occurs; he describes origins and consequences; he illuminates the relations of various groups of Populists to one another, and leaves moral and political speculation to others. His work is not an apologia either for Populism or its opponents. He does not praise or condemn, and seeks only to understand. Success in this task plainly needs no further reward. And yet one may, at moments, wonder whether Populism should be dismissed quite as easily as it still is today, both by communist and bourgeois historians. Were the populists so hopelessly in error? Were Chernyshevsky and Lavrov—and Marx who listened to them—totally deluded?

Was capitalism in fact inevitable in Russia? The consequences of accelerated industrialization prophesied by the neo-Populist economists in the 'nineties, namely a degree of social and economic misery as great as any undergone in the West during the Industrial Revolution, did occur, both before, and, at an increasing tempo, after the October revolution. Were they avoidable? Some writers on history consider this type of question to be absurd as such. What happened, happened. We are told that if we are not to deny causality in human affairs, we must suppose that what took place can only have done so precisely as it did; to ask what might have happened if the situation had been different is the idle play of the imagination, not worthy of serious historians. Yet this academic question is not without acute contemporary relevance. Some countries such, for example, as Turkey, India, and some states in the Middle East and Latin America, and even Yugoslavia, have adopted a slower tempo of industrialization and one less likely to bring immediate ruin to backward areas before they can be rehabilitated, and have done so in conscious preference to the forced marches of collectivization upon which, in our day, the Russians, and after them the Chinese, have embarked. Are these non-Marxist governments inescapably set upon a path to ruin? For it is Populist ideas which lie at the base of much of the socialist economic policy pursued by these and other countries today.

When Lenin organized the Bolshevik revolution in 1917, the technique that he adopted, *prima facie* at least, resembled those commended by the Russian Jacobins, Tkachev and his followers who had learnt them from Blanqui or Buonarroti, more than any to be found in the writings of Marx or Engels at any rate after 1851. It was not, after all, full-grown capitalism that was enthroned in Russia in 1917. Russian capitalism was a still growing force, not yet in power, struggling against the fetters imposed upon it by the monarchy and the bureaucracy, as it had done in eighteenth-century France. But Lenin acted as if the bankers and industrialists were already in control. He acted and spoke as if this was so, but his revolution succeeded not by taking over the centres of finance and industry (which history should already have undermined) but by a seizure of strictly political power by a determined and trained group of professional revolutionaries, precisely as had been advocated by Tkachev. If Russian capitalism had reached the stage, which, according to Marxist historical theory, it had to reach before a proletarian revolution could be successful, the seizure of power by a determined minority, and a very small one at that—a mere *Putsch*—could not, *ex hypothesi*, have retained it long. And this indeed is what Plekhanov said over and over again in his bitter denunciations of Lenin in 1917: ignoring his argument that much may be permitted in a backward country, provided that the results were duly saved by orthodox Marxist revolutions successfully carried out soon after in the industrially more advanced West. These conditions were not fulfilled; Lenin's hypothesis proved historically irrelevant; yet the Bolshevik revolution did not collapse. Could it be that the Marxist theory of history was mistaken? Or had the Mensheviks misunderstood it, and concealed from themselves the anti-democratic tendencies which had always been implicit in it? In which case were their charges against Mikhailovsky and his friends, after all, wholly just? By 1917 their own fears of the Bolshevik dictatorship rested upon the same basis. Moreover, the results of the October revolution turned out to be oddly similar to those which Tkachev's opponents had prophesied that his methods must inevitably produce: the emergence of an *élite*, wielding dictatorial power, designed in theory to wither away once the need for it had gone; but, as the Populist democrats had said over and over again, in practice more likely to grow in aggressiveness and strength, with a tendency towards self-perpetuation which no dictatorship seems able to resist. The Populists were convinced that the death of the peasant commune would mean death, or at any rate a vast setback, to freedom and equality in Russia; the Left Socialist-Revolutionaries, who were their direct descendants, transformed this into a demand for a form of decentralized, democratic self-government among the peasants, which Lenin adopted when he concluded his temporary alliance with them in October 1917. In due course the Bolsheviks repudiated this programme, and transformed the cells of dedicated revolutionaries—perhaps the most original contribution of Populism to revolutionary practice—into the hierarchy of centralized political power, which the Populists had steadily and fiercely denounced until they were themselves finally, in the form of the Socialist-Revolutionary party, proscribed and annihilated. Communist practice owed much, as Lenin was always ready to admit, to the Populist movement; for it borrowed the technique of its rival and adapted it with conspicuous success to serve the precise purpose which it had been invented to resist.

***What Is to Be Done?*, written in 1902, was Lenin's most forceful and influential formulation of his ideas about revolutionary organization and practice. It provided the theoretical foundation for the Bolshevik Party.**

What Is to Be Done?

V. I. LENIN

I. Dogmatism and "Freedom of Criticism"

A. WHAT DOES "FREEDOM OF CRITICISM" MEAN? . . . It is no secret for anyone that two trends have taken form in present-day international Social-Democracy. The conflict between these trends now flares up in a bright flame and now dies down and smoulders under the ashes of imposing "truce resolutions". The essence of the "new" trend, which adopts a "critical" attitude towards "obsolete dogmatic" Marxism, has been clearly enough *presented* by Bernstein. . . .

Social-Democracy must change from a party of social revolution into a democratic party of social reforms. Bernstein has surrounded this political demand with a whole battery of well-attuned "new" arguments and reasonings. Denied was the possibility of putting socialism on a scientific basis and of demonstrating its necessity and inevitability from the point of view of the materialist conception of history. Denied was the fact of growing impoverishment, the process of proletarisation, and the intensification of capitalist contradictions; the very concept, "*ultimate aim*", was declared to be unsound, and the idea of the dictatorship of the proletariat was completely rejected. Denied was the antithesis in principle between liberalism and socialism. Denied was *the theory of the class struggle,* on the alleged grounds that it could not be applied to a strictly democratic society governed according to the will of the majority, etc.

Thus, the demand for a decisive turn from revolutionary Social-Democracy to bourgeois social-reformism was accompanied by a no less decisive turn towards bourgeois criticism of all the fundamental ideas of Marxism. In view of the fact that this criticism of Marx-

Reprinted from *What Is to Be Done?* by V. I. Lenin. Progress Publishers, 1969, Moscow, U.S.S.R.

ism has long been directed from the political platform, from university chairs, in numerous pamphlets and in a series of learned treatises, in view of the fact that the entire younger generation of the educated classes has been systematically reared for decades on this criticism, it is not surprising that the "new critical" trend in Social-Democracy should spring up, all complete, like Minerva from the head of Jove. The content of this new trend did not have to grow and take shape, it was transferred bodily from bourgeois to socialist literature. . . .

He who does not deliberately close his eyes cannot fail to see that the new "critical" trend in socialism is nothing more nor less than a new variety of *opportunism*. And if we judge people, not by the glittering uniforms they don or by the high-sounding appellations they give themselves, but by their actions and by what they actually advocate, it will be clear that "freedom of criticism" means freedom for an opportunist trend in Social-Democracy, freedom to convert Social-Democracy into a democratic party of reform, freedom to introduce bourgeois ideas and bourgeois elements into socialism.

"Freedom" is a grand word, but under the banner of freedom for industry the most predatory wars were waged, under the banner of freedom of labour, the working people were robbed. The modern use of the term "freedom of criticism" contains the same inherent falsehood. Those who are really convinced that they have made progress in science would not demand freedom for the new views to continue side by side with the old, but the substitution of the new views for the old. The cry heard today, "Long live freedom of criticism", is too strongly reminiscent of the fable of the empty barrel.

We are marching in a compact group along a precipitous and difficult path, firmly holding each other by the hand. We are surrounded on all sides by enemies, and we have to advance almost constantly under their fire. We have combined, by a freely adopted decision, for the purpose of fighting the enemy, and not of retreating into the neighbouring marsh, the inhabitants of which, from the very outset, have reproached us with having separated ourselves into an exclusive group and with having chosen the path of struggle instead of the path of conciliation. And now some among us begin to cry out: Let us go into the marsh! And when we begin to shame them, they retort: What backward people you are! Are you not ashamed to deny us the liberty to invite you to take a better road! Oh, yes, gentlemen! You are free not only to invite us, but to go yourselves wherever you will, even into the marsh. In fact, we think that the marsh is your proper place, and we are prepared to render *you* every assistance to get there. Only let go of our hands, don't clutch at us and don't besmirch the grand word freedom, for we too are "free" to go where we please, free to fight not only against the marsh, but also against those who are turning towards the marsh!

. . . .

Thus, we see that high-sounding phrases against the ossification of thought, etc., conceal unconcern and helplessness with regard to the development of theoretical thought. The case of the Russian Social-Democrats manifestly illustrates the general European phenomenon (long ago noted also by the German Marxists) that the much vaunted freedom of criticism does not imply substitution of one theory for another, but freedom from all integral and pondered theory; it implies eclecticism and lack of principle. Those who have the slightest acquaintance with the actual state of our movement cannot but see that the wide spread of Marxism was accompanied by a certain lowering of the theoretical level. Quite a number of people with very little, and even a total lack of theoretical training joined the movement because of its practical significance and its practical successes. We can judge from that how tactless *Rabocheye Dyelo* is when, with an air of triumph, it quotes Marx's statement: "Every step of real movement is more important than a dozen programmes." To repeat these words in a period of theoretical disorder is like wishing mourners at a funeral many happy returns of the day. Moreover, these words of Marx are taken from his letter on the Gotha Programme, in which he *sharply condemns* eclecticism in the formulation of principles. If you must unite, Marx wrote to the party leaders, then enter into agreements to satisfy the practical aims of the movement, but do not allow any bargaining over principles, do not make theoretical "concessions". This was Marx's idea, and yet there are people among us who seek—in his name—to belittle the significance of theory!

Without revolutionary theory there can be no revolutionary movement. This idea cannot be insisted upon too strongly at a time when the fashionable preaching of opportunism goes hand in hand with an infatuation for the narrowest forms of practical activity. Yet, for Russian Social-Democrats the importance of theory is enhanced by three other circumstances, which are often forgotten: first, by the fact that our Party is only in process of formation, its features are only just becoming defined, and it has as yet far from settled accounts with the other trends of revolutionary thought that threaten to divert the movement from the correct path. On the contrary, precisely the very recent past was marked by a revival of non-Social-Democratic revolutionary trends (an eventuation regarding which Axelrod long ago warned the Economists). Under these circumstances, what at first sight appears to be an "unimportant" error may lead to most deplorable consequences, and only short-sighted people can consider factional disputes and a strict differentiation between shades of opinion inopportune or superfluous. The fate of Russian Social-Democracy for very many years to come may depend on the strengthening of one or the other "shade".

Secondly, the Social-Democratic movement is in its very essence an international movement. This means, not only that we must combat national chauvinism, but that an incipient movement in a young country can be successful only if it makes use of the experiences of other countries. In order to make use of these experiences it is not enough merely to be acquainted with them, or simply to copy out the latest resolutions. What is required is the ability to treat these experiences critically and to test them independently. He who realises how enormously the modern working-class movement has grown and branched out will understand what a reserve of theoretical forces and political (as well as revolutionary) experience is required to carry out this task.

Thirdly, the national tasks of Russian Social-Democracy are such as have never confronted any other socialist party in the world. We shall have occasion further on to deal with the political and organisational duties which the task of emancipating the whole people from the yoke of autocracy imposes upon us. At this point, we wish to state only that the *role of vanguard fighter can be fulfilled only by a party that is guided by the most advanced theory*. To have a concrete understanding of what this means, let the reader recall such predecessors of Russian Social-Democracy as Herzen, Belinsky, Chernyshevsky, and the brilliant galaxy of revolutionaries of the seventies; let him ponder over the world significance which Russian literature is now acquiring; let him . . . but be that enough!

Let us quote what Engels said in 1874 concerning the significance of theory in the Social-Democratic movement. Engels recognises, *not two* forms of the great struggle of Social-Democracy (political and economic), as is the fashion among us, *but three, placing the theoretical struggle on a par with the first two.* His recommendations to the German working-class movement, which had become strong, practically and politically, are so instructive from the standpoint of present-day problems and controversies, that we hope the reader will not be vexed with us for quoting a long passage from his prefatory note to *Der deutsche Bauernkrieg,*[1] which has long become a great bibliographical rarity:

"The German workers have two important advantages over those of the rest of Europe. First, they belong to the most theoretical people of Europe; and they have retained that sense of theory which the so-called 'educated' classes of Germany have almost completely lost. Without German philosophy, which preceded it, particularly that of Hegel, German scientific socialism—the only scientific socialism that has ever existed—would never have come into being. Without a sense of theory among the workers, this scientific socialism would never have entered their flesh and blood as much as is the case. What an immeasurable advantage this is may be seen, on the one hand, from the indifference towards all theory, which is one of the main reasons why the English working-class movement crawls along so slowly in spite of the splendid organisation of the individual unions; on the other hand, from the mischief and confusion wrought by Proudhonism, in its original form, among the French and Belgians, and, in the form further caricatured by Bakunin, among the Spaniards and Italians.

"The second advantage is that, chronologically speaking, the Germans were about the last to come into the workers' movement. Just as German theoretical socialism will never forget that it rests on the shoulders of Saint-Simon, Fourier, and Owen—three men who, in spite of all their fantastic notions and all their utopianism, have their place among the most eminent thinkers of all times, and whose genius anticipated innumerable things, the correctness of which is now being scientifically proved by us—so the practical workers' movement in Germany ought never to forget that it has developed on the shoulders of the English and French movements, that it was able simply to utilise their dearly bought experience, and could now avoid their mistakes, which in their time were mostly unavoidable. Without the precedent of the English trade unions and French workers' political struggles, without the gigantic impulse given especially by the Paris Commune, where would we be now?

"It must be said to the credit of the German workers that they have exploited the advantages of their situation with rare understanding. For the first time since a workers' movement has existed, the struggle is being conducted pursuant to its three sides—the theoretical, the political, and the practical-economic (resistance to the capitalists)—in harmony and in its interconnections, and in a systematic way. It is precisely in this, as it were, concentric attack, that the strength and invincibility of the German movement lies.

"Due to this advantageous situation, on the one hand, and to the insular peculiarities of the English and the forcible suppression of the French move-

[1] Dritter Abdruck, Leipzig, 1875. Verlag der Genossenschaftsbuchdruckerei. (*The Peasant War in Germany.* Third impression. Cooperative Publishers, Leipzig, 1875.—*Ed.*)

ment, on the other, the German workers have for the moment been placed in the vanguard of the proletarian struggle. How long events will allow them to occupy this post of honour cannot be foretold. But let us hope that as long as they occupy it, they will fill it fittingly. This demands redoubled efforts in every field of struggle and agitation. In particular, it will be the duty of the leaders to gain an ever clearer insight into all theoretical questions, to free themselves more and more from the influence of traditional phrases inherited from the old world outlook, and constantly to keep in mind that socialism, since it has become a science, demands that it be pursued as a science, i.e., that it be studied. The task will be to spread with increased zeal among the masses of the workers the ever more clarified understanding thus acquired, to knit together ever more firmly the organisation both of the party and of the trade unions. . . .

"If the German workers progress in this way, they will not be marching exactly at the head of the movement —it is not at all in the interest of this movement that the workers of any particular country should march at its head —but they will occupy an honourable place in the battle line; and they will stand armed for battle when either unexpectedly grave trials or momentous events demand of them increased courage, increased determination and energy."

Engels's words proved prophetic. Within a few years the German workers were subjected to unexpectedly grave trials in the form of the Exceptional Law Against the Socialists. And they met those trials armed for battle and succeeded in emerging from them victorious.

The Russian proletariat will have to undergo trials immeasurably graver; it will have to fight a monster compared with which an anti-socialist law in a constitutional country seems but a dwarf. History has now confronted us with an immediate task which is the *most revolutionary* of all the *immediate* tasks confronting the proletariat of any country. The fulfilment of this task, the destruction of the most powerful bulwark, not only of European, but (it may now be said) of Asiatic reaction, would make the Russian proletariat the vanguard of the international revolutionary proletariat. And we have the right to count upon acquiring this honourable title, already earned by our predecessors, the revolutionaries of the seventies, if we succeed in inspiring our movement, which is a thousand times broader and deeper, with the same devoted determination and vigour.

II. The Spontaneity of the Masses and the Consciousness of the Social-Democrats

We have said that our movement, much more extensive and deep than the movement of the seventies, must be inspired with the same devoted determination and energy that inspired the movement at that time. Indeed, no one, we think, has until now doubted that the strength of the present-day movement lies in the awakening of the masses (principally, the industrial proletariat) and that its weakness lies in the lack of consciousness and initiative among the revolutionary leaders. . . .

For this reason the question of the relation between consciousness and spontaneity is of such enormous general interest, and for this reason the question must be dealt with in great detail.

THE BEGINNING OF THE SPONTANEOUS UPSURGE. In the previous chapter we pointed out how *universally* absorbed the educated youth of Russia was in the theories of Marxism in the middle of the nineties. In the same period the strikes that followed the famous St. Petersburg industrial war of 1896 assumed a similar general character. Their spread over the whole of Russia clearly showed the depth of the newly awakening popular movement, and if we are to speak of the "spontaneous element" then, of course, it is this strike movement which, first and foremost, must be regarded as spontaneous. But there is spontaneity and spontaneity. Strikes occurred in Russia in the seventies and sixties (and even in the first half of the nineteenth century), and they were accompanied by the "spontaneous" destruction of machinery, etc. Compared with these "revolts", the strikes of the nineties might even be described as "conscious", to such an extent do they mark the progress which the working-class movement made in that period. This shows that the "spontaneous element", in essence, represents nothing more nor less than consciousness in an *embryonic form*. Even the primitive revolts expressed the awakening of consciousness to a certain extent. The workers were losing their age-long faith in the permanence of the system which oppressed them and began . . . I shall not say to understand, but to sense the necessity for collective resistance, definitely abandoning their slavish submission to the authorities. But this was, nevertheless, more in the nature of outbursts of desperation and vengeance than of *struggle*. The strikes of the nineties revealed far greater flashes of consciousness; definite demands were advanced, the strike was carefully timed, known cases and instances in other places were discussed, etc. The revolts were simply the resistance of the oppressed, whereas the systematic strikes represented the class struggle in embryo, but only in embryo. Taken by themselves, these strikes were simply trade-union struggles, not yet Social-Democratic struggles. They marked the awakening antagonisms between workers and employers; but the workers were not, and could not be, conscious of the irreconcilable antagonism of their interests to the whole of the modern political and social system, i.e., theirs was not yet Social-Democratic consciousness. In this sense, the strikes of the nineties, despite the enormous progress they represented as compared with the "revolts", remained a purely spontaneous movement.

We have said that *there could not have been* Social-Democratic consciousness among the workers. It would have to be brought to them from without. The history of all countries shows that the working class, exclusively by its own effort, is able to develop only trade-union consciousness, i.e., the conviction that it is necessary to combine in unions, fight the employers, and strive to compel the government to pass necessary labour legislation, etc.[2] The theory of socialism, however, grew out of the philosophic, historical, and economic theories elaborated by educated representatives of the propertied classes, by intellectuals. By their social status, the founders of modern scientific socialism, Marx and Engels, themselves belonged to the bourgeois intelligentsia. In the very same way, in Russia, the theoretical doctrine of Social-Democracy arose altogether independently of the spontaneous growth of the working-class movement; it arose as a natural and inevitable outcome of the development of thought among the revolutionary socialist intelligentsia. In the period under discussion, the middle nineties, this doctrine not only represented the completely formulated programme of the Emancipation of Labour group, but had already won over to its side the majority of the revolutionary youth in Russia.

[2] Trade-unionism does not exclude "politics" altogether, as some imagine. Trade unions have always conducted some political (but not Social-Democratic) agitation and struggle. We shall deal with the difference between trade-union politics and Social-Democratic politics in the next chapter.

Hence, we had both the spontaneous awakening of the working masses, their awakening to conscious life and conscious struggle, and a revolutionary youth, armed with Social-Democratic theory and straining towards the workers. In this connection it is particularly important to state the oft-forgotten (and comparatively little-known) fact that, although the *early* Social-Democrats of that period *zealously carried on economic agitation* (being guided in this activity by the truly useful indications contained in the pamphlet *On Agitation*, then still in manuscript), they did not regard this as their sole task. On the contrary, *from the very beginning* they set for Russian Social-Democracy the most far-reaching historical tasks, in general, and the task of overthrowing the autocracy, in particular. Thus, towards the end of 1895, the St. Petersburg group of Social-Democrats, which founded the League of Struggle for the Emancipation of the Working Class, prepared the first issue of a newspaper called *Rabocheye Dyelo*. This issue was ready to go to press when it was seized by the gendarmes, on the night of December 8, 1895, in a raid on the house of one of the members of the group, Anatoly Alexeyevich Vaneyev,[3] so that the first edition of *Rabocheye Dyelo* was not destined to see the light of day. The leading article in this issue (which perhaps thirty years hence some *Russkaya Starina* will unearth in the archives of the Department of Police) outlined the historical tasks of the working class in Russia and placed the achievement of political liberty at their head. The issue also contained an article entitled "What Are Our Ministers Thinking About?"[4] which dealt with the crushing of the elementary education committees by the police. In addition, there was some correspondence from St. Petersburg, and from other parts of Russia (e.g., a letter on the massacre of the workers in Yaroslavl Gubernia). This "first effort", if we are not mistaken, of the Russian Social-Democrats of the nineties was not a purely local, or less still "Economic", newspaper, but one that aimed to unite the strike movement with the revolutionary movement against the autocracy, and to win over to the side of Social-Democracy all who were oppressed by the policy of reactionary obscurantism. No one in the slightest degree acquainted with the state of the movement at that period could doubt that such a paper would have met with warm response among the workers of the capital and the revolutionary intelligentsia and would have had a wide circulation. The failure of the enterprise merely showed that the Social-Democrats of that period were unable to meet the immediate requirements of the time owing to their lack of revolutionary experience and practical training. . . . It is therefore highly important to establish the fact that a part (perhaps even a majority) of the Social-Democrats, active in the period of 1895–98, justly considered it possible even then, at the very beginning of the "spontaneous" movement, to come forward with a most extensive programme and a militant tactical line.[5] Lack of training of the

[3] A. A. Vaneyev died in Eastern Siberia in 1899 from consumption, which he contracted during solitary confinement in prison prior to his banishment. That is why we considered it possible to publish the above information, the authenticity of which we guarantee, for it comes from persons who were closely and directly acquainted with A. A. Vaneyev.

[4] See *Collected Works*, Vol. 2, pp. 87–92.—*Ed.*

[5] "In adopting a hostile attitude towards the activities of the Social-Democrats of the late nineties, *Iskra* ignores the absence at that time of conditions for any work other than the struggle for petty demands," declare the Economists in their "Letter to Russian Social-Democratic Organs" (*Iskra*, No. 12). The facts given above show that the assertion about "absence of conditions" *is diametrically opposed to the truth.* Not only at the end, but even in

majority of the revolutionaries, an entirely natural phenomenon, could not have roused any particular fears. Once the tasks were correctly defined, once the energy existed for repeated attempts to fulfil them, temporary failures represented only part misfortune. Revolutionary experience and organisational skill are things that can be acquired, provided the desire is there to acquire them, provided the shortcomings are recognised, which in revolutionary activity is more than half-way towards their removal.

But what was only part misfortune became full misfortune when this consciousness began to grow dim (it was very much alive among the members of the groups mentioned), when there appeared people—and even Social-Democratic organs—that were prepared to regard shortcomings as virtues, that even tried to invent a *theoretical* basis for their *slavish cringing before spontaneity*. It is time to draw conclusions from this trend, the content of which is incorrectly and too narrowly characterised as "Economism".

Since there can be no talk of an independent ideology formulated by the working masses themselves in the process of their movement,[6] the *only* choice is—either bourgeois or socialist ideology. There is no middle course (for mankind has not created a "third" ideology, and, moreover, in a society torn by class antagonisms there can never be a non-class or an above-class ideology). Hence, to belittle the socialist ideology *in any way, to turn aside from it in the slightest degree* means to strengthen bourgeois ideology. There is much talk of spontaneity. But the *spontaneous* development of the working-class movement leads to its subordination to bourgeois ideology, *to its development along the lines of the Credo programme;* for the spontaneous working-class movement is trade-unionism, is *Nur-Gewerkschaftlerei,* and trade-unionism means the ideological enslavement of the workers by the bourgeoisie. Hence, our task, the task of Social-Democracy, is *to combat spontaneity, to divert* the working-class movement from this spontaneous, trade-unionist striving to come under the wing of the bourgeoisie, and to bring it under the wing of revolutionary Social-Democracy. The sentence employed by the authors of the "Economist" letter published in *Iskra,* No. 12, that the efforts of the most inspired ideologists fail to divert the working-class movement from the path that is determined by the interaction of the material elements and the material environment *is* therefore *tantamount to renouncing socialism.* If these authors

---

the mid-nineties, all the conditions existed for *other* work, besides the struggle for petty demands—all the conditions except adequate training of leaders. Instead of frankly admitting that we, the ideologists, the leaders, lacked sufficient training—the "Economists" seek to shift the blame entirely upon the "absence of conditions", upon the effect of material environment that determines the road from which no ideologist will be able to divert the movement. What is this but slavish cringing before spontaneity, what but the infatuation of the "ideologists" with their own shortcomings?

[6] This does not mean, of course, that the workers have no part in creating such an ideology. They take part, however, not as workers, but as socialist theoreticians, as Proudhons and Weitlings; in other words, they take part only when they are able, and to the extent that they are able, more or less, to acquire the knowledge of their age and develop that knowledge. But in order that working men *may succeed in this more often,* every effort must be made to raise the level of the consciousness of the workers in general; it is necessary that the workers do not confine themselves to the artificially restricted limits of *"literature for workers"* but that they learn to an increasing degree to master *general literature.* It would be even truer to say "are not confined", instead of "do not confine themselves", because the workers themselves wish to read and do read all that is written for the intelligentsia, and only a few (bad) intellectuals believe that it is enough "for workers" to be told a few things about factory conditions and to have repeated to them over and over again what has long been known.

were capable of fearlessly, consistently, and thoroughly considering what they say, as everyone who enters the arena of literary and public activity should be, there would be nothing left for them but to "fold their useless arms over their empty breasts" and—surrender the field of action to the Struves and Prokopoviches, who are dragging the working-class movement "along the line of least resistance", i.e., along the line of bourgeois trade-unionism, or to the Zubatovs, who are dragging it along the line of clerical and gendarme "ideology".

Let us recall the example of Germany. What was the historic service Lassalle rendered to the German working-class movement? It was that he *diverted* that movement from the path of progressionist trade-unionism and cooperativism towards which it had been spontaneously moving (*with the benign assistance of Schulze-Delitzsch and his like*). To fulfil such a task it was necessary to do something quite different from talking of underrating the spontaneous element, of tactics-as-process, of the interaction between elements and environment, etc. *A fierce struggle against spontaneity* was necessary, and only after such a struggle, extending over many years, was it possible, for instance, to convert the working population of Berlin from a bulwark of the progressionist party into one of the finest strongholds of Social-Democracy. This struggle is by no means over even today (as might seem to those who learn the history of the German movement from Prokopovich, and its philosophy from Struve). Even now the German working class is, so to speak, split up among a number of ideologies. A section of the workers is organised in Catholic and monarchist trade unions; another section is organised in the Hirsch-Duncker unions, founded by the bourgeois worshippers of English trade-unionism; the third is organised in Social-Democratic trade unions. The last-named group is immeasurably more numerous than the rest, but the Social-Democratic ideology was able to achieve this superiority, and will be able to maintain it, only in an unswerving struggle against all other ideologies.

But why, the reader will ask, does the spontaneous movement, the movement along the line of least resistance, lead to the domination of bourgeois ideology? For the simple reason that bourgeois ideology is far older in origin than socialist ideology, that it is more fully developed, and that it has at its disposal *immeasurably* more means of dissemination.[7] And the younger the socialist movement in any given country, the more vigorously it must struggle against all attempts to entrench non-socialist ideology, and the more resolutely the workers must be warned against the bad counsellors who shout against "overrating the conscious element", etc.

And so, we have become convinced that the fundamental error committed by the "new trend" in Russian Social-Democracy is its bowing to spontaneity and its failure to understand that the spontaneity of the masses demands a high degree of consciousness from us Social-Democrats. The greater the spontaneous upsurge of the masses and the

[7] It is often said that the working class *spontaneously gravitates* towards socialism. This is perfectly true in the sense that socialist theory reveals the causes of the misery of the working class more profoundly and more correctly than any other theory, and for that reason the workers are able to assimilate it so easily, *provided,* however, this theory does not itself yield to spontaneity, *provided* it subordinates spontaneity to itself. Usually this is taken for granted, but it is precisely this which *Rabocheye Dyelo* forgets or distorts. The working class spontaneously gravitates towards socialism; nevertheless, most widespread (and continuously and diversely revived) bourgeois ideology spontaneously imposes itself upon the working class to a still greater degree.

more widespread the movement, the more rapid, incomparably so, the demand for greater consciousness in the theoretical, political, and organisational work of Social-Democracy.

The spontaneous upsurge of the masses in Russia proceeded (and continues) with such rapidity that the young Social-Democrats proved unprepared to meet these gigantic tasks. This unpreparedness is our common misfortune, the misfortune of *all* Russian Social-Democrats. The upsurge of the masses proceeded and spread with uninterrupted continuity; it not only continued in the places where it began, but spread to new localities and to new strata of the population (under the influence of the working-class movement, there was a renewed ferment among the student youth, among the intellectuals generally, and even among the peasantry). Revolutionaries, however, *lagged behind* this upsurge, both in their "theories" and in their activity; they failed to establish a constant and continuous organisation capable of *leading* the whole movement. . . .

The overwhelming majority of Russian Social-Democrats have of late been almost entirely absorbed by this work of organising the exposure of factory conditions. Suffice it to recall *Rabochaya Mysl* to see the extent to which they have been absorbed by it—so much so, indeed, that they have lost sight of the fact that this, *taken by itself*, is in essence still not Social-Democratic work, but merely trade-union work. As a matter of fact, the exposures merely dealt with the relations between the workers *in a given trade* and their employers, and all they achieved was that the sellers of labour-power learned to sell their "commodity" on better terms and to fight the purchasers over a purely commercial deal. These exposures could have served (if properly utilised by an organisation of revolutionaries) as a beginning and a component part of Social-Democratic activity; but they could also have led (and, given a worshipful attitude towards spontaneity, were bound to lead) to a "purely trade-union" struggle and to a non-Social-Democratic working-class movement. Social-Democracy leads the struggle of the working class, not only for better terms for the sale of labour-power, but for the abolition of the social system that compels the propertyless to sell themselves to the rich. Social-Democracy represents the working class, not in its relation to a given group of employers alone, but in its relation to all classes of modern society and to the state as an organised political force. Hence, it follows that not only must Social-Democrats not confine themselves exclusively to the economic struggle, but that they must not allow the organisation of economic exposures to become the predominant part of their activities. We must take up actively the political education of the working class and the development of its political consciousness. *Now* that *Zarya* and *Iskra* have made the first attack upon Economism, "all are agreed" on this (although some agree only in words, as we shall soon see).

The question arises, what should political education consist in? Can it be confined to the propaganda of working-class hostility to the autocracy? Of course not. It is not enough *to explain* to the workers that they are politically oppressed (any more than it is *to explain* to them that their interests are antagonistic to the interests of the employers). Agitation must be conducted with regard to every concrete example of this oppression (as we have begun to carry on agitation round concrete examples of economic oppression). Inasmuch as *this* oppression affects the most diverse classes of society, inasmuch as it manifests itself in the most varied spheres of life and activity—vocational, civic, personal, family, religious, scientific, etc., etc.—is it not evident that *we shall not be fulfilling our task* of developing the political consciousness of the workers if we do not *undertake* the organisation of the *political exposure* of the autocracy *in all its aspects?* In order to carry on agitation round concrete instances of oppression, these instances must be exposed (as it is necessary to expose factory abuses in order to carry on economic agitation).

POLITICAL EXPOSURES AND "TRAINING IN REVOLUTIONARY ACTIVITY." . . . In reality, it is possible to "raise the activity of the working masses" *only* when this activity *is not restricted* to "political agitation on an economic basis". A basic condition for the necessary expansion of political agitation is the organisation of *comprehensive* political exposure. *In no way* except by means of such exposures *can* the masses be trained in political consciousness and revolutionary activity. Hence, activity of this kind is one of the most important functions of international Social-Democracy as a whole, for even political freedom does not in any way eliminate exposures; it merely shifts somewhat their sphere of direction. Thus, the German party is especially strengthening its positions and spreading its influence, thanks particularly to the untiring energy with which it is conducting its campaign of political exposure. Working-class consciousness cannot be genuine political consciousness unless the workers are trained to respond to *all* cases of tyranny, oppression, violence, and abuse, no matter *what class* is affected—unless they are trained, moreover, to respond from a Social-Democratic point of view and no other. The consciousness of the working masses cannot be genuine class-consciousness, unless the workers learn, from concrete, and above all from topical, political facts and events to observe *every* other social class in *all* the manifestations of its intellectual, ethical, and political life; unless they learn to apply in practice the materialist analysis and the materialist estimate of *all* aspects of the life and activity of *all* classes, strata, and groups of the population. Those who concentrate the attention, observation, and consciousness of the working class exclusively, or even mainly, upon itself alone are not Social-Democrats; for the self-knowledge of the working class is indissolubly bound up, not solely with a fully clear theoretical understanding—it would be even truer to say, not so much with the theoretical, as with the practical, understanding—of the relationships between *all* the various classes of modern society, acquired through the experience of political life. For this reason the conception of the economic struggle as the most widely applicable means of drawing the masses into the political movement, which our Economists preach, is so extremely harmful and reactionary in its practical significance. In order to become a Social-Democrat, the worker must have a clear picture in his mind of the economic nature and the social and political features of the landlord and the priest, the high state official and the peasant, the student and the vagabond; he must know their strong and weak points; he must grasp the meaning of all the catchwords and sophisms by which each class and each stratum *camouflages* its selfish strivings and its real "inner workings"; he must understand what interests are reflected by certain institutions and certain laws and how they are reflected. But this "clear picture" cannot be obtained from any book. It can be obtained only from living examples and from exposures that follow close upon what is going on about us at a given moment; upon what is being discussed, in whispers perhaps, by each one in his own way; upon what finds expression in such and such events, in such and such statistics, in such and such court sentences, etc., etc. These comprehensive political exposures are an essential and *fundamental* condition for training the masses in revolutionary activity.

Why do the Russian workers still manifest little revolutionary activity in response to the brutal treatment of the people by the police, the persecution of religious sects, the flogging of peasants, the outrageous censorship, the torture of soldiers, the persecution of the most innocent cultural undertakings, etc.? Is it because the "economic struggle" does not "stimulate" them to this, because such activity does not "promise palpable results", because it produces little that is "positive"? To adopt such an opinion, we repeat, is merely to direct the charge where it does not belong, to blame the working masses for one's own philistinism (or Bernsteinism). We must blame ourselves, our lagging behind the mass movement, for still being unable to organise sufficiently wide, striking, and rapid exposures of all the shameful outrages. When we do that (and we must and can do it), the most backward worker will understand, *or will feel,* that the students and religious sects, the peasants and the authors are being abused and outraged by those same dark forces that are oppressing and crushing him at every step of his life. Feeling that, he himself will be filled with an irresistible desire to react, and he will know how to hoot the censors one day, on another day to demonstrate outside the house of a governor who has brutally suppressed a peasant uprising, on still another day to teach a lesson to the gendarmes in surplices who are doing the work of the Holy Inquisition, etc. As yet we have done very little, almost nothing, *to bring* before the working masses prompt exposures on all possible issues. Many of us as yet do not recognise this as our *bounden duty* but trail spontaneously in the wake of the "drab everyday struggle", in the narrow confines of factory life. Under such circumstances to say that "*Iskra* displays a tendency to minimise the significance of the forward march of the drab everyday struggle in comparison with the propaganda of brilliant and complete ideas" (Martynov) means to drag the Party back, to defend and glorify our unpreparedness and backwardness.

As for calling the masses to action, that will come of itself as soon as energetic political agitation, live and striking exposures come into play. To catch some criminal red-handed and immediately to brand him publicly in all places is of itself far more effective than any number of "calls"; the effect very often is such as will make it impossible to tell exactly who it was that "called" upon the masses and who suggested this or that plan of demonstration, etc. Calls for action, not in the general, but in the concrete, sense of the term can be made only at the place of action; only those who themselves go into action, and do so immediately, can sound such calls. Our business as Social-Democratic publicists is to deepen, expand, and intensify political exposures and political agitation. . . .

Class political consciousness can be brought to the workers *only from without,* that is, only from outside the economic struggle, from outside the sphere of relations between workers and employers. The sphere from which alone it is possible to obtain this knowledge is the sphere of relationships of *all* classes and strata to the state and the government, the sphere of the interrelations between *all* classes. For that reason, the reply to the question as to what must be done to bring political knowledge to the workers cannot be merely the answer with which, in the majority of cases, the practical workers, especially those inclined towards Economism, mostly content themselves, namely: "To go among the workers." To bring political knowledge to the *workers* the Social-Democrats must *go among all classes of the population;* they must dispatch units of their army *in all directions.* . . .

Let us return, however, to our thesis. We said that a Social-Democrat, if he really believes it necessary to develop comprehensively the political consciousness of the proletariat, must "go among all classes of the population". This gives rise to the questions: how is this to be done? have we enough forces to do this? is there a basis for such work among all the other classes? will this not mean a retreat, or lead to a retreat, from the class point of view? Let us deal with these questions.

We must "go among all classes of the population" as theoreticians, as propagandists, as agitators, and as organisers. No one doubts that the theoretical work of Social-Democrats should aim at studying all the specific features of the social and political condition of the various classes. But extremely little is done in this direction, as compared with the work that is done in studying the specific features of factory life. In the committees and study circles, one can meet people who are immersed in the study even of some special branch of the metal industry; but one can hardly ever find members of organisations (obliged, as often happens, for some reason or other to give up practical work) who are especially engaged in gathering material on some pressing question of social and political life in our country which could serve as a means for conducting Social-Democratic work among other strata of the population. In dwelling upon the fact that the majority of the present-day leaders of the working-class movement lack training, we cannot refrain from mentioning training in this respect also, for it too is bound up with the "Economist" conception of "close organic connection with the proletarian struggle". The principal thing, of course, is *propaganda* and *agitation* among all strata of the people. The work of the West-European Social-Democrat is in this respect facilitated by the public meetings and rallies which *all* are free to attend, and by the fact that in parliament he addresses the representatives of *all* classes. We have neither a parliament nor freedom of assembly; nevertheless, we are able to arrange meetings of workers who desire to listen to *a Social-Democrat*. We must also find ways and means of calling meetings of representatives of all social classes that desire to listen to *a democrat;* for he is no Social-Democrat who forgets in practice that "the Communists support every revolutionary movement", that we are obliged for that reason to expound and emphasise *general democratic tasks before the whole people,* without for a moment concealing our socialist convictions. He is no Social-Democrat who forgets in practice his obligation to be *ahead of all* in raising, accentuating, and solving *every* general democratic question.

In our time only a party that will *organise really nation-wide* exposures can become the vanguard of the revolutionary forces. The word "nation-wide" has a very profound meaning. The overwhelming majority of the non-working-class exposers (be it remembered that in order to become the vanguard, we must attract other classes) are sober politicians and level-headed men of affairs. They know perfectly well how dangerous it is to "complain" even against a minor official, let alone against the "omnipotent" Russian Government. And they will come *to us* with their complaints only when they see that these complaints can really have effect, and that we represent *a political force.* In order to become such a force in the eyes of outsiders, much persistent and stubborn work is required *to raise* our own consciousness, initiative, and energy. To accomplish this it is not enough to attach a "vanguard" label to rearguard theory and practice.

But if we have to undertake the organisation of a really nation-wide exposure of the government, in what way will then the class character of our movement be expressed?—the overzealous advocate of "close organic contact with the proletarian struggle" will ask us, as indeed he does. The reply is manifold: we Social-Democrats will organise these nation-wide exposures; all questions raised by the agitation will be explained in a consistently Social-Democratic spirit, without any concessions to deliberate or undeliberate distortions of Marxism; the all-round political agitation will be conducted by a party which unites into one inseparable whole the assault on the government in the name of the entire people, the revolutionary training of the proletariat, and the safeguarding of its political independence, the guidance of the economic struggle of the working class, and the utilisation of all its spontaneous conflicts with its exploiters which rouse and bring into our camp increasing numbers of the proletariat. . . .

Thus, we have reached the question of the relation between an organisation of professional revolutionaries and the labour movement pure and simple. Although this question has found little reflection in literature, it has greatly engaged us "politicians" in conversations and polemics with comrades who gravitate more or less towards Economism. It is a question meriting special treatment. . . .

ORGANISATION OF WORKERS AND ORGANISATION OF REVOLUTIONARIES. It is only natural to expect that for a Social-Democrat whose conception of the political struggle coincides with the conception of the "economic struggle against the employers and the government", the "organisation of revolutionaries" will more or less coincide with the "organisation of workers". This, in fact, is what actually happens; so that when we speak of organisation, we literally speak in different tongues. I vividly recall, for example, a conversation I once had with a fairly consistent Economist, with whom I had not been previously acquainted. We were discussing the pamphlet, *Who Will Bring About the Political Revolution?* and were soon of a mind that its principal defect was its ignoring of the question of organisation. We had begun to assume full agreement between us; but, as the conversation proceeded, it became evident that we were talking of different things. My interlocutor accused the author of ignoring strike funds, mutual benefit societies, etc., whereas I had in mind an organisation of revolutionaries as an essential factor in "bringing about" the political revolution. As soon as the disagreement became clear, there was hardly, as I remember, a single question of principle upon which I was in agreement with the Economist!

What was the source of our disagreement? It was the fact that on questions both of organisation and of politics the Economists are forever lapsing from Social-Democracy into trade-unionism. The political struggle of Social-Democracy is far more extensive and complex than the economic struggle of the workers against the employers and the government. Similarly (indeed for that reason), the organisation of the revolutionary Social-Democratic Party must inevitably be of *a kind different* from the organisation of the workers designed for this struggle. The workers' organisation must in the first place be a trade-union organisation; secondly, it must be as broad as possible; and thirdly, it must be as public as conditions will allow (here, and further on, of course, I refer only to absolutist Russia). On the other hand, the organisation of the revolutionaries must consist first and foremost of people who make revolutionary activity their profession (for which reason I speak of the organisation of *revolutionaries,* meaning revolutionary Social-Democrats). In view of this common characteristic of the members of such an organisation, *all distinctions as between workers and intellectuals,* not to speak of distinctions of trade and profession, in both categories, *must be effaced.* Such an organisation must perforce not be very extensive and must be as secret as possible. Let us examine this threefold distinction.

In countries where political liberty exists the distinction between a trade-union and a political organisation is clear enough, as is the distinction between trade unions and Social-Democracy. The relations between the latter and the former will naturally vary in each country according to historical, legal, and other conditions; they may be more or less close, complex, etc. (in our opinion they should be as close and as little complicated as possible); but there can be no question in free countries of the organisation of trade unions coinciding with the organisation of the Social-Democratic Party. In Russia, however, the yoke of the autocracy appears at first glance to obliterate all distinctions between the Social-Democratic organisation and the workers' associations, since *all* workers' associations and *all* study circles are prohibited, and since the principal manifestation and weapon of the workers' economic struggle—the strike—is regarded as a criminal (and sometimes even as a political!) offence. Conditions in our country, therefore, on the one hand, strongly "impel" the workers engaged in economic struggle to concern themselves with political questions, and, on the other, they "impel" Social-Democrats to confound trade-unionism with Social Democracy. . . .

A small, compact core of the most reliable, experienced, and hardened workers, with responsible representatives in the principal districts and connected by all the rules of strict secrecy with the organisation of revolutionaries, can, with the widest support of the masses and without any formal organisation, perform *all* the functions of a trade-union organisation, in a manner, moreover, desirable to Social-Democracy. Only in this way can we secure the *consolidation* and development of a *Social-Democratic* trade-union movement, despite all the gendarmes.

It may be objected that an organisation which is so *loose* that it is not even definitely formed, and which has not even an enrolled and registered membership, cannot be called an organisation at all. Perhaps so. Not the name is important. What is important is that this "organisation without members" shall do everything that is required, and from the very outset ensure a solid connection between our future trade unions and socialism. Only an incorrigible utopian would have a *broad* organisation of workers, with elections, reports, universal suffrage, etc., under the autocracy.

The moral to be drawn from this is simple. If we begin with the solid foundation of a strong organisation of revolutionaries, we can ensure the stability of the movement as a whole and carry out the aims both of Social-Democracy and of trade unions proper. If, however, we begin with a broad workers' organisation, which is supposedly most "accessible" to the masses (but which is actually most accessible to the gendarmes and makes revolutionaries most accessible to the police), we shall achieve neither the one aim nor the other; we shall not eliminate our rule-of-thumb methods, and, because we remain scattered and our forces are constantly broken up by the police, we shall only make trade unions of the Zubatov and Ozerov type the more accessible to the masses.

What, properly speaking, should be the functions of the organisation of revolutionaries? We shall deal with this question in detail. . . .

"A committee of students is of no use; it is not stable." Quite true. But the conclusion to be drawn from this is that we must have a committee of professional *revolutionaries*, and it is immaterial whether a student or a worker is capable of becoming a professional revolutionary. The conclusion you draw, however, is that the working-class movement must not be pushed on from outside! In your political innocence you fail to notice that you are playing into the hands of our Economists and fostering our amateurism. Wherein, may I ask, did our students "push on" our workers? *In the sense* that the student brought to the worker the fragments of political knowledge he himself possesses, the crumbs of socialist ideas he has managed to acquire (for the principal intellectual diet of the present-day student, legal Marxism, could furnish only the rudiments, only scraps of knowledge). There has never been too much of *such* "pushing on from outside"; on the contrary, there has so far been all too little of it in our movement, for we have been stewing too assiduously in our own juice; we have bowed far too slavishly to the elementary "economic struggle of the workers against the employers and the government". We professional revolutionaries must and will make it our business to engage in *this kind* of "pushing on" a hundred times more forcibly than we have done hitherto.

"A dozen wise men can be more easily wiped out than a hundred fools." This wonderful truth (for which the hundred fools will always applaud you) appears obvious only because in the very midst of the argument you have skipped from one question to another. You began by talking and continued to talk of the unearthing of a "committee", of the unearthing of an "organisation", and now you skip to the question of unearthing the movement's "roots" in their "depths". The fact is, of course, that our movement cannot be unearthed, for the very reason that it has countless thousands of roots deep down among the masses; but that is not the point at issue. As far as "deep roots" are concerned, we cannot be "unearthed" even now, despite all our amateurism, and yet we all complain, and cannot but complain, that the *"organisations"* are being unearthed and as a result it is impossible to maintain continuity in the movement. But since you raise the question of *organisations* being unearthed and persist in your opinion, I assert that it is far more difficult to unearth a dozen wise men than a hundred fools. This position I will defend, no matter how much you instigate the masses against me for my "anti-democratic" views, etc. As I have stated repeatedly, by "wise men", in connection with organisation, I mean *professional revolutionaries,* irrespective of whether they have developed from among students or working men. I assert: (1) that no revolutionary movement can endure without a stable organisation of leaders maintaining continuity; (2) that the broader the popular mass drawn spontaneously into the struggle, which forms the basis of the movement and participates in it, the more urgent the need for such an organisation, and the more solid this organisation must be (for it is much easier for all sorts of demagogues to side-track the more backward sections of the masses); (3) that such an organisation must consist chiefly of people professionally engaged in revolutionary activity; (4) that in an autocratic state, the more we *confine* the membership of such an organisation to people who are professionally engaged in revolutionary activity and who have been professionally trained in the art of combating the political police, the more difficult will it be to unearth the organisation; and (5) the *greater* will be the number of people from the working class and from the other social classes who will be able to join the movement and perform active work in it.

I invite our Economists, terrorists, and

"Economists-terrorists" to confute these propositions. At the moment, I shall deal only with the last two points. The question as to whether it is easier to wipe out "a dozen wise men" or "a hundred fools" reduces itself to the question, above considered, whether it is possible to have a mass *organisation* when the maintenance of strict secrecy is essential. We can never give a mass organisation that degree of secrecy without which there can be no question of persistent and continuous struggle against the government. To concentrate all secret functions in the hands of as small a number of professional revolutionaries as possible does not mean that the latter will "do the thinking for all" and that the rank and file will not take an active part in the *movement*. On the contrary, the membership will promote increasing numbers of the professional revolutionaries from its ranks; for it will know that it is not enough for a few students and for a few working men waging the economic struggle to gather in order to form a "committee", but that it takes years to train oneself to be a professional revolutionary; and the rank and file will "think", not only of amateurish methods, but of such training. Centralisation of the secret functions of the *organisation* by no means implies centralisation of all the functions of the *movement*. Active participation of the widest masses in the illegal press will not diminish because a "dozen" professional revolutionaries centralise the secret functions connected with this work; on the contrary, it will *increase* tenfold. In this way, and in this way alone, shall we ensure that reading the illegal press, writing for it, and to some extent even distributing it, will *almost cease to be secret work*, for the police will soon come to realise the folly and impossibility of judicial and administrative red-tape procedure over every copy of a publication that is being distributed in the thousands. This holds not only for the press, but for every function of the movement, even for demonstrations. The active and widespread participation of the masses will not suffer: on the contrary, it will benefit by the fact that a "dozen" experienced revolutionaries, trained professionally no less than the police, will centralise all the secret aspects of the work—the drawing up of leaflets, the working out of approximate plans; and the appointing of bodies of leaders for each urban district, for each factory district, and for each educational institution, etc. (I know that exception will be taken to my "undemocratic" views, but I shall reply below fully to this anything but intelligent objection.) Centralisation of the most secret functions in an organisation of revolutionaries will not diminish, but rather increase the extent and enhance the quality of the activity of a large number of other organisations, that are intended for a broad public and are therefore as loose and as non-secret as possible, such as workers' trade unions; workers' self-education circles and circles for reading illegal literature; and socialist, as well as democratic, circles among *all* other sections of the population; etc., etc. We must have such circles, trade unions, and organisations everywhere in *as large a number as possible* and with the widest variety of functions; but it would be absurd and harmful *to confound* them with the organisation of *revolutionaries*, to efface the border-line between them, to make still more hazy the all too faint recognition of the fact that in order to "serve" the mass movement we must have people who will devote themselves exclusively to Social-Democratic activities, and that such people must *train* themselves patiently and steadfastly to be professional revolutionaries.

Yes, this recognition is incredibly dim. Our worst sin with regard to organisation consists in the fact that *by our primitiveness we have lowered the prestige of revolutionaries in Russia.* A person who is flabby and shaky on questions of theory, who has a narrow outlook, who pleads the spontaneity of the masses as an excuse for his own sluggishness, who resembles a trade-union secretary more than a spokesman of the people, who is unable to conceive of a broad and bold plan that would command the respect even of opponents, and who is inexperienced and clumsy in his own professional art—the art of combating the political police—such a man is not a revolutionary, but a wretched amateur!

Let no active worker take offence at these frank remarks, for as far as insufficient training is concerned, I apply them first and foremost to myself. I used to work in a study circle that set itself very broad, all-embracing tasks; and all of us, members of that circle, suffered painfully and acutely from the realisation that we were acting as amateurs at a moment in history when we might have been able to say, varying a well-known statement: "Give us an organisation of revolutionaries, and we will overturn Russia!" The more I recall the burning sense of shame I then experienced, the bitterer become my feelings towards those pseudo-Social-Democrats whose preachings "bring disgrace on the calling of a revolutionary", who fail to understand that our task is not to champion the degrading of the revolutionary to the level of an amateur, but *to raise* the amateurs to the level of revolutionaries. . . .

"CONSPIRATORIAL" ORGANISATION AND "DEMOCRATISM." Yet there are many people among us who are so sensitive to the "voice of life" that they fear it more than anything in the world and charge the adherents of the views here expounded with following a Narodnaya Volya line, with failing to understand "democratism", etc. These accusations, which, of course, have been echoed by *Rabocheye Dyelo,* need to be dealt with.

The writer of these lines knows very well that the St. Petersburg Economists levelled the charge of Narodnaya Volya tendencies also against *Rabochaya Gazeta* (which is quite understandable when one compares it with *Rabochaya Mysl*). We were not in the least surprised, therefore, when, soon after the appearance of *Iskra,* a comrade informed us that the Social-Democrats in the town of X describe *Iskra* as a Narodnaya Volya organ. We, of course, were flattered by this accusation; for what decent Social-Democrat has not been accused by the Economists of being a Narodnaya Volya sympathiser?

These accusations are the result of a twofold misunderstanding. First, the history of the revolutionary movement is so little known among us that the name "Narodnaya Volya" is used to denote any idea of a militant centralised organisation which declares determined war upon tsarism. But the magnificent organisation that the revolutionaries had in the seventies, and that should serve us as a model, was not established by the Narodnaya Volya, but by the *Zemlya i Volya,* which split up into the Chorny Peredel and the Narodnaya Volya. Consequently, to regard a militant revolutionary organisation as something specifically Narodnaya Volya in character is absurd both historically and logically; for *no* revolutionary trend, if it seriously thinks of struggle, can dispense with such an organisation. The mistake the Narodnaya Volya committed was not in striving to enlist *all* the discontented in the organisation and to direct this organisation to resolute struggle against the autocracy; on the contrary, that was its great historical merit. The mistake was in relying on a theory which in substance was not a revolutionary theory at all, and the Narodnaya Volya members either did not know how, or were unable, to link their movement inseparably with the class struggle in the developing capitalist society. Only a gross failure to understand Marxism (or an "understanding" of it in the spirit of "Struveism") could prompt the opinion that the rise of a mass, spontaneous working-class movement *relieves* us of the duty of creating as good an organisation of revolutionaries as the Zemlya i Volya had, or, indeed, an incomparably better one. On the contrary, this movement *imposes* the duty upon us; for the spontaneous struggle of the proletariat will not become its genuine "class struggle" until this struggle is led by a strong organisation of revolutionaries. . . .

. . . We have always protested, and will, of course, continue to protest against *confining* the political struggle to conspiracy. But this does not, of course, mean that we deny the need for a strong revolutionary organisation. Thus, in the pamphlet mentioned in the preceding footnote, after the polemics against reducing the political struggle to a conspiracy, a description is given (as a Social-Democratic ideal) of an organisation so strong as to be able to "resort to . . . rebellion" and to every "other form of attack", in order to "deliver a smashing blow against absolutism". In *form* such a strong revolutionary organisation in an autocratic country may also be described as a "conspiratorial" organisation, because the French word "conspiration" is the equivalent of the Russian word "*zagovor*" ("conspiracy"), and such an organisation must have the utmost secrecy. Secrecy is such a necessary condition for this kind of organisation that all the other conditions (number and selection of members, functions, etc.) must be made to conform to it. It would be extremely naïve indeed, therefore, to fear the charge that we Social-Democrats desire to create a conspiratorial organisation. Such a charge should be as flattering to every opponent of Economism as the charge of following a Narodnaya Volya line.

The objection may be raised that such a powerful and strictly secret organisation, which concentrates in its hands all the threads of secret activities, an organisation which of necessity is centralised, may too easily rush into a premature attack, may thoughtlessly intensify the movement before the growth of political discontent, the intensity of the ferment and anger of the working class, etc., have made such an attack possible and necessary. Our reply to this is: Speaking abstractly, it cannot be denied, of course, that a militant organisation *may* thoughtlessly engage in battle, which *may* end in a defeat entirely avoidable under other conditions. But we cannot confine ourselves to abstract reasoning on such a question, because every battle bears within itself the abstract possibility of defeat, and there is no way of *reducing* this possibility except by organised preparation for battle. If, however, we proceed from the concrete conditions at present obtaining in Russia, we must come to the positive conclusion that a strong revolutionary organisation is absolutely necessary precisely for the purpose of giving stability to the movement and of *safeguarding* it against the possibility of making thoughtless attacks. Precisely at the present time, when no such organisation yet exists, and when the revolutionary movement is rapidly and spontaneously growing, we *already observe* two opposite extremes (which, as is to be expected, "meet"). These are: the utterly unsound Economism and the preaching of moderation, and the equally unsound "excitative terror", which strives "artificially to call forth symptoms of the end of the movement, which is developing and strengthening itself, when this movement is as yet nearer to the start than to the end" (V. Zasulich, in *Zarya*, No. 2–3, p. 353). And the instance of *Rabocheye Dyelo* shows that *there exist* Social-Democrats who give way to both these extremes. This is not surprising, for, apart from other reasons, the "economic struggle against the employers and the government" can *never* satisfy revolutionaries, and opposite extremes will therefore always appear here and there. Only a centralised, militant organisation that consistently carries out a Social-Democratic policy, that satisfies, so to speak, all revolutionary instincts and strivings, can safeguard the movement against making thoughtless attacks and prepare attacks that hold out the promise of success.

A further objection may be raised, that the views on organisation here expounded contradict the "democratic principle". Now, while the earlier accusation was specifically Russian in origin, this one is *specifically foreign* in character. And only an organisation abroad (the Union of Russian Social-Democrats Abroad) was capable of giving its Editorial Board instructions like the following:

"*Organisational Principle.* In order to secure the successful development and unification of Social-Democracy, the broad democratic principle of Party organisation must be emphasised, developed, and fought for; this is particularly necessary in view of the anti-democratic tendencies that have revealed themselves in the ranks of our Party" (*Two Conferences,* p. 18).

We shall see in the next chapter how *Rabocheye Dyelo* combats *Iskra*'s "anti-democratic tendencies". For the present, we shall examine more closely the "principle" that the Economists advance. Everyone will probably agree that "the broad democratic principle" presupposes the two following conditions: first, full publicity, and secondly, election to all offices. It would be absurd to speak of democracy without publicity, moreover, without a publicity that is not limited to the membership of the organisation. We call the German Socialist Party a democratic organisation because all its activities are carried out publicly; even its party congresses are held in public. But no one would call an organisation democratic that is hidden from every one but its members by a veil of secrecy. What is the use, then, of advancing "the *broad* democratic principle" when the fundamental condition for this principle *cannot be fulfilled* by a secret organisation? "The broad principle" proves itself simply to be a resounding but hollow phrase. Moreover, it reveals a total lack of understanding of the urgent tasks of the moment in regard to organisation. Everyone knows how great the lack of secrecy is among the "broad" masses of our revolutionaries. We have heard the bitter complaints of B—v on this score and his absolutely just demand for a "strict selection of members" (*Rabocheye Dyelo,* No. 6, p. 42). Yet, persons who boast a keen "sense of realities" *urge,* in a situation like this, not the strictest secrecy and the strictest (consequently, more restricted) selection of members, but "the *broad* democratic principle"! This is what you call being wide off the mark.

Nor is the situation any better with regard to the second attribute of democracy, the principle of election. In politically free countries, this condition is taken for granted. "They are members of the Party who accept the principles of the Party programme and render the Party all possible support," reads Clause 1 of the Rules of the German Social-Democratic Party. Since the entire political arena is as open to the public view as is a theatre stage to the audience, this acceptance or non-acceptance, support or opposition, is known to all from the press and from public meetings. Everyone knows that a certain political figure began in such and such a way, passed through such and such an evolution, behaved in a trying moment in such and such a manner, and possesses such and such qualities; consequently, *all* party members, knowing all the facts, can elect or refuse to elect this person to a particular party office. The general control (in the literal sense of the term) exercised over every act of a party man in the political field brings into existence an automatically operating mechanism which produces what in biology is called the "survival of the fittest". "Natural selection" by full publicity, election, and general control provides the assurance that, in the last analysis, every political figure will be "in his proper place", do the work for which he is best fitted by his powers and abilities, feel the effects of his mistakes on himself, and prove before all the world his ability to recognise mistakes and to avoid them.

Try to fit this picture into the frame of our autocracy! Is it conceivable in Russia for all "who accept the principles of the Party programme and render the Party all possible support" to control every action of the revolutionary working in secret? Is it possible for all to elect one of these revolutionaries to any particular office, when, in the very interests of the work, the revolutionary *must* conceal his identity from nine out of ten of these "all"? Reflect somewhat over the real meaning of the high-sounding phrases to which *Rabocheye Dyelo* gives utterance, and you will realise that "broad democracy" in Party organisation, amidst the gloom of the autocracy and the domination of gendarmerie, is nothing more than a *useless and harmful toy*. It is a useless toy because, in point of fact, no revolutionary organisation has ever practised, or could practise, *broad* democracy, however much it may have desired to do so. It is a harmful toy because any attempt to practise "the broad democratic principle" will simply facilitate the work of the police in carrying out large-scale raids, will perpetuate the prevailing primitiveness, and will divert the thoughts of the practical workers from the serious and pressing task of training themselves to become professional revolutionaries to that of drawing up detailed "paper" rules for election systems. Only abroad, where very often people with no opportunity for conducting really active work gather, could this "playing at democracy" develop here and there, especially in small groups.

Leon Trotsky was not only one of the key figures of the Russian Revolution but a masterful chronicler of that event. His monumental *History of the Russian Revolution*, notable among other things for being lucidly organized by a Marxist theory of history, was written while Trotsky lived in exile on the island of Prinkipo (off the Turkish coast) from 1929 to 1933.

The Proletariat and the Peasantry

LEON TROTSKY

The Russian proletariat learned its first steps in the political circumstances created by a despotic state. Strikes forbidden by law, underground circles, illegal proclamations, street demonstrations, encounters with the police and with troops—such was the school created by the combination of a swiftly developing capitalism with an absolutism slowly surrendering its positions. The concentration of the workers in colossal enterprises, the intense character of governmental persecution, and finally the impulsiveness of a young and fresh proletariat, brought it about that the political strike, so rare in western Europe, became in Russia the fundamental method of struggle. The figures of strikes from the beginning of the present century are a most impressive index of the political history of Russia. With every desire not to burden our text with figures, we cannot refrain from introducing a table of political strikes in Russia for the period 1903 to 1917. The figures, reduced to their simplest expression, relate only to enterprises undergoing factory inspection. The railroads, mining industries, mechanical and small enterprises in general, to say nothing of agriculture, for various reasons do not enter into the count. But the changes in the strike curve in the different periods emerge no less clearly for this.

We have before us a curve—the only one of its kind—of the political temperature of a nation carrying in its womb a great revolution. In a backward country with a small proletariat—for in all the enterprises undergoing factory inspection there were only about 1½ million workers in 1905, about 2 million in 1917—the strike movement attains such dimensions as it never knew before anywhere in the world. With the weakness of the petty bourgeois democracy, the scatteredness and political blindness of the peasant movement, the revolutionary strike of the workers becomes the battering ram which the awakening nation directs against the walls of absolutism. Participants in political strikes in 1905 numbering 1,843,000—workers participating in several strikes are here, of course counted twice—that number alone would permit us to put our finger on the revolutionary year in our table, if we knew nothing else about the Russian political calendar.

For 1904, the first year of the Russo-Japanese war, the factory inspection indicates in all only 25,000 strikers. In 1905, political and economic strikes to-

Year	Number in thousands of participants in political strikes
1903	87*
1904	25*
1905	1,843
1906	651
1907	540
1908	93
1909	8
1910	4
1911	8
1912	550
1913	502
1914 (first half)	1,059
1915	156
1916	310
1917 (January-February)	575

* The figures for 1903 and 1904 refer to all strikes, the economic undoubtedly predominating.

gether involved 2,863,000 men—115 times more than in the previous year. This remarkable fact by itself would suggest the thought that a proletariat, impelled by the course of events to improvise such unheard-of revolutionary activities, must at whatever cost produce from its depths an organization corresponding to the dimensions of the struggle and the colossal tasks. This organization was the soviets—brought into being by the first revolution, and made the instrument of the general strike and the struggle for power.

Beaten in the December uprising of 1905, the proletariat during the next two years makes heroic efforts to defend a part of the conquered positions. These years, as our strike figures show, still belong directly to the revolution, but they are the years of ebb. The four following years (1908–11) emerge in our mirror of strike statistics as the years of victorious counter-revolution. An industrial crisis coincident with this still further exhausts the proletariat, already bled white. The depth of the fall is symmetrical with the height of the rise. National convulsions find their reflection in these simple figures.

The industrial boom beginning in 1910 lifted the workers to their feet, and gave a new impulse to their energy. The figures for 1912–14 almost repeat those for 1905–07, but in the opposite order: not from above downwards, but from below up. On a new and higher historical basis—there are more workers now, and they have more experience—a new revolutionary offensive begins. The first half-year of 1914 clearly approaches in the number of political strikes the culminating point of the year of the first revolution. But war breaks out and sharply interrupts this process. The first war months are marked by political inertness in the working class, but already in the spring of 1915 the numbness begins to pass. A new cycle of political strikes opens, a cycle which in February 1917 will culminate in the insurrection of soldiers and workers.

The sharp ebbs and flows of the mass struggle had left the Russian proletariat after a few years almost unrecognizable. Factories which two or three years ago would strike unanimously over some single arbitrary police action, today have completely lost their revolutionary color, and accept the most monstrous crimes of the authorities without resistance. Great defeats discourage people for a long time. The consciously revolutionary elements lose their power over the masses. Prejudices and superstitions not yet burnt out come back to life. Gray immigrants from the village during these times dilute the workers' ranks. Sceptics ironically shake their heads. So it was in the years 1907–11. But molecular processes in the masses are healing the psychological wounds of defeat. A new turn of events, or an underlying economic impulse, opens a new political cycle. The revolutionary elements again find their audience. The struggle reopens on a higher level.

In order to understand the two chief tendencies in the Russian working class, it is important to have in mind that Menshevism finally took shape in the years of ebb and reaction. It relied chiefly upon a thin layer of workers who had broken with the revolution. Whereas Bolshevism, cruelly shattered in the period of the reaction, began to rise swiftly on the crest of a new revolutionary tide in the years before the war. "The most energetic and audacious element, ready for tireless struggle, for resistance and continual organization, is that element, those organizations, and those people who are concentrated around Lenin." In these words the Police Department estimated the work of the Bolsheviks during the years preceding the war.

In July 1914, while the diplomats were driving the last nail into the cross designed for the crucifixion of Europe, Petrograd was boiling like a revolutionary cauldron. The President of the French Republic, Poincaré, had to lay his wreath on the tomb of Alexander III amid the last echoes of a street fight and the first murmurs of a patriotic demonstration.

Would the mass offensive of 1912–14 have led directly to an overthrow of tzarism if the war had not broken out? It is hardly possible to answer that question with certainty. The process would inexorably have led to a revolution, but through what stages would the revolution in those circumstances have had to go? Would it not have experienced another defeat? How much time would have been needed by the workers in order to arouse the peasantry and win the army? In all these directions only guesses are possible. The war, at any rate, gave the process at first a backward movement, but only to accelerate it more powerfully in the next period and guarantee its overwhelming victory.

At the first sound of the drum the revolutionary movement died down. The more active layers of the workers were mobilized. The revolutionary elements were thrown from the factories to the front. Severe penalties were imposed for striking. The workers' press was swept away. Trade unions were strangled. Hundreds of thousands of women, boys, peasants, poured into the workshops. The war—combined with the wreck of the International—greatly disoriented the workers politically, and made it possible for the factory administration, then just lifting its head, to speak patriotically in the name of the factories, carrying with it a considerable part of the workers, and compelling the more bold and resolute to keep still and wait. The revolutionary ideas were barely kept glowing in small and hushed circles. In the factories in those days nobody dared to call himself "Bolshevik" for fear not only of arrest, but of a beating from the backward workers.

The Bolshevik faction in the Duma, weak in its personnel, had not risen at the outbreak of the war to the height of its task. Along with the Menshevik deputies, it introduced a declaration in which it promised "to defend the cultural weal of the people against all attacks wheresoever originating." The Duma underlined with applause this yielding of a position. Not one of the Russian organizations or groups of the party took the openly defeatist position which Lenin came out for abroad. The percentage of patriots among the Bolsheviks, however, was insignificant. In contrast to the Narodniks and Mensheviks, the Bolsheviks began in 1914 to develop among the masses a printed and oral agitation against the war. The Duma deputies soon recovered their poise and renewed their revolutionary work—about which the authorities were very closely informed, thanks to a highly developed system of provocation. It is sufficient to remark that out of seven members of the Petersburg committee of the party, three, on the eve of the war, were in the employ of the Secret Service. Thus tzarism played blind man's buff with the revolution. In November the Bolshevik deputies were arrested. There began a general smash-up of the party throughout the country. In February 1915 the case of the Duma faction was called in the courts. The deputies conducted themselves cautiously. Kamenev, theoretical instigator of the faction, stood apart from the defeatist position of Lenin; so did Petrovsky, the present president of the Central Committee in the Ukraine. The Police Department remarked with satisfaction that the severe sentences dealt out to the deputies did not evoke any movement of protest among the workers.

It seemed as though the war had produced a new working class. To a considerable extent this was the fact: in Petrograd the personnel of the workers had been renewed almost forty per cent. The revolutionary succession had been abruptly broken. All that existed before the war, including the Duma faction of the Bolsheviks, had suddenly retired to the background and almost disappeared in oblivion. But under cover of this quietness and patriotism—and to some extent even monarchism—the moods of a new explosion were gradually accumulating in the masses.

In August 1915 the tzarist ministers were telling each other that the workers "are everywhere hunting out treason, betrayal and sabotage in behalf of the Germans, and are enthusiastic in the search for those guilty of our unsuccesses at the front." It is true that in that period the awakening mass-criticism—in part sincerely and in part for the sake of defensive coloration—often adopted the standpoint of "defense of the fatherland." But that idea was only a point of departure. The discontent of the workers was digging a deeper and deeper course, silencing the masters, the Black Hundred workers, the servants of the administration, permitting the worker-Bolsheviks to raise their heads.

From criticism the masses pass over to action. Their indignation finds expression first of all in food disturbances, sometimes rising to the height of local riots. Women, old men and boys, in the market or on the open square, feel bolder and more independent than the workers on military duty in the factories. In Moscow in May the movement turns into a pogrom of Germans, although the participants in this are chiefly the scum of the town armed under police protection. Nevertheless, the very possibility of such a pogrom in industrial Moscow proves that the workers are not yet sufficiently awakened to impose their slogans and their discipline upon the disturbed small-town people. These food disorders, spreading over the whole country, broke the war hypnosis and laid the road to strikes.

The inflow of raw labor power to the factories and the greedy scramble for war-profits, brought everywhere a lowering of the conditions of labor, and gave rise to the crudest methods of exploitation. The rise in the cost of living automatically lowered wages. Economic strikes were the inevitable mass reflection—stormy in proportion as they had been delayed. The strikes were accompanied by meetings, adoption of political resolutions, scrimmages with the police, not infrequently by shots and casualties.

The struggle arose chiefly in the central textile district. On June 5 the police fire a volley at the weavers in Kostroma: 4 killed, 9 wounded. On August 10 the troops fire on the Ivanovo-Voznesensk workers: 16 killed, 30 wounded. In the movement of the textile workers some soldiers of a local battalion are involved. Protest strikes in various parts of the country give answer to the shootings at Ivanovo-Voznesensk. Parallel to this goes the economic struggle. The textile workers often march in the front rank.

In comparison with the first half of 1914 this movement, as regards strength of pressure and clarity of slogans, represents a big step backward. This is not surprising, since raw masses are to a large extent being drawn into the struggle, and there has been a complete disintegration of the guiding layer of the workers. Nevertheless even in these first strikes of the war the approach of great battles can be heard. The Minister of Justice, Khvostov, said on the 16th of August: "If there are at present no armed demonstrations of the workers, it is only because they have as yet no organization." Goremykin expressed himself more concisely: "The trouble among the workers' leaders is that they have no organization, since it was broken up by the arrest of the five members of the Duma." The Minister of the Interior added: "We must not amnesty the members of the Duma (Bolsheviks) —they are the organizing center of the movement in its most dangerous form." These people at least made no mistake as to who was the real enemy.

While the ministry, even at the moment of its greatest dismay and readiness for liberal concessions, deemed it necessary as before to pound the workers' revolution on the head—i.e. on the Bolsheviks—the big bourgeoisie was trying to fix up a cooperation with the Mensheviks. Frightened by the scope of the strike movement, the liberal industrialists made an attempt to impose patriotic discipline upon the workers by including their elected representatives in the staff of the Military Industrial Committees. The Minister of the Interior complained that it was very difficult to oppose this scheme, fathered by Guchkov. "The whole enterprise," he said, "is being carried out under a patriotic flag, and in the interests of the defense." We must remark, however, that even the police avoided arresting the social-patriots. seeing in them a side partner in the struggle against strikes and revolutionary "excesses." It was indeed upon their too great confidence in the strength of patriotic socialism, that the Secret Service based their conviction that no insurrection would occur while the war lasted.

In the elections to the Military-Industrial Committees the defensists, headed by an energetic metal worker, Gvozdev —we shall meet him later as Minister of Labor in the Coalition Government of the revolution—turned out to be a minority. They enjoyed the support, however, not only of the liberal bourgeoisie, but of the bureaucracy, in getting the better of those who, led by the Bolsheviks, wished to boycott the committees. They succeeded in imposing a representation in these organs of industrial patriotism upon the Petersburg proletariat. The position of the Mensheviks was clearly expressed in a speech one of their representatives later made to the industrialists in the Committee: "You ought to demand that the existing bureaucratic power retire from the scene, yielding its place to you as the inheritors of the present social structure." This young political friendship was growing by leaps and bounds. After the revolution it will bring forth its ripe fruit.

The war produced a dreadful desolation in the underground movement. After the arrest of the Duma faction the Bolsheviks had no centralized party organization at all. The local committees had an episodic existence, and often had no connections with the workers districts. Only scattered groups, circles and solitary individuals did anything. However, the reviving strike movement gave them some spirit and some strength in the factories. They gradually began to find each other and build up the district connections. The underground work revived. In the Police Department they wrote later: "Ever since the beginning of the war, the Leninists, who have behind them in Russia an overwhelming majority of the underground social-democratic organizations, have in their larger centers (such as Petrograd, Moscow, Kharkov, Kiev, Tula, Kostroma, Vladimir Province, Samara) been issuing in considerable numbers revolutionary appeals with a demand to stop the war, overthrow the existing government, and found a republic. And this work has had its palpable result in workers' strikes and disorders."

The traditional anniversary of the march of the workers to the Winter Palace, which had passed almost unnoticed the year before, produces a widespread strike on January 9, 1916. The strike movement doubles during this year. Encounters with the police accompany every big and prolonged strike. In contact with the troops, the workers conduct themselves with demonstrative friendliness, and the Secret Police more than once notice this alarming fact.

The war industries swelled out, devouring all resources around them and undermining their own foundation. The peacetime branches of production began to die away. In spite of all plannings, nothing came of the regulation of industry. The bureaucracy, incapable of taking this business in hand against the opposition of the powerful Military-Industrial Committees, at the same time refused to turn over the regulating rôle to the bourgeoisie. The chaos increased. Skilled workers were replaced by unskilled. The coal mines, shops and factories of Poland were soon lost. In the course of the first year of the war a fifth part of the industrial strength of the country was cut off. As much as 50 per cent of production went to supply the needs of the army and the war—including about 75 per cent of the textile production of the country. The overloaded transport proved incapable of supplying factories with the necessary quantity of fuel and raw material. The war not only swallowed up the whole current national income, but seriously began to cut into the basic capital of the country.

The industrialists grew less and less willing to grant anything to the workers, and the government, as usual, answered every strike with severe repressions. All this pushed the minds of the workers from the particular to the general, from economics to politics: "We must all strike at once." Thus arose the idea of the general strike. The process of radicalization of the masses is most convincingly reflected in the strike statistics. In 1915, two and a half times fewer workers participated in political strikes than in economic conflicts. In 1916, twice as few. In the first months of 1917, political strikes involved six times as many workers as economic. The role of Petrograd is portrayed in one figure: 72 per cent of the political strikers during the years of the war fall to her lot!

Many of the old beliefs are burned up in the fires of this struggle. The Secret Service reports, "with pain," that if they should react according to the dictates of the law to "every instance of insolence and open insult to His Majesty, the number of trials under Article 103 would reach an unheard-of figure." Nevertheless the consciousness of the masses is far behind their action. The terrible pressure of the war and the national ruin is accelerating the process of struggle to such a degree that broad masses of the workers, right up to the very revolution, have not freed themselves from many opinions and prejudices brought with them from the village or from the petty bourgeois family-circle in the town. This fact will set its stamp on the first stage of the February revolution.

By the end of 1916 prices are rising by leaps and bounds. To the inflation and the breakdown of transport, there is added an actual lack of goods. The demands of the population have been cut down by this time to one-half. The curve of the workers' movement rises sharply. In October the struggle enters its decisive phase, uniting all forms of discontent in one. Petrograd draws back for the February leap. A wave of meetings runs through the factories. The topics: food supplies, high cost of living, war, government. Bolshevik leaflets are distributed; political strikes begin; improvised demonstrations occur at factory gates; cases of fraternization between certain factories and the soldiers are observed; a stormy protest-strike flares up over the trial of the revolutionary sailors of the Baltic Fleet. The French ambassador calls Premier Stürmer's attention to the fact, become known to him, that some soldiers have shot at the police. Stürmer quiets the ambassador: "The repressions will be ruthless." In November a good-sized group of workers on military duty are removed from the Petrograd factories and sent to the front. The year ends in storm and thunder.

Comparing the situation with that in 1905, the director of the Police Department, Vassiliev, reaches a very uncomforting conclusion: "The mood of opposition has gone very far—far beyond anything to be seen in the broad masses during the above-mentioned period of disturbance." Vassiliev rests no hope in the garrison; even the police officers are not entirely reliable. The Intelligence Department reports a revival of the slogan of the general strike, the danger of a resurrection of the terror. Soldiers and officers arriving from the front say of the present situation: "What is there to wait for?—Why don't you take and bump off such-and-such a scoundrel? If we were here, we wouldn't waste much time thinking," etc. Shliapnikov, a member of the Bolshevik Central Committee, himself a former metal worker, describes how nervous the workers were in those days: "Sometimes a whistle would be enough, or any kind of noise—the workers would take it for a signal to stop the factory." This detail is equally remarkable both as a political symptom and as a psychological fact: the revolution is there in the nerves before it comes out on the street.

The provinces are passing through the same stages, only more slowly. The growth in massiveness of the movement and in fighting spirit shifts the center of gravity from the textile to the metalworkers, from economic strikes to political, from the provinces to Petrograd. The first two months of 1917 show 575,000 political strikers, the lion's share of them in the capital. In spite of new raids carried out by the police on the eve of January 9, 150,000 workers went on strike in the capital on that anniversary of blood. The mood was tense. The metal-workers were in the lead. The workers all felt that no retreat was possible. In every factory an active nucleus was forming, oftenest around the Bolsheviks. Strikes and meetings went on continuously throughout the first two weeks of February. On the 8th, at the Putilov factory, the police received "a hail of slag and old iron." On the 14th, the day the Duma opened, about 90,000 were on strike in Petrograd. Several plants also stopped work in Moscow. On the 16th, the authorities decided to introduce bread cards in Petrograd. This novelty rasped the nerves. On the 19th, a mass of people gathered around the food shops, especially women, all demanding bread. A day later bakeries were sacked in several parts of the city. These were the heat lightnings of the revolution, coming in a few days.

The Russian proletariat found its revolutionary audacity not only in itself. Its very position as minority of the nation suggests that it could not have given its struggle a sufficient scope—

certainly not enough to take its place at the head of the state—if it had not found a mighty support in the thick of the people. Such a support was guaranteed to it by the agrarian problem.

The belated half-liberation of the peasants in 1861 had found agricultural industry almost on the same level as two hundred years before. The preservation of the old area of communal land—somewhat filched from during the reform—together with the archaic methods of land culture, automatically sharpened a crisis caused by the rural excess population, which was at the same time a crisis in the three-field system. The peasantry felt still more caught in a trap because the process was not taking place in the seventeenth but in the nineteenth century—that is, in the conditions of an advanced money economy which made demands upon the wooden plow that could only be met by a tractor. Here too we see a drawing together of separate stages of the historic process, and as a result an extreme sharpening of contradictions. The learned agronomes and economists had been preaching that the old area with rational cultivation would be amply sufficient—that is to say, they proposed to the peasant to make a jump to a higher level of technique and culture without disturbing the landlord, the bailiff, or the tzar. But no economic régime, least of all an agricultural régime, the most tardy of all, has ever disappeared before exhausting all its possibilities. Before feeling compelled to pass over to a more intensive economic culture, the peasant had to make a last attempt to broaden his three fields. This could obviously be achieved only at the expense of non-peasant lands. Choking in the narrowness of his land area, under the smarting whip of the treasury and the market, the muzhik was inexorably forced to attempt to get rid of the landlord once for all.

On the eve of the first revolution the whole stretch of arable land within the limits of European Russia was estimated at 280 million dessiatins.[1] The communal allotments constituted about 140 million. The crown lands, above 5 million. Church and monastery lands, about 2½ million. Of the privately owned land, 70 million dessiatins belonged to the 30,000 great landlords, each of whom owned above 500 dessiatins. This 70 million was about what would have belonged to 10 million peasant families. These land statistics constitute the finished program of a peasant war.

The landlords were not settled with in the first revolution. Not all the peasants rose. The movement in the country did not coincide with that in the cities. The peasant army wavered, and finally supplied sufficient forces for putting down the workers. As soon as the Semenovsky Guard regiment had settled with the Moscow insurrection, the monarchy abandoned all thought of cutting down the landed estates, as also its own autocratic rights.

However, the defeated revolution did not pass without leaving traces in the village. The government abolished the old land redemption payments and opened the way to a broader colonization of Siberia. The frightened landlords not only made considerable concessions in the matter of rentals, but also began a large-scale selling of their landed estates. These fruits of the revolution were enjoyed by the better-off peasants, who were able to rent and buy the landlords' land.

However, the broadest gates were opened for the emerging of capitalist farmers from the peasant class by the law of November 9, 1906, the chief reform introduced by the victorious counter-revolution. Giving the right even to a small minority of the peasants of any commune, against the will of the

[1] A dessiatin is 2.702 English acres. [Trans.]

majority, to cut out from the communal land a section to be owned independently, the law of November 9 constituted an explosive capitalist shell directed against the commune. The president of the Council of Ministers, Stolypin, described the essence of this governmental policy towards the peasants as "banking on the strong ones." This meant: encourage the upper circles of the peasantry to get hold of the communal land by buying up these "liberated" sections, and convert these new capitalist farmers into a support for the existing régime. It was easier to propose such a task, however, than to achieve it. In this attempt to substitute the kulak [2] problem for the peasant problem, the counter-revolution was destined to break its neck.

By January 1, 1916, 2½ million home-owners had made good their personal possession of 17 million dessiatins. Two more million home-owners were demanding the allotment to them of 14 million dessiatins. This looked like a colossal success for the reform. But the majority of the homesteads were completely incapable of sustaining life, and represented only material for natural selection. At that time when the more backward landlords and small peasants were selling on a large scale—the former their estates, the latter their bits of land—there emerged in the capacity of principal purchaser a new peasant bourgeoisie. Agriculture entered upon a state of indubitable capitalist boom. The export of agricultural products from Russia rose between 1908 and 1912 from 1 billion roubles to 1½ billion. This meant that broad masses of the peasantry had been proletarianized, and the upper circles of the village were throwing on the market more and more grain.

To replace the compulsory communal ties of the peasantry, there developed very swiftly a voluntary coöperation, which succeeded in penetrating quite deeply into the peasant masses in the course of a few years, and immediately became a subject of liberal and democratic idealization. Real power in the coöperatives belonged, however, only to the rich peasants, whose interests in the last analysis they served. The Narodnik intelligentsia, by concentrating its chief forces in peasant coöperation, finally succeeded in shifting its love for the people on to good solid bourgeois rails. In this way was prepared, partially at least, the political bloc of the "anti-capitalist" party of the Social Revolutionaries with the Kadets, the capitalist party *par excellence*.

Liberalism, although preserving the appearance of opposition to the agrarian policy of the reaction, nevertheless looked with great hopes upon this capitalist destruction of the communes. "In the country a very powerful petty bourgeoisie is arising," wrote the liberal Prince Troubetskoy, "in its whole make and essence alien alike to the ideals of the united nobility and to the socialist dreams."

But this admirable medal had its other side. There was arising from the destroyed communes not only a "very powerful bourgeoisie," but also its antithesis. The number of peasants selling tracts of land they could not live on had risen by the beginning of the war to a million, which means no less than five million souls added to the proletarian population. A sufficiently explosive material was also supplied by the millions of peasant-paupers to whom nothing remained but to hang on to their hungry allotments. In consequence those contradictions kept reproducing themselves among the peasants which had so early undermined the development of bourgeois society as a whole in Russia. The

[2] *Kulak,* the Russian word for fist, is a nick-name for rich peasants—"land-grabbers," as we might say. [Trans.]

new rural bourgeoisie which was to create a support for the old and more powerful proprietors, turned out to be as hostilely opposed to the fundamental masses of the peasantry as the old proprietors had been to the people as a whole. Before it could become a support to the existing order, this peasant bourgeoisie had need of some order of its own wherewith to cling to its conquered positions. In these circumstances it is no wonder that the agrarian problem continued a sharp one in all the State Dumas. Everyone felt that the last word had not yet been spoken. The peasant deputy Petrichenko once declared from the tribune of the Duma: "No matter how long you debate you won't create a new planet—that means that you will have to give us the land." This peasant was neither a Bolshevik, nor a Social Revolutionary. On the contrary, he was a Right deputy, a monarchist.

The agrarian movement, having, like the strike movement of the workers, died down toward the end of 1907, partially revives in 1908, and grows stronger during the following years. The struggle, to be sure, is transferred to a considerable degree within the commune: that is just what the reaction had figured on politically. There are not infrequent armed conflicts among peasants during the division of the communal land. But the struggle against the landlord also does not disappear. The peasants are more frequently setting fire to the landlord's manors, harvests, haystacks, seizing on the way also those individual tracts which had been cut off against the will of the communal peasants.

The war found the peasantry in this condition. The government carried away from the country about 10 million workers and about 2 million horses. The weak homesteads grew still weaker. The number of peasants who could not sow their fields increased. But in the second year of the war the middle peasants also began to go under. Peasant hostility toward the war sharpened from month to month. In October 1916, the Petrograd Gendarme Administration reported that in the villages they had already ceased to believe in the success of the war—the report being based on the words of insurance agents, teachers, traders, etc. "All are waiting and impatiently demanding: When will this cursed war finally end?" And that is not all: "Political questions are being talked about everywhere and resolutions adopted directed against the landlords and merchants. Nuclei of various organizations are being formed. . . . As yet there is no uniting center, but there is reason to suppose that the peasants will unite by way of the co-operatives which are daily growing throughout all Russia." There is some exaggeration here. In some things the gendarme has run ahead a little, but the fundamentals are indubitably correct.

The possessing classes could not but foresee that the village was going to present its bill. But they drove away these black thoughts, hoping to wriggle out of it somehow. On this theme the inquisitive French ambassador Paléologue had a chat during the war days with the former Minister of Agriculture Krivoshein, the former Premier Kokovtsev, the great landlord Count Bobrinsky, the President of the State Duma Rodzianko, the great industrialist Putilov, and other distinguished people. Here is what was unveiled before him in this conversation: In order to carry into action a radical land reform it would require the work of a standing army of 300,000 surveyors for no less than fifteen years; but during this time the number of homesteads would increase to 30 million, and consequently all these preliminary calculations by the time they were made would prove invalid. To introduce a land reform thus seemed in the eyes of these landlords, officials and bankers something like squaring the circle. It is hardly necessary to say that a like mathematical scrupulousness was completely alien to the peasant. He thought that first of all the thing to do was to smoke out the landlord, and then see.

If the village nevertheless remained comparatively peaceful during the war, that was because its active forces were at the front. The soldiers did not forget about the land—whenever at least they were not thinking about death—and in the trenches the muzhik's thoughts about the future were saturated with the smell of powder. But all the same the peasantry, even after learning to handle firearms, could never of its own force have achieved the agrarian democratic revolution—that is, its own revolution. It had to have leadership. For the first time in world history the peasant was destined to find a leader in the person of the worker. In that lies the fundamental, and you may say the whole, difference between the Russian revolution and all those preceding it.

In England serfdom had disappeared in actual fact by the end of the fourteenth century—that is, two centuries before it arose in Russia, and four and a half centuries before it was abolished. The expropriation of the landed property of the peasants dragged along in England through one Reformation and two revolutions to the nineteenth century. The capitalist development, not forced from the outside, thus had sufficient time to liquidate the independent peasant long before the proletariat awoke to political life.

In France the struggle with royal absolutism, the aristocracy, and the princes of the church, compelled the bourgeoisie in various of its layers, and in several installments, to achieve a radical agrarian revolution at the beginning of the eighteenth century. For long after that an independent peasantry constituted the support of the bourgeois order, and in 1871 it helped the bourgeoisie put down the Paris Commune.

In Germany the bourgeoisie proved incapable of a revolutionary solution of the agrarian problem, and in 1848 betrayed the peasants to the landlords, just as Luther some three centuries before in the peasant wars had betrayed them to the princes. On the other hand, the German proletariat was still too weak in the middle of the nineteenth century to take the leadership of the peasantry. As a result the capitalist development of Germany got sufficient time, although not so long a period as in England, to subordinate agriculture, as it emerged from the uncompleted bourgeois revolution, to its own interests.

The peasant reform of 1861 was carried out in Russia by an aristocratic and bureaucratic monarchy under pressure of the demands of a bourgeois society, but with the bourgeoisie completely powerless politically. The character of this peasant emancipation was such that the forced capitalistic transformation of the country inevitably converted the agrarian problem into a problem of revolution. The Russian bourgeois dreamed of an agrarian evolution on the French plan, or the Danish, or the American—anything you want, only not the Russian. He neglected, however, to supply himself in good season with a French history or an American social structure. The democratic intelligentsia, notwithstanding its revolutionary past, took its stand in the decisive hour with the liberal bourgeoisie and the landlord, and not with the revolutionary village. In these circumstances only the working class could stand at the head of the peasant revolution.

The law of combined development of backward countries—in the sense of a peculiar mixture of backward elements with the most modern factors—here rises before us in its most finished form, and offers a key to the fundamental riddle of the Russian revolution. If the agrarian problem, as a heritage from the barbarism of the old Russian history, had been solved by the bourgeoisie, if it could have been solved by them, the Russian proletariat could not possibly have come to power in 1917. In order to realize the Soviet state, there was required a drawing together and mutual penetration of two factors belonging to completely different historic species: a peasant war—that is, a movement characteristic of the dawn of bourgeois development—and a proletarian insurrection, the movement signalizing its decline. That is the essence of 1917.

Reader in History at La Trobe University (Melbourne, Australia), Mr. Getzler is the author of *Martov: A Political Biography of a Russian Social Democrat.*

The Mensheviks

ISRAEL GETZLER

Menshevism had its origins in 1903–04 in the revolt of the large majority of the founders and leaders of the Russian Social Democratic Workers' Party (RSDWP) against Lenin's bid for personal domination of the party and for a hypercentralist scheme of organization which threatened to confine the party to an élite conspiracy of professional revolutionaries. The so-called "softs" of the Second RSDWP Congress—Julius Martov, A. N. Potresov, P. B. Akselrod, E. M. Aleksandrova, V. N. Krokhmal, Vera Zasulich, Lev Deich, Boris Koltsov, Lev Trotsky, and Rosa Galbershtadt of the *Iskra* group; and E. Ya. Levin, V. N. Rozanov, and E. S. Levina of the *Yuzhnyi rabochii* (Southern Worker) group—broke with Lenin in revulsion against the ruthless tactics he had adopted during and after the Congress in order to impose his leadership, and against the organizational concepts set forth in his *What is to be Done?* and *A Letter to a Comrade*. They also resented some of Lenin's "hards," an aggregation of close personal followers, tough and unscrupulous *Iskra* "agents," and young rank-and-filers from the provincial party organizations.

The ensuing debate between Lenin and his critics was acrimoniously argued out in terms of the latter's concept of a broad, inclusive party of *Parteigenossen* versus Lenin's idea of a narrow, exclusive party of professional revolutionaries; of the ethics of Lenin's attempts to gain mastery of the party by means of a ruthless purge of its institutions; and, above all, of that "personality cult" which soon became a permanent feature of Leninism and permanent anathema to the Mensheviks, who preached and practiced collective leadership. Soon after the Second Congress, Fiodor Dan voiced the Mensheviks' objection to Lenin's claim to a special place in the party by asking rhetorically:

From *Problems of Communism*, Vol. XVI, No. 6, Nov.–Dec. 1967, Courtesy of Press and Publications Service, United States Information Agency, Washington, D.C. Some footnotes omitted.

Can we tolerate a situation which ties the entire fate of the party, and consequently the fate of the Russian proletariat and of Russian liberty, to the fate of one person, however we may appreciate his mind, talents and energy? [1]

In the sphere of party power-politics, the Menshevik-Bolshevik ideological and personal conflict was complemented by a bitter struggle for control of the central party institutions—*i.e.*, the party's central organ, *Iskra*, which the Mensheviks captured in October 1903 when Lenin quit the editorial board after Plekhanov had taken the Mensheviks' side in a dispute over the board's composition; the Central Committee, which the Bolsheviks controlled; and the émigré Foreign League of Russian Revolutionary Social Democracy, which the Mensheviks controlled. Even the Central Committee slipped temporarily from Lenin's control in August 1904, when its "conciliatory" Bolshevik members (notably G. M. Krzhizhanovski and V. A. Noskov), who resented the "old man's" divisive venom and wanted a compromise with the Mensheviks, coopted Rozanov, Krokhmal and Rosa Galbershtadt onto the committee as representatives of Menshevism.

Yet, the Mensheviks were strangely remiss in exploiting their temporary advantages over Lenin in order to gain mastery of the party. Thus, when Lenin moved to reestablish his control in April 1905 by convoking in London a Bolshevik-dominated congress which arbitrarily proclaimed itself the Third Congress of the RSDWP and elected a new Central Committee, all the Mensheviks did to counter this provocation was to convene a separate "All-Russian Conference of Party Workers" which met in Geneva in April–May 1905 and elected an Organization Committee. The only effect of this was to continue the fiction of RSDWP unity after it had in fact been deliberately disrupted by Lenin. In short, the Mensheviks lost their opportunity to contain Lenin and gain control of the party by failing to translate their moral victory in the aftermath of the Second Congress into hard power positions.

The Revolution of 1905

The 1905 Revolution had the effect of diverting the attention of both rival factions from the "organizational question" to such immediate issues as what attitude the party should take toward the demands of liberal *zemstvo* (county assembly) groups for sweeping governmental reforms, toward the "Shidlovski Commission" which the Tsar appointed soon after "Bloody Sunday" to inquire into the causes of labor unrest, and toward the proposals advanced by Minister of Interior A. I. Bulygin, in August 1905, for a merely consultative Duma. Above all, the revolution placed the questions of an attempt to seize power (posed by Lenin) and of the composition of a postrevolutionary government (posed by Parvus and Trotsky) squarely on the Social Democratic agenda. If Tsarism toppled, who would form the provisional government? And what, in Marxist terms, should be the function of a social democratic workers' party after having played a vanguard role in a bourgeois revolution in a backward country where socialism could not yet be realized? Should it take its place in the government, or in opposition?

The Mensheviks did not allow themselves to be tempted by the alluring prospect of power. While Parvus and

[1] N. Riazanov, *Razbitye illiuzii. K voprosu o prichinakh krizisa v nashei partii,* Geneva, 1904, pp. 16, 144. (For a detailed discussion of the intraparty controversy preceding, during, and following the Second Congress in 1903, see Bertram D. Wolfe, *Three Who Made a Revolution,* New York, Dial Press, 1948.—Ed.)

Trotsky threw overboard altogether the doctrine of bourgeois revolution and Lenin discarded its complement—abstention from power—to advocate socialist participation in a postrevolutionary government, Mensheviks continued to regard it as an "incontestable proposition" that, until the advent of a *socialist* revolution (which could not yet be the order of the day in backward Russia),

> . . . social democracy is and must remain a *party of extreme opposition,* as distinct from all other parties which may consider, in one form or another, to one degree or another, participation in the state power of bourgeois society.[2]

True, the Mensheviks did not entirely exclude the possibility that the bourgeoisie might default on its "historical duty," and that the Social Democrats would then be forced, willy-nilly, to assume power in order to save the revolution. But in that event they predicted that they would have no other choice than to attempt to plunge their backward country into socialism, and that such an attempt would inevitably share the fate of the Paris Commune *unless* revolution were to spread to the West.[3]

A self-denying ordinance of abstention from power was made part of the Mensheviks' official doctrine by the Geneva "Conference of Party Workers," in April–May 1905. This meeting reaffirmed the "bourgeois" nature of the developing Russian revolution and enjoined the party not to capture or share power in a revolutionary provisional government, but to assume a role of "extreme revolutionary opposition." It allowed for a seizure of power only *for the purpose of building socialism* and in only one situation—if the revolution should "leap into the advanced countries of Europe."

There were a number of basic flaws in the Menshevik revolutionary scheme. The working class was cast in the role of "class emancipator," of "vanguard" and even "hegemon" of the "national liberation struggle," and was called upon to bear the brunt of the fight to topple Tsardom. Yet, once victory was achieved, this vanguard was expected to exercise self-restraint. It was to switch over to the role of a broadly-based social democratic *opposition* party which would content itself with acting as a gadfly to "exert revolutionary pressure on the will of the liberal and radical bourgeoisie" and thus compel the new bourgeois holders of state power, in spite of themselves, to carry the revolution forward to its "logical conclusion" —*i.e.*, to those farthest republican and democratic limits which, in due historical season, would serve as the starting point for a *socialist* revolution.

It was certainly too much to expect such self-abnegation from an ill-used and rebellious working class which hoped, as a contemporary workingmen's leaflet put it, to "topple the Tsarist government and set up our own." Nor was the Mensheviks' self-denying ordinance any more palatable to the many socialist intellectuals and professional revolutionaries who in 1905 swallowed their misgivings about the "hard" centralism and amoralism of the Bolsheviks and opted

[2] A. Martynov, *Dve diktatury,* Geneva, 1905, pp. 55, 57. For a more detailed account of the 1905 debate on this issue, see the author's "Marxist Revolutionaries and the Dilemma of Power," in the forthcoming volume, *In Memoriam B. I. Nicolaevsky,* edited by L. K. D. Kristof; also, Solomon M. Schwarz, *The Russian Revolution of 1905,* Chicago and London, 1967, pp. 8–28, 246–54.

[3] L. Martov, "Na ocheredi. Rabochaia partiia i zakhvat vlasti kak nasha blizhaishaia zadacha," *Iskra,* No. 93, March 17, 1905. (Martov's real name was Yulii Osipovich Tsederbaum. He adopted Martov as his pen and party name, signing himself sometimes as Julius Martov, and sometimes as L. Martov or L.M. "L" was the initial of his favorite sister, Lydia.)

for the latter's more revolutionary program calling for seizure of power *and* establishment of a revolutionary provisional government.[4] Indeed, in those heady "days of liberty," even good Mensheviks like Aleksandr Martynov and Fiodor Dan renounced their commitment to the principle of abstention from power and adopted views hardly distinguishable from those of Parvus and Trotsky.

But whatever the flaws in the Mensheviks' revolutionary strategy, their "resolution" of the dilemma of power—a dilemma which still seems to bedevil Marxist revolutionaries in backward countries [5]—was dictated to them by their understanding of peasant Russia, their Marxist theory of the state, and their democratic commitment. While they believed that Russia's vast millions of peasants, craftsmen and urban poor provided "ample fuel for revolution," they were even more convinced that these "petty bourgeois" masses did not want socialism. As Martynov observed in a 1905 article entitled "In the Struggle with the Marxist Conscience," this compelled Social Democrats to ask themselves whether they had the right to seize power and to "use the authority of state power to neutralize the resistance of the petty bourgeoisie to the socialist pretensions of the proletariat." It was thus "in struggle with their Marxist conscience" that the Mensheviks came to rule out a Social Democratic assumption of power in the emerging Russian revolution, except as a tragic necessity. Their perhaps overdogmatic adherence to a narrow Marxist "executive committee" theory of the state led them to take a position which would leave the Social Democrats, even after leading a successful revolution, with no better choice than abstention from power or a premature and suicidal plunge into socialism.

Revolutionary Tactics

Because they saw their future role as one not of ruling but of forming a militant opposition to the government which would issue from the revolution, the Mensheviks turned their energies in the latter half of 1905 to developing the concept of "revolutionary self-government." It was this concept rather than their orthodox and "democratic" justification of the taboo on assuming power which was the Mensheviks' most positive and significant contribution to the Marxist debate on the issue of power and to Social Democratic revolutionary tactics and practice in Russia.

The Mensheviks' idea of revolutionary self-government may have been inspired in part by strategy outlined in Marx's Address of the Central Bureau to the Communist League of 1850 and in part by the historical precedent of the Paris Commune. But it derived its immediate and greatest impetus from the "municipal revolutions" of early 1905 in Georgia and Latvia, where Tsarist police and officials were ousted from entire areas and replaced by local revolutionary authorities, and particularly from the action of the crew of the Tsarist battleship Potemkin, who mutinied and set up a "military republic" aboard their ship in June 1905. Spurred by these examples, the watchword "revolutionary self-government" and the organizational projects and forms it fathered stood in the center of Menshevik political thinking and agitation during the second half of 1905.

From this idea stemmed the Mensheviks' campaign for the creation of so-called "nonaffiliated workers' organiza-

[4] Based on author's interview with N. V. Volsky (Valentinov) in Paris, June 1961.

[5] See the author's "Marxist Revolutionaries and the Dilemma of Power," *loc. cit. supra.*

tions" in which workers would be united on the basis of social-economic and political needs common to the entire working class, regardless of their trade or industry, and Akselrod's plan for a "workers' congress"[6]—both these projects expressing the Mensheviks' concern with the task of organizing, educating and activating the vast and amorphous working masses which remained outside the party. But this was just one aspect of a broader strategy calling for the creation of a "network of organs of revolutionary self-government" in towns and villages, expanding "gradually all over the country with the perspective of an ultimate assault on the center of government." By this means the Mensheviks hoped to unleash a "people's revolution from below" against Tsarism. They envisaged the revolutionary process as taking the form of an intensifying conflict between aggressive organs of revolutionary self-government and a defensive central government.

These Menshevik ideas undoubtedly furnished the theoretical basis as well as the stimulus for the establishment of the Soviets of Workers' Deputies which sprang up in St. Petersburg and a number of provincial towns in the latter part of 1905. The nonaffiliated workers' organizations and "workers' agitational committees" advocated by the Mensheviks were intended initially to serve as a "point of departure for the political rallying of the working class" and as a recruiting ground and support for the accelerated building of "an independent workers' party under the banner of social democracy." They were then expected, under Social Democratic guidance, to become "permanent revolutionary organizations of the proletariat aiming at constant intervention in state and public affairs in the interests of the working class." It was also a Menshevik idea that the workers' organizations should elect an illegal "National Duma" representing the *pays réel* to confront and possibly supplant the State Duma of the *pays légal*.[7]

Small wonder, then, that Martov, upon his arrival in St. Petersburg at the end of October 1905, saw in the Soviets of Workers' Deputies "the embodiment of our ideas of revolutionary self-government." More than that, one can perhaps discern in the Menshevik concepts of revolutionary workers' organs intervening in state affairs in the interests of the working class, and of a National Duma representative of the working masses confronting and challenging the State Duma, a scheme of dual government not only consistent with the Mensheviks' conception of their own intended role as an irreconcilable, militant opposition to the government that would succeed Tsarism, but also curiously anticipatory of the "dual power" that was to emerge twelve years later during the short life of the Provisional Government of 1917.

The Mensheviks After 1905

The ultimate defeat of the 1905 Revolution temporarily shelved the dilemma of power and ushered in a period of revolutionary ebb during which the Mensheviks proved themselves better equipped than the Bolsheviks and the Socialist Revolutionaries to exploit the new opportunities for "open" political activity offered by the early post-1905 semi-constitutional regime and even—though on a reduced scale—by the subsequent Stolypin regime established in June 1907. While the Bolsheviks continued as a small, militarized under-

[6] J. L. H. Keep, *The Rise of Social Democracy in Russia*, Oxford, 1963, pp. 214–15.

[7] See the author's *Martov, Political Biography of a Russian Social Democrat*, London, Cambridge University Press, 1967, pp. 107–09.

ground harassed by the police, maintaining itself by criminal or shady methods, and keeping up the pretense that an armed uprising was still on the Russian agenda, the Mensheviks' "practical workers" (*praktiki*) engaged in constructive efforts to gain a foothold among the industrial working class through various kinds of aboveground organizations and projects. These included trade unions, workers' educational associations and clubs, insurance and medical schemes, crèches, legal journals, a committee of the Social Democratic members of the Duma, and even medical and scientific congresses.

The greater effectiveness of the Menshevik tactics as compared with those of the Bolsheviks was translated into party-political terms at the Fourth (Unification) Congress of the RSDWP held at Stockholm, Sweden, in April 1906, which reunited the two wings of the party and marked a clear-cut victory for Menshevism. Mensheviks constituted a majority of the delegates and elected a Central Committee consisting of seven Mensheviks and three Bolsheviks. Bolshevik resolutions in favor of "preparation for an armed uprising," the use of partisan tactics, and a boycott of the Duma were roundly defeated, while Menshevik resolutions calling for a positive attitude toward Duma elections, formation of a Social Democratic fraction in the Duma, and an agrarian program of "municipalization" were adopted. As opposed to the Bolsheviks' agrarian program demanding nationalization of all land (*including* peasant land), the Menshevik program envisaged the handing over of state and private land (*excluding* peasant land) to democratic organs of local government or municipalities for leasing to peasants on an individual basis (excepting large estates run on modern capitalist lines, which would be managed on a collective basis).

That the Menshevik *praktiki* were not more successful in the long run was due to a combination of factors. One was the fact that the Bolsheviks regained a demoralizing, if precarious, control over party institutions after their victory at the London Congress of the RSDWP in 1907. Others were the disillusionment of large sections of the intelligentsia with the revolutionary movement, the economic crisis which hit and cowed the working class, and above all, the savage repressive policies of the Stolypin regime. If some Social Democratic activity continued even during the dark period of Stolypin repression, it was thanks chiefly to the dogged efforts of the Menshevik "practical workers" in Russia, who ignored the Bolshevik-controlled party institutions and underground organizations and entrenched themselves in the Menshevik-sponsored front organizations. However, their exodus from the party organizations, which they abandoned to the Bolsheviks as "spy-ridden nests of provocation," and their dispersal into legal and semi-legal channels of marginal Social Democratic activity had the result that in the post-Stolypin era of heightened industrial conflict the Bolsheviks were able to bring many of the revived underground party organizations under their control, utilizing them as strongpoints from which to develop positions of strength in such legal areas of activity as the press, the trade unions, and the Social Democratic fraction in the Duma (which they had hitherto spurned). In this way, the Bolsheviks sought to outflank, dislodge, and defeat their Menshevik rivals.

True, Martov and such close followers as his brother Sergei (Yezhov), Yuri Larin and Eva Broido tried to rebuild a network of Menshevik underground party organizations, the so-called Initiative Groups, which were designed to underpin and integrate into the party the scattered and uncoordinated elements of the legal superstructure the *praktiki* had built. But they proved no match for the Bolshevik organizers, who had learned to make astute use of legal and illegal agitation. While the Mensheviks strove to educate the primitive Russian working class and to rally it behind limited but achievable objectives, the Bolsheviks laid stress on demagogical appeals to class hatred and millenarian illusions, leading the workers into futile strikes and bloody demonstrations in a reckless attempt to provoke a showdown with the regime and create a revolutionary situation.

The Decline of Menshevism

The Mensheviks' tactics of combined legal and illegal activities designed to gain as wide a foothold as possible among the working class made good sense as a method of survival during the Stolypin period (1907–10). They also made good sense in the four succeeding years up to 1914, which were characterized by industrial prosperity coupled with heightened labor conflicts, by the disintegration of Stolypin's political system, and by the radicalization of the Kadets and even the Octobrists.* Certainly these tactics were more responsible than the Bolsheviks' attempt to play upon the elemental and utopian yearnings of embittered Russian workers new to the cities and still tied to their village origins.

But in order to be effective, the Menshevik tactics required a party organization capable of coordinating the activities of the émigrés abroad and the "practical" and underground workers in Russia, a Social Democratic party proper in which the Bolsheviks—who disapproved of both the tactics and the strategic objective—could be made to submit or leave the party. Except for a precarious year between the Stockholm and London party congresses, however, the Mensheviks never had control of the party, nor did they make any determined effort to gain it. In fact, they had a final opportunity to capture the party and bring Lenin and his small Bolshevik faction in Russia (the "Bolshevik Center") and abroad (the editorial board of *Proletarii*) to heel in 1909–10, when the Bolsheviks were hopelessly divided into "Otzovists," "Conciliators"[8] and Leninists proper, with the Leninists seriously compromised by the "expropriation" scandals and a host of other shady deals.[9] But, at the Unification Plenum of the RSDWP Central Committee held

* *Kadets*—abbreviation for the Constitutional Democratic Party founded in 1905, a liberal middle-class party advocating a constitutional monarchy along English lines and various political and economic reforms. The *Oktiabristy* (Octobrists), whose party was also founded in 1905, were largely landowners and leading members of the bureaucracy. They favored a constitutional monarchy with a strong executive responsible to the monarch himself and were opposed to the Kadet program of land redistribution.

[8] In 1908, the ultra-left wing of the Bolsheviks, many of whom had called for total boycott of the Duma in 1907, split into two groups: the Otzovists (Recallers) and Ultimatists. The Otzovists demanded the immediate recall of delegates to the Duma; the Ultimatists wanted to order the delegates to obey unconditionally the instructions of the Central Committee. The Conciliators were those Bolsheviks who, at the January 1910 plenum of the Central Committee in Paris, pressed for reunification with the Mensheviks over Lenin's opposition.

[9] After 1906, the Bolsheviks and Maximalists (Left Socialist-Revolutionaries), in order to obtain funds for financing revolutionary activities, resorted to outright acts of robbery which they euphemistically called "expropriations." In June 1907, more than a quarter of a million rubles was stolen from the State Bank in Tiflis (Georgia). Information obtained by a Russian police spy in Lenin's confidence resulted in the arrest of several conspirators when they tried to change the ruble notes in Western Europe. The arrests and the indignation of the German Social Democratic newspaper *Vorwärts* at learning that its facilities had been used by the conspirators to transport the stolen funds touched off a great scandal in socialist circles.

in Paris in January–February 1910, the Mensheviks let their opportunity slip away. Though in a strong position, they failed to press home their advantage and accepted a compromise which gave them a moral victory plus some Bolshevik promises—but no control over the party institutions.[10]

The final upshot was that in 1912 a resolute Lenin confronted the Mensheviks and the rest of the party with still another coup by convoking a new "All-Russian Party Conference" at Prague which, though not attended by the Mensheviks, set itself up as representing the party and elected a new, purely Leninist Central Committee. The so-called "August Bloc" of non-Bolshevik Social Democrats, which met at Vienna in August 1912, could only register the fact that the Bolsheviks were forging ahead and beginning to make good their claim that they *were* the party. It is perhaps an index of the Mensheviks' failure to establish and preserve a genuine, broadly-based, Russian Social Democratic workers' party that they knew no better remedy for their frustration than to make a pathetic appeal to the Socialist International to discipline the Bolsheviks and impose party unity from above on those who did not care for social democracy.

Internal Divergences

In contrast with the Bolsheviks, whose favorite method of dealing with dissent was to purge the dissenters, the Mensheviks, like the German Social Democrats, allowed dissident factions to exist within their ranks and practiced collective leadership. This toleration of dissent and adherence to collective leadership gave the Menshevik wing of the party a more democratic and intellectual complexion, but at the same time a more amorphous type of organization. It was possibly its more permissive and richly intellectual atmosphere, as well as the high moral standards of its leaders and lieutenants, that attracted so many Russified Jewish and Georgian intellectuals and party workers into the Menshevik camp rather than into the fold of a monolithic and morally indifferent Bolshevism.[11]

A basic division developed in the Menshevik camp in the period 1906–12, between a right wing largely located in Russia and the more left-wing Menshevik leaders abroad. A group of party intellectuals associated with the *Nasha zaria* journal in St. Petersburg and led by A. N. Potresov and Vladimir Levitski (Martov's youngest brother) agreed with the leaders of the Menshevik "practical workers" in Russia—P. A. Garvi, K. M. Yermolaev and I. A. Isuv—on shifting party activity from underground into legal channels and overt front organizations; they wrote off the underground party as outmoded and demoralized and were firmly opposed to compromise with the Bolsheviks. On the other hand, the Menshevik leaders abroad—Martov, Dan and Martynov, who edited *Golos sotsialdemokrata* in Paris—while agreeing that the bulk of party effort should be shifted into legal and semi-legal activities, insisted on the need to link these activities with an underground party skeleton which would make sure that work in the open arena would not lose its social democratic character and objectives. The Menshevik leaders abroad therefore sponsored and supported the underground "Initiative Groups" which com-

[10] Leonard Schapiro, *The Communist Party of the Soviet Union*, London, 1960, pp. 117–20; also, Getzler, *Martov, Political Biography . . .* , pp. 127–32.

[11] Right from its inception, Menshevism seems to have been more attractive than Bolshevism to Russified Jews. Of the 25 Jews present at the Second Congress of the RSDWP in 1903, 6 were Bundists, 4 were Bolsheviks (out of 20), and 15 were Mensheviks (out of 17).

bined legal and illegal work. The émigré leaders also favored unity with the Bolsheviks and thus antagonized the champions of "practical work."

On the periphery of the Menshevik camp, sometimes inside it but more often outside, were Plekhanov's so-called "Party Mensheviks" and Trotsky's *Pravda* group. The former endorsed the Bolsheviks' denunciation of the Menshevik *praktiki* as "liquidators" who wished to bury the party, while the latter agreed with the Bolsheviks on revolutionary tactics and with the Mensheviks on principles of party organization, assuming a mediatory role in seeking party unity.

The émigré leaders and "practical worker" group became deeply estranged at the time of the RSDWP Central Committee Plenum of January 1910 in Paris, when the latter felt that their vital interests had been sacrificed by the leaders for the sake of an illusory unity with the Bolsheviks. True, by August 1912, the "practical worker" group, which bore the brunt of the Bolshevik onslaught on the Menshevik positions in Russia, became somewhat reconciled to the Menshevik leaders abroad; still it continued to remain close to the *Nasha zaria* group on the right wing of Menshevism.

Although the First World War gave rise to new divisions and alignments (the greatest surprise being Plekhanov's *Yedinstvo* group of patriotic social democratic "defensists"), the basic division in Menshevism between left and right wings remained more or less intact—but translated into terms of internationalism versus defensism. On the left were the émigré Menshevik-Internationalists led by Martov, Martynov and Akselrod, who were active in the Zimmerwald socialist peace movement. They were supported in Russia by the so-called "Siberian Zimmerwaldists" (Irakli G. Tseretelli and Dan), the "Initiative Groups," and the Menshevik fraction in the Duma, led by N. S. Chkheidze. On the right was Potresov's *Nasha zaria* group of "self-defensists," who gave full support to the workers' sections of the War Industries Commission led by Mensheviks Kuzma Gvozdev and B. O. Bogdanov. But the Menshevik Internationalists in Russia (as distinct from their comrades abroad) also gave conditional support to the workers' sections, though they did so for very different reasons, seeing in them a legal means of addressing, rallying and organizing the industrial working class at a time when savage police repression had driven both Bolshevik and Menshevik organizations either out of existence or into ineffective underground activity.

The February Revolution

When the February Revolution of 1917 came, the Mensheviks had good reason to feel jubilant and elated, for the chief tenets of their credo had been vindicated: the take-over was a spontaneous people's revolution in which the industrial working class had played a vanguard role, rather than a timetabled, armed uprising organized by a narrow party of professional revolutionaries. The predicted conflict between liberal bourgeois society and Tsardom, which the Mensheviks had included as a major factor in their revolutionary strategy, had been exemplified in the role the Progressive Bloc had played in the isolation of the Tsarist regime from society.

Moreover, the Mensheviks' tactics of entrenching themselves wherever and whenever possible in legal organizations, such as the workers' groups of the War Industries Commission, the Social Democratic fraction of the Duma, and the cooperatives, had maintained Social Democratic continuity during the dark war years. When Tsardom toppled, these were the organizations whose leaders took the initiative in forming the Petrograd Soviet, the Mensheviks' dream-come-true of "organs of revolutionary self-government."

The Menshevik originators and founders of the Petrograd Soviet thus had a substantial headstart over their Bolshevik rivals, who, caught napping by events and cut off from their leader abroad, displayed remarkably little initiative in the early days of the February Revolution. Similarly, while the Socialist Revolutionaries were more popular and more numerous than the Mensheviks, the latter's pre-planned policies and rich political and organizational experience made them the senior partners in the Menshevik-SR alliance that dominated the Soviets until the "October" (November) Revolution. That the Mensheviks in the early stages of the revolution formed the most influential political group in the camp of "democracy" (comprised of the parties which supported the Soviets) was reflected in their dominant position of leadership in the Executive Committee of Soviets: N. S. Chkheidze, who had led the Menshevik fraction in the Fourth Duma, was its formal chairman, while Irakli Tseretelli, the hero and martyr of the Second Duma, became its *de facto* and undisputed leader during the interval between his arrival in Petrograd from Siberia in March 1917 and his departure for Georgia early in October.

Yet by June the Mensheviks' prestige and influence was beginning to plummet, especially among the working class of Petrograd. The All-Petrograd Conference of Factory Committees, which met early in June, adopted a Bolshevik resolution by 297 to 21 votes (with 44 abstentions) and elected a Central Council with a Bolshevik majority.[12] On the eve of the October Revolution, only 8 out of 167 delegates attending the All-Russian Conference of Factory Committees were Mensheviks.[13] In the August elections to the Petrograd Duma the Mensheviks were wiped out as a political force when they got only 23,552 out of 549,379 votes, while in Moscow their vote dropped from 76,407 in June to 15,887 in September.[14] While at the First Congress of Soviets in June, 248 delegates had declared themselves to be Mensheviks as against 105 Bolsheviks, at the Second Congress of Soviets in October some 70–80 Mensheviks confronted 300 Bolshevik delegates.[15] Worse still, in the elections to the Constituent Assembly in November 1917, the Mensheviks received only 1,364,826 votes, as compared with 16 million votes for the Socialist Revolutionaries and 9.8 million for the Bolsheviks.[16] Even that Menshevik vote was largely due to the popularity of Menshevism in Georgia (569,362 votes) and to the support of the Jewish Bundists in the western areas. The Menshevik vote in Russia proper may have been little more than 500,000 all told.

Errors and Enigmas

The Mensheviks' *failure* in the period of the Provisional Government—unlike the *defeat* of the Socialist Revolutionaries, who succumbed to the brutal *force majeure* of the Bolshevik state power—is, then, a phenomenon which must be examined in its own right and not

[12] Oskar Anweiler, *Die Rätebewegung in Russland 1905–1921,* Leiden, 1958, p. 156.

[13] *Ibid.*

[14] O. H. Radkey, *The Election to the Russian Constituent Assembly of 1917,* Cambridge, Mass., 1950, p. 53; Vera Vladimirova, *Revoliutsiia 1917 goda. Khronika sobytii* Vol. IV, Moscow, 1924, p. 76.

[15] *Ibid.*, pp. 153, 323–24.

[16] Radkey, *op. cit.*, Appendix: "Election Results by Districts."

simply attributed to the Bolshevik coup. By November the Mensheviks already had thrown away their chances to be the leading force in the country. The present writer can find no better explanation for the Mensheviks' debacle in 1917 than their persistent refusal to assume supreme power. True, the Mensheviks' stand on the war, especially their support of the disastrous Kerensky offensive in June 1917, may have alienated some supporters; but even this is not certain since the latter probably switched their allegiance to the Menshevik-Internationalists led by Martov, who opposed the offensive and pressed for general peace negotiations and a universal armistice. It is certain, however, that in every government crisis—in the "April Days," in the "July Days," and in September following the Kornilov putsch—the working class of Petrograd urged the Soviet leaders to take over the government. All in vain. As Tseretelli, who bore major responsibility for the policy of the Executive Committee of Soviets, put it:

> History hardly knows another example of political parties who received so many proofs of confidence from the overwhelming majority of the population, yet showed so little inclination to take power.

What explains this reluctance of the Menshevik-dominated Soviet leadership to seize the reins? Was it their "Marxist blinkers"—the doctrine of "bourgeois revolution" and its self-denying ordinance—that determined Menshevik and Soviet political thinking in 1917? Were they "ruined by their pedantic Marxism" as John Plamenatz and E. H. Carr suggest? [17]

This may have been true of the period of the first Provisional Government. At the start all Mensheviks (including the Menshevik-Internationalists) agreed not to join the government or form a new one but instead to assume the role of opposition, using Soviet positions of strength to make the official "bourgeois" government pursue "democratic" policies. In other words, they tried to use the tactics of "dual government" which Marx had recommended to the German Communists in 1850 and which the Geneva conference of Menshevik "party workers" of 1905 had adopted as party policy. It is difficult to decide whether in March 1917 they acted as they did because of doctrine, as the Left Menshevik Sukhanov suggests, or because of other reasons: fear that the bourgeoisie and army might react against the "red specter" of a socialist government and join the counterrevolution, or simply lack of confidence in their own ability to run the war and the economy. Even the Bolsheviks, before the arrival of Lenin, were content to give conditional and critical support to the "bourgeois" government and did not yet urge the assumption of power.

If doctrine did at first determine Menshevik policy, it held brief sway. Early in May 1917, the Mensheviks —confronted with the April crisis of government and under pressure from their Socialist Revolutionary allies— agreed after much heart-searching to "make the great sacrifice," as Dan put it, and join a bourgeois coalition government as junior partners. They thus lapsed into that Millerandism which since the Paris and Amsterdam congresses of the Socialist International had been anathema to all orthodox Marxists, certainly to the Mensheviks; they also ignored the unequivocal warnings of Marx and Engels never to repeat the mistake of Louis Blanc and never to join

[17] John Plamenatz, *German Marxism and Russian Communism,* London, 1954, p. 211; E. H. Carr, *The Bolshevik Revolution 1917–1923,* Vol. I, London, 1950, p. 41.

a bourgeois government *"in a minority,"* for *"that is the greatest danger."* [18]

The Mensheviks' decision to join a coalition government was dictated by practical considerations, as Tseretelli concedes in his memoirs, and not by principle or doctrine—namely, the need for a national government supported by all the "living forces" of the country in order to deal with the problems caused by the war and the economic crisis. Perhaps their "acceptance" of the war and of the Kerensky offensive may have been an important reason why the Mensheviks allowed themselves to be lured into the first coalition government as minor partners and did not press for a majority position, as the "leftist coalitionists" Sukhanov, Yuri Steklov and J. P. Goldenberg urged.

The Mensheviks' first experiment in coalition, which ended on July 2 when four Kadet ministers resigned, may have made some practical sense, though it made no doctrinal sense. But why did they repeat the experiment of coalition with the bourgeoisie in July, and again in September after the Kornilov putsch, in defiance of mounting opposition in their own ranks? This is the more difficult to explain in view of the switch in position of Martov and his Menshevik-Internationalists in July; hitherto they had opposed both a coalition and a seizure of power, but on the morning of July 3, when the news of the Kadets' resignation from the government broke, they urged the formation of a government of the "democracy:" "History demands," Martov pleaded, "that we take power into our hands."

The July government crisis clearly offered a good opportunity to seize power and also to take the wind out of the sails of Bolshevism, which had been thriving on the "organized inactivity" of the coalition government. The Kadet ministers had walked out on that government—a most unpatriotic act coming at a time when the military offensive for which the Kadets had long clamored and which the government had done so much to launch, was going badly. The workers' section of the Petrograd Soviet by a vast majority voted on July 3 for the Soviets to take power; and a delegation of Menshevik workers urged Tseretelli and the Soviet leaders to form a government. Then came the Bolshevik-led armed demonstrations of workers, soldiers, and sailors from Kronstadt demanding that the Executive Committee of Soviets assume power; "Take power, you son of a bitch, when it is given to you," a worker is reported to have shouted at Viktor Chernov. Indeed, the Executive Committee of Soviets was at this time the *de facto* government: it put down the riots, restored order, brought troops to Petrograd, and received affirmations of loyalty from most garrison units even before the special task force which it had ordered from the Fifth Army had arrived. Yet the Soviet leaders, notably Tseretelli, and also Dan, refused to transform their *de facto* power into legal power, thereby enabling Kerensky to form another (the second) coalition government on July 24.

When the September crisis of government developed, opposition within the "camp of democracy" to coalition with the bourgeoisie was stronger than ever. At the Democratic Conference that was convoked to meet the crisis, a majority of both the Menshevik and the Soviet sections voted against coalition, and both sections elected Martov their spokesman; a clear majority of the conference voted against coalition with the

[18] Friedrich Engels letters to Filippo Turati, January 26, 1894, in Marx in Engels, *Selected Correspondence,* Moscow, 1965, pp. 471–72. (Italics added.)

Kadets. Yet Tseretelli took advantage of a third vote that negated the previous votes and made it possible for Kerensky to form still another (the third) coalition government. The last chance to stop Bolshevism was thus thrown away.

Why this stubborn pursuit of coalition, which Menshevik doctrine prohibited rather than prescribed? Was it due to the Mensheviks' acceptance of the war, which required bourgeois allies? Was it because of their fast-growing fear of Bolshevism and Tseretelli's conviction that a showdown with the Bolshevik "military apparatus" was inevitable? Or did the Menshevik leaders, who were urban worker-oriented socialist intellectuals, a majority of Jewish and Georgian origin, simply lack the confidence to confront and govern a post-revolutionary but still largely pre-industrial peasant Russia, where antisemitism was deeply rooted and distrust of non-Russians widespread? Here there are significant straws in the wind: it was, *e.g.*, precisely because he was a Jew that Dan refused to become a minister in the first coalition government and sent M. I. Skobelev instead.[19]

Whatever the explanations for the Mensheviks' persistent coalitionism, there can be little doubt that it facilitated the Bolshevik takeover in the name of "all power to the Soviets." For the real alternative in 1917, so it seems to this writer, was not Lenin or Kornilov —*i.e.*, a brutal choice between two forms of dictatorship—but a Soviet government under the *democratic* auspices of the Menshevik-SR alliance, legitimized by an early convocation of the Constituent Assembly or a Soviet government under Bolshevik auspices. If they had wished to preserve their early achievements in the February Revolution and to consolidate its gains, the Mensheviks would have had to assume power, to *be* the government. Only thus could they have ensured a speedy convocation of the Constituent Assembly and enaction of Menshevik solutions to the problems of land reform, nationalities, industrial relations, economic controls, and above all war and peace.

It was certainly no easy matter to reconcile Russia's burning interest in peace with the war policy of the Allies, which aimed at the knockout defeat of Germany. Yet whatever the merits or defects of Tseretelli's and Dan's "revolutionary defensism," they could argue that Russia had to stay in the war while pressure was put on the Allies directly (at the planned Paris conference) and indirectly (through the socialist parties of the belligerent and neutral nations at and after the Stockholm conference) to agree to a negotiated peace with the Central Powers on the basis of the Soviet formula, "peace without annexations and reparations." This, however, presupposed a government which was in sympathy with the Mensheviks' peace policy. Ironically enough, Menshevik coalitionism simply produced a succession of Kerensky governments whose permanent foreign minister, M. I. Tereshchenko, did his best to sabotage that policy.

Moreover, even if the Kerensky offensive of June 1917, which the Menshevik leaders supported, had made *military* sense (which, because of the poor condition of the army, it did not), it was badly timed to make *political* sense. The offensive was nothing less than Russia's trump card to make the Allies take account of her desperate need for peace. That card was thrown away when the offensive was launched *before* an agreement had been reached with the Allies.

It was, then, their underestimation of the importance of state power, their lack of understanding that the assump-

[19] Author's interview with Lydia Dan, New York, 1962.

tion of power is an integral part and consummation of revolution-making, which proved to be the Mensheviks' fatal flaw and gave the Bolsheviks their chance. As Saint-Just warned:

Ceux qui font des révolutions à demi ne font que creuser leurs tombeaux.

After November

While the Menshevik performance during the period of the Provisional Government adds up to a sad story of opportunities missed or thrown away, the Mensheviks did finally write a heroic chapter under the Bolshevik regime.

Confronted with the Bolshevik seizure of power, the Mensheviks, now led by Martov and Dan, tried their best to prevent the Bolsheviks from "going it alone" and establishing a minority dictatorship. During the so-called VIKZHEL negotiations of late October and early November 1917,[20] they campaigned for the creation of an all-socialist coalition government, ranging from the Popular Socialists to the Bolsheviks, and Martov and Raphael Abramovich played a leading part in bringing the Mensheviks, Socialist Revolutionaries and moderate Bolsheviks together. It is significant that the only "ultimative" condition which the Mensheviks set—and the Bolsheviks promptly rejected—was the "cessation of political terror." The negotiations thus foundered on the intransigence of Lenin and Trotsky, who, in a session described by Lenin as of "historical importance," called the moderate Bolsheviks to task and broke off the negotiations. When the Constituent Assembly was dispersed by armed force on January 18, 1918, the Mensheviks saw their last hopes dashed of mediating between the Bolsheviks, who held state power, and the Socialist Revolutionaries, who had received a majority of votes in the November elections to the Constituent Assembly. Soon the SR-Bolshevik conflict blazed into civil war.

Though in the first stage of the civil war, through the latter part of 1918, the Mensheviks' hearts were undoubtedly on the side of the Socialist Revolutionaries, they remained neutral and tried to halt the fighting, believing that regardless of the justified grievances and indignation of the SRs, "in the given political situation any armed struggle against the Bolshevik state power is adventurism, which can be of benefit only to counterrevolution."

After the civil war became a straight contest between Reds and Whites, the Mensheviks supported the Red Army. When Yudenich marched on Petrograd and Denikin on Moscow in 1919, and during the early defensive phase of the Russo-Polish war in 1920, the Menshevik Central Committee called on party members to volunteer for service in the Red Army. (A small right-wing section of the party, led by Mark Liber, showed considerable opposition to this policy. Liber advocated Menshevik participation in a "national struggle" against the Bolsheviks, who "were no longer a party which was liable to be shot at, but on the contrary a state power which had the power to shoot and execute." But this right wing was soon compelled to submit to party discipline or to leave the party.)

In the meantime—indeed right from the start—the Mensheviks fearlessly exposed and decried the Bolsheviks' use of terror. When in November 1917 the

[20] A few days after the November uprising, the VIKZHEL (National Committee of the Railway Workers' Union) demanded that the Bolsheviks negotiate with all the parties in the Petrograd Soviet for a multiparty, all-socialist government. The demand was backed up by a threat to call a strike and thus paralyze all Russian troop and supply movements—a threat to which Lenin reluctantly yielded only, as he later admitted, in order to gain time.

Kadets were imprisoned, some of their leaders murdered, and the "bourgeois" newspapers closed down, the Mensheviks spoke out in incensed protest. Thereafter Martov became the revolution's voice of conscience, denouncing Trotsky's threat of the guillotine, the trial of Admiral Shchastnyi (who was arraigned on fabricated charges of "treason" and sentenced to death after a manifestly rigged trial in June 1918), the Bolsheviks' system of hostages, and the murder of the royal family and the Grand Dukes (July 1918). In their persistent opposition to the Bolshevik terror, the Mensheviks' record remained unmarred and unmatched, to their enduring credit.

It is true that after the failure of their initial efforts to help restore democracy, the Mensheviks soon undertook to adapt to the Soviet constitution and system. But they did so reluctantly and critically, accepting the Bolshevik innovations "as a fact of life, though not in principle." They assumed the role of a semi-loyal semi-implacable opposition, trying to find a place for themselves in the Soviet regime without compromising their commitments to democracy and decency. They aimed, through combining the use of open institutions and platforms with semi-legal and illegal activities where open activity proved impossible, to broaden and strengthen their influence on the Russian working class and to civilize and democratize the regime.

Led by Martov, the small Menshevik fraction in the Executive Committee of Soviets put up a strenuous fight to be heard—and to educate the Bolsheviks into acceptance of an articulate and critical opposition. Wherever possible they participated in elections to local soviets, trade unions (they controlled the chemical workers' and printers' unions), cooperatives, insurance associations and cultural organizations. They also used public platforms and private channels in a desperate attempt to sway the Bolsheviks' consciences, to shame them into relinquishing the terror, restoring democratic and legal processes to the soviets, and abandoning the disastrous economic policies and practices of War Communism.

The Mensheviks' role of "legal" opposition in "Lenin's parliament" was played out when on June 14, 1918, they were expelled from the Executive Committee of Soviets and their newspapers *Novyi luch* and *Vperiod* were closed down. From then until 1921, when they were finally driven underground and into exile, the Bolsheviks were to keep them, somewhat as the Tsar had done, in an uncertain state of semi-legality marked by alternate periods of repression and relaxation. Yet it was a semi-legality with a Bolshevik difference. Under an anachronistic Tsarist regime, with a clumsy police apparatus legally limited in its powers, the Mensheviks' combined tactics of legal and illegal social democratic work had made good practical sense; but under the Soviet state power with its unrestricted and ubiquitous Cheka, underground activity was extremely hazardous. As Martov reported in a letter:

> . . . a section of ordinary citizens (Communists and those with a vested interest in the Soviet regime) regard denunciation, searches, and surveillance not only as proper but as the fulfilment of a supreme duty.[21]

Moreover, thorough Bolshevik *Gleichschaltung* of all organized activity, including the trade unions, cooperatives and insurance associations, prevented

[21] Unpublished letter, Martov to Alexander Stein, October 25, 1918, in Boris Nicolaevsky Collection, Hoover Institution on War, Revolution and Peace, Stanford University, Calif.

their use by the Mensheviks as front organizations.

The Mensheviks could, of course, have thrown in their lot with the Bolsheviks in the vain hope of reforming the Communist Party from within, and they would have been received with open arms. Indeed, a number of Mensheviks who did make their peace with the Bolshevik regime, such as Ivan Maiski, Aleksandr Martynov, G. V. Chicherin, A. I. Troianovski, L. M. Khinchuk and—last but not least—Andrei Vyshinski, became Soviet dignitaries, and some even survived under Stalin. But the leading Mensheviks would not even consider such "capitulation," [22] determined as they were to fight their losing battle to the bitter end. That end came when in 1921 the Menshevik leaders and activists were imprisoned and then exiled.

A Doomed Course

In view of the treatment they received, one wonders what made the Mensheviks support the Bolsheviks in the civil war and in the resistance against foreign intervention, in effect campaigning for the diplomatic recognition of a regime which they themselves denounced as a terrorist dictatorship; such loyalty the Bolshevik masters certainly did not deserve. The answer lies in the limited alternatives open to the Mensheviks. Unless they were prepared to compromise their democratic commitments and surrender to the Bolshevik state (and this was out of the question for a party which had elected Martov its leader), or to join the Socialist Revolutionaries, fighting the Bolsheviks and thus inviting counterrevolution (or so the Mensheviks believed), or to go out of existence as a political party, there was little else the Mensheviks could do but try to find themselves a place in the regime as a semi-loyal, semi-implacable opposition.

These tactics were also in tune with their interpretation of the October Revolution and of the regime that issued from it. They had disapproved of the Bolshevik seizure of power and had warned against the Bolsheviks' "maximalist-utopian" attempt to plunge a backward peasant country into socialism when all the necessary prerequisites were missing. Yet they did not interpret the Bolshevik minority dictatorship and the terror as the work of scoundrels and adventurers who lusted for power. They credited the Bolsheviks, whom they believed they knew intimately, with the determination to use the coercive power of the state to make up for and create the missing industrial and social base for the construction of a socialist order. They believed at the same time that the means which the Bolsheviks used, such as the dictatorship and the terror, doomed that experiment to failure. Still, the Mensheviks did not expect an imminent collapse of the Bolshevik regime, nor did they really wish for it. The only realistic alternative to the Bolshevik regime that the Mensheviks could discern was counterrevolution, and they detested this more than they feared Bolshevism, which, they hopefully believed, was not yet beyond redemption. Thus their only choice was to seek a place in the Soviet system as an opposition party and attempt to democratize it. By 1921 their valiant attempt had foundered on the rock of Soviet state power.

With the Civil War finally won but the country devastated, the Bolsheviks in 1921 adopted the essentials of Menshevik economic policy in the form of the NEP. This was the signal for the final crackdown on the long-harassed

[22] *Ibid.*

Menshevik leaders who were arrested and forced into exile.[23] It was a sad moment, and not only for the Mensheviks. It was now brutally clear for all to see that the one-party system and the terror were not the tragic necessity of a regime pressed to the wall and fighting for survival, but a new and permanent way of life. The Bolsheviks stood self-condemned when they showed they were incapable of tolerating even the loyal opposition of Martov, their "most sincere and honest opponent,"[24] and his band of talented and decent Mensheviks.

While a small underground survived in Russia until the early 1930's, the Menshevik exiles settled in Berlin and, after the advent of the Nazis to power, in Paris. Defeated but not disarmed, they were active in the European socialist movement, published the *Sotsialisticheskii vestnik,* observed and studied the Soviet scene with infinite care, and made their journal into a treasure house and archive of the Russian revolutionary movement and the Soviet Union.

Like Marx, their teacher, they had set out to change their world and in the end found themselves on the sidelines, condemned to merely interpreting the revolution which, "in the name of liberty," they had helped to make, and which their Bolshevik rivals had captured and changed beyond recognition. Through the years, as they saw many of their worst predictions come true, they were torn between fears that the "revolution" would utterly degenerate and hopes that it might somehow straighten itself out. In a sense, their hopes and fears are still with us.

[23] Martov himself was already out of the country, having left Russia in late 1920 to attend a conference in Germany. Long since ill with a serious disease, he died in a German sanatorium in 1923.

[24] See Martov's obituaries in *Pravda,* April 5, 1923 (unsigned), and in *Izvestia,* April 5, 1923 (signed by Karl Radek).

Alec Nove is Professor of Economics, University of Glasgow. Among his books on the Soviet Union are *Was Stalin Really Necessary?* and *An Economic History of the U.S.S.R.*

Was Stalin Really Necessary?

ALEC NOVE

Stalin has suffered a dramatic post-mortem demotion, and a monument to his victims is to be erected in Moscow. The present Soviet leadership is thus disassociating itself publicly from many of the highly disagreeable features of Stalin's rule, while claiming for the Party and the Soviet system the credit for making Russia a great economic and military power. Is this a logically con-

From *Encounter,* London, April 1962. Reprinted by permission of the author and the publisher.

sistent standpoint? How far was Stalin, or Stalinism, an integral, unavoidable, "necessary" part of the achievements of the period? How much of the evil associated with the Stalin system is attributable to the peculiar character of the late dictator, and how much was the consequence of the policies adopted by the large majority of the Bolshevik party, or of the effort of a small and dedicated minority to impose very rapid industrialisation on a peasant country?

To ask these questions is of interest from several standpoints. Firstly, in trying to answer them we might be able to see a little more clearly the meaning of such misused terms as "determinism," causality, or the role of personality in history, and so continue to explore some of the problems which E. H. Carr presented in so stimulating a way in his Trevelyan lectures. Secondly, an examination of the circumstances which brought Stalin to power and led to—or provided an opportunity for—crimes on a massive scale is surely of very practical interest, since it might help in understanding how to avoid a repetition of these circumstances, particularly in those under-developed countries which are being tempted by their very real difficulties to take the totalitarian road.

To some people, the word "necessary" smacks of "historicism," of a belief in inevitability, or suggests that the author wishes to find some historic justification, a whitewash to be applied to Stalin and his system. This is far from being my intention. "Necessity" is used here with no moral strings attached. If I say that to travel to Oxford it is necessary to go to Paddington station, this implies no approval, moral or otherwise, of the service provided by the Western Region of British Railways, still less of the project of making the journey to Oxford. It is simply that *if* I wish to do A, it involves doing B.

It is true that there may be alternatives. One might, for instance, do not B but C, or D. Thus I could go to Oxford by car, or by bus. However, it could be that these physically possible methods are not in fact open to me; I may not own a car, and shortage of time precludes taking the bus. Thus a judgment on the "necessity" or otherwise of an action in pursuit of a given purpose requires some consideration of what could have been done instead.

The range of choice is not, in practice, limited only by what is *physically* possible. There are also actions which are excluded by religious or ideological principle. For example, it is not in fact open to a rabbi to eat a ham sandwich or an orthodox Hindu to eat cow-meat. Thus if an "alternative" happens to involve such acts, it is not *for them* an alternative at all. This is because, were they to act otherwise, they would cease to be what they in fact are. A rabbi does not eat pork; were he to do so, he would not be a rabbi. The fact that he is a rabbi would also affect his outlook, his "freedom" to choose between alternative modes of conduct, where religious law is less strict: for instance, there is nothing in the Talmud or in Deuteronomy about smoking on the Sabbath, but rabbis would tend to be the kind of people who, faced with this "new" problem, would give the answer "no."

Thus, to come nearer our subject, there may have been a number of solutions to the problems posed by Russia of the 'twenties which the Communists could not have chosen because they were Communists, and in considering the practical alternatives before them we have to bear this in mind. In doing so, we are by no means driven to any generalisations about the "inevitability" of the Russian revolution or of the Bolshevik seizure of power, and *a fortiori* we need not assume that non-Bolsheviks could not have found some other ways of coping with the problems of the period. (Indeed, though the problems would still have been acute, they might in important respects have been different.) Before his assassination in 1911, the last intelligent Tsarist prime minister, Stolypin, expressed the belief that his land reform measures would create in about twenty years a prosperous peasantry which would provide a stable foundation for society and the throne. No one will know if he would have been right, if he had not been murdered, if the Tsar had been wise, if Rasputin had not existed, if the war had not broken out. . . . But of what use is it to indulge in such speculations? A 19th-century Russian blank-verse play provides, if somewhat inaccurately, a relevant comment:

> *If, if, if grandma had a beard,*
> *She would be grandpa. . . .*

In assessing the choices open to the Bolsheviks in, say, 1926, the events before that date must be taken as given. The real question, surely, is to consider the practical alternatives which Stalin and his colleagues had before them.

In doing so, we should certainly not assume that what happened was inevitable. "Necessity" and "inevitable" are quite distinct concepts, though some critics seem to confuse them. Two simple and probably uncontroversial propositions will illustrate this: it was necessary for 18th-century Poland to make drastic changes in its constitution if she were to survive as an independent state; and for China around 1890 a strong, modernising government was urgently necessary if many disasters were to be avoided. Yet the "necessary" steps were not taken and the disasters occurred. Unless we believe that whatever was not avoided was for that reason unavoidable, we would wish to examine the actions which men took, their choices between *available* alternatives, and see whether viable alternatives in fact existed.

At this point, many historians—at times one feels E. H. Carr is among them—tend to brush aside impatiently any talk of what might have been; they are concerned, they would claim, with chronicling and explaining what was. Curiously, this line is often taken both by those who believe in strict historical determinism, *i.e.*, that what happened *had* to happen, and by those who consider history to be merely a chronological series of events, *i.e.*, that by implication *anything* could have happened. Both these apparently opposite extremes agree in not examining the actual possibilities as they were seen by the statesmen of the period. Yet how can one speak meaningfully of the reasons for, or causes of, any political act unless one implicitly or explicitly considers what could have been done instead? In other words, we must be concerned with freedom of choice, or its converse, necessity, whether we like it or not, unless we hold either that freedom of choice is infinite or that it is non-existent.

There are several more things to be said on the subject of "necessity." One of these concerns what might be called consequences of consequences, or indirect effects. For example, it is difficult to marry a wife without simultaneously acquiring a mother-in-law. Or, moving nearer to our subject, a sergeant is an unavoidable element in an army, and the needs of discipline involve giving him powers over his men which he is likely to abuse. Bullying N.C.O.'s are likely to be found if an army exists, and so, given the necessity for an army, they become an inevitable consequence of its existence, just as the mother-in-law is an unavoidable appendage of a "necessary" wife. Thus, getting still nearer to the point, a situation which requires many bureaucrats, or which gives exceptional power to many policemen, may bring into action certain forces, certain behavioural tendencies, which are typical of bureaucrats or policemen and which, though not needed or desired as such, cannot in the circumstances be avoided.

The saying that "you cannot make omelettes without breaking eggs" (or its Russian equivalent: "if you chop trees, the chips fly") has been used so often as an excuse for excesses and crimes, that we sometimes forget that you really *cannot* make omelettes without breaking eggs. . . .

Now on to Stalin, or rather to Stalinism, since the idea of "necessity" does not of course mean that the leader had to be a Georgian with a long moustache, but rather a tough dictator ruling a totalitarian state of the Stalinist type. What were the practical alternatives before the Bolsheviks in the late 'twenties, which contributed to the creation of the Stalinist régime, or, if one prefers a different formulation, gave the opportunity to ambitious men to achieve so high a degree of absolutism?

The key problem before the Bolsheviks concerned the linked questions of industrialisation and political power. They felt they had to industrialise for several reasons, some of which they shared with non-Bolshevik predecessors. Thus the Tsarist minister, Count Witte, as well as Stalin, believed that to achieve national strength and maintain independence, Russia needed a modern industry, especially heavy industry. The national-defence argument, re-labelled "defence of the revolution," was greatly strengthened by the belief that the Russian revolution was in constant danger from a hostile capitalist environment, militarily and technically far stronger than the U.S.S.R. Then there was the belief that the building of socialism or communism involved industrialisation, and, more immediately, that a "proletarian dictatorship" was insecure so long as it ruled in an overwhelmingly petty-bourgeois, peasant, environment. There had to be a large increase in the number and importance of the proletariat, while the rise of a rich "kulak" class in the villages was regarded as a dangerous (or potentially dangerous) resurgence of capitalism. It was clear, by 1927, that it was useless to wait for "world revolution" to solve these problems. These propositions were common to the protagonists of the various platforms of the middle 'twenties. Thus even the "moderate" Bukharin wrote: "If there were a fall in the relative weight of the working class in its political and its social and class power, . . . this would subvert the basis of the proletarian dictatorship, the basis of our government." [1] He too spoke in principle of the "struggle against the kulak, against the capitalist road," and warned of the "kulak danger." [2] He too, even in the context of an attack on Zinoviev and the "left" opposition, argued the need for "changing the production relations of our country." [3]

Until about 1927, a rapid rise in industrial production resulted from (or, "was a result of") the reactivation of pre-revolutionary productive capacity, which fell into disuse and disrepair in the civil war period. However, it now became urgent to find material and financial means to expand the industrial base. This at once brought the peasant problem to the fore. The revolution had distributed land to 25 million families, most of whom were able or willing to provide only small marketable surpluses. Supplies of food to the towns and for ex-

[1] "The Results of the United Plenum of the Central and Control Commissions of the Party" (1927).

[2] Speech on "The Results of the 14th Party Congress" (5th January, 1926).

[3] Speech to the XXIII special conference of the Leningrad provincial party organisation (1926).

port fell, peasant consumption rose. Yet the off-farm surplus must grow rapidly to sustain industrialisation, especially where large-scale loans from abroad could scarcely be expected. As the "left" opposition vigorously pointed out, the peasant, the bulk of the population, had somehow to be made to contribute produce and money, to provide the bulk of "primitive Socialist accumulation."

The arguments around these problems were inextricably entangled in the political factional struggles of the 'twenties.[4] The moderate wing, led by Bukharin, believed that it was possible to advance slowly towards industrialisation "at the pace of a tortoise," [5] a pace severely limited by what the peasant was willing to do voluntarily. This was sometimes described as "riding towards socialism on a peasant nag." The logic of this policy demanded priority for developing consumers' goods industries, to make more cloth to encourage the peasants to sell more food. At first, Stalin sided with the moderates.

The case against the Bukharin line was of several different kinds. Firstly, free trade with the peasants could only provide adequate surpluses if the better-off peasants (*i.e.*, those known as *kulaks*) were allowed to expand, since they were the most efficient producers and provided a large part of the marketable produce. Yet all the Bolshevik leaders (including, despite momentary aberrations, Bukharin himself) found this ideologically and politically unacceptable. A strong group of independent, rich peasants was Stolypin's dream as a basis for Tsardom. It was the Bolsheviks' nightmare, as totally inconsistent in the long run with their rule or with a socialist transformation of "petty-bourgeois" Russia. But this made the Bukharin approach of doubtful internal consistency. This was understood at the time by intelligent non-party men. Thus the famous economist Kondratiev, later to perish in the purges, declared in 1927: "If you want a higher rate of accumulation . . . then the stronger elements of the village must be allowed to exploit (the weaker)," in other words that the "kulaks" must expand their holdings and employ landless labourers.[6] The "peasant nag" could not pull the cart; or it, and the peasant, would pull in the wrong direction.

A second reason concerned the pace of the tortoise. The Bolsheviks were in a hurry. They saw themselves threatened by "imperialist interventionists." Even though some war scares were manufactured for factional reasons, the Party as a whole believed that war against them would come before very long. This argued not merely for speed, but also for priority to *heavy* and not light industry, since it provided a basis for an arms industry. Still another reason was a less tangible but still very real one: the necessity of maintaining political *élan,* of not appearing to accept for an indefinite period a policy of gradualism based on the peasant, which would have demoralised the Party and so gravely weakened the régime. It was widely felt, in and out of Russia, that by 1927 the régime had reached a *cul-de-sac*. I have in front of me a contemporary Menshevik pamphlet published abroad, by P. A. Garvi,[7] which describes its dilemma quite clearly, and indeed the political and economic problem was extremely pressing: to justify its existence, to justify the Party dictatorship in the name

[4] See A. Erlich: *The Soviet Industrialisation Debate* (Harvard, 1960) for a most valuable account of the interaction between the debates and the economic realities of the period. The account given here is necessarily oversimplified.

[5] Paper read at a plenum of the Agricultural Economics Research Institute, Moscow, 1927.

[6] Bukharin's words, speech of 5th January, 1926.

[7] *Zakat bolshevisma* (Twilight of Bolshevism) (Riga, 1928).

of the proletariat, a rapid move forward was urgent; but such a move forward would hardly be consistent with the "alliance with the peasants" which was the foundation of the policy of the moderates in the 'twenties. Stalin at this point swung over towards the left, and his policy of all-out industrialisation and collectivisation was a means of breaking out of the *cul-de-sac,* of mobilising the Party to smash peasant resistance, to make possible the acquisition of farm surpluses without having to pay the price which any free peasants or free peasant associations would have demanded. He may well have felt he had little choice. It is worth quoting from the reminiscences of another Menshevik, who in the late 'twenties was working in the Soviet planning organs: "The financial base of the first five-year plan, *until Stalin found it in levying tribute on the peasants, in primitive accumulation by the methods of Tamerlane,* was extremely precarious. . . . (It seemed likely that) everything would go to the devil. . . . No wonder that no one, literally no one, of the well-informed economists, believed or could believe in the fulfilment (of the plan)." [8]

It does not matter in the present context whether Stalin made this shift through personal conviction of its necessity, or because this seemed to him to be a clever power-manœuvre. The cleverness in any case largely consisted in knowing that he would thus strengthen his position by becoming the spokesman of the view which was widely popular among Party activists. The "leftists," destroyed organisationally by Stalin in earlier years, had a considerable following. Stalin's left-turn brought many of them to his support—though this did not save them from being shot in due course on Stalin's orders. It is probably the case that he had at this time genuine majority support within the Party for his policy, though many had reservations about certain excesses, of which more will be said. But if this be so, the policy as such cannot be attributed to Stalin personally, and therefore the consequences which flowed from its adoption must be a matter of more than personal responsibility.

Let us examine some of these consequences. Collectivisation could not be voluntary. Rapid industrialisation, especially with priority for heavy industry, meant a reduction in living standards, despite contrary promises in the first five-year plans. This meant a sharp increase in the degree of coercion, in the powers of the police, in the unpopularity of the régime. The aims of the bulk of the people were bound to be in conflict with the aims of the Party. It should be added that this conflict is probably bound to arise in some form wherever *the state* is responsible for financing rapid industrialisation; the sacrifices are then imposed by political authority, and the masses of "small" people do not and cannot provide voluntarily the necessary savings, since in the nature of things their present abstinence cannot be linked with a future return which they as individuals can identify. However, this possibly unavoidable unpopularity was greatly increased in the U.S.S.R. by the sheer pace of the advance and by the attack on peasant property, and, as we shall see, both these factors reacted adversely on production of consumers' goods and so led to still further hardships and even greater unpopularity. The strains and priorities involved in a rapid move forward required a high degree of economic centralisation, to prevent resources from being diverted to satisfy needs which were urgent but of a non-priority character. In this situation, the Party was the one body capable of car-

[8] N. Valentinov, in *Sotsialisticheskii Vestnik* (New York), April, 1961. (Emphasis mine.)

rying out enormous changes and resisting social and economic pressures in a hostile environment; this was bound to affect its structure. For a number of years it had already been in process of transformation from a political into a power machine. The problems involved in the "revolution from above" intensified the process of turning it into an obedient instrument for changing, suppressing, controlling.

This, in turn, required hierarchical subordination, in suppression of discussion; therefore there had to be an unquestioned commander-in-chief. Below him, toughness in executing unpopular orders became the highest qualification for Party office. The emergence of Stalin, and of Stalin-type bullying officials of the sergeant-major species, was accompanied by the decline in the importance of the cosmopolitan journalist-intellectual type of party leader who had played so prominent a role earlier.

The rise of Stalin to supreme authority was surely connected with the belief among many Party members that he was the kind of man who could cope with this kind of situation. Of course, it could well be that Stalin tended to adopt policies which caused him and his type to be regarded as indispensable, and he promoted men to office in the Party because they were loyal to him. Personal ambition, a desire for power, were important factors in shaping events. But this is so obvious, so clearly visible on the surface, that the underlying problems, policy choices and logical consequences of policies need to be stressed.

Let us recapitulate: the Communists needed dictatorial power if they were to continue to rule; if they were to take effective steps towards industrialisation these steps were bound to give rise to problems which would require further tightening of political and economic control. While we cannot say, without much further research, whether a Bukharinite or other moderate policy was impossible, once the decision to move fast was taken this had very radical consequences; the need for a tough, coercive government correspondingly increased. Given the nature of the Party apparatus, the mental and political development of the Russian masses, the logic of police rule, these policies were bound to lead to a conflict with the peasantry and to excesses of various kinds. Thus, given the premises, certain elements of what may be called Stalinism followed, were objective "necessities." In this sense, and to this extent, Stalin was, so to speak, operating within the logical consequences of Leninism.

It is an essential part of Lenin's views that the Party was to seize power and use it to change Russian society; this is what distinguished him from the Mensheviks who believed that conditions for socialism should ripen within society. Lenin also suppressed opposition parties and required stern discipline from his own followers. (It is impossible to ban free speech outside the Party without purging the Party of those who express "wrong" views within it.) Indeed Lenin promoted Stalin because he knew he was tough, would "prepare peppery dishes," though he had last-minute regrets about it. While it would be going too far to describe Stalin as a true Leninist, if only because Lenin was neither personally brutal nor an oriental despot, Stalin undoubtedly carried through some of the logical consequences of Lenin's policies and ideas. This remains true even though Lenin thought that the peasant problem could be solved by voluntary inspiration, and would probably have recoiled at the conditions of forced collectivisation.

Is it necessary to stress that this does not make these actions right, or good? Yes, it is, because so many critics assume that to explain is to justify. So it must be said several times that no moral conclusions follow, that even the most vicious acts by politicians and others generally have causes which must be analysed. We are here only concerned to disentangle the special contribution of Stalin, the extent to which Stalinism was, so to speak, situation-determined. This is relevant, indeed, to one's picture of Stalin's personal responsibility, but in no way absolves him of such responsibility. If in order to do A it proves necessary to do B, we can, after all, refuse to do B, abandon or modify the aim of attaining A, or resign, or, in extreme circumstances—like Stalin's old comrade Ordzhonikidze—commit suicide.

But Stalin's personal responsibility goes far beyond his being the voice and leader of a party majority in a given historical situation. For one cannot possibly argue that all the immense evils of the Stalin era flowed inescapably from the policy decisions of 1928–29. In assessing Stalin's personal role in bringing these evils about, it is useful to approach the facts from two angles. There was, first, the category of evils which sprang from policy choices which Stalin made and which he need not have made; in other words we are here concerned with consequences (perhaps necessary) of unnecessary decisions. The other category consists of evil actions which can reasonably be attributed to Stalin and which are his direct responsibility.

Of course, these categories shade into one another, as do murder and manslaughter. In the first case, the evils were in a sense situation-determined, but Stalin had a large hand in determining the situation. In the second, his guilt is as clear as a politician's guilt can be.

The most obvious examples of the first category are: the brutality of collectivisation and the madly excessive pace of industrial development. In each case, we are dealing with "*excessive excesses,*" since we have already noted that collectivisation without coercion was impossible, and rapid industrialisation was bound to cause stresses and strains.

Take collectivisation first. Some overzealous officials were presumably bound to overdo things, especially since the typical Party man was a townsman with no understanding or sympathy for peasants and their problems. But these officials received orders to impose rapid collectivisation, to deport *kulaks,* to seize all livestock, and Stalin was surely the source of these orders. The deportation of the *kulaks* (which in reality meant anyone who voiced opposition to collectivisation) removed at one blow the most efficient farmers. There had been no serious preparation of the measures, no clear orders about how a collective farm should be run. Chinese experience, at least before the communes, suggests that milder ways of proceeding are possible. In any event, the attempt to collectivise all private livestock ended in disaster and a retreat. It is worth reproducing the figures from the official handbook of agricultural statistics:

LIVESTOCK POPULATION (MILLION OF HEAD)

	1928	*1934*
Horses	32.1	15.4
Cattle	60.1	33.5
Pigs	22.0	11.5
Sheep	97.3	32.9

Yet already by 1934 private livestock holdings were again permitted, and in 1938 over three-quarters of all cows, over two-thirds of all pigs, nearly two-thirds of all sheep, were in private hands. This is evidence of a disastrous error.

Its consequences were profound. Peasant hostility and bitterness were greatly intensified. For many years there were in fact no net investments in agriculture, since the new tractors merely went to replace some of the slaughtered horses. Acute food shortage made itself felt—though the state's control over produce ensured that most of those who died in the resulting famine were peasants and not townsmen. But once all this happened, the case for coercion was greatly strengthened, the need for police measures became more urgent than ever, the power of the censorship was increased, freedom of speech had still further to be curtailed, as part of the necessities of remaining in power and continuing the industrial revolution in an environment grown more hostile as a result of such policies. So Stalin's policy decisions led to events which contributed greatly to the further growth of totalitarianism and the police state.

The same is true of the attempt to do the impossible on the industrial front in the years of the first five-year plan. Much of the effort was simply wasted, as when food was taken from hungry peasants and exported to pay for machines which rusted in the open or were wrecked by untrained workmen. At the same time, the closing of many private workshops deprived the people of consumers' goods which the state, intent on building steelworks and machine-shops, was quite unable to provide. Again, living standards suffered, the hatred of many citizens for the régime increased, the N.K.V.D. had to be expanded and the logic of police rule followed. But Stalin had a big role in the initial decisions to jump too far too fast.[9] (It is interesting to note that Mao, who should have learnt the lessons of history, repeated many of these mistakes in China's "great leap forward" of 1958–59, which suggests that *there are certain errors which Communists repeatedly commit,* possibly due to the suppression, in "anti-rightist" campaigns, of the voices of moderation and common sense.)

One of the consequences of these acute hardships was isolation from foreign countries. Economists often speak of the "demonstration effect," *i.e.*, of the effect of the knowledge of higher living standards abroad on the citizens of poor and under-developed countries. This knowledge may act as a spur to effort —but it also generates resistance to sacrifice. Stalin and his régime systematically "shielded" Soviet citizens from knowledge of the outside world, by censorship, by cutting off personal contacts, by misinformation. The need to do so, in their eyes, was greatly increased by the extent of the drop in living standards in the early 'thirties.

But we must now come to Stalin's more direct contribution to the brutality and terrorism of the Stalin era.

There was, firstly, his needless cruelty which showed itself already in the methods used to impose collectivisation. The great purges were surely not "objectively necessary." To explain them one has to take into account Stalin's thirst for supreme power, his intense pathological suspiciousness, *i.e.*, matters pertaining to Stalin's personal position and character. These led him to massacre the majority of the "Stalinist" central committee elected in 1934, who had supported or at the very least tolerated Stalin's policies up to that date. The facts suggest that they believed that relaxation was possible and desirable; many of them seem to have died for the crime of saying so. Nor was there any "police logic" for the scale and drastic nature of the purges. Indeed, the police chiefs figured prominently among the victims. True, there was a kind of "snowballing" of arrests, which might have got out of control in 1938, but this was

[9] N. Jasny, in his *Soviet Industrialisation, 1938–52* (Chicago, 1961), has much to say about the chaotic planning of the early 'thirties.

due largely to the effect of the terror on the police, who had to show zeal or go under. Nor can any "necessity" explain the post-war repressions, the death of Voznesensky, the so-called "Leningrad affair," the shooting of the Jewish intellectuals, the "doctors' plot." Stalin played so prominently a personal role in establishing a reign of terror in the Party and the country that he must bear direct responsibility even where executions were the result of false information supplied to him by his subordinates for reasons of their own.

The atmosphere of terror had, of course, far-reaching consequences in every sphere of Soviet life. It became particularly grotesque and purposeless in the last years of Stalin, when the social and economic developments, plus victory in war, provided the Soviet régime with a much firmer base among the people, so that a considerable part of the discontent was the result, rather than the cause, of repressive measures. Many obviously overdue reforms had to await his death. As did Tsar Nicholas I, a century earlier, Stalin was able to delay "necessary" changes.

Many other examples can be given of the personal role of Stalin. On the economic front, the miserable state of the peasants in 1953 was due largely to Stalin's obstinate refusal to face the facts and listen to serious advice. He contributed greatly to wasteful and grandiose schemes to "transform nature," and to a wasteful and grandiose style of architecture. In the military field, history will, I think, support Khrushchev's accusation that Stalin's inability to see the signs of a German attack, his unwillingness to allow preparations, his massacre of the best Soviet officers, all made a personal contribution to the Russian disasters of 1941. Stalin personally insisted on his own deification, the rewriting of history, the creation of myths. Some myths were based on lies which he himself publicly uttered. For instance, in 1935 he announced: "We have had no poor for two or three years now"—and this when bread had reached the highest price, in relation to wages, that it had ever attained in Soviet history. Or equally ridiculous was his claim, in 1947, that Moscow "had completely abolished slums." In this personal way he made impossible all serious discussion either of living standards or the housing problem, just as his wildly false assertions about "Bukharin and Trotsky, agents of Hitler and the Mikado," made the writing of Soviet history impossible in Russia. One could argue that the myth about "voluntary collectivisation" was an objectively necessary lie, in the sense of transcending Stalin's personality; indeed, this lie figures in the Party programme adopted by the 22nd Congress last November. But Stalin's lies went very much beyond this, and beyond the distortions and myths which can be ascribed to other politicians in other countries.

Throughout Russia, officials at all levels modelled themselves on Stalin, and each succeeded in imposing more unnecessary misery on more subordinates, stultifying initiative, penalising intelligence, discouraging originality. The price of all this is still being paid.

The urgent need to prepare for war has often been advanced as an excuse for Stalin's industrial "tempos" and for the terror. This can hardly be accepted. In the worst years of social coercion and over-ambitious plans, *i.e.*, 1929–33, Hitler was only just climbing to power, and Comintern policy showed that he was not then regarded as the main enemy. It is possible that Stalin was liquidating all potential opponents in the Purges of 1936–38 as a precaution in case war broke out, though this seems doubtful for a variety of reasons. But it is quite false to use the result of the war as ex-post-factum justification of Stalinism.

Perhaps, with less harsh policies, the greater degree of loyalty in 1941 would have offset a smaller industrial base? In any event the Purges not only led to the slaughter of the best military officers but also halted the growth of heavy industry.

The attentive reader will have noticed that this analysis has some features in common with Khrushchev's. Before 1934, Stalin had been carrying out policies which commanded the assent of a majority of the Party and which, like collectivisation, had been accepted as necessary and irreversible by the bulk of Party members, whatever their reservations about particular mistakes and acts of brutality. However, after that date he took more and more personal, arbitrary measures, massacred much of the Party, behaved like an oriental despot. It is true that he was also arbitrary before 1934, and that he took some wise decisions after that date; but there is a case for placing a qualitative change around then.

But this is by no means the end of the matter. It is not only a question of making some obvious remarks concerning Khrushchev's own role during the terror. Of much more general significance is the fact that the events prior to 1934, including the building-up of Stalin into an all-powerful and infallible dictator (by men many of whom he afterwards massacred), cannot be disassociated with what followed; at the very least they provided Stalin with his opportunity. This is where the historian must avoid the twin and opposite pitfalls of regarding what happened as inevitable, and regarding it as a chapter of "personalised" accidents. At each stage there are choices to be made, though the range of possible choices is generally much narrower than people suppose. In 1928 any practicable Bolshevik programme would have been harsh and unpopular. It might not have been *so* harsh and unpopular but for choices which need not necessarily have been made. If before 1934, *i.e.*, in the very period of maximum social coercion, Stalin truly represented the will of the Party, and Khrushchev argues that he did, some totalitarian consequences logically follow. One of these, as already suggested, is the semi-militarised party led by a *Fuehrer*, a dictator, because without an unquestioned leader the consequences of the policies adopted could not be faced.

But, even if it is true that the triumph of a dictator may be explained by objective circumstances which certainly existed in the Soviet situation, the acts of a dictator once he has "arrived" involve a considerable (though of course not infinite) degree of personal choice. Those who gave him the opportunity to act in an arbitrary and cruel way, who adopted policies which involved arbitrariness and coercion on a big scale, cannot ascribe subsequent events to the wickedness of one man or his immediate associates and claim that their hands are clean, even indeed if they were shot themselves on Stalin's orders. The whole-hog Stalin, in other words, was not "necessary," but the possibility of a Stalin was a necessary consequence of the effort of a minority group to keep power and to carry out a vast social-economic revolution in a very short time. And *some* elements of Stalinism were, in those circumstances, scarcely avoidable.

The serious problem for us is to see how far certain elements of Stalinism, in the sense of purposefully-applied social coercion, imposed by a party in the name of an ideology, are likely or liable to accompany rapid economic development even in non-Communist countries.

For it is surely true that many of the problems tackled by Stalin so brutally are present elsewhere, though events in the U.S.S.R. were, of course, deeply affected by peculiar features of Russia and of Bolshevism. The West should indeed emphasise the high cost in human and material terms of a Stalin, and show that the rise of such a man to supreme power in the Soviet Union was, to use the familiar Soviet-Marxist jargon phrase, "not accidental." Indeed, some Western historians who normally write "personalist" and empiricist history will begin to see the virtues of an approach they normally deride as "historicist"; they will analyse Soviet history to establish patterns, regularities, "necessities" which lead to Stalin. By contrast, an embarrassed Khrushchev will be—is being—forced to give an un-Marxist emphasis to personal and accidental factors.

But, of course, we must not confine our search for "necessities" in history only to instances which happen to serve a propagandist purpose. This would be a typically Soviet approach to historiography, only in reverse. It is particularly important to think very seriously about the inter-relationship of coercion and industrialisation, about the nature of the obstacles and vicious circles which drive men to think in totalitarian terms. Unless we realise how complex are the problems which development brings, how irrelevant are many of our ideas to the practical possibilities open to statesmen in these countries, we may unconsciously drive them towards the road which led to Stalin. They cannot be satisfied with "the pace of a tortoise."

Zbigniew Brzezinski is Professor of Government and Director of the Research Institute for Communist Affairs at Columbia University. Among his books are *The Soviet Bloc: Unity and Conflict, Ideology and Power in Soviet Politics,* and (with Samuel Huntington) *Political Power, U.S.A. and U.S.S.R.*

Evolution of the U.S.S.R.: Two Paths

ZBIGNIEW BRZEZINSKI

The Soviet Union will soon celebrate its 50th anniversary. In this turbulent and rapidly changing world, for any political system to survive half a century is an accomplishment in its own right and obvious testimony to its durability. There are not many major political structures in the world today that can boast of such longevity. The approaching anniversary, however, provides an appropriate moment for a critical review of the changes that have taken place in the Soviet system, particularly in regard to such critical matters as the character of its top leadership, the methods by which its leaders acquire power, and the relationship of the Communist Party to society. Furthermore, the time is also ripe to inquire into the implications of these

From *Problems of Communism,* January–February 1966. Courtesy of Press and Publications Service, United States Information Agency, Washington, D.C.

changes, especially in regard to the stability and vitality of the system.

The Leaders

Today Soviet spokesmen would have us believe that the quality of the top Communist leadership in the USSR has been abysmal. Of the 45 years since Lenin, according to official Soviet history, power was exercised for approximately five years by leaders subsequently unmasked as traitors (although later the charge of treason was retroactively reduced to that of deviation); for almost 20 years it was wielded by a paranoiac mass-murderer who irrationally slew his best comrades and ignorantly guided Soviet war strategy by pointing his finger at a globe; and, most recently, for almost ten years, by a "harebrained" schemer given to tantrums and with a propensity for wild organizational experimentation. On the basis of that record, the present leadership lays claim to representing a remarkable departure from a historical pattern of singular depravity.

While Soviet criticism of former party leaders is now abundant, little intellectual effort is expended on analyzing the implications of the changes in leadership. Yet that, clearly, is the important question insofar as the political system is concerned.

Lenin was a rare type of political leader, fusing in his person several functions of key importance to the working of a political system: he acted as the chief ideologist of the system, the principal organizer of the party (indeed, the founder of the movement), and the top administrator of the state. It may be added that such personal fusion is typical of early revolutionary leaderships, and today it is exemplified by Mao Tse-tung. To his followers, Lenin was clearly a charismatic leader, and his power (like Hitler's or Mao Tse-tung's) depended less on institutions than on the force of his personality and intellect. Even after the Revolution, it was his personal authority that gave him enormous power, while the progressive institutionalization of Lenin's rule (the Cheka, the appearance of the *apparat*, etc.) reflected more the transformation of a revolutionary party into a ruling one than any significant change in the character of his leadership.

Lenin's biographers [1] agree that here was a man characterized by total political commitment, by self-righteous conviction, by tenacious determination and by an outstanding ability to formulate intellectually appealing principles of political action as well as popular slogans suitable for mass consumption. He was a typically revolutionary figure, a man whose genius can be consummated only at that critical juncture in history when the new breaks off—and not just evolves—from the old. Had he lived a generation earlier, he probably would have died in a Siberian *taiga;* a generation later, he probably would have been shot by Stalin.

Under Stalin, the fusion of leadership functions was continued, but this was due less to his personal qualities as such than to the fact that, with the passage of time and the growing toll of victims, his power became nearly total and was gradually translated also into personal authority. Only a mediocre ideologist—and certainly inferior in that respect to his chief rivals for power—Stalin became institutionally the ideologue of

[1] Angelica Balabanoff, *Impressions of Lenin,* Ann Arbor, Mich., University of Michigan Press, 1964. Louis Fischer, *Life of Lenin,* New York, Harper, 1964. S. Possony, *Lenin, the Compulsive Revolutionary,* Chicago, Regnery, 1964. Bertram D. Wolfe, *Three Who Made a Revolution,* New York, Dial Press, 1948.

the system. A dull speaker, he eventually acquired the "routinized charisma" [2] which, after Lenin's death, became invested in the Communist Party as a whole (much as the Pope at one time acquired the infallibility that for a long time had rested in the collective church). But his power was increasingly institutionalized bureaucratically, with decision-making centralized at the apex within his own secretariat, and its exercise involved a subtle balancing of the principal institutions of the political system: the secret police, the party, the state, and the army (roughly in that order of importance). Even the ostensibly principal organ of power, the Politburo, was split into minor groups, "the sextets," the "quartets," etc., with Stalin personally deciding who should participate in which subgroup and personally providing (and monopolizing) the function of integration.

If historical parallels for Lenin are to be found among the revolutionary tribunes, for Stalin they are to be sought among the Oriental despots.[3] Thriving on intrigue, shielded in mystery, and isolated from society, his immense power reflected the immense tasks he succeeded in imposing on his followers and subjects. Capitalizing on the revolutionary momentum and the ideological impetus inherited from Leninism, and wedding it to a systematic institutionalization of bureaucratic rule, he could set in motion a social and political revolution which weakened all existing institutions save Stalin's own secretariat and his chief executive arm, the secret police. His power grew in proportion to the degree to which the major established institutions declined in vitality and homogeneity.[4]

The war, however, as well as the postwar reconstruction, produced a paradox. While Stalin's personal prestige and authority were further enhanced, his institutional supremacy relatively declined. The military establishment naturally grew in importance; the enormous effort to transfer, reinstall, and later reconstruct the industrial economy invigorated the state machinery; the party apparat began to perform again the key functions of social mobilization and political integration. But the aging tyrant was neither unaware of this development nor apparently resigned to it. The Byzantine intrigues resulting in the liquidation of the Leningrad leadership and Voznesenski, the "doctors' plot" with its ominous implications for some top party, military and police chiefs, clearly augured an effort to weaken any institutional limits on Stalin's personal supremacy.

Khrushchev came to power ostensibly to save Stalinism, which he defined as safeguarding the traditional priority of heavy industry and restoring the primacy of the party. In fact, he presided over the dismantling of Stalinism. He rode to power by restoring the predominant position of the party apparat. But the complexities of governing (as contrasted to the priorities of the power struggle) caused him to dilute the party's position. While initially he suc-

[2] For a discussion of "routinized charisma," see Amitai Etzioni, *A Comparative Analysis of Complex Organizations*, Glencoe, Ill., Glencoe Free Press, 1961, pp. 26 ff.

[3] Compare the types discussed by J. L. Talmon in his *Political Messianism: the Romantic Phase*, New York, Praeger, 1960, with Barrington Moore, Jr., *Political Power and Social Theory*, Cambridge, Mass., Harvard University Press, 1958, especially Chapter 2 on "Totalitarian Elements in Pre-Industrial Societies," or Karl Wittfogel, *Oriental Despotism*, New Haven, Yale University Press, 1957.

[4] It seems that these considerations are as important to the understanding of the Stalinist system as the psychopathological traits of Stalin that Robert C. Tucker rightly emphasizes in his "The Dictator and Totalitarianism," *World Politics*, July 1965.

ceeded in diminishing the political role of the secret police and in weakening the state machinery, the military establishment grew in importance with the continuing tensions of the cold war.[5] By the time Khrushchev was removed, the economic priorities had become blurred because of pressures in agriculture and the consumer sector, while his own reorganization of the party into two separate industrial and rural hierarchies in November 1962 went far toward undermining the party's homogeneity of outlook, apart from splitting it institutionally. Consequently, the state bureaucracy recouped, almost by default, some of its integrative and administrative functions. Khrushchev thus, perhaps inadvertently, restored much of the institutional balance that had existed under Stalin, but without ever acquiring the full powers of the balancer.

Khrushchev lacked the authority of Lenin to generate personal power, or the power of Stalin to create personal authority—and the Soviet leadership under him became increasingly differentiated. The top leader was no longer the top ideologist, in spite of occasional efforts to present Khrushchev's elaborations as "a creative contribution to Marxism-Leninism." The ruling body now contained at least one professional specialist in ideological matters, and it was no secret that the presence of the professional ideologue was required because someone had to give professional ideological advice to the party's top leader. Similarly, technical-administrative specialization differentiated some top leaders from others. Increasingly Khrushchev's function—and presumably the primary source of his still considerable power—was that of providing political integration and impetus for new domestic or foreign initiatives in a political system otherwise too complex to be directed and administered by one man.

The differentiation of functions also made it more difficult for the top leader to inherit even the "routinized charisma" that Stalin had eventually transferred to himself from the party as a whole. Acquiring charisma was more difficult for a leader who (even apart from a personal style and vulgar appearance that did not lend themselves to "image building") had neither the great "theoretical" flare valued by a movement that still prided itself on being the embodiment of a messianic ideology, nor the technical expertise highly regarded in a state which equated technological advance with human progress. Moreover, occupying the posts of First Secretary and Chairman of the Council of Ministers was not enough to develop a charismatic appeal since neither post has been sufficiently institutionalized to endow its occupant with the special prestige and aura that, for example, the President of the United States automatically gains on assuming office.

Trying to cope with this lack of charismatic appeal, Khrushchev replaced Stalin's former colleagues. In the process, he gradually came to rely on a younger generation of bureaucratic leaders to whom orderliness of procedure was instinctively preferable to crash campaigns. Administratively, however, Khrushchev was a true product of the Stalinist school, with its marked proclivity for just such campaigns at the cost of all other considerations. In striving to develop his own style of leadership, Khrushchev tried to emulate Lenin in stimulating new fervor, and Stalin in mobilizing energies, but without the personal and institutional assets that

[5] For a good treatment of Soviet military debates, see Thomas Wolfe, *Soviet Strategy at the Crossroads,* Cambridge, Mass., Harvard University Press, 1964.

each had commanded. By the time he was removed, Khrushchev had become an anachronism in the new political context he himself had helped to create.

Brezhnev and Kosygin mark the coming to power of a new generation of leaders, irrespective of whether they will for long retain their present positions.[6] Lenin's, Stalin's, and Khrushchev's formative experience was the unsettled period of conspiratorial activity, revolution, and—in Khrushchev's case—civil war and the early phase of communism. The new leaders, beneficiaries of the revolution but no longer revolutionaries themselves, have matured in an established political setting in which the truly large issues of policy and leadership have been decided. Aspiring young bureaucrats, initially promoted during the purges, they could observe—but not suffer from—the debilitating consequences of political extremism and unpredictable personal rule. To this new generation of clerks, bureaucratic stability—indeed, bureaucratic dictatorship—must seem to be the only solid foundation for effective government.

Differentiation of functions to these bureaucrats is a norm, while personal charisma is ground for suspicion. The new Soviet leadership, therefore, is both bureaucratic in style and essentially impersonal in form. The curious emphasis on *kollektivnost rukovodstva* (collectivity of leadership) instead of the traditional *kollektivnoe rukovodstvo* (collective leadership)—a change in formulation used immediately after Khrushchev's fall—suggests a deliberate effort at achieving not only a personal but also an institutional collective leadership, designed to prevent any one leader from using a particular institution as a vehicle for obtaining political supremacy.

The question arises, however, whether this kind of leadership can prove effective in guiding the destiny of a major state. The Soviet system is now led by a bureaucratic leadership from the very top to the bottom. In that respect, it is unique. Even political systems with highly developed and skillful professional political bureaucracies, such as the British, the French, or that of the Catholic Church, have reserved some top policy-making and hence power-wielding positions for non-bureaucratic professional politicians, presumably on the assumption that a free-wheeling, generalizing and competitive political experience is of decisive importance in shaping effective national leadership.

To be sure, some top Soviet leaders do acquire such experience, even in the course of rising up the bureaucratic party ladder, especially when assigned to provincial or republican executive responsibilities. There they acquire the skills of initiative, direction, integration, as well as accommodation, compromise, and delegation of authority, which are the basic prerequisites for executive management of any complex organization.

Nonetheless, even when occupying territorial positions of responsibility, the *apparatchiki* are still part of an extremely centralized and rigidly hierarchical bureaucratic organization, increasingly set in its ways, politically corrupted by years of unchallenged power, and made even more confined in its outlook than is normally the case with a ruling body by its lingering and increasingly ritualized doctrinaire tradition. It is relevant to note here (from observations made in Soviet universities) that the young men who become active in the Komsomol organization and are presumably embarking on a professional political career are generally the dull

[6] See S. Bialer, "An Unstable Leadership," *Problems of Communism,* July–August 1965.

conformists. Clearly, in a highly bureaucratized political setting, conformity, caution and currying favor with superiors count for more in advancing a political career than personal courage and individual initiative.[7]

Such a condition poses a long-range danger to the vitality of any political system. Social evolution, it has been noted, depends not only on the availability of creative individuals, but on the existence of clusters of creators who collectively promote social innovation. "The ability of any gifted individual to exert leverage within a society . . . is partly a function of the exact composition of the group of those on whom he depends for day-to-day interaction and for the execution of his plans." [8] The revolutionary milieu of the 1920's and even the fanatical Stalinist commitment of the 1930's fostered such clusters of intellectual and political talent. It is doubtful that the CPSU party schools and the Central Committee personnel department encourage, in Margaret Mead's terms, the growth of clusters of creativity, and that is why the transition from Lenin to Stalin to Khrushchev to Brezhnev probably cannot be charted by an ascending line.

This has serious implications for the Soviet system as a whole. It is doubtful that any organization can long remain vital if it is so structured that in its personnel policy it becomes, almost unknowingly, inimical to talent and hostile to political innovation. Decay is bound to set in, while the stability of the political system may be endangered, if other social institutions succeed in attracting the society's talent and begin to chafe under the restraints imposed by the ruling but increasingly mediocre *apparatchiki*.

The Struggle for Power

The struggle for power in the Soviet political system has certainly become less violent. The question is, however: Has it become less debilitating for the political system? Has it become a more regularized process, capable of infusing the leadership with fresh blood? A closer look at the changes in the character of the competition for power may guide us to the answer.

Both Stalin and Khrushchev rode to power by skillfully manipulating issues as well as by taking full advantage of the organizational opportunities arising from their tenure of the post of party First Secretary. It must be stressed that the manipulation of issues was at least as important to their success as the organizational factor, which generally tends to receive priority in Western historical treatments. In Stalin's time, the issues facing the party were, indeed, on a grand scale: world revolution *vs.* socialism in one country; domestic evolution *vs.* social revolution; a factionalized *vs.* a monolithic party. Stalin succeeded because he instinctively perceived that the new *apparatchiki* were not prepared to sacrifice themselves in futile efforts to promote foreign revolutions but—being for the most part genuinely committed to revolutionary ideals—were becoming eager to get on with the job of creating a socialist society. (Moreover, had the NEP endured another ten years, would the Soviet Union be a Communist dictatorship today?)

[7] Writing about modern bureaucracy, V. A. Thompson (*Modern Organization*, New York, 1961, p. 91) observed: "In the formally structured group, the idea man is doubly dangerous. He endangers the established distribution of power and status, and he is a competitive threat to his peers. Consequently, he has to be suppressed." For a breezy treatment of some analogous experience, see also E. G. Hegarty, *How to Succeed in Company Politics*, New York, 1963.

[8] Margaret Mead, *Continuities in Cultural Evolution*, New Haven, Yale University Press, 1964, p. 181. See also the introduction, especially p. xx.

Stalin's choice of socialism in one country was a brilliant solution. It captivated, at least in part, the revolutionaries; and it satisfied, at least partially, the accommodators. It split the opposition, polarized it, and prepared the ground for the eventual liquidation of each segment with the other's support. The violence, the terror, and finally the Great Purges of 1936–1938 followed logically. Imbued with the Leninist tradition of intolerance for dissent, engaged in a vast undertaking of social revolution that taxed both the resources and the nerves of party members, guided by an unscrupulous and paranoiac but also reassuringly calm leader, governing a backward country surrounded by neighbors that were generally hostile to the Soviet experiment, and increasingly deriving its own membership strength from first-generation proletarians with all their susceptibility to simple explanations and dogmatic truths, the ruling party easily plunged down the path of increasing brutality. The leader both rode the crest of that violence and controlled it. The terror never degenerated into simple anarchy, and Stalin's power grew immeasurably because he effectively practiced the art of leadership according to his own definition:

> The art of leadership is a serious matter. One must not lag behind the movement, because to do so is to become isolated from the masses. But neither must one rush ahead, for to rush ahead is to lose contact with the masses. He who wants to lead a movement and at the same time keep in touch with the vast masses must wage a fight on two fronts—against those who lag behind and those who run ahead.[9]

Khrushchev, too, succeeded in becoming the top leader because he perceived the elite's predominant interests. Restoration of the primary position of the party, decapitation of the secret police, reduction of the privileges of the state bureaucrats while maintaining the traditional emphasis on heavy industrial development (which pleased both the industrial elite and the military establishment)—these were the issues which Khrushchev successfully utilized in the mid-1950's to mobilize the support of officials and accomplish the gradual isolation and eventual defeat of Malenkov.

But the analogy ends right there. The social and even the political system in which Khrushchev came to rule was relatively settled. Indeed, in some respects, it was stagnating, and Khrushchev's key problem, once he reached the political apex (but before he had had time to consolidate his position there) was how to get the country moving again. The effort to infuse new social and political dynamism into Soviet society, even while consolidating his power, led him to a public repudiation of Stalinism which certainly shocked some officials; to sweeping economic reforms which disgruntled many administrators; to a dramatic reorganization of the party which appalled the *apparatchiki;* and even to an attempt to circumvent the policy-making authority of the party Presidium by means of direct appeals to interested groups, which must have both outraged and frightened his colleagues. The elimination of violence as the decisive instrumentality of political competition—a move that was perhaps prompted by the greater institutional maturity of Soviet society, and which was in any case made inevitable by the downgrading of the secret police and the public disavowals of Stalinism —meant that Khrushchev, unlike Stalin, could not achieve both social dynamism and the stability of his power. Stalin magnified his power as he strove to change society; to change society Khrushchev had to risk his power.

[9] J. V. Stalin, *Problems of Leninism,* Moscow, 1940, p. 338.

The range of domestic disagreement involved in the post-Stalin struggles has also narrowed with the maturing of social commitments made earlier. For the moment, the era of grand alternatives is over in Soviet society. Even though any struggle tends to exaggerate differences, the issues that divided Khrushchev from his opponents, though of great import, appear pedestrian in comparison to those over which Stalin and his enemies crossed swords. In Khrushchev's case, they pertained primarily to policy alternatives; in the case of Stalin, they involved basic conceptions of historical development. Compare the post-Stalin debates about the allocation of resources among different branches of the economy, for example, with the debates of the 1920's about the character and pace of Soviet industrialization; or Khrushchev's homilies on the merits of corn—and even his undeniably bold and controversial virgin lands campaign—with the dilemma of whether to collectivize a hundred million reticent peasants, at what pace, and with what intensity in terms of resort to violence.

It is only in the realm of foreign affairs that one can perhaps argue that grand dilemmas still impose themselves on the Soviet political scene. The nuclear-war-or-peace debate of the 1950's and early 1960's is comparable in many respects to the earlier conflict over "permanent revolution" or "socialism in one country." Molotov's removal and Kozlov's political demise were to a large extent related to disagreements concerning foreign affairs; nonetheless, in spite of such occasional rumblings, it would appear that on the peace-or-war issue there is today more of a consensus among the Soviet elite than there was on the issue of permanent revolution in the 1920's. Although a wide spectrum of opinion does indeed exist in the international Communist movement on the crucial questions of war and peace, this situation, as far as one can judge, obtains to a considerably lesser degree in the USSR itself. Bukharin *vs.* Trotsky can be compared to Togliatti *vs.* Mao Tse-tung, but hardly to Khrushchev *vs.* Kozlov.

The narrowing of the range of disagreement is reflected in the changed character of the cast. In the earlier part of this discussion, some comparative comments were made about Stalin, Khrushchev, and Brezhnev. It is even more revealing, however, to examine their principal rivals. Take the men who opposed Stalin: Trotsky, Zinoviev, and Bukharin. What a range of political, historical, economic, and intellectual creativity, what talent, what a diversity of personal characteristics and backgrounds! Compare this diversity with the strikingly uniform personal training, narrowness of perspective, and poverty of intellect of Malenkov, Kozlov and Suslov.[10] A regime of the clerks cannot help but clash over clerical issues.

The narrowing of the range of disagreement and the cooling of ideological passions mean also the wane of political violence. The struggle tends to become less a matter of life or death, and more one in which the price of defeat is simply retirement and some personal disgrace. In turn, with the routinization of conflict, the political system develops even a body of precedents for handling fallen leaders. By now there must be a regular procedure, probably even some office, for handling pensions and apartments for former Presidium members, as well as a developing social etiquette

[10] One could hardly expect a historian to work up any enthusiasm for undertaking to write, say, Malenkov's biography: *The Apparatchik Promoted, The Apparatchik Triumphant, The Apparatchik Pensioned!*

for dealing with them publicly and privately.[11]

More important is the apparent development in the Soviet system of something which might be described as a regularly available "counter-elite." After Khrushchev's fall, his successors moved quickly to restore to important positions a number of individuals whom Khrushchev had purged,[12] while some of Khrushchev's supporters were demoted and transferred. Already for a number of years now, it has been fairly common practice to appoint party officials demoted from high office either to diplomatic posts abroad or to some obscure, out-of-the-way assignments at home. The total effect of this has been to create a growing body of official "outs" who are biding their time on the sidelines and presumably hoping someday to become the "ins" again. Moreover, they may not only hope; if sufficiently numerous, young, and vigorous, they may gradually begin to resemble something of a political alternative to those in power, and eventually to think and even act as such. This could be the starting point of informal factional activity, of intrigues and conspiracies when things go badly for those in power, and of organized efforts to seduce some part of the ruling elite in order to stage an internal change of guard.[13] In addition, the availability of an increasingly secure "counter-elite" is likely to make it more difficult for a leader to consolidate his power. This in turn might tend to promote more frequent changes in the top leadership, with policy failures affecting the power of incumbents instead of affecting—only retroactively—the reputation of former leaders, as has hitherto been the case.

The cumulative effect of these developments has been wide-ranging. First of all, the reduced importance of both ideological issues and personalities and the increasing weight of institutional interests in the periodic struggles for power a phenomenon which reflects the more structured quality of present-day Soviet life as compared with the situation under Stalin—tends to depersonalize political conflict and to make it a protracted bureaucratic struggle. Secondly, the curbing of violence makes it more likely that conflicts will be resolved by patched-up compromises rather than by drastic institutional redistributions of power and the reappearance of personal tyranny. Finally, the increasingly bureaucratic character of the struggle for power tends to transform it into a contest among high-level clerks and is therefore not conducive to attracting creative and innovating talent into the top leadership.

Khrushchev's fall provides a good il-

[11] Can Mikoyan, for example, invite Khrushchev to lunch? This is not a trivial question, for social mores and political style are interwoven. After all, Voroshilov, who had been publicly branded as a military idiot and a political sycophant, was subsequently invited to a Kremlin reception. Zhukov, against whom the Bonapartist charge still stands, appeared in full regalia at the 20th anniversary celebration of the Soviet victory in World War II.

[12] F. D. Kulakov, apparently blamed by Khrushchev in 1960 for agricultural failings in the RSFSR, was appointed in 1965 to direct the Soviet Union's new agricultural programs; V. V. Matskevich was restored as Minister of Agriculture and appointed Deputy Premier of the RSFSR in charge of agriculture; Marshal M. V. Zakharov was reappointed as Chief-of-Staff of the Armed Forces; even L. G. Melnikov reemerged from total obscurity as chairman of the industrial work safety committee of the RSFSR.

[13] Molotov's letter to the Central Committee on the eve of the 22nd Party Congress of October 1961, which bluntly and directly charged Khrushchev's program with revisionism, was presumably designed to stir up the *apparatchiki* against the First Secretary. It may be a portent of things to come.

lustration of the points made above, as well as an important precedent for the future. For the first time in Soviet history, the First Secretary has been toppled from power by his associates. This was done not in order to replace him with an alternative personal leader or to pursue genuinely alternative goals, but in order to depersonalize the leadership and to pursue more effectively many of the previous policies. In a word, the objectives were impersonal leadership and higher bureaucratic efficiency. Khrushchev's removal, however, also means that personal intrigues and cabals can work, that subordinate members of the leadership—or possibly, someday, a group of ex-leaders—can effectively conspire against a principal leader, with the result that any future First Secretary is bound to feel far less secure than Khrushchev must have felt at the beginning of October 1964.

The absence of an institutionalized top executive officer in the Soviet political system, in conjunction with the increased difficulties in the way of achieving personal dictatorship and the decreased personal cost of defeat in a political conflict, create a ready-made situation for group pressures and institutional clashes. In fact, although the range of disagreement may have narrowed, the scope of elite participation in power conflicts has already widened. Much of Khrushchev's exercise of power was preoccupied with mediating the demands of key institutions such as the army, or with overcoming the opposition of others, such as the objections of the administrators to economic decentralization or of the heavy industrial managers to non-industrial priorities. These interests were heavily involved in the Khrushchev-Malenkov conflict and in the "anti-party" episode of 1957.

At the present time, these pressures and clashes take place in an almost entirely amorphous context, without constitutional definition and established procedures. The somewhat greater role played by the Central Committee in recent years still does not suffice to give this process of bureaucratic conflict a stable institutional expression. As far as we know from existing evidence, the Central Committee still acted during the 1957 and 1964 crises primarily as a ratifying body, giving formal sanction to decisions already fought out in the Kremlin's corridors of power.[14] It did not act as either the arbiter or the supreme legislative body.

The competition for power, then, is changing from a death struggle among the few into a contest played by many more. But the decline of violence does not, as is often assumed, automatically benefit the Soviet political system; something more effective and stable has to take the place of violence. The "game" of politics that has replaced the former mafia-style struggles for power is no longer murderous, but it is still not a stable game played within an established arena, according to accepted rules, and involving more or less formal teams. It resembles more the anarchistic free-for-all of the playground and therefore could become, in some respects, even more debilitating to the system. Stalin encouraged institutional conflict below him so that he could wield his power with less restraint. Institutional conflict combined with mediocre and unstable personal leadership makes for ineffective and precarious power.

Party and Group Interests

In a stimulating study of political development and decay, Samuel Huntington has argued that stable political

[14] Roger Pethybridge, *A Key to Soviet Politics*, New York, Praeger, 1962. See also Myron Rush, *The Rise of Khrushchev*, Washington, DC, Public Affairs Press, 1958.

growth requires a balance between political "institutionalization" and political "participation": that merely increasing popular mobilization and participation in politics without achieving a corresponding degree of "institutionalization of political organization and procedures" results not in political development but in political decay.[15] Commenting in passing on the Soviet system, he therefore noted that "a strong party is in the Soviet public interest" because it provides a stable institutional framework.[16]

The Soviet political system has certainly achieved a high index of institutionalization. For almost five decades the ruling party has maintained unquestioned supremacy over the society, imposing its ideology at will. Traditionally, the Communist system has combined its high institutionalization with high pseudo-participation of individuals.[17] But a difficulty could arise if division within the top leadership of the political system weakened political "institutionalization" while simultaneously stimulating genuine public participation by groups and institutions. Could this new condition be given an effective and stable institutional framework and, if so, with what implications for the "strong" party?

Today the Soviet political system is again oligarchic, but its socio-economic setting is now quite different. Soviet society is far more developed and stable, far less *malleable* and atomized. In the past, the key groups that had to be considered as potential political participants were relatively few. Today, in addition to the vastly more entrenched institutional interests, such as the police, the military, and the state bureaucracy, the youth could become a source of ferment, the consumers could become more restless, the collective farmers more recalcitrant, the scientists more outspoken, the non-Russian nationalities more demanding. Prolonged competition among the oligarchs would certainly accelerate the assertiveness of such groups.

By now some of these groups have a degree of institutional cohesion, and occasionally they act in concert on some issues.[18] They certainly can lobby and, in turn, be courted by ambitious and opportunistic oligarchs. Some groups,

[15] Samuel P. Huntington, "Political Development and Political Decay," *World Politics* (Princeton, N. J.) April 1965.

[16] *Ibid.*, p. 414.

[17] The massive campaigns launching "public discussions" that involve millions of people, the periodic "elections" that decide nothing, were designed to develop participation without threat to the institutionalized political organization and procedures. The offical theory held that as Communist consciousness developed and new forms of social and public relations took root, political participation would become more meaningful and the public would come to govern itself.

[18] A schematic distribution of these groups is indicated by the following approximate figures: (A) amorphous social forces that in the main express passively broad social aspirations: workers and peasants, about 88 million; white collar and technical intelligentsia, about 21 million. (B) specific interest groups that promote their own particular interests: the literary and artistic community, about 75 thousand; higher-level scientists, about 150 thousand; physicians, about 380 thousand. (C) policy groups whose interests necessarily spill over into broad matters of national policy: industrial managers, about 200 thousand; state and collective farm chairmen, about 45 thousand; commanding military personnel, about 80 thousand; higher-level state bureaucrats, about 250 thousand. These groups are integrated by the professional *apparatchiki*, who number about 150–200 thousand. All of these groups in turn could be broken down into sub-units; *e.g.*, the literary community, institutionally built around several journals, can be divided into hard-liners, the centrists, and the progressives, etc. Similarly, the military. On some issues, there may be cross-interlocking of sub-groups, as well as more-or-less temporary coalitions of groups. See Z. Brzezinski and S. Huntington, *Political Power: USA–USSR*, New York, Viking Press, 1964, Ch. 4, for further discussion.

because of institutional cohesion, advantageous location, easy access to the top leadership, and ability to articulate their goals and interests, can be quite influential.[19] Taken together they represent a wide spectrum of opinion, and in the setting of oligarchical rule there is bound to be some correspondence between their respective stances and those of the top leaders. This spectrum is represented in simplified fashion by the chart on page 219, which takes cumulative account of the principal divisions, both on external and on domestic issues, that have perplexed Soviet political life during the last decade or so.[20] Obviously, the chart is somewhat arbitrary and also highly speculative. Individuals and groups cannot be categorized so simply, and some, clearly, could be shifted left or right with equal cause, as indeed they often shift themselves. Nonetheless, the chart illustrates the range of opinion that exists in the Soviet system and suggests the kind of alliances, group competition, and political courtship that probably prevail, cutting vertically through the party organization.

Not just Western but also Communist (although not as yet Soviet) political thinkers are coming to recognize more and more openly the existence of group conflict even in a Communist-dominated society. A Slovak jurist recently observed:

> The social interest in our society can be democratically formed only by the integration of group interests; in the process of this integration, the interest groups protect their own economic and other social interests; this is in no way altered by the fact that everything appears on the surface as a unity of interests.[21]

The author went on to stress that the key political problem facing the Communist system is that of achieving integration of group interests.

Traditionally, this function of integration has been monopolized by the party, resorting—since the discard of terror—to the means of *bureaucratic arbitration.* In the words of the author just cited, "the party as the leading and directing political force fulfills its functions by resolving intra-class and inter-class interests." In doing so, the party generally has preferred to deal with each group bilaterally, thereby preventing the formation of coalitions and informal group consensus. In this way the unity of political direction as well as the political supremacy of the ruling party have been maintained. The party has always been very jealous of its "integrative" prerogative, and the intrusion on the political scene of any other group

[19] An obvious example is the military command, bureaucratically cohesive and with a specific esprit de corps, located in Moscow, necessarily in frequent contact with the top leaders, and possessing its own journals of opinion (where strategic and hence also—indirectly—budgetary, foreign, and other issues can be discussed).

[20] The categories "systemic left," etc., are adapted from R. R. Levine's book, *The Arms Debate* (Cambridge, Mass., Harvard University Press, 1963), which contains a suggestive chart of American opinion on international issues. By "systemic left" is meant here a radical reformist outlook, challenging the predominant values of the existing system; by "systemic right" is meant an almost reactionary return to past values; the other three categories designate differences of degree within a dominant "mainstream."

In the chart opposite (unlike Levine's), the center position serves as a dividing line, and hence no one is listed directly under it. Malenkov is listed as "systemic left" because his proposals represented at the time a drastic departure from established positions. Molotov is labeled "systemic right" because of his inclination to defend the essentials of the Stalinist system in a setting which had changed profoundly since Stalin's death.

[21] M. Lakatos, "On Some Problems of the Structure of Our Political System," *Pravny obzor* (Bratislava), No. 1, 1965, as quoted in Gordon Skilling's illuminating paper, "Interest Groups and Communist Politics," read to the Canadian Political Science Association in June 1965.

Policy Spectrum USSR

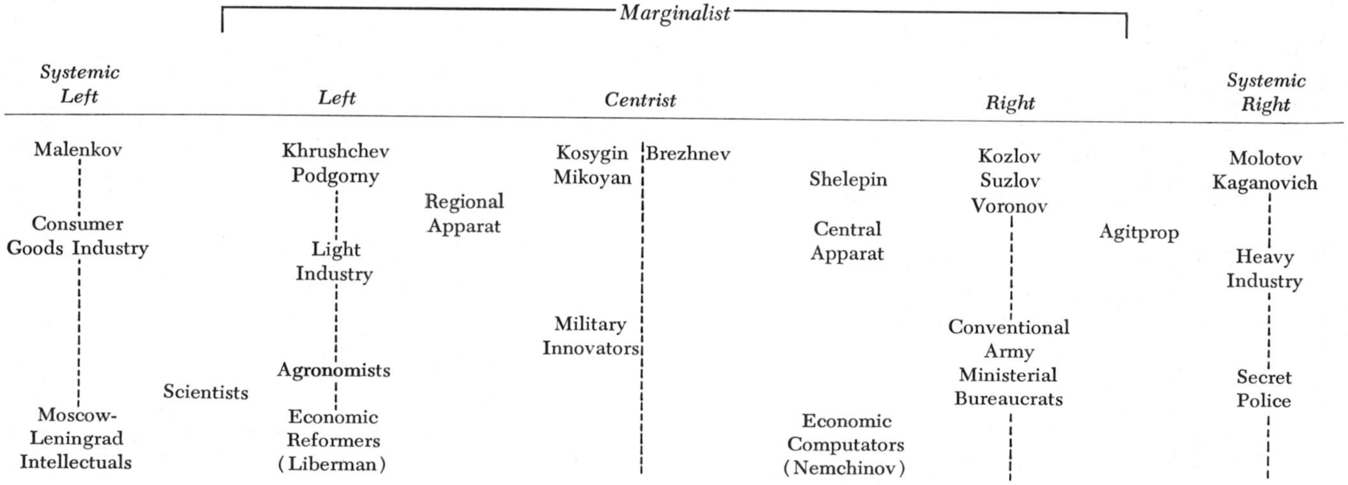

has been strongly resented. The party's institutional primacy has thus depended on limiting the real participation of other groups.

If, for one reason or another, the party were to weaken in the performance of this function, the only alternative to anarchy would be some *institutionalized process of mediation*, replacing the party's bureaucratic arbitration. Since, as noted, group participation has become more widespread, while the party's effectiveness in achieving integration has been lessened by the decline in the vigor of Soviet leadership and by the persistent divisions in the top echelon, the creation and eventual formal institutionalization of some such process of mediation is gaining in urgency. Otherwise participation could outrun institutionalization and result in a challenge to the party's integrative function.

Khrushchev's practice of holding enlarged Central Committee plenums, with representatives of other groups present, seems to have been a step towards formalizing a more regular consultative procedure. (It also had the politically expedient effect of bypassing Khrushchev's opponents in the central leadership.) Such enlarged plenums provided a consultative forum, where policies could be debated, views articulated, and even some contradictory interests resolved. Although the device still remained essentially non-institutionalized and only *ad hoc*, consultative and not legislative, still subject to domination by the party *apparat*, it was nonetheless a response to the new quest for real participation that Soviet society has manifested and which the Soviet system badly needs. It was also a compromise solution, attempting to wed the party's primacy to a procedure allowing group articulation.

However, the problem has become much more complex and fundamental because of the organizational and ideological crisis in the party over its relevance to the evolving Soviet system. For many years the party's monopoly of power and hence its active intervention in all spheres of Soviet life could indeed be said to be "in the Soviet public interest." The party provided social mobilization, leadership, and a dominant outlook for a rapidly changing and developing society. But, in the main, that society has now taken shape. It is no longer malleable, subject to simple mobilization, or susceptible to doctrinaire ideological manipulation.

As a result, Soviet history in the last few years has been dominated by the spectacle of a party in search of a role. What is to be the function of an ideocratic party in a relatively complex and industrialized society, in which the structure of social relationships generally reflects the party's ideological preferences? To be sure, like any large sociopolitical system, the Soviet system needs an integrative organ. But the question is, What is the most socially desirable way of achieving such integration? Is a "strong" party one that dominates and interferes in everything, and is this interference conducive to continued Soviet economic, political and intellectual growth?

In 1962 Khrushchev tried to provide a solution. The division of the party into two vertically parallel, functional organs was an attempt to make the party directly relevant to the economy and to wed the party's operations to production processes. It was a bold, dramatic and radical innovation, reflecting a recognition of the need to adapt the party's role to a new state of Soviet social development. But it was also a dangerous initiative; it carried within itself the potential of political disunity as well as the possibility that the party would become so absorbed in economic affairs that it would lose its political and ideological identity. That it was rapidly repudiated by Khrushchev's successors is testimony to the repugnance that the reorganization must have stimulated among the professional party bureaucrats.

His successors, having rejected Khrushchev's reorganization of the party, have been attempting a compromise solution—in effect, a policy of "muddling through." On the one hand, they recognize that the party can no longer direct the entire Soviet economy from the Kremlin and that major institutional reforms in the economic sphere, pointing towards more local autonomy and decision-making, are indispensable.[22] (Similar tendencies are apparent elsewhere—*e.g.*, the stress on professional self-management in the military establishment.) This constitutes a partial and implicit acknowledgment that in some respects a party of total control is today incompatible with the Soviet public interest.

On the other hand, since obviously inherent in the trend towards decentralization is the danger that the party will be gradually transformed from a directing, ideologically-oriented organization to a merely instrumental and pragmatic body specializing in adjustment and compromise of social group aspirations, the party functionaries, out of a sense of vested interest, have been attempting simultaneously to revive the ideological vitality of the CPSU. Hence the renewed stress on ideology and ideological training; hence the new importance attached to the work of the ideological commissions; and hence the categorical reminders that "Marxist education, Marxist-Leninist training, and the ideological tempering of CPSU members and candidate members is the primary concern of every party organization and committee." [23]

However, it is far from certain that economic decentralization and ideological "retempering" can be pushed forward hand in hand. The present leadership appears oblivious to the fact that established ideology remains vital only when ideologically motivated power is applied to achieve ideological goals. A gradual reduction in the directing role of the party cannot be compensated for by an increased emphasis on ideological semantics. Economic decentralization inescapably reduces the scope of the political-ideological and increases the realm of the pragmatic-instrumental. It strengthens the trend, publicly bemoaned by Soviet ideologists, toward depolitization of the Soviet elite.[24] A massive indoctrination campaign directed at the elite cannot operate in a "de-ideologized" socio-economic context, and major efforts to promote such a campaign could, indeed, prompt the social isolation of the party, making its dogmas even more irrelevant to the daily concerns of a Soviet scientist, factory director, or army general. That

[22] See the report delivered by A. Kosygin to the CC Plenum on Sept. 27, 1965, proposing the reorganization of the Soviet economy. Also his speech at a meeting of the USSR State Planning Committee, *Planovoe khoziaistvo* (Moscow) April 1965; and the frank discussion by A. E. Lunev, "Democratic Centralism in Soviet State Administration," *Sovetskoe gosudarstvo i pravo* (Moscow), No. 4, 1965.

[23] "Ideological Hardening of Communists" (editorial), *Pravda,* June 28, 1965. There have been a whole series of articles in this vein, stressing the inseparability of ideological and organizational work. For details of a proposed large-scale indoctrination campaign, see V. Stepakov, head of the Department of Propaganda and Agitation of the Central Committee of the CPSU, "Master the Great Teaching of Marxism-Leninism," *Pravda,* Aug. 4, 1965.

[24] Stepakov, *ibid.,* explicitly states that in recent years "many comrades" who have assumed leading posts in the "directive aktivs" of the party have inadequate ideological knowledge, even though they have excellent technical backgrounds; and he urges steps against the "replacement" of party training "by professional-technical education."

in turn would further reduce the ability of the party to provide effective integration in Soviet society, while underscoring the party *apparatchik's* functional irrelevance to the workings of Soviet administration and technology.

If the party rejects a return to ideological dogmas and renewed dogmatic indoctrination, it unavoidably faces the prospect of further internal change. It will gradually become a loose body, combining a vast variety of specialists, engineers, scientists, administrators, professional bureaucrats, agronomists, etc. Without a common dogma and without an active program, what will hold these people together? The party at this stage will face the same dilemma that the fascist and falange parties faced, and that currently confronts the Yugoslav and Polish Communists: in the absence of a large-scale domestic program of change, in the execution of which other groups and institutions become subordinated to the party, the party's domestic primacy declines and its ability to provide social-political integration is negated.

Moreover, the Soviet party leaders would be wrong to assume complacently that the narrowed range of disagreement over domestic policy alternatives could not again widen. Persistent difficulties in agriculture could some day prompt a political aspirant to question the value of collectivization; or the dissatisfaction of some nationalities could impose a major strain on the Soviet constitutional structure; or foreign affairs could again become the source of bitter internal conflicts. The ability of the system to withstand the combined impact of such divisive issues and of greater group intrusion into politics would much depend on the adaptations that it makes in its organization of leadership and in its processes of decision-making. Unless alternative mechanisms of integration are created, a situation could arise in which some group other than the top *apparat*—a group that had continued to attract talent into its top ranks and had not been beset by bureaucratically debilitating conflict at the top—could step forth to seek power; invoking the Soviet public interest in the name of established Communist ideals, and offering itself (probably in coalition with some section of the party leadership) as the only alternative to chaos, it would attempt to provide a new balance between institutionalization and participation.

The Threat of Degeneration

The Soviet leaders have recognized the need of institutional reforms in the economic sector in order to revitalize the national economy. The fact is that institutional reforms are just as badly needed—and even more overdue—in the political sector. Indeed, the effort to maintain a doctrinaire dictatorship over an increasingly modern and industrial society has already contributed to a reopening of the gap that existed in prerevolutionary Russia between the political system and the society, thereby posing the threat of the degeneration of the Soviet system.

A political system can be said to degenerate when there is a perceptible decline in the quality of the social talent that the political leadership attracts to itself in competition with other groups; when there is persistent division within the ruling elite, accompanied by a decline in its commitment to shared beliefs; when there is protracted instability in the top leadership; when there is a decline in the capacity of the ruling elite to define the purposes of the political system in relationship to society and to express them in effective institutional terms; when there is a fuzzing of institutional and hierarchical lines of command, resulting in the uncontrolled and unchanneled intrusion into politics of hitherto politically uninvolved groupings.[25] All of these indicators were discernible in the political systems of Tsarist Russia, the French Third Republic, Chiang Kai-shek's China and Rakosi's Hungary. Today, as already noted, at least several are apparent in the Soviet political system.

This is not to say, however, that the evolution of the Soviet system has inevitably turned into degeneration. Much still depends on how the ruling Soviet elite reacts. Policies of retrenchment, increasing dogmatism, and even violence, which—if now applied—would follow almost a decade of loosening up, could bring about a grave situation of tension, and the possibility of revolutionary outbreaks could not be discounted entirely. "Terror is indispensable to any dictatorship, but it cannot compensate for incompetent leaders and a defective organization of authority," observed a historian of the French revolution, writing of the Second Directory.[26] It is equally true of the Soviet political scene.

The threat of degeneration could be lessened through several adaptations designed to adjust the Soviet political system to the changes that have taken place in the now more mature society. First of all, the top policy-making organ of the Soviet system has been traditionally the exclusive preserve of the professional politician, and in many respects this has assured the Soviet political system of able and experienced leadership. However, since a professional bureaucracy is not prone to produce broad "generalizing" talents, and since the inherent differentiation of functions within it increases the likelihood of leaders with relatively much narrower specialization than hitherto was the case, the need for somewhat broader representation of social talent within the top political leadership, and not merely on secondary levels as hitherto, is becoming urgent. If several outstanding scientists, professional economists, industrial managers, and others were to be co-opted by lateral entry into the ruling Presidium, the progressive transformation of the leadership into a regime of clerks could thereby be averted, and the alienation of other groups from the political system perhaps halted.

Secondly, the Soviet leaders would have to institutionalize a chief executive office and strive to endow it with legitimacy and stability. This would eventually require the creation of a formal and open process of leadership selection, as well—probably—as a time limit on the tenure of the chief executive position. The time limit, if honored, would depersonalize power, while an institutionalized process of selection geared to a specific date—and therefore also limited in time—would reduce the debilitating effects of unchecked and protracted conflict in the top echelons of power.

The CPSU continues to be an ideocratic party with a strong tradition of dogmatic intolerance and organizational discipline. Today less militant and more bureaucratic in outlook, it still requires a top catalyst, though no longer a personal tyrant, for effective operations. The example of the papacy, or perhaps of Mexico, where a ruling party has created a reasonably effective system of presidential succession, offers a demonstration of how one-man rule can be combined with a formal office of the chief executive, endowed with legitimacy, tenure and a formally established pattern of selection.

[25] For a general discussion and a somewhat different formulation, see S. Huntington, "Political Development and Political Decay," pp. 15–17.

[26] G. Lefebvre, *The French Revolution*, New York, Columbia University Press, 1965, Vol. II, p. 205.

Any real institutionalization of power would have significant implications for the party. If its Central Committee were to become in effect an electoral college, selecting a ruler whom no one could threaten during his tenure, the process of selection would have to be endowed with considerable respectability. It would have to be much more than a mere ratification of an *a priori* decision reached by some bureaucratic cabal. The process would require tolerance for the expression of diverse opinions in a spirit free of dogmatism, a certain amount of open competition among rivals for power, and perhaps even the formation of informal coalitions—at least temporary ones. In a word, it would mean a break with the Leninist past, with consequences that would unavoidably spill over from the party into the entire system and society.

Thirdly, increased social participation in politics unavoidably creates the need for an institutionalized arena for the mediation of group interests, if tensions and conflicts, and eventually perhaps even anarchy, are to be avoided. The enlarged plenums of the Central Committee were a right beginning, but if the Committee is to mediate effectively among the variety of institutional and group interests that now exist in Soviet society, its membership will have to be made much more representative and the predominance of party bureaucrats watered down. Alternatively, the Soviet leaders might consider following the Yugoslav course of creating a new institution for the explicit purpose of providing group representation and reconciling different interests. In either case, an effective organ of mediation could not be merely a front for the party's continued bureaucratic arbitration of social interests, as that would simply perpetuate the present dilemmas.

Obviously, the implementation of such institutional reforms would eventually lead to a profound transformation of the Soviet system. But it is the absence of basic institutional development in the Soviet political system that has posed the danger of the system's degeneration. It is noteworthy that the Yugoslavs have been experimenting with political reforms, including new institutions, designed to meet precisely the problems and dangers discussed here. Indeed, in the long run, perhaps the ultimate contribution to Soviet political and social development that the CPSU can make is to adjust gracefully to the desirability, and perhaps even inevitability, of its own gradual withering away. In the meantime, the progressive transformation of the bureaucratic Communist dictatorship into a more pluralistic and institutionalized political system—even though still a system of one-party rule—seems essential if its degeneration is to be averted.

PART III

The Chinese Revolution

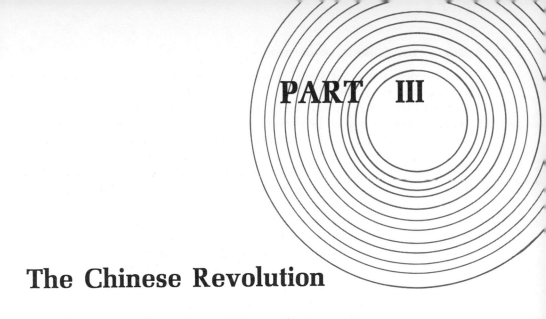

For most of the twentieth century China has been in the midst of a revolutionary upheaval that is unprecedented with regard to the number of people involved and the magnitude of the social transformation attempted. Yet until the victory of the Communist forces in 1949 and the subsequent proclamation of the Chinese People's Republic, the West was hardly aware of the Chinese Revolution, let alone capable of comprehending the profound causes underlying it. The Westerner, whether European or American, has never been much concerned with what has gone on in the Orient, but his ignorance here may also be reinforced by a certain conceptual blindness. Revolution has generally been considered as a phenomenon peculiar to the European, or at least Europeanized, world. That is to say, the conventional ideas as to what constitutes a revolution and the conventional theories used to analyze the dynamics of the revolutionary process have been drawn from the European experience. As a result, the great upheavals that have taken place in Asia, embodying a different constellation of social and political forces, have until recently been difficult to place within a familiar intellectual context. They have been, therefore, unclassifiable and little noticed.

The overthrow of the Manchu dynasty in 1911, following a century of increasingly precipitous decline, is usually taken as the start of the Chinese Revolution. We can quickly see, however, especially in the light of our earlier readings on the typology of revolution, that the time scale, the "definition," of the Chinese Revolution presents a difficult problem. In any case, this event, at first glance, was much like what had happened to almost every dynasty since the founding of the Empire two millennia before; but unlike dynastic collapses in the past, the disappearance of the Manchus, after a struggle between various factions, did not lead to the eventual emergence of a new ruling house governing within the framework of the traditional social order. Rather, it signaled the impending breakdown of that social order and of the system of moral values associated with it.

The Chinese Empire may well have been the most durable, and by that token successful, system of government on a large scale ever devised. For two thousand years, the inhabitants of the known world, i.e., the Chinese land mass and the areas immediately adjacent to it, lived under a theoretically monolithic political system with public affairs administered through a series of institutions remarkable for their permanence and their authority. This imperial system of government was but one, albeit salient, aspect of a coherent and stable civilization, one in which social behavior, ethical ideals, artistic vision, and economic activity were to an unusual degree integrated into a single, balanced synthesis. Within this civilization, every person from the poorest peasant to the emperor, the supreme ruler of the celestial empire, could in theory, and very often did in fact, find a meaningful and morally satisfying way of life. The nineteenth-century decline and twentieth-century collapse of so formidable a human achievement constitute a phenomenon of enormous significance, as does also the effort begun even before 1911, and still continuing, to evolve some kind of viable system with which to replace it.

How and why the traditional Chinese social order should have begun to break down when it did after functioning effectively for so many centuries is a question for which there is no simple answer. Many Chinese blame it primarily on the imperialist designs of the West. Certainly the confrontation with the West beginning in the 1830s and 1840s with the Opium Wars was a contributing factor. Still, the contact with the West in general involved relatively few people and disrupted life in only a small number of areas. One would be oversimplifying things to see it as the fundamental cause of so seismic an event as the Chinese Revolution. Yet small as was the actual extent of the Western penetration into China in the nineteenth century, it had profoundly disturbing implications for the country. The Westerners may have been uncultivated by Chinese standards, but they seemed serenely unaware of this fact. Satisfied with their own values and way of life, they had no desire, like past barbarians, to learn anything from the Chinese or to subjugate them. Rather, they sought to establish little enclaves in the midst of the Chinese and to exploit them economically in certain specific ways. The fact that so small a number of Western barbarians could do as they pleased within the Empire, to all intents and purposes ignoring the Chinese people around them, along with their culture, was a novel and unnerving experience. Even more disturbing was the realization that the Westerners were able to comport themselves in this fashion and to impose unequal treaties upon the government because they possessed tools and techniques, primarily of a military nature, whose efficacy the Chinese might well envy but to which they could not respond on the basis of their own technology and cultural attitudes. Having been for several millennia the preceptors in matters of culture and civilization to the barbarians, the Chinese were now faced with the necessity of having to learn from them, and it was profoundly humiliating to their sensibilities.

The ones most aware of China's technical inferiority to the West, and thus the ones most disturbed by the full implications of it, were the members of the governing elite, the so-called "scholar bureaucrats." For all its vast size, the Empire was administered as a single unit by a very small civil service. The members of this bureaucracy were for the most part recruited through a series of impartially administered examinations, the subject of which was the great Chinese classics, in particular the teachings of Confucius and his disciples. Confucianism was essentially a series of moral and ethical precepts concerning the relationships that should exist both within society and between man and nature. With their stress on harmony, order, and hierarchy, the precepts of Confucius would seem ideally suited to form the official ideology of a regime seeking stability above all. In few societies has learning been held in so high esteem as in Imperial China, if for no other reason than that it was the path to political power and influence. Imbued with the Confucian ideology through years of study and profoundly convinced of its correctness, the scholar bureaucrats of the late nineteenth century had to face the disquieting possibility that a society founded upon and functioning in accord with the teachings of Confucius might not be able to defend itself against the dynamic and culturally self-sufficient barbarians of the West. Added to this was the even more traumatic suspicion that within China itself the traditional ideology was losing its relevance.

We may surmise that the confrontation with the West would not have been so disruptive as it was if there were not already profound fissures in the structure of Chinese society. There had been in the remote past peasant revolts made in the name of an anti-Confucian ideology, but none of them rivaled the dimensions of the great Tai-Ping rebellion of the 1850s and 1860s, in which some fifteen million people are estimated to have perished. An uprising on this scale would indicate that a sizable sector of the population had begun to lose faith in the traditional verities of Chinese society. As to why this should be so, there are again no very certain answers, but it is probable that the dislocations in Chinese society must be approached in terms of the fundamental bedrock upon which it was originally built, the small peasant holding, farmed as a unit by one family. By the middle of the nineteenth century this bedrock was being seriously eroded, as individual holdings were proving incapable of supporting a family. The chief reason for this would seem to be that the population of China had, since at least 1700, been increasing at far too rapid a rate. This increase was inexorably undermining the ecological balance typical of traditional China, the balance whereby a large number of people were able to maintain themselves on a relatively small area of land through careful, intensive cultivation. As long as this balance existed, the fundamental bases of Chinese society were secure and the official ideology of the regime, with its stress on harmonious, hierarchical stability and the virtues of the patriarchal family, was almost universally applicable.

The overthrow of the Manchus was followed by a confused period of struggle between various factions in which the political unity of China threatened to disintegrate. A decade was to pass before a coherent force, potentially capable of establishing some kind of order, emerged—the Kuomintang originally founded in 1913. Under the leadership of Sun Yat-sen, one of the leaders in the struggle against the Manchus, the party took the Russian Communist Party as an organizational model, and sought to establish a single unitary body under whose auspices political developments in China could be guided and controlled and eventually a viable, stable regime set up. But whereas in Russia great stress was placed on ideological orthodoxy and unity, in the Kuomintang numerous ideological strains were present and in open competition with each other. Sun had originally seemed to envision an intellectual and political break with the past. But by the end of its reign, the Kuomintang, now under the leadership of Chiang Kai-shek, was sinking its ideological roots deep in the Chinese tradition and espousing a kind of neo-Confucianism (see Wright).

Founded to preserve the political unity of China, the Kuomintang first had to overcome the centrifugal forces personified by the so-called war lords. These local military chiefs had profited from the progressive breakdown of central authority to establish independent armed satrapies in various of the provinces. Their chief goal was to maintain their independent situation. But in the 1920s a tougher rival force took shape founded on an ideology opposed to that of the Kuomintang and seeking eventually to replace it as the governing elite of China—the Chinese Communist Party.

The most notable feature of Chinese intellectual life in the first decades of the twentieth century was the search by the heirs of the scholar bureaucrats for an explanation of what had happened to their society and for a new, more modern principle of social and political authority. Naturally enough, many of the rising young intellectuals looked to the West as the source of all that was apparently modern for guidance. None of the Western creeds was really applicable to the needs of the Chinese people, but Marxism seemed even less so than the others. With its assumption that revolution could take place only under the leadership of the proletariat, Marxism posited a crucial role for a class that was almost nonexistent in China in the 1920s. The Chinese Communist Party thus had few adherents in the early days, and consequently, on the orders of the Comintern, sought less to combat the Kuomintang than to advance its cause through cooperation with the party of Sun Yat-sen. It was only when Mao Tse-tung discovered the revolutionary potential of the peasantry and "creatively" incorporated this discovery into the Marxist canon that the creed of the Communists began to bear some relation to the realities of the Chinese situation (see Mao).

Whether what Mao preached may in any meaningful sense be classified as traditional Marxism is debatable. In any case his theories as to the necessity of a peasant-based revolution were not well received at first by his comrades within the party. Force of circumstances obliged them to accept his views, however, when in 1927 Chiang Kai-shek broke the alliance between the Kuomintang and the Communists. Driven from the cities, the Communists were obliged to seek a rural base for their activities. The first rural soviets were organized in Southern China in Hunan and Kwangsi provinces, but the persistent efforts by Chiang to exterminate them once and for all finally led Mao in 1934–35 to shift his base to the remote northwest province of Shensi after the epochal Long March of some 6,000 miles.

Among the revolutionary leaders of this century, Mao stands second only to Lenin. Yet despite his claims as an original Marxian theorist, there is considerable doubt as to how much of his revolutionary fervor has been motivated by some kind of vision of a classless society, and how much by the exacerbated national pride typical of his generation (see Schram). In the years when Mao was growing up, China had become virtually a cypher in international affairs, incapable of either promoting or protecting its own interests with regard to other powers and thus obliged to submit to their policies. Mao seems determined that China shall never again be placed in so humiliating a position. The nationalist and Marxist components in the Maoist vision can hardly be isolated from each other, but it does seem that the former played a vital role in bringing the Communists to power. In 1937, at the start of the Sino-Japanese War, they were a small, harassed force in a remote area of Northwest China, virtually reduced to the status of a war-lord faction. Eight years later they were in firm control of something like 20 per cent of the Chinese people and ready to launch a final assault on the faltering power of the Kuomintang. Much of the explanation for this remarkable improvement in their political fortunes may lie in the effective role they played in the war against the Japanese (see Johnson).

In any effort to comprehend and to explain the Chinese Revolution, one is tempted to draw analogies from the only other upheaval of the century of comparable enormity, the Russian Revolution. The analogy is all the more tempting since the victor in both cases has been an ostensibly Marxist party apparently seeking to build a viable modern society on the ruins of the old traditional way of life. Such analogies may be valid up to a point, but the two revolutions also differ in enough significant respects to lead one to wonder if the Chinese Revolution must not be analyzed as a case by itself. For example, the differences between the two revolutions can begin to be seen now that the Communists have been in power for more than two decades in China. By the time the Russian Communists had reached that milestone, their revolution had already entered its "bureaucratic" phase, which is to say that having effected a certain number of basic social and economic transformations they tacitly accepted the solidification, some would say the petrification, of state and society along these new lines and have done so ever since.

The Chinese Communists, or at least those supporting Mao, have not accepted the bureaucratization of the revolution and indeed are actively struggling against it. It is here then that analogies with the Russian Revolution break down. Rather than seeking to erect some kind of new but stable social order, Mao seems to be trying to perpetuate the fervor and enthusiasm that proved their efficacy in the years leading up to the defeat of the Kuomintang—although with what goal at present it is difficult to say. This last aspect more than anything else puzzles Western observers still trying to make sense of the Chinese Revolution in terms of the Western experience, and it may also be this that sets it apart from all previous revolutionary upheavals.

As the newest major revolution, the Chinese Revolution may well be the forerunner and/or the model for the revolutionary upheavals that may take place over the next generation or two. China, unlike Russia, was not, in its own eyes at least, at the bottom of a "cultural slope" starting in the West. Thus, China appears to have "Westernized" only to the extent necessary to reassert its own cultural uniqueness, not to new-model itself on the Western die. If this analysis is correct, then "modernization," at least on the Western scale, is something that China might enter upon with a very divided heart and psyche. Its Cultural Revolution, in that case, might be interpreted as, on one side, an effort to prevent the growth of a typical technological cum technocratic society, characterized by excessive urban growth, congestion, pollution, and the other attendant evils of many of the most advanced countries, and on the other side, an effort to ensure a pure and "permanent" revolution (see Pfeffer).

If future revolutions are to come from countries even less "developed," even more "rural" than China, then the Chinese Revolution may be their forerunner in the sense of showing how a revolution can occur in such a setting (see Lin Piao). If, however, future revolutions were to come in the most advanced countries, as some now advocate, and as Marx, originally predicted, then the Chinese Revolution might serve as a "model" of how to go beyond "modernization" as we have hitherto known it. More probably, new developments may occur beyond the models of either the Russian or Chinese Revolutions, but in which the latter especially may serve primarily as a "mythical" inspiration. All of these possibilities need to be discussed and analysed. Whatever the precise developments, we can be sure that the reverberations of the Chinese Revolution will be with us for a long time to come.

When the Manchu dynasty was finally overthrown in 1912, the event signaled the breakdown of traditional Chinese civilization. An analysis of how this remarkable civilization took shape and maintained itself more or less continuously for some twenty centuries is given in this selection, the opening chapter of *The Revolution in China* by Charles P. Fitzgerald.

The Origins of the Chinese Revolution

CHARLES P. FITZGERALD

Just inside the Ch'ien Men, the great south gate of the Northern City in Peking, there is a smaller gate, forming the most southerly entrance to the Imperial City which surrounds the still more secluded Forbidden City, the palace of the Emperors. This gate is called the Dynastic Gate, because it carried the name of the ruling dynasty. Thus, when it was built, it was 'Ta Ming Men', the 'Great Ming Gate', then 'Ta Ch'ing Men', 'Great Ch'ing (Manchu) Gate', and now 'Chung Hua Men', 'China Gate', since under the Republic, both the epithet 'great' and the distinctive dynastic title for a regime have been dropped.

It is related, in the gossip of the Peking people, that when the Republic was established in February 1912, workmen were sent with the new name tablet to take down the 'Ta Ch'ing Men' tablet and put up the 'Chung Hua Men'. The workman set up his ladder, took down the old tablet, fixed the new one and then said to the foreman down below, 'what shall I do with the old tablet?' The foreman, a humble official, thought for a moment. The Republic was very new, the idea strange, its duration perhaps uncertain. It would be awkward, should the Emperor regain power, if he, the foreman, should be held responsible for the loss or destruction of the old tablet. Better take no such risk. 'Put it up in the loft, there, under the roof', he replied.

The workman took the tablet up to the loft, and then called out in surprise, 'but there is one here already'. 'Bring it down and let us have a look,' said the foreman. The tablet found lying in the loft was brought down: the onlookers gathered around, the dust of ages was wiped off, and there was read the inscription 'Ta Ming Men'—'The Great Ming Gate'. Three hundred years before, another workman had had the same wisdom, and devised the same safeguard. No one seems to know whether both these fallen tablets still lie in the loft of the Chung Hua Men.

The Peking people like this kind of story: it appeals to their malicious contempt for all authority, the sophisticated, aloof indifference of the inhabitants of the capital—who see all regimes come and go, and see all their human frailties. Yet the foreman might, this time, have been more careless with impunity. This revolution was no mere change of dynasty, no simple change of name for the long-continuing Empire. This time not only the name but the structure itself must fall, for to wrench away the Throne is to pull out the king-pin of the Chinese civilization. The cloud of dust which obscured the col-

From Charles P. Fitzgerald, *The Revolution in China,* Cresset Press. London, 1952. Reprinted by permission of the Cresset Press, London, and of Frederick A. Praeger, Inc., New York.

lapse of that ancient fabric has only now begun to settle.

On October 10, 1911, the accidental explosion of a bomb in the home of some Chinese republican conspirators in Hankow precipitated the train of events which brought about the fall of the Manchu Dynasty, the rise and decay of the Republic, the Nationalist dictatorship, and finally the triumph of the Chinese Communist Party. So small a cause, so great a consequence; yet had not the landslide been ready to fall the movement of one small pebble would have been without significance. The Chinese Revolution was made possible by the long growth of elements of instability in Chinese society. The increasing maladjustment of institutions, the ever more apparent inadequacy of the ruling orthodox doctrines, the manifest decline in the prestige and power of the Empire both at home and abroad, all these factors had brought about a situation in which only a small agent was needed to bring the aged structure down in ruin.

Once that fall had begun it could not be stopped until the main constituent parts of the old society had been levelled with the ground and a firm basis found for the construction of a new order. The Revolution began, as it were, in slow motion, but its apparently erratic and spasmodic development was caused by the successive decay and fall of the bastions of the old society, the Throne, Confucian orthodoxy, the Civil Service, the land tenure system, the family system. Each phase of the Revolution saw the crumbling and collapse of some ancient institution, and in its fall the others were in turn shaken and successively overthrown. The Revolution which began with the simple elimination of an effete dynasty has progressively destroyed the fundamental concepts of the ancient civilization, and has substituted others, which seem, at least at first sight, to be wholly alien and diametrically opposed.

In 1911 the Manchu Dynasty ruled over an Empire which in all essentials was the Empire first unified by Ch'in Shih Huang Ti in 221 B.C. and perfected by the great Han Dynasty in the second century B.C. The Empire had been refounded, after foreign invasion and division, by the T'ang Dynasty in the seventh century A.D., refined and embellished by the Sung in the tenth century, usurped by the Mongols, restored by the Ming, and at last taken over, almost without change, by the Manchus; but during these centuries hardly any new institution or idea had modified the political system set up by the Han Emperors two hundred years before the birth of Christ. The T'ang had perfected the Civil Service system; Sung philosophy had brought the reigning Confucian orthodoxy into line with later thought; in the Ming and Manchu periods the development of the novel had produced the last literary form—even though this was considered heterodox and improper.

Nothing, it was often said, both by foreigners and Chinese, had changed; the Chinese civilization was and had been static for centuries. This view was not in fact correct, but the slow tempo of change in China, and the conservation of very ancient forms both in institutions and in material products, contributed to the belief that this was a stable and unchanging order of society. It is true that the European observers and Chinese scholars, although they agreed in the belief that China did not change, held opposite views on the value of this supposed immutability. To the Confucian scholar change could be only decay; the perfect system had been evolved in the remote past by the sage Emperors of antiquity and the best that the modern could hope for was to make some passable imitation of that

Golden Age. The Confucian therefore opposed all innovation as a further departure from the original and perfect pattern. The orthodoxy which gave him his rank, his outlook and his background constrained him to instinctive rejection of progress or change.

The European critic, usually in the early period a missionary, was often struck with admiration for the harmony and poise of Chinese civilization; his one complaint was that this was a pagan, not a Christian culture. In time, however, he came to realize that the seeming immutability and interdependence of all aspects of Chinese civilization was the real obstacle to the great reform which he lived to promote. The Gospel could not be dissociated from the culture and spirit of the West, yet these things were inimical to the Chinese civilization, and as such firmly rejected by the upholders of Confucian orthodoxy.

Gradually the missionary came to see that only by wide and sweeping changes could China be made accessible to his teaching; such changes would involve either the disappearance or the profound alteration of the culture; as the missionaries and their countrymen in lay life worked towards this end they encountered the ever sharper hostility of the defenders of ancient China. The foreign outlook triumphed, not through large conversions to Christianity, but by the spread of the secular ideas of the West. The Empire fell, Confucius was dethroned, political and ideological anarchy followed the collapse, but the Christian religion did not succeed in synthesizing this chaos and becoming the active principle of the new Chinese civilization.

In the late eighteenth and early nineteenth centuries the West was profoundly ignorant of the real character of Oriental society; neither its true strength nor its failings were detected; obsessed with the prevailing belief in the moral superiority of Christianity and the intellectual supremacy of Greek thought, the Oriental civilizations were dismissed as barbarous because they were manifestly polytheistic and ignorant of the conception of democracy. It was generally accepted that the mission of Europe was to lighten this darkness both by spreading Christianity and introducing the system of democratic government which was then gaining ascendancy in Western Europe and its overseas offshoots. It was hoped that once these changes had been made the Oriental cultures would progress in the European manner, keeping, perhaps, some picturesque native features. It was also confidently assumed that these changes would be speedily brought about, if not by persuasion, then by force.

History has not fulfilled these expectations, and some of the assumptions of the West are no longer widely held even in their lands of origin. The belief, even the hope, that large-scale conversions to some Christian church would transform the society of China or Japan, has long since faded. The expectation and the assurance that democracy as understood in the West was a necessary condition of all human progress and an inseparable characteristic of any modern State died harder, and indeed still lingers. The patent fact of new, powerful and technically all-too efficient authoritarian societies is unwelcome, and felt in some way to be a denial of truth, a travesty of the course of history.

If the real history of the great Oriental civilizations were better known and the true causes of their growth and stability appreciated these modern phenomena would be more easily understood. The conditions and the causes which brought democracy to the West are alike absent in the Far East; fundamental facts of geography, climate and economic circumstance determined the form which society took in China, and will continue to exercise their profound influence on all future change. These basic environmental circumstances differ very widely from those of Europe, in which continent, alone of all the five, the conception of individual liberty arose and flourished.

The great land mass of China is separated from the rest of Asia either by wide deserts or very high and difficult mountain country. It is in itself a fertile region, with a great variety of climate and soil, fit to nourish and sustain a great culture almost wholly isolated from any other. Eastward of China stretches the vast Pacific. A few small islands, the larger Japanese and Philippine groups, are all that early man could hope to reach by voyaging on that sea. The sea was the end of the world, leading nowhere and linking nothing. The Mediterranean, the central sea of the ancient western world, the bond and highway of the nations, has no counterpart in the Far East.

For very many centuries China was therefore a world apart, even when coasting voyages brought a slight link with southern Asia, and caravans could pass the Central Asiatic deserts; even then the contacts were few and their effects delayed. The Chinese people evolved the main features of their civilization alone, adapted themselves to their peculiar environment, and it was not until the adaptation had long been made, and its pattern set, that foreign influences seeped in to adorn and varify the uniform character of the Chinese culture. The basic elements of the great neolithic culture of the Western world are also found in China; but the next step, the advance to literacy, the organization of State and government, the development of abstract ideas and the conception of religion, all this was done in China, by Chinese alone, without contact with peoples of similar attainments.

For these reasons any observation of Chinese civilization shows at once two outstanding characteristics: the simple, fundamental arts, crafts, concepts and tools are similar to or identical with those of the rest of mankind; the elaborate work of art, the skilled craft, the advanced idea and the specialized instrument are always stamped with that indefinable but instantly recognizable quality which is Chinese, and which can be at once distinguished from the work of any other culture.

The Chinese peasant uses the hoe, the Yang Shao pottery of neolithic China is closely related to that of Turkestan and Eastern Russia; the Chinese clan system is familiar from other parts of the world. But the Chinese write with a brush, not a pen, their ideographs are wholly unlike other scripts; the cultivation of silk worms was a Chinese invention, and for centuries a monopoly; bronze came late to China but Chinese bronzes are in decoration and form purely Chinese, owing nothing to foreign influence. The Chinese conceptions which underlie the theory of government are unique; unlike any others, and evolved in China. The roots are deep and nourished in a soil alien to the West; the flower is therefore also strange, and hard to recognize.

When the Chinese people first become a distinct and recognizable group they are found in and around the Yellow River Valley. North of that region were barbarians, probably of nomadic culture. South of the Yellow River, in the Yang Tze Valley and what is now South China, there were peoples ethnically close to the Chinese, but culturally well below them. Chinese civilization gradually incorporated these peoples and raised them to its own level. To the north a different environment resisted for all time the spread of Chinese civilization, which with the cultivation of crops ended not far from the line of the Great Wall. The Chinese civilization thus arose in an area not, at first sight, particularly blessed by nature or easy to develop. The Yang Tze Valley and those of the South China rivers are fertile, mild in climate and far less subject to destructive floods or droughts than the Yellow River region. In those southern valleys the early inhabitants could find wild rice, and easily cultivate a variety of crops. Perhaps for this reason they were not inspired to do much more than that, like the primitive peoples of the remoter parts of South-East Asia today.

The Yellow River is a formidable and destructive stream. Flowing for hundreds of miles through the *loess* lands of North-West China it becomes silt laden and earns its name of 'Yellow'. In Western Honan it turns east, and soon enters the great plain of North-East China, where no hills confine the river, still four hundred miles from the sea. The current eases, the silt begins to settle, as the river moves east the silt deposit increases rapidly and can in a few years fill the bed. The river shifts its course and spreads like a vast marsh over the flat plains.

It was into this region, so unpromising in its primitive appearance, a wide plain covered with marshes, flooded periodically by the capricious river, but yet rich in the silt deposited by former floods, that the early Chinese first began to organize their communities into kingdoms and to evolve the early beginnings of their civilization.

Before cultivation could be carried on with any hope of security the spreading summer floods of the great river had to be confined by dykes. The marshes must be drained by canals; the dykes maintained, not for a few miles, but for scores, even for hundreds. Central control was essential. No local leader, head of clan or petty noble could find the men to build the great dykes, nor exercise authority over sufficient territory to carry out the work. The king of a large kingdom could alone command the support and control sufficient territory. Kingdoms therefore arose which were even in the earliest stage of considerable dimensions, some not much inferior to those of modern Europe.

At a very early period the states of the Chinese in the Yellow River Valley were grouped together in a loose federation, under the supreme leadership of a monarch who, strictly, was alone entitled to the rank which has been conventionally translated into English as 'king'. The king was both a ruler and a priest. He was the sole priest of the highest deities, and the authority of his inferior nobility was measured by the right to perform certain sacrifices to certain deities. Only the lord of a territory might perform those to the gods of the soil and the crops, only the supreme king those to the deity of heaven. The lesser nobility might sacrifice to their ancestors: the people, it would seem, were probably not allowed this right, and merely worshipped the spirits of the woods, rocks, springs and mountains, as indeed they still do. Thus far back in the beginnings arose the twin concepts of hierarchy and orthodox doctrine. The king was a priest, the director of irrigation and flood conservancy, the general, and the expounder of sacred matters; arbiter of heaven and earth.

Divine monarchy thus became at an early period the set pattern of Chinese government, nor was this form ever questioned until modern times. Chinese political philosophy concerned itself not with the form, but with the content of government. Monarchy was never in dispute: how to train the monarch to perform his proper duty, what system of rule he should follow, who should be the instruments of his government were the problems which for centuries were hotly debated by the Chinese philosophers. These thinkers, men whose speculations upon the nature and purpose of the universe closely paralleled those of their contemporaries the Greeks, never engaged, like the Greeks, in disputation upon forms of government. No ancient Chinese terms meaning 'democrary' or 'aristocracy' ever existed. But the Chinese sages did very actively contend for opposed systems of autocratic rule.

The Legists urged the full rigour of military despotism. 'Agriculture and war' were the purposes for which society existed; nothing that did not contribute to efficiency in agriculture and war should be tolerated by the king. The rule of this autocrat was to be upheld by a cruel and merciless code of criminal laws, to which all were to be equally subjected. Two thousand and more years before Hitler lived, the Legist statesman, the Lord of Shang, formulated the political philosophy of Fascism and put it into practice in the state of Ch'in.

Elsewhere, other doctrines were preached, and partly heeded. Confucius and his school taught that the sovereign must rule by benevolence and sincerity, using only the minimum of force. Every soldier he maintained was proof of a lack of these virtues. The perfect prince would have no need to issue orders, the perfect warrior would be victorious without fighting—because his virtue would so shine that he would be obeyed by spontaneous recognition of his merit. For man was born good and only corrupted by the evil of the world and society.

The Taoist sages despised the world, denied that government was anything but tyranny, advocated a completely passive approach to human relationships, and said that the very existence of institutions proved the decline of virtue, since when all men were sages no laws were needed. 'Govern a great state as you would cook a small fish'; i.e. hardly at all, advised one of the Taoist teachers. Mo Tze, a sublime figure, was the first pacifist statesman known to history. He taught the folly of war, deprecated the ceremony which the Confucians revered, and preached the unity of the human race. From all these diverse teachings the Chinese political system received something, but not one of them was concerned with the existence of monarchy or sought to justify or deny its value.

The Legists left to later China the theory of criminal law, harsh, severe and cruel, fit for the people but not for the scholars, except where treason to the throne was involved. By reason of the severity of this law, which was the sole concern of the State, no other law, civil, commercial or religious, flourished. Law meant what was done to vile criminals. No action not criminal was subject to law, nor concerned the State. All other disputes and causes were settled by custom wielded by the guilds, clans, associations and other bodies in which a citizen was enrolled.

The Confucians, the ultimately dominant party, gave the theory of moral government, the belief in a moral order to which the monarch must conform, and the corollary of unfailing loyalty by the subject to a just prince. From the Taoists came the Chinese conviction that government was a necessary evil, to be reduced to the minimum, and strictly confined to essential spheres of action. The Mohists, perhaps, left the military profession under that abiding stigma which it has endured in China for so many centuries. 'Good iron is not made into nails, nor good men into soldiers.'

This emphasis on content, on conduct and on doctrine, rather than on form, rank and law, marks the essential difference in spirit between Western and Chinese civilization. It is also the source of much error about Chinese history. Since the form of government was not in question it continued, very little changed for millennia. The spirit might alter, slow changes transform the character of absolute rule, but in history as formally recorded by the Chinese this was not made plain. Dynasty succeeds to dynasty; they rise, flourish and decline, and to the reader it might well seem that Amurath to Amurath succeeds with no change or advance. Yet closer study reveals that this was not at all the case. China before the Ch'in Dynasty was not an empire but a very loose federation of feudal states; power was held by hereditary aristocrats, who alone could exercise authority.

After the Ch'in and Han Revolution in 221–206 B.C., the first and still, perhaps, the greatest in Chinese history, a centralized Empire was formed governed by officers chosen by the Emperor and dismissed at his pleasure. Men of base origin rose to the highest posts. The Emperor who founded the Han was himself a peasant. The social system was transformed and wide changes in the economy took place. After the Han, in the period of weakness and partial foreign conquest, the forms of the old Empire were preserved but its power and control was gone. Dynasties rose and fell in two generations, a series of what were in fact military dictatorships are disguised as dynasties.

The Sui and the T'ang (A.D. 589–618) restored the Empire. Really they founded a new one which in many respects differed from its predecessor. The Civil Service, now recruited by public examination, replaced the haphazard choice of the earlier period. Under the Sung the Chinese Empire for a while lived under the rule of two rival parties who in turn received the patronage of the Throne, and when out of power were not slain but merely transferred to distant provinces.

The Mongols introduced a foreign bureaucracy of international adventurers—such as Marco Polo—and largely denied to their Chinese subjects the lucrative posts of authority. The Ming restored—or claimed to restore—the system of the T'ang but without its intellectual curiosity and freedom from prejudice. The Manchus, owning themselves as foreigners, and anxious to conciliate the Chinese, adopted everything that the Ming left, enshrined it with a veneration impervious to reform, and crystallized the Chinese Empire.

If even in the supposedly unchanging form of the absolute Empire there was in fact progress, regress, change and decline, so in the general civilization of China there were also great but slow alterations. Unlike Greek civilization Chinese culture did not flower at once in every field. Literature for many centuries lacked some of its greatest forms. Arts developed slowly over many periods. The drama is late in China, the art of painting very early, but not perfected until the tenth century. Poetry did not achieve its finest expression until the T'ang, architecture until the Ming. European observers first coming to China under the Manchus mistook much of what was really recent for high antiquity, since all alike was essentially so alien to their own culture, and by Chinese convention all alike was covered with the approval of Confucian orthodox doctrine.

The dynastic histories relate facts; they do not often theorize upon them, and they follow certain rigid conventions. Thus some of the most important and dynamic movements in Chinese history are disguised to make them conform with the established theory. The early foreign scholars of Chinese were easily deceived by these guides into the belief that all Chinese history had conformed to a pattern. That pattern was laid down by Confucian doctrine. The dynasty which ruled by the Mandate of Heaven was legitimate; rebellion against it, any movement of opposition, was wrong, both treasonable and wicked: unless such a rebellion succeeded. Then 'the Mandate of Heaven' had changed, and forthwith the successful rebel became the legitimate Emperor.

This theory was put forward by Mencius in a famous saying—that he had heard that a criminal had been executed, but not that a minister had assassinated his prince. The 'criminal' was the last king of the Shang Dynasty, the executioner, the first king of the succeeding Chou Dynasty, who had in fact held a post under the Shang. Thus an evil monarch, if slain or dethroned, is no longer a king, and can be treated as criminal. This is the theory of the Mandate of Heaven by which every Chinese Emperor reigned as the steward of the supreme deity, and could have his patent revoked if he did not carry out his duty.

The theory of the Mandate of Heaven has been called the Chinese Constitution, the Right of Rebellion, but it is important to see who exercised this right, who it was that rebelled successfully, and who failed to 'achieve the Mandate of Heaven'. Rebellions in China, from the foundation of the centralized Empire, fall into two classes; the great peasant risings, often associated with religious movements, and the insurrections of powerful generals. There have been many great peasant risings. There were two in the first Empire, the Han, another at the end of the T'ang Dynasty; the founder of the Ming was the leader of such a movement; another dethroned his descendants, and in the last century the T'ai P'ing rebellion conformed closely to the type. The Boxer movement at the beginning of the present century was essentially similar. Now with one exception all these great risings, which swept across the Empire, failed to overthrow the feeble and degenerate dynasties which they opposed. All were in the end defeated. They shook the Throne, but could not overturn it.

In each case the weakened dynasty a few years later succumbed to some military adventurer who had risen either in the ranks of rebellion or in the armies raised to suppress the rebels. This was the case with the Red Eyebrows and Yellow Turbans of the Han period, the rebellion of Huang Tsao in the T'ang; of Li Tze-ch'eng at the end of the Ming; and of the T'ai P'ing Heavenly King in the sixties of the last century. Only one exception occurs, the great rebellion which drove the Mongols from the throne of China and founded the Ming Dynasty.

The exception must therefore be examined to see why Ming Hung Wu succeeded when all the others failed. It was certainly not through superior education. Chu Yuan-chang, the man who reigned as Hung Wu of the Ming, was born in the poorest dregs of society. He was left a famine orphan at an early age, became a beggar, a Buddhist monk, a bandit, and then a leader of rebels. For many years he fought his way slowly to the forefront of the great movement of nationalist opposition which in the end drove out the Mongols. His success was in part due to military ability, to skilful alliances with other rebels, and above all to the fact that, leading a movement of peasants risen against the perennial injustices of landlord and official exactions, he welcomed to his standard the scholars who resented their exclusion from the government by the Mongol foreigners.

Ming Hung Wu, in fact, led more than a peasant rising, it was also a national rising, one of the very few in Chinese history before modern times. His success was due to the alliance of scholars and peasants, the two classes upon which all Chinese government must rest. The first by virtue of their education are essential to the workings of government. The second must give their consent to be governed; if they withhold it no regime can stand, if the scholars—the educated—withdraw, no system can work.

No other peasant rising commanded this dual support. The scholars drew back from the incantations and religious rites of the Red Eyebrows and Yellow Turbans. Huang Tsao failed to win their support, Li Tze-ch'eng was a bandit of renown, but no statesman; the T'ai P'ing Heavenly King by adopting a form of Christianity alienated the Confucian scholar class. Thus the scholars would always rally around the Throne, however bad, however weak, if the Throne was willing to use them. When the peasants were beaten some general could be allowed to usurp the Throne, since he would surely take over the Civil Service as a going concern, and the scholars would for their part ratify his act by declaring that the Mandate of Heaven had passed. The Mongols made the fatal mistake of both fleecing the peasants and excluding the scholars from employment and hopes of preferment. They thus raised up against them the irresistible combined force of both these classes, and were destroyed.

The Mandate of Heaven theory works out in practice as a justification for rebellions which succeed with the blessing of the literate class. Rebellions contrary to the interest of this class did not succeed. If the history of the successful founders of dynasties is examined the same rule holds true. Few of these men were peasants. Ming Hung Wu and the founder of the Han Dynasty are the exceptions. Most were generals, some few were governors or civil ministers. The great dynasties did not succeed each other immediately, but arose after an interval of some years during which power had been disputed between rival military leaders. In all cases the founders of enduring regimes were careful to conciliate the educated class and to relieve the worst distresses of the people. Those despots who seized power without the backing of the scholars did not retain it, those foreign invaders, such as the Mongols, who failed to use the scholars or relieve the peasants proved unable to endure.

The real character of Chinese rebellions is thus twofold; on the one hand there are peasant risings, which do not succeed in founding new regimes, on the other, military usurpations which obtain the backing of the Civil Service and treat the peasants with moderation. The Confucian scholar was certain that whatsoever king might reign he would be the Vicar of Bray, for he was essential to government, he was not merely the vicar of the Chinese Bray he was also the squire and the magistrate too. A Chinese change of dynasty was not a revolution; it was a change of government, sometimes carried out by force, more often by the constraint of superior power without bloodshed. Rebellions rarely overthrew dynasties, and when they did the scholars hastened to enlist under the banner of the victorious rebel and assure him of the Mandate of Heaven—provided he in turn was willing to use them and carry on the system of government they understood and served.

In the belief that this pattern of dynastic succession, which had endured so long, and so seldom suffered disturbance from the outside, would last for ever, the Confucian scholar official was content to serve even a decaying dynasty, knowing that in due course it, but not he, would be replaced. Even if nomadic invaders, such as the Manchus, should seize the Throne, they would rely on the Chinese official, and he would control their alien regime as much as he had the native one. The Mongols, who failed to play this game, paid for it with a very short term of power. The Manchus were very careful not to repeat the mistake.

When the Manchus had already held

the Throne of China for over one hundred years, and were now no longer in the full flush of their power, too satisfied, too rich, a little degenerate, less susceptible to new ideas than before, there occurred two momentous changes in the Chinese position in the world, and one far-reaching development in the internal situation. Under K'ang Hsi and his grandson Ch'ien Lung the Manchus achieved the final and definite conquest of the Mongol tribes of the north, who had for centuries raided China and at times conquered the Empire.

At the same time the advance of the Tsars across Siberia destroyed for the first time in history that great reservoir of nomadic peoples from which Europe and Asia had so long suffered. No Attila, no Tamerlane, no Genghiz Khan could evermore emerge from the steppes, 'threatening the world in high astounding terms and scourging kingdoms with his conquering sword'. The nomad power was for ever broken; neither China, India nor Europe would have to suffer the great invasions of the past. The Great Wall had become an historical monument.

The vast significance of this change, on which, for their part in it, the Manchu Emperors could justly congratulate themselves, was not understood either in China or in other countries. Gibbon could indeed, a century later, point out that barbarian invasions would no longer threaten Europe as they had threatened Rome, but the fact that China was now brought by way of Siberia into direct touch with a nation of European culture, Russia, was for long disregarded by Chinese as by Westerners. For the Chinese the end of the nomad menace appeared an unmixed blessing. The one frontier which had been in danger was now for ever quiet. The mountains to the west and south would, as before, keep off the weak and savage tribes beyond. The sea had never mattered. No enemies came from the sea; a few Japanese raids, but no real possibility of invasion or conquest. The Manchus and their Chinese subjects could well believe that peace was now certain and sure. It was hard to wrench the mind away from that northern frontier, so long the danger spot, and pay attention to the acts of a few Western ships from the unknown lands of Europe.

The first European (Portuguese) navigators to reach China had already arrived in the last years of the Ming Dynasty, and during the seventeenth and eighteenth centuries, the first two centuries of the Manchu Dynasty, they came in increasing numbers; the quality of their ships manifestly greatly improved, their military power was shown in the Philippines, in India and in the islands; yet none of these changes made any impression on the Manchus and their Chinese Confucian-trained officials. The conquest of India should have aroused the alarm of China; the size and strength of the Indiamen and ships of the line, with their guns and immense spread of sail, should have pointed a sharp contrast to the antique junks which were still the only ships the Chinese built or sailed. No such impression reached the Court. The Emperor reigned in Peking; the foreigners came only to Canton, two thousand miles away: the Court was pleased to receive gifts of clocks, watches and other ingenious products of Western manufacture. The Chinese, however, did not inquire why the 'barbarians' could make these things better than they could.

It is often argued that this strange indifference to a growing power and increasing danger was due to the effete indolence of the Manchu Court, sunk in degenerate luxury. But this picture is hardly compatible with the fact that under such Emperors as Ch'ien Lung, who reigned for sixty years in the last half of the eighteenth century, when the English were already conquering India and the great ships coming to

Canton, the Chinese armies, commanded by this active ruler, were completing a great historical task which had proved beyond the powers of the mightiest Emperors of the past—the final pacification and conquest of Mongolia.

Ch'ien Lung was no degenerate, and Chinese land power in his reign was probably greater than at any previous time. The Empire was then more populous and had had internal peace for a longer period than ever before; the reign of Ch'ien Lung was by all previous standards glorious and prosperous. Yet within a century of his death the dynasty was at its last gasp; within fifty years his successors saw the 'ocean devils'—the English in this case—invade the Empire, sack Canton, and impose the first of the Unequal Treaties.

So swift a decline, so unexpected a reversal of fortune must have some deep-seated cause. If the seaborne invaders had merely surprised an Empire unaccustomed to danger from that quarter, and thus gained some early transitory success before the Chinese could organize their defences, the history of the Far East would have been very different. But, on the contrary, the limited attacks of the European powers, their restricted objective of opening the ports to trade, their few missionaries and their still undeveloped but expanding mechanical science proved more than enough to overturn the whole Chinese society, Empire, economy and doctrine alike. Within a hundred years of the Opium War, China was in the last stages of revolution, and the rise of Communism was already the main issue.

The cause of this great upheaval therefore lay principally in China herself; the agency was Western imperialism, but the reaction was far more extensive than the force applied gave any reason to expect. The Westerners banged heavily upon the barred door of the Chinese world; to the amazement of all, within and without, the great structure, riddled by white ants, thereupon suddenly collapsed, leaving the surprised Europeans still holding the door handle.

The Chinese civilization rested, and had for centuries rested securely, on three pillars of support. First the universal Empire, which embraced the civilized world as known to the Chinese and beyond whose frontiers were only barbarians, and beyond them, faint and hardly known, remote peoples whose activities had no political significance and little cultural influence. The Empire had no official foreign relations; admitted no other State to equality, recognized no other monarch as sovereign. The Empire must be universal because it must be the only source of power, of orthodox doctrine and of civilization. Any rival or equal would be a competitor, 'two suns in one sky' and thus a source of war and disaster.

This idea had been evolved in China, in isolation; and for China in isolation it was true and valid. There is no real possibility of dividing China peacefully into two or more States. The attempt, repeated throughout history in times of confusion, has always led to war and the conquest of the weaker side. No adequate frontier between north and south can be found in the slow merging of millet lands and rice fields, without mountain barrier or desert to divide them. Deep-seated for two thousand years and rooted in their historical experience the belief that the Empire must be universal and co-extensive with civilization coloured all Chinese thinking and inhibited the establishment of normal relations with the Western powers.

The second base of the Chinese civilization was 'the fundamental occupation'—agriculture. Beyond the limits of possible farm land the Chinese neither sought to settle nor aspired to conquer. Throughout the long contest with the nomads of the Mongolian steppe the

Chinese debated the dilemma of these northern regions 'where not even a hair will grow'. Unless they were conquered and occupied the nomad menace would soon revive. If they were conquered, how could Chinese settle in a place where the soil yielded no crops? The possibility of Chinese settlers taking to the pastoral life was never regarded as a serious solution.

Chinese agriculture was, in the pre-industrial age, efficient. An immense labour conducted over centuries had transformed flood plains into farm lands, had terraced the hills and graded the valleys so that every field could be irrigated for rice cultivation. Huge works of embankment restrained the rivers. All this activity, directed by the central Empire and its officers, had made possible a large population. As the population grew in the northern plains emigrants moved south into the valleys of South China, or occupied the mountain country of the west. Even at an early time, the first centuries of the Christian era, the Chinese population was considerable.

As agriculture was the fundamental occupation, and taxation was collected in kind, the Empire very soon began to keep accurate records of the population and thus of the yield of the land. These figures, first collected during the Han period, and continued throughout the later dynasties, show that the Chinese population had already attained 46 millions in the third century A.D. By the year A.D. 754, the most prosperous period of the T'ang Dynasty, a very detailed census records the figure of 52,880,488. In 1578 a census of the Ming Dynasty gives a total of 63,601,046. Two hundred years later the annual census of 1778 gives the figure of 242,965,618 for the expressly stated total population, men, women and children.

In the Manchu period there was thus for the first time a heavy increase of population for which no new land was available. The Manchus restricted Chinese migration into the lands beyond the Wall, the original kingdom of the Manchu Dynasty, since they rightly feared that if permitted the Chinese flood would soon overwhelm the native population. The events of the last fifty years have shown that this was a correct view. Equally, since the Manchus were northern aliens and the native Ming Dynasty had found its last support in the far south, the Manchus were unwilling to see their Chinese subjects emigrate beyond the seas, fearing that such colonies would become the resort of the disaffected, and might, with foreign aid, stir up revolt at home. In this also they were correct; it was precisely in the overseas Chinese communities that the strength of the anti-Manchu movement grew and prospered, and it was such an emigrant, Dr Sun Yat-sen, who gave the movement leadership and a modern political objective—the establishment of a republic.

The Manchus were not able to prevent the growth of overseas Chinese settlement, although until the nineteenth century, when they were forced to concede the right of emigration to suit foreign interests, they did greatly restrict it. Nor was the restraint upon emigration the main cause of the very rapid growth of population during the seventeenth and eighteenth centuries. New crops had certainly some influence. The introduction of the sweet potato, of maize, and to a lesser extent of the potato had made possible the cultivation of lands unsuitable for rice or wheat.

The fact that the Manchu Empire expanded mainly by conquering nomad tribes whose habitat offered no scope for Chinese settlement was still more important. Under previous dynasties the newly-established regime found the best way to settle the soldiers and ease the pressure on the land was to send the army off to conquer and occupy new lands. The T'ang Dynasty had thus settled the south; the Ming had occupied the south-west. The Manchus excluded the Chinese from Manchuria and because their own army was required for garrison duty in the newly-conquered Empire made no conquests in the south, and in consequence little or no scope was provided for the expanding population.

Pressure of population rose steadily throughout the dynasty, and with the coming of seaborne trade the old economy was still further dislocated. The Chinese peasant had relied, apart from his fields, on the products of craftsmanship. In winter, at slack seasons, and at all times for the surplus hands, various handicrafts had provided a livelihood. With the import of manufactured goods from the West this rural industry was successively attacked, rendered unproductive, and at last in all the provinces accessible to the ports virtually extinguished.

The failure to develop a concurrent expansion of modern industry in China prevented the normal cycle of an industrial revolution from following its course. That failure was in part due to the tariff restrictions which the Western States imposed on China, preventing any protection for her nascent capitalism, but much more to the climate of opinion which formed the minds of the Chinese ruling class. The economic crisis which was swiftly approaching found the Chinese educated class wholly unprepared to meet the situation.

The third pillar of the old civilization, and the greatest of the three, was the orthodox doctrine of Confucian ethical and political teaching. Chinese civilization was for so many centuries the only higher culture known to the Chinese, Chinese thought the only field in which the powers of the intellect could be exercised, that the doctrines which enshrined this thought and which expressed this culture were *ipso facto* the only conceivable expression of civilization.

China had been both the Greece and the Rome of the Far Eastern world. She gave the thought, the arts, the laws and the system of government. Nothing essential to her civilization came from abroad, and when, many centuries after the mould had been formed, Indian Buddhism reached China, the pattern was too set to be remodelled. Buddhism, alone of all the foreign influences reaching China, made a deep impression, but Chinese culture transformed Buddhism more deeply still. India might have become the Holy Land for China, and Buddhism might have become the revealed religion reorientating the whole civilization as Christianity reformed that of the West. It did not happen.

Buddhism is not an organizing force, but a religion for the contemplative and the recluse. The Buddhist monastery is a retreat, set in the farther hills, not the centre of communal worship. Buddhism is a religion teaching the way of salvation for individuals through knowledge, not for a whole people through grace. Buddhism had no real desire to remould a culture, but merely to instruct the minds of those who were fit to receive knowledge. Moreover, even with this absence of evangelical fervour, this failure to condemn, not merely to ignore, the rival gods and the competitive ethical system, Buddhism had a harder task.

When Christianity captured the West the rival systems of polytheism and Greek philosophy were divided among themselves, without any unifying doctrine and coherent system. In China, Confucian order had long been imposed on the contest of the ancient philosophic schools. Taoism might still flourish as an esoteric sect given to the study of magic and astrology. Mohism, the Legists and many smaller sects were wholly extinct. The Confucian doctrine not only ruled the minds of men but also the Empire. To enter the Civil Service it was necessary to pass an examination concerned only to test proficiency in the Confucian philosophy and knowledge of its classical books. This system, not yet perfected when Buddhism first came to China, was one of the main contributions of the great T'ang Dynasty, which refounded and secured the Central Imperial State.

This fact, that at the very time when Buddhism was in full flood and at the height of its missionary zeal the divided Empire was once more united and stronger than ever, has had a profound influence on Chinese history. At a similar turning-point in the history of the West, it was not the Empire but the Papacy which obtained all and more than the ancient power, it was not the secular State but the theocratic Empire of the popes which arose on the ruins of the early Empire to salvage civilization and reshape the world. The rise of the T'ang Dynasty, the refounding of the Empire, stronger, more perfectly organized, and more extensive than the fallen Empire of the Han, left no room for the rise of theocracy. The Emperor was supreme: pope and king. The doctrine which served the Empire, which trained its officers, and which taught the duty of minister to prince, of prince to Emperor, and of Emperor to Heaven, this was inevitably the orthodox doctrine of the Imperial State. The Emperors of the T'ang and the people of China might, and did, devoutly follow the Buddhist teaching, but the State remained Confucian, secular and all powerful. Buddhism willingly left the world to its pomp and sought enlightenment in the hills. Confucianism secured the control of the Empire, contained Buddhism, and asserted its abiding identity with the theory and practice of the Empire.

Thus it had continued through all the changes of dynasty, which were in fact nothing but changes of government in the enduring Empire which the T'ang had built. With time and the deeply considered philosophy of the Sung thinkers to reinforce it, Confucianism had become so orthodox, so necessary and so accepted, that it was inconceivable to the Chinese that any civilization could exist without this orthodox doctrine to afford it the necessary ethical and spiritual foundation. Yet in the nineteenth century the Chinese became aware that this assumption was wrong. There were other worlds, technically superior, morally perhaps at least equal, and all animated by another philosophy.

At the time when the material power of the Empire was proved inadequate and antiquated, when its claim to universal sovereignty of the civilized world was manifestly disproved, and when the age-old economic balance of population and food supply was evidently being upset, then suddenly came the still more terrible realization that orthodoxy itself was neither infallible nor essential to civilization. There were whole worlds which knew not Confucius; great empires, more powerful than China, which derided her ethical and political system. The foreigner could point to defeat in war, to Chinese famine and poverty, and to the technical and scientific knowledge of the West, and say 'how do you justify your claim to civilization, let alone to superiority?'

The historian, writing centuries hence, will know the answer. He will suggest, perhaps, that technical skills are not good criteria of true civilization, that harmony and balance in a human society are better than restless change and the chimerical search for progress to some undefined goal. He may even decide that wide tolerance both of superstition and of unbelief is a higher good than any attempt to instil one creed, however sublime. Grace of living may seem to him better than material comfort, or even than hygiene. He may think that a system which gives men content, or even resignation, is better than one which gives them violent alternations between Utopian hopes and abysmal fear.

It did not appear to the Chinese of the second half of the nineteenth century in this light. All alike saw that the whole fabric of their culture and life was threatened by the innovations which the West either forced upon them at the cannon's mouth, or spread with the allures of commerce and education. Some thought that China must shut her doors more closely and make a supreme effort to expel the germ of change. Others, recognizing the inevitable, hoped to adopt just so much innovation as was necessary to resist the onrush of the rest. A few, a growing number, came to think that Chinese culture stood condemned; that all must be changed, that only by the outright adoption of every Western trait could the Chinese be saved. This view came to prevail. It was believed by the early revolutionaries that China must be entirely reshaped on the Western pattern, must become a nation State, and cease to pretend she was a universal Empire; must also become a democracy, because that was modern, too, and must be industrialized so as to have the strength to contend with the rest of the inhabitants of the political jungle.

These were, and perhaps to many Chinese still are, the aims of the Revolution, the imperative needs which any change must satisfy. Yet it may be asked, and perhaps the answer will explain some of the contradictions of the Chinese Revolution, whether these aims were attainable, or in the Chinese world really desirable. Could the Chinese Revolution, inevitable though it was, have made China a great democracy, and was such an end the proper aim of the Revolution?

The foundations of democracy in Western Europe and in its overseas daughter lands are not, except by later literary convention, built upon the city-state democracies of ancient Greece and Rome. Those democracies had long since perished, and the Roman World Empire that succeeded them had also collapsed before any sign of what can properly be called democracy had arisen in Western Europe, then a savage land. The origins of the institutions, as opposed to the ideas which were subsequently made to fit them, is much later. Freedom, the idea which preceded the application of democracy to European government, is not, as now understood, a classical concept. Freedom in the ancient world was the opposite of slavery, and democracy was the privilege of the free—a very small minority of the total population. Ancient democracy was more properly aristocracy.

The idea of freedom, applying to every man, not merely to a select category, would seem to have arisen in Western Europe as a consequence of the wars between different countries, and between Christian and Saracen. The English invasions of France, the Spanish war against the Moors, the Italian resistance to the German Holy Roman Emperors, from these national struggles, which to be won required the co-operation of all social classes, the sense of national freedom, freedom from foreign rule, was born and long preceded the idea of social or class freedoms. Yet once you have taught men the idea of resisting some sort of oppression, even though only foreign oppression, it is hard to make them forget the lesson. Oppressions nearer home, religious, social, political, will in turn be challenged and in turn overthrown. From wars of liberation against the Moors or the Germans it was but a step to wars for liberation of thought, or of freedom from feudal overlordship.

The idea of law, of human rights written in uncontestable covenants played a most significant part in the origin of Western democratic thinking.

So, too, in another way, did the Christian doctrine of the individual soul, the equal of any other soul. From these complex factors emerged the institutions which had in them the germs of democratic freedom. From the rediscovered literature of the classical past came a theory with which to adorn and justify these new liberties as a revival of the ancient democracy of Athens. And from the city-states, themselves a product of the Mediterranean environment, came that power of money as opposed to land which nourished the early growth of democracy, and later succumbed to the full-grown monster. The Western world came to accept this as a natural and indeed inevitable sequence of events; it was not perceived that it was in fact a series only possible in the peculiar setting of Europe, and wholly without application to other regions.

In China not one of the causes which gave birth to Western democracy operated. The universal Empire at a very early date, a date prior to the rise of the Roman Empire, extinguished for ever the rudimentary national States of the Far East and made each and all a province of the abiding Empire. War became civil war, and morally wrong. The rebel against the Empire was either a failure, in which case he was branded through history as a traitor, or successful, in which case he took over the Empire and became the legitimate ruler. In no case was he a patriot struggling for freedom. No sense of freedom as against tyranny animated the rebels of Chinese history. Their purpose was to capture the Empire, and then reform it, not to escape from it.

There were no foreign potentates against whom the Chinese struggled for liberation. The Tartars were either barbarians as long as they remained in Mongolia, or the legitimate rulers of China if they conquered the Empire in whole or in part. Only once, against the Mongols, can it be said that the Chinese rose as a people, in a national movement to win 'freedom'. The rising was successful and therefore set up once more the pattern of the Chinese Empire State with all the restoring conservative zeal of nationalism.

If no need for regaining national freedom urged the Chinese to resist absolutism, no question of religious faith or persecution ever imposed the obligation to fight for liberty of conscience. Buddhism, which ignores rather than opposes the other religions of China, did not demand from its votaries any denial of the old gods, or renunciation of Confucian ethics. The dominant state doctrine of Confucianism, which regards most supernatural beliefs as superstition, did not see any reason to demand that the people, who were not literate, nor studied the classics, should be asked to abandon their gods, or the Buddha. Confucian pedants and scholars upbraided the Court for favouring Buddhism, and at times urged the marriage of monks and nuns, as being necessary to the maintenance of the reproduction rate, but such milk and water persecutions would have been tolerance itself among the ferocious European Christians and their Moslem foes. Lacking any belief in a jealous God, the Chinese felt no jealousy towards a neighbour for his religion.

The concept of law in Chinese thought differs from its European counterpart. Law, in so far as it existed, meant criminal law; penalties, usually very harsh, inflicted on bandits, murderers, thieves and swindlers. Civil law was customary. The dispute over a contract was settled by the merchant guild; the dispute over land title or water right, by the village clan elders. Everyone was anxious to keep the official out of their business. There were no lawyers. Family jurisdiction ruled the problems of divorce, marriage, legitimacy and inheritance. Thus the government ignored the whole field of civil law, and left this to the subject and his proper and appropriate organization.

As no Church ever rose to power and influence so the question of foundations of organized benevolence and relief was also left to the private citizen and his associations. Temples were built and repaired by associations of merchants, of landowners, or by some rich official. The work of charity, which the Church first undertook in Europe before the State, was in China the responsibility of the clan or great family. If a workman sickened or lost his livelihood, he returned to his village, to claim and receive the support of his kin. If a poor boy showed promise his kin subscribed for his education so that he might become a scholar and official and so benefit the clan. The great official had his huge train of hangers-on, his relatives, clansmen and fellow countrymen who expected and received relief, employment and patronage from the great man. Few such men left huge fortunes to their descendants, for the obligation of clan support soon whittled away the largest accumulations.

There was no class of lawyers, and therefore no interpreters of rights, no claimants for greater liberty, no politicians. A Chinese official was a loyal servant of the Emperor, or else a scheming and intriguing traitor. He could not be a politician, because opposition was treason, and loyalty meant obedience. He could be, and often was a skilled and capable administrator, a wise counsellor, a perfectly devoted Civil Servant carefully guarding his precedents and citing his authorities, but never claiming rights or alleging laws.

Neither Buddhism, Confucianism, nor the ancient polytheism grouped under the name of Taoism taught with any assured voice on the life to come nor stressed the individuality of the soul, nor the importance of salvation. The concept of sin, as opposed to crime, is not known to the Far East. Therefore damnation was equally ignored. The Buddhist hell does indeed hold out a lively picture of the horrors which offenders against Buddha's rule must suffer for a long period of time. But these are penalties for crimes: for taking life, for slaying animals; and they are expiation, not damnation. All must in time rise, even from the lowest hell, to enlightenment and so to Buddhahood.

The idea of the individual, so essential to democracy, was blurred in China by the obligations and responsibility of the clan. If a man committed treason, all his kin suffered with him. If he rose to honour, all his kin rose too—'clinging to the hairs of the dragon'. Business, like government, tended to be a family matter. Men did not associate with strangers in a venture, but with their kin. Even in modern times every single person employed in the great banks, down to tea boys and coolies, was a relative of the proprietor and from his own village.

The city-State and the merchant prince were alike unknown in China. Commerce, though extensive on the great rivers and along the south coast, was at best secondary to agriculture, and mainly concerned in the exchange of luxuries. The government with its tribute system undertook the bulk transport of grain for the capital, or in time of famine. Merchants were not one of the esteemed social classes, and except in a few very large cities they catered for the needs of the adjacent country only. Early Chinese legislation, in the Han Dynasty, later often revived, was directed to restraining the rise of the merchant class, and curbing their wealth and luxury. The alliance between merchant and official which occurred to some degree tended to the enrichment and corruption of the official class rather than to the rise to political power of merchants.

The fundamental requisites for democracy were thus lacking, and to supply them would have required a revolution even more profound than that which has taken place. If the fragmentation of Europe into nation-States after the fall of Rome is the first cause of European ideas of liberty, the main preoccupation of the Chinese reformers, as of the conservatives, was how to preserve the Empire. If the Empire had been broken up, or reduced to some federal constitution, it would have at once become the prey of the imperialist powers, who eagerly anticipated such a development. The introduction of a legal system surrounded by the hoary veneration which law has acquired in Europe was obviously impossible. Any legal system had to be brand new. As such it was without sanction of custom, without prestige and without effect.

The growth of individualism in a nation which had thought in terms of clan responsibility for two or three thousand years meant a shedding of responsibility to the clan without the assumption of any duty to the community. Sun Yat-sen, thinking in political terms, compared China to a 'heap of sand', meaning that each man or family thought for themselves and had no national consciousness. This was in any case an exaggeration, but it is interesting to see that the great Chinese democrat himself saw individualism not as the necessary basis of democracy, but as a weakness in the nation-State. A heap of sand, each grain individual, but bound together by propinquity and in the mass forming a great entity is no bad simile for a democracy as understood in Europe. To Sun Yat-sen, a truer Chinese than he knew, it was an epitome of weakness, lacking the monolithic character which the authoritarian Empire should possess.

The overthrow of orthodoxy, of authoritarian doctrine, so essential if democracy is to be real, if the free play of ideas is to be allowed to form policy and advocate changes however sweeping, meant in China the simultaneous overthrow of moral standards. Confucianism was another monolith; ethics, morals, politics intricately bound together, inseparable, and clinging to the Empire like ivy to a tree. If Confucian doctrine was no longer sacred, then the bonds of filial obedience, of honesty and fair dealing were also deprived of sanctity; and if loyalty, the supreme Confucian virtue, were to be deprived of its object, the Throne, then no public virtue could survive.

The idea of patriotism, love of country, is not in China an ancient concept. Loyalty to the dynasty meant also, of course, loyalty to China, to civilization, and was so obvious a duty, so natural a sentiment of any thinking being, that it was not separated from its constituent ideas. The dynasty was China; China was the civilized world. No one would be loyal to barbarians rather than to China, and so the concept of patriotism lacked a contradiction and was left unexpressed.

Such were the causes which were leading the old Empire to destruction and revolution, and such were the obstacles in the way of a democratic State emerging from that revolution. It was thus inevitable that the revolution, which, once started by the changed circumstances of the Chinese world, could never be arrested half-way, must go through three main phases. First a period of increasing anarchy during which the pillars and bastions of the old order successively fell. Then a search, often enough down blind alleys, for a new pattern for society, a new theory of civilization. Finally, the search having shown that all other patterns were cut to suit very different communities, the reappearance of the fundamental concepts of Chinese society in a form fitted to the changed world.

These concepts are: a world sovereign authority, the old Empire, co-terminous with civilization; a balanced economy by which only luxuries and surplus products are exchanged, the basic industries and basic transportation being managed by the State; the establishment of an orthodox doctrine which harmonizes all the activities of the human being and provides a code of ethics, of politics, and of every other activity, including economics. This orthodox doctrine not only enshrines the aims and ideals of the Empire but also provides a means of selecting for its service the able and loyal members of the intellectual class.

In these old Chinese ideas, whether in their ancient form or in new guise, there is no place for freedom as the West understands it, no place for salvation as the Christian understands it, and no place for individualism as the Liberal would have it. But the old Chinese ideas fit very well to the new pattern. Loyalty to a doctrine, belief in the one world order which is civilization, and beyond which is either treason or barbarism, the duty to serve the sovereign authority, the importance of the clan—or the party—the subordinate role of the individual as such.

If it be true that the Chinese Revolution has ended in a new version of the ancient society, expanded beyond the limits of the Chinese Empire, embracing not Confucianism but Marxism, equally contemptuous of outer 'barbarians', and equally self-satisfied with the new orthodoxy which time has not yet proved inadequate, this is, seen in perspective, a very natural conclusion.

The Empire was forced into revolution not because the Chinese themselves were discontented with their way of life, but because outside changes, sea-power and navigation, the conquest of the steppes, altered the basic conditions of their autarchic world and made it too small to survive. Very well, the old Chinese world was too small, but nothing had happened to convince the Chinese of the inadequacy of their concept. The scale was too small; then make it bigger; the Chinese Communists, embracing a world authoritarian doctrine in place of one local to China, have enlarged the arena in which old Chinese ideas can once more be put into practice, in more modern guise, expanded to the new scale, but fundamentally the same ideas which inspired the builders of the Han Empire and the restorers of the T'ang.

The threatened breakdown of any political or social system and the consequent possibility of some kind of revolutionary upheaval can generally be sensed in advance. Whether they welcome or abhor the coming revolution, the ones most aware of its imminence are the more literate and intellectually acute members of a given society, the so-called "intelligentsia." In imperial China, the intelligentsia were the scholar bureaucrats. Although the emperor was the visible embodiment of the realm, they were the real keystone to its imposing political and administrative structure. Their skills guaranteed the continuity and effectiveness of the imperial system throughout the numerous dynasties that have ruled in China. No group had a greater vested interest in the survival of the traditional order and no group was more alarmed at its increasing dilapidation during the nineteenth century. In the following account, Professor Benjamin Schwartz describes the reaction of the scholar bureaucrats to the collapse of the imperial system, and the role that they and their spiritual successors played in the Chinese Revolution.

The Intelligentsia in Communist China

BENJAMIN SCHWARTZ

The word *intelligentsia,* while Russian in origin, has frequently been used with reference to Asian and other non-Western societies. Behind this usage there lurks the suggestion of some peculiar resemblance between groups in these societies and those to whom this word has been applied in Russia. Suggestive notions of this type generally are eagerly accepted and often achieve the status of journalistic clichés before being subjected to any sustained examination.

It is my own feeling that meaningful comparisons can indeed be drawn between the Russian intelligentsia and the various "intelligentsias" of Asia, but that comparison here as elsewhere involves an awareness of significant differences as well as of identities. It is precisely the juxtaposition of identity and difference which gives the comparative approach its value as a critique of generally accepted notions.

In the following pages I should like to make certain tentative comparisons between the Russian intelligentsia of the mid-nineteenth century and the Chinese intelligentsia of the twentieth century, with concluding reflections on the post-Communist situation in both countries.

Like all words of this type, the word intelligentsia has hardly been reduced to a crystalline precision, even as applied to the Russian scene. A survey of the literature on this subject indicates that the word is used with a wide range of meaning and that the outer limits of this range are by no means sharply defined. Often it seems to mean no more than the cultured stratum. All that can be said is that within this range there are certain characteristics and motifs

Reprinted by permission from *Daedalus,* Journal of the American Academy of Arts and Sciences, Boston, Mass., Vol. 89, No. 3 (Summer 1960).

[Editors' note] Notes for this selection appear at the end of the selection.

which are generally conceded by all to fit clearly within the category. Beyond this, the word refers to precisely those strata of the population in which individuality tends to be particularly well marked, so that any generalization about the "intelligentsia" as a whole, whether in Russia or China, can have no more validity than any generalization of a crude statistical type.

Finally, before we can attempt to transpose this term to China we must ask ourselves: what distinguishes the Russian intelligentsia in the narrow sense from those called intellectuals in the West? Probably it is precisely in its distinguishing features that the Russian intelligentsia is most comparable to the intelligentsias of Asia.

It is by no means easy to find these distinguishing characteristics. In the West, as in the case of the mid-nineteenth-century Russian intelligentsia, the word "intellectuals" is generally applied to that part of the educated class which claims to concern itself actively with what are considered the important issues of the age. In the West, also, the intellectuals tend to distinguish themselves from the common run of educated careerists and strictly professional men. Even the sense of alienation, which is often thought to distinguish the Russian intelligentsia, is of course an important part of the sensibility of the intellectuals in the West during the nineteenth and twentieth centuries. Finally, as has often been pointed out, the substantive ideas of the Russian intelligentsia are to a large extent the ideas of nineteenth-century Europe.

One of the obvious and most striking differences is the difference in the surrounding environment. The image of Russian society in the nineteenth century, as reflected in the writings of the *intelligenty* themselves (as here defined) is one of stark, almost melodramatic simplicity. On the one side, there is the anonymous and uniform peasant mass; on the other, the despotic state with its supporting nobility. Occasionally we find in the writings of the intelligentsia the idea of using the Tsar against the nobles or the nobles against the Tsar, or an occasional tendency to distinguish the various religious sectarian groups from the peasant mass as a whole. From the layman's point of view, however. Berdyaev's statement that "the intelligentsia was placed in a tragic position between the state and the people" holds generally true. Whether of noble, petty noble, or humble origin, the *intelligent* need not strive to achieve a stance of critical opposition—of "alienation"—from society: alienation is thrust upon him by an oppressive state and by a peasant mass which inhabits a different spiritual world. On the other hand, the Western intellectual operates in a much more complex, variegated and morally ambiguous environment. He may be vastly discontented, but he must struggle to locate the target of his animus, and he is likely to attack the status quo from many different vantage points—political, social, aesthetic, and religious.[1] Furthermore, those "conservatives" who defend the social order cannot be denied the quality of intellectuals. But in France, where the French revolutionary tradition had itself become part of the status quo, one could defend parts of the status quo in the very name of revolution.

One of the characteristics associated with this more clear-cut alienation is a tendency to "totalistic" attitudes. The nineteenth-century West, to be sure, was rich in monistic philosophic systems and totalistic socio-political theories which envisaged the total destruction of the social order and the utopian resolution of all human difficulties. As a matter of fact, the totalism of the Russian intelligentsia is set almost completely within a framework of current Western ideas, whatever may be its roots in Russian "national character" or the nature of Russian religion. Yet the Western advocates of a totalistic outlook have had considerable difficulty in relating their outlook in any clear-cut way to current social and political realities. In nineteenth-century Russia, where the "establishment" could be regarded without an excess of imagination as almost the incarnation of evil, where one could assume on Rousseauist grounds the essential goodness of the vast, silent, suffering peasantry, the expectation that a "root and branch" destruction of the establishment might lead to a total transformation of the conditions of human life recommended itself with particular force.

Such totalism is even to be found in a man like Herzen, whose major tendency, at least in the latter part of his life, seems to have been to regard all forms of authority as inherently vicious. In spite of his concern with individual liberty, he cannot easily be identified with Western "liberalism." Martin Malia draws an instructive parallel between Herzen and John Stuart Mill.[2] As Mr. Malia points out, both had an overriding concern with individual liberty, and both were concerned with the relations between liberty and social harmony. Yet Mill does not choose between a total acceptance or rejection of the whole complex socio-political machinery of Great Britain—a machinery which certainly embodied the principle of authority in various forms. Instead, he engages in a detailed and prosaic study of how the machinery of law, parliament, industrialism, etc., can be shaped to promote his ends. The pathos of Herzen, living in the same England, is quite different. To him, the whole social machinery, even in the "liberal" states of the West, is deeply interwoven with the hated authoritarianism of the past, albeit in mitigated form.

The machinery of parliaments, bureaucracy, law courts and industrial enterprise embodied the same mechanism of external authority as the hated machinery of the Petrine state.[3] Herzen would have swept away the whole evil incubus of the past. The very polarization of the Russian situation was an advantage, since one could see evil in all its stark nakedness without the disguises, mitigations and ambiguities of modern Western society.

Linked to this totalism, we find an aversion, not only for specialized, professional careers, but even for specialized and departmentalized modes of thinking. In a somewhat narrow way, the *intelligenty* of the nineteenth century (in sharp contrast to the specializing intellectuals of the twentieth) are nonprofessional universal men. If the generation of the 'sixties and 'seventies become specialists, it is mainly in the strategy and tactics of revolution. Here again, the repressive policies of the regime may have played as much of a role as did the subjective inclinations of the intelligentsia. Whatever the cause, an aversion to the demarcation of autonomous "pure" spheres of science and art seems to be one of the distinguishing characteristics of the nineteenth-century Russian intelligentsia, both in its earlier "philosophic" phase and its later social revolutionary phase.

Turning to the sphere of the "content of thought," one is struck by the dominance of certain strands of thought. (Again, this does not mean, either in the case of Russia or of China, that other ideas and other motifs are not to be found.) Mr. Karpovich, commenting on a discussion of nineteenth-century Russian thought, asks at one point, "To what extent are the ideas treated in the present discussion unique to Russia or even particularly characteristic of Russia?"[4] The same question might be asked with even greater emphasis concerning twentieth-century China. However, beyond this question there lurks another. Why are certain Western ideas received with greater enthusiasm than are others? The intellectual scene in nineteenth-century Europe is extremely complex and variegated. It abounds in mutually contradictory tendencies. One finds, however, that by some principle of selectivity certain strands of this thought find a much more fertile soil than do others. To the intellectual historian, the question, why do certain ideas enjoy more favor than others, may be just as significant as the question, is there anything uniquely Russian or Chinese in these ideas. For, behind this principle of selectivity, one may discern certain specific Russian and Chinese preoccupations. One may also legitimately speculate on the degree to which habits of thought derived from the past may have influenced the pattern of choice.

One of the dominant motifs of the thought of the nineteenth-century Russian intelligentsia is a chiliastic historicism. History was leading to a final apocalyptic event. The concept of a redemptive history, of course, is one of the most characteristic strands of nineteenth-century Western thought. In mid-nineteenth-century Russia, however, totalistic cataclysmic conceptions of history culminating in a redemptive revolution tend to dominate over gradualistic evolutionary views of historic "progress." Herzen and Belinsky, it is true, seem to have turned against their early Hegelianism, and to have rejected the authority of the "forces of history," along with other forms of authority, and to have reverted to something like the tradition of enlightenment. Yet Herzen continues to contemplate the total liberation of men from the whole social and cultural order of past and present. When one believes that a totally evil past and present can be replaced by a totally good future by means of some cataclysmic convulsion, the difference between "enlightenment" and "historicism" is somewhat reduced. In the one case, one believes in the working-out of historic forces; in the other, in the good will of enlightened men; but the mystique of the utopian revolution is shared by both.

Another dominant theme in the thought of the mid-nineteenth-century Russian intelligentsia is, of course, the theme of Populism. In Russia the peasant masses who make up the people are an entity apart from both the ruling classes and the intelligentsia, and it is easy to conceive of the people as a monolithic unity with a potential "general will" of its own. The Rousseauist conception of the people as a sort of collective whole recommends itself more than does any concept of the people as a sum total of widely differing individuals or of a plurality of varying groups. It is the people who are the victims of the present order, and it is the people who will be the object of historic redemption. There is, to be sure, a wide range of opinion as to whether the people themselves are the instrument of their own redemption. Anarchists like Bakunin would simply set loose the protean forces latent in the people. Those who participate in the movement "to the people" are also convinced that a modest educational stimulus will release such creative forces. At the other pole we have the Jacobinists, who believe that the general will of the people or the aspirations of the people must become incarnate in a guiding elite drawn from the intelligentsia itself.

The Marxism of the 'nineties, of course, rejects the concept of the united people in favor of class struggle. Instead of the "people," the urban proletariat becomes the agent of historic redemption. Yet, as has often been pointed out, the Marxist intelligentsia continues to manifest many of the tendencies we find among the Populists. As Mr. Haimson demonstrates in his *Russian Marxism and the Origins of Bolshevism*, many of the same divisions and polarities which existed in the Populist movement crop up again in Marxist guise. The two movements share a chiliastic view of history, a common espousal of "socialism" and a rejection of "capitalism." The notion of a collective general will is now attributed to the proletariat, rather than to the people as a whole, but in the Leninist transformation of Marxism we have again the Jacobinist notion of the general will incarnate in a vanguard elite. The concern of Marxism with the role of economic production would suggest a greater concern with economic development on the part of the Marxists than on the part of the Populists. (In Marxism, after all, it is the forces of production which bear the hopes of the future.) Alexander Gerschenkron [5] suggests that this was still not true of most of the pre-Soviet Marxists (with the exception of the Legal Marxists) who were much more concerned with overcoming capitalism than with economic development per se. Even if Russia did have to pass through the whole dirty work of capitalist industrialization, there was no reason for the Marxist *intelligent* to involve himself in the mess directly.

Common to most nineteenth-century intelligentsia, as already indicated, is an orientation toward socialism and a rejection of nineteenth-century economic liberalism in theory, and capitalism in practice. This is even true, as we have indicated, of the "individualist" Herzen. It is not easy to define the positive content of the word "socialism" as used by various individuals and groups. The very tendency of Populism to think of the people as a collective entity somehow places the collectivity on a higher plane than the individual. In general, collective forms of economic and social activity are associated with altruism, with social equality and humanity, and with other values. In nineteenth-century Russia this proclivity for collectivism comes, of course, to be linked with the idealization of the *obshchina*. Negatively, socialism implies a rejection of the capitalist ethic with its frank commitment to individual economic gain. Mr. Gerschenkron explains this bias toward "socialism" in terms of the confrontation of Russian "backwardness" with the humanitarian ideas of nineteenth-century Europe. Yet since the aversion to the "capitalist ethic" seems to be such a ubiquitous phenomenon, one wonders whether Weber's view that it is the emergence of the "capitalist ethic" in the West rather than its absence elsewhere which requires explanation, is not more cogent. In most cultures, ruling classes have tended to justify their existence in terms of some non-economic "service" ideal. In most cultures the systematic and rationalized pursuit of wealth has never achieved ethical respectability. Whether in addition a bias toward the "collective" exists in historic Russian culture is something the layman can hardly judge. One would hardly expect the *intelligenty*, who regarded themselves as men dedicated to universal human goals and ideal tasks, to turn their attention to industrial and mercantile activities, particularly since the emerging industrialism of nineteenth-century Russia was in their view closely linked to and supported by the whole "establishment." It is only slowly, and in the teeth of fierce opposition, that the notion of an automatic link between sheer economic growth and general cultural and political "progress" takes hold among twentieth-century liberals and Mensheviks.

In sum then, a messianic historicism, a Populism which later is channeled by some in a Marxist direction, and a general commitment to "socialism" are among the prominent strands of thought which make the outlook of the mid-nineteenth-century Russian intelligentsia eminently comparable to that of the twentieth-century Chinese intelligentsia.

Another feature of the development of the Russian intelligentsia which may be of some relevance in considering the modern intelligentsia in China is the concept of the "new man" which begins to emerge in Russia in the 'sixties. Here we have, in addition to certain general emotional attitudes and certain characteristic patterns of thought, a certain image of the ideal individual. The new man is the man who consciously converts himself into an instrument of his social and political goals, who allows no personal aims, no scruple, no sentiment or whims to deflect him from his historic role. He also has an unflagging faith in the purity of his own motives, in the rightness of his own ideas. As has often been pointed out, this image of the "new man" is probably the direct ancestor of the image of "Bolshevik man."

These, in short, are some of the characteristics of the Russian intelligentsia which strike the student of modern China as relevant for purposes of comparison.

Something must be said at the outset about the entirely different cultural backgrounds of the two "intelligentsias." Terms such as "backward" and "traditional" may be used to describe both cultures by those who judge everything by the yardstick of economic development. It flatters our "modernist" chauvinism to assume that the only important fact about premodern cultures is the fact of their non-modernity. Yet the differences in the concrete historic antecedents of the two intelligentsias are enormous. Whether the Russian intelligentsia has no tradition or is deeply rooted in Russia's religious tradition, it is certainly a new social fact in the nineteenth century (or, at the earliest, the late eighteenth century).

In China the twentieth-century intelligentsia is to a considerable extent spiritual as well as biological heir of the scholar-official class that has dominated the political and intellectual life of China for centuries. When one attempts to summarize some of the characteristics of the traditional Chinese elite, one finds some traits that remind us, curiously enough, of the Russian intelligentsia, as well as some significant differences. First of all, one notes that this elite is a small group hovering above a huge peasant mass—a group which very self-consciously distinguishes itself from the mass and tends to regard the "people" as a sort of monolithic entity. In sharp contrast to the Russian intelligentsia, the elite is also the state-service class. Its Confucian ideology inculcates an exaltation of public service, so that the class bears within itself centuries of bureaucratic experience.

Yet before one hastens to a too facile definition of the twentieth-century Chinese intelligentsia as simply a temporarily displaced bureaucratic class, it should also be noted that within the millennial history of China strong strands of alienation, withdrawal, and protest are evident. The image of Confucius himself is that of a man who cannot be "used" by any of the prevailing regimes of his time, in spite of his eminent qualifications for public vocation. The tradition of protest, withdrawal, and even of martyrdom is an integral part of the Confucian tradition. Furthermore, beyond the Confucian tradition, there lies the Taoist tradition with its derisively anarchistic contempt for the state and all its *Wichtigtuerei*, and its tradition of Buddhist withdrawal. None of this implies "democracy." However, it also does not necessarily imply a predisposition to modern totalitarianism.

Again it should be noted that within the Confucian tradition there is something like a concern for the minimal economic welfare of the masses—a certain idea of noblesse oblige vis-à-vis the "people" (*min*). This principle of obligation was, of course, unaccompanied by any concept of "popular sovereignty" or of the latent wisdom of the unenlightened masses. Political initiative could come only from the enlightened superior men. Nevertheless, the idea of obligation to the people provided a sort of traditional nucleus around which certain types of modern populism could grow.

Deeply engrained in the tradition we find an emphatic anti-mercantile orientation and an exaltation of the public service career over all private wealth-gathering activities. One even finds an equivalent to the dream of the *mir*. In spite of the fact that the organization of land tenure in China has been for centuries more or less "private," there has been a persistent tradition within the heart of Confucianism that this situation represented a falling away from the primeval communal organization of agriculture represented by the so-called "well-field" [6] system. The Confucian dream of utopia is of a docile peasant commune benignly supervised by the sage official. One must add that the "well-field" utopia had no anti-authoritarian or anti-hierarchic implications. On the contrary, it was an integral part of the idealization of the ancient Chou feudal order. None of this, however, implied a very favorable disposition toward any "capitalist ethic."

We are not attempting to suggest here any fundamental affinity between the scholar-official class of traditional China and the Russian intelligentsia of the nineteenth century. I am merely suggesting that there existed in the tradition of this class certain dispositions which may have favored the emergence in the Chinese intelligentsia of tendencies not unlike those of the Russian intelligentsia. Of course, many of the characteristics of the twentieth-century intelligentsia must be explained in terms of discontinuity with the past—in terms of the tragic situation within which this intelligentsia now finds itself.

For convenience, we may divide the twentieth-century Chinese intelligentsia into three generations. There is the transitional generation of the late nineteenth and early twentieth century—men whose roots lie deep in the old culture, who have undergone the regimen of a traditional education, but who are already deeply shaken by the desperate plight of their state and society. They are already prepared to consider new institutions and foreign ideas, and yet are in many ways still part of the older literati.[7] The crucial break comes with the student generation of the beginning of the twentieth century, many of whose members must be considered as the first truly "alienated" intellectuals of modern China. The third significant generation is the student generation of the May 4th period (1919), men now in their fifties and sixties. It is in this generation that the basic intellectual tendencies of recent decades crystallize.

The first generation is not yet alienated from the state. It still yearns to be "used," and still hopes to save the state from ruin. It is in the next generation that we see the emergence of the mystique of revolution. Only with this generation can we begin to speak with any assurance of a modern intelligentsia. It is also this generation which faces the enormous frustrations of the post-1911 period. There are many who enter political life in the sordid "warlord" period, but a clear cleavage appears between the "political opportunists" (*cheng k'o*) who serve, and the alienated intelligentsia who remain outside. The May 4th generation does become involved in the revolutionary activities of the Kuomintang-Communist alliance. Some of its members, in fact, become the bureaucracy of the Nationalist government. Yet many remain an alienated intelligentsia. The reasons for this are complex. The bulk of the intelligentsia had become committed in the period between 1919 and 1927 to a generally "left" and anti-traditional stance. There were, to be sure, individuals like Liang Sou-ming,

Feng Yu-Lan and others who may be considered the Chinese equivalents of the Russian Slavophiles. They continued to stress the validity, even the superiority, of certain Chinese values and often used Western conceptions to support their views. Like many of the Slavophiles, however, they carefully dissociated themselves from the official neo-traditionalism of the established regime and remained on the outside. The Nationalist government under Chiang K'ai-shek attempted to create a neo-traditional underpinning for its nationalism and regarded the stance of the intelligentsia with profound mistrust. With the growth of the Maoist phase of Chinese Communism, we have a small segment of the intelligentsia who, as it were, simultaneously became professional revolutionaries and acting functionaries of a Communist state within a state.

In this light one does not feel that the alienation of the Chinese intelligentsia from the state is as decisive or as profound as that of the mid-nineteenth-century Russian intelligentsia. During the period between the 1911 revolution and the rise of the Nationalist government, the intelligentsia does not confront the massive power of a state from which it feels alienated. It rather confronts the disintegration of the state. Under the Nationalist government it is indeed alienated, yet the officialdom of that government is drawn from a background identical with its own, and there are many elements who live in a twilight world between government and intelligentsia, in spite of their mutual hostility. With the rise of the Communist state many of the intelligentsia were prepared to serve without undergoing the enormous adjustment from the life of "professional revolutionary" to bureaucratic functionary which we find among the old Bolsheviks in Russia. One can speak of the alienation of the twentieth-century Chinese intelligentsia from the state. It is, however, a much more ambiguous and less decisive alienation than that of its Russian nineteenth-century counterpart.

Nevertheless, it is interesting to note that, as in the case of the Russian intelligentsia, the best of the Chinese intelligentsia do not turn their attention to the "practical" professions, in spite of a concerted effort on the part of the late Ch'ing government and later of the Nationalist government to channel it in this direction. A "bureaucratic" career, academic life or writing seem to be the major alternatives, and the choice determines one's future alignment as a conformist or as an alienated intellectual. To a considerable extent one must bear in mind the persistence of traditional habits of thought and behavior. Beyond this, we find, as in the Russian case, a reluctance among the more sensitive to commit themselves to specialized professions while the major agonizing problems of their society remain unsolved.

It is in terms of emotional attitudes and certain dominant strains of thought that the resemblance between the two intelligentsias becomes most striking. Thus the major general drift in the long run is toward "totalistic" attitudes. It is curious to note in this connection that the first important Western influences in China were preponderantly an Anglo-American liberalism running up through the philosophy of John Dewey, whose current Chinese spokesman, Hu Shih, has become in the Chinese view almost the embodiment of American liberalism. It is important to note that even Western liberalism, particularly if one includes certain French variants of that vague concept, can assume in a Chinese environment a totalistic coloration, and that this aspect is completely compatible with a total negation of the past. Some "Liberals" like the early Ch'en Tu-hsiu remind us more of Russian nihilists of the Pisarev variety than of

Western liberals. To Ch'en, "democracy" and "science" were corrosives for dissolving the traditional culture. Again, the mystique of the redemptive revolution is not incompatible with all forms of liberalism, and it is very much a part of Sun Yat-sen's early "liberalism." The very fact that the 1911 revolution in itself actually solved so little created a bias toward total solutions. In the early 'twenties, we find the famous controversy on "isms" and "problems," which deals most explicitly with the issue of total versus "pluralistic" solutions of China's difficulties. On the one side we have Hu Shih's espousal of Dewey's insistence on attention to concrete, discrete problems and on rejection of all-embracing nostrums. On the other side we have the new converts to Marxism-Leninism, who insist that the social order is a whole and who ardently look for an all-embracing solution. In the long run, the Marxist-Leninist claim to a monistic interpretation of the world and a monistic resolution of China's difficulties weighed heavily in its favor during the 'twenties and 'thirties. The widespread acceptance of a Marxist-Leninist world image, it must be added, however, did not imply a necessary commitment to the Communist party. To the very brink of 1949 a large part of the Chinese intelligentsia remained apart from the Communist movement itself. In China, however, as in Russia, the chiliastic view of "progress" was to dominate gradualistic, evolutionary views.

Something like a populist strain emerges quite early in China, although it is speedily overwhelmed by the influence of the Russian Revolution. The young nationalists of the early twentieth century were quick to add the rhetoric of Rousseau to the rhetoric of Mencius. At first this populism assumes a Western liberal coloration and is closely linked to political democracy. Later, in the case of Sun Yat-sen himself, this gives way to the notion of a "general will," which becomes embodied in a party elite. That anarchistic variety of populism which insists on the spontaneous initiative of the people itself does not become deeply entrenched in China. In seeking Chinese equivalents to the movement "to the people," one can only point to isolated instances such as T'ao Hsing-chih, Liang Sou-ming, James Yen, etc. These men, however, are basically gradualistic and wedded to an educationalist approach. One can perhaps discern something like a movement "to the people" within the framework of Chinese Communism during the Yenan period. Yet this takes place within a bureaucratized and institutionalized framework which makes the analogy quite specious. Whatever may be their subjective attitudes, the young cadres approach the peasants as functionaries of a regime. In general, it is the elitist rather than the anarchist brand of populism which wins in China. The notion that popular energies are to be tapped is certainly present, but it is linked to the conviction that their energies must be guided by those who know.

Although Marxism-Leninism after 1919 cuts short the emergence of a full-blown Populism, it would appear that Lenin's successes in China owe as much to those attitudes he shares with the Russian elitist Populists (e.g., Tkachev) as to those which divide him from them. In the long run, the notion of a vanguard elite embodying a general will is of more importance than the notion of the messianic role of the urban proletariat, although the dogma is retained. The Leninist theory of imperialism and the Leninist commitment to industrialism do indeed add something which is very relevant to the deep nationalist and social resentments of the Chinese intelligentsia, but the whole Maoist development of Chinese Communism might well have dispensed with Marxist class assumptions were it not for the international aspects of the movement.

The word "socialism" also won speedy approval in China. Sun Yat-sen begins to equate "socialism" with "the people's livelihood" at a very early point in his career, in spite of his Anglo-American background. At the same time he begins to turn his attention to the problem of "skipping the capitalist stage." Socialism had won general approval in the most diverse circles long before the October Revolution. One may assume that the same factors are operative here as in the Russian case, perhaps reinforced by the implicit anti-capitalism of the traditional culture.[8]

All of these similarities tend to support the thesis that the phenomenon of the intelligentsia is a universal concomitant of the confrontation of a "traditional" society with the modern West. There are, however, certain overriding differences which seem to me to loom quite as large as the similarities.

Viewed from the vantage point of China, Russian culture, even in its earliest form, must be viewed as an "affiliate" of the West. The Orthodox religion draws on the same Judaic and Hellenic sources as does the Christianity of the West.

Furthermore, the Russian enlightened nobility of the eighteenth century was in sustained contact with Western ideas, while the Petrine state had taken on many of the aspects of contemporary Western states. The language itself with its Indo-European structure and its heritage of Judeo-Hellenic concepts lends itself easily to the transposition of Western ideas. Thus, in spite of the gloomy social and political scene, the nineteenth-century Russian intellectual and literary development seem to mark the culmination of a slow growth, rather than a complete traumatic break. The intelligentsia may be in revolt, but it is in revolt within a continuous historic process. This feeling of culmination is most spectacularly manifest in the magnificent literature of the nineteenth century, with its universal appeal. Yet even the literature of ideas, whatever its lack of originality, is forceful, eloquent and self-assured. The Russian intelligentsia is reasonably at home in its intellectual and spiritual world.

In twentieth-century China we have not only a profound social and political crisis but also the seeming collapse of a culture and a whole system of values. The twentieth-century intelligentsia feverishly seeks Western values to fill the vacuum, and it must attempt to convey its ideas in a linguistic medium which is saturated with the categories of thought of an entirely different culture. It is no wonder that the writings of this intelligentsia frequently seem naïve and awkward to the Western eye. The Chinese *intelligent* is much less self-assured than his Russian counterpart, much less at home in the world of ideas he has come to embrace, much more in need of a new orientation.

One aspect of this cultural crisis is the burning need for a sense of national dignity. One of the striking aspects of the mid-nineteenth-century Russian intelligentsia is its disassociation from nationalistic aspirations. This intelligentsia may be nationalistic in certain senses of the word, but it is entirely divorced [9] from the aspirations and ambitions of the Russian state. On the contrary, it deplores the success of Russian arms and the oppressive extension of the influence of the Tsarist state abroad. (The sense of deprivation of dignity deriving from the loss of a sense of identification with state power does not exist for this intelligentsia.) In China, the preoccupation with the weakness and decay of the state is a common denominator uniting the last generation of the literati with the "alienated" generations of the twentieth century. To use the old Chinese phrase, "enriching the state and strengthening the military" [10] is an aim shared by the most diverse ideological commitments. The deep resentment and sense of deprivation of dignity which accompany China's political humiliation become the personal resentments of the whole articulate class.

This difference reflects an enormous difference in the objective situation of the two societies. In spite of Russian backwardness, the Petrine reforms had made Russia one of the great powers of nineteenth-century Europe. The economic bases of this power may have been woefully weak, but this did not prevent the chancelleries of Europe from dreading the expansion of Russia's might. At the very end of the nineteenth century, the Chinese reformer K'ang Yu-wei could still offer Peter the Great as a model for his emperor. Not until the rise of Stalin in the twentieth century did a new sense of Russia's weakness as a world power become felt, and this sense was closely associated with a consciousness of her economic backwardness. The spokesmen of Stalinism are acutely and morbidly concerned with building up the power and prestige of the Russian state. In this light, the new ruling class hardly resemble the spiritual descendants of the nineteenth-century intelligentsia. Even Lenin, in spite of his strategic use of nationalism, in this respect still seems to belong to the older intelligentsia.

In China, the growing success of Marxism-Leninism owed much to the appeal of the Leninist theory of imperialism, particularly those parts that are related most directly to national resentments. While Marxism had been accepted in Russia in its original cosmopolitan garb, Marxism-Leninism was widely received in China only after it had already been bent to the uses of a resentful nationalism.

Most of the factors discussed above would seem to argue for a more compliant attitude toward totalitarianism on the part of the Chinese intelligentsia. The ardent cravings for a sense of national dignity, the deep spiritual insecurity, the long tradition of authoritarianism, the orientation toward state service, the rejection of "capitalist" values, etc., would all appear to have created preconditions for a complaisant attitude toward the Communist state.

While such a conclusion would provide a neat ending to this paper and conform to our usual expectations concerning "Asia," life continues to be richer than gray theory, and the intelligentsia in China tends to betray the unpredictable qualities of the intelligentsia elsewhere.

It is true that a considerable portion of this intelligentsia either actively welcomed the Communist assumption of power in 1949 or acquiesced in it. This is in striking contrast to the situation in Russia during the October Revolution. There, a large part of the political intelligentsia was anti-Bolshevik, and a considerable body of nonpolitical intellectuals was also anti-Bolshevik. These facts, of course, reflect the enormous changes in the intellectual evolution of Russia during the late nineteenth and early twentieth centuries, which are discussed by Mr. Pipes in this issue. In twentieth-century Russia, the intelligentsia as here defined had become only one strand in a variegated intellectual stratum that included nonpolitical intellectuals, professionals who certainly considered themselves *intelligenty*, and groups advocating a wide gamut of opinion among the more politically minded intelligentsia. There was certainly no automatic polarization toward Leninism. Whatever similar tendencies existed in twentieth-century China, they were inhibited by the dire conditions created by the Japanese War and by the polarization of power toward the two political forces which enjoyed a military base. Efforts on the part of intellectuals to create "third force" groups were rendered ineffectual by this situation.

It must also be emphasized that in committing itself to the new regime the Chinese intelligentsia as a whole had not necessarily committed itself to the type of totalitarianism which subsequently emerged. It had committed itself to the acceptance of certain Marxist-Leninist premises. Many hoped that the totalism of the new regime would remain within a more moderate "new democratic" framework. It is doubtful whether they anticipated the whole fantastic "thought reform" experience.

The regime itself directed some of its most concentrated efforts to the psychological transformation of the intelligentsia. The whole "thought reform" experiment would seem to reflect an ambition to achieve by new methods a form of monolithic "internalized" consensus such as the Soviet Union has never achieved. On the other hand, the fact that much of this effort has been focused on the intelligentsia would indicate a deep and abiding suspicion of that stratum in spite of its complaisant attitude.

In certain respects the present situations in Russia and China cannot be compared. In the forty years since the October Revolution there has emerged in the Soviet Union a new professional and managerial class that hardly remembers the past. The Soviet Union has attempted with some success to appropriate the word intelligentsia to designate this class. A similar attempt is taking place in China, but as of the present, the word intelligentsia still refers to the older intelligentsia, and whatever professional class exists is still drawn from "older cadres," who, in the view of the regime, share many of the shortcomings of the intelligentsia as a whole.

It has perhaps not been sufficiently noted that the redefinition of the term intelligentsia has not solved all problems even in the Soviet Union. The professional classes may be acquiescent but they nevertheless lay claim to private preserves of specialized knowledge which, in some sense, place them beyond the pale of party omniscience. There is, of course, a long history of efforts to "bolshevize" the professionals in the Soviet Union. At the moment, the regime would seem to have made a tacit surrender to the expertise of those professions it regards as essential, in return for unquestioning political loyalty.

In China, on the other hand, the renewed attack on the intelligentsia since 1957 has involved an attack on the pretensions of experts and professionals as one of its integral ingredients. At the moment, the Chinese regime is rather more impressed with the "defects" common to the literary and academic intelligentsia and the professionals than with the differences between them. Both groups have dared to pit their judgments against the judgments of the Party on the basis of criteria external to the Party line. At the moment a concerted effort is under way to reduce the stature of both the professional and the nonprofessional intelligentsia.

The particular animus of the regime toward the intelligentsia, however defined, reflects of course the shocking revelations of the "Hundred Flowers" episode of 1956–1957. This is hardly the place to consider the reasons behind this episode or the intentions of the Communist Party leadership. For our purposes it is sufficient to note that the official slogan, "Let the hundred flowers bloom, let the hundred schools contend," was meant to suggest to the intelligentsia that a certain undefined area of free discussion was now open to them. What emerged was highly revealing. Not only were the literary and cultural policies of the regime attacked; not only did professionals challenge the authority of the Party within their areas of competence; but there were even those who raised the dread question of power itself. The very grounds on which the Communist Party claimed political infallibility were challenged. In raising the question of political power, the "civism" of the Chinese intelligentsia went beyond anything that has occurred in the Soviet Union since the inauguration of the "Khrushchev era." The numbers involved were, of course, small. One may surmise, however, that those who had the courage to speak represented many more who were silent. It is also true that this is still the older pre-1949 intelligentsia.[11] Yet it was also the intelligentsia who had embraced the new regime and gone through all the ardors of "thought reform." Any notion of a natural proclivity on their part for limitless dosages of totalitarianism must certainly be rejected after this episode. The regime may ultimately reduce this older intelligentsia to complete silence and create a completely conditioned "new intelligentsia." One can no longer speak, however, of any unlimited receptivity on its part to totalitarian control.

In the end, the intelligentsia in China as in Russia remains an incalculable and unknown quantity. Chinese totalitarianism, like Russian totalitarianism, may have had one of its roots in the past propensities of the intelligentsia of these countries.[12] In China, in fact, the top leadership of the Communist party itself derives from that stratum. Yet the relations of the intelligentsia as a whole to the regime remain a problem. A rejection of Western liberalism does not necessarily imply a willing acceptance of totalitarian extremism in all its forms. Between the two lies a whole spectrum of possibilities. If the intelligentsia in twentieth-century China dreamed of "totalistic" solutions, this does not mean that the form of totalism that actually emerged has proven completely palatable. If it rejected Western liberalism, its exposure to certain habits of thought derived from liberalism has made a certain impression on it.

Finally, as to the extent that the traditional culture of China has shaped the present scene, it must be pointed out that this culture contained many conflicting tendencies. It is easy enough to draw up a list of such predispositions as may have facilitated the acceptance of totalitarianism, yet within the older culture one can also discern predispositions that run in quite another direction. These tendencies were not "liberal," or "democratic," or "individualistic," and it would be wrong to romanticize them. They did involve, however, the concept of moral norms that transcend the arbitrary will of the ruler, and even the concept of what might be called the civic obligation of the literati to defend these norms. In China, as elsewhere, the intelligentsia remains an unpredictable variable.

REFERENCES

[1] One may say that the "alienation" of Kafka and Kierkegaard is essentially more radical than anything one can find among the Russian intelligentsia. It is, however, different in kind.

[2] Martin E. Malia, "Herzen and the Peasant Commune," in *Continuity and Change in Russian and Soviet Thought* (Cambridge: The Harvard University Press, 1955), pp. 214–215.

[3] The unenthusiastic attitude of many of the intelligentsia toward modern Western political, economic and social development may spring in part from their implicit awareness that, in a sense, the Petrine state with its bureaucratic, military, and police machine was the most "modern" and "rationalized" sector of Russian society.

[4] Michael Karpovich, "Review," in *Continuity and Change,* p. 279.

[5] Alexander Gerschenkron, "Nineteenth Century Intellectual History," in *Continuity and Change,* p. 33.

[6] The "well-field" in the idealized schematic account of Mencius consists of eight plots of land assigned to eight families surrounding a ninth plot, the yield of which sustained the lord. Presumably the plots were cultivated collectively.

[7] Men such as K'ang Yu-wei, Yen Fu, Liang Ch'i-ch'ao, Chang Ping-lin, etc.

[8] This account of trends in China is extremely crude. Economic liberalism, Chinese equivalents of Slavophilism, and all sorts of other tendencies are to be found. We are here simply isolating certain major tendencies.

[9] Here again we are excluding such men as Aksakov and Katkov from our definition of intelligentsia.

[10] An aim, incidentally, rejected by the main line of Confucian orthodoxy. This intelligentsia does not suffer from the sense of loss of dignity that marks the Chinese intelligentsia after the collapse of the Chinese Imperial State.

[11] Actually, however, an astonishing number of students became deeply involved in these criticisms.

[12] I continue to believe that this was one of the roots of totalitarianism, and to reject the currently fashionable theory that totalitarianism is merely a "function" of the "industrialization process."

The Chinese Communist Party, in the years immediately after its founding in 1921, took its tactical and ideological cues from the Third International, essentially the organ of the Russian state concerned with supporting revolutionary movements in foreign countries. According to the then current Bolshevik theory of revolution in the underdeveloped countries of Asia, as this theory was propounded by Lenin himself, the leading revolutionary element was at that time not the small, often embryonic proletariat, but rather the emerging nationalistic bourgeoisie. And in China the nationalist bourgeoisie were represented by the Kuomintang. The Chinese Communists were thus instructed to cooperate closely with the Kuomintang and even to join it in an effort to accelerate the pace of China's political and economic development to a point where a working-class revolution would be feasible.

As for the peasantry, constituting the vast majority of the population, their revolutionary potential was discounted by all. Thus when Mao Tse-tung, one of the founders of the Chinese Communist Party, discovered, in the course of a visit to Hunan Province in 1925, that the peasants there were capable of taking revolutionary political action quite on their own initiative, it was in the nature of a revelation for him. His consequent efforts to develop a revolutionary strategy based on the peasantry were rejected by his comrades even after Chiang Kai-shek broke the alliance with the Communists, thus ending the possibility of cooperating with the bourgeoisie and demonstrating the incorrectness of the strategy advocated by the Third International. Several years were to pass before Mao's ascendancy within the party was such that his theories could become the basis for its official strategy. As the first coherent statement on the revolutionary potential of the peasantry in an underdeveloped country, the "Report on an Investigation of the Peasant Movement in Hunan," is one of the truly significant documents on revolution in the twentieth century.

Report on an Investigation of the Peasant Movement in Hunan, March 1927

MAO TSE-TUNG

[Translator's note.] This article was written as a reply to the carping criticisms both inside and outside the Party then being levelled at the peasants' revolutionary struggle. Comrade Mao Tse-tung spent thirty-two days in Hunan Province making an investigation and wrote this report in order to answer these criticisms. The Right opportunists in the Party, headed by Chen Tu-hsiu, would not accept his views and stuck to their own wrong ideas. Their chief error was that, frightened by the reactionary trend in the Kuomintang, they dared not support the great revolutionary struggles of the peasants which had erupted or were erupting. To appease the Kuomintang, they preferred to desert the peasantry, the chief ally in the revolution, and thus left the working class and the Communist Party isolated and without help. It was mainly because it was able to exploit this weakness within the Communist Party that the Kuomintang dared to betray the revolution, launch its "party purge" and make war on the people in the summer of 1927.

From *The Selected Works of Mao Tse-tung,* Vol. I, Peking Foreign Language Press, 1965.

The Importance of the Peasant Problem

During my recent visit to Hunan I made a first-hand investigation of conditions in the five counties of Hsiangtan, Hsianghsiang, Hengshan, Liling and Changsha. In the thirty-two days from January 4 to February 5, I called together fact-finding conferences in villages and county towns, which were attended by experienced peasants and by comrades working in the peasant movement, and I listened attentively to their reports and collected a great deal of material. Many of the hows and whys of the peasant movement were the exact opposite of what the gentry in Hankow and Changsha are saying. I saw and heard of many strange things of which I had hitherto been unaware. I believe the same is true of many other places, too. All talk directed against the peasant movement must be speedily set right. All the wrong measures taken by the revolutionary authorities concerning the peasant movement must be speedily changed. Only thus can the future of the revolution be benefited. For the present upsurge of the peasant movement is a colossal event. In a very short time, in China's central, southern and northern provinces, several hundred million peasants will rise like a mighty storm, like a hurricane, a force so swift and violent that no power, however great, will be able to hold it back. They will smash all the trammels that bind them and rush forward along the road to liberation. They will sweep all the imperialists, warlords, corrupt officials, local tyrants and evil gentry into their graves. Every revolutionary party and every revolutionary comrade will be put to the test, to be accepted or rejected as they decide. There are three alternatives. To march at their head and lead them? To trail behind them, gesticulating and criticizing? Or to stand in their way and oppose them? Every Chinese is free to choose, but events will force you to make the choice quickly.

Get Organized!

The development of the peasant movement in Hunan may be divided roughly into two periods with respect to the counties in the province's central and southern parts where the movement has already made much headway. The first, from January to September of last year, was one of organization. In this period, January to June was a time of underground activity, and July to September, when the revolutionary army was driving out Chao Heng-ti, one of open activity. During this period, the membership of the peasant associations did not exceed 300,000–400,000, the masses directly under their leadership numbered little more than a million, there was as yet hardly any struggle in the rural areas, and consequently there was very little criticism of the associations in other circles. Since its members served as guides, scouts and carriers of the Northern Expeditionary Army, even some of the officers had a good word to say for the peasant associations. The second period, from last October to January of this year, was one of revolutionary action. The membership of the associations jumped to two million and the masses directly under their leadership increased to ten million. Since the peasants generally enter only one name for the whole family on joining a peasant association, a membership of two million means a mass following of about ten million. Almost half the peasants in Hunan are now organized. In counties like Hsiangtan, Hsianghsiang, Liuyang, Changsha, Liling, Ninghsiang, Pingkiang, Hsiangyin, Hengshan, Hengyang, Leiyang, Chenhsien and Anhua, nearly all the peasants have combined in the peasant associations or have come under their leadership. It was on the strength of their extensive organization that the peasants went into action and within four months brought about a great revolution in the countryside, a revolution without parallel in history.

Down with the Local Tyrants and Evil Gentry! All Power to the Peasant Associations!

The main targets of attack by the peasants are the local tyrants, the evil gentry and the lawless landlords, but in passing they also hit out against patriarchal ideas and institutions, against the corrupt officials in the cities and against bad practices and customs in the rural areas. In force and momentum the attack is tempestuous; those who bow before it survive and those who resist perish. As a result, the privileges which the feudal landlords enjoyed for thousands of years are being shattered to pieces. Every bit of the dignity and prestige built up by the landlords is being swept into the dust. With the collapse of the power of the landlords, the peasant associations have now become the sole organs of authority and the popular slogan "All power to the peasant associations" has become a reality. Even trifles such as a quarrel between husband and wife are brought to the peasant association. Nothing can be settled unless someone from the peasant association is present. The association actually dictates all rural affairs, and, quite literally, "whatever it says, goes". Those who are outside the associations can only speak well of them and cannot say anything against them. The local tyrants, evil gentry and lawless landlords have been deprived of all right to speak, and none of them dares even mutter dissent. In the face of the peasant associations' power and pressure, the top local tyrants and evil gentry have fled to Shanghai, those of the second rank to Hankow, those of the third to Changsha and those of the fourth to the county towns, while the fifth rank and the still lesser fry surrender to the peasant associations in the villages.

"Here's ten yuan. Please let me join the peasant association," one of the smaller of the evil gentry will say.

"Ugh! Who wants your filthy money?" the peasants reply.

Many middle and small landlords and rich peasants and even some middle peasants, who were all formerly opposed to the peasant associations, are now vainly seeking admission. Visiting various places, I often came across such people who pleaded with me, "Mr. Committeeman from the provincial capital, please be my sponsor!"

In the Ching Dynasty, the household census compiled by the local authorities consisted of a regular register and "the other" register, the former for honest people and the latter for burglars, bandits and similar undesirables. In some places the peasants now use this method to scare those who formerly opposed the associations. They say, "Put their names down in the other register!"

Afraid of being entered in the other register, such people try various devices to gain admission into the peasant associations, on which their minds are so set that they do not feel safe until their names are entered. But more often than not they are turned down flat, and so they are always on tenterhooks; with the doors of the association barred to them, they are like tramps without a home or, in rural parlance, "mere trash". In short, what was looked down upon four months ago as a "gang of peasants" has now become a most honourable institution. Those who formerly prostrated themselves before the power of the gentry now bow before the power of the peasants. No matter what their identity, all admit that the world since last October is a different one.

"It's Terrible!" or "It's Fine!"

The peasants' revolt disturbed the gentry's sweet dreams. When the news from the countryside reached the cities, it caused immediate uproar among the gentry. Soon after my arrival in Changsha, I met all sorts of people and picked up a good deal of gossip. From the middle social strata upwards to the Kuomintang right-wingers, there was not a single person who did not sum up the whole business in the phrase, "It's terrible!" Under the impact of the views of the "It's terrible!" school then flooding the city, even quite revolutionary-minded people became down-hearted as they pictured the events in the countryside in their mind's eye; and they were unable to deny the word "terrible". Even quite progressive people said, "Though terrible, it is inevitable in a revolution." In short, nobody could altogether deny the word "terrible". But, as already mentioned, the fact is that the great peasant masses have risen to fulfil their historic mission and that the forces of rural democracy have risen to overthrow the forces of rural feudalism. The patriarchal-feudal class of local tyrants, evil gentry and lawless landlords has formed the basis of autocratic government for thousands of years and is the cornerstone of imperialism, warlordism and corrupt officialdom. To overthrow these feudal forces is the real objective of the national revolution. In a few months the peasants have accomplished what Dr. Sun Yat-sen wanted, but failed, to accomplish in the forty years he devoted to the national revolution. This is a marvellous feat never before achieved, not just in forty, but in thousands of years. It's fine. It is not "terrible" at all. It is anything but "terrible". "It's terrible!" is obviously a theory for combating the rise of the peasants in the interests of the landlords; it is obviously a theory of the landlord class for preserving the old order of feudalism and obstructing the establishment of the new order of democracy, it is obviously a counterrevolutionary theory. No revolutionary comrade should echo this nonsense. If your revolutionary viewpoint is firmly established and if you have been to the villages and looked around, you will undoubtedly feel thrilled as never before. Countless thousands of the enslaved—the peasants—are striking down the enemies who battened on their flesh. What the peasants are doing is absolutely right; what they are doing is fine! "It's fine!" is the theory of the peasants and of all other revolutionaries. Every revolutionary comrade should know that the national revolution requires a great change in the countryside. The Revolution of 1911 did not bring about this change, hence its failure. This change is now taking place, and it is an important factor for the completion of the revolution. Every revolutionary comrade must support it, or he will be taking the stand of counter-revolution.

The Question of "Going Too Far"

Then there is another section of people who say, "Yes, peasant associations are necessary, but they are going rather too far." This is the opinion of the middle-of-the-roaders. But what is the actual situation? True, the peasants are in a sense "unruly" in the countryside. Supreme in authority, the peasant association allows the landlord no say and sweeps away his prestige. This amounts to striking the landlord down to the dust and keeping him there. The peasants threaten, "We will put you in the other register!" They fine the local tyrants and evil gentry, they demand contributions from them, and they smash their sedan-chairs. People swarm into the houses of local tyrants and evil gentry who are against the peasant association, slaughter their pigs and consume their grain. They even loll for a minute or two on the ivory-inlaid beds belonging to the young ladies in the households of the local tyrants and evil gentry. At the slightest provocation they make arrests, crown the arrested with tall paper-hats, and parade them through the villages, saying, "You dirty landlords, now you know who we are!" Doing whatever they like and turning everything upside down, they have created a kind of terror in the countryside. This is what some people call "going too far", or "exceeding the proper limits in righting a wrong", or "really too much". Such talk may seem plausible, but in fact it is wrong. First, the local tyrants, evil gentry and lawless landlords have themselves driven the peasants to this. For ages they have used their power to tyrannize over the peasants and trample them underfoot; that is why the peasants have reacted so strongly. The most violent revolts and the most serious disorders have invariably occurred in places where the local tyrants, evil gentry and lawless landlords perpetrated the worst outrages. The peasants are clear-sighted. Who is bad and who is not, who is the worst and who is not quite so vicious, who deserves severe punishment and who deserves to be let off lightly—the peasants keep clear accounts, and very seldom has the punishment exceeded the crime. Secondly, a revolution is not a dinner party, or writing an essay, or painting a picture, or doing embroidery; it cannot be so refined, so leisurely and gentle, so temperate, kind, courteous, restrained and magnanimous. A revolution is an insurrection, an act of violence by which one class overthrows another. A rural revolution is a revolution by which the peasantry overthrows the power of the feudal landlord class. Without using the greatest force, the peasants cannot possibly overthrow the deep-rooted authority of the landlords which has lasted for thousands of years. The rural areas need a mighty revolutionary upsurge, for it alone can rouse the people in their millions to become a powerful force. All the actions mentioned here which have been labelled as "going too far" flow from the power of the peasants, which has been called forth by the mighty revolutionary upsurge in the countryside. It was highly necessary for such things to be done in the second period of the peasant movement, the period of revolutionary action. In this period it was necessary to establish the absolute authority of the peasants. It was necessary to forbid malicious criticism of the peasant associations. It was necessary to overthrow the whole authority of the gentry, to strike them to the ground and keep them there. There is revolutionary significance in all the actions which were labelled as "going too far" in this period. To put it bluntly, it is necessary to create terror for a while in every rural area, or otherwise it would be impossible to suppress the activities of the counter-revolutionaries in the countryside or overthrow the authority of the gentry. Proper limits have to be exceeded in order to right a wrong, or else the wrong cannot be righted. Those who talk about the peasants "going too far" seem at first sight to be different from those who say "It's terrible!" as mentioned earlier, but in essence they proceed from the same standpoint and likewise voice a landlord theory that upholds the interests of the privileged classes. Since this theory impedes the rise of the peasant movement and so disrupts the revolution, we must firmly oppose it.

The "Movement of the Riffraff"

The right-wing of the Kuomintang says, "The peasant movement is a movement of the riffraff, of the lazy peasants." This view is current in Changsha.

When I was in the countryside, I heard the gentry say, "It is all right to set up peasant associations, but the people now running them are no good. They ought to be replaced!" This opinion comes to the same thing as what the right-wingers are saying; according to both it is all right to have a peasant movement (the movement is already in being and no one dare say otherwise), but they say that the people running it are no good and they particularly hate those in charge of the associations at the lower levels, calling them "riffraff". In short, all those whom the gentry had despised, those whom they had trodden into the dirt, people with no place in society, people with no right to speak, have now audaciously lifted up their heads. They have not only lifted up their heads but taken power into their hands. They are now running the township peasant associations (at the lowest level), which they have turned into something fierce and formidable. They have raised their rough, work-soiled hands and laid them on the gentry. They tether the evil gentry with ropes, crown them with tall paper-hats and parade them through the villages. (In Hsiangtan and Hsianghsiang they call this "parading through the township" and in Liling "parading through the fields".) Not a day passes but they drum some harsh, pitiless words of denunciation into these gentry's ears. They are issuing orders and are running everything. Those who used to rank lowest now rank above everybody else; and so this is called "turning things upside down".

Vanguards of the Revolution

Where there are two opposite approaches to things and people, two opposite views emerge. "It's terrible!" and "It's fine!", "riffraff" and "vanguards of the revolution"—here are apt examples.

We said above that the peasants have accomplished a revolutionary task which had been left unaccomplished for many years and have done an important job for the national revolution. But has this great revolutionary task, this important revolutionary work, been performed by all the peasants? No. There are three kinds of peasants, the rich, the middle and the poor peasants. The three live in different circumstances and so have different views about the revolution. In the first period, what appealed to the rich peasants was the talk about the Northern Expeditionary Army's sustaining a crushing defeat in Kiangsi, about Chiang Kai-shek's being wounded in the leg and flying back to Kwangtung, and about Wu Pei-fu's recapturing Yuehchow. The peasant associations would certainly not last and the Three People's Principles could never prevail, because they had never been heard of before. Thus an official of the township peasant association (generally one of the "riffraff" type) would walk into the house of a rich peasant, register in hand, and say, "Will you please join the peasant association?" How would the rich peasant answer? A tolerably well-behaved one would say, "Peasant association? I have lived here for decades, tilling my land. I never heard of such a thing before, yet I've managed to live all right. I advise you to give it up!" A really vicious rich peasant would say, "Peasant association! Nonsense! Association for getting your head chopped off! Don't get people into trouble!" Yet, surprisingly enough, the peasant associations have now been established several months, and have even dared to stand up to the gentry. The gentry of the neighbourhood who refused to surrender their opium pipes were arrested by the associations and paraded through the villages. In the county towns, moreover, some big landlords were put to death, like Yen Jung-chiu of Hsiangtan and Yang Chih-tse of Ninghsiang. On the anniversary of the October Revolution, at the time of the anti-British rally and of the great celebrations of the victory of the Northern Expedition, tens of thousands of peasants in every township, holding high their banners, big and small, along with their carrying-poles and hoes, demonstrated in massive, streaming columns. It was only then that the rich peasants began to get perplexed and alarmed. During the great victory celebrations of the Northern Expedition, they learned that Kiukiang had been taken, that Chiang Kai-shek had not been wounded in the leg and that Wu Pei-fu had been defeated after all. What is more, they saw such slogans as "Long live the Three People's Principles!" "Long live the peasant associations!" and "Long live the peasants!" clearly written on the "red and green proclamations". "What?" wondered the rich peasants, greatly perplexed and alarmed, " 'Long live the peasants!' Are these people now to be regarded as emperors?" So the peasant associations are putting on grand airs. People from the associations say to the rich peasants, "We'll enter you in the other register," or, "In another month, the admission fee will be ten yuan a head!" Only under the impact of all this are the rich peasants tardily joining the associations, some paying fifty cents or a yuan for admission (the regular fee being a mere ten coppers), some securing admission only after asking other people to put in a good word for them. But there are quite a number of die-hards who have not joined to this day. When the rich peasants join the associations, they generally enter the name of some sixty or seventy year-old member of the family, for they are in constant dread of "conscription". After joining, the rich peasants are not keen on doing any work for the associations. They remain inactive throughout.

How about the middle peasants? Theirs is a vacillating attitude. They think that the revolution will not bring them much good. They have rice cooking in their pots and no creditors knocking on their doors at midnight. They, too, judging a thing by whether it ever existed before, knit their brows and think to themselves, "Can the peasant association really last?" "Can the Three People's Principles prevail?" Their conclusion is, "Afraid not!" They imagine it all depends on the will of Heaven and think, "A peasant association? Who knows if Heaven wills it or not?" In the first period, people from the association would call on a middle peasant, register in hand, and say, "Will you please join the peasant association?" The middle peasant would reply, "There's no hurry!" It was not until the second period, when the peasant associations were already exercising great power, that the middle peasants came in. They show up better in the associations than the rich peasants but are not as yet very enthusiastic; they still want to wait and see. It is essential for the peasant associations to get the middle peasants to join and to do a good deal more explanatory work among them.

The poor peasants have always been the main force in the bitter fight in the countryside. They have fought militantly through the two periods of underground work and of open activity. They are the most responsive to Communist Party leadership. They are deadly enemies of the camp of the local tyrants and evil gentry and attack it without the slightest hesitation. "We joined the peasant association long ago," they say to the rich peasants, "why are you still hesitating?" The rich peasants answer mockingly, "What is there to keep you from joining? You people have neither a tile over your heads nor a speck of land under your feet!" It is true the poor peasants are not afraid of losing anything. Many of them really have "neither a tile over their heads nor a speck of land under their feet". What, indeed, is there to keep them from joining the associations? According to the survey of Changsha County, the poor peasants comprise 70 per cent, the middle peasants 20 per cent, and the landlords and the rich peasants 10 per cent of the population in the rural areas. The 70 per cent, the poor peasants, may be sub-divided into two categories, the utterly destitute and the less destitute. The utterly destitute, comprising 20 per cent, are the completely dispossessed, that is, people who have neither land nor money, are without any means of livelihood, and are forced to leave home and become mercenaries or hired labourers or wandering beggars. The less destitute, the other 50 per cent, are the partially dispossessed, that is, people with just a little land or a little money who eat up more than they earn and live in toil and distress the year round, such as the handicraftsmen, the tenant-peasants (not including the rich tenant-peasants) and the semi-owner-peasants. This great mass of poor peasants, or altogether 70 per cent of the rural population, are the backbone of the peasant associations, the vanguard in the overthrow of the feudal forces and the heroes who have performed the great revolutionary task which for long years was left undone. Without the poor peasant class (the "riffraff", as the gentry call them), it would have been impossible to bring about the present revolutionary situation in the countryside, or to overthrow the local tyrants and evil gentry and complete the democratic revolution. The poor peasants, being the most revolutionary group, have gained the leadership of the peasant associations. In both the first and second periods almost all the chairmen and committee members in the peasant associations at the lowest level were poor peasants (of the officials in the township associations in Hengshan County the utterly destitute comprise 50 per cent, the less destitute 40 per cent, and poverty-stricken intellectuals 10 per cent). Leadership by the poor peasants is absolutely necessary. Without the poor peasants there would be no revolution. To deny their role is to deny the revolution. To attack them is to attack the revolution. They have never been wrong on the general direction of the revolution. They have discredited the local tyrants and evil gentry. They have beaten down the local tyrants and evil gentry, big and small, and kept them underfoot. Many of their deeds in the period of revolutionary action, which were labelled as "going too far", were in fact the very things the revolution required. Some county governments, county headquarters of the Kuomintang and county peasant associations in Hunan have already made a number of mistakes; some have even sent soldiers to arrest officials of the lower-level associations at the landlords' request. A good many chairmen and committee members of township associations in Hengshan and Hsianghsiang Counties have been thrown in jail. This mistake is very serious and feeds the arrogance of the reactionaries. To judge whether or not it is a mistake, you have only to see how joyful the lawless landlords become and how reactionary sentiments grow, wherever the chairmen or committee members of local peasant associations are arrested. We must combat the counter-revolutionary talk of a "movement of riffraff" and a "movement of lazy peasants" and must be especially careful not to commit the error of helping the local tyrants and evil gentry in their attacks on the poor peasant class. Though a few of the poor peasant leaders undoubtedly did have shortcomings, most of them have changed by now. They themselves are energetically prohibiting gambling and suppressing banditry. Where the peasant association is powerful, gambling has stopped altogether and banditry has vanished. In some places it is literally true that people do not take any articles left by the wayside and that doors are not bolted at night. According to the Hengshan survey, 85 per cent of the poor peasant leaders have made great progress and have proved themselves capable and hard-working. Only 15 per cent retain some bad habits. The most one can call these is "an unhealthy minority", and we must not echo the local tyrants and evil gentry in undiscriminatingly condemning them as "riff-raff". This problem of the "unhealthy minority" can be tackled only under the peasant associations' own slogan of "strengthen discipline", by carrying on propaganda among the masses, by educating the "unhealthy minority", and by tightening the associations' discipline; in no circumstances should soldiers be arbitrarily sent to make such arrests as would damage the prestige of the poor peasants and feed the arrogance of the local tyrants and evil gentry. This point requires particular attention.

Fourteen Great Achievements

Most critics of the peasant associations allege that they have done a great many bad things. I have already pointed out that the peasants' attack on the local tyrants and evil gentry is entirely revolutionary behaviour and in no way blameworthy. The peasants have done a great many things, and in order to answer people's criticism we must closely examine all their activities, one by one, to see what they have actually done. I have classified and summed up their activities of the last few months; in all, the peasants under the leadership of the peasant associations have the following fourteen great achievements to their credit.

1. **Organizing the peasants into peasant associations.** This is the first great achievement of the peasants. In counties like Hsiangtan, Hsianghsiang and Hengshan, nearly all the peasants are organized and there is hardly a remote corner where they are not on the move; these are the best places. In some counties, like Yiyang and Huajung, the bulk of the peasants are organized, with only a small section remaining unorganized; these places are in the second grade. In other counties, like Chengpu and Lingling, while a small section is organized, the bulk of the peasants remain unorganized; these places are in the third grade. Western Hunan, which is under the control of Yuan Tsu-ming, has not yet been reached by the associations' propaganda, and in many of its counties the peasants are completely unorganized; these form a fourth grade. Roughly speaking, the counties in central Hunan, with Changsha as the centre, are the most advanced, those in southern Hunan come second, and western Hunan is only just beginning to organize. According to the figures compiled by the provincial peasant association last November, organizations with a total membership of 1,367,727 have been set up in thirty-seven of the province's seventy-five counties. Of these members about one million were organized during October and November when the power of the associations rose high, while up to September the membership had only been 300,000–400,000. Then came the two months of December and January, and the peasant movement continued its brisk growth. By the end of January the membership must have reached at least two million. As a family generally enters only one name when joining and has an average of five members, the mass following must be about ten million. This astonishing and accelerating rate of expansion explains why the local tyrants, evil gentry and corrupt officials have been isolated, why the public has been amazed at how completely the world has changed since the peasant movement, and why a great revolution has been wrought in the countryside. This

is the first great achievement of the peasants under the leadership of their associations.

2. **HITTING THE LANDLORDS POLITICALLY.** Once the peasants have their organization, the first thing they do is to smash the political prestige and power of the landlord class, and especially of the local tyrants and evil gentry, that is, to pull down landlord authority and build up peasant authority in rural society. This is a most serious and vital struggle. It is the pivotal struggle in the second period, the period of revolutionary action. Without victory in this struggle, no victory is possible in the economic struggle to reduce rent and interest, to secure land and other means of production, and so on. In many places in Hunan like Hsianghsiang, Hengshan and Hsiangtan Counties, this is of course no problem since the authority of the landlords has been overturned and the peasants constitute the sole authority. But in counties like Liling there are still some places (such as Liling's western and southern districts) where the authority of the landlords seems weaker than that of the peasants but, because the political struggle has not been sharp, is in fact surreptitiously competing with it. In such places it is still too early to say that the peasants have gained political victory; they must wage the political struggle more vigorously until the landlords' authority is completely smashed. All in all, the methods used by the peasants to hit the landlords politically are as follows:

Checking the accounts. More often than not the local tyrants and evil gentry have helped themselves to public money passing through their hands, and their books are not in order. Now the peasants are using the checking of accounts as an occasion to bring down a great many of the local tyrants and evil gentry. In many places committees for checking accounts have been established for the express purpose of settling financial scores with them, and the first sign of such a committee makes them shudder. Campaigns of this kind have been carried out in all the counties where the peasant movement is active; they are important not so much for recovering money as for publicizing the crimes of the local tyrants and evil gentry and for knocking them down from their political and social positions.

Imposing fines. The peasants work out fines for such offences as irregularities revealed by the checking of accounts, past outrages against the peasants, current activities which undermine the peasant associations, violations of the ban on gambling and refusal to surrender opium pipes. This local tyrant must pay so much, that member of the evil gentry so much, the sums ranging from tens to thousands of yuan. Naturally, a man who has been fined by the peasants completely loses face.

Levying contributions. The unscrupulous rich landlords are made to contribute for poor relief, for the organization of co-operatives or peasant credit societies, or for other purposes. Though milder than fines, these contributions are also a form of punishment. To avoid trouble, quite a number of landlords make voluntary contributions to the peasant associations.

Minor protests. When someone harms a peasant association by word or deed and the offence is a minor one, the peasants collect in a crowd and swarm into the offender's house to remonstrate with him. He is usually let off after writing a pledge to "cease and desist", in which he explicitly undertakes to stop defaming the peasant association in the future.

Major demonstrations. A big crowd is rallied to demonstrate against a local tyrant or one of the evil gentry who is an enemy of the association. The demonstrators eat at the offender's house, slaughtering his pigs and consuming his grain as a matter of course. Quite a few such cases have occurred. There was a case recently at Machiaho, Hsiangtan County, where a crowd of fifteen thousand peasants went to the houses of six of the evil gentry and demonstrated; the whole affair lasted four days during which more than 130 pigs were killed and eaten. After such demonstrations, the peasants usually impose fines.

"Crowning" the landlords and parading them through the villages. This sort of thing is very common. A tall paper-hat is stuck on the head of one of the local tyrants or evil gentry, bearing the words "Local tyrant so-and-so" or "So-and-so of the evil gentry". He is led by a rope and escorted with big crowds in front and behind. Sometimes brass gongs are beaten and flags waved to attract people's attention. This form of punishment more than any other makes the local tyrants and evil gentry tremble. Anyone who has once been crowned with a tall paper-hat loses face altogether and can never again hold up his head. Hence many of the rich prefer being fined to wearing the tall hat. But wear it they must, if the peasants insist. One ingenious township peasant association arrested an obnoxious member of the gentry and announced that he was to be crowned that very day. The man turned blue with fear. Then the association decided not to crown him that day. They argued that if he were crowned right away, he would become case-hardened and no longer afraid, and that it would be better to let him go home and crown him some other day. Not knowing when he would be crowned, the man was in daily suspense, unable to sit down or sleep at ease.

Locking up the landlords in the county jail. This is a heavier punishment than wearing the tall paper-hat. A local tyrant or one of the evil gentry is arrested and sent to the county jail; he is locked up and the county magistrate has to try him and punish him. Today the people who are locked up are no longer the same. Formerly it was the gentry who sent peasants to be locked up, now it is the other way round.

"Banishment". The peasants have no desire to banish the most notorious criminals among the local tyrants and evil gentry, but would rather arrest or execute them. Afraid of being arrested or executed, they run away. In counties where the peasant movement is well developed, almost all the important local tyrants and evil gentry have fled, and this amounts to banishment. Among them, the top ones have fled to Shanghai, those of the second rank to Hankow, those of the third to Changsha, and of the fourth to the county towns. Of all the fugitive local tyrants and evil gentry, those who have fled to Shanghai are the safest. Some of those who fled to Hankow, like the three from Huajung, were eventually captured and brought back. Those who fled to Changsha are in still greater danger of being seized at any moment by students in the provincial capital who hail from their counties; I myself saw two captured in Changsha. Those who have taken refuge in the county towns are only of the fourth rank, and the peasantry, having many eyes and ears, can easily track them down. The financial authorities once explained the difficulties encountered by the Hunan Provincial Government in raising money by the fact that the peasants were banishing the well-to-do, which gives some idea of the extent to which the local tyrants and evil gentry are not tolerated in their home villages.

Execution. This is confined to the worst local tyrants and evil gentry and is carried out by the peasants jointly with other sections of the people. For instance, Yang Chih-tse of Ninghsiang, Chou Chia-kan of Yuehyang and Fu Tao-nan and Sun Po-chu of Huajung were shot by the government authorities at the insistence of the peasants and other sections of the people. In the case of Yen Jung-chiu of Hsiangtan, the peasants and other sections of the people compelled the magistrate to agree to hand him over, and the peasants themselves executed him. Liu Chao of Ninghsiang was killed by the peasants. The execution of Peng Chih-fan of Liling and Chou Tien-chueh and Tsao Yun of Yiyang is pending, subject to the decision of the "special tribunal for trying local tyrants and evil gentry". The execution of one such big landlord reverberates through a whole county and is very effective in eradicating the remaining evils of feudalism. Every county has these major tyrants, some as many as several dozen and others at least a few, and the only effective way of suppressing the reactionaries is to execute at least a few in each county who are guilty of the most heinous crimes. When the local tyrants and evil gentry were at the height of their power, they literally slaughtered peasants without batting an eyelid. Ho Mai-chuan, for ten years head of the defence corps in the town of Hsinkang, Changsha County, was personally responsible for killing almost a thousand poverty-stricken peasants, which he euphemistically described as "executing bandits". In my native county of Hsiangtan, Tang Chun-yen and Lo Shu-lin who headed the defence corps in the town of Yintien have killed more than fifty people and buried four alive in the fourteen years since 1913. Of the more than fifty they murdered, the first two were perfectly innocent beggars. Tang Chun-yen said, "Let me make a start by killing a couple of beggars!" and so these two lives were snuffed out. Such was the cruelty of the local tyrants and evil gentry in former days, such was the White terror they created in the countryside, and now that the peasants have risen and shot a few and created just a little terror in suppressing the counter-revolutionaries, is there any reason for saying they should not do so?

. . . .

7. **OVERTHROWING THE CLAN AUTHORITY OF THE ANCESTRAL TEMPLES AND CLAN ELDERS, THE RELIGIOUS AUTHORITY OF TOWN AND VILLAGE GODS, AND THE MASCULINE AUTHORITY OF HUSBANDS.** A man in China is usually subjected to the domination of three systems of authority: (1) the state system (political authority), ranging from the national, provincial and county government down to that of the township; (2) the clan system (clan authority), ranging from the central ancestral temple and its branch temples down to the head of the household; and (3) the supernatural system (religious authority), ranging from the King of Hell down to the town and village gods belonging to the nether world, and from the Emperor of Heaven down to all the various gods and spirits belonging to the celestial world. As for women, in addition to being dominated by these three systems of authority, they are also dominated by the men (the authority of the husband). These four authorities—political, clan, religious and masculine—are the embodiment of the whole feudal-patriarchal system and ideology, and are the four thick ropes binding the Chinese people, particularly the peasants. How the peasants have overthrown the political authority of the landlords in the countryside has been described above. The political authority of the landlords is the backbone of all the other systems of authority. With that overturned, the clan authority, the religious authority and the authority of the husband all begin to totter. Where the peasant association is powerful, the clan elders and administrators of temple funds no longer dare oppress those lower in the clan hierarchy or embezzle

clan funds. The worst clan elders and administrators, being local tyrants, have been thrown out. No one any longer dares to practise the cruel corporal and capital punishments that used to be inflicted in the ancestral temples, such as flogging, drowning and burying alive. The old rule barring women and poor people from the banquets in the ancestral temples has also been broken. The women of Paikuo in Hengshan County gathered in force and swarmed into their ancestral temple, firmly planted their backsides in the seats and joined in the eating and drinking, while the venerable clan bigwigs had willy-nilly to let them do as they pleased. At another place, where poor peasants had been excluded from temple banquets, a group of them flocked in and ate and drank their fill, while the local tyrants and evil gentry and other long-gowned gentlemen all took to their heels in fright. Everywhere religious authority totters as the peasant movement develops. In many places the peasant associations have taken over the temples of the gods as their offices. Everywhere they advocate the appropriation of temple property in order to start peasant schools and to defray the expenses of the associations, calling it "public revenue from superstition". In Liling County, prohibiting superstitious practices and smashing idols have become quite the vogue. In its northern districts the peasants have prohibited the incense-burning processions to propitiate the god of pestilence. There were many idols in the Taoist temple at Fupoling in Lukou, but when extra room was needed for the district headquarters of the Kuomintang, they were all piled up in a corner, big and small together, and no peasant raised any objection. Since then, sacrifices to the gods, the performance of religious rites and the offering of sacred lamps have rarely been practised when a death occurs in a family. Because the initiative in this matter was taken by the chairman of the peasant association, Sun Hsiao-shan, he is hated by the local Taoist priests. In the Lungfeng Nunnery in the North Third District, the peasants and primary school teachers chopped up the wooden idols and actually used the wood to cook meat. More than thirty idols in the Tungfu Monastery in the Southern District were burned by the students and peasants together, and only two small images of Lord Pao were snatched up by an old peasant who said, "Don't commit a sin!" In places where the power of the peasants is predominant, only the older peasants and the women still believe in the gods, the younger peasants no longer doing so. Since the latter control the associations, the overthrow of religious authority and the eradication of superstition are going on everywhere. As to the authority of the husband, this has always been weaker among the poor peasants because, out of economic necessity, their womenfolk have to do more manual labour than the women of the richer classes and therefore have more say and greater power of decision in family matters. With the increasing bankruptcy of the rural economy in recent years, the basis for men's domination over women has already been weakened. With the rise of the peasant movement, the women in many places have now begun to organize rural women's associations; the opportunity has come for them to lift up their heads, and the authority of the husband is getting shakier every day. In a word, the whole feudal-patriarchal system and ideology is tottering with the growth of the peasants' power. At the present time, however, the peasants are concentrating on destroying the landlords' political authority. Wherever it has been wholly destroyed, they are beginning to press their attack in the three other spheres of the clan, the gods and male domination. But such attacks have only just begun, and there can be no thorough overthrow of all three until the peasants have won complete victory in the economic struggle. Therefore, our present task is to lead the peasants to put their greatest efforts into the political struggle, so that the landlords' authority is entirely overthrown. The economic struggle should follow immediately, so that the land problem and the other economic problems of the poor peasants may be fundamentally solved. As for the clan system, superstition, and inequality between men and women, their abolition will follow as a natural consequence of victory in the political and economic struggles. If too much of an effort is made, arbitrarily and prematurely, to abolish these things, the local tyrants and evil gentry will seize the pretext to put about such counter-revolutionary propaganda as "the peasant association has no piety towards ancestors", "the peasant association is blasphemous and is destroying religion" and "the peasant association stands for the communization of wives", all for the purpose of undermining the peasant movement. A case in point is the recent events at Hsianghsiang in Hunan and Yanghsin in Hupeh, where the landlords exploited the opposition of some peasants to smashing idols. It is the peasants who made the idols, and when the time comes they will cast the idols aside with their own hands; there is no need for anyone else to do it for them prematurely. The Communist Party's propaganda policy in such matters should be, "Draw the bow without shooting, just indicate the motions." It is for the peasants themselves to cast aside the idols, pull down the temples to the martyred virgins and the arches to the chaste and faithful widows; it is wrong for anybody else to do it for them. . . .

8. SPREADING POLITICAL PROPAGANDA. Even if ten thousand schools of law and political science had been opened, could they have brought as much political education to the people, men and women, young and old, all the way into the remotest corners of the countryside, as the peasant associations have done in so short a time? I don't think they could. "Down with imperialism!" "Down with the warlords!" "Down with the corrupt officials!" "Down with the local tyrants and evil gentry!"—these political slogans have grown wings, they have found their way to the young, the middle-aged and the old, to the women and children in countless villages, they have penetrated into their minds and are on their lips. For instance, watch a group of children at play. If one gets angry with another, if he glares, stamps his foot and shakes his fist, you will then immediately hear from the other the shrill cry of "Down with imperialism!"

. . . .

Some of the peasants can also recite Dr. Sun Yat-sen's Testament. They pick out the terms "freedom", "equality", "the Three People's Principles" and "unequal treaties" and apply them, if rather crudely, in their daily life. When somebody who looks like one of the gentry encounters a peasant and stands on his dignity, refusing to make way along a pathway, the peasant will say angrily, "Hey, you local tyrant, don't you know the Three People's Principles?" Formerly when the peasants from the vegetable farms on the outskirts of Changsha entered the city to sell their produce, they used to be pushed around by the police. Now they have found a weapon, which is none other than the Three People's Principles. When a policeman strikes or swears at a peasant selling vegetables, the peasant immediately answers back by invoking the Three People's Principles and that shuts the policeman up.

Once in Hsiangtan when a district peasant association and a township peasant association could not see eye to eye, the chairman of the township association declared, "Down with the district peasant association's unequal treaties!"

The spread of political propaganda throughout the rural areas is entirely an achievement of the Communist Party and the peasant associations. Simple slogans, cartoons and speeches have produced such a widespread and speedy effect among the peasants that every one of them seems to have been through a political school. According to the reports of comrades engaged in rural work, political propaganda was very extensive at the time of the three great mass rallies, the anti-British demonstration, the celebration of the October Revolution and the victory celebration for the Northern Expedition. On these occasions, political propaganda was conducted extensively wherever there were peasant associations, arousing the whole countryside with tremendous effect. From now on care should be taken to use every opportunity gradually to enrich the content and clarify the meaning of those simple slogans.

9. **PEASANT BANS AND PROHIBITIONS.** When the peasant associations, under Communist Party leadership, establish their authority in the countryside, the peasants begin to prohibit or restrict the things they dislike. Gaming, gambling and opium-smoking are the three things that are most strictly forbidden.

Gaming. Where the peasant association is powerful, mahjong, dominoes and card games are completely banned.

The peasant association in the 14th District of Hsianghsiang burned two basketfuls of mahjong sets.

If you go to the countryside, you will find none of these games played; anyone who violates the ban is promptly and strictly punished.

Gambling. Former hardened gamblers are now themselves suppressing gambling; this abuse, too, has been swept away in places where the peasant association is powerful.

Opium-smoking. The prohibition is extremely strict. When the peasant association orders the surrender of opium pipes, no one dares to raise the least objection. In Liling County one of the evil gentry who did not surrender his pipes was arrested and paraded through the villages.

The peasants' campaign to "disarm the opium-smokers" is no less impressive than the disarming of the troops of Wu Pei-fu and Sun Chuan-fang by the Northern Expeditionary Army. Quite a number of venerable fathers of officers in the revolutionary army, old men who were opium-addicts and inseparable from their pipes, have been disarmed by the "emperors" (as the peasants are called derisively by the evil gentry). The "emperors" have banned not only the growing and smoking of opium, but also trafficking in it. A great deal of the opium transported from Kweichow to Kiangsi via the counties of Paoching, Hsianghsiang, Yuhsien and Liling has been intercepted on the way and burned. This has affected government revenues. As a result, out of consideration for the army's need for funds in the Northern Expedition, the provincial peasant association ordered the associations at the lower levels "temporarily to postpone the ban on opium traffic". This, however, has upset and displeased the peasants.

There are many other things besides these three which the peasants have prohibited or restricted, the following being some examples:

The flower drum. Vulgar performances are forbidden in many places.

Sedan-chairs. In many counties, especially Hsianghsiang, there have been cases of smashing sedan-chairs. The peasants, detesting the people who use this conveyance, are always ready to smash the chairs, but the peasant associations forbid them to do so. Association officials tell the peasants, "If you smash the chairs, you only save the rich money and lose the carriers their jobs. Will that not hurt our own people?" Seeing the point, the peasants have worked out a new tactic—considerably to increase the fares charged by the chair-carriers so as to penalize the rich.

Distilling and sugar-making. The use of grain for distilling spirits and making sugar is everywhere prohibited, and the distillers and sugar-refiners are constantly complaining. Distilling is not banned in Futienpu, Hengshan County, but prices are fixed very low, and the wine and spirits dealers, seeing no prospect of profit, have had to stop it.

Pigs. The number of pigs a family can keep is limited, for pigs consume grain.

Chickens and ducks. In Hsianghsiang County the raising of chickens and ducks is prohibited, but the women object. In Hengshan County, each family in Yangtang is allowed to keep only three, and in Futienpu five. In many places the raising of ducks is completely banned, for ducks not only consume grain but also ruin the rice plants and so are worse than chickens.

Feasts. Sumptuous feasts are generally forbidden. In Shaoshan, Hsiangtan County, it has been decided that guests are to be served with only three kinds of animal food, namely, chicken, fish and pork. It is also forbidden to serve bamboo shoots, kelp and lentil noodles. In Hengshan County it has been resolved that eight dishes and no more may be served at a banquet. Only five dishes are allowed in the East Third District in Liling County, and only three meat and three vegetable dishes in the North Second District, while in the West Third District New Year feasts are forbidden entirely. In Hsianghsiang County, there is a ban on all "egg-cake feasts", which are by no means sumptuous. When a family in the Second District of Hsianghsiang gave an "egg-cake feast" at a son's wedding, the peasants, seeing the ban violated, swarmed into the house and broke up the celebration. In the town of Chiamo, Hsianghsiang County, the people have refrained from eating expensive foods and use only fruit when offering ancestral sacrifices.

Oxen. Oxen are a treasured possession of the peasants. "Slaughter an ox in this life and you will be an ox in the next" has become almost a religious tenet; oxen must never be killed. Before the peasants had power, they could only appeal to religious taboo in opposing the slaughter of cattle and had no means of banning it. Since the rise of the peasant associations their jurisdiction has extended even to the cattle, and they have prohibited the slaughter of cattle in the towns. Of the six butcheries in the county town of Hsiangtan, five are now closed and the remaining one slaughters only enfeebled or disabled animals. The slaughter of cattle is totally prohibited throughout the county of Hengshan. A peasant whose ox broke a leg consulted the peasant association before he dared kill it. When the Chamber of Commerce of Chuchow rashly slaughtered a cow, the peasants came into town and demanded an explanation, and the chamber, besides paying a fine, had to let off firecrackers by way of apology.

Tramps and vagabonds. A resolution passed in Liling County prohibited the drumming of New Year greetings or the chanting of praises to the local deities or the singing of lotus rhymes. Various other counties have similar prohibitions, or these practices have disappeared of themselves, as no one observes them any more. The "beggar-bullies" or "vagabonds" who used to be extremely aggressive now have no alternative but to submit to the peasant associations. In Shaoshan, Hsiangtan County, the vagabonds used to make the temple of the Rain God their regular haunt and feared nobody, but since the rise of the associations they have stolen away. The peasant association in Huti Township in the same county caught three such tramps and made them carry clay for the brick kilns. Resolutions have been passed prohibiting the wasteful customs associated with New Year calls and gifts.

Besides these, many other minor prohibitions have been introduced in various places, such as the Liling prohibitions on incense-burning processions to propitiate the god of pestilence, on buying preserves and fruit for ritual presents, burning ritual paper garments during the Festival of Spirits and pasting up good-luck posters at the New Year. At Kushui in Hsianghsiang County, there is a prohibition even on smoking water-pipes. In the Second District, letting off firecrackers and ceremonial guns is forbidden, with a fine of 1.20 yuan for the former and 2.40 yuan for the latter. Religious rites for the dead are prohibited in the 7th and 20th Districts. In the 18th District, it is forbidden to make funeral gifts of money. Things like these, which defy enumeration, may be generally called peasant bans and prohibitions.

. . . .

12. THE MOVEMENT FOR EDUCATION. In China education has always been the exclusive preserve of the landlords, and the peasants have had no access to it. But the landlords' culture is created by the peasants, for its sole source is the peasants' sweat and blood. In China 90 per cent of the people have had no education, and of these the overwhelming majority are peasants. The moment the power of the landlords was overthrown in the rural areas, the peasants' movement for education began. See how the peasants who hitherto detested the schools are today zealously setting up evening classes! They always disliked the "foreign-style school". In my student days, when I went back to the village and saw that the peasants were against the "foreign-style school", I, too, used to identify myself with the general run of "foreign-style students and teachers" and stand up for it, feeling that the peasants were somehow wrong. It was not until 1925, when I lived in the countryside for six months and was already a Communist and had acquired the Marxist viewpoint, that I realized I had been wrong and the peasants right. The texts used in the rural primary schools were entirely about urban things and unsuited to rural needs. Besides, the attitude of the primary school teachers towards the peasants was very bad and, far from being helpful to the peasants, they became objects of dislike. Hence the peasants preferred the old-style schools ("Chinese classes", as they called them) to the modern schools (which they called "foreign classes") and the old-style teachers to the ones in the primary schools. Now the peasants are enthusiastically establishing evening classes, which they call peasant schools. Some have already been opened, others are being organized, and on the average there is one school per township. The peasants are very enthusiastic about these schools, and regard them, and only them, as their own. The funds for the evening schools come from the "public revenue from superstition", from ancestral temple funds, and from other idle public funds or property. The county education boards wanted to use this money to establish primary schools, that is, "foreign-style schools" not suited to the needs of the peasants, while the latter wanted to use it for peasant schools, and the outcome of the dispute was that both got some of the money, though there are places where the peasants got it all. The development of the peasant

movement has resulted in a rapid rise in their cultural level. Before long tens of thousands of schools will have sprung up in the villages throughout the province; this is quite different from the empty talk about "universal education", which the intelligentsia and the so-called "educationalists" have been bandying back and forth and which after all this time remains an empty phrase.

Pride in the exceptional achievements of the Chinese people has always been a central element in the thought of Mao Tse-tung, as can be seen in the following selection, written in 1939, where he provides a purportedly Marxian analysis of the nature of Chinese society.

The Chinese Revolution and the Chinese Communist Party, December 1939

MAO TSE-TUNG

Chapter 1: Chinese Society

1. THE CHINESE NATION. China is one of the largest countries in the world, her territory being about the size of the whole of Europe. In this vast country of ours there are large areas of fertile land which provide us with food and clothing; mountain ranges across its length and breadth with extensive forests and rich mineral deposits; many rivers and lakes which provide us with water transport and irrigation; and a long coastline which facilitates communication with nations beyond the seas. From ancient times our forefathers have laboured, lived and multiplied on this vast territory.

China borders on the Union of Soviet Socialist Republics in the northeast, the northwest and part of the west; the Mongolian People's Republic in the north; Afghanistan, India, Bhutan and Nepal in the southwest and part of the west; Burma and Indo-China in the south; and Korea in the east, where she is also a close neighbour of Japan and the Philippines. China's geographical setting has its advantages and disadvantages for the Chinese people's revo-

From Mao Tse-tung, *Selected Works,* Vol. II (Peking: Foreign Language Press, 1961). The translation is by Peking.

[Translator's note.] *The Chinese Revolution and the Chinese Communist Party* is a textbook which was written jointly by Comrade Mao Tse-tung and several other comrades in Yenan in the winter of 1939. The first chapter, "Chinese Society", was drafted by other comrades and revised by Comrade Mao Tse-tung. The second chapter, "The Chinese Revolution", was written by Comrade Mao Tse-tung himself. Another chapter, scheduled to deal with "Party Building", was left unfinished by the comrades working on it. The two published chapters, and especially Chapter 2, have played a great educational role in the Chinese Communist Party and among the Chinese people. The views on New Democracy set out by Comrade Mao Tse-tung in Chapter 2 were considerably developed in his "On New Democracy", written in January 1940.

lution. It is an advantage to be adjacent to the Soviet Union and fairly distant from the major imperialist countries in Europe and America, and to have many colonial or semi-colonial countries around us. It is a disadvantage that Japanese imperialism, making use of its geographical proximity, is constantly threatening the very existence of all China's nationalities and the Chinese people's revolution.

China has a population of 450 million, or almost a quarter of the world total. Over nine-tenths of her inhabitants belong to the Han nationality. There are also scores of minority nationalities, including the Mongol, Hui, Tibetan, Uighur, Miao, Yi, Chuang, Chungchia and Korean nationalities, all with long histories though at different levels of cultural development. Thus China is a country with a very large population composed of many nationalities.

Developing along the same lines as many other nations of the world, the Chinese people (here we refer mainly to the Hans) went through many thousands of years of life in classless primitive communes. Some 4,000 years have gone by since the collapse of these primitive communes and the transition to class society, which took the form first of slave and then of feudal society. Throughout the history of Chinese civilization its agriculture and handicrafts have been renowned for their high level of development; there have been many great thinkers, scientists, inventors, statesmen, soldiers, men of letters and artists, and we have a rich store of classical works. The compass was invented in China very long ago.[1] The art of paper-making was discovered as early as 1,800 years ago.[2] Block-printing was invented 1,300 years ago,[3] and movable type 800 years ago.[4] The use of gunpowder was known to the Chinese before the Europeans.[5] Thus China has one of the oldest civilizations in the world; she has a recorded history of nearly 4,000 years.

The Chinese nation is known throughout the world not only for its industriousness and stamina, but also for its ardent love of freedom and its rich revolutionary traditions. The history of the Han people, for instance, demonstrates that the Chinese never submit to tyrannical rule but invariably use revolutionary means to overthrow or change it. In the thousands of years of Han history, there have been hundreds of peasant uprisings, great and small, against the dark rule of the landlords and the nobility. And most dynastic changes came about as a result of such peasant uprisings. All the nationalities of China have resisted foreign oppression and have invariably resorted to rebellion to shake it off. They favour a union on the basis of equality but are against the oppression of one nationality by another. During the thousands of years of recorded history, the Chinese nation has given birth to many national heroes and revolutionary leaders. Thus the Chinese nation has a glorious revolutionary tradition and a splendid historical heritage.

2. THE OLD FEUDAL SOCIETY. Although China is a great nation and although she is a vast country with an immense population, a long history, a rich revolutionary tradition and a splendid historical heritage, her economic, political and cultural development was sluggish for a long time after the transition from slave to feudal society. This feudal society, beginning with the Chou and Chin Dynasties, lasted about 3,000 years.

. . . .

It was under such feudal economic exploitation and political oppression that the Chinese peasants lived like slaves, in poverty and suffering, through the ages. Under the bondage of feudalism they had no freedom of person. The landlord had the right to beat, abuse or even kill them at will, and they had no political rights whatsoever. The extreme poverty and backwardness of the peasants resulting from ruthless landlord exploitation and oppression is the basic reason why Chinese society remained at the same stage of socio-economic development for several thousand years.

The principal contradiction in feudal society was between the peasantry and the landlord class.

The peasants and the handicraft workers were the basic classes which created the wealth and culture of this society.

The ruthless economic exploitation and political oppression of the Chinese peasants forced them into numerous uprisings against landlord rule. There were hundreds of uprisings, great and small, all of them peasant revolts or peasant revolutionary wars. . . .

. . . The scale of peasant uprisings and peasant wars in Chinese history has no parallel anywhere else. The class struggles of the peasants, the peasant uprisings and peasant wars constituted the real motive force of historical development in Chinese feudal society. For each of the major peasant uprisings and wars dealt a blow to the feudal regime of the time, and hence more or less furthered the growth of the social productive forces. However, since neither new productive forces, nor new relations of production, nor new class forces, nor any advanced political party existed in those days, the peasant uprisings and wars did not have correct leadership such as the proletariat and the Communist Party provide today; every peasant revolution failed, and the peasantry was invariably used by the landlords and the nobility, either during or after the revolution, as a lever for bringing about dynastic change. Therefore, although some social progress was made after each great peasant revolutionary struggle, the feudal economic relations and political system remained basically unchanged.

It is only in the last hundred years that a change of a different order has taken place.

3. **PRESENT-DAY COLONIAL, SEMI-COLONIAL AND SEMI-FEUDAL SOCIETY.** As explained above, Chinese society remained feudal for 3,000 years. But is it still completely feudal today? No, China has changed. After the Opium War of 1840 China gradually changed into a semi-colonial and semi-feudal society. Since the Incident of September 18, 1931, when the Japanese imperialists started their armed aggression, China has changed further into a colonial, semi-colonial and semi-feudal society. We shall now describe the course of this change. . . .

However, the emergence and development of capitalism is only one aspect of the change that has taken place since the imperialist penetration of China. There is another concomitant and obstructive aspect, namely, the collusion of imperialism with the Chinese feudal forces to arrest the development of Chinese capitalism.

It is certainly not the purpose of the imperialist powers invading China to transform feudal China into capitalist China. On the contrary, their purpose is to transform China into their own semi-colony or colony.

To this end the imperialist powers have used and continue to use military, political, economic and cultural means of oppression, so that China has gradually become a semi-colony and colony. . . .

It is thus clear that in their aggression against China the imperialist powers have on the one hand hastened the disintegration of feudal society and the growth of elements of capitalism, thereby transforming a feudal into a semi-feudal society, and on the other imposed their ruthless rule on China, reducing an independent country to a semi-colonial and colonial country.

Taking both these aspects together, we can see that China's colonial, semi-colonial and semi-feudal society possesses the following characteristics:

(1) The foundations of the self-sufficient natural economy of feudal times have been destroyed, but the exploitation of the peasantry by the landlord class, which is the basis of the system of feudal exploitation, not only remains intact but, linked as it is with exploitation by comprador and usurer capital, clearly dominates China's social and economic life.

(2) National capitalism has developed to a certain extent and has played a considerable part in China's political and cultural life, but it has not become the principal pattern in China's social economy; it is flabby and is mostly associated with foreign imperialism and domestic feudalism in varying degrees.

(3) The autocratic rule of the emperors and nobility has been overthrown, and in its place there have arisen first the warlord-bureaucrat rule of the landlord class and then the joint dictatorship of the landlord class and the big bourgeoisie. In the occupied areas there is the rule of Japanese imperialism and its puppets.

(4) Imperialism controls not only China's vital financial and economic arteries but also her political and military power. In the occupied areas everything is in the hands of Japanese imperialism.

(5) China's economic, political and cultural development is very uneven, because she has been under the complete or partial domination of many imperialist powers, because she has actually been in a state of disunity for a long time, and because her territory is immense.

(6) Under the twofold oppression of imperialism and feudalism, and especially as a result of the large-scale invasion of Japanese imperialism, the Chinese people, and particularly the peasants, have become more and more impoverished and have even been pauperized in large numbers, living in hunger and cold and without any political rights. The poverty and lack of freedom among the Chinese people are on a scale seldom found elsewhere.

Such are the characteristics of China's colonial, semi-colonial and semi-feudal society.

This situation has in the main been determined by the Japanese and other imperialist forces; it is the result of the collusion of foreign imperialism and domestic feudalism.

The contradiction between imperialism and the Chinese nation and the contradiction between feudalism and the great masses of the people are the basic contradictions in modern Chinese society. Of course, there are others, such as the contradiction between the bourgeoisie and the proletariat and the contradictions within the reactionary ruling classes themselves. But the contradiction between imperialism and the Chinese nation is the principal one. These contradictions and their intensification must inevitably result in the incessant growth of revolutionary movements. The great revolutions in modern and contemporary China have emerged and grown on the basis of these basic contradictions.

Chapter 2: The Chinese Revolution

1. THE REVOLUTIONARY MOVEMENTS IN THE LAST HUNDRED YEARS. The history of China's transformation into a semi-colony and colony by imperialism in collusion with Chinese feudalism is at the same time a history of struggle by the Chinese people against imperialism and its lackeys. The Opium War, the Movement of the Taiping Heavenly Kingdom, the Sino-French War, the Sino-Japanese War, the Reform Movement of 1898, the Yi Ho Tuan Movement, the Revolution of 1911, the May 4th Movement, the May 30th Move-

ment, the Northern Expedition, the Agrarian Revolutionary War and the present War of Resistance Against Japan —all testify to the Chinese people's indomitable spirit in fighting imperialism and its lackeys.

The national revolutionary struggle of the Chinese people has a history of fully one hundred years counting from the Opium War of 1840, or of thirty years counting from the Revolution of 1911. It has not yet run its full course, nor has it yet performed its tasks with any signal success; therefore the Chinese people, and above all the Communist Party, must shoulder the responsibility of resolutely fighting on.

What are the targets of the revolution? What are its tasks? What are its motive forces? What is its character? And what are its perspectives? These are the questions we shall now deal with.

2. THE TARGETS OF THE CHINESE REVOLUTION. From our analysis in the third section of Chapter I, we know that present-day Chinese society is a colonial, semi-colonial and semi-feudal society. Only when we grasp the nature of Chinese society will we be able clearly to understand the targets, tasks, motive forces and character of the Chinese revolution and its perspectives and future transition. A clear understanding of the nature of Chinese society, that is, of Chinese conditions, is therefore the key to a clear understanding of all the problems of the revolution.

Since the nature of present-day Chinese society is colonial, semi-colonial and semi-feudal, what are the chief targets or enemies at this stage of the Chinese revolution?

They are imperialism and feudalism, the bourgeoisie of the imperialist countries and the landlord class of our country. For it is these two that are the chief oppressors, the chief obstacles to the progress of Chinese society at the present stage. The two collude with each other in oppressing the Chinese people, and imperialism is the foremost and most ferocious enemy of the Chinese people, because national oppression by imperialism is the more onerous.

It is evident, then, that the enemies of the Chinese revolution are very powerful. They include not only powerful imperialists and powerful feudal forces, but also, at times, the bourgeois reactionaries who collaborate with the imperialist and feudal forces to oppose the people. Therefore, it is wrong to underestimate the strength of the enemies of the revolutionary Chinese people.

In the face of such enemies, the Chinese revolution cannot be other than protracted and ruthless. With such powerful enemies, the revolutionary forces cannot be built up and tempered into a power capable of crushing them except over a long period of time. With enemies who so ruthlessly suppress the Chinese revolution, the revolutionary forces cannot hold their own positions, let alone capture those of the enemy, unless they steel themselves and display their tenacity to the full. It is therefore wrong to think that the forces of the Chinese revolution can be built up in the twinkling of an eye, or that China's revolutionary struggle can triumph overnight.

In the face of such enemies, the principal means or form of the Chinese revolution must be armed struggle, not peaceful struggle. For our enemies have made peaceful activity impossible for the Chinese people and have deprived them of all political freedom and democratic rights. Stalin says, "In China the armed revolution is fighting the armed counter-revolution. That is one of the specific features and one of the advantages of the Chinese revolution." This formulation is perfectly correct. Therefore, it is wrong to belittle armed struggle, revolutionary war, guerrilla war and army work.

In the face of such enemies, there

arises the question of revolutionary base areas. Since China's key cities have long been occupied by the powerful imperialists and their reactionary Chinese allies, it is imperative for the revolutionary ranks to turn the backward villages into advanced, consolidated base areas, into great military, political, economic and cultural bastions of the revolution from which to fight their vicious enemies who are using the cities for attacks on the rural districts, and in this way gradually to achieve the complete victory of the revolution through protracted fighting; it is imperative for them to do so if they do not wish to compromise with imperialism and its lackeys but are determined to fight on, and if they intend to build up and temper their forces, and avoid decisive battles with a powerful enemy while their own strength is inadequate. Such being the case, victory in the Chinese revolution can be won first in the rural areas, and this is possible because China's economic development is uneven (her economy not being a unified capitalist economy), because her territory is extensive (which gives the revolutionary forces room to manoeuvre), because the counter-revolutionary camp is disunited and full of contradictions, and because the struggle of the peasants who are the main force in the revolution is led by the Communist Party, the party of the proletariat; but on the other hand, these very circumstances make the revolution uneven and render the task of winning complete victory protracted and arduous. Clearly then the protracted revolutionary struggle in the revolutionary base areas consists mainly in peasant guerrilla warfare led by the Chinese Communist Party. Therefore, it is wrong to ignore the necessity of using rural districts as revolutionary base areas, to neglect painstaking work among the peasants, and to neglect guerrilla warfare.

However, stressing armed struggle does not mean abandoning other forms of struggle; on the contrary, armed struggle cannot succeed unless co-ordinated with other forms of struggle. And stressing the work in the rural base areas does not mean abandoning our work in the cities and in the other vast rural areas which are still under the enemy's rule; on the contrary, without the work in the cities and in these other rural areas, our own rural base areas would be isolated and the revolution would suffer defeat. Moreover, the final objective of the revolution is the capture of the cities, the enemy's main bases, and this objective cannot be achieved without adequate work in the cities.

3. THE TASKS OF THE CHINESE REVOLUTION. Imperialism and the feudal landlord class being the chief enemies of the Chinese revolution at this stage, what are the present tasks of the revolution?

Unquestionably, the main tasks are to strike at these two enemies, to carry out a national revolution to overthrow foreign imperialist oppression and a democratic revolution to overthrow feudal landlord oppression, the primary and foremost task being the national revolution to overthrow imperialism.

. . . .

In fact, the two revolutionary tasks are already linked, since the main immediate task of the national revolution is to resist the Japanese imperialist invaders and since the democratic revolution must be accomplished in order to win the war. It is wrong to regard the national revolution and the democratic revolution as two entirely different stages of the revolution.

4. THE MOTIVE FORCES OF THE CHINESE REVOLUTION. Given the nature of Chinese society and the present targets and tasks of the Chinese revolution as analysed and defined above, what are the motive forces of the Chinese revolution?

Since Chinese society is colonial, semi-colonial and semi-feudal, since the targets of the revolution are mainly foreign imperialist rule and domestic feudalism, and since its tasks are to overthrow these two oppressors, which of the various classes and strata in Chinese society constitute the forces capable of fighting them? This is the question of the motive forces of the Chinese revolution at the present stage. A clear understanding of this question is indispensable to a correct solution of the problem of the basic tactics of the Chinese revolution.

What classes are there in present-day Chinese society? There are the landlord class and the bourgeoisie, the landlord class and the upper stratum of the bourgeoisie constituting the ruling classes in Chinese society. And there are the proletariat, the peasantry, and the different sections of the petty bourgeoisie other than the peasantry, all of which are still the subject classes in vast areas of China.

The attitude and the stand of these classes towards the Chinese revolution are entirely determined by their economic status in society. Thus the motive forces as well as the targets and tasks of the revolution are determined by the nature of China's socio-economic system.

Let us now analyse the different classes in Chinese society. . . .

5. THE PROLETARIAT. Among the Chinese proletariat, the modern industrial workers number from 2,500,000 to 3,000,000, the workers in small-scale industry and in handicrafts and the shop assistants in the cities total about 12,000,000, and in addition there are great numbers of rural proletarians (the farm labourers) and other propertyless people in the cities and the countryside.

In addition to the basic qualities it shares with the proletariat everywhere—its association with the most advanced form of economy, its strong sense of organization and discipline and its lack of private means of production—the Chinese proletariat has many other outstanding qualities.

What are they?

First, the Chinese proletariat is more resolute and thoroughgoing in revolutionary struggle than any other class because it is subjected to a threefold oppression (imperialist, bourgeois and feudal) which is marked by a severity and cruelty seldom found in other countries. Since there is no economic basis for social reformism in colonial and semi-colonial China as there is in Europe, the whole proletariat, with the exception of a few scabs, is most revolutionary.

Secondly, from the moment it appeared on the revolutionary scene, the Chinese proletariat came under the leadership of its own revolutionary party—the Communist Party of China—and became the most politically conscious class in Chinese society.

Thirdly, because the Chinese proletariat by origin is largely made up of bankrupted peasants, it has natural ties with the peasant masses, which facilitates its forming a close alliance with them.

Therefore, in spite of certain unavoidable weaknesses, for instance, its smallness (as compared with the peasantry), its youth (as compared with the proletariat in the capitalist countries) and its low educational level (as compared with the bourgeoisie), the Chinese proletariat is nonetheless the basic motive force of the Chinese revolution. Unless it is led by the proletariat, the Chinese revolution cannot possibly succeed. To take an example from the past, the Revolution of 1911 miscarried because the proletariat did not consciously participate in it and the Communist Party was not yet in existence. More recently, the revolution of 1924–27 achieved great success for a time because the proletariat consciously participated and exercised leadership and the Communist Party was already in existence; it ended in defeat because the big bourgeoisie betrayed its alliance with the proletariat and abandoned the common revolutionary programme, and also because the Chinese proletariat and its political party did not yet have enough revolutionary experience.

. . . .

The Chinese proletariat should understand that although it is the class with the highest political consciousness and sense of organization, it cannot win victory by its own strength alone. In order to win, it must unite, according to varying circumstances, with all classes and strata that can take part in the revolution, and must organize a revolutionary united front. Among all the classes in Chinese society, the peasantry is a firm ally of the working class, the urban petty bourgeoisie is a reliable ally, and the national bourgeoisie is an ally in certain periods and to a certain extent. This is one of the fundamental laws established by China's modern revolutionary history.

Since Chinese society is colonial, semi-colonial and semi-feudal, since the principal enemies of the Chinese revolution are imperialism and feudalism, since the tasks of the revolution are to overthrow these two enemies by means of a national and democratic revolution in which the bourgeoisie sometimes takes part, and since the edge of the revolution is directed against imperialism and feudalism and not against capitalism and capitalist private property in general even if the big bourgeoisie betrays the revolution and becomes its enemy—since all this is true, the character of the Chinese revolution at the present stage is not proletarian-socialist but bourgeois-democratic.

However, in present-day China the bourgeois-democratic revolution is no longer of the old general type, which is now obsolete, but one of a new special type. We call this type the new-democratic revolution and it is developing in all other colonial and semi-colonial countries as well as in China. The new-democratic revolution is part of the world proletarian-socialist revolution, for it resolutely opposes imperialism, *i.e.*, international capitalism. Politically, it strives for the joint dictatorship of the revolutionary classes over the imperialists, traitors and reactionaries, and opposes the transformation of Chinese society into a society under bourgeois dictatorship. Economically, it aims at the nationalization of all the big enterprises and capital of the imperialists, traitors and reactionaries, and the distribution among the peasants of the land held by the landlords, while preserving private capitalist enterprise in general and not eliminating the rich-peasant economy. Thus, the new type of democratic revolution clears the way for capitalism on the one hand and creates the prerequisites for socialism on the other. The present stage of the Chinese revolution is a stage of transition between the abolition of the colonial, semi-colonial and semi-feudal society and the establishment of a socialist society, *i.e.*, it is a process of new-democratic revolution. This process, begun only after the First World War and the Russian October Revolution, started in China with the May 4th Movement of 1919. A new-democratic revolution is an anti-imperialist and anti-feudal revolution of the broad masses of the people under the leadership of the proletariat. Chinese society can advance to socialism only through such a revolution; there is no other way.

The new-democratic revolution is vastly different from the democratic revolutions of Europe and America in that it results not in a dictatorship of the bourgeoisie but in a dictatorship of the united front of all the revolutionary classes under the leadership of the proletariat.

The new-democratic revolution also differs from a socialist revolution in that it overthrows the rule of the imperialists, traitors and reactionaries in China but does not destroy any section of capitalism which is capable of contributing to the anti-imperialist, anti-feudal struggle.

The new-democratic revolution is basically in line with the revolution envisaged in the Three People's Principles as advocated by Dr. Sun Yat-sen in 1924. In the Manifesto of the First National Congress of the Kuomintang issued in that year, Dr. Sun stated:

> The so-called democratic system in modern states is usually monopolized by the bourgeoisie and has become simply an instrument for oppressing the common people. On the other hand, the Kuomintang's Principle of Democracy means a democratic system shared by all the common people and not privately owned by the few.

He added:

> Enterprises, such as banks, railways and airlines, whether Chinese-owned or foreign-owned, which are either monopolistic in character or too big for private management, shall be operated and administered by the state, so that private capital cannot dominate the livelihood of the people: this is the main principle of the regulation of capital.

Thus, the role of the proletariat, the peasantry and the other sections of the petty bourgeoisie in China's bourgeois-democratic revolution cannot be ignored, either in the alignment of forces for the struggle (that is, in the united front) or in the organization of state power. Anyone who tries to bypass these classes will certainly be unable to solve the problem of the destiny of the Chinese nation or indeed any of China's problems. The Chinese revolution at the present stage must strive to create a democratic republic in which the workers, the peasants and the other sections of the petty bourgeoisie all occupy a definite position and play a definite role. In other words, it must be a democratic republic based on a revolutionary alliance of the workers, peasants, urban petty bourgeoisie and all others who are against imperialism and feudalism. Only under the leadership of the proletariat can such a republic be completely realized.

. . . .

However, it is not at all surprising but entirely to be expected that a capitalist economy will develop to a certain extent within Chinese society with the sweeping away of the obstacles to the development of capitalism after the victory of the revolution, since the purpose of the Chinese revolution at the present stage is to change the existing colonial, semi-colonial and semi-feudal state of society, *i.e.*, to strive for the completion of the new-democratic revolution. A certain degree of capitalist development will be an inevitable result of the victory of the democratic revolution in economically backward China. But that will be only one aspect of the outcome of the Chinese revolution and not the whole picture. The whole picture will show the development of socialist as well as capitalist factors. What will the socialist factors be? The increasing relative importance of the proletariat and the Communist Party among the political forces in the country; leadership by the proletariat and the Communist Party which the peasantry, intelligentsia and the urban petty bourgeoisie already accept or are likely to accept; and the state sector of the economy owned by the democratic republic, and the co-operative sector of the economy owned by the working people. All these will be socialist factors. With the addition of a favourable international environment, these factors render it highly probable that China's bourgeois-democratic revolution will ultimately avoid a capitalist future and enjoy a socialist future.

7. THE TWOFOLD TASK OF THE CHINESE REVOLUTION AND THE CHINESE COMMUNIST PARTY. Summing up the foregoing sections of this chapter, we can see that the Chinese revolution taken as a whole involves a twofold task. That is to say, it embraces both the bourgeois-democratic revolution (the new-democratic revolution) and the proletarian-socialist revolution, *i.e.*, both the present and future stages of the revolution. The leadership in this twofold revolutionary task devolves on the Chinese Communist Party, the party of the proletariat, without whose leadership no revolution can succeed.

To complete China's bourgeois-democratic revolution (the new-democratic revolution) and to transform it into a socialist revolution when all the necessary conditions are ripe—such is the sum total of the great and glorious revolutionary task of the Chinese Communist Party. Every Party member must strive for its accomplishment and must under no circumstances give up halfway. Some immature Communists think that our task is confined to the present democratic revolution and does not include the future socialist revolution, or that the present revolution or the Agrarian Revolution is actually a socialist revolution. It must be emphatically pointed out that these views are wrong. Every Communist ought to know that, taken as a whole, the Chinese revolutionary movement led by the Communist Party embraces the two stages, *i.e.*, the democratic and the socialist revolutions, which are two essentially different revolutionary processes, and that the second process can be carried through only after the first has been completed. The democratic revolution is the necessary preparation for the socialist revolution, and the socialist revolution is the inevitable sequel to the democratic revolution. The ultimate aim for which all communists strive is to bring about a socialist and communist society. A clear understanding of both the differences and the interconnections between the democratic and the socialist revolutions is indispensable to correct leadership in the Chinese revolution.

Except for the Communist Party, no political party (bourgeois or petty-bourgeois) is equal to the task of leading China's two great revolutions, the democratic and the socialist revolutions, to complete fulfilment. From the very day of its birth, the Communist Party has taken this twofold task on its own shoulders and for eighteen years has fought strenuously for its accomplishment.

It is a task at once glorious and arduous. And it cannot be accomplished without a bolshevized Chinese Communist Party which is national in scale and has a broad mass character, a party fully consolidated ideologically, politically and organizationally. Therefore every Communist has the duty of playing an active part in building up such a Communist Party.

NOTES

[1] With reference to the invention of the compass, the magnetic power of the loadstone was mentioned as early as the 3rd century B.C. by Lu Pu-wei in his *Almanac,* and at the beginning of the 1st century A.D., Wang Chung, the materialist philosopher, observed in his *Lun Heng* that the loadstone points to the south, which indicates that magnetic polarity was known by then. Works of travel written at the beginning of the 12th century show that the compass was already in general use among Chinese navigators at that time.

[2] It is recorded in ancient documents that Tsai Lun, a eunuch of the Eastern Han Dynasty (A.D. 25–220), invented paper, which he had made from bark, hemp, rags and worn-out fishing nets. In A.D. 105 (the last year of the reign of Emperor Ho Ti), Tsai Lun presented

his invention to the emperor, and subsequently this method of making paper from plant fibre gradually spread in China.

[3] Block-printing was invented about A.D. 600, in the Sui Dynasty.

[4] Movable type was invented by Pi Sheng in the Sung Dynasty between 1041 and 1048.

[5] According to tradition, gunpowder was invented in China in the 9th century, and by the 11th century it was already in use for firing cannon.

Revolution in the twentieth century has generally been made in the name of the internationalist creed expounded by Karl Marx. Nevertheless the goals of the revolutionaries tend to be either avowedly or implicitly nationalistic. Mao Tse-tung, second only to Lenin in the theory and practice of Marxian revolution in this century, is no exception to this paradox. How these two apparently antagonistic strains can coexist in Mao and which is the stronger are here discussed by Professor Stuart R. Schram.

Professor Schram is Professor of Politics in the University of London and Head of the Contemporary China Institute of the School of Oriental and African Studies, and author of *The Political Thought of Mao Tse-tung.*

Mao: The Man and His Doctrines

STUART R. SCHRAM

This article is an attempt to define the essential characteristics of Mao's personal contribution to the ideas and methods of Communist China. In it I shall employ certain generalizations—some might say "abstractions"—regarding the nature of Mao's thought and its historical role. There are those who consider all such discussions as airy speculations, and who recommend limiting the analysis of Mao's ideas to his "operational code" and the immediate experience from which it emerges. Unfortunately, this approach often leads those who adopt it to conclude simultaneously 1) that Mao is a hard-bitten revolutionary and nothing else, and 2) that he is above all a "chauvinist." It will be for the reader to judge whether the speculations in which I shall now indulge throw any light on the links between these apparently unrelated attitudes.

The starting point for any attempt to elucidate the nature and significance of Mao's thought must be the fact that he is *both* a Leninist revolutionary and an Afro-Asian nationalist. On the one hand, he pursues radical social change as an end in itself; on the other hand, he is intent on the restoration of national independence and national dignity after the humiliation of Western domination.

From *Problems of Communism,* September–October, 1966. Courtesy of Press and Publications Service, United States Information Agency, Washington, D.C.

Being simultaneously a revolutionary and a nationalist, he finds a further justification for revolution in the belief that the nation can be restored and made to flourish only by a change in the social and political system. His aims are thus broader and more radical than those of such revolutionary nationalists as, say, Nasser, Sukarno, or Nkrumah, who do not subscribe to Leninism, and who regard revolution merely as a means of strengthening the nation, and not as an end in itself. But psychologically he also has a great deal in common with them.

The above abstractions do not carry us very far in the understanding of Mao's thought, but they do guide us toward certain basic questions: 1) What is the precise nature of Mao's "nationalist" and "revolutionary" tendencies? 2) How do these strains combine, and what is their relative importance in his thought and action?

These are not easy questions to answer. But to ignore either of the two aspects of Mao's personality, to treat him on one hand as a new Liu Pang or Genghis Khan, or on the other as a "pure" Leninist revolutionary (whatever that may be), is to make certain in advance that everything one says will be at least half false.

Chinese and Leninist Traits

Contrary to what might be assumed at first glance, this is not merely another way of formulating the problem of the relation between the revolutionary and nationalist aspects of Mao's thought. Mao's "Chineseness" is not the same thing as his nationalism. Chinese traditions and Chinese patterns of thought frequently color and shape his modes of reasoning even when his conscious concern is with problems of Leninist theory or with the world proletarian revolution. And conversely, his image of China and his evaluation of the Chinese heritage are cast to a large extent in Leninist categories. There is thus a subtle counterpoint and not a simple coincidence between the dichotomies "Chinese-Leninist" and "nationalist-revolutionary."

Leaving till the next section a discussion of Mao's "Chineseness"—understood in the sense of an identification with China above all, and therefore as another name for nationalism—what is the importance of the Chinese *form* of Mao's thought in general? Is it merely a matter of folklore and local color, of Chinese decorations pasted on an intellectual edifice basically similar to that of any Russian or European Leninist, with due allowance for the differences resulting from the peculiar tactical problems with which Mao has had to deal?

Undoubtedly there *is*, in Mao's writings, an element of *mere* local color, a conscious exploitation of traditional metaphors and examples, because he knows this will appeal to his countrymen and make it easier for them to assimilate a foreign system of thought. But there is much more to the problem than this. If Mao adapts his mode of expression to the habits of thought of his compatriots, he does so not merely to please them, but also to please himself. An extreme but nonetheless significant example is his composition of poems in classical forms, some of which I analyzed in an earlier issue of this review.[1] Mao could clearly have made himself far more accessible to the majority of today's citizens by writing his poems in the modern spoken language, as others have been doing for nearly half a century, and as he himself advises young Chinese to do. If he did not follow his own advice, it is because he *likes* to write in these forms, and also possibly because in this way he strengthens his image as a leader set apart from his con-

[1] "Mao as a Poet," *Problems of Communism*, Sept.–Oct. 1964, p. 38.

temporaries, speaking through barely comprehensible oracles. Neither of these motives could be justified in terms of Leninist ideology.

Nor is it merely a matter of the forms of expression which Mao chooses to employ. Not only the form but the substance of his thought is profoundly affected by his Chinese background. One example is the concept of *fu-ch'iang* (literally "rich and powerful"—a contraction of a phrase meaning "to enrich the country and make it strong militarily") which Mao absorbed from the late 19th-century nationalists who influenced him as an adolescent. As recently as 1957, during his visit to Moscow, he hailed the October Revolution for having shown China the road to "emancipation and *fu-ch'iang*." Both he and Liu Shao-ch'i have often indulged in a type of moralizing which owes more to the Confucian ideal of self-cultivation than to Lenin, for whom that which was moral was simply that which was useful to the revolution. The idea, launched by Mao in 1958, that it was a good thing the Chinese people were "poor and blank" because they could thus be reshaped at will, is totally foreign to the spirit of Marxism, with its insistence on the unique value of Western culture and the importance of a high level of social and intellectual development as a precondition for socialism. While I cannot attempt in this small space to define the antecedents of this notion with any precision, it is certainly more compatible with the traditional Chinese dialectics according to which extremes are transformed into one another, than with Marxist dialectics even as interpreted by Mao. Moreover, the very style in which the Chinese "apply" Marxism—as exemplified by the use of a few sentences from Marx quoted out of context to justify the totally un-Marxist enterprise of the communes—is not unrelated to the handling of quotations from the classics in the Chinese tradition.

Operative Factors

First on the list of the basic operative factors in Mao's thought must be placed his nationalism, not because it is necessarily the most important, but because it is chronologically and psychologically primary in Mao's thought. That it is chronologically primary is clear: Mao was a nationalist (and a relatively conservative one) long before he was a Communist or revolutionary of any kind. But, to a large extent, it is also psychologically primary, both for Mao and for the millions of Chinese who take his thought as their guide. In the complex structure of Mao's mind and personality as a whole, the nationalist components are to be found more or less on the visceral, and the revolutionary components on the cerebral, side. It has been affirmed that to emphasize Mao's nationalism is meaningless, inasmuch as all national leaders in this world are nationalists. Since World War II, France has been governed both by General de Gaulle and by, say, M. René Pleven. Would anyone suggest that the kind and degree of nationalism manifested by the one and the other was of no practical importance?

Another fundamental concept in Mao's intellectual world, which is at the same time a symbol for mobilizing political support, is that of the "people." Mao's "populist" tendency—the notion that the overwhelming majority of the Chinese are basically progressive and capable of participating in the revolution—is probably the most important single device by which he reconciles the nationalist and revolutionary halves of his personality. It is, of course, true that Lenin showed him the way by developing the idea that the bourgeoisie, in backward and dependent countries, could collaborate in the revolution during a certain period. But Mao enormously enlarged the scope of this thesis. On the one hand, he extended the definition of the forces in Chinese society which might play a positive role to include, at certain times, not only the whole of the bourgeoisie ("compradores" as well as national bourgeoisie), but even "patriotic landlords." He has repeatedly affirmed, in a series of utterances stretching over the last 40 years, that 90 or 95 percent of the Chinese people were on the side of the revolution. Secondly, he has proclaimed that collaboration among the four classes (proletariat, peasantry, petty bourgeoisie, and national bourgeoisie) constituting the "people," as defined since 1949, can continue throughout the whole period of the socialist revolution until all class differences finally disappear. Even if, since 1955, this formula no longer corresponds to any significant reality, it has an important symbolic function. For if virtually all Chinese (except for a handful of reactionaries and traitors) are basically revolutionary, then in defending the cause of China one is in fact advancing the world revolution. This is clearly what Mao and his disciples do believe today.

Another key factor in Mao's thought is an insistence on the importance of changing the mentality of the Chinese people as an indispensable condition for the modernization of China. Although Mao is proud of the achievements of traditional Chinese culture, and although his own mind is deeply marked by traditional modes of thought, he has been, for nearly half a century, in violent revolt against the stifling effects of such Confucian principles as submission to the authority of the family or the notion that man should adapt himself to the forces of nature rather than seeking to dominate nature. For a brief period in his youth, his revolt against the tyranny of nature and authority took an individualist form. The idea of the emancipation of the individual has, of course, long since been subordinated in his thinking to that of the collective emancipation of the Chinese people, but he has never lost sight of the importance of the individual. The citizen must act in the way required by the exigencies of the system and the aims of the government, but at the same time he must act consciously and not merely by rote.

The revolution which Mao has undertaken to carry out in the mentality of his compatriots in order to fit the Chinese nation for survival in the modern world has two aspects which are summed up in the famous phrase "red and expert," used since the period of the "Great Leap Forward" to define the ideal of excellence in China today. On one hand, Mao wants his compatriots to be expert—that is, to master modern ways of thinking about nature and modern techniques for dealing with nature, as developed in the West. But on the other hand, he wants them to be "red" —that is, filled with revolutionary passion and animated by the conviction that the action of the masses can ultimately triumph over all objective difficulties. To use Mao's own language, the flagrant opposition between these two exigencies is no doubt the "principal contradiction" in his thought.

Mao's Leadership Style

The principal traits in Mao's leadership style grow out of his personality and experience. Perhaps the most important and most characteristic is linked to what I have called his "military romanticism." By this term, I mean to designate not only Mao's fondness for warfare as such, but his tendency to envisage political, economic, and even philosophical problems as forms of combat. It is in warfare, he declared in 1938, that men give the full measure of themselves. He would like to infuse the same qualities of heroism and drama into every aspect of human activity.

This attitude has naturally been

shaped by Mao's twenty-year experience of guerrilla warfare, but it also corresponds to the orientation of his personality from the beginning. In the earliest authoritative document available, the article on physical culture which he published in 1917, he appears already as first and foremost a warrior. Mao's taste and talent for this type of pathos and this style of leadership were unquestionably of immense value to him in the course of the struggle for power. Since 1949, they have been of more dubious utility, at least as regards internal affairs. In the present context, when it is desired to mobilize the population, and to rely on China's own efforts and resources for modernization in the face of the denial of Soviet aid, this ethic may again be of some use; but at the same time, like the emphasis on "redness," it may be a hindrance to rational economic construction. There are apparently those in the Chinese Communist Party who realize this. Mao himself stated in 1958 that a certain number of comrades regarded the effort to make steel by relying on mass enthusiasm as a "guerrilla habit." But he has given no sign that he is capable, or even desirous, of modifying his personality and outlook.

For the rest, Mao's style of leadership is in large part a projection of the emphasis on conscious action which marks his thought as a whole. While Mao is resolved that all Chinese shall think alike, and think as he wishes, he wants them to do so spontaneously. To the outside observer, this ambition seems contradictory and absurd, but it is nevertheless a reality in Mao's mind. It perhaps reflects a nostalgia for the ideal of individual liberation which he espoused in his youth; most certainly, it is inspired by the belief that human beings act effectively only when they act with conviction.

Mao's recipe for achieving the desired combination of spontaneity and discipline consists, of course, in transforming the attitudes of his fellow-citizens by methods which vary considerably according to the situation at a given moment, the social category involved, and the aims pursued, but which can be broadly designated by the term "thought reform." As is well known, violence is by no means absent from the techniques employed to change the thinking of the Chinese, but it is a means rather than an end. Ideally, the citizens should not be kept in line indefinitely by sheer fear of police terror; terror is used, in conjunction with various methods of indoctrination, in order to transform their minds and personalities to such an extent that the desired modifications in their behavior will be enforced by internal rather than external sanctions.

This enterprise has so far been neither a total success nor a total failure. Terror and constraint are by no means absent from China today. "Mao Tse-tung's thought" has certainly not been adequately assimilated by all Chinese, and at various times, notably in the difficult years after the failure of the "Great Leap Forward," there has clearly been considerable opposition and hostility to the regime. But at the same time, there is probably more consensus, and less blind obedience, than in the Soviet Union at the corresponding stage in its development.

A technique related to Mao's emphasis on "conscious action," and to his desire to show that he enjoys the enthusiastic support of the masses, is his practice of allowing policy decisions to filter out at first only partially and indirectly, through anonymous newspaper editorials summarizing the essential points of his speeches and directives, and his parallel practice of publishing his own words only after a delay of weeks, months, or even years, during which an attempt is made to give the appearance that a movement is developing spontaneously. Examples of this aspect of his leadership style are legion. To cite only two, his speech of February 27, 1957, on the correct manner of resolving contradictions among the people was not published until June of that year, and then in a form revised to take account of the intervening developments; similarly, his speech on art and literature, delivered in May 1942, was not published until October 1943. To be sure, delays in the publication of important documents are not unknown in other countries, particularly the Soviet Union, but they are usually explicable in terms of a desire for secrecy rather than as a deliberate technique for encouraging apparently spontaneous action by the masses to give the impression that the regime is acting in harmony with the masses.

The Role of Intellectuals

"Intellectuals" is here understood in the sense usually employed in talking about Communist countries, that is, to mean any more or less educated and technically competent person. Mao's attitude toward this category is intimately bound up with his desire to effect a cultural revolution which will make the Chinese both "red" and "expert." As the carriers of expertness, intellectuals are indispensable if China is to be turned into a powerful modern nation. But in a great many instances expertness does not go hand in hand with redness, and those who are more red than expert may come into conflict with those who are more expert than red. For the moment, it is necessary to live with this "contradiction" in the reality of Chinese society—a contradiction which reflects a similar contradiction in Mao's thought. Though, on the whole, authority belongs to those who are "red," the hard lessons of 1959–61 have taught Mao and his colleagues that experts must have a certain amount of freedom to do their job. In the long run, however, such a compromise, such a sacrifice of principle to efficiency, is certainly intolerable to Mao. To admit that managers and engineers are (1) inherently skeptical, and (2) inclined to seek comfortable lives for themselves, to admit that they must be humored indefinitely to some extent in order to keep them working efficiently, would be for him the height of immorality—a surrender to that very restoration of capitalism which he denounces in the USSR and which he has declared must be fought to the bitter end in China itself.

As for intellectuals in the narrow sense of the word—writers, artists, philosophers, historians, etc.—Mao finds the dilemma even harder. More than average citizens, people in these categories must act consciously and with conviction if they are to play an effective role in society. At the same time, they cannot be allowed to plant "poisonous weeds" instead of flowers in the socialist garden. In the course of the past decade, Mao has repeatedly swung from one extreme to the other, from the liberalism of the "Hundred Flowers" to the extreme regimentation prevailing in recent years, in an effort to find a method of reconciling individual awareness with social harmony. It does not appear that a solution is in sight, but Mao is certainly not prepared to admit defeat. Whenever the choice is between stifling opposition, with force if necessary, and tolerating dissidence which challenges such basic principles of the regime as the predominance of the Communist Party, Mao will choose repression, as his reaction in the latter half of 1957 made perfectly clear. Yet he will never abandon his efforts to persuade people to believe what in his view they ought to believe, so as to avoid having to constrain them to act as though they believed it.

Mao and the World

It is perhaps in the field of global strategy that the interaction between revolutionary and nationalist impulses in Mao's personality weaves the most fascinating counterpoint. A decisive question that poses itself here is whether we are in fact dealing with only two factors, or with three. It is clear that Mao has three concentric loyalties: to China; to the liberation of the peoples of Asia, Africa, and Latin America; and to world revolution as the joint enterprise of the proletariat of the developed countries and the "oppressed peoples" of the underdeveloped countries. Should this concern with national liberation movements be regarded as a partially independent factor in Mao's thought? Or is it a projection of his commitment to Chinese nationalism, to world revolution, or to both? No doubt, it is all of these things at the same time. Mao's feeling of solidarity with other non-European peoples struggling against "imperialism" undoubtedly exists in its own right as a spontaneous reaction. But his formulation of the principle of solidarity, and his application of it, are shaped by both nationalist and revolutionary considerations. His attitude is marked by nationalism, because to support revolutionary movements in Asia, Africa, and Latin America means to extend Chinese influence in these areas. It is transmuted and rendered more virulent by Mao's commitment to revolution everywhere as a value in itself.

But just how abstract and general is Mao's love of revolution? On the face of it, the anti-imperialist theme appears to be an example of perfect harmony between nationalist and revolutionary motives, for it is at once a basic tenet of Leninism and an emotional necessity for the peoples of Asia and Africa. Yet, though Mao has been a believer in Marxism-Leninism for some forty years and has had a fairly good knowledge of it for some twenty-five, it is not easy to say what this ideological commitment actually means to him. He has given us a clue by affirming: "There is no such thing as abstract Marxism, but only concrete Marxism. What we call concrete Marxism is Marxism that has taken on a national form. . . ."[2] If Mao now proposes to encircle the "cities" of Europe and America from the "countryside" of Asia, Africa, and Latin America, is this out of abstract devotion to world revolution—or to gain final revenge for the humiliation which, for over a century, the "cities" inflicted on the "countryside," and on China in particular? Does he really have a feeling of comradeship with the workers of Europe and the United States, and hope for their support at a later stage? Or does he regard them as hopelessly degenerate, cowardly, and *embourgeoisés*, paying lip service to their role in the world revolution only in order to give revolutionary legitimacy and wider appeal to an enterprise which in fact owes more to Chinese tradition than to Lenin?

Some clues regarding these questions can be obtained by considering the actual Chinese attitude toward the Soviet role in the world revolution and comparing it with the attitude that would result from a "leftist" position rooted in fidelity to the letter of Marxist doctrine. Recent Chinese statements do not merely criticize the Soviet leaders for their "revisionism" and betrayal of Marxist principles; they virtually exclude the Soviet Union from estimates

[2] Mao's report of October 1938, as translated in the author's *The Political Thought of Mao Tse-tung*, New York, Praeger, 1963, p. 114. (This passage has been removed from the current edition of Mao's *Selected Works*.)

regarding the future course of events. Mao and his comrades regularly denounce the Soviet Union for failing to support "national liberation" movements in Vietnam and elsewhere, but they show no signs of genuinely desiring such action on the part of Moscow, either now or in the future, for it might jeopardize their own professed position as the sole hope and sole guiding center of the oppressed peoples throughout the world. This attitude is in sharp contrast to that of Trotsky, who continued right to his death to denounce in the most scathing terms the "Thermidorean Reaction" existing under Stalin's dictatorship, but who nevertheless affirmed that the Soviet Union was a "workers' and peasants' state," however degenerate, and must therefore be supported in all circumstances. It seems clear that an ultra-leftist view inspired by doctrine alone would today take this same line, proclaiming that the Soviet Union, however timid and selfish its leadership, remains the principal bulwark of the "anti-imperialist" struggle on the world scene. If Mao does not reason in this way, it is because his view of the world is rooted less in theory than in emotion. The assault on "modern revisionism" is a Marxist-Leninist justification for Chinese resentment over the arrogant and high-handed treatment inflicted on China by the Soviet leaders and their refusal to be guided by Chinese counsels, just as anti-imperialism is the expression in ideological terms of resentment against the West.

This does not imply that Mao's ultra-revolutionary verbiage is *nothing* but a fig leaf for the visceral reactions of a Chinese and/or an Asian. In recent years, there has been a tendency, in the interpretation of Chinese communism and the Sino-Soviet dispute, to move from one extreme, which held that ideology was everything, to the opposite extreme, according to which it is nothing. As emphasized at the beginning of this article, I do not subscribe to either view. Nationalist and revolutionary impulses must both be taken into account. In terms of their relative weight, it seems clear that on the world scene, even more than in internal affairs, nationalist passion comes first and revolutionary ideology second. But ideology nevertheless serves a double and important function. It provides a justification in abstract terms for anti-western sentiment, and thereby makes it more virulent. And it dresses up Chinese experience and aspirations in a garb of universality, thereby making it possible for Mao to appeal not only to his compatriots but to the peoples of Asia, Africa, and Latin America as a whole.

In both these roles, Mao's version of Leninism is effective to a certain, no doubt considerable, extent. But in both roles its ultimate effect is problematical. As regards the appeal to other non-European countries, the "Sinification" of Marxism, while bringing it closer to the traditions and experience of the Chinese, may make it more foreign to other peoples. Even more important in this respect than the Sinocentrism of Mao's thought is the Sinocentrism of his action. The open pursuit of specifically Chinese goals may produce a disillusionment on the part of other Asians and Africans anent the purity of Mao's anti-imperialist motives, doing even more to undermine his pretentions to universality than the citations from the Chinese classics with which Peking's ideological utterances are studded.

Is Mao's thinking about foreign policy sufficiently coherent and consistent at the present time to enable one to sum it up in a few clear sentences? I have already said that China is at the center of his world, and I have suggested that the advanced countries of Europe and North America play very little part in his calculations except as enemies to be struggled against or played off against one another. But how does Mao conceive of the relation between China and the other peoples of Asia, Africa, and Latin America? Does he regard Peking first and foremost as a revolutionary Mecca, even though, consciously or unconsciously, he may wish to propagate revolution primarily in order to increase Chinese influence in the world and not merely out of abstract devotion to "proletarian internationalism"? Or is he inspired by nostalgia for China's traditional position as an empire surrounded by client states?

In the long run, the two goals are obviously related in his mind, for only a Communist state (run, of course, by a genuine, non-revisionist Communist party) could be expected to maintain unwavering solidarity with China as the leader of the genuinely revolutionary forces in the world. But both the ideological line and the actual policies that Mao has pursued over the past fifteen years have tended to indicate that for a relatively long time he would be satisfied with "bourgeois" governments provided they were oriented toward Peking. Last fall's unsuccessful coup in Indonesia, it is true, raised new doubts on this score. If Peking wanted to overthrow Sukarno, the champion of the "New Emerging Forces," what non-Communist Asian or African leader, however revolutionary, could consider himself safe? The contradiction between this action and Mao's foreign policy as a whole is so flagrant, however, that one is led to wonder whether the Indonesian events were not in fact the result of a miscalculation inspired by Sukarno's very bad health rather than the first manifestation of a new ultra-left line in Peking. This interpretation is supported by China's consistent support of Marshal Ayub Khan's Pakistan as a revolutionary force in the world.

In fact, the foreign policy of Mao's China, like its domestic policy, suffers from an acute contradiction between the style and the substance. In internal affairs, a frantic insistence on the study of Mao Tse-tung's thought as the key to everything has recently gone hand in hand with a relatively realistic economic policy. In foreign affairs, the constant affirmation of implacable hostility to "US imperialism" has not led to any large-scale involvement in the Vietnamese conflict, and Mao appears to be guided primarily by considerations of Chinese interest and Chinese dignity. Of the two, dignity would appear to be the more important to him. But even this may conceivably be changing. An interesting and suggestive example is that of Chinese policy toward Cuba. At first sight, the clumsy and tactless handling of Fidel Castro would appear to reflect above all an exaggerated susceptibility to behavior which Peking judges to be disrespectful. But the decision to reduce sugar purchases may also have been motivated by a desire to bring China's foreign aid commitments into line with her economic capacity. Any such tendency to be guided at least in part by interests rationally understood rather than by nationalist passion or revolutionary zeal would be a hopeful development both for China and for the world.

The Chinese Communist Party, in the decade and a half between its founding and the outbreak of the Sino-Japanese War in 1937, succeeded in winning the effective allegiance of only a very small fraction of the Chinese people, despite its determined efforts and its program of agrarian revolution. At the end of the war, eight years later, the fortunes of the party had changed to such an extent that it was ready to launch a full-scale armed assault on the Kuomintang government of Chiang Kai-shek, an assault that was to end in victory in 1949. In the following selection, Professor Chalmers A. Johnson suggests that an explanation for this remarkable improvement in the situation of the party should be sought in the awakening nationalism of the Chinese peasantry caused by the Japanese invasion and in the peculiar ability of the Communists to take political advantage of it.

Chalmers Johnson is Professor of Political Science at Berkeley, and author of *Peasant Nationalism and Communist Power* and *Revolutionary Change*, among other books.

Peasant Nationalism in China

CHALMERS A. JOHNSON

The Communist government of China was formally proclaimed on October 1, 1949, and it is this date that is celebrated today as the national anniversary of its accession to power. However, to regard 1949 as the beginning of Communist government in China obscures the fact that the Communist Party actually ruled a large part of China for at least ten years before that time. Following the outbreak of the Sino-Japanese War in 1937, the Communist Party enlarged the territory under its control to a degree previously unimagined even by the Communist leaders themselves. This enlargement took the form of "guerrilla bases," which were established in rural areas behind the Japanese lines. Before Japan's capitulation in 1945, one-fifth of the population of China was living in these guerrilla bases and following the leadership of the Communist Party. Thus, it is from the early stages of the Sino-Japanese War that we should date the Chinese Communists' true rise to power.

The Communists' success during the war was in marked contrast to their experiences in the decade preceding the war, when they first undertook seriously to organize the peasantry. Although the Communists were in effective control of various small enclaves in the Chinese countryside from 1927 on, their painful efforts during that period to set up rural "soviets" were incomparably less successful than their activities during the blackest period of the Sino-Japanese War. The Party's prewar failure was not the result of a lack of effort. From the first Communist-led jacqueries in 1927 until the beginning of the Long March

[Editors' note:] Notes for this selection are grouped at the end of the selection.

in 1934, the Communists utilized every available economic, ideological, and military tool to establish a durable political order in the territories defended by their army. In 1938, however, using essentially the same organizational techniques they had used in the past, the Chinese Communists were successful in rural China as they had never been before. An understanding of the factors that brought about this development is crucial to an assessment of Chinese politics today and to an appreciation of what a "Communist" China means in the twentieth century.

Peasant Mobilization

The critical difference between the two periods was that the Communist Party failed to obtain mass support in the Kiangsi period, but did achieve such a following during the Resistance War.[1] Prior to 1937, although the peasantry collaborated half-heartedly with the Communists (the Communists purchased peasant support of the Red Army with their anti-landlord economic policy), the relationship established between the two was contingent upon Communist military successes and the failure of other contenders to make the peasants a better offer. As we know, the Communists were not successful militarily in the Kiangsi period, and the Kuomintang did make the peasantry at least an equally good offer.[2]

However, after the outbreak of the war the situation changed; it became much more fluid, much more dynamic. The politically illiterate masses of China were awakened by the Japanese invasion and its aftermath; wartime conditions made them receptive to a new kind of political appeal—namely, the defense of the fatherland. The war presented the peasantry with a challenge to its security of such immediacy that the peasants could not ignore it. Prewar pressures on the peasantry—such as economic exploitation, Communist ideology, warlord wars, and natural calamities—had never been sufficiently widespread or sufficiently intense to give rise to a peasant-based mass movement. But after July 7, 1937, the peasants spontaneously created resistance organizations in many areas of China; and they felt a heightened sensitivity to proposals for defensive organization throughout the entire occupied area. There were several specific influences that promoted this new activity among the peasants.

First, as the armies of the Central Government retreated from north China and the lower Yangtze Valley after the Japanese invasion, and as the majority of the officials and other agents of the existing establishment retreated with them, anarchy settled on the Chinese villages. The U.S. War Department has described the situation in the occupied areas as follows:

> While the Japanese set up a Chinese puppet administration, and through this and their army authorities maintained a measure of order in their occupied zones in North China, the rural areas around these zones fell prey to ravaging hordes of Japanese soldiers engaged in grain confiscations and "mopping up" operations against Communists and remnants of Chinese provincial forces, roving units of disorganized Chinese soldiers who had turned bandits, and bandit groups formed out of peasants who had collected arms on various battlefields.[3]

The rural villages responded to this situation by establishing self-defense forces and, in some cases, guerrilla corps. In their efforts at defensive organization, the villagers welcomed whatever capable military and political leadership they could find—Communist, Nationalist, Sacrifice League (Shansi), secret society, KMT Army remnants, or purely local leaders. Hundreds of new, anti-Japanese popular governments were set up behind the Japanese lines at the basic level of Chinese local government —the hsien, or county.[4] These rear-area governments, led by local men or Partisans of battle-proved integrity, filled the vacuum left by the retreat of the former authorities. Such governments provided for self-defense, education, agricultural cooperation, support for full-time guerrillas, and other needs of the villages; most important, they served as instruments for helping the rural masses attain a political understanding of the war to serve as a gloss on their personal experience. While mining a road, or guarding a village, or attending a meeting of one of the mass associations (some of the many activities sponsored by the guerrilla governments), the rural "common man" learned that his peril was also China's peril.

Many of these governments were, of course, sponsored by or under the influence of the Communist Party; but, as William G. Carleton has put it, "Under Communism, the mass of Asiatics in some countries may come into close contact with their governments for the first time in their history; and this contact, because of the many functions exercised by Communist governments, will be far more intimate than the contacts of the mass of Europeans with their national governments in the days when European nationalism was emerging."[5] These wartime governments were not democratic (there was virtually no opposition), but the masses did participate on an enormous scale in "governmental" activities via the so-called "mass movement" (*min-chung yün-tung*). The feeling of belonging and of having a stake in government that grew up in this period was entirely novel to the Chinese masses; and it brought with it an exhilarating sense of self-determination. At the same time, villages in which the population decided to cooperate with the Japanese generally suffered for their decision, and this also had its educative effect. Thus, the very setting of the war proved favorable to Communist propaganda.

A second factor that influenced the peasants after 1937 was the propaganda and educational effort launched by the Communist Party. This propaganda was remarkably free of a "Communist" quality; it stressed *chiu-kuo*, or national salvation. The Communists had, of course, used patriotic and anti-Japanese appeals in their propaganda since the Manchurian Incident (1931). What was actually new in the propaganda field after 1937 was that the Japanese Army had created a huge ready-made audience for Communist propaganda as a result of its conduct of the invasion. The Communists themselves took no chances on repeating their failure to unite the masses in the Kiangsi Soviet; they eschewed their old slogans of class warfare and violent redistribution of property in their post-1937 propaganda and concentrated solely on national salvation. As one example of the wartime orientation of this propaganda, here is part of a leaflet prepared by the CCP-dominated Shansi Sacrifice League and captured by the Japanese Army in Chiehhsiu hsien, Shansi, in September 1938.[6] It reads:

> Exterminate the Traitor Peace Preservation Committees! Comrades! Japan has invaded our Shansi, killed large numbers of our people, burned thousands of our houses, raped our women in countless numbers, robbed us of our food and wealth, trampled on the graves of our ancestors, forced our wives and children to flee, destroyed our famous places, . . . and made the joy of peace impossible. . . . Everybody! Rise up and join a guerrilla self-defense unit! Exterminate the Peace Maintenance Committee which sells out the nation! Defend our anti-Japanese patriotic people's government! Assist the all-out resistance of Commander Yen [Hsi-shan]! Act in unison with Army and people to overthrow Japanese imperialism![7]

This is merely one sample of the propaganda—itself only one tool of the total Communist effort—employed by the Party behind the lines to help the peasantry help themselves, and also to obtain from them assistance for the Communist Army in its efforts to hamper the invasion. These activities promoted mobilization in the countryside and, at the same time, fed upon the spontaneous peasant unrest. Nationalistic propaganda from Communist sources fell on fertile ground, where it both furthered the mobilization of the masses and helped determine the form this mobilization took.

Still another component in the complex of forces that assaulted the Chinese peasant after 1937 was the policy of Japanese reprisals. Because the Japanese Army was suffering from Communist military pressure and from a situation in which it could not distinguish a guerrilla from a villager, the Japanese and puppet forces took ruthless action against the rural population, action that resulted in the depopulation of several areas.[8] The effect of this policy—as in Yugsoslavia under similar circumstances—was to arouse even the most parochial of village dwellers to the fact that politics could no longer be ignored. The "mop-ups" (Chinese *sao-tang;* Japanese *sōtō*) tended to confirm the charges made against the Japanese by the Communists, notably that there was no way of accommodating to Japanese rule short of slavery. Peasants who survived the mopping-up campaigns were forced to conclude that their only hope lay in resistance, and the Communists were widely regarded as the most competent organizers of resistance. The question of whether or not Communist activity provoked Japanese reprisals will be considered in a later chapter; the point to be stressed here is that the peasants of the occupied areas faced the continuous threat of military attack from the Japanese Army throughout the eight years of the Sino-Japanese War. The dislocations produced by the invasion itself were relatively minor compared with the destruction caused by the mopping-up campaigns, for example those of 1941 and 1942 in Hopei and Shansi provinces.

All these forces—the evacuation, the establishment of *ad hoc* governments, Communist propaganda, and Japanese reprisals (plus other influences, such as the policies of the puppets and the incipient KMT-CCP civil war, which we shall discuss subsequently)—broke the hold of parochialism on the Chinese peasant. Before the Japanese invasion the Chinese peasantry was indifferent to "Chinese" politics, being wholly absorbed in local affairs. The war totally destroyed the traditional rural social order and sensitized the Chinese peasantry to a new spectrum of possible associations, identities, and purposes. Foremost among the new political concepts were those of "China" and "Chinese nationality" (as distinct from one's normal identity as a mere resident of the warlord satrapy of, for example, Han Fu-ch'ü). During the war, the peasants began to hear and use such terms as *Han-chien* (Chinese traitor), *wei-chün* (bogus army, i.e., the puppet forces), *wan-chün* (reactionary army, i.e., the KMT forces as seen by Yenan), and *Jih-k'ou* (Japanese bandits). The intrusion of these terms into the peasants' vocabulary signified the spread of a force that hitherto was prevalent only among the intelligentsia and city-bred people—namely, nationalism.[9]

Like all illiterate populations in such circumstances, the Chinese masses themselves—the peasants [10]—have left no record of the transformation wrought in their lives and thoughts when they were assaulted from the east by the Japanese and invaded from the west and north by the Communists. This study attempts to reveal the nature of that transformation as it is unwittingly disclosed in the archives of the Japanese government. Later on in this chapter I offer an abstract explanation, in terms of a theory of nationalism, of what the Chinese peasants experienced during the war; and in succeeding chapters I shall detail the actual experiences that support such a theory. Before we proceed to these subjects, however, it is necessary to discuss the Communist victory, which was one of the products of the transformation of the peasant masses.

The Role of the Communist Party

If one were to make a diagram of the fortunes of the Communist Party of China in terms of its popular following, the result would be an undulating line. Starting with the Party's foundation in 1921, a slowly ascending curve rises to 1927; then, with the Nationalist-Communist split and the Kuomintang's purge of the Communists, the line descends precipitously. Next comes the ascent from approximately 1929 to 1934, representing the growth of the Kiangsi Soviet, followed by the sharp dive when the victorious Kuomintang armies drove the Communists from south China. Starting after the period of the Long March, the line begins again from the bottom of the graph, ascends slowly to the peak of 1940, dips sharply in 1941 and 1942 (recording the effect of the Japanese mopping-up campaigns) and then rises from an already fairly high level up and off the top of the page. In the first hump, the Party made a strong economic appeal to the urban workers and shared with the Kuomintang the leadership of the early anti-imperialist, anti-Japanese nationalist movement among the intellectual and urban classes. In the second period, the Party sought to profit from the endemic land hunger of the Chinese tenants and farm laborers and promised them a radical redistribution of farmlands. In the third period, the Party joined its experienced guerrilla cadres with the violently uprooted peasants of the Japanese-occupied areas in tactical alliances against the invader and his puppets. This last period was the one in which the Chinese Communist Party won the Chinese masses to its cause.

Again, we might view this 25-year history in terms of a metaphor from the laboratory. If we think of the Chinese population as a culture plate and of the Communist Party as a colony of viruses growing on its surface, we may suggest various ways in which the Party and the population influenced each other. In the periods before the Japanese invasion, the culture nourished the Communist virus scarcely at all and only sustained the life of other viruses in specific and atypical patches. The Party attempted to adapt itself to its environment and in the process displayed the entire spectrum of Leninist and Comintern disguises, in addition to a few that it created itself. However, it failed and was in its worst straits just prior to the Japanese invasion. After the invasion of 1937, large patches of the culture plate that had previously inhibited political growths of any variety became highly receptive to a particular kind: one that was anti-Japanese, possessed organizational and military abilities, and recognized that a change had occurred in the culture. In other words, from 1921 to 1937 Communism failed in China because the Chinese people, in general, were indifferent to what the Communist Party had to offer. After 1937, it succeeded because the population became receptive to one particular kind of political appeal; and the Communist Party—in one of its many disguises—made precisely that appeal: it offered to meet the needs of the people for leadership in organizing resistance to the invader and in alleviating war-induced anarchy in the rural areas.

A similar process brought the Yugoslav Communist Party to power at the end of World War II, and a study of the better documented and more realistically observed Yugoslav revolution accordingly offers us useful comparative insights into the dynamics of the Chinese revolution. (The Yugoslav comparison is taken up in detail in Chapter Six; for the present we are interested only in the general similarities.) There were two forms of Communist territorial expansion in the 1940's. The first was by means of the Soviet Red Army (Czechoslovakia, although not invaded, was included in the sphere of influence created by the Red Army); the second was by means of Communist-led, rural-recruited partisan armies united under banners of defense of the fatherland and anti-fascism.

There are only two cases in which the second method was employed successfully: China and Yugoslavia. The rise to power of the YCP was remarkably similar to that of the Chinese Communist Party. The Yugoslav Party enjoyed only a limited base of popular support in the 1920's and 1930's, and this situation became reversed during World War II. Forces similar to those in China operated to bring about a situation favorable to the Yugoslav Communists. The German invaders carried out unenlightened occupation policies. The war offered an opportunity for the Communist Party to discredit the "legal" wartime government of Drazha Mihailović, first by gaining access to the realm of nationalist sentiment in which the Chetniks had claimed a monopoly, then by emasculating the Chetniks' remnant claims to the mantle of nationalism, and finally by denouncing them as traitors. And, above all, the political role of the peasantry was drastically increased—a result of the dislocations produced by invasion and of Communist engineering. As in China, the Yugoslav Partisans participated in the resistance movement as defenders of Yugoslav national integrity and set aside, for the duration of the war, elements of Marxist dogma that would have conflicted with the interests of the mass movement. As one of the leading non-Communist analysts of the Yugoslav revolution has observed:

> The Yugoslav Communists appealed to the peasants with slogans that were not economic but purely patriotic. The peasants had no idea what would happen to them in the event of a Communist victory. For example, in the locality of Srem [the region between the Danube and the Sava in Serbia], one of the most fertile regions, they fought valiantly in the ranks of the Partisans without ever reflecting that the next day their property might be redistributed or collectivized by Tito.[11]

Thus Communism and nationalism were fused in wartime China and Yugoslavia as a result of the identification of the CCP and YCP, respectively, with the resistance movements of the two countries—movements that the Communist parties themselves were not primarily responsible for setting into motion. The result of this fusion was the creation of Communist nation-states that were not subordinate to the Soviet Union, specifically because the traditional party allegiance to Moscow counted for less than the national unity created between the agricultural masses and the Party by their close cooperation in wartime. Milovan Djilas stresses the difference between the Yugoslav-Chinese experience and the cases of the Soviet satellites in his discussion of national Communism:

> The differences between Communist countries will, as a rule, be as great as the extent to which the Communists were independent in coming to power. Concretely speaking, only the Communists of three countries—the Soviet Union, China, and Yugoslavia—independently carried out revolutions or, in their own way and at their own speed, attained power and began "the

building of socialism." These three countries remained independent Communist states even in the period when Yugoslavia was—as China is today—under the most extreme influence of the Soviet Union; that is, in "brotherly love" and in "eternal friendship" with it. In a report at a closed session of the Twentieth Congress, Khrushchev revealed that a clash between Stalin and the Chinese government had barely been averted. The case of the clash with Yugoslavia was not an isolated case, but only the most drastic and the first to occur. In other Communist countries the Soviet government enforced Communism by "armed missionaries"—its army.[12]

The fact that wartime alliances between uprooted peasants and the preexisting Communist parties of China and Yugoslavia brought the second and third independent Communist governments into being presents many different problems of analysis. Our primary concern in this study is with the origin of the alliances themselves and particularly with the peasants' side in these alliances. To place such concerns in their correct context, however, it is first necessary to consider what this particular mode of political success meant to the Communist movement, and to discuss certain aspects of postwar Communist government that cause many people in the West to doubt that the Chinese or Yugoslav governments could possess a popular basis of support. Among the various problems that require mention are those of the "Leninist party," Comintern direction, and the United Front. We might call the first problem that of "totalitarianism and legitimacy."

In both China and Yugoslavia, Communist governments came to power after the collapse of the Axis governments and proceeded to implement a broad program of national reconstruction. Although this was undertaken in the name of Communist ideology and the historical mission of the Communist parties as the vanguard of the working class, both parties' popular basis of support in fact derived from peasant armies whose chief and almost sole concern had been successful resistance against fascist invaders. Did the peasants, therefore, regard their postwar governments as a betrayal of the wartime alliances with the Communists? There is every indication that they did not. Although it is true that the Communist parties eschewed Marxist-Leninist dogmatism in their efforts at wartime mass organization, they nevertheless transmitted their ultimate objectives and their world view to the population by means of propaganda and education, particularly in the later periods of the war, when victory was in sight. This ideology was, in turn, given legitimacy by the fact that the Communist parties were proving their ability to lead and govern during the resistance. The peasants thus did not question the nature of their postwar governments, because the Communist parties had achieved not only power but also authority.

A relation between ruler and subject based solely on power implies nothing more than the possession of superior coercive instruments in the hands of the ruler, regardless of the attitudes of the ruled. A relation based on authority is another matter: here a dialogue of mutual interest exists between ruler and subject. Superior means of coercion may still be present (in fact, such means are part of the definition of a "state"); but a government possessing authority can execute its policies without an overt show of force because the citizens feel that it is to their advantage to follow governmental directives, and because they feel that the government itself was legitimately placed in its position of command. On authority in general, Max Weber has written: "The motives of obedience to commands . . . can rest on considerations varying over a wide range from case to case; all the way from a simple habituation to the most purely rational calculation of advantage. A criterion of every true relation of imperative control, however, is a certain minimum of voluntary submission; thus an interest (based on ulterior motives or genuine acceptance) in obedience." [13]

What were the interests of the Chinese masses at the time that they accepted the leadership of the Chinese Communists? Their interests lay with plans and abilities that offered a means to cope with conditions of mass destruction and anarchy. The Chinese Communists had such plans, had veteran guerrilla cadres to put them into effect, and possessed the imagination to offer their leadership to the peasants. By 1945, the peasants of north and central China had experienced at least six years of life and work in the Communist-led anti-Japanese guerrilla bases. With the victory, for which the Communists logically took credit, the interest of the masses in continuing Communist leadership was further strengthened. The Communists had proved their abilities through years of difficult war; far from questioning the value of the Communists' newly unfurled ideology, the peasant felt that his own experience during the war indicated a need for him to learn the new ideas which promised so much and which, viewed retrospectively, had already succeeded in defeating the Japanese Army.[14]

The distinction here is between the usurpation of power and the achievement of a position in which power is exercised in pursuit of goals shared by the entire community. War provided the means by which the Communist Party re-entered Chinese political life; its war record made its Communist ideology legitimate (although the ideology itself may have been altered in major respects in the process—a subject to which we shall return later). In what sense "legitimate"? In the sense that the Chinese Communist Party came to power on the basis of a loyal constituency of about 100,000,000 peasants *during* the war, and that this constituency was still further expanded as a result of Japan's capitulation and the Communists' successful discrediting on nationalist grounds of the semi-exiled government of Chiang Kai-shek during and after the war. (Many peasants of north China were scarcely aware of the Chungking government's existence during the war; or they confused it with the Nanking puppets, who also called themselves the "Kuomintang.")

All this is not to ignore that the Chinese Communist government is totalitarian—i.e., that it is committed to the wholesale reorganization of society under conscious direction from above, and that it has enlisted all the institutions of the society (particularly the state) in the service of this single aim. Moreover, as we shall see, even during the war the Chinese Communist Party showed its Leninist virtuosity in organizing mass associations for ensuring total involvement of the peasants in the war effort and for isolating dissenters. The point, however, is that the Chinese masses—at least during the war and at the beginning of the regime—placed themselves at the disposal of the Communist Party to be used for nationalistic purposes. The travesties of individual human dignity perpetrated by totalitarianism were accepted during the war and in the first years of the regime (no one can speak authoritatively of contemporary internal conditions) as the necessary labor pains of China's renaissance. It was not totalitarian instruments of mass manipulation that originally led the Chinese masses into their pact with the Communist elite; it was, rather, the effects of the war and the national awakening that the war induced. Regardless of how well a Communist party masters Leninist theory, it is destined to remain a minor party without a mass following unless at some point it brings its interests into correspondence with those of the people (even if it subsequently reorients the interests of those people). Communist "organizational weapons" are important, but they scarcely account for the entire dynamic of a Communist society, or for that matter any other totalitarian society.

Totalitarianism is not incompatible with legitimacy, or nationalism, or the self-appraised interests of the masses; in fact, totalitarianism usually seems to depend upon the existence of these factors. As George Lichtheim has observed, "Since it is of the essence of a totalitarian regime to be dynamic, it cannot function in an atmosphere of public indifference." [15] We run the danger in contemporary Western studies of Chinese Communism of elevating "organization"—the party structure, communes, the cult of Mao, brainwashing, and so forth—to the level of a sociological secret weapon and, as a result, of accepting the "manipulation hypothesis" as a satisfactory explanation for the entire Chinese Communist work ethic. The present study is not concerned with the policies of the Communist government in power; but as for the *origin* of Communist power, this was simply the mutual interest of the Party and the masses in fighting the Japanese, and this interest developed in a normal fashion to the point at which the Party's directives were obeyed as those of a legitimate authority.

There are those, of course, who believe that the Communist rise to power in China can be explained without reference to the peasantry. Such persons pay little attention to the problems of the mass basis of Communist power and focus directly on Moscow's leadership of the international Communist movement. According to this view, if one possesses a knowledge of the "classical" Comintern-directed (i.e., Moscow-directed) Communist revolution, the formulas for which have been given wide publicity, the idea that indigenous forces could bear any responsibility for the revolution becomes absurd. As Jules Monnerot has described it, "What is happening . . . can be compared to what the situation would have been in the Roman world of the third century if there had been *international* and *preconcerted* synchronization between the Christian refusal of obedience and the successive thrusts of barbarian invasion; in other words, if a *single general staff*, devoted to the ruin of the ancient world, had had command of both the Christian church and the barbarians." [16] Clearly, the emphasis here is upon a "general staff" that plans the entire operation. To extend the analogy, the Chinese peasantry, which supported the Communist armies with men and provisions but denied them to the Nationalists, would be the Christian subversives in the grip of a foreign religion, while the Soviet's Far East General Army under Marshal A. M. Vassilievsky, which invaded Manchuria on August 9, 1945, becomes the barbarian horde. The general staff, needless to say, is the Comintern and its successors.

One of the difficulties of this theory is in proving that communications existed between the two control centers, Moscow and Yenan.[17] It may be argued, of course, that whether contacts existed or not the Chinese Communist leaders were still Communists. Although the success of the Communist Party may have been based upon an alliance with a nationalistically aroused peasantry, this does not—in and of itself—make the Communist Party any less Communist. Article I of the Party statutes of 1928 states that, "The Chinese Communist Party is a part of the Communist International"—that is, subject to Moscow—and the Party did not repudiate this tie during the period under study. It may also be advanced that the essence of Leninist theory and of Maoist practice is the use of professional revolutionaries to capitalize on mass discontent, regardless of its origin. Thus, one may ask, what difference does it make whether or not the Communists manipulated the symbols of nationalism or of any other sufficiently widespread ideology, so long as they were successful? They were and still are Bolsheviks.

The major feature of the Sino-Japanese War which supports the contention that the Communist Party acted as a Soviet tool was the creation of the KMT-CCP "United Front" against Japan. As is well known, the United Front tactic was ordered at the Comintern Congress in 1935 and was successfully implemented in China following the Sian Incident.[18] But one can scarcely regard the United Front as the vehicle by which the Communists came to power. In the first place, the United Front between the KMT and CCP was clearly a sham after the establishment of the blockade against Shen-Kan-Ning in 1939, and ceased to exist after the New Fourth Army Incident of January 1941. Despite this, Communist forces continued to expand their territories and popular following. Moreover, this expansion was not into areas in which the United Front had been strongest, such as the Hankow area, or into areas in which the facade of the United Front was still maintained (it is doubtful whether the publication of the Communist *Hsin-Hua jih-pao* in wartime Chungking can be credited with converting anyone to the Communist side, except possibly some Western journalists). The expansion was, instead, into areas that the Japanese armies had overrun.

In the second place, use of the United Front tactic in China had developed prior to and independent of the Seventh Comintern Congress; in the pre-1937 period it was predominantly an anti-KMT device used in the cities.[19] Party propaganda of that period was not an actual call to the colors for war with Japan, but a way of developing popular pressure on Chiang to call off his Communist-suppression campaigns. Least of all was the United Front used to legitimatize the Communist Party in the eyes of the peasantry—the only group whose support was of lasting importance to the Communists.

In actual fact, the United Front was irrelevant to the peasantry. The so-called "three-thirds" system—the practice whereby the Communists occupied no more than one-third of the posts in the guerrilla area governments—was not a "United Front" in any functional sense, i.e., in the sense of its being necessary for peasant support. Unity between the peasants and the Party was not based upon the three-thirds system, because the peasants actually supported the Communists through the mass organizations and the army.[20] The three-thirds system was a device for incorporating local non-Communist leaders, landlords, rich peasants, and other well-known people into the regional governments; it was similar to the system of "democratic parties" adopted in post-1949 Communist China.

The only concrete benefit obtained by the Communist Party as a result of its implementing the Moscow line on the United Front was that it permitted the recruitment, for a short period of time, of comparatively large numbers of students from urban areas. These students, after completing the course at Yenan's Anti-Japanese Military-Political University (K'ang-jih Chün-cheng Tahsüeh, abbreviated K'angta), generally served in the Communist forces as lower-level political officers. The existence of the United Front thus gave one important advantage to the Communists. However, other features of the United Front that the Communists viewed as desirable prior to 1937, such as the calling off of Nationalist attacks on Communist areas, all evaporated with the advance of the Japanese armies.

In short, we must conclude that the

United Front was not the basis upon which the Communist Party built its strength in China. It did not prevent continual armed clashes between KMT and CCP troops; it did not facilitate the large-scale supply of arms by the Western Allies to the Communists; and it did not allow the Communists to subvert the legitimate government from within (as in Spain). Most important, it did not promote acceptance of Communist Party leadership in the north China guerrilla bases (north China was a traditionally conservative area where even the KMT was almost unknown); yet it was in the guerrilla bases of north China that the Communist Party came to power.

The Economics of the Communist-Peasant Alliance

Among the many scholars who have recognized that the ranks of the victorious Communist armies were filled with peasants, there exists a great deal of confusion about the nature of the Communist-peasant partnership. Much of this confusion derives from the view that Communism should be understood solely or chiefly as an economic doctrine and that the peasant-based Communist revolutions should be regarded as a rural analogue of the Marxist proletarian revolution. This view has promoted two different kinds of erroneous interpretations. On the one hand, some writers see the impoverishment of the Chinese peasantry as the primary motivating force that drove them into alliance with the Communists, who are, in turn, regarded as agrarian reformers. On the other hand, those who regard the twentieth-century Communist movement as an elitist conspiracy primed to capitalize upon any crisis or fissure in the society that it hopes to capture are at pains to expose how little Communist parties promote the class interests of their followers. Although the latter theorists object, correctly, to regarding the Chinese Communist revolution as a "peasant rebellion," they ignore the possibility that the peasants had other motives than the economic interests of their class; and they insist that the Communists won over the peasantry by manipulation and fraud.

This failure to consider the basis of the wartime Communist-peasant alliances reflects the general lack of attention paid to the wartime resistance movements (by which the Communists of China and of Yugoslavia actually came to power) and the lack of inquiry into the origins of the nationalistic policies pursued by the Communist governments that achieved power independently of the Soviet Union. As examples of these policies, one need mention only the Soviet-Yugoslav dispute beginning in 1948 and the Sino-Soviet controversy of the early 1960's. We shall return in a later chapter to the problems of "national Communism"; for the present we must deal at greater length with the question of economic determinants in the Communist-peasant wartime alliances.

"Pure" peasant rebellions, in the sense of sporadic outbursts against local misery, are commonly met with in the histories of agricultural societies. Rarely, however, have they had any significant political effects. Thus, when the interpreters of the rise of Communism in China refer to the Communist revolution as a "peasant rebellion," they do not mean by that term merely a spontaneous demonstration or a local rebellion. The reference in the following remarks by Professor Mary Wright is not to a small-scale effort or to a movement lacking purpose or direction. She observes:

> The Chinese Revolution of which the Communists have secured leadership was and is a peasant revolution. . . . There [in the countryside prior to 1930] Mao Tse-tung's

group survived because it found the key to peasant support and control, land reform and a host of subordinate policies designed to mobilize the peasantry, improve agrarian production, and secure its fruits. . . . Communists do not have to fabricate figures to prove the poverty of the Chinese peasant. In actual fact, conditions are intolerable, and peasant revolt has long been endemic.[21]

The inspiration for these remarks comes predominantly from a knowledge of Chinese social history. Large-scale peasant rebellion in response to intolerable conditions of land tenure, food shortage, natural calamities, excessive taxation, usurious moneylending, and general misery in the villages has long been identified as the crucial event in the spectacular upheavals associated with changes of regime in China. The most recent of these disturbances occurred slightly more than a century ago, when the Taiping Rebellion erupted across south China as a reaction to population pressure and to the great famines of 1847 and 1849. That rebellion combined a quasi-Christian religious movement with a movement for agrarian reform. The result was a revolutionary effort of such scale that its ultimate failure seems more remarkable today than its successes. Professor Wright characterizes the Taiping Rebellion as an "agrarian revolution," i.e., one in which economic conditions were the primary determinants, and places it squarely in the history of the Communist revolution: "Today's agrarian revolution began a century ago when the Chinese peasantry rose against the existing order in the great Taiping Rebellion."[22] Even if Mao's effort does not actually span the century and link with the "long-haired thieves" (*ch'ang mao tsei*) of the Taiping leader Hung Hsiu-ch'üan, persons who agree with the peasant-rebellion theory argue that the Communist Party of China, after slowly coming to an appreciation of the potentialities of rural revolution, abandoned its futile attempts at urban insurrection and won the support of the peasantry by transforming itself into the scourge-of-the-landlords. Certainly Mao Tse-tung's Communism was as adaptable to this purpose as Hung's Christianity.

The essence of this analysis is the identification of rural economic distress as the cause of peasant rebelliousness. Although this may have been the crucial inducement to rebellion during certain periods of Chinese history, it fails to explain the success of the Communist-rural coalition of World War II. During the war the Communists did not contemplate the redistribution of land or any other class-oriented measures that would have radically altered the pattern of land ownership. Instead, the economic policies implemented by the Communist Party during the Sino-Japanese War were designed to create maximum unity—"to protect everybody from everybody else."[23] As Mao has put it, "The agrarian policy is a dual policy of demanding that the landlords reduce rent and interest, stipulating that the peasants pay this reduced amount of rent and interest."[24] This moderate wartime policy did not, of course, necessarily alienate the peasantry; but the Communists' success in winning peasant support cannot be attributed to their carrying out an "agrarian revolution."

It is in fact very difficult to apply economic criteria to either the Taiping or the Communist revolution. No answer can be given to a specific question dealing with the course of these revolutions in terms of economic forces alone. In the case of the Taipings, the desperately poor Hakka and Miao inhabitants of south China, who were the first to join Hung, came not out of economic motives but as converts to his religion.[25] The majority of peasants joined him as the rebellion gained momentum and after traditional rebels and local leaders had allied themselves with the Taiping objectives. Economic motives certainly underlay specific decisions to rebel, but they can be understood only as necessary, not as sufficient, causes. Relative economic deprivation came to a head in the Tao-kuang period (1821–50) and was a constant circumstance in various areas of China thereafter; however, it influenced but did not direct rebellion. The economic variable does not account for particular targets of rebellion (the dynasty, foreigners, invaders, or traitors); and it does not explain why rebellion occurs in one area, and then in another, but not in all places that have grievances and have given expression to them in the recent past. Underlying economic pressures also existed during the resistance war and exist today, but again an analysis purely in terms of economic forces leaves most political questions unanswered. Why is it that the peasantry did not support the Japanese and their puppets after 1937? Why did huge numbers of north China peasants volunteer for the Communist armies only after the Japanese invasion? Obviously, an argument based solely on the economic situation in China ignores the influence of the Japanese invasion, and thereby misinterprets the role of the Communist Party as leader of the anti-Japanese peasant armies.

This is not to argue that if the Japanese invasion of China or the German invasion of Yugoslavia had not occurred, the prewar governments could have continued to exist unassailed or that the process of social change associated with the Communist governments would never have begun. If the invasions had never occurred, a severe economic catastrophe in the future, or a prolongation of the rural depression of the 1930's, might well have produced revolutionary mobilization. But a constant, or slowly evolving, rate of economic deprivation would still have constituted only a conditioning factor in the subsequent revolutionary movements; and it is unlikely that such revolutionary movements would have confined themselves to economic reforms, just as the Chinese Communist government aims at more ambitious goals than the relief of rural misery. The movement of Fidel Castro in Cuba, for example, can hardly be accounted for by reference solely to the economic conditions of the Cuban peasants—conditions that have existed for decades. An economic analysis alone offers no insights into the potentiality of success of a revolutionary movement, and commonly distorts attempts at political analysis of the policies pursued by postrevolutionary governments.

There are other critics of Professor Wright's views, but, paradoxically enough, they seem to accept her idea that economic hardship is the only logical motive for peasant rebelliousness. Their argument with her turns on the question of whether the Chinese Communists were true agrarian reformers; they accurately point out that the CCP did not offer to advance the economic interests of the peasants during the war. Thus, they conclude (very like those who consider Chinese Communism the result of a Moscow-directed conspiracy), the Communists cynically manipulated the peasantry, and the peasants had no stake, real or imagined, in Communist leadership. Professor Franz Michael, for example, has stated:

> The fact that the Communist armies were enlarged by recruiting from the peasantry does not make them any more or less peasant armies than the nationalist troops with which they are contrasted and which drew their recruits from the same source. That the Communists had a land policy which in different forms favored the small peasants does not alter the fact that the Communists and not the peasants commanded the army. The term "peasant armies" implies an expression of the peasant will and peasant control which obviously did not exist, and the term "peasant

leader" implies a man who represents the peasants rather than the Communist Party and its policies.[26]

This type of analysis does not, of course, explain what the basis of the Communist-peasant alliance was, nor does it in any way account for the development of national Communist states. Professor Michael implies that the peasantry played no role in the revolution other than to provide soldiers and services for the armies of either the Kuomintang or the Communists (ignoring, among other things, the fact that the KMT had to utilize conscription from March 1936 on, whereas the Communists, in the main, relied upon volunteers both for their regular forces and for what was surely the world's largest militia system).

The major difficulty, as Professor Michael sees it, is the lack of correspondence between the "peasant will" and the "Communist Party and its policies." This use of the term "peasant will," and the implication that the peasant will is not equatable with Communist policies, suggests a confusion between the Communist Party's acting on the *side* of the peasantry and their acting for the *sake* of the peasantry. "For the sake of the peasantry" refers specifically to Communist policies that appealed directly to the economic interests and class-consciousness of the landless farm laborers, and that were directed against landlords and middle and rich peasants. This type of land policy was on the statute books in the Kiangsi Soviet Republic, but it was unsuccessful in creating a mass basis for the Party. The Party faced a dilemma in Kiangsi that became more difficult as the Party tried to deal with it. If the "radical" agrarian reform law were strictly implemented, it would alienate all but the poorest section of the peasantry, thereby defeating its purpose, which was to gain general rural support. On the other hand, if it were honored in the breach, as was the common practice in Kiangsi, it not only failed to gain supporters, but also left the Communist Party open to invidious comparison with the Kuomintang's announced land program.[27] The failure to resolve these questions of mass support was one of the strategic weaknesses of the Kiangsi Soviet, and thereby contributed to its military failure.

During the Anti-Japanese War period the Party abandoned the "radical" land program altogether and carried out a policy designed to create maximum unity for national defense.[28] All plans for agrarian reform were abrogated during the war while a mild policy of rent reduction and general rationalization of debts was carried out. Despite this, the Communists achieved their greatest popular following precisely during the period in which their unity policy was in effect. Clearly, their acting on the *side* of the peasantry—i.e., their successful opposition to the Japanese invaders—had become more important than their actions for the *sake* of the peasantry. In retrospect, the Communist Party was successful only when it ceased acting solely for the sake of the peasantry and began acting on the side of the peasantry instead. The interesting question, of course, is how the peasantry came to have a side at all.[29]

Mass Nationalism in China

It is the thesis of this study that the rise to power of the CCP and YCP in collaboration with the peasantry of the two countries can best be understood as a species of nationalism. A definition is necessary here because so many different usages for the term "nationalism" exist. In the past "nationalism" has been employed to refer to the postfeudal monarchies of western Europe, to certain romantic doctrines of the nineteenth century, and to the underlying dynamic of Communist Russia. The word has been equated with "a daily plebiscite," "political *bovarysme*," and a form of tribalism; persons as different as Theodore Roosevelt, Mahatma Gandhi, and Fidel Castro have been called "nationalists." Thus, in order to avoid confusion, it is necessary to consider at some length the meaning of nationalism in general and, more particularly, of nationalism in China during the period under investigation.

The first distinction to be made in the use of the term involves its altered scope over time. There has been a long-range trend toward the expansion of the numbers of persons subject to nationalism; and, as a result, the use of the term in 1960 is very different from its use in 1789. E. H. Carr's periodization of this expansion is standard: originally, national "populations" consisted of only the ruler and the nobility, and "the first period begins with the gradual dissolution of the mediaeval unity of empire and church and the establishment of the national state and the national church."[30] The second period occupies the century of the "Third Estate" (1789–1914), during which nationalism spread to the bourgeoisie; the contemporary third period is characterized by "the bringing of new social strata within the effective membership of the nation, the visible reunion of economic with political power, and the increase in the number of nations."[31] Contemporary studies of nationalism are concerned with mass nationalism, i.e., the third period; in China, this means peasant nationalism. A successful nationalist movement today—one that succeeds in founding a nation state—must be a mass movement; and a regime that rules a people indifferent to or unaware of government, such as that of Chiang Kai-shek or of the late Rafael Trujillo, cannot properly be called "nationalist."

A second distinction must be made between two analytical uses of the term nationalism: nationalism understood as a condition already in existence, and nationalism understood as a process of coming into being. An example of nationalism understood as a condition occurs in the work of the historian Carlton J. H. Hayes. He writes: "I would define nationality as a cultural group of people who speak a common language (or closely related dialects) and who possess a community of historical traditions (religious, territorial, political, military, economic, artistic, and intellectual)."[32] Many students of nationalism would take exception to this definition, particularly to the insistence upon linguistic homogeneity; however, the important point here is that Hayes considers nationalism as a static condition—namely, as consciousness of nationality.[33] How people become conscious of their national characteristics, or what their self-image was before they were conscious of nationality, is not considered.

The deficiency of this definition lies in its lack of differentiation between "national movement" and "nationalism." Hayes's definition will not help us to explain why, for example, the Japanese were more nationalistic in 1930 than in 1830, since at both times they spoke the same language, held roughly the same religious views, and painted the same kinds of pictures. Professor Hayes mentions the importance of political, military, and economic traditions; but by not asking what lies behind these traditions or why certain traditions are honored over others, he is considering only the plumage of nationalism. For purposes of studying the spread or onset of nationalism, we must identify the forces that cause populations to form nation states and isolate the circumstances under which groups of human beings are transformed into national citizens. Also, in order to understand why the particular traditions and characteristics mentioned by Hayes are valued by a given national community, we must relate these elements of "national plumage" to a functional model of the nation.

Karl W. Deutsch has summed up the failure of writers to use functional concepts in early studies of nationalism: "The dangerous result was that nationalism came to be widely accepted as a mere 'state of mind' with *few tangible roots.*"[34] Deutsch himself has done much to correct this deficiency by developing a functional definition of nationalism—one that is helpful in understanding nationalism among the peasantry in China. Deutsch's central concept is that of a "people," which he defines in the following way:

> The community which permits a common history to be experienced as common is a community of complementary habits and facilities of communication. . . . A large group of persons linked by such complementary habits and facilities of communication we may call a people. . . . All the usual descriptions of a people in terms of a community of languages, or character, or memories, or past history, are open to exception. For what counts is not the presence or absence of any single factor, but merely the presence of sufficient communications facilities with enough complementarity to produce the over-all result.[35]

Thus Deutsch regards the ability of members of one large group to communicate with each other as the basic "root" of nationalism. "The essential aspect of the unity of a people . . . is the complementarity or relative efficiency of communication among individuals—something that is in some ways similar to mutual rapport, but on a larger scale."[36] The important question is how does such a mutual rapport (identity of interest, intermingling of wills, sharing of responsibility, and so forth) come into existence among a specific population at a given time and place?

"Social mobilization" is the shorthand term generally used to describe the dynamic process whereby pre-national peoples enter into political community with their fellows. This is the primary conceptual tool in contemporary studies of nationalism.[37] Social mobilization refers to the pressures that cause populations to form political communities—in other words, the changes that cause people of towns, villages, and regions to knit together into new political orders which transcend these areas as their inhabitants realize that their mutual interests extend beyond daily contacts. The pressures that cause social mobilization may be evolutionary, revolutionary, or both. Deutsch, in his study of social communication, is concerned primarily with how national communities developed out of European feudal society; he points particularly to the importance of the growth of towns, the shift from a subsistence economy to an exchange economy, and the enlargement of basic communications grids in promoting this development. However, although the evolutionary growth of physical links was an important mobilizing agent in early modern Europe, it is not the only source of effective social mobilization; and towns, regional communications, and markets all emerged in China many centuries ago without producing a nation state. In the twentieth century, evolutionary pressure has been accelerated and supplemented by more immediate and violent ways of mobilizing a population.

E. J. Hobsbawm in his study of pre-national mass movements (particularly among peasants) describes some of these other, more immediate, forces that may mobilize populations:

> [Pre-political] men and women . . . form the large majority in many, perhaps in most, countries even today, and their acquisition of political consciousness has made our century the most revolutionary in history. . . . They come into it [the modern political world] as first-generation

> immigrants, or what is even more catastrophic, it comes to them from outside, insidiously by the operation of economic forces which they do not understand and over which they have no control, or brazenly by conquest, revolutions and fundamental changes of law whose consequences they may not understand, even when they have helped to bring them about.[38]

Among the forces listed by Hobsbawm, foreign invasion and internal resistance organization have taken, in recent years, a predominant role in mobilizing prepolitical populations. World War II, in particular, unleashed forces of mass awakening in countries such as China and Yugoslavia, where previous "national movements" had appealed only to educated elites. War-induced anarchy and the organization of guerrilla resistance gave the Chinese and Yugoslav peasant masses new experiences and a new history. Their common action in defending and governing large areas of occupied territory and in solving specific political, economic, and military problems laid the foundation for social communication.[39] That is to say, the masses of China and Yugoslavia were socially mobilized by the war.

In making this observation we are not overlooking the prewar movement in China that centered upon the Kuomintang. Nationalism in China did not, of course, make its first appearance during the Sino-Japanese war; at the time of the invasion a nationalist movement had already existed for at least forty years. However, the National Movement (with capital letters) that began with Sun Yat-sen and developed among the students and educators in Peking after May 4, 1919, was not a mass movement; it was confined almost entirely to the socially mobilized but unassimilated intelligentsia and to the small middle classes that grew up in the treaty ports. Sun himself acknowledged the popular weakness of his party when he sought alliance with the CCP, and when he initiated the KMT reorganization as an elite association in 1924. Early Kuomintang nationalism bears a strong resemblance to nineteenth-century nationalism among central European intellectuals and to the formative periods of colonial or non-European nationalism in this century—for example, the movements in Egypt, Tunisia, and Turkey. Because of this similarity, the term "nationalist" has commonly been used to characterize the activities of intellectuals in their creative search for doctrines of national identity and uniqueness. Although this usage has been bolstered by general acceptance, it must be clearly understood that nationalism among intellectual elites and mass nationalism are two distinct, if related, phenomena.

Such early intellectual nationalism in China was peculiarly the product of Westernized, or cosmopolitan, educated Chinese. They sought a new understanding of Chinese culture and history that would facilitate the acceptance of China into the modern world and rationalize their own discontent at China's backwardness. It is not surprising that the various doctrines to emerge from this intellectual ferment were amalgams of Western revolutionary thought, violent reactions to contemporary Japan, and drastic revisions of traditional Chinese philosophy.[40] For a century Chinese culture had been under continuous assault both from abroad by missionaries and merchants and from within by native iconoclasts; during this time Chinese intellectuals consulted a broad range of social theorists (from Henry George to Japanese militarists) in order to explain and to overcome China's political backwardness. Equally important, prewar intellectual nationalists were concerned with the obstructions to China's reform created by imperialism and the unequal treaties. The wars, humiliations, and material and territorial losses suffered by the Ch'ing empire and the still-born Republic during the century of contact with modern imperialist states were continuous sources of outrage and inspiration to the new nationalist ideologues.

For all the political activities of the prewar Chinese educated elites, theirs was a nationalist movement with a head and no body. The Chinese peasantry was isolated from the long-standing Chinese nationalist movement, having neither a stake in Chinese literati culture nor any direct contact with the imperialists. The humiliations to China were largely meaningless to the agricultural masses; and when imperialism did impinge upon their lives in a direct way, as at the time of the Boxer Rebellion, their reaction was essentially nativistic and pre-political.[41] The peasants did not share the intellectuals' idealized vision of the Chinese state; they had no theory of tutelage by which it should be achieved, no "Three Principles of the People" which, if fully implemented, would restore China to a position of equality as a sovereign nation.

If this indifference of the Chinese masses to prewar politics is ignored, a realistic appraisal of the Nanking Government (1928–37) cannot be made. That is to say, if we characterize Chiang Kai-shek's government as nationalistic, we overlook the opportunistic alliances among military leaders that underlay Chiang's power, and we disregard the ceaseless efforts made by Nanking to unify the country after 1928 by direct military action. Prior to 1937, nationalism in China was a powerful sentiment among many leadership groups, but the social milieu in which they acted was not nationalistic. When, during the war, the peasants were mobilized and the Communist Party identified itself with Chinese nationalism, the Nationalist Government was slow to recognize the implications that this development had for its own future. The failure of the wartime KMT to understand that its own claims to nationalist leadership were not accepted by the whole population and that it was vulnerable to an attack on purely nationalist grounds contributed directly to its defeat by the Communist-peasant alliance.

Mention of the fact that prewar Chinese nationalism was primarily an ideological phenomenon restricted to educated elites raises further questions in the definition of nationalism. In the past, particularly in the nineteenth century, nationalist activities appeared to be confined exclusively to the sort of ideological controversy that we associate with the May Fourth period in China. Nationalist intellectuals sought, in their polemical and creative activities, to identify the peculiar characteristics of a particular people (usually their own) or to establish a historical, linguistic, or racial tradition that would support a claim for these people to form a nation-state—for example, early German claims of linguistic unity, Slavic claims of religious uniqueness. As a result of the predominance of ideological disputation in nationalist movements, the study of nationalism has often become the province of the intellectual historian; and the establishment of an intellectual claim to "self-determination" (or to "manifest destiny") was often thought to constitute all that was meant by nationalism.

An exclusive concern with nationalism as nationalists themselves define it is of almost no use for purposes of general analysis; and it ignores the question of timing in the onset of a particular search for nationalist doctrine by given intellectual circles. Today such nationalist activity is understood as a product of the social mobilization of nationalist intellectuals—usually prior to the mobilization of the general population and as a result of causes different from those that affect total populations. Education, or foreign residence, is a common mobilizing agent among intellectual elites—particularly when colonial domination, racial discrimination, or other circumstances prevent the people concerned from achieving a social status commensurate with their education. The origins of the early twentieth-century Chinese nationalists, in these terms, are well known: Sun Yat-sen's intimate association with overseas Chinese and his extensive foreign travel, the creation of the T'ung Meng Hui among Chinese students in Japan, the peculiarly elevated position of Peking University students at the time of World War I, and the extensive European travel and education of the early Chinese Communist leaders.[42] Thus, in recognizing the existence of a nationalist movement in China before the wartime peasant mobilization, we are not recognizing a different kind of nationalism, but only one that was prior to the mass movement, restricted to specific types of people, and energized by different but analogous forces. It is perfectly possible that an intellectual nationalist movement will not ever possess a mass nationalist following: or that a later mass nationalist mobilization will unseat a pre-existing nationalist elite and install its own leadership; or that intellectual nationalists may guide and control, particularly by education, the subsequent development of mass nationalism. China offers an example of a mass nationalist movement unseating a previously mobilized and installed nationalist elite.

So far in this discussion of the meaning of nationalism, we have stressed the central importance of the process by which a people become a nation. We have labeled this process "social mobilization," and we have indicated that a variety of forces may be responsible for bringing it about—particularly a social cataclysm such as war, or the collapse of a colonial government, which acts as a catalyst for more general pressures of social change. Many years ago Max Weber noted the important fact that nations and nationalism do have a beginning and suggested the need for studying the activating forces in nationalism. His observation, interestingly enough (although erroneously) based on a Chinese example, was: "Only fifteen years ago [from c. 1914], men knowing the Far East, still denied that the Chinese qualified as a 'nation'; they held them to be only a 'race.' Yet today, not only the Chinese political leaders but also the very same observers would judge differently. Thus it seems that a group of people under certain conditions may attain the quality of a nation through specific behavior, or that they may claim this quality as an 'attainment' —and within short spans of time at that."[43] Despite the fact that Weber, along with Sun Yat-sen and many other Chinese, was to be disappointed by the 1911 revolution, his point is very valuable. Social mobilization, as we have used it, corresponds to Weber's "certain conditions" under which a given people attain the quality of a nation; on the basis of evidence presented in subsequent chapters, it is advanced here that the peasants of the occupied areas in China were socially mobilized by war and resistance organization, and thereby became a national population.[44]

However, social mobilization itself is not all that is meant by nationalism; it is, rather, the crucial occurrence in the onset of nationalism. There is another constituent in mass nationalist movements, which usually appears simultaneously with or shortly after mobilization; this is ideology. Following upon a given national mobilization, the newly mobilized people will commonly receive from their leadership a more or less elaborate doctrine that serves to idealize the activities undertaken by the people in common. In model form, such a doctrine will provide an ideological framework within which the mobilized people may understand and express their behavior as a nation. Often it will portray the given nationalist movement as undertaken in behalf of an ultimately triumphant cause; and it will draw upon allegedly universal religions or philosophical systems for "proof" of the justness or inevitability of nationalist activities.[45] Such a national myth usually exalts the leadership elite that directs the work of the mobilized population and places an ideological support under the claims to legitimacy that the elite enjoys.

The content of these national myths ranges widely over the entire spectrum of human thought; "racial science" or "geopolitics" may support certain national communities, enlightenment philosophy supports others. Buddhism is enlisted in the service of Burmese nationalism, Islam in the Middle Eastern states, Catholicism in Ireland, and an undifferentiated protestantism in the United States. Professional exponents of particular religions as well as *bona fide* scientists may, and often do, object to the use of religion or science in the service of nationalist doctrines. It must be understood, however, that national myths drawn from nonnationalist systems of belief or analysis do not have the effect of placing the nation-state under the guidance of popes or scientists; rather, they are intended to reinforce the legitimacy of the nation by incorporating the legitimacy of priests, scientists, or philosophers into it. In other words, myth draws from doctrines that are independently respected in society and reinterprets such doctrines so that they will tend to mobilize popular imagination in support of national government—a government that in all probability is already supported on the basis of interest.

Although national myth is constructed by nationalist intellectuals from among all the diverse historical, religious, and philosophical influences present in a people's past, a given myth is not, of course, selected at random. The study of both the transmission of myth to nationalist ideologues and the current intellectual and philosophical trends that dictate "choice" among national myths is of great importance. As Professor Hatfield has observed in connection with Nazi myth, "Did these dogmas actually determine events, or were they a mere ideological façade? Even if they were only that, it would remain a matter of some importance to discover why one facade was chosen rather than another, and why it impressed so many people, not all of them Germans, by any means."[46] This observation is true, but it must be clearly understood that the subject of ideological inquiry is a national myth overlaying the social mobilization of a given people. Failure to bear this in mind has produced, for example, the plethora of uniformly ineffectual anti-Marxist books that aim at "meeting Communism on its own terms"; and it likewise explains the weakness of the counterideological approach to Communism—for example, that of Moral Rearmament.

With regard to the question, raised by Professor Hatfield, of a functional role for myth in determining events, this is found as a general rule not to be the case. Myth is most often an *ex post facto* revision either of written history or of the nonnationalist ideology that is being used as the basis of the myth. This is not to say that national myth does not exist prior to the victory of a mass nationalist movement; of course it does. But ideology itself—whether fascism, communism, or only a belief in a glorious ancestral history—does not in and of itself mobilize either intellectual elites or nationalist masses. Such mobilization is produced by other more immediate and less abstract pressures, as discussed earlier. Myth exists before mass mobilization because the elite is usually mobilized before the masses. A nationalist elite will acquire or create a fairly well developed "explanation" of its "mission," looking to the time when mass mobilization might occur. However, as the two cases of China and Yugoslavia strongly suggest, the prewar elite ideology itself will probably undergo an extensive process of renovation and "nationalization" at the time when elite mobilization is translated into mass mobilization. Thus we commonly find that the ideological history of an elite group prior to the time it comes to power is largely irrelevant to its subsequent ideological activities and pretensions. In such cases, it is convenient to distinguish pre-mobilization ideology and post-mobilization ideology as two separate entities—for example, to distinguish the Yugoslav Communist Party's Stalinism of 1939 from its Titoism of 1948 and after.

This general idea of national myth following upon and supplementing social mobilization is useful in understanding the political history of the national Communist states. When we assert that the Chinese and Yugoslav Communist movements can best be understood as a species of nationalism, we have in mind other considerations than just the two movements' wartime origins. Most important of these considerations is the marked eccentricity displayed by China and Yugoslavia in their relations with the other eleven Communist governments.[47] This eccentricity goes beyond the possibility that China and Yugoslavia merely consider Moscow's leadership to have been faulty in particular instances; both states have broken with the USSR in response to different types of Soviet leadership, and the Soviet Union has been unable to reconcile its differences with the two nations by either enticement or discipline. Although it is possible to maintain that national Communism in China and Yugoslavia represents simply a reaction to national Communism in the USSR, one must still account for the fact that only the Chinese and Yugoslav parties have successfully given expression to their resentment.

We observe the emergence in both China and Yugoslavia of indigenous brands of Communism. The propounders of these new formulations claim that Chinese and Yugoslav revolutionary experiences, respectively, constitute an advance over Soviet revolutionary tradition, and at the same time insist that they are squarely in the line of development predicted by "scientific socialism." In view of the existence of the wartime resistance movements in both Communist China and Yugoslavia, as well as the subsequent development of national Communism in both states, it is necessary to reexamine their particular histories from the point of view of nationalism. It appears today that China and Yugoslavia, from the time of the invasions to the present, offer typical examples of mass nationalist movements in which Communism serves as an official rationale for nationalist policies.

Communism, in the sense of the philosophy of Marx and Lenin, is remarkably well suited to the role of national myth. In addition to proclaiming the inevitability of success in the work of national construction under Communist auspices, it also partakes of the single most widely accepted ideology of the present age—science. With the necessary revisions, Communism legitimatizes the totalitarian rule of the national directorate ("the vanguard of the working class"), and it provides a Manichaean identification of the nation's enemies ("the imperialists") to be used as an ever-present scapegoat in case of nationalist setbacks.

Although we often read that the "Chinese Communists have stood Marx on his head," [48] we rarely consider why Marxism has such a grip on the Chinese. We do not consider how revised Marxism eases the tremendous sacrifices required for national construction, or how it reinforces the desire of many Chinese to make China a powerful nation. We do not contemplate the demands of Chinese nationalism or the place of Communism in its support; as a result, we are astonished when the Communist leaders resort to ideological pedantry to explain reverses in the development program. The defense of Chinese Communist ideology is as important to Chinese nationalism as the successful raising of bumper crops. It is because he is a nationalist that the Communist leader claims Marxist legitimacy: "While revising Marxism in accordance with the national environment and his own beliefs . . . the local leader always claims that he is not revising Marxism, but is only 'applying it creatively.' Furthermore, he usually asserts that his interpretation of Marxism is the only correct one and might well be imitated by other countries. For this reason, national Communists refuse to admit that they are national Communists." [49] Obviously, if a national Communist declared that his revisions diverged from Marxism as a consistent system, he would forfeit the advantage he obtains from being a Marxist—the participation in a widely accepted theory that underwrites his actions as "scientific."

In a later chapter of this study we shall review certain of the nationalist manifestations in Chinese and Yugoslav Communist ideology. For the present, my intention is only to introduce the concept of national myth as complementary to social mobilization in the present use of the term "nationalism." In essence, I understand a mass nationalist movement as a combination of the concepts of social mobilization and national myth. My purpose in advancing this hypothesis is not to offer a general theory of nationalism describing the basic circumstances in which all nations have been formed. It is, rather, to seek an understanding of the remarkable change in fortunes experienced by the Chinese Communist Party during World War II —a question that has been ignored in the past largely because of insufficient data. On the importance of the war, Fitzroy Maclean, Commander of the British mission to the Yugoslav Partisans, once wrote: "At the bottom of their dispute with the Kremlin lay Tito's claim that 'the Jugoslav brand of Communism was not something imported from Moscow but had its origin in the forests and mountains of Jugoslavia.'" [50] Similarly, I suggest that the origins of the Sino-Soviet dispute are to be found in the plains of central Hopei and in the mountains of Shantung at the time of the Japanese invasion.

NOTES

[1] The maximum populations of the various districts under the direct control of the Soviet Central Government in 1934 were estimated by Mao Tse-tung for Edgar Snow in 1936 as follows:

Kiangsi Soviet	3,000,000
Hupeh-Anhwei-Honan	2,000,000
Hunan-Kiangsi-Hupeh	1,000,000
Kiangsi-Hunan	1,000,000
Chekiang-Fukien	1,000,000
Hunan-Hupeh	1,000,000
Total	9,000,000

Snow recalled that "Mao laughed when I quoted him the figure of '80,000,000' people living under the Chinese Soviets, and said that when they had that big an area the revolution would be practically won." *Red Star Over China* (New York: Modern Library ed., 1938), p. 73. By April 24, 1945, at the Seventh Chinese Communist Party Congress, Mao Tse-tung could announce that "China's liberated areas under the leadership of the Chinese Communist Party have now a population of 95,500,000." "On Coalition Government," *Selected Works of Mao Tse-tung* (London: Lawrence and Wishart, 1956), IV, 259. On August 13, 1945, Mao claimed 200,000,000 inhabitants for the Communist-controlled Great Rear Area (*Ta-hou-fang*). *Mao Tse-tung hsüan-chi* IV (Peking, 1960), 1124. This last figure reflects the great expansion of Communist territories that accompanied the Japanese collapse; actually only about 100,000,000 had been securely organized in Communist bases.

[2] Chiang Kai-shek's first speech calling for a movement to achieve a "new life" was made in Nanch'ang, Kiangsi, February 19, 1934. Chiang launched the New Life Movement (Hsin Sheng-huo Yün-tung) in conjunction with the final annihilation drive against the Communists. As Samuel Chu notes, "The Movement was an outgrowth of the immediate problem of reconstructing and rehabilitating those areas of Kiangsi taken from the Communists, but soon became a movement on a national scale." "The New Life Movement, 1934–1937," in John E. Lane, ed., *Researches in the Social Sciences on China* (New York: Columbia University East Asian Institute Studies, No. 3, 1957), p. 2. It is of no immediate concern whether the New Life Movement actually helped the peasantry of Kiangsi or not (it certainly did not aid the peasants of other provinces); the point is that it competed economically with the Communists' program, offered peace, and was vigorously presented to the peasantry.

The assertion that the basis of peasant-Communist collaboration in the Kiangsi period was economic is, of course, an abstraction. In the actual village context, influences such as the peasants' lack of physical mobility, personal feuds, the history of banditry in the area, and the strength of secret societies would all enter into decisions for or against the Red Army. But, as one contemporary account puts it, "To unravel these criss-cross relationships [the sources of popular support for the Communists in the Soviet Republic] is almost impossible. The fact remains that economic inequities and iniquities have much to do with them. People who are economically secure or contented rarely respond to the enticements of Reds or any other revolutionary movement. In the territory held by the 'China Soviet State' the government is promoting a campaign to relieve these economic stresses—to improve upon the aims of the 'Soviet State.'" "The Red Hegira to Szechuan Province and the Future of the Movement," *China Weekly Review* (Shanghai, February 16, 1935), p. 382.

[3] U.S. War Department, Military Intelligence Division, "The Chinese Communist Movement" (July 5, 1945) (declassified August 23, 1949). This useful report is published in U.S. Senate, 82d Congress, 2d Session, Committee on the Judiciary, *Institute of Pacific Relations* (Washington: Government Printing Office, 1952), as Part 7A, Appendix II. The quotation is from p. 2332.

[4] According to Niijima Sunayoshi, the following numbers of "democratic political authorities" had been set up in the guerrilla areas by the end of the war: 22 Administrative Offices (*hsing-cheng hsing-shu*); 90 Inspectorates (*chuan-yüan kung-shu*); and 635 hsien governments. See his article "Kaihō-kū" (Liberated Areas), in Chūgoku Kenkyū-sho, *Gendai Chūgoku jiten* (Dictionary of Modern China) (Tokyo, 1959), pp. 46–49. The first two types of administrative agencies were located at the subprefectural level; their functions varied according to locality. According to Ch'ien Tuan-sheng, there were a total of 1,949 hsien in 28 provinces at the start of the war. "Wartime Local Government in China," *Pacific Affairs,* XVI (1943), 441–60.

The rates of growth in hsien governments established by the Communist forces were compiled in a Japanese study of 1942 as follows:

(a) Numbers of hsien in north China with magistracies set up under the sponsorship of the Chinese Communist forces.

January 1938	18
August 1939	130
July 1941	355
(plus 23 estimated to be in Shen-Kan-Ning)	

(b) Central China (New Fourth Army)

October 1941	104

See "Chūgoku kyōsantō no genkyō, dōkō narabi ni taisaku" (The Present Condition of the Chinese Communist Party: Trends and Countermeasures) in Kōain (Asia Development Board), *Jōhō* (Intelligence), No. 57 (January 1, 1942), p. 5. (*Jōhō,* an invaluable source for the study of modern China, was a classified, bimonthly publication of the Political Affairs Bureau of the

Asia Development Board (Kain Seimubu) in Tokyo (first published September 1, 1939). The Kōain was founded December 16, 1938, in accordance with Imperial Ordinance No. 758; it became a part of the Greater East Asia Ministry when that agency was established on November 1, 1942. The Kōain's head office was in Tokyo with branch offices in Shanghai, Peiping, Amoy, and Kalgan; and with subbranch offices in Canton and Tsingtao. There were four divisions in Tokyo: political, economic, cultural, and technical. The Premier was President of the Kōain. Since its affairs dealt exclusively with China, it was commonly known in English as the China Affairs Board, but this is a mistranslation. See affidavit of Oikawa Genshichi, International Military Tribunal for the Far East (IMTFE), *Proceedings*, pp. 4761–62.)

[5] "The New Nationalism," *Virginia Quarterly Review*, XXVI (1950), 436–37.

[6] To facilitate the accurate location of places named in this study, an appendix has been provided in which hsien are identified both by name and by the number given in U.S. Central Intelligence Agency, *China, Provisional Atlas of Communist Administrative Units* (Washington: Department of Commerce, 1959). Although this atlas is not contemporary with the period Chinese characters, a uniform Wade-Giles system of romanization is used throughout, the index is superior to any other in present use, and the atlas is readily available in libraries.

[7] Printed in Chief of Staff, Terauchi Corps, *Kyōsangun no seijibu ni tsuite* (Concerning the Political Department of the Communist Army), November 8, 1938, *Rikushi mitsu dai nikki* (Army, China, Secret Diary) [Rikugunshō (War Ministry) Archives], Vol. 64 (of 73 vols.), 1938, No. 3. The Japanese Army archives have been catalogued by John Young in his *Checklist of Microfilm Reproductions of Selected Archives of the Japanese Army, Navy, and Other Government Agencies, 1868–1945* (Washington: Georgetown University Press, 1959). Young's "T" (title) numbers are given in this study for works from this particular collection (original films located in the Library of Congress) as an aid to identification. In future citations the Rikugunshō series title and volume numbers will be omitted; full citations can be found in the Bibliography. The Terauchi Corps work, a collection of captured Chinese materials, is T912. The Japanese Army archives were returned to Japan by the U.S. government in 1957 and are at present housed at the Bōeichō Senshishitsu (Defense Agency, War History Office), Tokyo.

[8] See the article "Sankō-seisaku" (The "Three-All" Policy) by Fujita Masatsune in *Gendai Chūgoku jiten*, pp. 209–10. The three components of this policy were "kill all, burn all, loot all." The Japanese began serious "mopping-up" campaigns following the so-called "Hundred Regiments Offensive" (August 20–December 5, 1940) of the Eighth Route Army. The first known mop-up was carried out in central Shansi and in the Foup'ing area of Hopei by the 108th division (Maj. Gen. Tomabechi Shiro), First Army, between March 10 and the end of April, 1938. One Japanese report reads: "Although the enemy suffered heavy losses during these operations the desired result was not achieved. Communist troops, particularly in the vicinity of Wut'ai and the area north of Ch'angchih, were not completely wiped out and powerful forces continued to roam the countryside harassing the Japanese rear. It was evident that the need existed for more aggressive campaigns and mopping-up operations in order to establish peace and order in the area. This was especially true as, with the withdrawal of various First Army units during the latter part of April for the T'ungshan Operation [Battle of Hsüchou; city fell May 19, 1938], enemy guerrilla activity within the Army's jurisdictional area increased markedly." U.S. Army, Forces in the Far East, *North China Area Operations Record, July 1937–May 1941* (Tokyo: Military History Section; Headquarters, Army Forces Far East, 1955), pp. 137–38. ["Japanese Monograph 178."] This document was written by Lt. Gen. Shimoyama Takuma, former staff officer, North China Area Army, and Lt. Gen. Hashimoto Gun, former Chief of Staff, First Army.

[9] The term "peasant nationalism" was first used to describe the Chinese resistance by Professor George E. Taylor in his study of Japanese occupation policies. He wrote: "The peasants, as usual, stayed on their fields and the village headmen, local gentry, and even district magistrates failed to retreat with the Chinese armies. It was not that they welcomed the invader; they were merely unaccustomed to resisting by force the exchange of one tax collector for another. . . . The village was a collection of impoverished and leaderless farmers, at least at the beginning of the war. That the peasantry of North China did not prove such an easy problem in government, and later emerged as the chief obstacle to the extension of Japanese-sponsored administration, was due to the development of a peasant nationalism on a scale broad enough to constitute a political revolution. The main contribution of the Japanese to this development of peasant nationalism lay in their conduct of the war, but the chief responsibility rests with the Chinese leadership which emerged in the hinterland." *The Struggle for North China* (New York: International Secretariat, Institute of Pacific Relations, 1940), pp. 41–42.

[10] Of China's total population in 1949, which has been estimated at 557,010,000, village dwellers accounted for 480,720,000, or 89.65 per cent. *Gendai Chūgoku jiten*, p. 302.

[11] Branko Lazitch, *Tito et la révolution yougoslave* (Paris, 1957), p. 65. (All translations from the French, as well as those from Chinese and Japanese, are by the author unless otherwise indicated.) In regard to the social composition of the Partisan units, Lazitch (Lazić) remarks (p. 63), "The Communist insurrection combined two forces: the members of the Party, who executed Moscow's directives, and the population, which wanted to help sustain the fight against the Germans and which had to defend itself against the extermination policy of the Independent State of Croatia. The former constituted the leadership, and the latter *the bulk of the Partisans*. From the point of view of social origins, the former consisted largely of young intellectuals and the latter of *peasants*." Italics mine.

[12] Milovan Djilas, *The New Class, An Analysis of the Communist System* (New York, 1957), pp. 174–75.

[13] *The Theory of Social and Economic Organization*, Henderson and Parsons, trans. (Glencoe, Ill., 1947), p. 324.

[14] Lucian W. Pye's distinctions among the various "appeals" of Communism are different from, but parallel to, the interpretation of Chinese Communism offered here. He records (1) a Communist appeal by the British and American parties to intellectuals alienated from the general society, and (2) an appeal by the French and Italian parties to the interests of distinct classes in the total society. His third type of "appeal" is that made by "People's Liberation Communism." "[In Asia] large numbers of people are losing their sense of identity with their traditional ways of life and are seeking restlessly to realize a modern way. . . . These people see the Communist organization as a stable element in their otherwise highly unstable societies. In modern times, these societies have generally been subjected to war and violence to an extreme degree. . . . The structure of Communism is something to which these people can hitch their ambitions. In the hierarchy of the party they can discover potentialities for advancement. They come to believe that in the structure of the party they can find a closer relationship between effort and reward than in anything they have known in either the static old society or the unstable, unpredictable, new one. . . . Communism also offers to such persons a means for understanding and explaining the social realities that have been disturbing them. Events and developments that they have had to accept as the workings of an unknown fate become comprehensible through Communism. The promise of knowledge is also a promise of action; a sense of futility can be replaced by the spirit of the activist. Thus, it seems that People's Liberation Communism can best be explained by the role it has assumed in an acculturation process involving whole societies." *Guerrilla Communism in Malaya* (Princeton, N.J., 1956), pp. 7–8. This role taken by Communism in Asian societies can equally well be understood as a species of nationalism.

[15] *Marxism, An Historical and Critical Study* (London, 1961), p. 378.

[16] Jules Monnerot, *Sociology and Psychology of Communism* (Boston: Beacon ed., 1960), p. 21. Italics mine. (Translation of Monnerot's *Sociologie du communisme*, Paris, 1949).

[17] The authoritative study of precisely this question is Charles B. McLane, *Soviet Policy and the Chinese Communists 1931–1946* (New York, 1958). McLane (p. 9) finds that "The Fourth Plenum [January 1931] is primarily significant, not because it marked another change in the Party leadership, but because it is the last identifiable instance of outright Soviet intervention in the internal affairs of the Chinese Communist Party." Contacts between Mao and Stalin in this period were fragmentary, if they existed at all.

[18] For a reappraisal of the Seventh Comintern Congress, see Kermit E. McKenzie, "The Soviet Union, the Comintern, and World Revolution: 1935," *Political Science Quarterly*, LXV (1950), 214–37. The most carefully reasoned analysis of the Sian Incident is Ishikawa Tadao, "Shian-jiken no ikkōsatsu; Mosukō to Chūgoku kyōsantō to no kankei ni tsuite" (An Inquiry into the Sian Incident: Concerning the Relations Between Moscow and the Chinese Communist Party), in his *Chūgoku kyōsantō shi kenkyū* (Studies in the History of the Chinese Communist Party) (Tokyo, 1959), pp. 217–45. As we shall see, the true significance of the Sian Incident lies not in its giving rise to the United Front, but in its compelling Chiang Kai-shek and his government to adopt an anti-Japanese policy.

[19] "On 10 January 1933 the Chinese Red Army offered a united front to any armed force that would join it in battle against Japan." U.S. War Dept., "The Chinese Communist Movement," p. 2327. In the pre-1935 period, however, the united front propaganda of the CCP did not envisage collaboration with the *Kuomintang* against Japan. It was a call for a "popular front from below." Despite the existence of anti-Japanese sentiment in China, the Communists' anti-Japanese pronouncements from as early as April 1932 were dismissed by the public at

large as transparent attempts to undermine the Kuomintang's anti-Communist campaign. The Chinese Communist attitude toward a KMT-led United Front was changed by the Seventh Comintern Congress (1935). The CCP acquiesced in Russian demands for a Sino-Russian alliance against Japan in response to the obvious Japanese threat to Russia's borders. (The Soviet Union and Nanking had re-established diplomatic relations in December 1932.) Thus, although Russian influence on United Front policy in China was important, the United Front cannot be understood wholly in terms of Comintern directives. For Chinese Communist United Front policy, see McLane, *Soviet Policy and the Chinese Communists,* pp. 62–63; and Ishikawa Tadao, "Kōsei soveto ki ni okeru kōnichi hantei tōitsu sensen no shomondai" (Various Questions Concerning the Anti-Japanese, Anti-Imperialist United Front in the Period of the Kiangsi Soviet), *Chūgoku kyōsantō shi kenkyū,* pp. 198–216. For an excellent discussion of the dangers of deducing all wartime actions of individual Communist parties from the Seventh Comintern Congress, see David T. Cattell, *Communism and the Spanish Civil War* (Berkeley, Calif., 1955), pp. 28–56 and *passim.*

20 "[The three-thirds] system supports the claims of the Communists that they are maintaining a democratic, united front government. But no real opposition toward the Communists could, it appears, develop from any other party or class or group, since the electoral vote is controlled by the masses and the masses are controlled by the Communists. Anyone is free to stand as a candidate, but in practice nearly all the candidates are proposed by the mass movement associations and the choice offered the electors is usually limited. . . . The Communists' control of (or loyalty from) the masses, combined with universal suffrage, is the chief cause of Communist power and political and military control." U.S. War Dept., "The Chinese Communist Movement," p. 2338.

21 Mary C. Wright, "The Chinese Peasant and Communism," *Pacific Affairs,* XXIV (1951), 258–59.

22 *Ibid.,* p. 257.

23 Sidney Klein, *The Pattern of Land Tenure Reform in East Asia After World War II* (New York, 1958), p. 142.

24 Mao Tse-tung, April 19, 1941, in *Selected Works,* IV, 11.

25 See the article "Hung Hsiu-ch'üan," by Teng Ssu-yü in A. W. Hummel, ed., *Eminent Chinese of the Ch'ing Period* (Washington, 1943), I, 362.

26 Franz Michael, "The Fall of China," *World Politics,* VIII (1956), 303.

27 The land problem in Kiangsi is fully discussed in Brandt, *et al., A Documentary History of Chinese Communism* (London, 1952), pp. 218–19; for agrarian policy in Kiangsi and during the Sino-Japanese war period, also see Chao Kuo-chun, *Agrarian Policy of the Chinese Communist Party 1921–1959* (Bombay, 1960), pp. 38–74. On April 19, 1941, Mao Tse-tung wrote, "In agrarian policy [in Kiangsi] we also made a mistake in repudiating the correct policy adopted in the earlier and middle periods of the Ten-year Civil War [the Chingkangshan period and after–late 1927 to the autumn of 1931], i.e., allotting the same amount of land to the landlords as to the peasants, so that the landlords could engage in farming and would not become displaced or turn to banditry to disturb peace and order." "Postscript to Rural Survey," *Selected Works,* IV, 10. Even this "correct policy" did not win a mass following for the Communist Party; that is one of the reasons why it was abandoned.

28 Brandt, *et al.,* pp. 275–76.

29 It might be argued that the peasants' subordination of economic interests to nationalism was only temporary, for they reverted to a violently anti-landlord policy in the land confiscations of 1947. However, an aspect of the postwar anti-landlord struggle that is commonly overlooked is its nationalistic coloration. The landlords were attacked not solely as rentiers, but also as collaborators with the enemy. Frank C. Lee has observed, "As a rule, most of the collaborationists were landlords, or, if not landlords originally, they had fared so well under the protection of the Japanese Army that they had accumulated large fortunes, mainly in land, at the expense of the local peasants." "Land Redistribution in Communist China," *Pacific Affairs,* XXI (1948), 22–23. Thus, the economic interests of the peasantry in these activities cannot be discounted, but neither can they be taken as the sole determinants.

30 Edward H. Carr, *Nationalism and After* (London, 1945), p. 2.

31 *Ibid.,* p. 18.

32 Carlton Hayes, *Nationalism: A Religion* (New York, 1960), p. 5.

33 Hayes: "In simplest terms, nationalism may be defined as a fusion of patriotism with a consciousness of nationality." *Ibid.,* p. 2.

34 *Nationalism and Social Communication, An Inquiry into the Foundations of Nationality* (New York, 1953), p. 2. Italics mine.

[35] *Ibid.*, pp. 70–71.

[36] *Ibid.*, p. 162.

[37] Cf. Karl W. Deutsch, "Social Mobilization and Political Development," *American Political Science Review*, LV (1961), 493–514. In Deutsch's view, "Social mobilization can be defined . . . as the process in which major clusters of old social, economic, and psychological commitments are eroded or broken and people become available for new patterns of socialization and behavior" (p. 494).

[38] Eric J. Hobsbawm, *Social Bandits and Primitive Rebels, Studies in Archaic Forms of Social Movement in the 19th and 20th Centuries* (Glencoe, Ill., 1959), pp. 2–3.

[39] Although he mistakenly regards joint action as the sole characteristic of nationalism, Ernest Renan stresses its importance as follows: "What constitutes a nation is not speaking the same tongue or belonging to the same ethnic group, but having accomplished great things in common in the past and the wish to accomplish them in the future." *Qu'est-ce qu'une nation?* (1882), quoted in Louis Snyder, *The Meaning of Nationalism* (New Brunswick, N.J., 1954), p. 14.

[40] For the development of nationalism in Chinese intellectual circles, see Chow Tse-tsung, *The May Fourth Movement* (Cambridge, Mass., 1960); John De Francis, *Nationalism and Language Reform in China* (Princeton, N.J., 1950); Kiang Wen-han, *The Chinese Student Movement* (New York, 1948); Joseph R. Levenson, *Confucian China and its Modern Fate* (Berkeley, Calif., 1958); and Robert A. Scalapino and George Yu, *The Chinese Anarchist Movement* (Berkeley: Center for Chinese Studies, University of California, 1961).

[41] The Boxer Rebellion could be compared to the Mau Mau uprising in Kenya in the early 1950's in the sense that both were pre-national, atavistic rebellions against aliens and their native followers.

[42] Cf. Y. C. Wang, "Intellectuals and Society in China 1860–1949," *Comparative Studies in Society and History* (July 1961), pp. 395–426.

[43] "The Nation," *From Max Weber: Essays in Sociology*, Gerth and Mills, eds. (New York, Oxford Galaxy ed., 1958), p. 174.

[44] For a revealing illustration of the political backwardness of the peasantry in an area untouched by either the war or the Communist Party, see G. William Skinner, "Aftermath of Communist Liberation in the Chengtu Plain," *Pacific Affairs*, XXIV (1951), 61–76.

[45] Cf. Salo Wittmayer Baron, *Modern Nationalism and Religion* (New York, 1960). On this point, Elie Kedourie observes, "Nationalist historiography operates, in fact, a subtle but unmistakable change in traditional conceptions. In Zionism, Judaism ceases to be the *raison d'être* of the Jew, and becomes, instead, a product of Jewish national consciousness. In the doctrine of Pakistan, Islam is transformed into a political ideology and used in order to mobilize Muslims against Hindus; more than that it cannot do since an Islamic state on classical lines is today an impossible anachronism. In the doctrine of the *Action Française* Catholicism becomes one of the attributes which define a true Frenchman and exclude a spurious one. This transformation of religion into nationalist ideology is all the more convenient in that nationalists can thereby utilize the powerful and tenacious loyalties which a faith held in common for centuries creates." *Nationalism* (London, 1960), p. 76. For an insight into Israeli national myth, see Alfred Kazin, "Eichmann and the New Israelis," *The Reporter* (April 27, 1961), pp. 24–25.

[46] Henry Hatfield (professor of German at Harvard), "The Myth of Nazism," in *Myth and Mythmaking*, Henry A. Murray, ed. (New York, 1960), p. 199.

[47] The thirteen Communist states are Albania, Bulgaria, China, Czechoslovakia, East Germany, Hungary, Mongolia, North Korea, North Vietnam, Poland, Rumania, USSR and Yugoslavia. If Cuba is included, the number, of course, is fourteen.

[48] Lichtheim, *Marxism*, p. 364, for example.

[49] Thomas T. Hammond, "The Origins of National Communism," *Virginia Quarterly Review*, XXXIV (1958), 278.

[50] Fitzroy Maclean, *Tito* (New York, 1957), p. 355.

The Kuomintang at the moment of its founding, two years after the Manchu dynasty had been overthrown, was the party of revolution and its adherents were the advocates of radical change in Chinese society. Three decades later, most of the original revolutionaries, having gained what they wanted from the revolution, were now advocates of the status quo. As Professor Mary Wright here demonstrates, this evolution, typical of what has taken place in other revolutions, is reflected in the change in the ideology of the party. Mary Wright was Professor of History at Yale University.

From Revolution to Restoration: The Transformation of Kuomintang Ideology

MARY C. WRIGHT

The accession to power of the Kuomintang in 1927–1928 marked the end of the era in which revolutionary strains had been dominant in the party's program and the beginning of one of the most interesting and instructive of the many efforts in history to make a revolution the heir of ancient tradition. The Kuomintang effort was noteworthy for four reasons: (1) the rapidity with which its course was reversed; (2) the magnitude of the gulf between the Confucian political and social system which the Kuomintang sought to restore and the national and social revolution which the party had lately led to victory; (3) the full and uninhibited adherence of Chiang Kai-shek and other leaders not only to the values of the traditional society but to the specific institutions in which these had been embodied; and (4) a well-documented, persistent and self-conscious effort on the part of these leaders to win the competition with the Communists by detailed application in the mid-twentieth century of precisely the means which the Imperial Chinese Government had applied against the Taiping Rebellion in the mid-nineteenth.

As the new rulers of China, Kuomintang leaders searched China's past for ways of dealing with economic decline, social dissolution, political incapacity and armed uprisings; and they seized upon the T'ung-chih Restoration of the 1860's as a model. While the Kuomintang in its revolutionary days had regarded itself as the heir of the great Taiping Rebellion, the Kuomintang in power identified itself with the Imperial Government and its apparently successful Restoration.

In brief, the T'ung-chih Restoration had saved the Ch'ing dynasty and the traditional social order in the face of domestic and foreign threats apparently greater than those with which the Kuomintang was confronted. In 1860 a weak monarch had been in flight in Jehol while foreign troops roamed the streets of his capital and burned his Summer Palace. The Taiping forces with their capital at Nanking had been in control of the richest and most populous areas of the country and straddled its economic life lines. The Nien rebels

Reprinted from *The Far Eastern Quarterly*, Vol. 14, No. 4 (1955), pp. 515–32. Copyright by the Association for Asian Studies, Inc. Reprinted with permission. Footnotes deleted.

were enlarging their sphere of activity and there were Moslem uprisings in both the Northwest and the Southwest. In these circumstances it had been widely assumed that total collapse was in sight. And yet within a matter of months a new government had come to power in the capital, and provincial leaders and local gentry had rallied around the alien monarchy as the defender of the Confucian society. In the following years, the tide of Western encroachment had been stayed, new instruments for the handling of foreign affairs had been created, the rebellions had been put down and rather remarkable headway had been made toward rehabilitation of the agricultural economy, reassertion of local control, revival and modernization of the armed forces, and restoration of the Confucian system of cheap and effective civil government through an intricately balanced bureaucracy of able and thoroughly indoctrinated officials over a passive and thoroughly indoctrinated populace. In appraising this achievement, Chinese statesmen and historians of the time used the ancient term *chung-hsing*—"revival" or "restoration."

Chiang Kai-shek and his colleagues attributed the achievements of the T'ung-chih Restoration to the stern moral character and insight into the working of the Confucian social process which had characterized the heroes of the age, notably Prince Kung, Tseng Kuo-fan, Tso Tsung-t'ang and Hu Lin-i. They saw that the Restoration had involved not politics alone but the whole of Chinese life; not only the suppression of rebellion, the selection and control of officials and the training of armies, but also the norms of behavior in ordinary social life, personal relations outside as well as within the family, the role of women, the relation between the generations, the choice of jobs, the demand for goods, the forms of recreation. Kuomintang leaders saw in the T'ung-chih Restoration Confucian ideas in a form which appeared relevant to twentieth century problems of domestic tranquillity and international security. They did not see that the T'ung-chih Restoration, for all its brilliance, had in the end failed precisely because the requirements for maintaining the Confucian social order and the requirements for ensuring China's survival in the modern world had proved quite fundamentally opposed.

The issue of Confucianism as a social principle and of the T'ung-chih Restoration as a guide to its revival were squarely joined in the Kuomintang-Communist struggle for the control of China's destiny. According to the cofounder of the Chinese Communist Party Ch'en Tu-hsiu: ". . . the question of Confucianism relates not only to the Constitution; it is the basic question of our people's actual life and ethical thought. The essence of Confucianism is that the 'principles of social usage' (*li*) are the basis of our country's ethics and politics. Their preservation or destruction is a question which our country must soon resolve, and it should be resolved before questions of the form of state or of the constitution." The Communists studied the lessons of the T'ung-chih Restoration almost as carefully as did the Nationalists, and dubbed it "a counter-revolution achieved with foreign support." In the Communist view, the Kuomintang exaltation of the Restoration and the virtual canonization of Tseng Kuo-fan were fraudulent and futile efforts to anesthetize youth, the fabrication of a legend out of whole cloth by fascist theoreticians.

As they made their bid for power, the Communists called the conflict in the interpretation of Tseng's character and career one of the battle-fronts in the struggle between the "democracy-demanding Chinese people and the property-owning classes." They insisted that Sun Yat-sen, like all true revolutionaries of the early Kuomintang, had repudiated Tseng and had considered himself the younger brother of the Taiping leader Hung Hsiu-ch'uan.

In contrast to Communist doctrinal consistency in implacable opposition to Confucianism in general and to the T'ung-chih Restoration in particular, dominant Kuomintang views shifted and varied in the years preceding the party's accession to power, for the issues of a Confucian society vs. a modern society, of restoration vs. revolution, had not been sharply posed until the years of heightened intellectual and social ferment after 1916. Among early Kuomintang leaders, including Sun Yat-sen and Chang T'ai-yen, the issue of nationalism had been primary and the establishment of the republican capital at Nanking a vindication of the Ming Dynasty rather than of the Taiping Rebellion. Indeed Chang's views seem to have differed from those of his monarchist political opponents largely on the question of the nationality of the chief of state. And while Sun himself was sharply critical of those who saw nothing but the nationality issue, he did not consider the revolution of 1911 a break in the main course of Chinese history but as a continuation of five thousand years of glory.

As late as 1915, when Yüan Shih-k'ai assumed autocratic powers, the Kuomintang's own argument against the pretender to the Confucian monarchy and the "stabilizing" figure of the age rested on essentially Confucian grounds. The leaders of the uncompromising armed opposition to Yüan, "Martyr of the Revolution Ts'ai Sung-p'o" (Ts'ai O) himself selected maxims from the works of the heroes of the Restoration, Tseng Kuo-fan and Hu Lin-i, and issued them to his revolutionary forces as basic indoctrination material. In his preface Ts'ai wrote that where values and morale were concerned, discussion of the present was less useful than transmission of the teachings of antiquity; that while antiquity was sometimes too remote to be directly relevant, Tseng and Hu had lived only a half-century ago, so that what they had to say was of urgent importance today.

After 1915, however, Chinese history moved rapidly and in the years following the May 4th movement of 1919 a Communist-Nationalist coalition centered at Canton gained strength. In 1924 the first congress of the reorganized Kuomintang issued a radical declaration which provided the basis of a common program with the Communists. Borodin was at the height of his influence and the young Chiang Kai-shek, recently returned from the Soviet Union, was commander of the revolutionary Whampoa Military Academy with Chou En-lai as director of the political department. It was in these extraordinary circumstances that Chiang selected for the Academy's textbook his own enlarged version of Ts'ai O's selections from the maxims of Tseng Kuo-fan and Hu Lin-i and it was to this step that Chiang's later success was subsequently attributed.

In his preface Chiang wrote that the reason for the success of the Restoration and the failure of the Taiping Rebellion was not difference in ability, for in ability the Taiping heroes Hung Hsiu-ch'uan, Shih Ta-k'ai and Li Hsiu-ch'eng were the equals of the Restoration heroes Tseng Kuo-fan, Hu Lin-i and Tso Tsung-t'ang. In Chiang's view, Tseng had been the leader of the age because he acclaimed virtue and embodied proper personal conduct. It was because of this that Chiang took Tseng for his master.

Chiang continued that he himself had been studying the works of Tseng and Hu for some time, and had earlier decided to "postpone" writing the history of the Taiping Rebellion he had once intended as a guide to his comrades, and to compile instead a selection of the works of Tseng and Hu as their guide. For convenience he was using Ts'ai O's compilation as a basis, but he had made certain additions, particularly with reference to mental discipline, and had included selections from the works of Tso Tsung-t'ang as well. And Chiang concluded: "Alack! The words of Tseng, Hu and Tso are the voice of true experience in governing men, the things I wish to say but cannot put into words . . . I wish to present a copy to each of my comrades in the Academy so that in future there will be a foundation for the command of the army and the government of the country."

In 1924 Chiang Kai-shek's view of the army of the revolution as the stabilizer of Chinese society along Restoration lines contrasted sharply with most of the published statements of the Party's position. There were a few like Tai Chi-t'ao who were already urging the use of the party organization "to restore the spirit of our ancestors and thus cause the country to flourish." But Chiang's own position was still ambivalent. In 1924 at Whampoa he lectured on Tseng and stability but he also lectured on revolution. There was nothing about the Confucian order in his manifesto to the nation of August 1926. In 1933–1934 he lectured only on stability and the Confucian code of behavior. In 1924, while Chiang extolled Tseng, his references to the Taiping Rebellion were polite. In 1932 he spat upon it. And in 1933–1934 at Lushan Chiang took his stand not only against the Communists and the Taiping Rebellion but against all the rebellions in Chinese history, going back to the Red Eyebrows and the Yellow Turbans. His cause was one with the cause of Hu Lin-i, he proclaimed, because: "If we do not exterminate the red bandits, we cannot preserve the old morals and ancient wisdom handed down from our ancestors . . ."

The full turn in the Kuomintang position took place between 1924 and 1928, and Chiang was always ahead of the party. The proclamations of the first two congresses of the Kuomintang were revolutionary documents. In the first (1924), the enemies of the party were specified as the constitutional clique, the federal autonomy clique, the compromisers, and the groups dominated by business men. The manifesto of the second congress (1926) was similar but more sharply anti-imperialist in the Marxist sense. The enemies of the party were the warlords, the bureaucrats, the compradors and the local bosses. With the third congress in 1929 the picture changed and the enemies of the party became the "agents of red imperialism." Radicals now either reformed their outlook or left the party, while many of those purged in earlier years returned to the fold.

Even at the high-tide of the northern expedition there were already those who called Chiang Kai-shek today's Tseng, who compared T'ang Sheng-chih to Hu Lin-i. When the Communist Propaganda Corps called on Generalissimo Chiang, its leader was struck by the fact that the phrases, the procedure, the whole atmosphere already suggested the traditional rulers of China. The Communist view of the alternatives before the Kuomintang late in 1926 was illustrated in a poster hung at the Peasants' Association in a small town near Nan-ch'ang. On one side was a Confucian Temple, on the other the "World Park," featuring Marx, Lenin and a vacant third position. In the center a man in Chinese Nationalist uniform was carrying the portrait of Sun Yat-sen toward the Confucian Temple. The legend read: "Sun ought to be in the world park but Tai (Chi-t'ao) wants him in the Confucian Temple."

Public and avowed veneration for Confucius was resumed in 1928. As late as 1927 a mob had dragged a straw effigy of Confucius through the streets of Changsha and beat and burned it, and the National Government itself had on February 15 ordered the abolition of official Confucian rites and turned the funds over to public education on the grounds that "The principles of Confucius were despotic. For more than twenty centuries they have served to oppress the people and to enslave thought. . . . As to the cult of Confucius, it is superstitious and out of place in the modern world . . . China is now a Republic. These vestiges of absolutism should be effaced from the memory of citizens." The vestiges were not effaced for long. On November 6, 1928 Chiang Kai-shek was urging his officers to spend their leisure in the study of the Four Books. In 1931 Confucius' birthday became a national holiday. Nationalist troops were ordered to give special protection to all local Confucian temples. Recognition increased by degrees, culminating in the recanonization of Confucius in 1934 when Yeh Ch'u-ts'ang was sent as the official delegate of the National Government to take part in the ceremonies at the Confucian Temple at Ch'ü-fu.

The Kuomintang never ceased talking about revolution. It merely redefined the term in a precisely opposite sense. As Ch'en Li-fu said in 1935, the "new" to which the revolution must lead was new in the sense that the Chou dynasty was new, new in the sense of slow adjustment and renewal of ancient and unchanging principles. The official party history declared that Taiping thought was contrary to the spirit of Chinese culture, of which the Kuomintang was the true revolutionary carrier. The party elder Chang Chi told the party's Central Training Corps in 1943 that the rejection of the sage kings and loyal ministers of the past which had characterized the early period of the revolution had been an error of youth, one which the party had long since corrected. In these circumstances, T'ao Hsi-sheng wrote, as well he might, that the historic origins of the Kuomintang were subtle and confused, for the party was "the heir of both the Taiping Rebellion and of Tseng Kuo-fan." By 1953 the confusion had disappeared and reversal in the meaning of revolution was complete. According to T'ao: "Revolutionaries are scholars who take the *ching-shih* (statesmanship) studies of the late Ming and early Ch'ing as their basis, but who have also imbibed Western thought."

The change in the orientation of the Kuomintang was marked by a growing cult of Tseng Kuo-fan. In 1922 it had been difficult to believe that Tseng had been dead only fifty years, so much had Chinese life apparently changed. By 1932 he seemed very much alive again, as his works were reissued in large volume and discussions of his life and its meaning filled the new books and magazines. Again and again Tseng was described as the leading meritorious official of the Restoration of the Ch'ing house and the pillar of the Restoration; the greatest man in modern Chinese history because he preserved not only the Ch'ing house but China; the greatest statesman of the Restoration, even greater as a thinker; a man of grand vision who renovated the old society.

After 1928, *The Maxims of Tseng and Hu* became virtually part of the Kuomintang Party canon. New compilations and new editions of Ts'ai O's original compilation poured from the presses. Orders to study the maxims became a routine part of lectures by Party leaders to army officers. Ts'ai himself was increasingly identified with the Restoration and he became a "model for youth" because he combined Tseng's "capacity" (*tu*), Tso's ability and Chiang Chung-yüan's courage.

This apotheosis of Tseng, and of Chiang Kai-shek as a greater Tseng, was not unprotested but the critics had little effect. Repeatedly in times of crisis Chiang called on the nation to rise taking Tseng as its model. Tseng was everything: the symbol of "spiritual mobilization" in the war against Japan, the consummate military commander, the embodiment of party discipline, the arbiter of the academic world, the proof incarnate that every man might through diligence and moral firmness rise to the heights.

The choice of the Restoration as a model was logical enough once the Kuomintang leaders had ceased to consider the party a spearhead of revolution and come to regard it as an instrument for restoring order. With their new outlook, they declared that the new period of revolutionary construction required qualities opposite to those needed in the preceding period of revolutionary destruction. The revolution could now go forward only if the party purged itself in one sweep of the evil tendencies left over from its earlier history and concentrated on re-establishing the fixed and secure relationships of the Confucian order. And the main and obvious feature of the Restoration was that these Confucian relationships had been re-established in the face of a revolutionary threat, and that order had thereby been restored.

The new Confucians of the Kuomintang were men of action, not philosophers. Chiang Kai-shek might quote the whole of the "great harmony" passage of the *Li chi* to the People's Political Conference, and other leaders might refer in passing to any appropriate classical dictum, but Kuomintang leaders did not attempt to expound the Confucianism of the party in theoretical terms. They pulled from Confucianism, on an *ad hoc* basis, whatever seemed likely to promote internal order. Reasonably enough, their chief emphasis, like that of the Restoration leaders, was on the principles of social usage (*li*) and the associated virtues of *i, lien* and *ch'ih*.

There is little point in attempting a systematic analysis of exactly what the Kuomintang meant by *li, i, lien* and *ch'ih*. They were discussed incessantly in party literature, but never very precisely or reflectively. Chiang Kai-shek instructed party workers that *li*—the principles of social usage—meant precise and meticulous behavior in accordance with the unchanging principles of nature, society and the state. He told army officers that *li* and the associated virtues of *i, lien* and *ch'ih* were the only sources of order, discipline, vision and courage in the army, the best defense against the loss of loyalty which, as Tseng Kuo-fan had pointed out, was the great cause of all rebellions. He told the general public not what these virtues were in positive terms, but what their absence entailed: in the absence of *li*, there was inattention to order, discipline and rules; in the absence of *i*, there was lack of good faith and neglect of duty; in the absence of *lien* there was confusion between right and wrong, between public and private; in the absence of *ch'ih* there was imperceptiveness and irresolution.

If to the shadowy negative connotations which Chiang gave to these four terms we add Ch'en Li-fu's positive connotations, we are further than ever from a definition. According to Ch'en, when *li* is present the standards of civilized and barbaric are clear; with *i*, the distinctions of true and false are clear; with *lien*, the distinctions of taking and receiving are clear; with *ch'ih*, the criteria of good and evil are clear.

While the philosophic meaning of this version of the doctrine of the rites is confused and scarcely worth discussion, its political and social meaning is clear enough, and worth careful attention. The thing that is really being discussed all the time is the means of insuring social stability and popular discipline. In the view of the Kuomintang ideologists, Confucianism was the most effective and cheapest means ever devised by man for this purpose. They saw that the Confucian order had held together because certain canons of behavior had been hammered in by precept and example so effectively that deviation was nearly impossible. In their view the content of these canons mattered less than reviving the habit of behaving in accordance with fixed and unquestioned rules. This it was hoped would end the opposition to Kuomintang control. That the disciplinary effectiveness of the canon was dependent on its whole content and its whole context seems never to have occurred to them.

What has sometimes been called Chiang Kai-shek's idealism stemmed from this belief that indoctrination and habit are more effective than physical force in social control. In the mid-1930's, as economic crises and Japanese threats mounted, he stated that if the classic virtues of *li, i, lien,* and *ch'ih* had been more assiduously cultivated in recent years, China would not then be facing either domestic or foreign difficulties. As his armies fell back before the advancing Japanese in 1939, he blamed neglect of the doctrine of the rites and urged salvation of the nation through renewed emphasis on loyalty and filial piety. And when, in 1950, his armies had retreated to Formosa, he attributed the Communist victory primarily to Kuomintang loss of morale. He replaced the morally discredited Central Executive Committee with a new Central Reform Committee with the charge: "We must inherit our five thousand year old culture and make it a guide in human progress."

Chiang's insistence that the decisive element in human affairs, and in the flourishing and decay of civilizations, is the moral purpose of men, is good Confucian doctrine and more particularly good Restoration doctrine. But in Chiang's conception of this moral purpose and of the legacy from which it springs there is an important new element. For Chiang the Confucian way of life has lost its traditional rational and universal qualities and it has become imbued with a romantic nationalism. It has supreme value because it is Chinese, the source of *our* great past, the promise of *our* great future. There are not one but two anomalies in the statement that the task of the revolution is "to revive our Chinese culture, to restore our people's ancient virtues, to proclaim our Chinese national soul."

Out of all these five thousand years of which the Generalissimo talked, it was the T'ung-chih Restoration which held his attention. As he took command of the anti-Communist forces in the critical battles in Hupeh in 1932 his thoughts turned to Hu Lin-i, whom he eventually came to consider as even greater than Tseng Kuo-fan. The Communists, he reflected, were nothing like so formidable a foe as the Taipings had been. He meditated about the way in which Hu had pacified the area, turned defeat into victory and overcome his environment. If Hu's principles could be mastered they could become "the ultimate guiding principles for our suppression of the Communists today."

While in theory the new Kuomintang policy was modelled on Restoration policy in all fields, in practice the Kuomintang emphasized Restoration lessons with respect to local control, military leadership and strategy, and revival of the Confucian ideology. Restoration principles in other fields—notably economics—were almost entirely ignored. It is true that Chiang quoted with unreserved approval Hu Lin-i's version of the classic principle: "If civil government is weakened, then the people's livelihood has nothing on which to depend. Even though you kill a thousand bandits a day, you will not remedy the general situation." But Chiang also instructed party workers that it was an error to quote the classics to the effect that adequate food and clothing were prerequisite to virtue. On the contrary, Chiang stated, the people must first be virtuous; only then will they have the moral strength to obtain food and clothing.

For the Kuomintang, agriculture was the basis of the state in theory, but the Kuomintang documentation lacks the Restoration emphasis on water control, public works, reduction of the land tax, and control of currency and speculation in the interest of the agrarian economy. And evidently Kuomintang leaders did not agree with Restoration leaders that the Confucian virtues flourish only in an agrarian society, that industry and commerce are profoundly disruptive of the traditional way of life. For as the "Confucian" governor of Kwangtung put it in a stormy interview with Hu Shih: "In building production, we may use foreign machines, foreign sciences, even foreign engineers. But for building men we must have roots; and these roots must be sought within China's ancient culture."

By contrast with its relative neglect of Restoration precedents in economic policy, the Kuomintang gave close attention to certain aspects of Restoration local control. In 1930 in Kiangsi, where the Red armies had their bases, it seemed to the Kuomintang that control could best be reasserted by applying Tseng Kuo-fan's three basic principles: strict law enforcement, revival of the *pao-chia* system and organization of the gentry. This was "the best model in history for learning how to exterminate Communists."

Chiang and other leaders reiterated these principles and repeatedly tried to put them into effect. Logically enough, they tried to build up the position of the gentry. Old privileges were restored and new ones added in the hope that the gentry might once again play its traditional role of maintaining local order and indoctrinating the peasantry. In 1939 Chiang Kai-shek wired all regional and local government and party officials to remind the gentry throughout the country that, in the words of the *Lun-yü*, when the wind moves, the grass bends; that the gentry could educate beyond where government orders could reach; that the country could be saved only if they recovered their "true national spirit" and remembered that "for several thousand years our country has considered loyalty and filial piety as the basis of the state."

Revival of the *pao-chia* system of collective responsibility and the related militia system was as important in the Kuomintang program of local control as was reinstatement of the gentry. Ch'ing statements on the *pao-chia* were carefully studied and reissued for the guidance of army officers and local officials, with particular attention to the plan of "strengthening the walls and clearing out the countryside" which was first developed for the suppression of the White Lotus Rebellion. The compilations reissued by the Kuomintang emphasized such points as: "The villages of the *chou* and *hsien* are like the leaves and branches of a tree; if the leaves and branches are damaged, the root and trunk have nothing to shelter them." For this reason, "To defend cities is not as good as to defend villages." In the defense of villages, the *pao-chia* and the militia must function together, the one preventing traitors from operating within the area, the other warding off outside attack. In this, "the poor serve with their strength, the rich contribute money, and separate families are banded together in large groups." This last, the party noted, is the very essence of the system.

The Kuomintang evidently accepted the Ch'ing arguments without reservation, and ordered the full re-institution of the *pao-chia* system against which they as revolutionaries had once railed, with particular attention to its use in Communist-infested areas.

The Kuomintang gave less emphasis to good local government in connection with local control than the Restoration leaders gave to this subject. In the Kuomintang sources, there is relatively little attention to the slowness of justice, the interference of the clerks and other abuses which Restoration leaders considered major causes of local dissatisfaction and revolt. While the Kuomintang in theory considered the quality of officials to be a matter of major importance, the Restoration emphasis on the quality of local officials was lacking. Moreover since the actual machinery through which these men of ability were supposed to be selected, trained and controlled had long since collapsed, Kuomintang discussions of the subject often lacked practical point.

The second field in which the Kuomintang modelled itself closely on the Restoration was military leadership and strategy. From the time when Chiang first used Ts'ai O's book as a text at the Whampoa Military Academy in 1924, Nationalist army officers were lectured to about the principles to be learned from studying the careers of Restoration leaders. As Ts'ai O put it, and others have repeated, the Restoration experience shows that the essential qualities of a good commander are: (1) a sense of public duty and in consequence of this a respect for the troops; (2) fearlessness in the face of death; and (3) indifference to fame. Ts'ai noted that while Westerners valued genius in military men, Tseng and Hu emphasized the good heart and thereby transformed an era of catastrophic rebellion into an era of immortal glory.

If the officers of the Nationalist army have fallen short of this goal, it has not been for want of instruction.

Restoration precedents also dominated Kuomintang thinking about strategy. While the campaigns against the Taiping furnished the chief lessons, those against the Nienfei were not neglected. In analyzing the various campaigns, the Kuomintang consistently drew the lessons from the Ch'ing side. The Party was not interested in learning how the Nienfei might have avoided being trapped, but in mastering the relentless *hua-ho ch'uan-ti* hemming-in strategy by which the Ch'ing trapped the rebels. In 1930 Chiang Kai-shek ordered the compilation of all the proclamations and reports—even the troop songs—of the Ch'ing campaign against the Nienfei, for the specific purpose of using similar methods against the Communists. In 1948, researchers in the Ministry of National Defense were still hopefully studying this problem. Interestingly enough, the conclusion was drawn that the secret of Ch'ing success lay less in superior fire-power than in the attention which Tseng Kuo-fan and others devoted to the appointment of good local officials and to the discipline of troops so that popular support of the Government would be assured.

The Kuomintang effort to use Restoration models in local control and in military affairs obviously required an intensified campaign to revive the Confucian ideology. To the Kuomintang the question of education was the most critical of all, for according to the training manual for party political workers: "During several decades of revolutionary war, the old culture has collapsed in most areas, and a new culture has not yet been created."

The Kuomintang indoctrination program took many forms: reprinting of the works of Tseng Kuo-fan and their assignment in the schools; publicity to all Confucian ceremonies; a flood of books and articles on the traditional virtues; manifestoes by selected professors on the preservation of the Chinese heritage; and a government-ordered "read the classics" movement, promulgated from the "cradle of the Nationalist revolution,

Canton." Liberal comment might be scathing, but Hu Shih was expelled from Kwangtung for lecturing against this movement and threatened with loss of his civil rights. To counter the left-wing pamphlets and the learned Marxist treatises which offered new solutions for the country's ills, special popular editions of traditional works were released in the most disturbed areas, and books in conflict with the doctrine of the rites (*li-chiao*) were banned.

With the movement to revive the classics went its corollary—a movement to discourage education in the modern humanities and social sciences. With Chinese studies as the basis, it was argued, only science and technology need be borrowed from the West. This was of course not a new idea. As T. F. Tsiang pointed out, it was a reversion to the policy of the T'ung-chih Restoration and history had proved that the Restoration formula was unworkable.

Kuomintang leaders thought otherwise. In their view, history had *not* discredited the T'ung-chih Restoration. In Chiang Kai-shek's view, a little science might be useful, but Chinese education, like Chinese civilization, had a special basic character, and this could best be preserved through studies of Tseng Kuo-fan and Hu Lin-i.

The whole of the neo-Restoration of the Kuomintang was a dismal failure; a far sadder spectacle than the T'ung-chih Restoration which it tried to copy. Local control was not reasserted. Army morale was not restored. There was never really any effort to revive the Confucian economy. And above all there was no general resurgence of Confucian values and mores. All this is scarcely surprising. The principles which the Kuomintang tried to use had long since been tried under far more hopeful circumstances and found wanting.

Yet this Restorationism of the Kuomintang cannot be dismissed as a joke. For all its foolishness, it was the ideology of the only political movement which ever had a chance of successfully competing with the Communists, and the character of the competition was gravely affected by the persistence of the doctrine of the rites. While the Kuomintang was not a monolith, criticism on this point of the primacy of the doctrine of the rites and of the lessons to be learned from the T'ung-chih Restoration came largely from the party's opponents. On this point there was little protest either from the splinter parties associated with the Kuomintang, or from the partially independent regional military leaders.

Within the Kuomintang itself there were fissures but not on this point. Li Tsung-jen, leader of the Free China opposition to Chiang Kai-shek, declared from New York in 1950: "After Chiang Kai-shek, it was thought any change was for the better. But after one year of trial, the people found that whereas Chiang Kai-shek was only interested in money and in depriving the people of their material well being, the Communists aim at depriving them of their soul." But Li, like Chiang, went on to reassert the hard core of the Confucian social doctrine: "For over 4000 years the Chinese people were knitted together by a moral code, apart from a common written language, the same blood strain and a cultural heritage. The code of morals expounded by Confucius and the rest of our sages is the only reason Chinese exist as a people and as a country. This code of morals distinguishes Chinese from other people by defining the correct relationship between parents and children, husband and wife, brother and sister, teacher and student, friend and friend." As Vice-president and then Acting President of the Chinese National Government, Li offered a program of opposition to Chiang for failing to fulfill the responsibilities of a Confucian head of state, but of even greater opposition to the Communists for their denial of the very aims of the Confucian state. Li might easily be Prince Kung writing on the principles of social usage as the basis of the state.

Formerly the Communists were not the only outspoken critics of the neo-restorationism of the Kuomintang. As has been indicated above, the leading liberals of the twenties and thirties noted the successive waves of reaction and voiced their views with vigor. Long ago Hu Shih warned the new Confucians that they were doing what the leaders of the T'ung-chih Restoration had done, and he urged them to study the reasons for the Restoration's failure and to take warning. In Hu's view at that time, the leaders of the Restoration had failed because in their attempt to preserve the Chinese basis while selectively adapting from the West, they tried to preserve too much. They could not bring themselves to relinquish what had to be relinquished. Hu pointed out that again and again in the history of the twentieth century, whenever it appeared that the decision had at last been taken to initiate long-overdue reforms, a conservative clique had always re-emerged and had succeeded in blocking change on the ground that the precious "Chinese heritage" was being threatened. For Hu, their arguments were spurious: "They buy airplanes and artillery; naturally they can select the newest 1935 automobile; they merely want to use 2500 year old classics to teach men to be men."

Hu was arguing against superficial modernization, urging fundamental modernization, and he thought that the Restoration, to which it had become so fashionable to refer, taught a lesson opposite to that currently drawn; for Hu the T'ung-chih Restoration taught that limited, controlled, conservative modernization was simply impossible. And yet fundamentally, the difference between Hu and those whom he criticized was a matter of degree. He was willing to relinquish more than they, but by no means everything. He was optimistic; he considered that Chinese tradition was so strong and vigorous that radical adjustments could be made without danger of its loss.

It is nearly meaningless to say of a twentieth century Chinese thinker or politician that he is striving to select from the Chinese past the principles of enduring value and to adapt them to meet the problems of the modern world, for in various ways that is what they all have done with the exception of the leadership of the Communist party. For all the others, the hold of the traditional has been too powerful for the most ardent modernizer to escape, and the demands of the modern too compelling for the most confirmed traditionalist to ignore. The core of all intellectual and political controversy in China's turbulent twentieth century has been the restatement of Chang Chih-tung's formula: *Chung-hsüeh wei-t'i; hsi-hsüeh wei-yung* (Chinese studies as the basis; Western studies for practical use).

Faced with this dilemma, intellectual and political leaders of three decades professed optimism about the possibility of a viable compromise. They argued hotly, but their arguments could be reduced to disagreement about the elements of the two civilizations which it was desirable and feasible to blend. A man might attack his opponent as a compromiser, as limited to the Restoration mentality, but his own solution nearly always proved in the end another version of *chung-hsüeh wei-t'i; hsi-hsüeh wei-yung*.

During the past twenty years this lingering optimism, this hope that with new proportions this formula might somehow work has nearly disappeared in the face of a polarization of Chinese opinion. Those who have wanted a strong, modern China, even at the cost of the "Chinese basis" have drifted toward the Communists, who have been the only consistent advocates of fundamental social change. Those who have believed that there was something of enduring value in the Confucian tradition have had no practicable alternative to the neo-restorationism of the Kuomintang.

In these circumstances interpretations have been extreme. The Restoration has been taken to prove either that the traditional society it sought to restore was an evil and ugly thing, or that that society was a splendid thing which must govern China's future. Fung Yu-lan is one of the few who have recently urged "sympathetic understanding" of traditional China without urging that it be revived: "In saying this I have no intention of supporting it as a working social system in present day China. In order to live in the modern world in a position worthy of her past China must be industrialized. Where there is industrialization there is no place for the traditional family system and the traditional social structure."

But Fung is now with the Communists. From Formosa it is still said that the spirit of Chinese culture is everlasting, that it is at work today on the mainland and within the Communist Party; that Communism was accepted because of certain superficial similarities to Confucianism; that sooner or later the mainland population will recognize that they are two opposed systems and will reject Communism and modernization in favor of the Confucian social order. The controversy is not over, and as long as men dispute the relation of China's future to China's past they will probably continue to dispute the true meaning of the T'ung-chih Restoration.

Mr. Pfeffer is Assistant Professor of Political Science at Johns Hopkins University (Baltimore, Maryland) and editor of *No More Vietnams? The War and the Future of American Foreign Policy*, New York, Harper and Row, 1968.

The Pursuit of Purity: Mao's Cultural Revolution

RICHARD M. PFEFFER

China's "Great Proletarian Cultural Revolution" is too complex and too diffuse a configuration of phenomena to be "explained" within the confines of any single perspective. It has been described, derisively, as "really three things in one: an enigmatic multiple power struggle, wrapped in a crusade, and superimposed on a scattering of more or less spontaneous, more or less politicized student riots, strikes, peasant uprisings, mutinies, and palace coups." [1]

Reprinted from *Problems of Communism*, November–December 1969, Courtesy of Press and Publications Service, United States Information Agency, Washington, D.C.

[1] W. A. C. Adie, "China's 'Second Liberation' in Perspective," *Bulletin of the Atomic Scientists* (Chicago), February 1969, p. 14.

Quite clearly, the Cultural Revolution, unlike Pallas Athena, did not spring full-blown from anyone's brow. While Mao appears to have fathered it, various groupings within the elite, the masses, and the middle levels of power have, for their own reasons, contributed to its development. Individual interpretations of its motive forces, focusing on one or more of its aspects and levels of relevant "facts," vary widely.[2]

We are not yet, and perhaps never shall be, at a stage where we can systematically appreciate all the facets of so momentous a complex of events as the Cultural Revolution. But if it is too early to set down refined theoretical frameworks for understanding the CR as a whole, we can at least begin to formulate tentative approaches toward understanding each of its levels of reality and the nature of the relationships among certain of those levels. This article focuses on what Mao Tse-tung has been attempting to accomplish through the CR. The assumptions behind this focus are twofold: 1) Mao's intentions are significant in shaping the events of the CR; and 2) Mao's "intentions" are, in some sense, knowable.

If the assumption that Mao planned the CR in advance and deftly manipulated it to his own taste requires a near-deification of the man, the contrary assumption that Mao simply played events by ear and in fact exercised little influence over their development trivializes one of the great men of the 20th century. The reality doubtless lies somewhere in between. Mao probably had no detailed plan for developing the CR; but, on the basis of his ideology, his personality, his experience as a revolutionary, and the actual course of events as seen in retrospect, it seems fair to conclude that Mao had a vision of what he sought to accomplish and an intuitive conception of the means appropriate to those ends. Moreover, although Mao's power to determine events is limited, the CR has reminded the world of the immense power of ideology and of a supreme leader who, to a large degree, can shape ideology, through propaganda, to fit his needs.

Undoubtedly Mao provoked the CR for a variety of reasons: he sought to achieve multiple goals, some minimal, others maximal. The minimal goals might be said to include the purge of particular individuals, the shake-up of the bureaucracy (in the manner of past but less intense campaigns), and even the temporary breakup of the party machine.[3] The maximal goals seem to have included the training of a suc-

[2] See, *e.g.*, Benjamin Schwartz, "The Reign of Virtue: Some Broad Perspectives on Leader and Party in the Cultural Revolution," *The China Quarterly* (London), July–September 1968, pp. 1–17; Franz Schurmann, "What's Happening in China?," *The New York Review of Books*, Oct. 20, 1966, pp. 18–25; and Richard D. Baum, "Ideology Redivivus," *Problems of Communism*, May–June 1967, pp. 1–11. Baum's excellent analysis, which in part argues a "functional nexus between revisionism and modernization," suggests at least that Mao's concern over the deterioration of revolutionary values and spirit in the CCP is well founded. Much of my argument is in line with Baum's analysis, but Baum, like most American social scientists today, appears to assume the "rationality" of modernization and the "revivalist" irrationality of Mao's Cultural Revolution (see also footnote 11).

[3] Regarding the last, see Charles Neuhauser, "The Impact of the Cultural Revolution on the Chinese Communist Party Machine," *Asian Survey*, June 1968, pp. 465–88. The present author disagrees with Neuhauser's view that "the party as such has not been under attack . . . in the . . . Cultural Revolution"—that it is not the party as such and its "central legitimizing role as the 'vanguard of the proletariat' and the font of political authority in China," but rather the "party machine, the organizational command structure," which has come under Maoist attack. While I accept the validity of Neuhauser's analytic distinction between "party" and "party machine," I argue in this paper that Mao has attacked the party as such, not to destroy it, but to transform it. It is precisely the party's exclusive legitimizing role that has been brought into question.

cessor generation in revolution by allowing and encouraging youth to wage "revolution from below" (*i.e.*, without the disciplined control from above characteristic of past intraparty rectification movements); the creation of a new morality and "superstructure" in China; and, more specifically, the reinstatement in practice of the revolutionary ideals of equality and mass participation, and the transformation of the nature of the Communist Party.

This article concerns itself almost exclusively with Mao's maximal goals, in large part because the dimensions of the CR and Mao's role in it seem hardly intelligible in terms of his more minimal goals.

Dimensions of the CR

Viewed from Mao's perspective, the CR may be taken as the latest and most striking manifestation of the historical dialectic involving leader, party, and masses that is at the heart of Maoism and the Chinese Communist Revolution. It represents part of the continuing search for a Chinese way—more particularly, a Maoist way—to carry on that revolution.

Few analysts to date have begun to take the CR seriously as a revolution.[4] Yet it seems appropriate to understand it as such. For while it is true that the CR is not a comprehensive socio-political revolution in the sense of the earlier Communist Revolution in China, it clearly goes beyond the limits of any lesser category of socio-political change. Through the CR Mao has sought to transform a whole culture and its central legitimating institution. If he has not attempted, in the classical mode of great revolutions, to eliminate physically the members of a ruling class, he appears at least to have tried to prevent members of the post-1949 elite from becoming entrenched to the point where they take on the characteristics of such a class. If he has not attempted a fundamental change in the economic relations of Chinese society, he has tried to an unprecedented degree to delegitimize, on the level of ideals, the individual pursuit of material gain. If in short, the CR has not embodied several of the core elements of the major social revolutions in history, the reason is simply that the CR is the progeny of such a revolution, and its function is not to repeat the earlier revolution but to revitalize it.

Franz Schurmann, placing the CR in the historical perspective of a continuing Chinese revolution, writes:[5] ". . . for decades now, elite upon elite has been dragged into the mire of discreditation. . . . Today the new elite of the party is sharing their fate." In this sense, the CR is a testament to the fact that social revolutions which are not permanent revolutions tend to eliminate one mode of inequality—*e.g.*, the inequality of traditional societies—only to establish another mode of inequality. The events in China suggest that Mao, the visionary, is no longer satisfied with such a substitution.

The CR was directed against Communist China's "New Class," to use

[4] One notable exception is William Hinton, who appears to have become a straightforward Maoist. He writes in his most recent article: "The world has never witnessed anything to approach, not to mention equal, this mass mobilization . . . as hundreds of millions entered the arena of political action" ("Hinton Re-examines 'Fanshen'," *Progressive Labor,* February 1969, p. 107).

[5] "The Attack of the Cultural Revolution on Ideology and Organization," in Ping-ti Ho and Tang Tsou, eds.; *China in Crisis,* Chicago, University of Chicago Press, 1968, Vol. I, Book 2, p. 551.

Djilas' term. Its first-stated aim, "to struggle against and crush those persons in authority who are taking the capitalist road," [6] can be meaningfully understood only in this sense. In Mao's view, the growth of such an "increasingly privileged and powerful social stratum in command of . . . [China's] politico-economic apparatus" [7]—paralleling developments in other socialist countries—posed the threat of death to the Chinese Revolution.[8]

Inextricably related to the growth of this stratum has been a decline in the Chinese popular spirit of revolutionary solidarity and sacrifice. To quote two sympathetic yet perceptive American observers of recent Chinese Communist development,

> . . . life has become "privatized," especially among the youth, who tend increasingly to concentrate on their careers and to neglect social responsibilities; admiration for the material achievements and the supposedly freer ways of the affluent capitalist societies has grown; an abyss has opened up between the style of life and modes of thought of the leading stratum on the one hand and the still poor, toiling masses on the other.[9]

Mao and his supporters have increasingly come to believe that these trends, if unrestrained, will sooner or later result in the "restoration of capitalism."

Revolution Against History

But viewed in this light, the CR also seems to be a revolution against history—that is, against what appears to be the inevitable development of a privileged stratum in the process of economic development, or, even more boldly, against modernization itself.[10] Never in history has there been a revolution that has continued to place the same high ideal and practical value on egalitarianism and mass participation once the mobilization and destructive phases of the revolution were completed. As every major social revolution became institutionalized, egalitarianism and mass participation have been substantially sacrificed in favor of other goals such as national power or modernization. It is this historical pattern—again repeating itself in post-1949 China—that Mao has sought to combat through the CR.

It is not clear whether Mao still embraces modernization as a major goal of the Chinese Revolution. If he does, then—in the words of the observers quoted above—"it makes no sense to talk about completely preventing the growth of a privileged stratum" since "that is part of the necessary price of economic development," but "it [still] does make sense to talk about limiting the power of this stratum, keeping its privileges to the necessary minimum, and preventing it from solidifying its position and trans-

[6] "Decision of the Central Committee of the Chinese Communist Party Concerning the Great Proletarian Cultural Revolution," *Peking Review*, Aug. 12, 1966, p. 6.

[7] Leo Huberman and Paul Sweezy, "The Cultural Revolution in China," *Monthly Review* (New York), January 1967, as reprinted by the Radical Education Project, p. 11.

[8] The use of the death imagery is suggested by Robert J. Lifton's *Revolutionary Immortality*, New York, Random House, 1968.

[9] Huberman and Sweezy, *loc. cit.*, p. 11.

[10] Insofar as the CR appears to be a revolution against modernization, it is no wonder that many American social scientists have tended to deride it. In the United States today, modernization has come to be worshipped as a kind of new Hegelianism combining the "is" and the "ought" in history. Despite reservations, American social scientists generally tend to treat it as both inevitable and good. Even so perceptive an observer as Robert Lifton concludes that Mao, in trying to confront some of the problems connected with modernization, is out of touch with reality and guilty of "psychism" (Lifton, *op. cit.*). Also see Baum, *loc. cit.*

forming its vested interests into [the equivalent of] inheritable property rights." [11] If this, indeed, has been one of Mao's aims in the CR, his decision to make allies of the very young—particularly those below college age who are neither dominated by traditional mores nor tainted by careerism—is readily understandable. For one of the difficulties of preventing the development of a new ruling class is that many members of the very groups that have the greatest interest in preventing it too frequently "still live under the influence of old moral and religious ideas which sanction and sanctify the privileges of the few and confer legitimacy on their rule." [12] This problem has been compounded in China since 1949 by the elitist and careerist element in the Communist Party. The thinking of Mao and his allies is probably well summarized by Huberman and Sweezy when they point out that the initiative in preventing the emergence of a new ruling class therefore devolved upon

> those, both in the leadership and in the rank and file, who made the revolution and remain uncorrupted by the temptations of actual or potential privilege. It is up to them to lead the struggle and to enlist as much support as possible from the ranks of the underprivileged and the uncorrupted. If those who made the revolution fail in this task, or if they do not understand its necessity . . . then they will have put their country firmly on what the Chinese [*i.e.*, the Maoists] call the capitalist road, and their successors who never had their revolutionary experience and understanding will almost certainly not be able, and in all probability will not want, to divert it from that road.[13]

In the 1950's and 1960's, the Chinese party leadership, as it turned to the task of reconstruction and economic development, undertook a series of campaigns aimed in part at maintaining the revolutionary elan. The CR, viewed in this perspective, might be understood as a bigger and more ambitious campaign to protect certain revolutionary goals while continuing the drive toward modernization. In this interpretation, the Maoists are seen as continuing to embrace the goals of modernization but hoping, through the CR, to minimize the negative social implications of the modernization process. Thus, according to Huberman and Sweezy:

> Mao and his colleagues are realists enough to know that it will be a long . . . time before China can hope to wipe out substantial inequalities. The target [of the CR] is the privileged ones who are misusing their power to promote special and private interests. . . . The method of dealing with them is not terror [selectively] wielded by a secret police . . . but the mobilization of [certain of] the unprivileged and particularly the youth who have not yet been exposed to the temptations of privilege and power. The [Maoist] . . . leadership evidently believes that if the privileged stratum can be contained and controlled and the young . . . won for the Revolution . . . , then the country can be kept from taking the capitalist road for at least one more generation while economic development brings closer the day when general abundance will make possible the real elimination of inequality and privilege.[14]

But if the CR, in one sense, was just a bigger and better campaign against the regularized abuses of the new privileged stratum, it was also more than that. Besides being an attack on those

[11] Huberman and Sweezy, *op. cit.*, p. 13 (italics deleted).
[12] *Ibid.*
[13] *Ibid.*, pp. 13–14.
[14] *Ibid.*, pp. 15–16. See also Carl Riskin, "The Chinese Economy in 1967," in *The Cultural Revolution: 1967 in Review*, Ann Arbor, University of Michigan, 1968, p. 60.

who abused their privileged positions, it was at the same time an attack on the legitimacy of the institutions and organizations from which privilege in Communist China arose. And it also appears to have entailed the relegation of modernization as a national goal to a lower priority. Seen in this broader context, the CR seems to have been an extremely radical attempt to establish what might be called counter-institutions capable both of limiting the drift towards hierarchy and privilege and of reasserting the revolutionary goals of egalitarianism and mass participation. The three central counter-institutions—none of which requires a high degree of disciplined organization, and all of which are therefore relatively free at least of the inflexibilities toward which organizations are prone—are: 1) the supreme leader; 2) the Thought of Mao Tse-tung; and 3) "the masses" as participants (the role of the masses being legitimized, in part, in much the same way as peasant rebellions were legitimized in China's traditional political system by the concept of the passing of the mandate of heaven).[15]

Leader, Party and Masses

The Chinese Communist political system since the mid-1930's has been characterized by a dialectical process involving leader, masses, and organization, a process that can be personified partially in the historical relation between Mao and Liu. In that relationship Mao functioned primarily as the radical initiator, the leader who set general directions, stimulated the release of mass energies, and worked to prevent the ossification of institutions. Liu, on the other hand, functioned more in the role of coordinator and consolidator of gains, the relatively conservative "organization man," the implementer on the ground.[16] Generally speaking, the mutuality and tension between the two roles has been healthy for the ongoing revolution.

Mao, the great leader, has been consistently ambivalent about large-scale bureaucratic organizations. In part, this may simply reflect his personal and historical awareness, as a 20th-century Chinese, of China's two major pre-Communist examples of such organizations. Born in 1893, at the end of the Ch'ing dynasty, Mao grew up while the traditional Chinese bureaucracy disintegrated. He also saw at first hand the efforts of the Kuomintang to build its own bureaucracy in Republican China, and he observed its rapid corruption. Thus, Ezra F. Vogel is probably right in observing that "Chinese Maoists are preoccupied with a vision from their past —the vision of the moral degeneration of a bureaucracy which is out of touch with the people, the core problem which led to the decline and fall of the

[15] Ray Wylie ("Revolution Within a Revolution," *Bulletin of the Atomic Scientists*, February 1969, p. 32) sees the role of the masses in the CR as setting a possible pattern for the future: "The Maoist press has declared that there will probably be more Cultural Revolutions in the future. That is, the people have in Mao Tse-tung's thought the theoretical basis—and in the present Cultural Revolution the historical precedent—by which to justify an attack on any future regime that loses its revolutionary elan and begins to drift toward despotism . . . Above all, it is an endeavour . . . to impart to them the ideal of a 'new China' and the idea that it is 'right to rebel' if a future regime betrays that ideal." In this perspective, Mao Tse-tung becomes Chinese communism's own John Locke.

[16] The perspective of Mao as radical initiator and Liu as consolidator was suggested to the author by Professor Tang Tsou's "The Cultural Revolution and the Chinese Political System," *The China Quarterly* (London), April–June 1969, pp. 63–91. I am grateful to Professor Tsou for having allowed me to read the manuscript prior to its publication.

Kuomintang".[17] However, this interpretation, by itself, fails to explain why Mao (and the Maoists) should be so much more preoccupied than other elements in China's leadership with the problematic nature of bureaucracy as an instrument for achieving goals—especially revolutionary goals.[18]

To understand Mao's particular ambivalence toward bureaucratic organization, it is also necessary to recognize the relevance of Mao's special experience in Yenan during the revolutionary war—an experience which some observers have seen as responsible for the so-called "Yenan syndrome" or, more derisively, for Mao's attachment to a "primitive political system." During the Yenan days of 1935–45, as John W. Lewis has pointed out, Mao functioned in the role of distant, charismatic leader of the highly decentralized guerrilla war.[19] In that role, he emphasized the positive function of the masses [20] and the critical importance of relatively unlimited struggle in maintaining a revolutionary environment; and he was habitually suspicious of elitist bureaucratic organization as the primary medium for waging revolution.

By contrast, Lewis argues, Liu Shao-ch'i operated in those days as chief political commissar (today's "party bureaucrat"), "fashioning a strong party-army wherein only limited forms of struggle were tolerated".[21] He ritualized these limited forms of struggle in tightly organized local party units, concentrated on the elitist organization of the party, and after the establishment of Communist rule in 1949 played a leading role in building the centralizing party bureaucracy. The result was that, by 1956, China's Yenan-type, flexible, decentralized revolutionary warfare organization had been effectively replaced:

> Guided and dominated by party structure, that [Maoist] system had made the initial transition to an elite system according priority to the goals of modernization and the requisite recruitment from scientific and technical sectors of the society. The party apparatus was at its zenith, and the term "thought of Mao" [since resurrected and enshrined in the CR] was dropped from the 1956 party constitution. Charisma, now routinized, had shifted from Mao to the party, and with Leninism supplanting "the thought of Mao Tse-tung," the Chairman had subsumed his image under the party and lent it his authority.[22]

Having basically eliminated, neutralized, and/or delegitimized all hostile

[17] "The Structure of Conflict: China in 1967," in *The Cultural Revolution: 1967 in Review*, *op. cit.*, p. 102. Vogel's analysis is deeply informed and frequently brilliant, but it tends to ignore the significance of Mao's maximal goals, mentioning Mao's "major objectives" almost in passing, and treating the CR simply as a great and sophisticated Maoist-type purge. Power is the name of the game, and the relevance of ultimate values, if assumed, is obscured.

[18] Chalmers Johnson ("China: The Cultural Revolution in Structural Perspective," *Asian Survey*, January 1968, pp. 3–4) touches on problems of bureaucratic ossification and goal displacement in China. His description of the inefficiencies of bureaucracies, said to be particularly serious in Communist countries, drives another nail into the coffin in which theories of totalitarianism are destined to be buried.

[19] John W. Lewis, "Leader, Commissar, and Bureaucrat: The Chinese Political System in the Last Days of the Revolution," in Ho and Tsou, *op. cit.* The following discussion of the roles of Mao and Liu in Yenan is based on Lewis' stimulating piece, but in stressing the different experiences of the two men, I do not mean to imply that other factors may not be equally important in explaining their divergent orientations towards revolution.

[20] For a discussion of Mao's "populism" and "his 'mystical faith' . . . in the rural masses," see Lifton, *op. cit.*, pp. 83–85 and 110.

[21] Lewis, *loc. cit.*, p. 453.

[22] *Ibid.*, pp. 464–65.

competing power elites, the CCP itself became what Professor Tang Tsou has aptly termed "the establishment *par excellence.*"[23] The party allied itself with leaders in all segments of Chinese life to form a privileged stratum which kept "the levers of power in various fields in their hands and [lived] fairly comfortably amidst the general poverty of China even during the years of agricultural crisis. . . . The party organization's sensitivity to the material interests of the various social groups and its ability to work with the privileged groups" enabled this stratum to operate quite effectively in modernizing China, but it also built up repressed dissatisfaction among the Maoists and among some dominated or underprivileged groups.[24]

Thus, the Chinese political system before the CR was dominated by a centralized, hierarchical, incredibly pervasive party-cum-privileged stratum, which has been described—again in the words of Tang Tsou—as "one of the purest forms found in human experience of a type of association in which there is a clear-cut separation between the elite and the masses".[25] In this light, the CR and, to a lesser degree, many of the earlier Maoist-type mass campaigns can be viewed as a critique of, and reaction against, this elitist type of political system.

The Mission of the Party

But with the perspective of the dialectical process between leader and party in mind, Mao's Great Proletarian Cultural Revolution seems to have been less purely anti-organizational in character than has been generally assumed. The CR appears rather to have been aimed at reasserting, on a greater scale and in the face of intense resistance, the earlier balance between leader, masses, and party organization that prevailed in the 1940's. As such, it may also be said to represent Mao's attempt to reestablish the distinctive quality of the party organization—which is one key to any organization's survival and continued success.

The distinctive quality of the CCP historically has lain in the content and diffuseness of its goals and in its style. As Professor Schurmann has observed, the Chinese party, unlike organizations with narrower goals, has made its broad objective "not to produce organizational expertise but to make men into committed leaders who can command [other] men in a variety of concrete problems to be resolved."[26] The Chinese Communist movement has also been committed to achieving modernization, national power, and the ideal Communist society of the future, but increasingly after taking power the party found that it had little distinctive to offer with regard to the first two of these goals. Writes Schurmann:

> The state administrative bureaucracy planned and operated the economy and seems to have acquitted itself well. The army was doing its best to provide for

[23] Tsou, *loc. cit.*

[24] *Ibid.*

[25] *Ibid.* This emphasis on the relatively elitist nature of the Chinese political system in the mid-1950's should not, however, obscure the complex reality of politics within that system. For an excellent and provocative article which begins to sketch out the contours of reciprocity in Chinese politics in the mid-1960's, see Michel Oksenberg, "Occupational Groups in Chinese Society and the Cultural Revolution," in *The Cultural Revolution: 1967 in Review, op. cit.*, pp. 1–44.

[26] Schurmann, "The Attack of the Cultural Revolution . . ." *loc. cit.*, p. 538.

China's defense. . . . [And] looking at these . . . segments of the trinity of state power, one cannot but have the feeling that the role of the party was becoming increasingly unclear.[27]

The more the emphasis shifted toward modernization, professionalism, pragmatism, and the use of material incentives rather than spiritual ones, the more the party found itself deprived of a valid leadership role. It was left with its ideology, but without organizations for which the application of that ideology had any real practical value. At the risk of exaggeration, Schurmann writes that "during the period of liberalization in the early 1960's before the Tenth Plenum of September 1962, the 17 million party members had nothing to do except what they had to do otherwise in their practical roles (for example, as factory directors)." And he concludes that "to compensate for this, China's leaders decided to launch a campaign of ideological indoctrination designed to preserve the party member's leadership role in the realm of ideology, even if practically there wasn't much for him to do."[28]

But surely, given a continued concentration on goals related to modernization, such campaigns would simply establish more firmly the "trained incapacity" of party members to exercise meaningful leadership. If this is true, then only by reestablishing the primacy of the Maoist vision of the good society—a society that requires for its realization the transformation of human nature, requiring in turn a continuing cultural revolution—could the party hope to perform again a unique and significant leadership role.

The same point can be made with respect to the party's distinctive style, a critical element of which is the organizational technique known as the "mass line." As ideally conceived, this technique is a sophisticated method for encouraging participation by those at the bottom of the organization (*e.g.*, the peasants), for gathering information, and for translating high-level policy decisions (made partly on the basis of this information) into operational decisions on the ground. It is predicated upon a continuing process of interaction between leaders and led, the purposes of which are to stimulate initiative below, to reduce the feedback problem common to highly authoritarian or so-called "totalitarian" societies, and simultaneously, within the limits of practicability, to tutor the masses. Ideally, the mass line functions to avoid the twin extremes of "tailism"—responding primarily to the short-term demands of the masses—and "commandism"—simply ordering from above, without consideration for the desires of the masses.

With the regularization of party bureaucratic procedures and the increased emphasis on professional expertise in the early and middle 1950's, however, the elitist element in the party character tended to dominate patterns of decision-making, and participation by the masses came to be looked upon by organization men as regressive. As a consequence, instead of becoming firmly institutionalized as part of routine decision-making, mass-line techniques

[27] *Ibid.*, p. 546. See also the same author's "China's 'New Economic Policy'—Transition or Beginning," *The China Quarterly*, January–March 1964, pp. 65–91, especially after p. 83.

[28] Schurmann, "The Attack of the Cultural Revolution . . . ," *loc. cit.*, p. 543. Schurmann's vision of the party in the early 1960's ties in nicely with the theory later set forth by Baum (see footnote 2). On the other hand, Oksenberg (in Ho and Tsou, *op. cit.*, pp. 494–96) diverges from Schurmann and Baum in wondering whether the attitudes and values of the Liu Shao-ch'i/Teng Hsiao-p'ing grouping might not be *less* conducive to modernization than those of the Red Guards. Several economists have also begun to raise such questions: *e.g.*, Riskin, *loc. cit.*, pp. 60–64; and Jack Gray, "The Economics of Maoism," *Bulletin of the Atomic Scientists*, February 1969, pp. 42–51.

tended to be more and more embodied in periodic waves of mass campaigns which the organization men in turn viewed increasingly as antagonistic to party regularity. Such campaigns became *ad hoc* mechanisms for temporarily de-regularizing procedures and shaking up the bureaucracy. But in view of the hostility which the campaigns generated within the bureaucracy, the mass line tended to be employed erratically and without the organizational discipline and balance required for its successful functioning.

Leader Above Party

In the CR, Mao seems to have attempted to revive the distinctive attributes of the party described above. It can be seen that in some sense this required an assault on the party as then constituted, as a preparatory step toward re-instilling in it a sense of its sacred mission and special competence. The party, if it is to maintain its institutional integrity, cannot be concerned primarily with modernization, for it has shown no distinctive competence in this realm. Rather, the party has to concern itself primarily with the quality of life in China as measured, for example, by the standards of the Maoist ideal society. Such a concern may prompt the party to act at times as a counterbalance to the modernization process. If the likelihood of the party's success in moving counter to such forces can be regarded as less than certain, the long-run consequence of an abdication in this regard would be to assure the party's own irrelevance.

In recognizing and acting upon these facts of organizational life, Mao, in his assault on the party, ironically was acting as the great party leader. As Philip Selznick points out in his analysis of leadership, it is the function of "leadership in administration" to "define the mission of the enterprise" and to build "special values and distinctive competence into the organization." [29] He goes on to say:

> It is in the realm of policy—including the areas where policy formation and organization-building meet—that the distinctive quality of institutional leadership is found. Ultimately, *this is the quality of statesmanship which deals with current issues, not for themselves alone, but according to their long-run implications for the role and meaning of the group.* Group leadership is far more than the capacity to mobilize personal support; it is more than the maintenance of equilibrium through the routine solution of everyday problems; it is the function of the leader statesman . . . to define the ends of group existence, to design an enterprise distinctively adapted to these ends, and to see that that design becomes a living reality.[30]

Using Selznick's analytic distinction between "organizations" (technical instruments which are expendable, are designed to achieve relatively definite goals, and can therefore be judged on "engineering premises") and "institutions" (which are "infused with value" beyond their mere utility as a means and are therefore more resistant to change even if they are inefficient),[31]

[29] Philip Selznick, *Leadership in Administration,* Evanston, Ill., Row, Peterson, 1957, pp. 26–27.

[30] *Ibid.*, p. 37 (italics added). Mao, as leader, can be seen as the receptacle of ultimate values. Dick Wilson refers to Mao as China's "conscience" in his "Where China Stands Now: An Introduction," *Bulletin of the Atomic Scientists,* February 1969, p. 5.

[31] Elsewhere in this paper, the terms "organization" and "institution" are not used in the technical sense in which Selznick uses them. Selznick treats these terms as ideal types. In the concrete, the relationship between the organizational and institutional components in a particular unit is complex and a matter of process.

and as Franz Schurmann has pointed out, one can say that Mao has tried to de-institutionalize the party so that it can be judged by Maoist standards as an expendable instrument. Realistically, one also can say that Mao, aware that the process of institutionalization is a recurring one, has attempted to set leader above party, to elevate the Thought of Mao Tse-tung to the level of the highest moral standard, and to establish the precedent of discovering vanguard elements outside the party in order to counter the natural tendencies within the party toward institutionalization.[32]

The cult of personality, which was used in the early 1950's to legitimize roles and institutions through association with a beloved and respected leader (thus, Chinese children's songs praise *Chairman* Mao), has in the 1960's been raised to new heights and used to place leader above institutions. The cult was thus forged into a weapon for assaulting the party and government.[33] Similarly, the Thought of Mao—which the 1956 party constitution relegated to second place by substituting the statement that "the CCP takes Marxism-Leninism as its guide to action" for the sentence in the 1945 party constitution that the CCP "guides its entire work" by the Thought of Mao Tse-tung—has increasingly been treated in the 1960's as a quasi-sacred, magical body of norms.

Mao's extreme reliance in recent years on his own personal authority and ideology reflects the seriousness of his predicament. As Tang Tsou points out, Mao has been "confronted with the very difficult problem of justifying his revolution and legitimizing his attack on the party organization," whose authority had hitherto been accepted as axiomatic.[34] Moreover, the pragmatic policies initiated by the party in the early 1960's have been highly successful. Mao therefore felt it necessary to use all his non-organizational weapons in order both to attack the still sacred aura of party authority and to "override pragmatic standards." [35] Mao's thought was elevated to a new peak higher than that occupied by the thought of Marx, Engels and Lenin, and therefore higher than the party or any ideology upon which the party might base a claim to legitimacy in opposition to Mao. This, notes Professor Tsou, served a definite political purpose by setting "a new standard of legitimacy and correctness with which the actions and opinions of many top leaders were to be judged." [36]

At the same time, Mao's strategy deprived his opponents of the capacity to attack him openly, forcing them in effect "to hide under the Maoist cover [and to] 'fight the Red Flag by waving the Red Flag'." [37] In other words, even when opposing Mao, the opposition found itself obliged to rely publicly for

[32] In the author's view, Mao is aware that his own personal authority and charisma cannot be bestowed with great effectiveness on another and has therefore sought to establish counter-institutions to protect his value concerns after his death (see below).

[33] The author's hypothesis that Mao has consciously used his personal authority, earlier institutionalized in the cult of personality, for grand political purposes is in contrast to the view that Mao is a supervain megalomaniac. While one may disagree with Mao's goals and methods, neither are, in my view, pathological. The "growing personalization of the Mao cult" (noted by Stuart Schram in his *Mao Tse-tung*, Baltimore, Penguin, 1967, revised paperback ed., p. 340) has been part of Mao's effort to play an active leadership role in the CR. By deliberately repersonalizing the cult of personality and recreating it as charisma—for example, by his numerous appearances at huge mass rallies—Mao has heightened his own capacity to evoke great emotion and to manipulate that emotion.

[34] Tsou, *loc. cit.*

[35] *Ibid.*

[36] *Ibid.*

[37] See Vogel, *loc. cit.*, p. 106.

its legitimacy upon Mao's thought, thereby reinforcing his primacy. Thus, Professor Tsou rightly observes, the party organization had "to defend itself under the major premises and rules of the game laid down by Mao. All . . . organizations pledged allegiance to Mao and his thought. All . . . said that they supported the Cultural Revolution. . . ." [38] In short, the party organization was disarmed by Mao's capacity as supreme leader to manipulate political ideology.

Countervailing Institutions

The proposition that Mao sought through the CR to establish counter-institutions that would assure the realization of his vision of the Chinese revolution finds support in the new CCP constitution adopted by the Ninth Party Congress on April 14, 1969. In startling contrast to the 1956 party constitution, which lauded Marxism-Leninism without even mentioning the Thought of Mao in its preamble (general program section), the new constitution proclaims:

> The Communist Party of China takes Marxism, Leninism, and the Thought of Mao Tse-tung as the theoretical basis guiding its thinking. The thought of Mao Tse-tung *is* Marxism-Leninism of the era in which . . . socialism is advancing to worldwide victory.[39]

The document goes on to credit Mao with integrating "the universal truth of Marxism-Leninism with the concrete practice of revolution" and bringing Marxism-Leninism "to a higher and completely new stage." Thus, Mao's thought is once more enshrined in the party constitution.

By contrast, the references to the party in the new constitution are less grand than those in the preceding constitution, which called the CCP "the vanguard of the Chinese working class [and] the highest form of its class organization." The new constitution simply states that "the Communist Party of China is the political party of the proletariat." The text, it is true, later refers to the party in more eulogistic terms, but only in conjunction with Mao's leadership: "The Communist Party of China with Comrade Mao Tse-tung as its leader is a great, glorious, and correct party and is the core of leadership of the Chinese people." Thus, the party as a separate entity is downgraded.

In line with the explicit emphasis on Mao's thought and leadership, the new constitution also praises Lin Piao as a most loyal and resolute defender of Mao's "revolutionary line" and, in a departure from past precedent, specifically designates him as Mao's "successor." The constitution thus takes the authority to determine the succession to the post of party chairman out of the hands of the party Central Committee, where it would normally reside, and assures Mao of a successor acceptable to him. Moreover, Articles 5 and 9, by comparison with the 1956 constitution, place heavier stress on the leadership role of the party chairman and vice-chairman relative to the rest of the party organization. In particular, Article 5 provides that if a party member disagrees with the decisions or directive of a party organization, he "has the right to *bypass the immediate leadership* and report directly to higher levels up to and including the Central Committee *and the Chairman* of the Central Committee" (italics added). Thus, the Maoist

[38] Tsou, *loc. cit.*

[39] This and other passages are quoted from the text as reported in English by *New China News Agency*, April 28, 1969; italics added.

leadership is upgraded at the expense of the party hierarchy.

Finally, the constitution fully endorses the "Great Proletarian Cultural Revolution" and exhorts party members and party organization to "consult with the masses" (Article 3) and to "constantly listen to the opinions of the masses both inside *and outside* the party and accept their supervision" (Article 5; italics added).[40]

Thus, taken as a whole, the new constitution appears to formalize Mao's effort to set up countervailing institutions above and below the party. Mao's thought, Mao's leadership—or, more generally, Maoist leadership—and the role of the masses are all upgraded, while the monopoly role of the party is downgraded.

Mao, Marx and Rousseau

Mao's experience in Yenan and since, his image of himself as leader, and his conceptions of the nature of the party and the masses all contribute towards an understanding of his goals in the CR. Beyond this, Mao's goals since the mid-1950's may in some sense best be comprehended in terms of an increasingly observable rejection of Marxism-Leninism, accompanied by an increasing affirmation of Rousseauean concerns and methods.[41]

Although Mao earlier seems to have believed, with Marx, that economic development and moral progress were indissolubly and positively linked—that industrialization would produce the "Communist man"—there is little evidence that Mao today continues to embrace this convenient rationalization for withholding concern for moral progress while focusing on material progress. Like Rousseau, and buttressed by world history since Marx, in particular by the experience of having observed the processes and consequences of the institutionalization of the Chinese revolution, Mao appears to have concluded that "the arts and sciences (technico-economic progress) as they . . . developed . . . [after the Great Leap] . . . actually . . . [ran] counter to moral progress and contributed to all the corruptions of society"[42] and of the revolution.

And the parallels to Rousseau do not stop there. Mao's vision of the ideal society is very similar to that of Rousseau. Mao's good society is a kind of Christian utopia, collectivist, austere, egalitarian, and without the need for coercive institutions because it is composed of virtuous men who have internalized such values as self-sacrifice in the common good, and who directly and actively participate as a solidary mass in determining the course of politics. And like Rousseau, Mao focuses on the demand for a new society, the importance of education, and the role of the great charismatic leader who understands the needs of the masses, epitomizes the na-

[40] Just what "supervision" by "the masses" will mean in practice is unclear. The revolutionary committees which have been set up throughout China at all levels may well represent, in part, an attempt to institutionalize the role of "the masses," but the nature and permanency of these committees and their relationship to other institutions are problematical. Whatever is meant by "supervision," the vision of an active role for "the masses" will be an empty one if there is no institutional facility through which they can make their power felt.

[41] Marx's philosophy, especially his early work, obviously owes much to Rousseau. In this sense, Mao may be said to be rejecting elements of Marxism while selectively reaffirming the concerns of the early Marx. The following discussion of Mao and Rousseau draws to a considerable extent upon the work of Benjamin I. Schwartz, especially his brilliant "The Reign of Virtue . . . (*loc. cit.*, footnote 2) and his earlier "Modernization and the Maoist Vision—Some Reflections on Chinese Communist Goals" (*The China Quarterly*, Jan.–March 1965.)

[42] Schwartz, "The Reign of Virtue . . . ," *loc. cit.*, p. 9.

tional character, and at the same time embodies their highest moral concerns. It is the leader who "liberates" the masses from their narrow particularity as individuals so that they can realize their human potential.

But there is a vital difference between Mao and Rousseau which is central to an understanding of Mao's role in the Cultural Revolution. Rousseau was a radical theorist without power. His primary goal, historically conditioned, was to eliminate the sort of immobile particularism associated with feudalism, thereby freeing man to understand the broader potentiality of his nature. Rousseau's mechanism for this miraculous transformation is the "great legislator," who arrives Messiah-like, fuses the people into a moral unity, extirpates traditional institutions which obstruct that fusion, and establishes laws and institutions to perpetuate the good society. Rousseau's whole scheme has frequently and correctly been described as an evasion of the central political problem of how the desired transformation of society is to be effected—an evasion accomplished by the invocation of a *deus ex machina*, the great legislator.

But Mao *is* the great legislator, *a radical in power*—perhaps the first in history who has substantially retained his radical purity after being in power for over a generation.[43] As such he must deal with political problems, the foremost of which is that there will be no Messiah to produce the ultimate ideal state. The cultural revolution required to "liberate" man must be accomplished through, not in evasion of, politics. The great leader must act in history. The problems of institutions cannot be avoided—neither the present problem of how to transform old institutions and men, nor the continuing problem of how to ensure the future integrity of those transformed.

In going beyond Rousseau, Mao has also gone beyond Marxism-Leninism and Stalinism in his effort to resolve institutional problems. He has sought in the CR to transform the most powerful institution in China, the Communist Party. As Benjamin Schwartz brilliantly argues, Mao has declared that the sacred moral values previously associated exclusively with the party are most purely found in himself and his thought, and that these qualities "may be shared by groups, institutions and individuals which lie *outside* of the party. Indeed, the party as such, when considered apart from . . . [the leader and his thought], may wholly degenerate. . . ."[44] It is the leader, his ideology, and the masses whom he can directly inspire, that offer hope of becoming a counterforce to over-institutionalization and the problems of organizational goal displacement.

Polarization of the Elite

But how and why did Mao determine to follow this strategy? In the 1950's, despite important differences of opinion within the Chinese leadership group over the priorities to be given to various revolutionary goals, there was a shared belief that these goals were compatible —a belief, in short, that by working for China's modernization and strengthen-

[43] It appears that as 20th-century Americans we may be peculiarly unable to appreciate Mao as a radical in power and as a great man. We tend to view politics as "the art of the possible"—an implicitly conservative formulation. Radicals at home and abroad tend to frighten and annoy us. Moreover, while in the 19th century we had our voluntarist heroes—*e.g.*, self-made men and captains of industry—today we increasingly have come to disbelieve in the power of man's will in the face of overwhelming technological forces. Bereft of white, middle-class heroes at home, we may even resent great men abroad.

[44] Schwartz, "The Reign of Virtue . . . ," *loc. cit.*, p. 13.

ing, one was simultaneously working for a Maoist-Communist China. Here again, the role of ideology, this time as a cohesive force, can hardly be overestimated. For Marxism-Leninism, the commonly accepted ideology of the leadership elite, combined a technological approach to history with a moral one. By promising simultaneous fulfillment of technological and moral goals through history, Marxism-Leninism strengthened the Chinese leadership consensus. Particularly in the early stages after 1949, the obvious tensions between professionalism ("expert") and Maoist politics ("red") did not seem unmanageable. Even the Great Leap of 1958 appears to have been conceived and implemented, in large part, on the assumption that the different revolutionary goals were not fundamentally incompatible: it was, to some degree, an attempt to harness the power of "redness" in the service of modernization, an attempt to accelerate economic development through mass mobilization and ideological exhortation, with politics in control.

But the failure of the Great Leap in the immediate economic and organizational sense (there were severe food shortages and breakdowns in organizational control) and the recriminations that followed that failure in 1959–61, including Marshal P'eng Te-huai's attack on Mao's leadership at the August 1959 Lushan Plenum, tended to polarize China's political elite into two groupings. One diffuse grouping, headed—we can say in retrospect—by Liu Shao'ch'i, P'eng Chen, Teng Hsiao-p'ing and others, concentrated their attention primarily on organization-building, regularity and modernization. These men, the "organization men," were in operational control of China after 1959 and built up vested interests in the party and state organizations. In general, it was their view that economic development directed by the party and government bureaucracies would ultimately produce the desired Communist society. The other grouping, headed by Mao, was more radical and increasingly lost faith in bureaucratic procedures and in the Marxist notion that economic development would lead to the good society. As the two groups tended to polarize, the struggle between them became more and more a struggle for power—for the power to determine the course of China's development.

In the early 1960's, with the organization men in control of party, government, and economy and pursuing pragmatic policies, Mao moved rapidly to maximize his influence in the People's Liberation Army (PLA) through a series of internal campaigns to reindoctrinate the army with Maoist goals and techniques. Mao's decision to make the PLA the opening wedge in what he probably envisaged even then as a long-range and vitally needed campaign was natural. In many ways the PLA was the easiest of the three basic organizational hierarchies of China—army, party, and government—to politicize in Maoist modes of thought and action. In the context of the break with the Soviet Union and China's increasing desire to find a "Chinese path" of socialist development, and given the fact that of the three hierarchies the PLA had the least need to "produce" from day to day, Mao seemed best able to establish his model in the army. Despite some opposition from professionally-oriented officers, Mao succeeded in the early 1960's in fashioning the PLA into his most reliable organizational support.

In the years just prior to the launching of the Cultural Revolution, the prestige and power of the PLA's top and second-echelon officers increased rapidly under the tutelage of Mao and Lin Piao, at the expense primarily of the party and secondarily of the government. The PLA became the embodiment of Maoist virtue, thereby subtly undermining the party's prestige. PLA leaders assumed important political roles in the government and economy. And as the battle between Mao and the leaders of the Peking party organization became more intense in late 1965, the PLA's official organ, *Chieh-fang Chün Pao* (Liberation Army Daily) became for a time the most authoritative voice among the mass media, superseding even the party's own *Jen-min Jih-pao* (People's Daily).

On the other hand, too much should not be made of Maoist control of the army. While the PLA has probably been the most loyal organizational support of the Maoists, the events of the CR have made clear that its support has been substantially limited. If Mao hoped in the early 1960's to fashion the PLA into a truly revolutionary force, the prospects for success seemed dim by 1966. The key question has always been: *PLA support to do what?* The upgrading of the PLA to the role of Mao's staunchest ally appears to have been feasible precisely because Maoist demands for its support remained relatively restricted. Until late January of 1967, the PLA was significant primarily as a proclaimed model and as a reserve force which all sides were probably pleased to see remain on the sidelines—in part because of uncertainty as to what action it might take. In short, its role in support of Mao did not directly involve the use of its coercive powers. Nor was Mao's most vocal supporter, Defense Minister Lin Piao, called upon to test on any national scale the solidity and unity of this support.

Red Guards and the PLA

As the CR evolved out of elite polarization and certain mass dissatisfactions, Mao came to rely basically on two groups—the Red Guards (and Revolutionary Rebels) and the PLA. In retrospect, it can be said that these two groups functioned—ironically enough—in relatively specialized ways: the Maoist Red Guard and Revolutionary Rebel movement constituted the force for seizing power from below, while the PLA substantially embodied the tendency to impose order from above.[45]

As the CR intensified in 1966–67, reaching its peak perhaps in August 1967,[46] it went through alternating cycles of attack and retrenchment—*i.e.*, of revolution from below and control from above. The attack phases were not fully controllable by the Maoist faction, not only because their intensity and duration depended in large part on the de-

[45] The Red Guard and Rebel groups were by no means all responsive to Mao's desires. According to John Gittings ("The Prospects of the Cultural Revolution in 1969," *Bulletin of the Atomic Scientists,* February 1969, p. 24), "the real rebels were the 'have nots' of China—the unemployed students, contract laborers, unskilled workers, and others who looked on rebellion as the way to remedy their lot." But even many of these "rebels" were more concerned with the material improvement of their lot than with Maoist values: see Evelyn Anderson, "Shanghai: The Masses Unleashed," *Problems of Communism,* January–February 1968 pp. 12–21. In addition, other conservative groups were set up by "local establishment figures" in self-defense: see Allen S. Whiting, "Mao's Troubled Ark," *Life,* February 21, 1969, pp. 62 f. Naturally, all groups, whatever their motives, called themselves "Maoists."

[46] It is arguable whether the violence and dislocation of the CR reached their peak in August 1967 or at certain times in 1968, but August 1967 still appears to have been the major turning point. After that, as Ezra Vogel notes (*loc. cit.,* p. 118), "there was a serious attempt to rebuild local political structures," and the subsequent struggles "should be viewed in the context of rebuilding the organizations." Gittings also observes ("The Prospects . . . ," *loc. cit.,* pp. 24–27) that struggles in 1968 generally involved a jockeying for power in "the whole process of political consolidation and restoration of order." It became necessary at times for the radicals to demonstrate their strength in order to keep from being frozen out in the division and restructuring of power.

gree of resistance encountered, but also because, by the very nature of the CR, the capacity to exercise internal operational control over highly decentralized Red Guard activities was limited. Moreover, even where that capacity may have existed, its exercise often would not have been legitimated by the primary goals of the CR itself. Within the parameters prescribed by the exigencies of the power balance in China and the need to avoid excessive disruption of agricultural and industrial production and distribution, the Maoist central Cultural Revolution Group found it difficult both organizationally and on ideological grounds to impose internal control from above on a revolution they were trying to stimulate from below. As for external controls, the usual instruments of such control—the party and the government—were themselves the prime targets of attack by the Maoist revolutionaries, leaving only the PLA as a potential restraining force.

In the first phase of the CR, from its inception up to January 1967, the PLA played a relatively minor role. In fact, most of the events of this phase took place outside and independently of any well-structured national organization. The shift from institutionalized procedures to mass meetings in Peking between revolutionary youth and the supreme leader was more than simply symbolic. The shift was central to the meaning of the CR as an assault on hierarchically structured control mechanisms. In this centrality lie both the peculiar strengths and weaknesses of the CR.

When the CR shifted in 1966 from attacks on relatively defenseless members of the bourgeoisie, shopkeepers, and tourists to an assault on leading party personnel at all levels throughout China, it encountered expectable resistance. Red Guard units were disorganized and inexperienced. Organizational power, experience in political infighting, and vested interests were all on the side of the entrenched party apparatus. Even Mao's attempt to legitimize the onslaught and to delegitimize resistance to it could not compensate for these realities. Moreover, in the nature of the situation, the proper targets for attack frequently were unclear. The directives from the central Cultural Revolution Group in Peking—lacking as they did the organizational apparatus required to translate their vaguely stated and even contradictory goals into practical action—were subject at least to honest misinterpretation. As a result, the Red Guard units—moved by enthusiasm and/or self-interest—often acted erratically, indiscriminately, and too intensely. Once again, Mao could not have the best of both worlds: he could not, on the one hand, encourage spontaneity and broad-gauged attacks from below on bureaucratic organizations and traditional institutions in the hope that this would teach youth the meaning of revolution by encouraging them to wage revolution, and, on the other hand, expect to be able to exercise definitive control even over his own forces in the struggle. As Mao's ideology was severed from organization, ideology manipulated by the leader inspired attacks that led to confusion and chaos.

Mao's Dilemma

In January 1967, the turmoil caused both by the Maoist drive to "seize power from below" through the Red Guard (student) and Revolutionary Rebel (adult worker) movements and by the subsequent inability of the radical Maoist factions to unify and stabilize the situation made it necessary to call upon the PLA to intervene in support of the left and restore order. But as the military, during February, stepped into the virtual organizational vacuum that had been created throughout the country, it became clear that PLA loyalty to Mao did not mean comprehensive and unified support for his radical goals. In fact, as might have been expected of a military organization trained to keep order —or, for that matter, of almost any large, hierarchical, national organization—the PLA intervened, in terms of practical effect, more on the side of order than of the revolutionary Left. And the more it expanded its governing activities, the greater its stake became in maintaining production and order.

Thus, despite his extensive earlier efforts to radicalize the PLA, Mao found himself confronted, in the final analysis, by a contradiction inherent in the thrust of the Cultural Revolution. The spearhead of the CR was the youth movement and its "assault" from below on the establishment. But when that assault led to excessive disruption or faced defeat, it became necessary, temporarily at least, to impose order from above through the only organization that remained relatively effective—the PLA. Insofar as the latter retained its integrity as a hierarchically organized and still relatively centralized and disciplined organization, it was capable of imposing order on a national scale in response to Maoist demands from Peking, but as such it was likely to favor order rather than revolution, and its very use interfered with the goal of revolution from below. On the other hand, insofar as the hierarchical military structure tended to become decentralized and disunited—as actually happened during the summer of 1967—the PLA inevitably became less responsive to Maoist demands and more likely to be controlled by regional or provincial military leaders who had their own local interests and organizations to protect and were generally antagonistic towards the disruptive activities of the revolutionary youth.

Mao, in short, was faced by a paradox. He needed an organization to wage permanent revolution, but found that organizations tend, at some point in the process of institutionalization, to become counterrevolutionary. There appears to be no single organizational form appropriate to permanent revolution. Hence, the tenuous "division of labor" in the CR between the Red Guards and the PLA; but in that division, final power lay with the PLA.

The CR in Perspective

The major exploits of Mao's life, and the Cultural Revolution in particular, are events which outside observers (and perhaps many Chinese as well) have had great difficulty in appreciating. The sheer intensity of emotions that has marked these events, combined with the not infrequent use of coercive and violent methods and the masses of people involved, has tended to arouse anxieties and antagonisms in much of the world outside China. Generally speaking, revolutions tend to appear less costly and awesome the farther they recede into the past, becoming abstractions in the process; revolutions in the present tend to repel or disturb us.[47] How much more is this the case when the sort of revolution at issue seems incomprehensible, even in terms of our past understanding of revolutions? We were not prepared by that understanding to appreciate Mao's Cultural Revolution. In terms of classical revolutions, the CR seems "artificial," or even superfluous, and therefore obviously excessive and romantic.

Yet, many observers sense that something of historic significance has happened in China. Even if we do not pretend to understand its implications, we sense that a great leader has fused explosive idealism and intense power in uneasy union and, in the process, has

[47] Of course, the frequently hidden costs of maintaining the status quo can also be awesome.

released tremendous energies. In a meaningful sense, the CR has been a struggle waged by the Maoists both to reopen in the most comprehensive manner the issue of China's goals and to determine the issue in favor of their own objectives. The central question for Maoists, in the author's view, is the nature of the society (quality of life) that should be the "end" of the Chinese Communist Revolution. Mao reopened the issue because it became increasingly clear to him that the dominant means employed to institutionalize the Chinese Revolution, while conducive to achieving certain of the Revolution's values, simultaneously appeared to preclude the realization of other values more deeply held by him and others. To a much greater degree than in the Great Leap, the core issue in the CR has been structured dramatically in terms of a choice of priorities—a choice, in short, between "modernization" and the Maoist vision of the good society.

Viewed in this light, the CR should not be dismissed simply as an aberration, as just another succession crisis characteristic of "totalitarian systems," or even as a kind of transition crisis peculiar to a certain stage of a society's development—it appears to be much more than a developmental watershed. In the final analysis, the CR seems to epitomize the tension between reality and ideals (in this case, Maoist ideals). It involves conflicts between societal values, social change, group and individual attitudes and interests, and social organizations and institutions. As such, it may have meaning for the world.

China's Cultural Revolution, in this sense, is part of a worldwide pattern of movement-type challenges to established authority and to related bureaucratic structures, challenges based fundamentally on the stated ideals of the very social systems whose authority structures are under assault. This worldwide pattern transcends stages of development and particular cultures, and it increasingly articulates a worldwide consciousness and sharing of certain values, particularly among the young. While one may point out that the challenge in China differed from analogous movements elsewhere (*e.g.*, in France, Mexico, and the United States) in that it was initiated from above and developed in the context of a power struggle within the elite, the fact remains that the Chinese movement also forged a life of its own: it gained believers, developed with considerable spontaneity, proved exceedingly difficult to control, and sought to realize—too often by methods difficult for most Western minds to accept—a vision of a more humane existence.

China's Cultural Revolution is also part of a worldwide historical tradition having its own vision of how men should relate to one another and to their society—namely, the tradition supported by theorists and practitioners of anarchism and permanent revolution. As Michel Oksenberg observes:

> Mao's policy may . . . be seen as an effort to secure the commitment particularly of the younger generation to the building of a more just society, a commitment that arises from participation in the revolutionary act of defying authority. Mao would rather delay China's industrialization than have its industrialization serve the purposes of an entrenched bureaucratic elite. In this respect, Mao continues to be true to his revolutionary heritage. At the same time, Mao shares with many the belief that bureaucracy and industrialization do not necessarily lead to an improved quality of life. To the extent that Mao's desire is to insure that industrialization serves the interests of his society, he is dealing with the central . . . problem of our age. Seen in this light, Mao cannot be discussed in terms of "success" or "failure." To call his system "primitive" is to do him injustice, for in many ways we are reduced to value judgments. And we can be sure that the faith in voluntarism, egalitarianism, and

permanent revolution which captured a long line of revolutionaries before Mao, and which [has] . . . gripped Mao in his life, will continue to attract political figures who come after him.[48]

In the opinion of this author, the problem of permanent revolution is not, as is often argued, only of interest to political theorists and intellectual historians. Nor is the concept of permanent revolution merely a romantic ideal of abnormal personalities ("romantic revolutionaries"). Rather, to an increasing extent throughout the world and—ironically—in advanced industrial societies particularly, permanent revolution is a fact. The motor for permanent revolution in advanced industrial societies is technology. But the problems presented are more universal: how to create flexible institutions which are responsive to popular interests, encourage direct mass participation, and are capable of controlling development on the basis of values meaningfully determined by the people.

The challenge of creating participatory institutions to deal with these problems is, in the author's view, at the core of the Chinese Cultural Revolution. Only time will tell what Mao has been able to achieve in facing this challenge and what those achievements may mean in the concrete for China and for the world.

[48] Oksenberg, in Ho and Tsou, *op. cit.*, pp. 493–94.

Lin Piao is Minister of National Defense and Mao Tse-tung's heir-apparent in the Chinese People's Republic. The following selection consists of excerpts from his famous elaboration of the Chinese Communist myth of the coming death of world capitalism-imperialism-fascism at the hands of agrarian "People's Revolutions."

Long Live the Victory of People's War

LIN PIAO

History shows that when confronted by ruthless imperialist aggression, a Communist Party must hold aloft the national banner and, using the weapon of the united front, rally around itself the masses and the patriotic and anti-imperialist people who form more than 90 per cent of a country's population, so as to mobilize all positive factors, unite with all the forces that can be united and isolate to the maximum the common enemy of the whole nation. If we abandon the national banner, adopt a line of "closed-doorism" and thus isolate ourselves, it is out of the question to exercise leadership and develop the

This speech was given in 1965 "In Commemoration of the Twentieth Anniversary of Victory in the Chinese People's War of Resistance Against Japan." The translation is Peking's.

people's revolutionary cause, and this in reality amounts to helping the enemy and bringing defeat on ourselves.

History shows that within the united front the Communist Party must maintain its ideological, political and organizational independence, adhere to the principle of independence and initiative, and insist on its leading role. Since there are class differences among the various classes in the united front, the Party must have a correct policy in order to develop the progressive forces, win over the middle forces and oppose the die-hard forces. The Party's work must centre on developing the progressive forces and expanding the people's revolutionary forces. This is the only way to maintain and strengthen the united front. "If unity is sought through struggle, it will live; if unity is sought through yielding, it will perish." This is the chief experience gained in our struggle against the die-hard forces.

History shows that during the national-democratic revolution there must be two kinds of alliance within this united front, first, the worker-peasant alliance and second, the alliance of the working people with the bourgeoisie and other non-working people. The worker-peasant alliance is an alliance of the working class with the peasants and all other working people in town and country. It is the foundation of the united front. Whether the working class can gain leadership of the national-democratic revolution depends on whether it can lead the broad masses of the peasants in struggle and rally them around itself. Only when the working class gains leadership of the peasants, and only on the basis of the worker-peasant alliance, is it possible to establish the second alliance, form a broad united front and wage a people's war victoriously. Otherwise, everything that is done is unreliable, like castles in the air or so much empty talk.

Rely on the Peasants and Establish Rural Base Areas

The peasantry constituted more than 80 per cent of the entire population of semi-colonial and semi-feudal China. They were subjected to threefold oppression and exploitation by imperialism, feudalism and bureaucrat-capitalism, and they were eager for resistance against Japan and for revolution. It was essential to rely mainly on the peasants if the people's war was to be won.

But at the outset not all comrades in our Party saw this point. The history of our Party shows that in the period of the First Revolutionary Civil War, one of the major errors of the Right opportunists, represented by Chen Tu-hsiu, was their failure to recognize the importance of the peasant question and their opposition to arousing and arming the peasants. In the period of the Second Revolutionary Civil War, one of the major errors of the "Left" opportunists, represented by Wang Ming, was likewise their failure to recognize the importance of the peasant question. They did not realize that it was essential to undertake long-term and pains-taking work among the peasants and establish revolutionary base areas in the countryside; they were under the illusion that they could rapidly seize the big cities and quickly win nation-wide victory in the revolution. The errors of both the Right and the "Left" opportunists brought serious setbacks and defeats to the Chinese revolution.

As far back as the period of the First Revolutionary Civil War, Comrade Mao Tse-tung had pointed out that the peasant question occupied an extremely important position in the Chinese revolution, that the bourgeois-democratic revolution against imperialism and feudalism was in essence a peasant revolution and that the basic task of the Chinese proletariat in the bourgeois-democratic revolution was to give leadership to the peasants' struggle.

In the period of the War of Resistance Against Japan, Comrade Mao Tse-tung again stressed that the peasants were the most reliable and the most numerous ally of the proletariat and constituted the main force in the War of Resistance. The peasants were the main source of manpower for China's armies. The funds and the supplies needed for a protracted war came chiefly from the peasants. In the anti-Japanese war it was imperative to rely mainly on the peasants and to arouse them to participate in the war on the broadest scale.

The War of Resistance Against Japan was in essence a peasant revolutionary war led by our Party. By arousing and organizing the peasant masses and integrating them with the proletariat, our Party created a powerful force capable of defeating the strongest enemy.

To rely on the peasants, build rural base areas and use the countryside to encircle and finally capture the cities—such was the way to victory in the Chinese revolution.

Basing himself on the characteristics of the Chinese revolution, Comrade Mao Tse-tung pointed out the importance of building rural revolutionary base areas.

> Since China's key cities have long been occupied by the powerful imperialists and their reactionary Chinese allies, it is imperative for the revolutionary ranks to turn the backward villages into advanced, consolidated base areas, into great military, political, economic and cultural bastions of the revolution from which to fight their vicious enemies who are using the cities for attacks on the rural districts, and in this way gradually to achieve the complete victory of the revolution through protracted fighting; it is imperative for them to do so if they do not wish to compromise with imperialism and its lackeys but are determined to fight on, and if they intend to build up and temper their forces, and avoid decisive battles with a powerful enemy while their own strength is inadequate.

Experience in the period of the Second Revolutionary Civil War showed that, when this strategic concept of Comrade Mao Tse-tung's was applied, there was an immense growth in the revolutionary forces and one Red base area after another was built. Conversely, when it was violated and the nonsense of the "Left" opportunists was applied, the revolutionary forces suffered severe damage, with losses of nearly 100 per cent in the cities and 90 per cent in the rural areas.

During the War of Resistance Against Japan, the Japanese imperialist forces occupied many of China's big cities and the main lines of communication, but owing to the shortage of troops they were unable to occupy the vast countryside, which remained the vulnerable sector of the enemy's rule. Consequently, the possibility of building rural base areas became even greater. Shortly after the beginning of the War of Resistance, when the Japanese forces surged into China's hinterland and the Kuomintang forces crumbled and fled in one defeat after another, the Eighth Route and New Fourth Armies led by our Party followed the wise policy laid down by Comrade Mao Tse-tung and boldly drove into the areas behind the enemy lines in small contingents and established base areas throughout the countryside. During the eight years of the war, we established nineteen anti-Japanese base areas in northern, central and southern China. With the exception of the big cities and the main lines of communication, the vast territory in the enemy's rear was in the hands of the people.

In the anti-Japanese base areas, we

carried out democratic reforms, improved the livelihood of the people, and mobilized and organized the peasant masses. Organs of anti-Japanese democratic political power were established on an extensive scale and the masses of the people enjoyed the democratic right to run their own affairs; at the same time we carried out the policies of "a reasonable burden" and "the reduction of rent and interest," which weakened the feudal system of exploitation and improved the people's livelihood. As a result, the enthusiasm of the peasant masses was deeply aroused, while the various anti-Japanese strata were given due consideration and were thus united. In formulating our policies for the base areas, we also took care that these policies should facilitate our work in the enemy-occupied areas.

. . . .

"Without a people's army the people have nothing." This is the conclusion drawn by Comrade Mao Tse-tung from the Chinese people's experience in their long years of revolutionary struggle, experience that was bought in blood. This is a universal truth of Marxism-Leninism.

Guided by Comrade Mao Tse-tung's theory on building a people's army, our army was under the absolute leadership of the Chinese Communist Party and most loyally carried out the Party's Marxist-Leninist line and policies. It had a high degree of conscious discipline and was heroically inspired to destroy all enemies and conquer all difficulties. Internally there was full unity between cadres and fighters, between those in higher and those in lower positions of responsibility, between the different departments and between the various fraternal army units. Externally, there was similarly full unity between the army and the people and between the army and the local government.

During the anti-Japanese war our army staunchly performed the three tasks set by Comrade Mao Tse-tung, namely, fighting, mass work, and production, and it was at the same time a fighting force, a political work force and a production corps. Everywhere it went, it did propaganda work among the masses, organized and armed them and helped them set up revolutionary political power. Our armymen strictly observed the Three Main Rules of Discipline and the Eight Points for Attention, carried out campaigns to "support the government and cherish the people", and did good deeds for the people everywhere. They also made use of every possibility to engage in production themselves so as to overcome economic difficulties, better their own livelihood and lighten the people's burden. By their exemplary conduct they won the whole-hearted support of the masses, who affectionately called them "our own boys".

Our army consisted of local forces as well as of regular forces; moreover, it energetically built and developed the militia, thus practising the system of combining the three military formations, i.e., the regular forces, the local forces and the militia.

Our army also pursued correct policies in winning over enemy officers and men and in giving lenient treatment to prisoners of war. During the anti-Japanese war we not only brought about the revolt and surrender of large numbers of puppet troops, but succeeded in converting not a few Japanese prisoners, who had been badly poisoned by fascist ideology. After they were politically awakened, they organized themselves into anti-war organizations such as the League for the Liberation of the Japanese People, the Anti-War League of the Japanese in China and the League of Awakened Japanese, helped us to disintegrate the Japanese army and cooperated with us in opposing Japanese militarism. Comrade Sanzo Nosaka, the leader of the Japanese Communist

Party, who was then in Yenan, gave us great help in this work.

The essence of Comrade Mao Tse-tung's theory of army building is that in building a people's army prominence must be given to politics, i.e., the army must first and foremost be built on a political basis. Politics is the commander, politics is the soul of everything. Political work is the lifeline of our army. True, a people's army must pay attention to the constant improvement of its weapons and equipment and its military technique, but in its fighting it does not rely purely on weapons and technique, it relies mainly on politics, on the proletarian revolutionary consciousness and courage of the commanders and fighters, on the support and backing of the masses.

Owing to the application of Comrade Mao Tse-tung's line on army building, there has prevailed in our army at all times a high level of proletarian political consciousness, an atmosphere of keenness to study the thought of Mao Tse-tung, an excellent morale, a solid unity and a deep hatred for the enemy, and thus a gigantic moral force has been brought into being. In battle it has feared neither hardships nor death, it has been able to charge or hold its ground as the conditions require. One man can play the role of several, dozens or even hundreds, and miracles can be performed.

All this makes the people's army led by the Chinese Communist Party fundamentally different from any bourgeois army, and from all the armies of the old type which served the exploiting classes and were driven and utilized by a handful of people. The experience of the people's war in China shows that a people's army created in accordance with Comrade Mao Tse-tung's theory of army building is incomparably strong and invincible.

. . . .

In his celebrated ten cardinal military principles Comrade Mao Tse-tung pointed out:

> In every battle, concentrate an absolutely superior force (two, three, four and sometimes even five or six times the enemy's strength), encircle the enemy forces completely, strive to wipe them out thoroughly and do not let any escape from the net. In special circumstances, use the method of dealing crushing blows to the enemy, that is, concentrate all our strength to make a frontal attack and also to attack one or both of his flanks, with the aim of wiping out one part and routing another so that our army can swiftly move its troops to smash other enemy forces. Strive to avoid battles of attrition in which we lose more than we gain or only break even. In this way, although we are inferior as a whole (in terms of numbers), we are absolutely superior in every part and every specific campaign, and this ensures victory in the campaign. As time goes on, we shall become superior as a whole and eventually wipe out all the enemy.

At the same time, he said that we should first attack dispersed or isolated enemy forces and only attack concentrated and strong enemy forces later; that we should strive to wipe out the enemy through mobile warfare; that we should fight no battle unprepared and fight no battle we are not sure of winning; and that in any battle we fight we should develop our army's strong points and its excellent style of fighting. These are the major principles of fighting a war of annihilation.

In order to annihilate the enemy, we must adopt the policy of luring him in deep and abandon some cities and districts of our own accord in a planned way, so as to let him in. It is only after letting the enemy in that the people can take part in the war in various ways and that the power of a people's war can be fully exerted. It is only after letting the enemy in that he can be compelled to divide up his forces, take on heavy burdens and commit mistakes. In other words, we must let the enemy become elated, stretch out all his ten fingers and become hopelessly bogged down. Thus, we can concentrate superior forces to destroy the enemy forces one by one, to eat them up mouthful by mouthful. Only by wiping out the enemy's effective strength can cities and localities be finally held or seized. We are firmly against dividing up our forces to defend all positions and putting up resistance at every place for fear that our territory might be lost and our pots and pans smashed, since this can neither wipe out the enemy forces nor hold cities or localities.

Comrade Mao Tse-tung has provided a masterly summary of the strategy and tactics of people's war: You fight in your way and we fight in ours; we fight when we can win and move away when we can't.

In other words, you rely on modern weapons and we rely on highly conscious revolutionary people; you give full play to your superiority and we give full play to ours; you have your way of fighting and we have ours. When you want to fight us, we don't let you and you can't even find us. But when we want to fight you, we make sure that you can't get away and we hit you squarely on the chin and wipe you out. When we are able to wipe you out, we do so with a vengeance; when we can't, we see to it that you don't wipe us out. It is opportunism if one won't fight when one can win. It is adventurism if one insists on fighting when one can't win. Fighting is the pivot of all our strategy and tactics. It is because of the necessity of fighting that we admit the necessity of moving away. The sole purpose of moving away is to fight and bring about the final and complete destruction of the enemy. This strategy and these tactics can be applied only when one relies on the broad masses of the people, and such application brings the superiority of people's war into full play. However superior he may be in technical equipment and whatever tricks he may resort to, the enemy will find himself in the passive position of having to receive blows, and the initiative will always be in our hands.

We grew from a small and weak to a large and strong force and finally defeated formidable enemies at home and abroad because we carried out the strategy and tactics of people's war. During the eight years of the War of Resistance Against Japan, the people's army led by the Chinese Communist Party fought more than 125,000 engagements with the enemy and put out of action more than 1,700,000 Japanese and puppet troops. In the three years of the War of Liberation, we put eight million of the Kuomintang's reactionary troops out of action and won the great victory of the people's revolution.

. . . .

Difficulties are not invincible monsters. If everyone co-operates and fights them, they will be overcome. The Kuomintang reactionaries thought that it could starve us to death by cutting off allowances and imposing an economic blockade, but in fact it helped us by stimulating us to rely on our own efforts to surmount our difficulties. While launching the great campaign for production, we applied the policy of "better troops and simpler administration" and economized in the use of manpower and material resources; thus we not only surmounted the severe material difficulties and successfully met the crisis, but lightened the people's burden, improved their livelihood and laid the material foundations for victory in the anti-Japanese war.

The problem of military equipment was solved mainly by relying on the capture of arms from the enemy, though we did turn out some weapons too. Chiang Kai-shek, the Japanese imperialists and the U.S. imperialists have all been our "chiefs of transportation corps". The arsenals of the imperialists always provide the oppressed peoples and nations with arms.

The people's armed forces led by our Party independently waged people's war on a large scale and won great victories without any material aid from outside, both during the more than eight years of the anti-Japanese war and during the more than three years of the People's War of Liberation.

Comrade Mao Tse-tung has said that our fundamental policy should rest on the foundation of our own strength. Only by relying on our own efforts can we in all circumstances remain invincible.

The peoples of the world invariably support each other in their struggles against imperialism and its lackeys. Those countries which have won victory are duty bound to support and aid the peoples who have not yet done so. Nevertheless, foreign aid can only play a supplementary role.

In order to make a revolution and to fight a people's war and be victorious, it is imperative to adhere to the policy of self-reliance, rely on the strength of the masses in one's own country and prepare to carry on the fight independently even when all material aid from outside is cut off. If one does not operate by one's own efforts, does not independently ponder and solve the problems of the revolution in one's own country and does not rely on the strength of the masses, but leans wholly on foreign aid—even though this be aid from socialist countries which persist in revolution—no victory can be won, or be consolidated even if it is won.

THE INTERNATIONAL SIGNIFICANCE OF COMRADE MAO TSE-TUNG'S THEORY OF PEOPLE'S WAR

The Chinese revolution is a continuation of the Great October Revolution. The road of the October Revolution is the common road for all people's revolutions. The Chinese revolution and the October Revolution have in common the following basic characteristics: (1) Both were led by the working class with a Marxist-Leninist party as its nucleus. (2) Both were based on the worker-peasant alliance. (3) In both cases state power was seized through violent revolution and the dictatorship of the proletariat was established. (4) In both cases the socialist system was built after victory in the revolution. (5) Both were component parts of the proletarian world revolution.

Naturally, the Chinese revolution had its own peculiar characteristics. The October Revolution took place in imperialist Russia, but the Chinese revolution broke out in a semi-colonial and semifeudal country. The former was a proletarian socialist revolution, while the latter developed into a socialist revolution after the complete victory of the new-democratic revolution. The October Revolution began with armed uprisings in the cities and then spread to the countryside, while the Chinese revolution won nation-wide victory through the encirclement of the cities from the rural areas and the final capture of the cities.

Comrade Mao Tse-tung's great merit lies in the fact that he has succeeded in integrating the universal truth of Marxism-Leninism with the concrete practice of the Chinese revolution and has enriched and developed Marxism-Leninism by his masterly generalization and summation of the experience gained during the Chinese people's protracted revolutionary struggle.

Comrade Mao Tse-tung's theory of people's war has been proved by the long practice of the Chinese revolution to be in accord with the objective laws of such wars and to be invincible. It has not only been valid for China, it is a great contribution to the revolutionary struggles of the oppressed nations and peoples throughout the world.

The people's war led by the Chinese Communist Party, comprising the War of Resistance and the Revolutionary Civil Wars, lasted for twenty-two years. It constitutes the most drawn-out and most complex people's war led by the proletariat in modern history, and it has been the richest in experience.

In the last analysis, the Marxist-Leninist theory of proletarian revolution is the theory of the seizure of state power by revolutionary violence, the theory of countering war against the people by people's war. As Marx so aptly put it, "Force is the midwife of every old society pregnant with a new one."

It was on the basis of the lessons derived from the people's wars in China that comrade Mao Tse-tung, using the simplest and the most vivid language, advanced the famous thesis that "political power grows out of the barrel of a gun."

He clearly pointed out:

> The seizure of power by armed force, the settlement of the issue by war, is the central task and the highest form of revolution. This Marxist-Leninist principle of revolution holds good universally, for China and for all other countries.

War is the product of imperialism and the system of exploitation of man by man. Lenin said that "war is always and everywhere begun by the exploiters themselves, by the ruling and oppressing classes." So long as imperialism and the system of exploitation of man by man exist, the imperialists and reactionaries will invariably rely on armed force to maintain their reactionary rule and impose war on the oppressed nations and peoples. This is an objective law independent of man's will.

In the world today, all the imperialists headed by the United States and their lackeys, without exception, are strengthening their state machinery, and especially their armed forces. U.S. imperialism, in particular, is carrying out armed aggression and suppression everywhere.

What should the oppressed nations and the oppressed people do in the face of wars of aggression and armed suppression by the imperialists and their lackeys? Should they submit and remain slaves in perpetuity? Or should they rise in resistance and fight for their liberation?

Comrade Mao Tse-tung answered this question in vivid terms. He said that after long investigation and study the Chinese people discovered that all the imperialists and their lackeys "have swords in their hands and are out to kill. The people have come to understand this and so act after the same fashion." This is called doing unto them what they do unto us.

In the last analysis, whether one dares to wage a tit-for-tat struggle against armed aggression and suppression by the imperialists and their lackeys, whether one dares to fight a people's war against them, is tantamount to whether one dares to embark on revolution. This is the most effective touchstone for distinguishing genuine from fake revolutionaries and Marxist-Leninists.

In view of the fact that some people were afflicted with the fear of the imperialists and reactionaries, Comrade Mao Tse-tung put forward his famous thesis that "the imperialists and all reactionaries are paper tigers." He said,

> All reactionaries are paper tigers. In appearance, the reactionaries are terrifying, but in reality they are not so powerful. From a long-term point of view, it is not the reactionaries but the people who are really powerful.

The history of people's war in China and other countries provides conclusive evidence that the growth of the people's revolutionary forces from weak and small beginnings into strong and large forces is a universal law of development of class struggle, a universal law of development of people's war. A people's war inevitably meets with many difficulties, with ups and downs and setbacks in the course of its development, but no force can alter its general trend towards inevitable triumph.

. . . .

It must be emphasized that Comrade Mao Tse-tung's theory of the establishment of rural revolutionary base areas and the encirclement of the cities from the countryside is of outstanding and universal practical importance for the present revolutionary struggles of all the oppressed nations and peoples, and particularly for the revolutionary struggles of the oppressed nations and peoples in Asia, Africa and Latin America against imperialism and its lackeys.

Many countries and peoples in Asia, Africa and Latin America are now being subjected to aggression and enslavement on a serious scale by the imperialists headed by the United States and their lackeys. The basic political and economic conditions in many of these countries have many similarities to those that prevailed in old China. As in China, the peasant question is extremely important in these regions. The peasants constitute the main force of the national-democratic revolution against the imperialists and their lackeys. In committing aggression against these countries, the imperialists usually begin by seizing the big cities and the main lines of communication, but they are unable to bring the vast countryside completely under their control. The countryside, and the countryside alone, can provide the broad areas in which the revolutionaries can manoeuvre freely. The countryside, and the countryside alone, can provide the revolutionary bases from which the revolutionaries can go forward to final victory. Precisely for this reason, Comrade Mao Tse-tung's theory of establishing revolutionary base areas in the rural districts and encircling the cities from the countryside is attracting more and more attention among the people in these regions.

Taking the entire globe, if North America and Western Europe can be called "the cities of the world," then Asia, Africa and Latin America constitute "the rural areas of the world." Since World War II, the proletarian revolutionary movement has for various reasons been temporarily held back in the North American and West European capitalist countries, while the people's revolutionary movement in Asia, Africa and Latin America has been growing vigorously. In a sense, the contemporary world revolution also presents a picture of the encirclement of cities by the rural areas. In the final analysis, the whole cause of world revolution hinges on the revolutionary struggles of the Asian, African and Latin American peoples who make up the overwhelming majority of the world's population. The socialist countries should regard it as their internationalist duty to support the people's revolutionary struggles in Asia, Africa and Latin America.

The October Revolution opened up a new era in the revolution of the oppressed nations. The victory of the October Revolution built a bridge between the socialist revolution of the proletariat of the West and the national-democratic revolution of the colonial and semi-colonial countries of the East. The Chinese revolution has successfully solved the problem of how to link up the national-democratic with the socialist revolution in the colonial and semi-colonial countries.

Comrade Mao Tse-tung has pointed out that, in the epoch since the October Revolution, anti-imperialist revolution in any colonial or semi-colonial country is no longer part of the old bourgeois, or capitalist world revolution, but is part of the new world revolution, the proletarian-socialist world revolution.

Comrade Mao Tse-tung has formulated a complete theory of the new-democratic revolution. He indicated that this revolution, which is different from all others, can only be, nay must be, a revolution against imperialism, feudalism and bureaucrat-capitalism waged by the broad masses of the people under the leadership of the proletariat.

This means that the revolution can only be, nay must be, led by the proletariat and the genuinely revolutionary party armed with Marxism-Leninism, and by no other class or party.

This means that the revolution embraces in its ranks not only the workers, peasants and the urban petty bourgeoisie, but also the national bourgeoisie and other patriotic and anti-imperialist democrats.

This means, finally, that the revolution is directed against imperialism, feudalism and bureaucrat-capitalism.

The new-democratic revolution leads to socialism, and not to capitalism.

Comrade Mao Tse-tung's theory of the new-democratic revolution is the Marxist-Leninist theory of revolution by stages as well as the Marxist-Leninist theory of uninterrupted revolution.

Comrade Mao Tse-tung made a correct distinction between the two revolutionary stages, i.e., the national-democratic and the socialist revolutions; at the same time he correctly and closely linked the two. The national-democratic revolution is the necessary preparation for the socialist revolution, and the socialist revolution is the inevitable sequel to the national-democratic revolution. There is no Great Wall between the two revolutionary stages. But the socialist revolution is only possible after the completion of the national-democratic revolution. The more thorough the national-democratic revolution, the better the conditions for the socialist revolution.

The experience of the Chinese revolution shows that the tasks of the national-democratic revolution can be fulfilled only through long and tortuous struggles. In this stage of revolution, imperialism and its lackeys are the principal enemy. In the struggle against imperialism and its lackeys, it is necessary to rally all anti-imperialist patriotic forces, including the national bourgeoisie and all patriotic personages. All those patriotic personages from among the bourgeoisie and other exploiting classes who join the anti-imperialist struggle play a progressive historical role; they are not tolerated by imperialism but welcomed by the proletariat.

It is very harmful to confuse the two stages, that is, the national-democratic and the socialist revolutions. Comrade Mao Tse-tung criticized the wrong idea of "accomplishing both at one stroke," and pointed out that this utopian idea could only weaken the struggle against imperialism and its lackeys, the most urgent task at that time. The Kuomintang reactionaries and the Trotskyites they hired during the War of Resistance deliberately confused these two stages of the Chinese revolution, proclaiming the "theory of a single revolution" and preaching so-called "socialism" without any Communist Party. With this preposterous theory they attempted to swallow up the Communist Party, wipe out any revolution and prevent the advance of the national-democratic revolution, and they used it as a pretext for their non-resistance and capitulation to imperialism. This reactionary theory was buried long ago by the history of the Chinese revolution.

The Khrushchov [*sic*] revisionists are now actively preaching that socialism can be built without the proletariat and without a genuinely revolutionary party armed with the advanced proletarian ideology, and they have cast the fundamental tenets of Marxism-Leninism to the four winds. The revisionists' purpose is solely to divert the oppressed nations from their struggle against imperialism and sabotage their national-democratic revolution, all in the service of imperialism.

The Chinese revolution provides a successful lesson for making a thoroughgoing national-democratic revolution under the leadership of the proletariat; it likewise provides a successful lesson for the timely transition from the national-democratic revolution to the socialist revolution under the leadership of the proletariat.

Mao Tse-tung's thought has been the guide to the victory of the Chinese revolution. It has integrated the universal truth of Marxism-Leninism with the concrete practice of the Chinese revolution and creatively developed Marxism-Leninism, thus adding new weapons to the arsenal of Marxism-Leninism.

Ours is the epoch in which world capitalism and imperialism are heading for their doom and socialism and communism are marching to victory. Comrade Mao Tse-tung's theory of people's war is not only a product of the Chinese revolution, but has also the characteristics of our epoch. The new experience gained in the people's revolutionary struggles in various countries since World War II has provided continuous evidence that Mao Tse-tung's thought is a common asset of the revolutionary people of the whole world. This is the great international significance of the thought of Mao Tse-tung.

Defeat U.S. Imperialism and Its Lackeys by People's War

Since World War II, U.S. imperialism has stepped into the shoes of German, Japanese and Italian fascism and has been trying to build a great American empire by dominating and enslaving the whole world. It is actively fostering Japanese and West German militarism as its chief accomplices in unleashing a world war. Like a vicious wolf, it is bullying and enslaving various peoples, plundering their wealth, encroaching upon their countries' sovereignty and interfering in their internal affairs. It is the most rabid aggressor in human history and the most ferocious common enemy of the people of the world. Every people or country in the world that wants revolution, independence and peace cannot but direct the spearhead of its struggle against U.S. imperialism.

Just as the Japanese imperialists' policy of subjugating China made it possible for the Chinese people to form the broadest possible united front against them, so the U.S. imperialists' policy of seeking world domination makes it possible for the people throughout the world to unite all the forces that can be united and form the broadest possible united front for a converging attack on U.S. imperialism.

At present, the main battlefield of the fierce struggle between the people of the world on the one side and U.S. imperialism and its lackeys on the other is the vast area of Asia, Africa and Latin America. In the world as a whole, this is the area where the people suffer worst from imperialist oppression and where imperialist rule is most vulnerable. Since World War II, revolutionary storms have been rising in this area, and today they have become the most important force directly pounding U.S. imperialism. The contradiction between the revolutionary peoples of Asia, Africa and Latin America and the imperialists headed by the United States is the principal contradiction in the contemporary world. The development of this contradiction is promoting the struggle of the people of the whole world against U.S. imperialism and its lackeys.

Since World War II, people's war has increasingly demonstrated its power in

Asia, Africa and Latin America. The peoples of China, Korea, Viet Nam, Laos, Cuba, Indonesia, Algeria and other countries have waged people's wars against the imperialists and their lackeys and won great victories. The classes leading these people's wars may vary, and so may the breadth and depth of mass mobilization and the extent of victory, but the victories in these people's wars have very much weakened and pinned down the forces of imperialism, upset the U.S. imperialist plan to launch a world war, and become mighty factors defending world peace.

Today, the conditions are more favourable than ever before for the waging of people's wars by the revolutionary peoples of Asia, Africa and Latin America against U.S. imperialism and its lackeys.

Since World War II and the succeeding years of revolutionary upsurge, there has been a great rise in the level of political consciousness and the degree of organization of the people in all countries, and the resources available to them for mutual support and aid have greatly increased. The whole capitalist-imperialist system has become drastically weaker and is in the process of increasing convulsion and disintegration. After World War I, the imperialists lacked the power to destroy the new-born socialist Soviet state, but they were still able to suppress the people's revolutionary movements in some countries in some parts of the world under their own rule and so maintain a short period of comparative stability. Since World War II, however, not only have they been unable to stop a number of countries from taking the socialist road, but they are no longer capable of holding back the surging tide of the people's revolutionary movements in the areas under their own rule.

U.S. imperialism is stronger, but also more vulnerable, than any imperialism of the past. It sets itself against the people of the whole world, including the people of the United States. Its human, military, material and financial resources are far from sufficient for the realization of its ambition of dominating the whole world. U.S. imperialism has further weakened itself by occupying so many places in the world, overreaching itself, stretching its fingers out wide and dispersing its strength, with its rear so far away and its supply lines so long. As Comrade Mao Tse-tung has said, "Wherever it commits aggression, it puts a new noose around its neck. It is besieged ring upon ring by the people of the whole world."

When committing aggression in a foreign country, U.S. imperialism can only employ part of its forces, which are sent to fight an unjust war far from their native land and therefore have a low morale, and so U.S. imperialism is beset with great difficulties. The people subjected to its aggression are having a trial of strength with U.S. imperialism neither in Washington nor New York, neither in Honolulu nor Florida, but are fighting for independence and freedom on their own soil. Once they are mobilized on a broad scale, they will have inexhaustible strength. Thus superiority will belong not to the United States but to the people subjected to its aggression. The latter, though apparently weak and small, are really more powerful than U.S. imperialism.

The struggles waged by the different peoples against U.S. imperialism reinforce each other and merge into a torrential world-wide tide of opposition to U.S. imperialism. The more successful the development of people's war in a given region, the larger the number of U.S. imperialist forces that can be pinned down and depleted there. When the U.S. aggressors are hard pressed in one place, they have no alternative but to loosen their grip on others. Therefore, the conditions become more favourable for the people elsewhere to wage struggles against U.S. imperialism and its lackeys.

Everything is divisible. And so is this colossus of U.S. imperialism. It can be split up and defeated. The peoples of Asia, Africa, Latin America and other regions can destroy it piece by piece, some striking at its head and others at its feet. That is why the greatest fear of U.S. imperialism is that people's wars will be launched in different parts of the world, and particularly in Asia, Africa, and Latin America, and why it regards people's war as a mortal danger.

U.S. imperialism relies solely on its nuclear weapons to intimidate people. But these weapons cannot save U.S. imperialism from its doom. Nuclear weapons cannot be used lightly. U.S. imperialism has been condemned by the people of the whole world for its towering crime of dropping two atom bombs on Japan. If it uses nuclear weapons again, it will become isolated in the extreme. Moreover, the U.S. monopoly of nuclear weapons has long been broken; U.S. imperialism has these weapons, but others have them too. If it threatens other countries with nuclear weapons, U.S. imperialism will expose its own country to the same threat. For this reason, it will meet with strong opposition not only from the people elsewhere but also inevitably from the people in its own country. Even if U.S. imperialism brazenly uses nuclear weapons, it cannot conquer the people, who are indomitable.

However highly developed modern weapons and technical equipment may be and however complicated the methods of modern warfare, in the final analysis the outcome of a war will be decided by the sustained fighting of the ground forces, by the fighting at close quarters on battlefields, by the political consciousness of the men, by their courage and spirit of sacrifice. Here the weak points of U.S. imperialism will be completely laid bare, while the superiority of the revolutionary people will be brought into full play. The reactionary troops of U.S. imperialism cannot possibly be endowed with the courage and the spirit of sacrifice possessed by the revolutionary people. The spiritual atom bomb which the revolutionary people possess is a far more powerful and useful weapon than the physical atom bomb.

Viet Nam is the most convincing current example of a victim of aggression defeating U.S. imperialism by a people's war. The United States has made south Viet Nam a testing ground for the suppression of people's war. It has carried on this experiment for many years, and everybody can now see that the U.S. aggressors are unable to find a way of coping with people's war. On the other hand, the Vietnamese people have brought the power of people's war into full play in their struggle against the U.S. aggressors. The U.S. aggressors are in danger of being swamped in the people's war in Viet Nam. They are deeply worried that their defeat in Viet Nam will lead to a chain reaction. They are expanding the war in an attempt to save themselves from defeat. But the more they expand the war, the greater will be the chain reaction. The more they escalate the war, the heavier will be their fall and the more disastrous their defeat. The people in other parts of the world will see still more clearly that U.S. imperialism can be defeated, and that what the Vietnamese people can do, they can do too.

History has proved and will go on proving that people's war is the most effective weapon against U.S. imperialism and its lackeys. All revolutionary people will learn to wage people's war against U.S. imperialism and its lackeys. They will take up arms, learn to fight battles and become skilled in waging people's war, though they have not done so before. U.S. imperialism, like a mad bull dashing from place to place, will finally be burned to ashes in the blazing fires of the people's wars it has provoked by its own actions.

The Khrushchov Revisionists Are Betrayers of People's War

The Khrushchov revisionists have come to the rescue of U.S. imperialism just when it is most panic-stricken and helpless in its efforts to cope with people's war. Working hand in glove with the U.S. imperialists, they are doing their utmost to spread all kinds of arguments against people's war and, wherever they can, they are scheming to undermine it by overt or covert means.

The fundamental reason why the Khrushchov revisionists are opposed to people's war is that they have no faith in the masses and are afraid of U.S. imperialism, of war and of revolution. Like all other opportunists, they are blind to the power of the masses and do not believe that the revolutionary people are capable of defeating imperialism. They submit to the nuclear blackmail of the U.S. imperialists and are afraid that, if the oppressed peoples and nations rise up to fight people's wars or the people of socialist countries repulse U.S. imperialist aggression, U.S. imperialism will become incensed, they themselves will become involved and their fond dream of Soviet-U.S. co-operation to dominate the world will be spoiled.

Ever since Lenin led the Great October Revolution to victory, the experience of innumerable revolutionary wars has borne out the truth that a revolutionary people who rise up with only their bare hands at the outset finally succeed in defeating the ruling classes who are armed to the teeth. The poorly armed have defeated the better armed. People's armed forces, beginning with only primitive swords, spears, rifles and hand-grenades, have in the end defeated the imperialist forces armed with modern aeroplanes, tanks, heavy artillery and atom bombs. Guerrilla forces have ultimately defeated regular armies. "Amateurs" who were never trained in any military schools have eventually defeated "professionals" graduated from military academies. And so on and so forth. Things stubbornly develop in a way that runs counter to the assertions of the revisionists, and facts are slapping them in the face.

The Khrushchov revisionists insist that a nation without nuclear weapons is incapable of defeating an enemy with nuclear weapons, whatever methods of fighting it may adopt. This is tantamount to saying that anyone without nuclear weapons is destined to come to grief, destined to be bullied and annihilated, and must either capitulate to the enemy when confronted with his nuclear weapons or come under the "protection" of some other nuclear power and submit to its beck and call. Isn't this the jungle law of survival par excellence? Isn't this helping the imperialists in their nuclear blackmail? Isn't this openly forbidding people to make revolution?

The Khrushchov revisionists assert that nuclear weapons and strategic rocket units are decisive while conventional forces are insignificant, and that a militia is just a heap of human flesh. For ridiculous reasons such as these, they oppose the mobilization of and reliance on the masses in the socialist countries to get prepared to use people's war against imperialist aggression. They have staked the whole future of their country on nuclear weapons and are engaged in a nuclear gamble with U.S. imperialism, with which they are trying to strike a political deal. Their theory of military strategy is the theory that nuclear weapons decide everything. Their line in army building is the bourgeois line which ignores the human factor and sees only the material factor and which regards technique as everything and politics as nothing.

The Khrushchov revisionists maintain that a single spark in any part of the globe may touch off a world nuclear conflagration and bring destruction to mankind. If this were true, our planet would have been destroyed time and time again. There have been wars of national liberation throughout the twenty years since World War II. But has any single one of them developed into a world war? Isn't it true that the U.S. imperialists' plans for a world war have been upset precisely thanks to the wars of national liberation in Asia, Africa and Latin America? By contrast, those who have done their utmost to stamp out the "sparks" of people's war have in fact encouraged U.S. imperialism in its aggressions and wars.

The Khrushchov revisionists claim that if their general line of "peaceful coexistence, peaceful transition and peaceful competition" is followed, the oppressed will be liberated and "a world without weapons, without armed forces and without wars" will come into being. But the inexorable fact is that imperialism and reaction headed by the United States are zealously priming their war machine and are daily engaged in sanguinary suppression of the revolutionary peoples and in the threat and use of armed force against independent countries. The kind of rubbish peddled by the Khrushchov revisionists has already taken a great toll of lives in a number of countries. Are these painful lessons, paid for in blood, still insufficient? The essence of the general line of the Khrushchov revisionists is nothing other than the demand that all the oppressed peoples and nations and all the countries which have won independence should lay down their arms and place themselves at the mercy of the U.S. imperialists and their lackeys who are armed to the teeth.

"While magistrates are allowed to burn down houses the common people are forbidden even to light lamps." Such is the way of the imperialists and reactionaries. Subscribing to this imperialist philosophy, the Khrushchov revisionists shout at the Chinese people standing in the forefront of the fight for world peace: "You are bellicose!" Gentlemen, your abuse adds to our credit. It is this very "bellicosity" of ours that helps to prevent imperialism from unleashing a world war. The people are "bellicose" because they have to defend themselves and because the imperialists and reactionaries force them to be so. It is also the imperialists and reactionaries who have taught the people the arts of war. We are simply using revolutionary "bellicosity" to cope with counter-revolutionary bellicosity. How can it be argued that the imperialists and their lackeys may kill people everywhere, while the people must not strike back in self-defence or help one another? What kind of logic is this? The Khrushchov revisionists regard imperialists like Kennedy and Johnson as "sensible" and describe us together with all those who dare to carry out armed defence against imperialist aggression as "bellicose." This has revealed the Khrushchov revisionists in their true colors as the accomplices of imperialist gangsters.

We know that war brings destruction, sacrifice and suffering on the people. But the destruction, sacrifice and suffering will be much greater if no resistance is offered to imperialist armed aggression and the people become willing slaves. The sacrifice of a small number of people in revolutionary wars is repaid by security for whole nations, whole countries and even the whole of mankind; temporary suffering is repaid by lasting or even perpetual peace and happiness. War can temper the people and push history forward. In this sense, war is a great school.

When discussing World War I, Lenin said,

The war has brought hunger to the most civilized countries, to those most culturally developed. On the other hand, the war, as a tremendous historical process, has accelerated social development to an unheard-of degree.

He added,

War has shaken up the masses, its untold horrors and suffering have awakened them. War has given history momentum and it is now flying with locomotive speed.

If the arguments of the Khrushchov revisionists are to be believed, would not that make Lenin the worst of all "bellicose elements"?

In diametrical opposition to the Khrushchov revisionists, the Marxist-Leninists and revolutionary people never take a gloomy view of war. Our attitude towards imperialist wars of aggression has always been clearcut. First, we are against them, and secondly, we are not afraid of them. We will destroy whoever attacks us. As for revolutionary wars waged by the oppressed nations and peoples, so far from opposing them, we invariably give them firm support and active aid. It has been so in the past, it remains so in the present and, when we grow in strength as time goes on, we will give them still more support and aid in the future. It is sheer day-dreaming for anyone to think that, since our revolution has been victorious, our national construction is forging ahead, our national wealth is increasing and our living conditions are improving, we too will lose our revolutionary fighting will, abandon the cause of world revolution and discard Marxism-Leninism and proletarian internationalism. Of course, every revolution in a country stems from the demands of its own people. Only when the people in a country are awakened, mobilized, organized and armed can they overthrow the reactionary rule of imperialism and its lackeys through struggle; their role cannot be replaced or taken over by any people from outside. In this sense, revolution cannot be imported. But this does not exclude mutual sympathy and support on the part of revolutionary peoples in their struggles against the imperialists and their lackeys. Our support and aid to other revolutionary peoples serves precisely to help their self-reliant struggle.

The propaganda of the Khrushchov revisionists against people's war and the publicity they give to defeatism and capitulationism tend to demoralize and spiritually disarm revolutionary people everywhere. These revisionists are doing what the U.S. imperialists are unable to do themselves and are rendering them great service. They have greatly encouraged U.S. imperialism in its war adventures. They have completely betrayed the Marxist-Leninist revolutionary theory of war and have become betrayers of people's war.

. . . .

The peoples of the world now have the lessons of the October Revolution, the Anti-Fascist War, the Chinese people's War of Resistance and War of Liberation, the Korean people's War of Resistance to U.S. Aggression, the Vietnamese people's War of Liberation and their War of Resistance to U.S. Aggression, and the people's revolutionary armed struggles in many other countries. Provided each people studies these lessons well and creatively integrates them with the concrete practice of revolution in their own country, there is no doubt that the revolutionary peoples of the world will stage still more powerful and splendid dramas in the theatre of people's war in their countries and that they will wipe off the earth once and for all the common enemy of all the peoples, U.S. imperialism, and its lackeys.

. . . .

The U.S. imperialists are now clamouring for another trial of strength with the Chinese people, for another large-scale ground war on the Asian mainland. If they insist on following in the footsteps of the Japanese fascists, well then, they may do so, if they please. The Chinese people definitely have ways of their own for coping with a U.S. imperialist war of aggression. Our methods are no secret. The most important one is still mobilization of the people, reliance on the people, making everyone a soldier and waging a people's war.

We want to tell the U.S. imperialists once again that the vast ocean of several hundred million Chinese people in arms will be more than enough to submerge your few million aggressor troops. If you dare to impose war on us, we shall gain freedom of action. It will then not be up to you to decide how the war will be fought. We shall fight in the ways most advantageous to us to destroy the enemy and wherever the enemy can be most easily destroyed. Since the Chinese people were able to destroy the Japanese aggressors twenty years ago, they are certainly still more capable of finishing off the U.S. aggressors today. The naval and air superiority you boast about cannot intimidate the Chinese people, and neither can the atom bomb you brandish at us. If you want to send troops, go ahead, the more the better. We will annihilate as many as you can send, and can even give you receipts. The Chinese people are a great, valiant people. We have the courage to shoulder the heavy burden of combating U.S. imperialism and to contribute our share in the struggle for final victory over this most ferocious enemy of the people of the world.

. . . .

U.S. imperialism is preparing a world war. But can this save it from its doom? World War I was followed by the birth of the socialist Soviet Union. World War II was followed by the emergence of a series of socialist countries and many nationally independent countries. If the U.S. imperialists should insist on launching a third world war, it can be stated categorically that many more hundreds of millions of people will turn to socialism; the imperialists will then have little room left on the globe; and it is possible that the whole structure of imperialism will collapse.

We are optimistic about the future of the world. We are confident that the people will bring to an end the epoch of wars in human history. Comrade Mao Tse-tung pointed out long ago that war, this monster, "will be finally eliminated by the progress of human society, and in the not too distant future too. But there is only one way to eliminate it and that is to oppose war with war, to oppose counter-revolutionary war with revolutionary war."

All peoples suffering from U.S. imperialist aggression, oppression and plunder unite! Hold aloft the just banner of people's war and fight for the cause of world peace, national liberation, people's democracy and socialism! Victory will certainly go to the people of the world!

Long live the victory of people's war!

PART IV

The Cuban Revolution

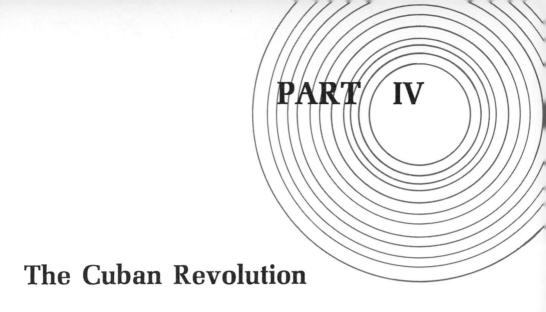

Though Cuba cannot compare with Russia or China in power, resources, and influence, the Cuban Revolution nonetheless is of great significance. In the first place, it is by all criteria a major revolution. That is, it has resulted not only in a transfer of power from one political elite to another, but also in the transformation of almost every aspect of life in Cuba. At the same time, it has developed in a way that has added something new for us to understand about revolution in our time, and it has done so with a most extraordinary self-consciousness and sense of twentieth-century revolutionary history. Moreover, its international impact has been enormous in that it quickly became yet another front of the "international civil war" between the "socialist" and "capitalist" powers.

To a degree this was inevitable. In the era of international ideological conflict a domestic upheaval in any country, no matter how small, is bound to be of international concern. Furthermore, Cuba's proximity to the United States and the fact that Castro's revolution was the first successful socialist revolution in the Western hemisphere—hitherto an almost impregnable American domain—ensured that responses to the revolution would be especially intense. Finally, in another respect the Cuban revolution is of international significance, in that it has been held by some ideologists and analysts to be a possible model for revolution in "third-world" societies, especially in other Latin American countries where its impact has already undoubtedly been great.

To the student of revolutions, Cuba poses a series of important questions. For a decade now, scholars have been striving to understand precisely why the revolution occurred when and how it did and why it took the course it eventually did; and the difficulty we have in comprehending the Cuban Revolution—as visible, well-scrutinized, and (initially) as "open" as it was—

reminds us of how much more difficult it is to understand revolution in more closed or distant societies. For the fact is that in large measure the Cuban Revolution has seemed to be *sui generis* and has resisted efforts at categorization. It does not seem to have been a "peasant," nor a "proletarian," nor even a "middle class" revolution.[1] Its path of development has appeared unpredictable, governed by realities unique to the Cuban situation. Even the revolutionaries themselves seem initially to have had difficulty explaining themselves and their movement. They seem slowly to have evolved a coherent ideology, slowly to have understood the forces that made their triumph possible, and only gradually to have focused their ideas about the kind of society they wanted to build. They seem not to have fully anticipated the direction in which the revolution would move. And that is true of students of the revolution as well as of its leaders.

Yet if the dynamics of the Cuban Revolution have been in some measure a puzzle for both scholar and revolutionary, still it can be seen to have grown out of certain historic instabilities and conditions of Cuban life. Cuba from the time of its liberation from Spanish rule had suffered from chronic political instability, and the *coup* was as familiar a mode of political transition as were elections. The tradition of revolutionary violence of course extended back far beyond 1898; and the Cuban Revolution can be seen as the last step in the process of nation building in a manner to which the Cubans had by force of circumstance become accustomed. Irresponsible political leadership throughout the twentieth century had done nothing to enhance the legitimacy of existing institutions. These were also undermined by the fact that American power, often quite crudely, played such an important role in Cuban political life.

Socially, Cuba was fragmented, the major split being between a very large landless rural proletariat and a small (but significant and growing) urban middle class. The styles of life, and the economic and social prospects of these groups, were widely disparate. Economically, Cuba was by no means backward, but her economy was in many ways unhealthy—much too dependent on tourism and on one export staple (sugar) for income, and thus vulnerable to fluctuations on the international market. Land was concentrated in a small number of huge holdings, with the result that Cuba's landless rural workers, dependent on the seasonal sugar industry for work and income, suffered long periods of unemployment and lived in deep poverty and deprivation. Much of the economy was controlled by foreign investors, and though in the '50s the proportion of foreign investment did slightly decrease, Cuba was still very much a United States colony.

The undiversified economy meant that Cuba's considerable resources were underutilized; and the economy by the '50s, after a wartime boom, had become stagnant, much to the dissatisfaction of Cuba's middle class, which

[1] See Theodore Draper's "Castro's Cuba: A Revolution Betrayed?" in *Encounter* (March 1961), for an analysis of early theories about the Cuban Revolution. Draper's "The Declassé Revolution" in his *Castroism, Theory and Practice* (New York, Praeger, 1965) is an interesting extension of his effort to find a class basis for the revolution.

felt increasingly constricted by lack of opportunity. Unimaginative and corrupt political leadership with no interest in reconstructing the Cuban economy (the Agrarian Reform Act of 1940 had never been implemented) was largely responsible for this situation. The increasingly restless middle class found Castro's promise of economic rejuvenation an attractive contrast to the sterility of Batista and his predecessors. Under Batista, the future looked economically almost as bleak to the urban businessman as it did to the rural worker. As one student of Cuban history, Robert F. Smith, has summarized the prerevolutionary situation,

> Pre-Castro Cuba had a solid modern infrastructure of roads and communications, a developed agricultural industry in sugar, and a capital-generating economy. In comparison with other Latin American countries Cuba was relatively well off. With appropriate allocation of resources, the output of the economy could have increased considerably. But many Cubans were living on the margins of existence, especially in rural areas. And many of the rest lived in a twilight zone of semipoverty, fluctuating between degrees of quasi-affluence and hard times. Cubans were living in a consumer market cash economy, and their appetites were conditioned by the prosperous periods. Even those at the bottom of the economic ladder had enough contact with society at large to see that poverty was neither inevitable nor immutable. Cubans could see about them a paradox of "progress and poverty." New expectations and frustrations, brought about by Cuba's development and economic fluctuation, produced greater dissatisfaction than centuries-old conditions of abject poverty.[2]

Castro sounded very much like a middle-class reformer in his initial explanation of the revolution. (See *History Will Absolve Me.*) While he spoke eloquently of social justice, he emphasized especially those aims that would appeal strongly to the urban middle class: economic progress, government of law and not of men, national pride. Though there are suggestions in the early Castro that he thought socialism, or at least a rigorously regulated economy, was necessary for Cuba, one could not have predicted—even as late as 1959 —simply by listening to Castro explain himself, in which direction the revolution would move. In early 1959 he rejected communism as the answer for Cuba. (He was still *persona grata* in the United States at the time and even visited Washington.) Why then did the revolution take the turn it did? No wholly satisfactory answer has yet been fashioned for this question, but a few things seem clear. Historians have rejected as conspiratorial fantasy the thesis that Castro had all along been a communist. There is no evidence that Castro himself was a communist; the Cuban Communist Party itself played little or no role in the revolution, even denouncing Castro as a bourgeois reformer and becoming a part of the revolutionary government only late in 1959.

It seems to have been not ideology but circumstances that propelled the revolution increasingly to the left. For example, certain features of the economy—a highly concentrated, largely absentee-owner capitalism—made

[2] Robert F. Smith, "Castro's Revolution, Domestic Sources and Consequences," in John N. Plank, ed., *Cuba and the United States: Long-Range Perspectives* (Washington, D.C., Brookings Institution, 1967), pp. 50–51.

easy a swift transition to socialism. This was especially true after, as Maurice Zeitlin puts it, "a leadership came to power in Cuba that was really committed to a national solution to her problems—once revolutionaries committed to economic development and independent national existence took power. . . ."[3] And of course, though it is difficult to measure, the role of the United States in radicalizing the revolution must be considered. If every revolution needs a foreign enemy as a means of ensuring some unity during stressful and conflict-producing social change, the United States was fated to play that role. For generations, nationalistic Cuban intellectuals had been assailing imperial America as the source of Cuba's woes. The hostile American response to developments in Cuba, especially after 1959, contributed to the phenomenon we are seeking to understand. With a capitalist oppressor, Cuba's revolutionary ideology was bound to turn left. Of course other factors, internal (increasing opposition from middle-class Cubans) and external (Soviet diplomacy) also pushed the revolution to the left.

These developments, as well as the increasing radicalism of the Cuban revolution—from its first "humanist" phase (as it was described by the leaders of the revolution) to the present efforts to create a true socialist society—are reflected in the thought of the late Ernesto "Che" Guevara, from whose writings we have selected some representative pieces in which he seeks to explain the nature and the tasks of the revolution and in which he touches on issues important to the student of revolution concerning the role of ideology in revolutionary movements.

Above all, we see Guevara (in *Socialism and Man in Cuba*) wrestling with the problems of how to achieve a cooperative society and avoid the hazards of bureaucracy and *embourgeoisement;* that is, of how to keep alive loyalty to and enthusiasm for the revolution. Some other revolutions have produced unhappy answers to that problem. Conscious of the failures as well as of the achievements of other great socialist revolutions (the historicity of the Cuban Revolution is remarkable) the Cubans have given deep attention to the task of creating a moral climate that will support and perpetuate the revolution. In his analysis of the need for a cultural transformation as well as a socialist restructuring of society and of the role of conscience in revolution, Guevara has greatly elaborated a theme of revolutionary thought that goes back at least as far as Lenin: that of the need to create a new kind of man if we are to have a new kind of society.

If the Cuban Revolution slowly evolved an ideology, what then is the function of ideology in revolutionary movements? And if the Cuban Revolution had no clear basis in any one class (despite the fact that, initially at least, most of the revolutionary leadership was of middle-class origin), what then was the social basis of the revolution? What is the role of leadership—of a revolutionary elite—in a revolution the central aim of which is social equality? These questions, too, Guevara touches on. His own answers must

[3] Maurice Zeitlin, "Cuba, Revolution Without a Blueprint," *Transaction*, Vol. 6, No. 6 (April 1969), p. 61.

be carefully considered by students of the Cuban Revolution. (See also Boris Goldenberg's essay.)

Successful revolutions invariably exhibit a kind of missionary zeal that manifests itself usually in the export of revolutionary ideas but occasionally even in efforts to ignite revolutions elsewhere. In part this is the result of a natural desire to secure the revolution by undermining hostile neighbors, in part it is a consequence of the tendency of revolutionary ideologies to claim universal applicability. The Cuban Revolution is no exception to this pattern. In his early attempts to export the revolution Castro spoke in Caracas and Buenos Aires and sent *guerrilleros* to Haiti, Nicaragua, the Dominican Republic, and Panama. These activities were later followed by efforts to train Latin American revolutionaries in Cuba and by Che Guevara's ill-fated attempt to organize a guerrilla movement in Bolivia.

Despite the failure of the Cuban Revolution to reproduce itself, the question of the applicability of the Cuban model to other countries in Latin America and elsewhere in the "third world" remains a matter of debate and deep interest. Clearly, social conditions in most Latin American societies are explosive. Will Cuba, so similar in many ways to those societies, provide a pattern for revolution, or will it prove unique? Régis Debray argued that the genius of the Cuban Revolution lay in its pragmatic adjustment to the realities of the Cuban situation and in its refusal to be slave to any model, a lesson Guevara inexplicably seemed to forget during his Bolivian misadventure. But if the same kind of rural-based insurrection is unlikely to be successful elsewhere in Latin America (see Gall) does this mean that Cuba will provide no inspiration, no lessons for revolutionaries elsewhere? In the answer to these questions, and to those earlier asked, lies the full meaning and significance of the Cuban Revolution.

Castro made this speech while on trial for the famous 26th of July, 1953 attack on the Moncada Barracks in Santiago de Cuba. It was his first major exposition of his ideas about the causes and purposes of the revolutionary movement he was leading and is especially important as an early formulation of the objectives of that movement. Castro was 26 at the time. The speech was printed by the Cuban underground in 1954 and was broadly circulated after Dec. 31, 1958, as the fundamental text of the Revolution.

History Will Absolve Me

FIDEL CASTRO

. . . .

As soon as Santiago de Cuba was in our hands, we would immediately have readied the people for war. Bayamo was attacked precisely to situate our advance forces along the Cauto River. Never forget that this province which has a million and a half inhabitants today, provides without a doubt the best resistance and the most patriotic men of Cuba. It was this province that continued the fight for independence for thirty years and paid the highest tribute in blood, sacrifice and heroism. In Oriente, you can still breathe the air of that glorious epoch. At dawn, when the cocks crow as if they were bugles calling soldiers to reveille, and when the sun rises, radiant, over the rugged mountains, it seems that once again we will hear the cry of Yara or Baire.[1]

I stated that the second consideration on which we based our chances for success was one of social order because we were assured of the people's support. When we speak of the people we do not mean the comfortable ones, the conservative elements of the nation, who welcome any regime of oppression, any dictatorship, any despotism, prostrating themselves before the master of the moment until they grind their foreheads into the ground. When we speak of struggle, the *people* means the vast unredeemed masses, to whom all make promises and whom all deceive; we mean the people who yearn for a better, more dignified and more just nation; who are moved by ancestral aspirations of justice, for they have suffered injustice and mockery, generation after generation; who long for great and wise changes in all aspects of their life; people, who, to attain these changes, are ready to give even the very last breath of their lives—when they believe in something or in someone, especially when they believe in themselves. In stating a purpose, the first condition of sincerity and good faith, is to do precisely what nobody else ever does, that is, to speak with absolute clarity, without fear. The demagogues and professional politicians who manage to perform the miracle of being right in every-

From The Political, Economic and Social Thought of Fidel Castro (Editorial Lex, Havana, 1959). The translation is Havana's.

[1] *Yara and Baíre.* "Yara" on October 10, 1868, was the first battlecry for independence. The cry of "Baíre" on February 24, 1895, announced the final drive to liberate Cuba from Spanish rule.

thing and in pleasing everyone, are, of necessity, deceiving everyone about everything. The revolutionaries must proclaim their ideas courageously, define their principles and express their intentions so that no one is deceived, neither friend nor foe.

The people we counted on in our struggle were these:

Seven hundred thousand Cubans without work, who desire to earn their daily bread honestly without having to emigrate in search of livelihood.

Five hundred thousand farm laborers inhabiting miserable shacks, who work four months of the year and starve for the rest of the year, sharing their misery with their children, who have not an inch of land to cultivate, and whose existence inspires compassion in any heart not made of stone.

Four hundred thousand industrial laborers and stevedores whose retirement funds have been embezzled, whose benefits are being taken away, whose homes are wretched quarters, whose salaries pass from the hands of the boss to those of the usurer, whose future is a pay reduction and dismissal, whose life is eternal work and whose only rest is in the tomb.

One hundred thousand small farmers who live and die working on land that is not theirs, looking at it with sadness as Moses did the promised land, to die without possessing it; who, like feudal serfs, have to pay for the use of their parcel of land by giving up a portion of their products; who cannot love it, improve it, beautify it or plant a lemon or an orange tree on it, because they never know when a sheriff will come with the rural guard to evict them from it.

Thirty thousand teachers and professors who are so devoted, dedicated and necessary to the better destiny of future generations and who are so badly treated and paid.

Twenty thousand small business men weighted down by debts, ruined by the crisis and harangued by a plague of filibusters and venal officials.

Ten thousand young professionals: doctors, engineers, lawyers, veterinarians, school teachers, dentists, pharmacists, newspapermen, painters, sculptors, etc., who come forth from school with their degrees, anxious to work and full of hope, only to find themselves at a dead end with all doors closed, and where no ear hears their clamor or supplication.

These are the people, the ones who know misfortune and, therefore, are capable of fighting with limitless courage!

To the people whose desperate roads through life have been paved with the brick of betrayals and false promises, we were not going to say: "we will eventually give you what you need, but rather—Here you have it, fight for it with all your might so that liberty and happiness may be yours!"

In the brief of this cause there must be recorded the five revolutionary laws that would have been proclaimed immediately after the capture of the Moncada barracks and would have been broadcast to the nation by radio. It is possible that Colonel Chaviano may deliberately have destroyed these documents, but even if he has done so, I conserve them in my memory.

The First Revolutionary Law would have returned power to the people and proclaimed the Constitution of 1940 the supreme Law of the land, until such time as the people should decide to modify or change it. And, in order to effect its implementation and punish those who had violated it—there being no organization for holding elections to accomplish this—the revolutionary movement, as the momentous incarnation of this sovereignty, the only source of legitimate power, would have assumed all the faculties inherent to it, except that of modifying the Constitution itself: In other words it would have assumed the legislative, executive and judicial powers.

This approach could not be more crystal clear nor more free of vacillation and sterile charlatanry. A government acclaimed by the mass of rebel people would be vested with every power, everything necessary in order to proceed with the effective implementation of the popular will and true justice. From that moment, the Judicial Power, which since March 10th has placed itself *against* the Constitution and *outside* the Constitution, would cease to exist and we would proceed to its immediate and total reform before it would again assume the power granted to it by the Supreme Law of the Republic. Without our first taking those previous measures, a return to legality by putting the custody of the courts back into the hands that have crippled the system so dishonorably would constitute a fraud, a deceit, and one more betrayal.

The Second Revolutionary Law would have granted property, not mortgageable and not transferable, to all planters, sub-planters, lessees, partners and squatters who hold parcels of five or less "caballeria" [2] of land, and the state would indemnify the former owners on the basis of the rental which they would have received for these parcels over a period of ten years.

The Third Revolutionary Law would have granted workers and employees the right to share 30% of the profits of all the large industrial, mercantile and mining enterprises, including the sugar mills. The strictly agricultural enterprises would be exempt in consideration of other agrarian laws which would have been implemented.

The Fourth Revolutionary Law would have granted all planters the right to share 55% of the sugar production and a minimum quota of forty thousand "arrobas" [2] for all small planters who have been established for three or more years.

The Fifth Revolutionary Law would have ordered the confiscation of all holdings and ill-gotten gains of those who had committed frauds during previous regimes, as well as the holdings and ill-gotten gains of all their legatees and heirs. To implement this, special courts with full powers would gain access to all records of all corporations registered or operating in this country [in order] to investigate concealed funds of illegal origin, and to request that foreign governments extradite persons and attach holdings [rightfully belonging to the Cuban people]. Half of the property recovered would be used to subsidize retirement funds for workers and the other half would be used for hospitals, asylums and charitable organizations.

Furthermore, it was to be declared that the Cuban policy in the Americas would be one of close solidarity with the democratic people of this continent, and that those politically persecuted by bloody tyrants oppressing our sister nations would find generous asylum, brotherhood, and bread in the land of Marti. Not the persecution, hunger and treason that they find today. Cuba should be the bulwark of liberty and not a shameful link in the chain of despotism.

These laws would have been proclaimed immediately, as soon as the up-

[2] *Caballeria.* tract of land, about 33⅓ acres. *Arroba.* 25 pounds.

heaval was ended and prior to a detailed and far-reaching study, they would have been followed by another series of laws and fundamental measures, such as, the Agrarian Reform, Integral Reform of Education, nationalization of the Utilities Trust and the Telephone Trust, refund to the people of the illegal excessive rates this company has charged, and payment to the Treasury of all taxes brazenly evaded in the past.

All these laws and others would be inspired in the exact fulfillment of two essential articles of our Constitution. One of these orders the outlawing of feudal estates by indicating the maximum area of land any person or entity can possess for each type of agricultural enterprise, by adopting measures which would tend to revert the land to the Cubans. The other categorically orders the State to use all means at its disposal to provide employment to all those who lack it and to insure a decent livelihood to each manual laborer or intellectual.

None of these articles may be called unconstitutional. The first popularly elected government would have to respect these laws, not only because of moral obligation to the nation, but because when people achieve something they have yearned for throughout generations, no force in the world is capable of taking it away again.

The problems concerning land, the problem of industrialization, the problem of housing, the problem of unemployment, the problem of education and the problem of the health of the people; these are the six problems we would take immediate steps to resolve, along with the restoration of public liberties and political democracy.

Perhaps this exposition appears cold and theoretical if one does not know the shocking and tragic conditions of the country with regard to these six problems, to say nothing of the most humiliating political oppression.

85% of the small farmers in Cuba pay rent and live under the constant threat of being dispossessed from the land that they cultivate. More than half the best cultivated land belongs to foreigners. In *Oriente*, the largest province, the lands of the United Fruit Company and West Indian Company join the north coast to the southern one. There are two hundred thousand peasant families who do not have a single acre of land to cultivate to provide food for their starving children. On the other hand, nearly three hundred thousand "caballerias" of productive land owned by powerful interests remain uncultivated.

Cuba is above all an agricultural state. Its population is largely rural. The city depends on these rural areas. The rural people won the Independence. The greatness and prosperity of our country depends on a healthy and vigorous rural population that loves the land and knows how to cultivate it, within the framework of a state that protects and guides them. Considering all this, how can the present state of affairs be tolerated any longer?

With the exception of a few food, lumber and textile industries, Cuba continues to be a producer of raw materials. We export sugar to import candy, we export hides to import shoes, we export iron to import plows. Everybody agrees that the need to industrialize the country is urgent, that we need steel industries, paper and chemical industries; that we must improve cattle and grain products, the technique and the processing in our food industry, in order to balance the ruinous competition of the Europeans in cheese products, condensed milk, liquors and oil, and that of the Americans in canned goods; that we need merchant ships; that tourism should be an enormous source of revenue. But the capitalists insist that the workers remain under a Claudian [3] yoke; the State folds its arms and industrialization can wait for the Greek calends.

Just as serious or even worse is the housing problem. There are two hundred thousand huts and hovels in Cuba; four hundred thousand families in the country and in the cities live cramped into barracks and tenements without even the minimum sanitary requirements; two million two hundred thousand of our urban population pay rents which absorb between one fifth and one third of their income; and two million eight hundred thousand of our rural and suburban population lack electricity. If the State proposes lowering rents, landlords threaten to freeze all construction; if the State does not interfere, construction goes on so long as the landlords get high rents, otherwise, they would not lay a single brick even though the rest of the population should have to live exposed to the elements. The utilities monopoly is no better: they extend lines as far as it is profitable and beyond that point, they don't care if the people have to live in darkness for the rest of their lives. The State folds its arms and the people have neither homes nor electricity.

Our educational system is perfectly compatible with the rest of our national situation. Where the *guajiro* [4] is not the owner of his land, what need is there for agricultural schools? Where there are no industries what need is there for technical or industrial schools? Everything falls within the same absurd logic: there is neither one thing nor the other. In any small European country there are more than 200 technical and industrial arts schools; in Cuba, there are only six such schools, and the boys graduate without having anywhere to use their skills. The little rural schools are attended by only half the school-age children—barefoot, half-naked and undernourished—and frequently the teacher must buy necessary materials from his own salary. Is this the way to make a nation great?

Only death can liberate one from so much misery. In this, however,—early death—the state is most helpful. 90% of rural children are consumed by parasites which filter through their bare feet from the earth. Society is moved to compassion upon hearing of the kidnapping or murder of one child, but they are criminally indifferent to the mass murder of so many thousands of children who die every year from lack of facilities, agonizing with pain. Their innocent eyes—death already shining in them—seem to look into infinity as if entreating forgiveness for human selfishness, as if asking God to stay his wrath. When the head of a family works only four months a year, with what can he purchase clothing and medicine for his children? They will grow up with rickets, with not a single good tooth in their mouths by the time they reach thirty; they will have heard ten million speeches and will finally die of misery and deception. Public hospitals, which are always full, accept only patients recommended by some powerful politician who, in turn, demands the electoral votes of the unfortunate one and his family so that Cuba may continue forever the same or worse.

With this background, is it not understandable that from May to December

[3] *Claudius Caecus.* refers to Roman Emperor who so oppressed the plebeians that they left Rome.

[4] *Guajiro.* term usually refers to modest and underprivileged farmers in *Oriente* province.

over a million persons lost their jobs, and that Cuba, with a population of five and a half million, has a greater percentage of unemployed than France or Italy with a population of forty million each?

When you judge a defendant for robbery, Your Honors, do you ask him how long he has been unemployed? Do you ask him how many children he has, which days of the week he ate and which he didn't, do you concern yourselves with his environment at all? You send him to jail without further thought. But those who burn warehouses and stores to collect insurance do not go to jail, even though a few human beings should have happened to [be cremated with the property insured]. The insured have money to hire lawyers and bribe judges. You jail the poor wretch who steals because he is hungry; but none of the hundreds who steal from the Government has ever spent a night in jail; you dine with them at the end of the year in some elegant place and they enjoy your respect.

In Cuba when a bureaucrat becomes a millionaire overnight and enters the fraternity of the rich, he could very well be greeted with the words of that opulent Balzac character, Taillefer, who, in his toast to the young heir to an enormous fortune, said: "Gentlemen, let us drink to the power of gold! Mr. Valentine, a millionaire six times over has just ascended the throne. He is king, can do everything, is above everything—like all the rich. Henceforward, equality before the law, before the Constitution, will be a myth for him; for he will not be subject to laws, the laws will be subject to him. There are no courts or sentences for millionaires."

The future of the country and the solution of its problems cannot continue to depend on the selfish interests of a dozen financiers, nor on the cold calculations of profits that ten or twelve magnates draw up in their air-conditioned offices. The country cannot continue begging on its knees for miracles from a few golden calves, similar to the Biblical one destroyed by the fury of a prophet. Golden calves cannot perform miracles of any kind. The problems of the Republic can be solved only if we dedicate ourselves to fight for that Republic with the same energy, honesty and patriotism our liberators had when they created it.

It is not by statesmen such as Carlos Saladrigas,[5] whose statesmanship consists of preserving the status quo and mouthing phrases like the "absolute freedom of enterprise," "guarantees to investment capital" and "the law of supply and demand," that we will solve these problems. Those ministers can chat gaily in a mansion on Fifth Avenue [6] until there remains not even the dust of the bones of those whose problems required immediate solution. In this present-day world, social problems are not solved by spontaneous generation.

A revolutionary government with the backing of the people and the respect of the nation, after cleaning the various institutions of all venal and corrupt officials, would proceed immediately to industrialize the country, mobilizing all inactive capital, currently estimated at about 1500 million dollars, through the National Bank and the Agricultural, Industrial and Development Bank, and submitting this mammoth task to experts and men of absolute competence, completely removed from all political

[5] *Carlos Saladrigas.* Batista's presidential candidate in 1944 elections, Saladrigas was defeated.

[6] *Fifth Avenue.* located in Miramar residential district of Havana.

machinations, for study, direction, planning and realization.

After settling the one hundred thousand small farmers as owners on land which they previously rented, a revolutionary government would proceed immediately to settle the land problem. First, as the Constitution orders we would establish the maximum amount of land to be held by each type of agricultural enterprise and would acquire the excess acres by: expropriation, recovery of the lands stolen from the State, improvement of swampland, planting of large nurseries and reserving of zones for reforestation. Secondly, we would distribute the remaining land among peasant families with priority given to the larger ones, and would promote agricultural cooperatives with a single technical, professional direction in farming and cattle raising. Finally, we would provide resources, equipment, protection and useful guidance to the peasants.

A revolutionary government would solve the housing problem by cutting all rents in half, by providing tax exemptions on homes inhabited by the owners; by tripling taxes on rented homes; by tearing down hovels and replacing them with modern multiple-dwelling buildings; and by financing housing all over the island on a scale heretofore unheard of; with the criterion that, just as each rural family should possess its own tract of land, each city family should own its home or apartment. There is plenty of building material and more than enough manpower to make a decent home for every Cuban. But if we continue to wait for the miracle of the golden calf, a thousand years will have gone by and the problem will still be the same. On the other hand, today there are greater than ever possibilities of bringing electricity to the remotest corner of the island. The use of nuclear energy in this field is now a reality and will greatly reduce the cost of producing electricity.

With these three projects and reforms, the problem of unemployment would automatically disappear and the work to improve public health and to fight against disease would be made much less difficult.

Finally, a revolutionary government would undertake the integral reform of the educational system, bringing it in line with the foregoing projects, with the idea of educating those generations who will have the privilege of living in a happy land. Do not forget the words of the Apóstol [7]: "A serious error is being made in Latin America: where the inhabitants depend almost exclusively on the products of the soil for their livelihood, the education stress, contradictorially, is on urban rather than farm life." "The happiest people are the ones whose children are well-educated and instructed in philosophy; whose sentiments are directed into noble channels." "A well-educated people will always be strong and free."

The spirit of education lies, however, in the teacher himself and in Cuba the teaching profession is miserably underpaid. Despite this, no one is more dedicated than the Cuban teacher. Who among us has not learned his ABC's in the little public schoolhouse? It is time we stopped paying pittances to these young men and women who are entrusted with the sacred task of teaching the young. No teacher should earn less than \$200, no secondary professor should get less than \$350, if they are to devote themselves exclusively to their high calling without suffering want. Moreover, all rural teachers should have free use of the various systems of transportation; and, at least every five years, all teachers should enjoy a sabbatical leave of six months with pay so they

[7] *Apóstol.* Refers to Jose Martí.

may attend special refresher courses at home and abroad to keep abreast of the latest developments in their field. In this way, the curriculum and the teaching system may be constantly improved.

Where will the money be found for all this? When there is an end to rife embezzlement of government funds, when public officials stop taking graft from the large companies who owe taxes to the State, when the enormous resources of the country are brought into full use, when we no longer buy tanks, bombers and guns for this country (which has no frontiers to defend and where these instruments of war, now being purchased, are used against the people), when there is more interest in educating the people than in killing them—then there will be more than enough money.

Cuba could easily provide for a population three times as great as it now has, so there is no excuse for the abject poverty of a single one of its present inhabitants. The markets should be overflowing with produce, pantries should be full, all hands should be working. This is not an inconceivable thought. What is inconceivable is that anyone should go to bed hungry, that children should die for lack of medical attention; what is inconceivable is that 30% of our farm people cannot write their names and that 99% of them know nothing of Cuba's history. What is inconceivable is that the majority of our rural people are now living in worse circumstances than were the Indians Columbus discovered living in the fairest land that human eyes had ever seen.

To those who would call me a dreamer, I quote the words of Marti: "A true man does not seek the path where advantage lies, but rather, the path where duty lies, and this is the only practical man, whose dream of today will be the law of tomorrow, because he who has looked back on the upheavals of history and has seen civilizations going up in flames, crying out in bloody struggle, throughout the centuries, knows that the future well-being of man, without exception, lies on the side of duty."

Only when we understand that such high ideals inspired them, can we conceive of the heroism of the young men who fell in Santiago.

The meager material means at our disposal was all that prevented our certain success. When the soldiers were told that Prío [8] had given a million dollars to us, they were told this in the regime's attempt to distort the most serious fact—the fact that our movement had no link with past politicians. The regime [was trying] to prevent the soldiers from learning that this movement is a new Cuban generation with its own ideas, rising up against tyranny; that this movement is made up of young men who were barely seven years old when Batista committed the first of his crimes in 1934.

The lie about the million dollars could not have been more absurd. If, with less than $20,000, we armed 165 men and attacked one regiment and one squadron, then with a million dollars we could have armed 8,000 men to attack 50 regiments and 50 squadrons—and Ugalde Carrillo [9] would not have found out until Sunday, July 26th, at 5:15 a.m. I assure you that for every man

[8] *Dr. Carlos Prio Socarras.* Participated in overthrow of Machado, later becoming member of Grau San Martin's cabinet, finally was elected President of Cuba in 1948.

[9] *Ugalde Carrillo.* Colonel Ugalde Carrillo, Commander of Batista's armed forces in the region neighboring the town of Nicaro.

who fought, twenty well-trained men were unable to fight, for lack of arms. When these men paraded along the streets of Havana with the student demonstration on the Centenary of Marti, they solidly packed six city blocks. If even 200 more men had been able to fight [at Moncada] or had we possessed 20 more hand-grenades, perhaps this honorable court would have been spared all this bother.

The politicians spent millions of dollars buying off consciences, whereas, a handful of Cubans who wanted to save their country's honor, had to face death—bare-handed, for lack of funds. This explains why the country, to this very day, has been governed not by generous and dedicated men, but by political racketeers, the scum of our public life.

With pride, therefore, I say that, in accord with our principles, we have asked no past or present politician for a penny. Those who gave us funds for the cause did so with sacrifice beyond compare. For example, Elpidio Sosa who gave up his job and came to me one day with $300 for the cause; Fernando Chenard, who sold the photographic equipment with which he earned his livelihood; Pedro Marrero, who contributed several months' salary and who had to be stopped from actually selling the very furniture in his house; Oscar Alcalde, who sold his pharmaceutical laboratory, and Jesús Montané, who gave his five years' savings, and so on, with many others, each giving the little he had.

One must have great faith in his country to do such a thing. . . .

Boris Goldenberg is a sociologist who lived for many years in Cuba and who has written widely on Latin American affairs. The argument of this essay—in which he tests the applicability of certain categories of analysis to the Cuban Revolution, and examines its pertinence for the rest of Latin America—has been elaborated in his book *The Cuban Revolution and Latin America.*

The Cuban Revolution: An Analysis

BORIS GOLDENBERG

The Cuban revolution has many unique aspects—as do all historical phenomena—but it also belongs to a class of happenings. Insofar as it is unique, it can be explained only by means of historical description. Insofar as it is one of a general type, it can be analyzed in sociological terms. Both kinds of investigation are necessary, but both have been difficult due to lack of factual knowledge, to political and emotional preconceptions, to the myths built up by the revolution's friends as well as its opponents, and finally to the impossibil-

From *Problems of Communism,* September–October, 1963, courtesy of Press and Publications Service, United States Information Service, Washington, D.C.

ity of explaining it inside the framework of either liberal or Marxist concepts. What follows is a schematic outline of a thesis in keeping with the facts of the case.

Considered from the standpoint of political dynamics, the Cuban revolution is a "permanent" one. It began as the democratic revolution of one country, but it was transformed into a "socialist" revolution which has tried to overspill its national boundaries and which has established close relations with the Communist bloc. Referring to this transformation as Castro's "betrayal" of the revolution's original aims is not really very helpful, since most revolutions turn out to be quite different from what their original protagonists wanted and proclaimed.

The Revolution as a "Leninist" Type

In terms of its general type, the Cuban revolution can be classified as "Leninist" and belongs to a sub-class of transformations distinctive in that they arose from inner developments and were not imposed by direct intervention of a foreign power. Russia, Yugoslavia, Albania, China, and perhaps North Vietnam are the other members of this sub-class.

All "Leninist" revolutions have claimed Marx as their inspiration, but have contradicted the main tenets of mature Marxism. All have been brought about by a radical elite in underdeveloped countries; in none has the purpose been to break the fetters which an overmature capitalism had imposed on further social progress; in none did the preconditions exist which Marx considered essential for the establishment of socialism; and in none did the revolution arise from the more or less conscious will of a popular majority composed of impoverished and embittered proletarians. Introduced with the object of furthering industrialization and modernization, this kind of "socialism" has been a substitute for rather than an heir to capitalism.

Because such revolutions have run counter to the spontaneous historical tendencies of the countries concerned, and because they have not been based on either the abilities or the desires of the population at large, the revolutionary elites have established a totalitarian system of rule. The term "totalitarianism" does not imply the total absence of consent on the part of the ruled. No man or group of men can rule for any length of time without the consent, freely given or induced, of a considerable part of the population. What is meant is a social and political system imposed, shaped and controlled by a revolutionary elite, which finds its legitimization in some ideology, monopolizes all power, prohibits all opposition, reduces the private sphere of men's lives, indoctrinates the population and maintains it in a state of constant mobilization.

Some Concepts That Don't Apply

According to liberal beliefs about the causes of Leninist revolutions—beliefs which underly the "Alliance for Progress"—such upheavals and transformations result from the activity of Communist parties which are able to exploit popular discontent caused mainly by poverty and by huge economic inequalities. They occur mainly in predominantly agrarian countries with archaic and semi-feudal structures, in which the middle class is weak and frustrated, in which representative democracy lacks popular appeal, and in which the impact of beginning industrialization causes severe disruption.

This explanation does not fit the Cuban revolution.

Cuba was certainly poor. But all economic and social indicators show that its population enjoyed a higher standard of living than that of southern Italy or Spain, and that in terms of per capita assets Cuba rated among the upper fifth of the Latin American countries.[1] This fact has occasionally been recognized by Cuban leaders:

> Cuba was not one of the countries with the lowest standard of living of the masses in America, but, on the contrary, one of those with the highest standard of living.[2]

Although social and economic inequalities were very great, they were probably less pronounced than in most of Latin America, and had diminished rather than increased in the course of recent decades—as we are told by another revolutionary source:

> Cuban distributive policy since 1933, with its higher salaries, eight-hour day, paid vacations, social security, etc., had produced a more just division of "national income." . . . Previously this income went into the hands of a few. . . .[3]

Only a minority of Cubans were engaged in agriculture, which could not be described as feudal. It was dominated by sugar-mills, and its latifundia (landed estates) had nothing in common with the haciendas of many Latin American countries. The majority of agriculturalists were not peasants but wage-earners—poor largely because of their underemployment due to the seasonal character of the sugar crop. The peasants, mostly tenants of various kinds, suffered from ignorance, from a lack of roads, credits, decent houses, and implements, and also from exploitation by commercial intermediaries and by local stores, often owned by big companies to which many peasants were chronically in debt. But their rents were not exorbitant and there was little land-hunger because most of them were protected by law and by custom against eviction—the main exception being those who lived in the remoter areas.

The "middle classes," insofar as such an ambiguous and confused term can be applied to Latin American realities, were rather numerous and were on the increase. While there are no reliable measures or statistics on their proportion in the population, evidence of a growing and more or less stable lower middle-class element was to be found in the mushrooming areas of urban and suburban dwellers holding steady jobs, leading relatively comfortable lives, buying their own homes, and so on. The higher strata, ranging from technicians and small businessmen through profes-

[1] While per capita comparisons of the different countries are admittedly unreliable, they are useful as indicators. Recently it has been shown that even the rather high figures of per capita national product in Cuba had been seriously undervalued (see Harry T. Oshima, *The National Income and Product of Cuba,* 1953, Food Research Institute Studies, Stanford University, November 1961). One has to complement such data by other indicators—*e.g.*, the number of population employed in agriculture, energy consumption per head, the number of private cars, radio and television sets, the rate of illiteracy, etc.—factors which this writer examines in his book.

[2] Anibal Escalante in *Verde Olivo* (Havana), July 30, 1961. Escalante, it will be remembered, later became the key figure of a shake-up within the new "Marxist-Leninist" party amalgamating the PSP (Cuban Communist Party) with Castro's revolutionaries. Latent dissensions came to a head in March 1962, when Castro violently denounced Escalante, long a top PSP leader, and charged the "old" Communists with attempting to assume controlling power in the party and government. Escalante quickly left the country for Eastern Europe. By his actions, Castro made clear that he intended to remain in control of the "Marxist-Leninist" course in Cuba, and so far Moscow has given him complete backing.

[3] "Lex," Ed., *Political, Economic, and Social Thought of Fidel Castro.* Havana, 1959, p. 153.

sionals, managers, bankers and bigger entrepreneurs, were of course much fewer in number but were also growing.

Representative democracy, as enshrined in the Constitution of 1940, had gained tremendous popularity in the Cuban nation. This constitution, virtually the Magna Carta for a Cuban "welfare-state democracy," had been the product of a freely-elected Constitutional Assembly in which all political parties were represented. In this period Fulgencio Batista, already the strongman of Cuba, had seemed to be veering toward support of a democratic system; prior to the Assembly he had legalized the Communist Party and condoned legal activity by his major adversaries, the "Autenticos." [4] Under the new constitution he was elected president of Cuba, serving until 1944. After his illegal reseizure of power in 1952 the entire struggle against him was to be conducted under the banner of the constitution.

The Communists had never constituted more than a small minority in Cuba and had little appeal. Even in the years they enjoyed legal status and participated in the government, they used to get hardly 10 percent of the vote in free elections. They did not make or direct the revolution in its first stage and had to submit to Castro in the second. Even those revolutionaries who had sympathies for communism—if not for the Communist Party—refrained from proclaiming it:

> Sure—if at this time, when we were only a handful, we had proclaimed from the top of the Pico Turquino [the highest mountain of the Sierra Maestra] that we were Marxist-Leninists, we might never have been able to come down to the plains.[5]

The unpopularity of the Communists did not decrease but rather increased after Castro's victory, as he himself has stated:

> The anti-Communist prejudices were so strong that a wave of protests used to arise each time a Communist was appointed to even a very modest post.[6]

Thus, the Cuban example shows that a Communist-type revolution can be successful where there is no feudalism, little conscious misery, no general popular despair, no mass desire for a "socialist" transformation, and no strong Communist Party.

The Pitfalls of Class Analyses

According to Marxist ideas—shared by many non-Marxists—revolutions must be explained as the outcome of class struggles and must be classified according to their class character. During 1959 the official Communists described the Cuban revolution as a "progressive, democratic, anti-imperialist" revolution led by the petty bourgeoisie and "national bourgeoisie,"—*i.e.*, as a fundamentally *bourgeois* revolution. Some authors classified it in its first stage, before it turned socialist, as a *peasant* revolution, while not a few analyzed it as a revolution of the *intellectuals*. The present "socialist" stage must, from the Marxist standpoint, be classified as *proletarian* revolution.

In the writer's view, however, any analysis framed in terms of social classes is utterly misleading and befogs the character of the Cuban revolution, as much in its first (democratic) as in its final ("socialist") stage.

[4] The Cuban "Autenticos," organized as a party by Grau Sau Martin, pursued a radical, pro-"welfare state," anti-imperialist line and were violently opposed to dictatorship in any form. The party won the elections of 1944 and remained in power until Batista's *coup d'êtat* in 1952.

[5] Speech of Dec. 21, 1961, in *El Mundo* (Havana), Dec. 22.

[6] *El Mundo,* Dec. 2, 1961.

The revolution against Batista cannot be understood as a bourgeois or middle-class revolution. It is true that most—though by no means all—of its leaders and very many of its active participants were young intellectuals of middle-class extraction. Yet this has been the case in most modern revolutions and cannot serve to differentiate them. It is also true that the widest if not always most active support for the struggle against the Batista regime came from those groups of people who can be called middle-class—precisely because this label is used to cover the totality of diverse and heterogeneous strata found between the "rich" and the "poor". But in no way can it be inferred that the revolution was conducted on behalf of the bourgeoisie and for the attainment of its class aims. In Cuba there existed neither feudalism nor absolutism. There was no fundamental opposition between the landed interests of an oligarchy and the bourgeois "capitalists"—both groups were mixed and intimately related to each other. The landowners participated in capitalist enterprise and the bourgeoisie invested in land. Batista favored the bourgeoisie and encouraged industrialization, although his record was marred by terrorism and corruption.

Just as important, imperialistic interests were no longer hindering the development of a Cuban bourgeoisie, as had been the case up to the 1930's. Local industries had developed under the protection of tariffs, and many of them were either in Cuban hands or operating partly with Cuban capital. The proportion of Cuban capital to foreign capital was constantly growing, as shown by the increasing number of Cuban-owned sugar mills and banks. Cuban capitalists were participating in business ventures with North Americans. As a result there had been a decline in anti-imperialist sentiment in the course of recent decades—hence the great effort of the Communists and other radicals to revive this issue by hurling "pro-American" charges at the representatives of the Cuban progressive bourgeoisie who were ministers in the first postrevolutionary government.

Neither can the Cuban revolution be classified as a peasant revolution. The peasants formed only a small minority of the total population, and even those whose lot was most miserable were not revolutionary. Cuba was no land of "*jaqueries*"—there was no peasant unrest comparable to that which preceded and accompanied the revolutions of Mexico and Bolivia or to that now apparent in northeastern Brazil and Peru. Most of the population of the countryside remained passive throughout the struggle against Batista. A small minority of young peasants joined the guerrillas in the mountains of the Sierra Maestra, mainly because, like young men from other social classes, they had to flee from police and army persecution, which was particularly marked in the regions where the guerrillas were active. This group was not in the least representative of the Cuban agricultural population; moreover, it was not in any sense inclined towards socialist solutions for Cuba:

> The first territory occupied by the Rebel Army . . . was inhabited by a class of peasants different in its cultural and social roots from those that dwell in the regions of extensive, semi-mechanized Cuban agriculture. . . . The soldiers that made up our first guerrilla army of country people came from that part of . . . [the peasant] social class which shows its love for the possession of land most aggressively, which expresses most perfectly the spirit catalogued as petty bourgeois; the *campesino* fights because he wants land, for himself, for his children. He wants to manage it, sell it, and make himself rich through his work.[7]

[7] Che Guevara in *Monthly Review* (New York), July–August 1961.

Finally, neither in its first (democratic) nor in its final ("socialist") stage can the Cuban revolution be characterized as "proletarian." Indeed, the workers as a whole were the most passive section of the population during the struggle against Batista. Strikes were called for economic reasons, but wherever political strikes were attempted they failed to arouse the mass of the workers—as demonstrated most notably in the "general strike" of April 9, 1958. This passivity of the "proletariat" was—at least initially—admitted by the official Communists, who attributed it not only to fear of persecution and the subservience of the trade unions to Batista, but also to the materialistic attitude of workers interested in mere economic betterment and expecting to achieve it through actions of the government in power.[8] Later, Fidel Castro accused the better-paid urban workers in particular of having sacrificed their birthright to rule the country for a miserable pot of lentil soup.[9]

There is nothing astonishing in this passivity. Cuban economic conditions were good in 1956–58. The benefits which successive governments (including that of Batista) had conferred on various elements of the working class were quite substantial, and in fact had been carried so far that they contributed in some degree to the relative stagnation of the Cuban economy.[10] In order to develop the country more rapidly, Castro's government—once it had reached its "socialist" phase—tried to force the workers to work harder for less pay, annulled many of their former benefits, introduced "voluntary" work and "socialist emulation," and transformed the trade unions into organs of the state with the job of increasing production. The results have been described by a pro-Castro author:

> The revolution has faced a difficult and potentially dangerous problem in the attitude of city workers. While for the most part they love Fidel as the orator and guerrilla-fighter . . . they have been slow to acquire a consciousness of their own indispensable role in the revolution, with its burdens and opportunities. The *initiative for the transition to a workers' state has come from the bourgeois leaders* of the revolution, not from a politically conscious working class.[11]

All efforts of the revolutionary leaders to get the voluntary cooperation of the workers failed, as Che Guevara noted bitterly when speaking about the introduction of advisory workers' councils in the factories:

> The main sin [*pecado*] of the advisory technical councils is that they have not arisen out of the pressure of the masses. They are a bureaucratic creation, introduced from above in order to give the masses a vehicle for which they had not asked—and in this consists the sin of the masses.[12]

While opposition to revolutionary measures came originally from urban workers, it soon spread to the countryside, as has been evident from the constant complaints of leading members of the government, the poor results of agriculture, the introduction of piecework and "norms" for agricultural work, and the transformation of the former "cooperatives" into state farms.

There remains to be noted a "Marxist" interpretation of the revolution which, in a certain sense, evades the problem of class characterization. Ac-

[8] Blas Roca in *World Marxist Review* (Prague), No. 8, August 1961.

[9] *Obra Revolucionaria* (Havana), No. 32, Dec. 15, 1960.

[10] On this subject see *Report on Cuba,* Mission of the International Bank, Washington, D. C., 1951.

[11] J. P. Murray in *Monthly Review,* July–August 1961. My italics.

[12] *Obra Revolucionaria,* No. 17, May 15, 1961.

cording to one analyst, the Cuban revolution in its *first* phase was essentially a "*popular*" revolution, as had been the Paris Commune of 1871 and the Russian revolution of 1905–07. He quotes Lenin's remarks calling these revolutions "popular" because the masses of the people intervened actively and in an autonomous manner, pushing their own political and economic aims.[13]

But neither will this interpretation do for Cuba. The revolution against Batista was the work of a small minority, supported by the sympathies of a growing majority. There was little active participation of the masses, and certainly they did not behave in the manner described by Lenin.

The Social (vs. Class) Base

To reject a class analysis of the revolution does not eliminate the need to look for a social basis in those parts of the population which, because of their economic and social situation, could expect most from its victory and even from its socialist transformation. There were such people, but they did not form a social class.

Social classes arise, in the last analysis, out of a social division of labor. But in Cuba—as in most Latin American countries whose economies are growing too slowly—there was a huge number of persons who had no real "work," who therefore stood outside the social division of labor. An investigation conducted by the Consejo Nacional de Economia (National Council of Economy) during the economically favorable period of May 1956 to April 1957 showed that out of a labor force of 2,200,000, some 361,000 (16.3 percent) were totally unemployed and 134,000 "underemployed" [14]—without taking into consideration "hidden" unemployment, the people classified under "services" or as "independents" who in fact were underemployed, or the many superfluous "civil servants" filling the governmental offices.

The majority of these persons have had no real roots in the economy of their nation and are, in some respects, comparable to the *Lumpenproletariat*. Because of their rootlessness they have frequently been inclined toward social radicalism; since they could expect little from reforms of the existing system, they have been favorably disposed towards its substitution by another in which they might be able to take root. Because of its utter heterogeneity, this mass of people has never been able to develop a common consciousness or to form a common political organization. As a conglomeration of rootless individuals, unaccustomed to work, they have resisted strict discipline and have been prone to corruption of all kinds—their hopes being pinned on some "caudillo," or benefactor. Since they have not worked, they more than others have been able to participate in terroristic and guerrilla activities. These are the people who may be said to have given something like a social basis to the Cuban revolution as a whole. A closer look at the social composition of the anti-Batista rebels reveals that, rather than the middle-class extraction of their leaders, it is this rootlessness which has been the common denominator tying them together. They were recruited from the young unemployed and underemployed of the cities and the countryside, as well as from university and high-school students and from frustrated intellectuals of all de-

[13] Jacques Arnault, "Cuba et le marxisme," *La Nouvelle critique* (Paris), Special number of 1962, esp. pp. 53–54.

[14] *Resultados de la encuesta sobre empleo, sub-empleo y desempleo en Cuba,* Consejo Nacional de Economia, Havana, January 1958.

scriptions who, with a lot of time on their hands, had only their rootlessness to lose and a world to conquer. Whether the regime will now be able to mold these people into workers for "socialist reconstruction" is quite another matter; given their social and psychological characteristics, the task would appear formidable.

The Uniqueness of Cuba

There seem to be three main peculiarities of the Cuban revolution which distinguish it from other "Leninist" revolutions: (1) it was initiated and led not by a Communist Party, but by a charismatic leader; (2) it passed through a "humanist" phase characterized by the bestowal of immediate benefits on the majority of the underprivileged; (3) its transformation from the democratic to the totalitarian phase was continuous, peaceful, and made without change of leadership.

The first peculiarity is well known and has been referred to earlier. Suffice it to add that during the whole process of the anti-Batista struggle and even during the first months of 1959, the Communist Party, which had considered Castro a petty-bourgeois putchist and had only come to an understanding with him in the fall of 1958, continued to be as distrustful of him as he was suspicious of their "old guard." These mutual suspicions were not entirely dispelled even at the beginning of the "socialist" phase; they led to a power struggle within the embryonic form of the future unitary party of the revolution, resulting in a purge of the "old" Communists and the submission of the party to Castro (see footnote 2).

The outcome of this struggle was never in question. From the first to the last phase of the revolution virtually all power resided with Castro. If ever there has been in history a charismatic leader, Castro embodies the type in almost chemical purity. It was Castro who appointed the first revolutionary president and gave him a free hand to choose ministers—only to assume the premiership himself six weeks after his entry into Havana. It was just as easy for him to dismiss the president and various other ministers when he later wanted to do it.

It is therefore utterly misleading to talk of a period of "dual government" in Cuba analogous to the duality of the English Revolution (Cromwell's army *vs.* Long Parliament), the French Revolution (the Paris Commune *vs.* the Legislative Assembly and Convention) or the Russian revolution (the Soviets *vs.* the Provisional Government). If the "bourgeois" government under Urrutia had no independent power, neither was there any counterbalancing power opposing it.

To cast the rebel army in this role is to overestimate its numerical strength, to ascribe to it a particular will, and to overlook its inner differentiations. Although the army grew quickly during the last weeks of the anti-Batista struggle, and even more rapidly in the first days after victory, its kernel was exceedingly small. There were less than some 2,000 guerrilla fighters, even including the members of the "Second Front" of Escambray who soon fell out with Castro. Castro's own forces at the end of December 1958 can be estimated at about 1,000, and the great majority of them had joined him only during the previous six months (as late as April 1958, according to Castro himself, his men numbered only 180).[15] Moreover, the members of the Rebel Army had no common political opinion; many of them were soon purged, while those openly

[15] Figure of 180 cited in Castro's speech of Dec. 21, 1961, *loc. cit.* Other figures are not exact but are estimated on the basis of various pieces of evidence.

opposing the turn towards the Communists were arrested.

The INRA, the organization created to direct the agrarian reform, for a time enjoyed wide power, but it does not fit into the concept of "dual government" either. It is true that during the second half of 1959 and the first half of 1960 the staff of the INRA largely ran affairs behind the back of the official government—but both arms of authority were headed by Fidel Castro, who at no time relinquished his power over either.

The second peculiarity of the Cuban revolution was the heyday of what might be called its "humanist" phase. Marked by an increase in mass consumption, a trend to disinvestment and an atmosphere of general enthusiasm (as well as general disorganization), this phase was in keeping with the political necessities of a revolutionary leadership that had not yet established its own apparatus of power. Castro's policies in this period went contrary to economic reason, necessitating the postponement of "socialist reconstruction" and in fact increasing the difficulties of such a transformation later on. The largesse of the regime was possible because the revolution had succeeded without Cuba's experiencing either a period of economic crisis or the destruction of a real fighting war. The economy was intact, with ample and underutilized resources of almost every description:

> During the first year of the revolution there was an abundance of everything. The warehouses were full . . . on the other hand, there were many people without work. Almost all building had stopped and one had to occupy the people. . . . From this period we inherited the legacy of unproductive labor.[16]

Many leading revolutionaries were conscious of the danger of this economic policy. Guevara, for example, stated in a television speech in early 1961 (when the humanist phase was already waning):

> We are consciously retarding our development by creating workers' circles, day nurseries, playgrounds for children, in order that everybody may enjoy benefits which other peoples have gotten only after forty years of hard toil. . . . We are building a thousand houses, knowing quite well that from the economic standpoint it would be much better to build a factory. But we desire the people to feel that a revolution like this one is made to benefit the great majority.[17]

Thus the leaders knew that in a certain sense they were sacrificing the future to the immediate present. And so it turned out: this period was short and the difficulties it created drove the revolution along totalitarian paths.

Contrary to Castro's later declarations, the second stage of the revolution was brought about without any major violence. Confiscations were carried out peacefully, both in the cities and in the countryside. While growing opposition became apparent, it was ineffectual; for the most part it took the form of verbal protests against the introduction of totalitarian measures, resulting in the arrest or in the flight of opponents—but there was hardly any real struggle. Hence it can be said that the revolution, insofar as it was violent (in the phase of the struggle against Batista) was not socialist, and insofar as it was socialist was not violent.

Castro—Master of His Fate?

The transformation of the democratic into the socialist-totalitarian revolution was the result of the interaction between the personal decisions of the su-

[16] Castro, speech quoted in *Obra Revolucionaria,* No. 30, Aug. 26, 1961, p. 215.
[17] Speech reproduced in *Bohemia* (Havana), Jan. 15, 1961.

preme leader and their consequences—consequences which, in turn, forced him into new decisions.

Castro was a typical revolutionary intellectual—voluntaristic, romantic, impatient, and unwilling to enter into compromises. He was not a Communist; in fact he distrusted and to some extent despised the old opportunistic and bureaucratic leaders who were creatures of Moscow, who for many years had collaborated with Batista, and who had not taken part in the armed struggle. Being a revolutionary pragmatist who had read very little "Marxist" literature, he at first had no clear program for Cuba, although he was certainly more radical than he chose to pretend—and in many respects more radical than the Communists. *"On s'engage, puis on voit,"* the formula of Napoleon, also fits Castro, whose ideas changed (or developed) with the change of circumstances. When he came to power he was free to do what he wanted, as few historical personalities have been. He may have wanted to establish a system of mixed economy and a society which combined social justice with individual freedom, but the changes inaugurated by his decisions made such an outcome impossible. They imposed on Castro, who was ever reluctant to pause or to retreat, further decisions that made any form of capitalism or mixed economy and any representative form of government as unfeasible as the maintenance of more or less friendly relations with the USA; on the contrary, they drove him towards totalitarianism and dependence on the Soviet Union.

This became clear even in the "humanist" phase of the revolution, in the course of 1959. Massive confiscations of the properties of "Batistianos" and of almost everybody connected with the dictatorship led to the emergence of a huge, heterogeneous state sector of the economy. Wage increases, price reductions, the promise of a vigorous collection of taxes, and a general climate of legal insecurity combined to make the functioning of private enterprise virtually impossible. The halving of rents and the decree devaluating land values stopped private building, sapped the wealth of the middle classes, and forced the government to undertake its own building program.

The agrarian "reform" was impelled along a similar course. As originally formulated, the reform was quite radical but by no means socialist in character. While liquidating the vast latifundia—already prohibited in principle by the Constitution of 1940—it permitted agricultural units up to 30 and in some cases up to 100 caballerias in size to remain in private hands (one cab. = 33.5 acres). The land was to be redistributed gradually, with the subdivision of state-owned property (including that seized from the Batistianos) taking place before the expropriation of first the unproductive and finally all other latifundias. Adequate indemnities payable in bonds were promised, based on a careful evaluation of land values, and independent tribunals were to be set up to decide conflicts. Homes, machinery, implements, cattle, etc., were exempted from forcible expropriation. The land was to be redivided either in private plots or in larger units owned collectively by "cooperatives."

In practice, however, almost none of this program was honored. Indeed, the agrarian "reform" was rapidly transformed into a chaotic agrarian revolution, led by impetuous youths in uniform who confiscated any properties they wanted, including the houses on the land, cattle and implements. Nothing was done about evaluation and indemnification, no "bonds" were ever even printed, and no tribunals established. Finally, a number of state farms were set up, and the new "cooperatives" were soon remodeled into state units in everything but name.

The effect of all of these developments virtually rendered any form of "capitalism" or even of a "mixed economy" out of the question, whatever Castro initially had in mind. The course of events also provoked growing opposition in Cuba, which in turn led to the progressive curtailment and disappearance of civil liberties, the freeze in US-Cuban relations, and Castro's rapprochement with Moscow.

Why the Revolution Was Possible

That Castro was able to proceed along this course without a major breakdown of the revolution was due on one hand to the existence of certain favorable circumstances in Cuba, and on the other to the absence of major obstacles.

Among the factors in his favor were the relative richness of the country, the fact that its economy was intact and at the same time under-utilized, the weakness of the independent peasantry, and the prevalence of big agricultural enterprises which could be easily nationalized. The first two of these factors made possible the freehanded distribution of benefits to the masses in the "humanist" period, winning enormous support for Castro, especially among the vast numbers of "rootless" people disposed to "getting along" through gifts from a "*caudillo*". This mass support far outweighed the opposition that began to grow as the revolution progressed to its second stage. In the atmosphere created by the regime's initial largesse, it was not difficult to convince the masses that their former poverty had been due to capitalist and imperialist exploitation. With the help of popular simplifications, and through a clever use of semantic devices which cloaked the second stage of revolution in appealing slogans, it was possible to win over a considerable part of the population to support of a "Marxist-Leninist" ideology which probably very few understood.[18] Simultaneously, the slogans of "anti-Yanquism," playing on latent resentment of the rich neighbor to the north, provided Castro with a rallying call for national unity and a basis of appeal to the "have-nots" in other Latin American countries.[19]

The success—or better, the non-failure

[18] The revolutionary leaders have at times been quite frank about the use of such simplifications and semantic devices. Castro, for example, discussing in retrospect the language that had been used in the agrarian "reform" law, remarked: "It was discussed if the ground should be given as property or in usufruct. Then we said, well, in reality it will be the same, but let us not put down 'usufruct,' let us write—precisely so that the enemies cannot take advantage of it—'property' of . . . the cooperative. This property is entirely equivalent to usufruct . . . because the cooperative cannot sell the land." (Speech of Dec. 21, 1961, in *El Mundo* Dec. 22.) When the peasants became so afraid of "cooperatives" that, as Castro said, "they could not even hear the word mentioned" (*Revolucion,* Nov. 11, 1961), the new name "agricultural society" was substituted.

The Communist leader Blas Roca has best summed up the importance of such semantic devices: "Many things done in Cuba are called with new, strange names. But this has many advantages. If one had used high-sounding words, when the forces [of the revolution] were not yet consolidated, when consciousness was not yet developed, nothing would have been achieved. Herein consists . . . the cunning of [the revolutionaries], that the necessary tasks have been done under new names and with new methods." (Speech printed in the records of the Eighth National Assembly of the PSP, Havana, Ediciones Populares, 1960, p. 388.)

[19] One of Castro's sympathizers (Jean Paul Sartre) has remarked, rightly, that Castro would have had to invent the "Yanquis" if they had not existed. Although the evidence suggests that he initially wavered on the question of accepting US financial aid (a fact which he later denied —*e.g.,* in a speech of Dec. 1, 1961, reprinted in *El Mundo* Dec. 2), he soon came around to the view of the Communist-oriented Castroites (including his brother Raul) that "anti-Yanqui" propaganda would help him more than US economic help, which might have put a brake on the radicalism of his revolution.

—of Castro's course is also explained by the lack of any serious obstacles in his path. There were simply no brakes that could have slowed down the process of radicalization. The old state apparatus had been destroyed; the former parties were prevented from reorganizing, with the single exception of the Communist Party; and repeated purges destroyed any chance of effective opposition in such institutions as the trade unions. The Church was weak: there were only some 700 priests in the country and most of them were non-Cubans. Finally, there was a lack of unity and direction among foreign opponents of Castro. As Guevara has remarked:

> The condition that we could call exceptional is that North American imperialism was disoriented and could not measure the true depth of the Cuban revolution. . . . When imperialism wanted to react . . . it was already too late.[20]

To sum up, when one discards the myths, abandons the use of irrelevant social categories and misleading historical analogies, and looks dispassionately at the historical events, the Cuban revolution ceases to be so incomprehensible. Its "uniqueness" far outbalances its typicality as a "Leninist" revolution—and it will probably remain unique because nowhere else in Latin America do we see the same constellation of factors as those that existed in Cuba from 1958 to 1960. Its outcome did not even conform to what Castro had originally wanted—a sort of socialism that would combine "freedom, independence, and bread." But impatient radicalism leads to extreme solutions, and totalitarianism arises because such "solutions" must be applied forcibly since they inevitably meet with some opposition and resistance. Such resistance seems to be innate in human nature; when it is directed against "socialist" solutions, the Marxist-Leninists attribute it to persisting "capitalist" influences in the society. However they wish to explain it, human nature still constitutes one of the main dangers along the road to the "socialist" utopia.

Castro himself knows this and feels it. Hence his strange outcry—so contrary to any genuinely Marxist conception:

> In the Communist Manifesto Marx says that capitalism is digging its own grave—but capitalism digs two graves, one for itself and the other for the society which comes after it. What we must do is to fill the hole rapidly, so that the legacy of capitalism may not destroy and bury socialism.[21]

[20] *Monthly Review*, July–August 1961.
[21] Speech delivered in Camaguey, reported in *Hoy* (Havana), May 15, 1962.

The following excerpts from the writings of Ernesto "Che" Guevara provide us with an early postrevolutionary analysis of the development, the nature, and the prospects of the Cuban Revolution. Guevara was not only one of the major leaders of that revolution but its chief ideologist as well.

Notes for the Study of the Ideology of the Cuban Revolution

ERNESTO "CHE" GUEVARA

This is a unique Revolution which some people maintain contradicts one of the most orthodox premises of the revolutionary movement, expressed by Lenin: "Without a revolutionary theory there is no revolutionary movement." It would be suitable to say that revolutionary theory, as the expression of a social truth, surpasses any declaration of it; that is to say, even if the theory is not known, the revolution can succeed if historical reality is interpreted correctly and if the forces involved are utilized correctly. Every revolution always incorporates elements of very different tendencies which, nevertheless, coincide in action and in the revolution's most immediate objectives.

It is clear that if the leaders have an adequate theoretical knowledge prior to the action, they can avoid trial and error whenever the adopted theory corresponds to the reality.

The principal actors of this revolution had no coherent theoretical criteria; but it can not be said that they were ignorant of the various concepts of history, society, economics, and revolution which are being discussed in the world today.

Profound knowledge of reality, a close relationship with the people, the firmness of the liberator's objective, and the practical revolutionary experience gave to those leaders the chance to form a more complete theoretical concept.

The foregoing should be considered an introduction to the explication of this curious phenomenon which has intrigued the entire world: the Cuban Revolution. It is a deed worthy of study in contemporary world history: the how and the why of a group of men who, shattered by an army enormously superior in technique and equipment, managed first to survive, soon became strong, later became stronger than the enemy in the battle zones, still later moved into new zones of combat, and finally defeated that enemy on the battlefield even though their troops were still very inferior in number.

Naturally, we who often do not show the requisite concern for theory, will not run the risk of expounding the truth of the Cuban Revolution as though we were its masters. We will simply try to give the bases from which one can interpret this truth. In fact, the Cuban Revolution must be separated into two absolutely distinct stages: that of the armed action up to January 1, 1959, and the political, economic and social transformations since then.

From *Studies on the Left,* 1960, Vol. 1, No. 3. Reprinted by permission of Agenda Publishing Company, San Francisco.

Even these two stages deserve further subdivisions; however, we will not take them from the viewpoint of historical exposition, but from the viewpoint of the evolution of the revolutionary thought of its leaders through their contact with the people. Incidentally, here one must introduce a general attitude toward one of the most controversial terms of the modern world: Marxism. When asked whether or not we are Marxists, our position is the same as that of a physicist or a biologist when asked if he is a "Newtonian," or if he is a "Pasteurian."

There are truths so evident, so much a part of people's knowledge, that it is now useless to discuss them. One ought to be "Marxist" with the same naturalness with which one is "Newtonian" in physics, or "Pasteurian" in biology, considering that if facts determine new concepts, these new concepts will never divest themselves of that portion of truth possessed by the older concepts they have outdated. Such is the case, for example, of Einsteinian relativity or of Planck's "quantum" theory with respect to the discoveries of Newton; they take nothing at all away from the greatness of the learned Englishman. Thanks to Newton, physics was able to advance until it had achieved new concepts of space. The learned Englishman provided the necessary steppingstone for them.

The advances in social and political science, as in other fields, belong to a long historical process whose links are connecting, adding up, molding and constantly perfecting themselves. In the origin of peoples, there exists a Chinese, Arab or Hindu mathematics; today, mathematics has no frontiers. In the course of history there was a Greek Pythagoras, an Italian Galileo, an English Newton, a German Gauss, a Russian Lobatschevsky, an Einstein, etc. Thus in the field of social and political sciences, from Democritus to Marx, a long series of thinkers added their original investigations and accumulated a body of experience and of doctrines.

The merit of Marx is that he suddenly produces a qualitative change in the history of social thought. He interprets history, understands its dynamic, predicts the future, but in addition to predicting it (which would satisfy his scientific obligation), he expresses a revolutionary concept: the world must not only be interpreted, it must be transformed. Man ceases to be the slave and tool of his environment and converts himself into the architect of his own destiny. At that moment Marx puts himself in a position where he becomes the necessary target of all who have a special interest in maintaining the old—similar to Democritus before him, whose work was burned by Plato and his disciples, the ideologues of Athenian slave aristocracy. Beginning with the revolutionary Marx, a political group with concrete ideas establishes itself. Basing itself on the giants, Marx and Engels, and developing through successive steps with personalities like Lenin, Stalin, Mao Tse-tung and the new Soviet and Chinese rulers, it establishes a body of doctrine and, let us say, examples to follow.

The Cuban Revolution takes up Marx at the point where he himself left science to shoulder his revolutionary rifle. And it takes him up at that point, not in a revisionist spirit, of struggling against that which follows Marx, of reviving "pure" Marx, but simply because up to that point Marx, the scientist, placed himself outside of the History he studied and predicted. From then on Marx the revolutionary could fight within History. We, practical revolutionaries, initiating our own struggle, simply fulfill laws foreseen by Marx the scientist. We are simply adjusting ourselves to the predictions of the scientific Marx as we travel this road of rebellion, struggling against the old structure of power, supporting ourselves in the people for the destruction of this structure, and having the happiness of this people as the basis of our struggle. That is to say, and it is well to emphasize this once again: the laws of Marxism are present in the events of the Cuban Revolution, independently of what its leaders profess or fully know of those laws from a theoretical point of view. . . .

Each of those brief historical moments in the guerilla [*sic*] warfare framed distinct social concepts and distinct appreciations of the Cuban reality; they outlined the thought of the military leaders of the Revolution—those who in time would also take their position as political leaders.

Before the landing of the "Granma," a mentality predominated that, to some degree, might be called "subjectivist": blind confidence in a rapid popular explosion, enthusiasm and faith in the power to liquidate the Batista regime by a swift, armed uprising combined with spontaneous revolutionary strikes, and the subsequent fall of the dictator. . . .

After the landing comes the defeat, the almost total destruction of the forces and their regrouping and integration as guerillas. Characteristic of those few survivors, imbued with the spirit of struggle, was the understanding that to count upon spontaneous outbursts throughout the island was a falsehood, an illusion. They understood also that the fight would have to be a long one and that it would need vast *campesino* participation. At this point, the *campesinos* entered the guerilla war for the first time. Two events—hardly important in terms of the number of combatants, but of great psychological value—were unleashed. First, antagonism that the city people, who comprised the central guerilla group, felt towards the *campesinos* was erased. The *campesinos*, in turn, distrusted the group and, above all, feared barbarous reprisals of the government. Two things demonstrated themselves at this stage, both very important for the interrelated factors: to the *campesinos*, the bestialities of the army and all the persecution would not be sufficient to put an end to the guerilla war, even though the army was certainly capable of liquidating the *campesinos'* homes, crops, and families. To take refuge with those in hiding was a good solution. In turn, the guerilla fighters learned the necessity, each time more pointed, of winning the *campesino* masses. . . .

[Following the failure of Batista's major assault on the Rebel Army,] the war shows a new characteristic: the correlation of forces turns toward the Revolution. Within a month and a half, two small columns of eighty and of a hundred forty men, constantly surrounded and harassed by an army which mobilized thousands of soldiers, crossed the plains of Camagüey, arrived at Las Villas, and began the job of cutting the island in two.

It may seem strange, incomprehensible, and even incredible that two columns of such small size—without communications, without mobility, without the most elemental arms of modern warfare—could fight against well trained, and above all, well armed troops.

Basic [to the victory] is the characteristic of each group: the more uncomfortable the guerilla fighter is, and the more he is initiated into the rigors of nature, the more he feels himself at home; his morale is higher, his sense of security greater. At the same time, he has learned to risk his life in every circumstance that might arise, to trust it to luck like a tossed coin; and in general, as a final result of this kind of combat, it matters little to the individual guerilla whether or not he survives.

The enemy soldier in the Cuban example which presently concerns us, is the junior partner of the dictator; he is the man who gets the last crumbs left to him in a long line of profiteers that begins in Wall Street and ends with him. He is disposed to defend his privileges, but he is disposed to defend them only to the degree that they are important to him. His salary and his pension are worth some suffering and some dangers, but they are never worth his life: if the price of maintaining them will cost it, he is better off giving them up; that is to say, withdrawing from the face of guerilla danger. From these two concepts and these two morals springs the difference which would cause the crisis of December 31, 1958. . . .[1]

Here ends the insurrection. But the men who arrive in Havana after two years of arduous struggle in the mountains and plains of Oriente, in the plains of Camagüey, and in the mountains, plains, and cities of Las Villas, are not the same men, ideologically, that landed on the beaches of Las Coloradas, or who took part in the first phase of the struggle. Their distrust of the *campesino* has been converted into affection and respect for his virtues; their total ignorance of life in the country has been converted into a knowledge of the needs of our *guajiros;* their flirtations with statistics and with theory have been fixed by the cement which is practice.

With the banner of Agrarian Reform, the execution of which begins in the Sierra Maestre, these men confront imperialism. They know that the Agrarian Reform is the basis upon which the new Cuba must build itself. They know also that the Agrarian Reform will give land to all the dispossessed, but that it will dispossess its unjust possessors; and they know that the greatest of the unjust possessors are also influential men in the State Department or in the Government of the United States of America. But they have learned to conquer difficulties with bravery, with audacity, and above all, with the support of the people; and they have now seen the future of liberation which awaits us on the other side of our sufferings.

From "Analysis of the Cuban Situation" in *La Guerra de Guerillas*, Published in Early 1960

More than a year has passed now since the flight of the dictator, corollary to a long civil and armed struggle of the Cuban people. The achievements of the Government in the social, economic and political fields are enormous; nevertheless, we need to analyze, to give to each term its proper meaning; and to show the people the exact dimensions of our Cuban revolution. This is because our national revolution (fundamentally agrarian, but with the enthusiastic participation of workers, people of the middle class, and today even with the support of industrialists) has acquired continental and even world importance, sheltered as it is by the unshakable decision of its people and the peculiar features which animate it.

We are not attempting a synthesis, however much one may be needed, of the sum total of laws passed, all of them of undeniable popular benefit. It will suffice to place upon some of them the needed emphasis, showing at the same time the logical sequence which from first to last leads us, in a progressive and necessary scale, from affairs of state to the necessities of the Cuban people.

Attention was first directed against the hopes of the parasitic classes of our country, when there were decreed, in rapid succession, the rent regulation law, the lowering of electrical rates, and the intervention of the telephone company with the subsequent lowering of rates. Those who hoped to see in Fidel Castro and in the men who made this revolution only some politicians of the old school, or some manageable dolts

[1] The day Batista was overthrown.

whose beards were their only distinctive trait, began to suspect that there was something deeper emerging from the depths of the Cuban people and that their prerogatives were in danger of disappearing. The word Communism began to hover about the figures of the leaders, the figures of the triumphant guerillas, and as a consequence, the word Anti-Communism as the dialectically contrary position began to nuclearize all those whose unjust sinecures were hampered or taken away. . . .

The Agrarian Reform law was a tremendous shock; now the majority of those affected saw clearly. Before they did, the voice of reaction, Gastón Baquero, had pointed out in no uncertain terms what would happen and had retired to the more tranquil waters of the Spanish dictatorship. Some still thought that "the law is the law," and that other governments had promulgated some which were theoretically good for the people; the enforcement of the laws was another matter. And that naughty and complex lad who had as his nickname the abbreviation INRA was looked upon at first with displeased and touching paternalism, from the high walls of a science which was infused with social doctrines and with respectable theories of public finance—inaccessible of course to the untutored and absurd mentality of guerilla fighters. But the INRA advanced like a tractor or a tank of war, since it is both tractor and tank, breaking down in its passage the barriers of the *latifundia* and creating new social relationships out of land tenure. This Cuban Agrarian Reform has emerged with several characteristics important in America. It was indeed antifeudal, for besides eliminating the *latifundia*—under Cuban conditions—it suppressed all contracts which required that land rent be paid in specie, and liquidated the conditions of serfdom which were primarily maintained among our great agricultural products of coffee and tobacco. But this was also an Agrarian Reform which was made in a capitalist environment in order to destroy the pressures of monopoly which work against the potentialities of human beings, isolated or collectively, to work their land honorably and to be productive without fear of creditor or master. It had the characteristic from the very first of assuring the *campesinos* and agricultural workers, those to whom the land was given, of necessary technical support, capable personnel and machinery, as well as financial support by means of credits granted by INRA or sympathetic banks; and the great support of the "Association of Stores of the People," which has developed extensively in Oriente Province and is in the process of developing in other provinces, where state graineries are replacing the ancient *garrotero*, paying a just price for crops and giving a fair return as well.

Of all the characteristics which differentiate the Cuban from the other three great agrarian reforms in America (Mexico, Guatemala and Bolivia), that which appears most important is the decision to carry it through to the end, without leniencies or concessions of any sort. This integral Agrarian Reform respects no right which is not the right of the people, nor is it directed against any particular class or nationality; the scales of the law tip alike for the United Fruit Company or the King Ranch, and for the Creole *latifundistas*.

Under these conditions, the production of the materials most important for the country, such as rice, oleaginous grains and cotton, is being developed intensively and is being made central in the planning process; but the Nation is not satisfied and it is going to redeem all its conculcated [*sic*] wealth. Its rich subsoil, the site of monopolists' struggle and pasture for their voracity, has for all practical purposes been rescued by the petroleum law. This law, like the Agrarian Reform and all the others dictated by the revolution, responds to the undeniable needs of Cuba, to the inescapable urgencies of a people which wants to be free, which wants to be master of its economy, which wants to prosper and to achieve progressively higher goals of social development. But for this very reason it is a continental example which is feared by the petroleum monopolies. It is not that Cuba harms the petroleum monopoly substantially or directly, for there is no reason to consider our country an emporium of that precious combustible, although there are reasonable hopes of obtaining a sufficient amount to satisfy internal needs. On the other hand, the palpable example of Cuba's law is seen by the sister nations of America, many of whom are the grazing-land of those monopolies, while others are impelled to internal wars in order to satisfy the necessities or appetites of competing trusts. It shows to them what is possible, indicating likewise the exact hour when one may think of carrying it out. The great monopolies turn their inquiet gaze once more to Cuba; not only has that little island in the Caribbean dared to liquidate Mr. Foster Dulles' legacy to his heirs, the United Fruit Company; but it has also dealt a blow to Señor Rockefeller, and the Dutch group suffers as well from the intervention of the Cuban popular revolution.

By a simple law of gravity, the small island of 114,000 square kilometers and 6,500,000 inhabitants is assuming the leadership of the anticolonial struggle in America, for there are important conditions which permit it to take the glorious, heroic and dangerous lead. The nations of colonial America which are economically less weak, those which are developing their national capitalism by fits and starts in a continual struggle, at times violent and without quarter, against the foreign monopolies, are gradually relinquishing their place to this small new power for liberty, since their governments do not find themselves with sufficient strength to carry the struggle to the finish. This is because the struggle is no simple matter, nor is it free of dangers nor exempt from difficulties. It is essential to have the backing of an entire people, and an enormous amount of idealism and the spirit of sacrifice, to carry it out to the end under the almost isolated conditions in which we are doing it in America. Small countries have previously tried to maintain this position; Guatemala, the Guatemala of the quetzal bird which dies when it is imprisoned in a cage, the Guatemala of the Indian Tecum Uman who fell before the direct aggression of the colonialists; and Bolivia, the Bolivia of Morillo, the prototype of martyrs for American independence, who yielded before the terrible difficulties of the struggle, in spite of having initiated it and having given three examples which are fundamental to the Cuban revolution: suppression of the army, the Agrarian Reform, and the nationalization of mines—a maximum source of wealth as well as of tragedy.

Cuba knows the previous examples, it knows the failures and the difficulties, but it knows also that it stands at the dawn of a new era in the world; the colonial pillars have been swept away before the impulse of the national and popular struggle, in Asia as in Africa. Now the tendencies to unification of the peoples are no longer given by their religions, by their customs, by their appetites, by their racial affinities or lack of them; it is given by the economic similarities of their social conditions and by the similarity of their desire for progress and recovery. Asia and Africa have shaken hands at Bandung, Asia and Africa are coming to shake hands with colonial and indigenous America by means of Cuba, here in Havana.

On the other hand, the great colonial powers have given ground before the struggle of the peoples. Belgium and Holland are but two caricatures of empire; Germany and Italy have lost their colonies. France debates in the midst of a war she has lost, and England, diplomatic and skilled, liquidates her political power while maintaining economic connections.

North American capitalism has replaced some of the old colonial capitalisms in those countries which have initiated their independent life; but it knows that this is transitory and that there is no real rest to be found in the new territory of its financial speculations. The claws of the imperial eagle have been blunted. Colonialism has died in all those places of the world or is in process of natural death.

America is another matter. It was some time ago that the English lion removed his greedy paws from our America, and the nice young Yankee capitalists installed the "democratic" version of the English clubs and imposed their sovereign domination in every one of the twenty republics.

These nations are the colonial feudal-estate of North American monopoly, "right in its own backyard"; at the present moment this is their *raison d'être* and the only possibility they have. If all the Latin American peoples were to raise the banner of dignity, as has Cuba, monopoly would tremble; it would have to accommodate itself to a new politico-economic situation and to substantial cuts in its profits. But monopoly does not like to cut its profits and the Cuban example—this "bad example" of national and international dignity—is spreading among the American countries. Every time that an upstart people sets up a cry of liberation, Cuba is accused; somehow or other Cuba is guilty, guilty because it has shown a way, the way of armed popular struggle against the supposedly invincible armies, the way of struggle in difficult terrain in order to exhaust and destroy the enemy away from his bases; in short, the way of dignity.

. . . .

"It may be that they attack us as 'Communists', but they are not going to eliminate us as 'imbeciles'," said someone in our Government.

. . . .

One may outline then, the necessity of a direct aggression on the part of the monopolies, and there are many possibilities which will be shuffled and studied in the IBM machines with all their calculating processes. It occurs to us at this moment that one possibility is the Spanish variation. The Spanish variation would be that in which an initial pretext will be seized upon: exiles, with the aid of volunteers, volunteers who for example might be mercenaries or simply soldiers of a foreign power, well supported by water and air; very well supported in order to insure success, let us say. It might be also the direct aggression of a state, such as Santo Domingo, which will ask some of its people, our brothers, and many mercenaries to die on these beaches in order to provoke the act of war, the act which will obligate the candid fathers of monopoly to declare that they do not wish to intervene in this "disastrous" struggle between brothers, that they will concentrate on freezing and limiting it to its present dimensions, that their battleships, cruisers, destroyers, aircraft carriers, submarines, minesweepers, torpedo boats, and airplanes as well will keep guard over the seas and skies of this part of America. And it could happen that, unbeknownst to the zealous guardians of continental peace, a single ship will get past them which will bring nothing good for Cuba, which will manage to "elude" the "iron" vigilance. Also intervention might take place through some "prestige" organ of the Americas, in order to put an end to the "crazy war" which "Communism" will unleash in our island; or, if this mechanism of this American "prestige" organ will not suffice, there might be direct intervention in its name in order to bring peace and to protect the interests of citizens, creating the variant of Korea. . . .

Many things might be asserted against the feasibility of enemy victory, but two of them are fundamental: one external, which is the year 1960, the year of the underdeveloped peoples, the year of the free peoples, the year in which at last and for always the voices of the millions of beings who do not have the luck to be governed by the possessors of the means of death and payment are going to make themselves respected; but a further, and even more weighty reason, is that an army of six million Cubans will reach for their weapons as a single individual to defend their territory and their revolution, and that this will be a field of battle where the army will be nothing other than a part of the people armed, and that following destruction in a frontal attack, hundreds of guerillas with dynamic command, with a single central orientation, will carry on the battle in every part of the country, and that in the cities the workers will carry death from the walls of their factories or centers of work, and in the fields the *campesinos* will carry death to the invader from behind every palm or from every furrow dug by the new mechanical plows which the revolution gave them.

And throughout the world, international solidarity will create a barricade of millions protesting against the aggression. Monopoly will see how its rotted pillars tremble and how its curtain of lies elaborated by the press will be swept away in a breath like a spider web.

. . . .

From a Speech Delivered August 19, 1960

It would be well for you who are present, the inhabitants of Havana, to turn over this idea in your minds: the idea that in Cuba a new type of human is being created, a fact which cannot be adequately appreciated in the capital, but which may be seen in every corner of the country. Those of you who went to the Sierra Maestra on the 26th of July will have seen two things absolutely unheard-of: an army with picks and poles, an army whose great pride it was to march in the patriotic festivities in Oriente Province in columns and bearing pick and pole, while their companions of the militia marched with their rifles. But you will also have seen something even more important; you will have seen some children whose physiques made you think that they were 8 or 9 years old, and who nevertheless were almost all 13 or 14 years old. They are the most authentic children of the Sierra Maestra, the most authentic children of hunger and misery in all their forms. They are the creatures of malnutrition.

In this small Cuba, with its four or five television channels and its hundreds of radio stations, with all of the advances of modern science, when those children went to school by night for the first time and saw the shining of the electric lights, they exclaimed: "The stars are very low tonight." And those children, whom some of you will have seen, are learning in the collective schools everything from the ABCs to a trade, and even the most difficult science: of being revolutionaries. These are the new human types which are being born in Cuba. They are being born in some isolated spot, at distant points in the Sierra Maestra, and also in the cooperatives and the work centers.

. . . .

From a Speech Delivered September 17, 1960

The more that the imperialist forces (which act from without) and the reactionary forces (who are their natural allies from within) increase their pressure against the Cuban revolution, the more profound will it become, responding to the voice of the people and adopting measures each time more drastic. . . . The ink is still fresh with which we have just finished printing Resolution Number Two in our Gazette, by which the North American banks are nationalized. And while it is still fresh, our *companero* Fidel is packing his knapsack to go to New York. And I say that he is packing his knapsack, first of all, because that is a fighting job and therefore merits such a literary figure of speech. But he is also packing it because the North American imperialists, submerged in barbarism, wish to deprive him even of the right of all members of the United Nations to live in the place where the United Nations is located, in the United States of America. And Fidel Castro has clearly announced that he is taking his knapsack and his hammock with the nylon awning, and we ought not to be surprised if tomorrow we see a photo of our delegation slinging its hammocks in the Central Park of the most barbarous nation on earth.

And it is logical that way. We slung our hammocks up in the mountains when Cuba was submerged in barbarism and we fought for her liberation. Therefore we can sling our hammocks today in the center of that barbarous civilization, defending the right of all peoples to achieve their liberty, their total economic independence and their freely chosen path.

But he will go preceded by this new measure which will deepen the struggle, a measure which will bring economic problems, but which we have adopted precisely in order to defend our dignity and our right to be free. For many years now imperialism has based its economic power on money, on the bank, and has little by little taken possession of the peoples and has twisted their economy, until it has converted these peoples into a simple appendage of the greater economy of imperialism.

That is how our potent sugar industry has developed; it did not fall from the sky, nor did it develop because of North American goodness, but because they dominated the great *centrales,* those of greatest productivity, and dominated the entire market and paid us a preferential price. This last they did because, sheltered by these prices, they would introduce into our country, by means of a law falsely called the law of reciprocity, all of the manufactured consumers' articles used by this people; the conditions were such that the competition of other countries, also producers of consumer goods, was impossible.

. . . .

But the North American form of action requires accomplices. They could not, as in the ancient times of the Roman Empire, hurl their legions upon a conquered country and have there a proconsul representing the Empire. They needed a proconsul, but one with special characteristics, outfitted in the modern manner and at times suave of demeanor, but revealing always his imperialist entrails. And those proconsuls were at times ambassadors, sometimes they were bank presidents, and sometimes they were the heads of military missions; but always they spoke English.

It was precisely in the dark epoch of

the sugar depression that the task of the banks was very important, since all depressions are always felt by the mass of the people, and in the moments of depression is when the great monopolies see their profits increased and when they consolidate their economic empire, absorbing all the small fry, all the sardines in this sea of economic struggle. Thus in that epoch the North American banks had an important task. It was the task of foreclosing for debts, according to the laws of the country, all those who could not resist the force of the depression; and they rapidly consolidated their empires. Always they belong to the vanguard of the great financial groups which in the United States dispute for power.

They belong to the Rockefellers, to the Mellons, to the Morgans and to all those who have deployed their tentacles among the three branches which sustain the power of the United States: finance, the army, and as a simple younger brother, the government. For the government of the United States represents, as its army also does, the finances of the United States; but these finances do not represent the North American people, they represent a small group of financiers, the owners of all the big enterprises, the owners of money, who also exploit the North American people. Clearly they do not exploit them in the same manner that they exploit us, the human beings of inferior races, the *mestizos* of America, Africa and Asia, for we have not had the good fortune of being born from blonde, Anglo-Saxon parents. But they do exploit them and divide them; they too are divided into blacks and whites, and they too are divided into men and women, union and non-union, employed and unemployed. . . .

Because of this it is good to see that here the first stage of imperial division, of disunion, has been absolutely conquered; that we no longer need to be ashamed of the color of our skin; that we no longer need to fear because of our sex or our social status that we will or will not obtain a job more or less remunerative. When the working class united, when the agricultural laborers of the country united, the first step toward definitive liberation was taken. For the old, the very old imperial maxim of "divide and conquer" remains, today as yesterday, the basis of imperialist strategy.

This letter sent in 1965 by Guevara to a Uruguayan journalist offers a deeper and later view of his thinking about the tasks and the future of the Cuban Revolution. It is especially interesting for its elaboration of a universal revolutionary theme: the need to create a new man with a new kind of social consciousness before a genuine cooperative society will be possible.

Socialism and Man in Cuba

ERNESTO "CHE" GUEVARA

Dear *Compañero:*

I am finishing these notes during my trip through Africa, stimulated by the desire to fulfill, though tardily, my promise to you. I shall deal with the theme of the title as I believe it will be interesting to your Uruguayan readers.

It is common to hear from capitalistic spokesmen, as an argument in the ideological struggle against socialism, the statement that this social system or the period of socialist construction which Cuba has entered is characterized by the abolition of the individual for the sake of the state. I shall not try to refute this assertion on a merely theoretical basis, but shall attempt to establish the facts as they are experienced in Cuba and to add some general comments of my own. . . .

For one who has not lived the revolutionary experience, it is difficult to understand the close dialectical unity that exists between the individual and the mass, in which both are interrelated, and the mass, as a whole composed of individuals, is in turn interrelated with the leader.

Under capitalism, phenomena of this sort are observed when politicians appear who are capable of popular mobilization; but if it is not an authentic social movement, in which case it is not completely accurate to speak of capitalism, the movement will have the same lifespan as its promoter or until the popular illusions imposed by the rigors of capitalism are ended. In this type of society, man is directed by a cold mechanism which habitually escapes his comprehension. The alienated man has an invisible umbilical cord which ties him to the whole society: the law of value. It acts on all facets of his life, shaping his road and destiny.

The laws of capitalism, invisible and blind for most people, act on the individual even though he is not aware of them. He sees only a horizon that appears infinite. This is how capitalistic propaganda presents it, pretending to extract from the "Rockefeller" story—whether it is true or not—a lesson of the possibility of success. Yet the misery which necessarily accumulates in order that an example of this sort arise and the sum total of vileness resulting from a fortune of this magnitude do not appear in the picture. It is not always possible to clarify these concepts for the popular forces. (It would be fitting at this point to study how the workers of the imperialist countries gradually

From *Che: Selected Works of Ernesto Guevara,* Bonachea and Valdes (eds.), The M.I.T. Press, Cambridge, Mass. Translation by Bonachea and Valdes.

lose their international class spirit under the influence of a certain complicity in the exploitation of the dependent countries and how this fact at the same time wears away the masses' spirit of struggle within their own country, but this is a topic which is not within the intention of these notes.)

In any case the path is very difficult and apparently an individual with the proper qualities can overcome it to achieve the final goal. The prize is glimpsed in the distance; the road is solitary. Moreover, this is a race of wolves: One can only arrive by means of the failure of others.

I shall now attempt to define the individual, this actor in the strange and passionate drama that is the building of socialism, in his twofold existence as a unique being and as a member of the community.

I believe that the simplest way to begin is to recognize his unmade quality: man as an unfinished product. The prejudices of the past are carried into the present in the individual's consciousness and a continual effort has to be made in order to eradicate them. It is a twofold process. On the one hand, society acts with its direct and indirect education; and on the other, the individual submits himself to a conscious process of self-education.

The newly forming society has a hard competition with the past. This is so not only on the level of individual consciousness, with the residue of a systematic education oriented toward the isolation of the individual, but also on the economic level where, because of the very nature of the transitional period, mercantile relationships persist. *Mercancía* is the economic cell of capitalistic society; as long as it exists, its effects will be felt in the organization of production and, hence, in the individual's consciousness.

In Marx's scheme, the period of transition was conceived as the result of the explosive transformation of the capitalist system destroyed by its own contradictions; subsequent reality has shown how some countries which constitute the weak branches detach themselves from the capitalist tree, a phenomenon foreseen by Lenin. In those countries, capitalism has developed sufficiently for its effects to be felt in one way or another on the people, but it is not its own inner contradictions that explode the system after having exhausted all of its possibilities. The struggle for liberation against a foreign oppressor, misery provoked by strange accidents such as war, whose consequences make the privileged classes fall upon the exploited, and liberation movements to overthrow neocolonial regimes are the habitual unchaining factors. Conscious action does the rest.

In these countries there has not been a complete education, for social work and wealth through the simple process of appropriation is far away from the reach of the masses. Underdevelopment on the one hand and the usual flight of capital to the "civilized" countries on the other make a rapid change impossible without sacrifice. There is still a long stretch to be covered in the construction of an economic base, and the temptation to take the beaten path of material interest as the lever of accelerated development is very great.

There is the danger of not seeing the forest because of the trees. Pursuing the wild idea of trying to realize socialism with the aid of the worn-out weapons left by capitalism (the market place as the basic economic cell, profit making, individual material incentives, and so forth), one can arrive at a dead end. And one arrives there after having traveled a long distance with many forked roads where it is difficult to perceive the moment when the wrong path was taken. Meanwhile, the adapted economic base has undermined the development of consciousness. To construct communism simultaneously with the material base of our society, we must create a new man.

This is why it is so important to choose correctly the instrument for the mobilization of the masses. That instrument must be of a fundamentally moral nature, without forgetting the correct utilization of material incentives, especially those of a social nature.

As I have stated before, it is easy to activate moral incentives in times of extreme danger. To maintain their permanence, it is necessary to develop a consciousness in which values acquire new categories. Society as a whole must become a gigantic school.

In general the phenomenon is similar to the process of the formation of a capitalist consciousness in the system's first stage. Capitalism resorts to force but also educates the people in the system. Direct propaganda is carried out by those who explain to the people the inevitability of the class system, whether it be of divine origin or due to the imposition of nature as a mechanical entity. This appeases the masses, who find themselves oppressed by an evil impossible to fight.

This is followed by hope, which differentiates capitalism from the previous caste regimes that offered no way out.

For some, the caste system continues in force: the obedient will be rewarded in the afterlife by the arrival in other wonderful worlds where the good are requited, and thus the old tradition is continued. For others, innovation: the division of classes is a matter of fate, but individuals can leave the class to which they belong through work, initiative, and so on. This process, and that of self-education for success, must be deeply hypocritical; it is the interested demonstration that a lie is true.

In our case, direct education acquires much greater importance. Explanations are convincing because they are true; there is no need for subterfuge. It is carried out through the state's educational apparatus in the form of general, technical, and ideological culture, by means of bodies such as the Ministry of Education and the party's information apparatus. Education takes among the masses, and the new attitude that is patronized tends to become a habit; the masses incorporate the attitude as their own and exert pressure on those who still have not become educated. This is the indirect way of educating the masses, as powerful as the other one.

But the process is a conscious one; the individual receives a continuous impact from the new social power and perceives that he is not completely adequate to it. Under the influence of the pressure implied in indirect education, the individual tries to accommodate to a situation which he feels is just while recognizing that his lack of development has impeded him in doing so until now. He educates himself.

In this period of the construction of socialism, we can see the new man being born. His image is as yet unfinished; in fact, it will never be finished, for the process advances parallel to the development of new economic forms. Discounting those whose lack of education makes them tend toward the solitary road, toward the satisfaction of their ambitions, there are others who, even within this new panorama of overall advances, tend to march in isolation from the accompanying mass. What is important is that men acquire more awareness every day of the need to incorporate themselves into society, and, at the same time, of their importance as motors of that society.

They no longer march in complete solitude along lost paths toward distant longings. They follow their vanguard constituted of the party, of the most advanced workers, of the advanced men who move along bound in close communion to the masses. The vanguard has their sight on the future and its rewards, but these are not envisioned as something individual; the reward is the new society where men will have different characteristics—the society of communist man.

The road is long and full of difficulties. Sometimes it is necessary to retreat, having lost the way; at times, because of a rapid pace, we separate ourselves from the masses; and on occasion, because of our slow pace, we feel the close breath of those who follow on our heels. In our ambition as revolutionaries, we try to move as quickly as possible, clearing the path, understanding that we receive our nourishment from the masses and that they will advance more rapidly if we encourage them by our example.

In spite of the importance given to moral incentives, the fact that there exist two principal groups (excluding, of course, the minority fraction of those who do not participate for one reason or another in the construction of socialism) indicates the relative lack of development of social consciousness. The vanguard groups are ideologically more advanced than the mass. The latter is acquainted with the new values, but insufficiently. Whereas in the former a qualitative change occurs which permits them to make sacrifices as a function of their vanguard character, the latter see only by halves and must be subjected to incentives and pressures of some intensity; it is the dictatorship of the proletariat operating not only over the defeated class but also individually over the victorious class.

All of this entails, for its total success, a series of revolutionary institutions. The image of the multitudes marching toward the future fits the concept of institutionalization as a harmonic unit of canals, steps, dams, well-oiled apparatus which make the march possible, which will permit the natural selection of those who are destined to march in the vanguard and who will dispense rewards and punishments to those who fulfill their duty or act against the society under construction.

The institutionalization of the Revolution has still not been achieved. We are searching for something new which will allow perfect identification between the government and the community as a whole, adjusted to the peculiar conditions of the building of socialism and avoiding to the utmost the commonplaces of bourgeois democracy transplanted to the society in formation (such as legislative houses, for example). Some experiments have been carried out with the aim of gradually creating the institutionalization of the Revolution, but without too much hurry. Our greatest restraint has been the fear that any formal aspect might separate us from the masses and the individual, making us lose sight of the ultimate and most important revolutionary ambition: to see man liberated from his alienation.

Notwithstanding the lack of institutions (which must be overcome gradually), the masses now make history as a conscious aggregate of individuals who struggle for the same cause. The individual's possibilities for expressing himself and making himself heard in the social apparatus are infinitely greater, in spite of the lack of a perfect mechanism to do so.

It is still necessary to accentuate his conscious, individual, and collective participation in all the mechanisms of direction and production and tie them in with the idea of the need for technical and ideological education, so that the individual will grasp how these processes are closely interdependent and their advances parallel. He will thus achieve total awareness of his social being, which is equivalent to his full realization as a human creature, having broken the chains of alienation.

This will be translated concretely into the reappropriation of his nature through freed work and the expression of his own human condition through culture and art.

In order for it to attain the characteristic of being freed, work must acquire a new condition; man as a commodity ceases to exist and a system is established which grants a quota for the fulfillment of social duty. The means of production belong to society and the machine is only the front line where duty is performed. Man begins to liberate his thought from the bothersome fact that presupposes the need to satisfy his animal needs through work. He begins to see himself portrayed in his work and to understand its human magnitude through the created object, through the work carried out. This no longer entails leaving a part of his being in the form of labor, power, soul, which no longer belong to him, but rather it signifies an emanation from himself, a contribution to the life of society in which he is reflected, the fulfillment of his social duty.

We are doing everything possible to give work this new category of social duty and to unite it to the development of technology, on the one hand, which will provide the conditions for greater freedom, and to voluntary labor on the other, based on the Marxist concept that man truly achieves his full human condition when he produces without being compelled by the physical necessity of selling himself as a commodity.

It is clear that work still has coercive aspects, even when it is voluntary; man as yet has not transformed all the coercion surrounding him into conditioned reflexes of a social nature, and in many cases he still produces under the pressure of the environment (Fidel calls this moral compulsion). He still has to achieve complete spiritual re-creation in the presence of his own work, without the direct pressure of the social environment but bound to it by new habits. That will be communism.

The change in consciousness is not produced automatically, just as it is not produced in the economy. The variations are slow and not rhythmic; there are periods of acceleration, others are measured, and some even involve a retreat.

We must also consider, as we have already pointed out, that we are not before a pure transition period such as that envisioned by Marx in the *Critique of the Gotha Program*, but rather a new phase not foreseen by him—the first period in the transition to communism or in the construction of socialism.

This process takes place in the midst of a violent class struggle; and elements of capitalism are present within it, which obscure the complete understanding of the essence of the process.

If to this be added the scholasticism that has delayed the development of Marxist philosophy and impeded the systematic treatment of the period in which the political economy has as yet not been developed, we must agree that we are still in diapers and it is urgent to investigate all the primordial characteristics of the period before elaborating a far-reaching economic and political theory.

The resulting theory will necessarily give preeminence to the two pillars of socialist construction: the formation of the new man and the development of technology. In both aspects we have a great deal to accomplish still, but the delay is less justifiable regarding the conception of technology as the basis: here it is not a matter of advancing blindly, but rather of following for a considerable stretch the road opened up by the most advanced countries of the world. This is why Fidel harps with so much insistency on the necessity of the technological and scientific formation of all of our people and especially of the vanguard.

In the field of ideas that lead to nonproductive activities, it is easier to see the division between material and spiritual needs. For a long time man has been trying to free himself from alienation through culture and art. He dies daily in the eight and more hours during which he performs as a commodity in order to be resuscitated in his spiritual creation. But this remedy bears the germs of the same disease: He is a solitary being who seeks communion with nature. He defends his oppressed individuality from the environment and reacts to esthetic ideas as a unique being whose aspiration is to remain immaculate.

It is only an attempt at flight. The law of value is no longer a mere reflection of production relations; the monopoly capitalists have surrounded it with a complicated scaffolding which makes of it a docile servant, even when the methods employed are purely empirical. The superstructure imposes a type of art in which the artist must be educated. The rebels are dominated by the apparatus, and only exceptional talents are able to create their own work. The remaining ones become shamefaced wageworkers, or they are crushed.

Artistic experimentation is invented and is taken as the definition of freedom. But this "experimentation" has limits which are imperceptible until they are clashed with, that is to say, when the real problems of man and his alienation are dealt with. Senseless anguish or vulgar pastimes are comfortable safety valves for human uneasiness; the idea of making art a weapon of denunciation and accusation is combatted.

If the rules of the game are respected, all honors are obtained—the honors that might be granted to a pirouette-creating monkey. The condition is to not attempt to escape from the invisible cage.

When the Revolution took power, the exodus of the totally domesticated took place; the others, revolutionaries or not, saw a new road. Artistic experimentation gained new impulse. However, the roots were more or less traced, and the concept of flight was the hidden meaning behind the word freedom. This attitude, which was a reflection in consciousness of bourgeois idealism, was frequently maintained in the revolutionaries themselves.

In countries which have gone through a similar process, there was an attempt made to combat these tendencies with an exaggerated dogmatism. General culture became something like a taboo, and a formally exact representation of nature was proclaimed as the height of cultural aspiration. This later became a mechanical representation of social reality created by wishful thinking, the ideal society, almost without conflict or contradiction, that man was seeking to create.

Socialism is young and makes mistakes. We revolutionaries many times lack the knowledge and the necessary intellectual audacity to face the task of the development of the new human being by methods distinct from the conventional ones, and the conventional methods suffer from the influence of the society that created them. (Once again the topic of the relation between form and content appears.) Disorientation is great, and the problems of material construction absorb us. There are no artists of great authority who also have great revolutionary authority.

The men of the party must take this task on themselves and seek the achievements of the critical objective: to educate the people.

What is then sought is simplification, what everyone understands, what the functionaries understand. True artistic experimentation is annulled and the problem of general culture is reduced to the assimilation of the socialist present and the dead (and therefore not dangerous) past. As such, socialist realism is born on the foundation of the art of the last century.

But the realistic art of the nineteenth

century is also class art, perhaps more purely capitalist than the decadent art of the twentieth century, where the anguish of alienated man shows through. In culture, capitalism has given all that it has to give and all that remains of it is the announcement of a bad-smelling corpse—in art, its present decadence. But why endeavor to seek in the frozen forms of socialist realism the only valid recipe? "Freedom" cannot be set against socialist realism because the former does not yet exist and it will not come into existence until the complete development of the new society. But at all costs let us not attempt to condemn all post-mid-nineteenth-century art forms from the pontifical throne of realism. That would mean committing the Proudhonian error of the return to the past, and strait-jacketing the artistic expression of the man who is being born and constructed today.

An ideological and cultural mechanism which will permit experimentation and clear out the weeds that shoot up so easily in the fertilized soil of state subsidization is lacking.

In our country, the error of mechanical realism has not appeared, but rather the contrary. This has been because of the lack of understanding of the need to create the new man who will represent neither nineteenth-century ideas nor those of our decadent and morbid century. It is the twenty-first-century man whom we must create, although this is still a subjective and unsystematic aspiration. This is precisely one of the fundamental points of our studies and our work; to the extent that we make concrete achievements on a theoretical base or vice versa, that we come to theoretical conclusions of a broad character on the basis of our concrete studies, we will have made a valuable contribution to Marxism-Leninism, to the cause of mankind.

The reaction against nineteenth-century man has brought a recurrence of twentieth-century decadence. It is not a very grave error, but we must overcome it so as not to leave the doors wide open to revisionism.

The large multitudes of people are developing themselves, the new ideas are acquiring an adequate impetus within society, the material possibilities of the integral development of each and every one of its members make the task ever more fruitful. The present is one of struggle; the future is ours.

To summarize, the culpability of many of our intellectuals and artists lies in their original sin; they are not authentic revolutionaries. We can attempt to graft elm trees so they bear pears, but simultaneously we must plant pear trees. The new generations will arrive free of original sin. The possibility that exceptional artists will arise will be that much greater because of the enlargement of the cultural field and the possibilities for expression. Our task is to keep the present generation, maladjusted by its conflicts, from becoming perverted and perverting the new generations. We do not want to create salaried workers docile to official thinking or "scholars" who live under the wing of the budget, exercising a freedom in quotation marks. Revolutionaries will come to sing the song of the new man with the authentic voice of the people. It is a process that requires time.

In our society the youth and the party play a large role. The former is particularly important because it is malleable clay with which the new man, without any of the previous defects, can be constructed.

They receive treatment which is in consonance with our ambitions. Education is increasingly more complete, and we do not forget the incorporation of the students into work from the very first. Our scholarship students do physical work during vacation or simultaneously with their studies. In some cases work is a prize, in others it is an educational tool; it is never a punishment. A new generation is being born.

The party is a vanguard organization. The best workers are proposed by their comrades for membership. The party is a minority, but the quality of its cadres gives it great authority. Our aspiration is that the party become a mass one, but only when the masses have attained the level of development of the vanguard, that is, when they are educated for communism. Our work is aimed at providing that education. The party is the living example; its cadres must be lecturers of assiduity and sacrifice; with their acts they must lead the masses to end the revolutionary task, which entails years of struggle against the difficulties of construction, class enemies, the defects of the past, imperialism.

I would like to explain now the role played by the personality, man as the individual who leads the masses that make history. This is our experience, and not a recipe.

Fidel gave impulse to the Revolution in its first years, he has given leadership to it always and has set the tone; but there is a good group of revolutionaries developing in the same direction as the maximum leader and a great mass that follows its leaders because it has faith in them. It has faith in them because these leaders have known how to interpret the longings of the masses.

It is not a question of how many kilograms of meat are eaten or how many times a year someone may go on holiday to the seashore or how many pretty imported things can be bought with present wages. It is rather that the individual feels greater fulfillment, that he has greater inner wealth and many more responsibilities. In our country the individual knows that the glorious period in which it has fallen to him to live is one of sacrifice; he is familiar with sacrifice.

The first ones came to know it in the Sierra Maestra and wherever there was fighting; later we have known it in all Cuba. Cuba is the vanguard of America and must make sacrifices because it occupies the advance position, because it points out to the masses of Latin America the road to full freedom.

Within the country the leaders must fulfill their vanguard role; and it must be said with all sincerity that in a true revolution, to which one gives oneself completely, from which one expects no material compensation, the task of the vanguard revolutionary is both magnificent and anguishing.

Let me say, with the risk of appearing ridiculous, that the true revolutionary is guided by strong feelings of love. It is impossible to think of an authentic revolutionary without this quality. This is perhaps one of the greatest dramas of a leader; he must combine an impassioned spirit with a cold mind and make painful decisions without flinching one muscle. Our vanguard revolutionaries must idealize their love for the people, for the most sacred causes, and make it one and indivisible. They cannot descend, with small doses of daily affection, to the places where ordinary men put their love into practice.

The leaders of the Revolution have children who do not learn to call their father with their first faltering words; they have wives who must be part of the general sacrifice of their lives to carry the Revolution to its destiny; their friends are strictly limited to their comrades in revolution. There is no life outside it.

In these conditions, one must have a large dose of humanity, a large dose of a sense of justice and truth, to avoid falling in dogmatic extremes, into cold scholasticism, into isolation from the masses. Every day we must struggle so that this love of living humanity is transformed into concrete facts, into acts that will serve as an example, as a mobilizing factor.

The revolutionary, ideological motor

of the Revolution within his party, is consumed by this uninterrupted activity that has no other end but death, unless construction be achieved on a world-wide scale. If his revolutionary eagerness becomes dulled when the most urgent tasks are realized on a local scale, and if he forgets about proletarian internationalism, the revolution that he leads ceases to be a driving force and it becomes a comfortable drowsiness which is taken advantage of by our irreconcilable enemy, by imperialism, which gains ground. Proletarian internationalism is a duty, but it is also a revolutionary need. This is how we educate our people.

It is clear that there are dangers in the present circumstances. Not only that of dogmatism, not only that of the freezing up of relations with the masses in the midst of the great task, but there also exists the danger of weaknesses in which it is possible to fall. If a man thinks that in order to dedicate his entire life to the Revolution, he cannot be distracted by the worry that one of his children lacks a certain product, that the children's shoes are in poor condition, that his family lacks some very necessary item, beneath this reasoning the germs of future corruption are allowed to filter through.

In our case we have maintained that our children must have, or lack, what the children of the ordinary citizen have or lack; our family must understand this and struggle for it. The Revolution is made through man, but man must forge day by day his revolutionary spirit.

Thus we go forward. At the head of the immense column—we are neither ashamed nor afraid to say so—is Fidel, followed by the best party cadres and, immediately after, so close that their great strength is felt, come the people as a whole, a solid conglomeration of individualities moving toward a common objective: individuals who have achieved the awareness of what must be done, men who struggle to leave the domain of necessity and enter that of freedom.

That immense multitude is ordering itself; its order responds to an awareness of the need for order; it is no more a dispersed force, divisible in thousands of fractions shot into space like the fragments of a grenade, trying through any means, in a fierce struggle with their equals, to attain a position that would give them support in the face of an uncertain future.

We know that we have sacrifices ahead of us and that we must pay a price for the heroic act of constituting a vanguard as a nation. We, the leaders, know that we must pay a price for having the right to say that we are at the head of the people who are at the head of America.

Each and every one of us punctually pays his quota of sacrifice, aware of receiving our reward in the satisfaction of fulfilling our duty, conscious of advancing with everyone toward the new man who is glimpsed on the horizon.

Allow me to attempt to come to some conclusions:

We socialists are more free because we are more fulfilled; we are more fulfilled because we are more free.

The skeleton of our freedom is formed, but it lacks the protein substance and the draperies; we shall create them.

Our freedom and its daily sustenance are the color of blood and are swollen with sacrifice.

Our sacrifice is a conscious one; it is the payment for the freedom we are constructing.

The road is long and unknown in part; we are aware of our limitations. We shall make the twenty-first-century man, we ourselves.

We shall be forged in daily action, creating a new man with a new technology.

The personality plays the role of mobilization and leadership insofar as it incarnates the highest virtues and aspirations of the people and is not detoured.

The road is opened up by the vanguard group, the best among the good, the party.

The fundamental clay of our work is the youth; in it we have deposited our hopes and we are preparing it to take the banner from our hands.

If this faltering letter has made some things clear, it will have fulfilled my purpose in sending it.

Accept our ritual greetings, as a handshake or an "Ave María Purísima."

Patria o muerte

Norman Gall is an American journalist and scholar who knows Latin America intimately and is currently writing a book on the Andean Revolution. His essay explores the reasons for Guevara's failure in Bolivia and evaluates Régis Debray's celebrated prescription for revolution in Latin America in terms of the political and social realities of that part of the world.

The Legacy of Che Guevara

NORMAN GALL

To the memory of Father John Higgins (1925–1967) of Nashville and La Paz, a servant of the Bolivian people who understood their revolution.

Ernesto "Che" Guevara, who had come to be Latin America's most feared and famous professional revolutionary, died this October on the southern fringe of the Amazon basin, in a jungle area of tortured ravines where a thousand streams make their way from the Andean highlands into the wild continental heartland below. The circumstances of his death are still unclear. There is some reason to suspect that considerable time elapsed between his capture by the Bolivian army and the day he "died of his wounds." It may also be that the guerrillas he led had been infiltrated by agents since the beginning of their Bolivian operations a year ago. This possibility is supported by the unusually high quality of documentary evidence, intended to prove Cuban "foreign intervention" in Bolivia, that was presented by Bolivian Foreign Minister Walter Guevara Arce (no relation) before a meeting of the Organization of American States in Washington last September 22—evidence which included a false Uruguayan passport, comparative fingerprints, a guerrilla diary, and excellent photos of "Che" in the guerrilla camp.

These suspicions may never be resolved. One thing, however, *is* clear: Che's death at age thirty-nine at the hands of the ragged Bolivian army, after less than six months of guerrilla combat,

Reprinted from *Commentary,* December 1967, by permission;

testifies less to one man's failure than to the profound weakness and incompetence of the current wave of "Marxist" revolutionary struggle in Latin America. In his last manifesto, published in April 1967 as an article in the Cuban magazine *Tricontinental*, Guevara declared: "Fresh outbursts of warfare will arise in the American countries, as has already occurred in Bolivia. They will continue to grow with all the vicissitudes involved in this dangerous business of a modern revolutionary. Many will die, the victims of their errors. [But] new fighters and new leaders will emerge in the heat of the revolutionary struggle. . . . We must wage a general-type action with the tactical goal of drawing the [U.S.] enemy out of his surroundings, forcing him to fight in places where his living habits clash with the actual situation." But Che's guerrilla diary, captured by the Bolivian army, contrasts strongly with this prophecy; it contains bitter complaints in his own handwriting about the indifference of the local peasants to revolution: "The inhabitants of this region are as impenetrable as rocks. You speak to them, but in the deepness of their eyes you note they do not believe you." Indeed, in the seven years since Che wrote *Guerrilla Warfare*, there has been no proof of the "three fundamental lessons that the Cuban Revolution contributed to the conduct of revolutionary movements in America: (1) Popular forces can win a war against an army; (2) It is not necessary to wait until all conditions for making a revolution exist, [since] the insurrection can create them; (3) In underdeveloped America the countryside is the basic area for armed fighting." Instead, the chronicle of guerrilla disasters so far is a tale of hardship, failure, and wasted idealism.

Just a few examples will illustrate this point. In Ecuador, some forty students of the Revolutionary Union of Ecuadorean Youth were captured in 1962 by army paratroopers near Santo Domingo de los Colorados, just two days after the youths arrived to set up a guerrilla camp. In Paraguay, since 1959, at least three guerrilla movements have been dismantled by the authorities before they carried out a single action. In the Dominican Republic in 1963, members of the Castroite June 14th Movement were supplied with defective arms from a government munitions factory by a German-born CIA collaborator (who fled the country a few days later); seventeen of them were killed in cold blood when they found their weapons useless, and surrendered.[1] In Argentina, police in December 1964 raided key training camps and underground supply depots of the "People's Guerrilla Army" (which police agents had previously infiltrated), killing six guerrillas and capturing twelve others before the "army," after six months of training and preliminary contacts with the rural population, could even begin operations. In Peru, three Castroite guerrilla bands, which in 1965–66 had tried to establish themselves along the eastern slopes of the Andes, were knocked out of action within seven months of their first ambush. In the La Convencion Valley of southern Peru, the guerrilla band of Luis de la Puente Uceda, an old friend of Castro, was literally destroyed by internal quarrels; de la Puente himself was shot by the army a few days after

[1] These unfortunate youths constituted a sufficient "Communist menace" for the Johnson administration, then barely three weeks in power, to reverse President Kennedy's policy of denying recognition to the provisional regime which, in a September 1963 military coup, had deposed President Juan Bosch, the first freely-elected Dominican ruler in 38 years; however, the puppet head of the new provisional government resigned in protest a few days later when it was learned that his nephew was among the guerrillas slain.

he was captured without resistance.[2] In Guatemala, two rival insurgency movements that were gaining ground steadily for four years have been inactivated over the past year by an army campaign of rural slaughter in which peasants have been impressed into right-wing vigilante organizations (using weapons supplied in the U.S. military aid program).

The death of Ernesto Guevara in Bolivia seems to fall quite naturally into place in this general history of failure and rout. But the Bolivian disaster is also compounded by the fact that that country seemed to be a relatively comfortable theater for guerrilla operations. It is a country with a strong revolutionary tradition; its army has been twice defeated by popular uprisings since World War II; and its sparsely-populated national territory contains vast areas of lowland jungle and savannah—abundant in water and game animals—capable of hiding and supporting a small guerrilla movement for many years. In his 1965 article, "Castroism: The Long March in Latin America,"[3] Régis Debray, the young French theorist of Castroism, rhapsodized: "Bolivia is the country with the best subjective and objective conditions, the only South American nation where revolution is the order of the day, despite the reconstitution of an army totally destroyed [in battles with the workers and miners] in the 1952 revolution. It is also the only country where the revolution can restore the classic Bolshevik form—the proof is the 1952 proletarian insurrection—on the basis of soviets, that burst the state apparatus with a short and decisive armed struggle." The U.S. Army Area Handbook for Bolivia (1963) noted that in the fifteen-thousand-man Bolivian army "conscripts (mainly Indians speaking little Spanish) receive no regular pay for their services. Instead they are provided with food, clothing, and lodging and, on rare occasions when funds are available, they may be awarded small monetary gratuities or issues of alcohol. The details of the defense budget are not made known publicly, but a probably valid assumption is that rates of pay for officers and noncommissioned officers . . . range from the equivalent of $18 a month for colonel to about $8 for the lowest noncommissioned officer grade. For that reason it is officially approved that service personnel are given sufficient free time to earn a supplementary income." The morale of the Bolivian army is such that officers often earn this "supplementary income" by selling the food raised for army rations on the open market, and by letting recruits go home months before completion of the usual one-year hitch in order to capitalize on their maintenance allotments and to reduce the "political risks" of barracks revolts.

The Bolivian army, it should be noted, has become the nation's leading political party since the November 1964 coup which ousted President Victor Paz Estenssoro and the *Movimiento Nacional Revolucionario* (MNR) and installed René Barrientos, the former Vice President and air force chief of staff and a kind of Latin American Captain Marvel. Between 1964 and 1965 the military budget was doubled, army officers were named to key administrative posts, and General Barrientos's incumbency was formalized in rigged elections twenty months after the coup. An astute and glamorous loudmouth who, a Uruguayan journalist once wrote, "even

[2] See my "Letter from Peru," in *Commentary*, June 1964, and "Peru's Misfired Guerrilla Campaign," *The Reporter*, January 26, 1967.

[3] In *Les Temps Modernes*, January 1965.

looks like an American," Barrientos has maintained a popular base by buying off the leaders of the peasant *sindicatos* created by the 1952 revolution, and by being very kind to the faction-ridden officers' corps. He reacted to the outbreak of guerrilla warfare by screaming for $1 million worth of modern U.S. military hardware: mortars, jeeps, jet aircraft, tanks, napalm, helicopters, and automatic weapons. This equipment was meant to replace the old Mauser rifles from the Chaco War with Paraguay (1932–35) with which his army had been combating the guerrillas. In turn, U.S. Ambassador Douglas Henderson initially cabled Washington that Barrientos was exaggerating the guerrilla emergency to exploit it for his own purposes. One U.S. official said: "We are certainly not going to supply the means for Bolivian army hotheads to start bombing and napalming villages or even suspected guerrilla jungle hideaways. Civilians would inevitably be killed and we have a long experience that this inevitably produces a stream of recruits for the guerrillas." [4] Shortly thereafter, Barrientos complained publicly that Bolivia was fighting "all America's war," in the long-range interests of the United States, without adequate support. (His problems were complicated during the guerrilla insurrection by the sudden need to send troops into the nationalized tin mines to suppress a rebellion by the miners, who had expelled the police from the two biggest mining areas and declared them "free territory.")

All in all, the Bolivian army was so unprepared for guerrilla warfare, according to one Bolivian colonel, "that our officers dressed differently and wore different arms than the soldiers when out on patrol, so that the guerrillas killed the officers first in the early ambushes. The soldiers, with their old rifles, could not respond to the fire of the guerrillas, who had automatic weapons, so we lost many men at first." [5] To bolster flagging morale, Barrientos himself went to the guerrilla zone on a few occasions to spend the night with army patrols. At the start of hostilities, a dark comedy of blunders prevailed on both sides. The guerrilla operation was discovered prematurely on March 23 when a guerrilla column—headed, the Bolivian government said, by a Cuban named "Marcos"—disobeyed orders to hold fire and ambushed an army patrol, killing seven, wounding five, and capturing two officers and several more soldiers, who were then stripped of their uniforms and arms and set free forty-eight hours later. Most of the dead were conscripts who had been in the army less than a week. According to the government, guerrilla defectors said that "Marcos" was stripped of his rank as "Comandante" for this act of disobedience. At any rate, the ambush led the army to find the guerrillas' main base, a cattle hacienda called "Casa Calamina." According to the army, Casa Calamina had been bought by Roberto Paredo Leigue—a known member of the Bolivian Communist party and a leader of the guerrilla band—and registered in his own name only a few months before the opening ambush,[6] about the time Che was said to have entered the country

[4] The New York *Times*, April 12, 1967.

[5] The following reconstruction of events in Bolivia comes largely from the press and from statements of Bolivian and Cuban leaders. Unfortunately, very few foreign journalists ventured into the guerrilla zone to corroborate official reports of individual raids and ambushes. However, what seems to be an incisive and richly-detailed series of dispatches was filed by Edwin Chacon of the La Paz Catholic-leftist daily, *Presencia.*

[6] Some aspects of this story are strange, if not totally absurd: for example, the official contention that Paredo openly scouted the villages of the area looking for a suitable farm to buy. Or the claim that the guerrillas left behind, in a cave clothing with the label *"Casa Albion de*

on a false Uruguayan passport. According to Defense Minister Alfredo Ovando, the "defectors" said the guerrillas were not scheduled to begin combat operations until August. However, it is also possible that Casa Calamina was never intended to be more than a relatively permanent training base, like several others the Cubans have been trying to establish along the eastern slopes of the Andes, with the Cuban army officers acting as guerrilla instructors. (This seems to be the explanation for the presence of Cuban guerrilla warfare specialists in Venezuela about the same time, after the Venezuelan Communist party withdrew its trained cadres and switched to electoral tactics.)

The official version cites the following incidents after the first ambush this year: army patrol waylaid at Iripiti on April 10, eleven soldiers dead, seven wounded, and a Major Sanchez taken prisoner; an ambush (no date given) at El Meson, killing a guide, a policeman, and a police dog; at the end of April, at Taperilla, two soldiers were killed by guerrillas; a few days later, another army patrol was ambushed at Ñancahuazu, with three more dead and three injured. Further clashes are subsequently reported, with three guerrillas dead and "several wounded," after the guerrillas had split into three groups, the principal one—led by Che—heading north for the country's only paved highway, which connects the cities of Cochabamba and Santa Cruz. After a few weeks without fresh battle reports, the guerrillas' apparent ascendancy reached its peak on July 7, with what the army calls an "audacious raid" on the town of Samaipata on the main highway. Before seizing control of the town for an hour, the guerrillas barricaded the highway, cut telephone lines, and halted several vehicles. They also wired beforehand, in military code, to Samaipata's small army garrison, sending the soldiers away in another direction. Around 11:15 P.M. they entered the town, disarmed and undressed the twenty remaining soldiers in the garrison, who offered no resistance. They entered the town's stores to stock up on food, clothing, and antibiotics, paying the merchants two and three times the normal prices. (Most of the town slept through the raid.) The guerrillas then commandeered a Gulf Oil truck (which they later returned) and drove to another town, La Tranca, where they took nearly all the local officials hostage and killed a soldier who resisted their entry. Then they disappeared before dawn, without a single loss.

In late July, the Fourth and Eighth Divisions of the Bolivian army were reinforced with specially-trained anti-guerrilla units brought in from the interior. This signalled the beginning of two counter-insurgency drives, "Operation Cynthia" in the southern part of the guerrilla zone, and "Operation Parabano" in the north. On July 20, four guerrillas were killed when an army patrol surprised the camp of Guevara's column, seizing ten knapsacks, small radios, a short-wave receiver, weapons, and some audiotapes. On August 31, an army patrol ambushed a column of ten guerrillas heading north across the Rio Grande river, which divides the Depart-

---

Havana." But one must accept most of this story, though it reflects an almost incredible stupidity on the part of the guerrillas that is bound to be most damaging to Castro in his disagreements with Moscow and the Latin American Communists. For to fabricate such a story out of whole cloth would necessarily involve a conspiracy among Fidel Castro, President Johnson, the Bolivian government, Régis Debray, and from thirty to fifty persons in the guerrilla zone, not to speak of the prisoners, "defectors," and the families of some of the thirty-odd Bolivian soldiers said to have died. As Castro said himself in his October 16 speech confirming Che's death, such a fraud would be very hard to bring off.

ments of Chuquisaca and Santa Cruz. According to the army, the guerrillas had impressed an Indian peasant as a guide, and sent him across the Rio Grande to see if any trouble awaited them on the other side. He was caught by an army patrol, which forced him to betray the guerrillas' intention to cross the river that day. "The guerrillas were frightened because the guide did not return," an army officer said. "The army patrol waited for sixteen hours on the river bank before the guerrillas decided to cross. They held their fire until the whole guerrilla column of nine men and one woman were deep in the water. The army patrol was made up of Indian recruits, and it took a lot of discipline to hold their fire until the guerrillas were helplessly deep in the water. Nine of the guerrillas were killed and the tenth taken prisoner."

On September 2, a further clash occurred in Yajo Pampa; four guerrillas and one soldier died. A few days later, an army patrol stumbled on a larger group of twenty-five guerrillas, who withdrew from the scene leaving behind one dead and deposits of arms and documents. These and other captured documents, together with information gleaned from the interrogation of prisoners, led to a large roundup of political suspects in La Paz, after which the army claimed to have destroyed the guerrillas' logistical "rear-guard" support organization. By September 26, about six hundred Bolivian "Ranger" troops, who had been rushed through an intensive course taught by U.S. Special Forces instructors, had joined the final hunt for the guerrilla columns, which had been reduced from some fifty-four men to between twenty-five and thirty. It is possible that the reason the "Rangers" were sent in so precipitously was a strange event that had occurred a few days earlier, on September 22. At 4 A.M. on the morning of that Friday, a column of about twenty-five guerrillas had marched into the mountain village of Alto Seco while its three hundred inhabitants were still asleep. Alto Seco lies at the edge of a desert mountain area that forms the principal natural barrier to an escape route from the eastern jungle in the direction of the highland city of Cochabamba, the tin mines, and the Pacific coast. At 5 A.M. the villagers began emerging from their houses to find the guerrillas waiting for them. The guerrillas asked the location of the community's only telephone and then cut the line, although the phone had not been working for weeks. Apparently in no great hurry, the guerrillas dug trenches and built barricades near the cemetery which lies on the only trail leading to the village. They then asked for the village headman, whose wife said he had gone away. (He was hiding in a neighbor's house.)

Then "El Che" himself appeared. The peasants subsequently told Edwin Chacon of the La Paz newspaper *Presencia* that "the chief" arrived on a mule. "He was a man of medium height with long chestnut hair. . . . It seems he was sick, because they helped him to dismount." He wore army camouflage pants and red socks and carried an olive-green windbreaker and a worker's leather cap. Some of these clothes were changed when the guerrillas bought new provisions from the villagers and burned their old garments. The guerrillas called a town meeting, attended by only thirty-five peasants, at which a speech was given by the Bolivian leader of the group, Roberto "Coco" Paredo, who was killed in a clash with the army a few days later. Paredo asked for volunteers, saying, "Here you have no drinking water or electricity. You are abandoned, like all Bolivians. This is why we are fighting here." According to the peasants, Che then intervened: "We would like you to come voluntarily, not by force. The army says it killed Joaquin and other comrades, but this is a lie, all army propaganda. The corpses they showed in Vallegrande were taken from a cemetery. They haven't killed any guerrillas, and this I assure you because only two days ago I communicated with Joaquin." The peasants were frightened and did not volunteer. After they had rested and changed clothes, the guerrillas began leaving in three different groups. They had stayed in Alto Seco for three days.

One of the last pages of Che's handwritten diary, transmitted in facsimile by wirephoto throughout the world, contained this entry: "The eleven-month anniversary of our guerrilla organization has arrived without complications. Early in the day we descended with the mules, past some precipices that caused a spectacular plunge of the *macho*. . . . The trail was longer than we thought, and only at 8:15 we realized that we were near the brook, which Miguel followed at full speed, but could only reach the *camino real* [highway], since it was already completely dark. . . . We advance with precaution, and note nothing abnormal, for we occupied an empty house. The army hadn't come any closer, losing its chance. We find flour, oats, salt, and goats, killing two of them, making for a little feast together with the flour, although . . . we consumed the night expecting something. In the morning. . . ." In his October 16 speech, Castro read the last entry (October 7) of the diary: "At noon, an old lady grazing her goats entered the canyon where we had camped, and we had to hold her. The woman would not give any reliable information about the soldiers. To every question, she replies that she does not know, that she has not been there for some time. She only gave information about the roads. From the report of the old lady, we learn we are roughly one league from Lleras and another from Haguey, and six from Pusara. They give the old woman fifty pesos with orders to say nothing, but with little hope she will keep her word. Seventeen of us went out with a very small moon; the march was very dangerous, leaving many signs along the canyons. There are no houses nearby, but only potato plots along the ravine, as we advance between two high ridges without vegetation. The army has a report that there are 250 revolutionaries."

Colonel Joaquin Zenteno Anaya, commander of the Bolivian army's Eighth Division, said at a crowded press conference on October 10 that Ernesto Guevara had been gravely wounded two days before at the junction of two narrow ravines in a battle with an army patrol that lasted at least two hours. Five more guerrillas were killed (a Peruvian, two Cubans, and two Bolivians, Zenteno said), with four soldiers also dead and four wounded. In his speech of October 16, Fidel Castro reconstructed the incident to say that, instead of withdrawing quickly as guerrillas normally do when confronted with superior numbers, the members of the band chose to make a desperate last stand around the body of their wounded leader. The army said Che was taken in a coma to Vallegrande, where his body was exhibited October 10. A Bolivian medical examiner, Dr. José Martinez Cazo, subsequently told reporters that the fatal bullet wound—which pierced the heart and lung—had killed Guevara instantly only five hours before he, Martinez, examined the corpse on Monday afternoon, October 9. Then the Bolivian government suddenly announced that the body had been cremated, with two fingers severed beforehand for purposes of fingerprint identification. And this is all we know.

Are we to believe the official story? It is of course possible that the telltale photos of the guerrillas could have been taken by an infiltrator, or that some U.S. Special Forces troops out of uniform could have played a key role in hunting down Che and his men. (The Americans did assemble most of the impressive montage of evidence presented by Bolivia to the OAS.) But even if these possibilities were proved to be true, they would not change the essential nature of the disaster. Some doubts were relieved by Fidel Castro's October 16 speech to the Cuban people confirming the news of Che's death:

In other words, the diary [found in Che's knapsack] is authentic in our judgment. The photographs are authentic. It seems to us to be utterly impossible to organize all this on false grounds. Many forgeries can be made but it is impossible to forge the most subtle features of the personality, the bearing, and the facial features of a person. And having analyzed all the data, all the details, all the angles—diary, photographs, news reports, the manner in which the news breaks—in our judgment it was technically impossible to fabricate these facts.

But let us go further afield. In the bosom of the Bolivian regime there are so many rivalries and problems that it becomes absolutely impossible for them to get together and agree even to tell a lie. They could tell some lie or give some news that they killed some guerrillas and their bodies never turned up. But many of these reports are usually given by reactionary governments and they have not the slightest importance. From the technical standpoint, [a fraud] would require a quantity of resources that does not exist there.

II

"El Che" was the only member of the Cuban Revolution's high command with extensive experience in South America, and the one most concerned—aside from Fidel—with the revolution's world role. The big billboard portraits of Che throughout post-revolution Cuba displayed him in the likeness of a soulful, husky movie star, with dark, distant eyes and a flowing mane, in a black beret and olive green uniform open romantically at the throat to expose his manly chest. (In reality, he was lean and asthmatic, with a catlike irony and quick, impish eyes.) A large portrait of him was also hung over the speaker's rostrum at the Chaplin Theater in Havana last August during sessions of the LASO (Latin American Solidarity Organization) conference, at which a kind of Castroite Comintern for Latin America was formally established. Che was the conference's "honorary president"; he was so much Fidel's other self that his mysterious "disappearance" [7] enabled Castro figuratively to be at once in Cuba and in many other places throughout Latin America.

The rumors generated by the Che mystery placed him at different times in the Dominican Republic, Brazil, Venezuela, Colombia, Peru, Bolivia, Chile, and Guatemala—as well as in the Congo, China, and Vietnam—always plotting revolution with some menacing and inscrutable bunch of desperadoes. Che's "disappearance" may be seen as a ploy to buy time to resolve a political conflict with the Russians over guerrilla warfare; at the same time, it generated a cheap and flattering windfall of publicity in the speculations over Che's whereabouts; in any case, it provides a telling example of Castro's propaganda genius. John Gerassi, an American writer who often reflects the hopes of the Cuban leaders, reported in an August 22 dispatch from Havana appearing in the October *Ramparts:*

Like a revolutionary phoenix, Che Guevara is rising from the ashes of his own, self-imposed obscurity. Long thought by the

[7] The last time he was seen publicly was at Havana's Rancho Boyeros airport on March 15, 1965, when he returned from a three-month journey to Africa and Asia. There he had spoken in a way that foreshadowed a hardening of Castro's foreign-policy line.

American press to have been killed or betrayed by the very Cuban revolutionary regime he had helped to create, Che has once again assumed a clear role as the world's foremost proponent of a revolutionary internationalism which knows no allegiances to state power or political party. And Che, by his independent vision of revolution, also haunts the Kremlin policymakers, complicating diplomacy within the Communist world and frustrating Russian hopes for a secure detente with Washington. The revolutionary spirit symbolized by Guevara is everywhere undercutting the influence and the dynamism of old-line Communist parties. . . .

It is always interesting to know how one acquires such revolutionary credentials. Guevara's road to Marxism began when he left his family home in Cordoba, Argentina, in 1952 (at age twenty-four) to cross the Andes on a motorbike to Peru via Chile. By coincidence, this writer happened on his path two years ago while covering a Castroite guerrilla insurrection based on the Hacienda Chapi in the mountains of central Peru—a wild and vast cattle estate at the approaches to the Amazon basin, requiring a week to cross on foot and situated at two days' walk from the nearest road. Neighbors in the area recalled that Che had worked on the hacienda in an anti-leprosy campaign headed by a Peruvian Communist physician, Dr. Hugo Pesce. (Childhood friends of his from Cordoba recently told me that, as an adolescent, Ernesto used to ride fifty miles by bike during his summer vacation to spend a few days at a leper hospital in the town of San Francisco, where he read Goethe's *Faust* aloud to the patients. As a guerrilla leader in the Sierra Maestra, he gave literacy classes to his peasant recruits, reading aloud to them from Cervantes, Robert Louis Stevenson, and the poetry of Pablo Neruda.)

In Peru, Che fell in with the youth of the (then) leftist and outlawed APRA party, some of whom later said they had supported him during hard days in Lima. He went to Bolivia to look for a job—he didn't find one—in the government created by the convulsive revolution of 1952, a revolution which destroyed the Bolivian army, abolished serfdom, and nationalized the tin mines. Then he went to Guatemala and got a minor post in the land-reform agency a few months before the overthrow of the Communist-dominated regime of Col. Jacobo Arbenz—by a CIA-backed invasion from Honduras which the Guatemalan army refused to oppose. After two months of asylum in the Argentine embassy in Guatemala City, he went to Mexico City where he soon became a friend of Fidel and Raul Castro, who had just been released from jail for staging the abortive and suicidal attack on the Moncada army barracks at Santiago de Cuba on July 26, 1953. Guevara joined the group of young Cubans being trained in guerrilla warfare by General Alberto Bayo, an elderly Republican émigré from the Spanish Civil War, who had been born in Cuba; along with eighty-one of these youths, he took part in the "invasion" of Cuba in December 1956 under the command of Fidel Castro.

A Cuban exile who worked with Che for a year after he became President of the Cuban National Bank in October 1959, recalled recently how Che would enter the bank daily at 1 P.M.—in his olive drab uniform and paratroop boots—to begin office hours that would last until 6 A.M. the next day. (Three nights a week, between 2 A.M. and 4 A.M., he would take tutorial classes in economics and mathematics as a self-imposed measure to compensate for his lack of training in these subjects. At the same time he required his bodyguards, peasant boys from his guerrilla column in the Sierra Maestra, to take literacy instruction; when they slacked off, he sent them to jail.) As Minister of Industries (1961–65), he involved himself in a long and acrimonious ideological debate with Carlos Rafael Rodriguez, an old-line Cuban Communist who had once served in the cabinet of Batista, Che arguing for "moral incentives" as against "material incentives" to increase production and efficiency in the Cuban economy. (Ultimately, in typical fashion, Fidel relieved Che of his ministerial post and Rodriguez of his job as director of INRA [*Instituto Nacional de la Reforma Agraria*] while temporarily deciding to use both pay incentives and psychological rewards to stimulate better work performance.)

Che's reading in Marxism was so meager at the time the rebel army of the July 26th Movement descended victoriously on Havana in 1959, that he, like Fidel, had to start becoming a Communist virtually from scratch. In both of these young men, the common denominator was anti-Yankeeism, an emotion of which Communism seemed to be the most extreme and dramatic form. This anti-Yankeeism has also been the *logos* of Cuban ambitions for Latin America, which is why Fidel's kind of "Marxism" has had so little positive ideological thrust, and has been so far confined—with a few exceptions—to the student circles that have adopted Castroism as a cult of adolescence.

Che emerged again this year as the ideal example—second only to Fidel himself—of a new revolutionary personality defined by Castro in his acrid debate with the Venezuelan Communist party (VCP) over the VCP's "cowardice and repugnant opportunism" in abandoning the "armed struggle" (*lucha armada*) in the face of crushing military and police repression, as well as the growing viability of the Venezuelan democratic system. On March 13, the anniversary of the suicidal 1957 attack on the National Palace led by Havana University students in an effort to kill Batista, an anniversary used repeatedly by Castro to attack "orthodox" Communists in Cuba and elsewhere, Castro made what is perhaps the most daring theoretical statement of his career:

> Our position toward Communist parties will be based on strictly revolutionary principles. To the parties without vacillation or contradiction in their line and that, in our judgment, take a consistently revolutionary position, we will give total support. But in any country where those who call themselves Communists do not know how to fulfill their [revolutionary] duties, we will support those who, though not labeled Communists, behave like true Communists in action and struggle. Because all true revolutionaries, who carry within themselves revolutionary vocation and spirit, will always terminate in Marxism!

This could provoke a parting of the ways between insurrectional "Castroism" and official "Socialism" as molded by Lenin, Stalin, and Khrushchev, with the future role of Communist parties everywhere in dispute. The role of Che Guevara as a new kind of revolutionary —and the manner of his death—may help to shape this struggle.[8]

[8] The recriminations have already begun. In an October 25 *Pravda* article, Rudolfo Ghioldi, a Politburo member of the Argentine Communist party wrote: "Along with rejection of the international importance of Marxism-Leninism, petty bourgeois nationalists are creating the concept of local or continental exception in order to justify deviations from Marxist-Leninist teaching. . . . Maoism and related currents advertise extreme adventurism, adapting offensive theory to any situation regardless of the presence of objective conditions. They propose that a revolution can be initiated from the outside and artificially stimulated across the borders, considering the nature of revolution isolated from the process of class struggle in the countries involved." A few days later, a relatively unimportant Cuban functionary, Minister of Health José Ramon Machado Ventura, replaced President Osvaldo Dorticos as head of the Cuban delegation to the 50th anniversary of the Bolshevik Revolution.

III

Che Guevara was an inspiration to insurgents all over Latin America. His romantic portrait of the guerrilla fighter as social reformer, written in terse and graceful prose in his 1960 manual, *Guerrilla Warfare,* represented an attempt to elaborate upon Lenin's concept of the professional revolutionary. It was aimed at the idealism of Latin America's alienated population of students, ex-students, and non-students as truly as had been Lenin's appeal to the same class in Russia:

> The guerrilla fighter . . . must have a moral conduct that shows him to be a true priest of the reform to which he aspires. To the stoicism imposed by the difficult conditions of warfare should be added an austerity born of rigid self-control that will prevent a single excess, a single slip, whatever the circumstances. The guerrilla soldier should be an ascetic. . . . The peasant must always be helped technically, economically, morally, and culturally. The guerrilla fighter will be a sort of guiding angel who has fallen into the zone, helping the poor always and bothering the rich as little as possible in the first phases of the war. But this war will continue on its course; contradictions will continuously become sharper; the moment will arrive when many of those who regarded the revolution with a certain sympathy at the outset will place themselves in a position diametrically opposed; and they will take the first step into battle against the popular forces. At that moment the guerrilla fighter should act to make himself the standard-bearer of the people's cause, punishing every betrayal with justice. Private property should acquire in the war zones its social function. For example, excess land and livestock not essential for the maintenance of a wealthy family should pass into the hands of the people and be distributed equitably and justly.

One of the cardinal tenets of what may be called the Castroite theory of guerrilla warfare, insisted upon by Castro and Guevara alike, is the impossibility of "exporting revolution." This point was brought home by Castro in a talk he had on June 13, 1964 with a small group of foreign reporters (myself included): "You cannot export revolution," he remarked, "just as you cannot export counterrevolution." The same idea was expressed privately by Guevara to Marcos Antonio Yon Sosa, a young guerrilla leader whom I interviewed two years later in the dry, hungry, hillbilly country of the Guatemalan Oriente:

> Before we really organized our movement, five of us went to Havana in September 1962, and stayed through the October missile crisis. It was arranged after a lawyer in Guatemala City called us and said Che Guevara wanted to see us. We met with Che four or five times and talked with Fidel once from 3 P.M. until 2 A.M. the next morning. The first time we met Che was when he walked into our house unannounced. We didn't know who he was until one of his aides finally told us. He had just come in without any fanfare or pretensions and just started chatting. We asked him later about how to organize our guerrilla movement and what would be the best part of Guatemala to start guerrilla operations in. Che told us very modestly that he couldn't answer these questions, that the Guatemalans have to make their own revolution and decide these things for themselves.

All guerrilla strategy in Latin America over the past nine years has been founded on Guevara's contention that "a nucleus of thirty to fifty men . . . is sufficient to initiate an armed struggle in any country of the Americas with their conditions of favorable territory for operations, [peasant] land hunger, repeated injustices, etc." This assumption has been further developed, by Régis Debray and others, into a full-fledged "Leninist" theory of the insurrectional *foco* (a Spanish word used to describe the unitary focus or base of guerrilla operations). The *foco* theory was formulated by Debray in his 1965 article, "Castroism: The Long March in Latin America":

> Although at the start it is a tiny group (ten to thirty persons, professional revolutionaries entirely dedicated to the cause and seeking the conquest of power), the *foco* does not intend to conquer power by itself, through an audacious strike. Nor would it seek power through war or a military defeat of the enemy. It seeks only to prepare the masses to overthrow established power by themselves. [It is] a minority which, embedded in the most vulnerable part of the national territory, will extend slowly, like an oil stain, propagating concentric waves in the peasant masses, then in the cities, and finally over the capital. . . . The first contact with the peasants that inhabit the wilderness where the guerrillas install themselves for reasons of security and natural protection is the hardest to establish and consolidate. These isolated peasants, small owners of dry parcels . . . are also the most closed to political consciousness, the most difficult to guide and organize, because of their dispersion, illiteracy, and initial suspicion toward these strangers whom they believe will bring bombardment, looting, and blind repression. But later, when this sector is conquered, the guerrilla *foco*—already consolidated in provisions, intelligence, and recruits—will enter into contact with agricultural workers in the lowlands (sugar cane cutters, etc.), a social level much more receptive and prepared because of its concentration, chronic unemployment, vulnerability to market fluctuation, etc. And in neighboring cities, contact will finally be made with small concentrations of industrial workers who are already interested in politics, without the need of the slow work of approach so indispensable in the wilderness. . . . The *foco* installs itself as a detonator in the least-watched point of the explosive charge and in the most favorable moment for the explosion. By itself, the *foco* will not change a given social situation, nor even—in a single action—a political situation. It cannot have an active part if it does not find a point of insertion within the contradictions in development. In space: where class contradictions are the most violent and less evident politically, in the core area of agrarian feudalism, far from the repressive apparatus of the cities. In time: there is the *quid*. It is sure that a guerrilla *foco* cannot be born in tranquil times, but should be instead the culmination of a political crisis.

The long-term cost and political implications for a Latin American government in combating a guerrilla insurrection is an integral part of this strategy. A 1964 clandestine guerrilla handbook of the Venezuelan FALN (*Fuerzas Armadas de Liberacion Nacional*) put it this way: "The uncontrolled increase in the armed forces would break the equilibrium of forces guaranteeing the stability of the government. In other words, a civil government cannot sustain itself in a Spartan Venezuela. When revolutionary operations constantly strike the reactionary military vanguard, it is probable that the military will insist on certain political controls for 'pacification' and finally will decide on a coup d'état." [9]

And yet, despite the tactical validity of such analyses, the Castroite insurgencies in Latin America are not succeeding. Quite apart from the stiffer and more intelligent resistance which they have been encountering from the U.S. and from Latin American military establishments, they have also violated some of the fundamental strategic precepts of their own revolutionary theory. Che himself wrote that guerrilla insurgencies cannot be successful against governments able to make a pretense of democratic legitimacy, but the Cubans have in fact spurred Castroite "National Liberation" movements against governments of precisely this kind in Peru, Venezuela, and Colombia. Castro him-

[9] Yoboso, "*Las FALN Venceran: Notas Para una Tactica Militar Revolucionaria*," 1964.

self voiced the fear privately to foreigners this summer that when the United States frees itself from its Vietnam commitment, it will turn full-force on Cuba, and that Cuba's only defense in that case will be to foment as many new "Vietnams" as possible, to commit American power elsewhere as well as to recoup the faltering prestige of her strategy of revolutionary "armed struggle" in the hemisphere.

Earlier this year, a few American officials privately expressed the belief that Cuba was making an all-out effort, after many defeats, to prove the efficacy of its guerrilla warfare theory by sending its own men to join insurgents in South America. This view was supported by the Cubans themselves; both Castro and the Cuban Vice Minister of Defense, Juan Almeida (who substituted for Castro as speaker at Havana's May Day parade), hinted broadly at Cuban participation in the Bolivian and Venezuelan guerrilla movements. (On May 8, Venezuelan authorities captured two Cuban military men in a guerrilla landing operation; a third was caught in a Caracas penthouse on August 24, after having participated in a terrorist bank robbery.) When Régis Debray was arrested with two other foreigners after leaving Che's guerrilla camp, he claimed that he had entered Bolivia on his own French passport and had obtained press accreditation from the Bolivian Foreign Ministry as a correspondent for the Mexican magazine *Sucesos*, a pictorial bi-weekly which is widely believed to enjoy a Castro subsidy and which has won special fame in Latin American journalism for its glamorous photo-interviews with Castroite guerrilla leaders.[10] The photos showing Che and the Cubans in the guerrilla camp—exhibited by the Bolivians at the OAS ministerial conference on September 22—are very much in the style of these pictorial reports.

It appears, then, that a desperate hunger for publicity severely prejudiced the security of the guerrilla operation while it still should have been in the secret stages of gestation. It seems too that a deficient recruitment procedure led to several early defections, which gave the Bolivian army enough information to seek out the guerrillas when they were not yet prepared for action. Most important, the presence of a large proportion of foreigners (including former Cuban sub-cabinet officers and at least three former members of the Central Committee of the Cuban Communist party, according to photographic identification offered by the Bolivians) severely burdened the political thrust of Bolivia's "War of National Liberation." What is worse, this foreign presence flew in the face of Che's advice to younger guerrilla leaders that such wars must be fought by indigenous patriots and, preferably, by peasants from the guerrilla zone itself.

But in assessing the full significance of the failure of the Bolivian guerrilla insurrection, one is lured beyond the errors of the guerrillas themselves to view the spectacular ecological changes that have been occurring recently at the fringes of the Amazon basin. Many of the basic conditions of life have been changed by the introduction into the area of new roads, cheap airplane travel, small electric generators, out-

[10] These *Sucesos* specials usually appear in series with color photos and a text that gives a very flattering estimate of the guerrillas' political and military strength. Just before Debray's arrest, the editor of *Sucesos*, Mario Menendez Rodriguez, was jailed for several days in Bogota after a guerrilla band staged a train robbery and a raid on a police post (leaving thirteen dead) for him to photograph and describe. By tracing Menendez's travels, police were able to dismantle the guerrillas' urban support organization. Menendez gave police additional details after his arrest.

board motors, canned food, radio transmitters, and—most important—malaria control. The impact of these innovations has been felt most strongly over the past decade. Along the eastern Andean slopes of Bolivia and Peru, many thousands of Quechua-speaking Indian families from the highlands are descending to build "spontaneous settlements" alongside the new but still primitive dirt roads which penetrate trackless and unsurveyed areas. These Indians will go wherever there is a road; their tenacity is making a mockery of the small and shoddy government colonization schemes that have so far been tried.

Perhaps the most significant factor of all, however, in the recent history of the jungle frontier, has been the pervasive American presence in some of those areas where the national governments are unable to finance and execute development programs. This American presence is articulated in many ways. Since the closing of China in 1949, Latin America has become the main field of American missionary work. There are now relatively few aboriginal peoples that have not been reached by missionaries, many of whom have specialized in building schools and recording primitive languages. In jungle towns nowadays it is not unusual to see an American missionary fly in alone in a single-engine plane (with perhaps three or four aborigines in need of medical treatment) to buy supplies and then fly back into the jungle an hour or two later.[11]

In some areas the new tropical economies have been growing so fast that they have literally leapt out of their isolation. For example, the tiny jungle airstrip serving the Peruvian town of Tarapoto is the country's busiest air terminal outside of Lima, shipping out the foodstuffs produced in the nearby tropical valleys that are heavily settled by highland peasant migrants. To reach Tarapoto with a road (a project fitting into President Fernando Belaunde's grandiose scheme for a $300 million Marginal Jungle Highway running north-south along the eastern slopes of the Andes through four nations), Peruvian army engineers in 1965 had to appeal to the U.S. air force to airlift in five hundred tons of heavy construction equipment, too heavy for Peruvian military planes to carry. An American engineering firm solved the same problem by bringing its equipment into Peru on barges over more than two thousand miles from the Atlantic Coast of Brazil along the Amazon River and its minor tributaries. (In recent years the Brazilian air force has been dropping paratroops into Amazon jungle clearings to build small airstrips, which can later be expanded to accommodate C-47's for scheduled airline service.)

The revolutionary thrust of the United States in creating new conditions of life has been most apparent in the Santa

[11] Two years ago, a Castroite guerrilla insurrection occurred in the Peruvian jungle area of the semi-aboriginal Campa Indians, who had wiped out several Franciscan missions in the 17th and 18th centuries. The leader of the insurrection was Guillermo Lobaton, who reportedly had been to China and Vietnam before returning to Peru and was apparently attempting to work with the warlike Campas the way General Vo Nguyen Giap worked with the mountain tribes of northeastern Vietnam during World War II. The difference, however, is that Giap worked *politically* with his tribesmen for two years before entering into combat; the Peruvian guerrillas worked with the Campas for less than six months in a very desultory fashion before ambushing a rural police patrol (killing seven), and provoking a repression by the Peruvian army that wiped out the guerrillas in six months and led to the death of hundreds of Campas. American missionaries working in the zone reported that the Peruvian air force had bombed a number of Campa villages. While the guerrilla insurgency was still alive, however, a special school was set up under AID auspices in the area to train the Peruvian rural police in counter-insurgency operations.

Cruz area of Bolivia—less than one hundred miles from where Che was killed. Here the U.S. government has invested close to $100 million since 1956, in what is now one of the few notable successes of the Alliance for Progress in regional development. This investment has financed the construction of all-weather roads, three sugar mills, and numerous schools; the clearing of twenty-five thousand acres of virgin land between 1955 and 1959 alone; and the providing of cattle, poultry, and supervised farm credit and loans for purchase of industrial and farm machinery—all this as part of the $400 million in U.S. aid to Bolivia since the 1952 revolution. The investment was sufficient to consolidate the currency (at a time of wild inflation) to the point where the country's Indian peasants were able to retain enough purchasing power to acquire, over the past fifteen years, a wide range of imported goods: shoes, bicycles, trucks, transistor radios, etc. In the Bolivian Oriente, the investment has laid important economic foundations, reinforced by the discovery of oil and natural gas in the area after Gulf Oil obtained an export concession in 1956. Both rice and sugar production have doubled between 1960 and 1964, converting Bolivia from an importer of these tropical products to a hard-pressed searcher for export markets. At the time Che's guerrilla operation was discovered last March, there were Peace Corps volunteers working in the guerrilla zone itself. Debray paid this American presence a rather stirring tribute earlier this year: [12]

> The armed guerrilla unit and the people's vanguard are not dealing with a foreign expeditionary force, with limited manpower, but with a well-established system of local domination. They [the guerrillas] themselves are the foreigners, lacking status, who at the beginning can offer the populace nothing but bloodshed and pain. Furthermore, channels of communication are increasing; airports and landing fields are being built in the most remote areas, heretofore inaccessible by land routes. On the other side of the Andes, for example, between the mountains and the Amazon basin, there is a famous highway that is meant to skirt the jungle and link up the tropical zones of Venezuela, Colombia, Peru, and Bolivia, as well as join each with its respective capital. As for North American imperialism, it has increased its forces in the field and is making every effort to present itself, not in repressive guise but in the shape of social and technical assistance: we are familiar with all the sociological projects now under way, staffed with international personnel. . . . Thousands of Peace Corpsmen have succeeded in integrating themselves in rural areas—some of them by dint of hard work, patience, and at times real sacrifices—*where they profit by the lack of political work by left-wing organizations* (my italics—N.G.). Even the most remote regions are today teeming with Catholic, Evangelical, Methodist, and Seventh Day Adventist missionaries. In a word, all of these close-knit networks of control strengthen the national machinery of domination. Without exaggerating the depth or scope of their penetration, we can say that they have indeed changed the scene.

IV

The last years of Ernesto Guevara's life were identified with two bitter causes: the creation of "two, three, many Vietnams" to pin down North American imperialism in long and debilitating struggles in as many places as possible in Latin America and elsewhere, and the parallel economic struggle between the rich nations and poor nations. In his last public speech, at an Afro-Asian economic conference in Al-

[12] Régis Debray, "Revolution in the Revolution?" *Monthly Review,* July–August 1967, pp. 52–53.

giers just before he returned to Cuba and dropped out of sight, he made a modest proposal concerning the burdens of progress within the socialist camp: [13]

> The development of the countries that now begin the road of liberation should cost the socialist countries. We say it thus, without the least spirit of blackmail or theatricality, nor for a facile appeal for greater closeness to the grouping of Afro-Asiatic countries; it is a profound conviction. Socialism cannot exist if a new collective and individual attitude is not provoked by a change in conscience of a worldwide character toward the peoples that suffer imperialist oppression. . . . How can "mutual benefit" meaning selling at world market prices the primary materials that cost limitless sweat and suffering for the backward countries, and buying at world market prices the machines produced in modern automated factories? If we establish this type of relationship between the two groups of nations, we should agree that the socialist countries are, in a certain way, accomplices of imperial exploitation. . . . The truths of socialism, and more so the crude truth of imperialism, have shaped the Cuban people and showed them the road toward Communism that later was taken voluntarily. The peoples of Asia and Africa proceeding toward their final liberation should begin the same route; they will take this road sooner or later. Although their socialism today takes one or another descriptive adjective, there is no other valid definition of socialism for us than the abolition of exploitation of man by man. . . . Our reasoning is that investments of socialist states in their own territories weigh directly on the state budget and are not recovered save through use at the end of the long manufacturing process. Our proposition is that investments of this type should be made in the underdeveloped countries. An immense force should be put in motion in our miserably exploited continents . . . to begin a new stage of the authentic international division of labor, based not in the history of what has been done until now, but in the future history of what can be done. The states in whose territories the new investments will be placed would have all the inherent rights of sovereign property over them (without any payment or credit attached), remaining obligated as possessors to supply [goods for] a determined number of years at determined prices.

The Russians must have been delighted with this proposal, having spent $1 million daily over the past six years just to keep the Cuban economy afloat, and having learned many lessons from the Cubans just by watching the marvels of their manufacturing processes! The East European People's Republics have largely begged off from diverting significant amounts of their resources to the goal of Cuba's survival, save for straight cash and barter deals and for Czech and Bulgarian technical aid programs. And the shrinking foreign aid budgets of Western governments also reflect an increasing disbelief in the revolutionary rhetoric of the "Third World"; "Westerners" are becoming peeved and bored at the incapacity of aid recipients to improvise for their own survival, and at the extraordinary variety of bastard socialisms that always seem to be stuck in the mud. The failure up to now of planned (as opposed to spontaneous) guerrilla insurrections in Latin America can only reenforce the impression left by the Chinese fiasco in Indonesia and the disarray created by the "Cultural Revolution" inside China itself. On the latter event, the *Economist* editorialized: [14]

> What has been happening in China since the summer is the end of the road that started in Paris in 1789. We are seeing the last stages of the revolutionary cycle that began in France, was checked in central Europe in 1848, and picked up impetus

[13] *Politica* (Mexico) March 1, 1965.
[14] "The Last Revolution," January 14, 1967.

again in Russia in 1917. It continued its eastward march in 1949, when it reached China, and it is in China that it finally seems to be working itself out. The ideas behind the social revolutions of the past two hundred years have changed their shape as the center of the storm has moved steadily eastward. The revolutionary doctrine first picked up Marxism, and now Mao Tse-tung's reinterpretation of Marxism. But the assumption shared by all revolutionaries throughout the whole period has been their belief that a radical act of violence will burst open the door to a better society: that the way to a juster form of government necessarily lies over the exploded ruins of the old order. It is this belief that Chairman Mao has now finally and perhaps decisively put in doubt.

If this editorial is any sort of guide to emergent "Western" attitudes, what we seem to be heading toward in the very near future is an exchange of the social evangelism of the first half of this century for a perversion of the old Calvinist doctrine of the Elect. This "social Calvinism" represents the belief that a large portion of humanity—a clear majority—is naturally and irremediably condemned to the lower depths of poverty and misery, and that the more powerful elect of mankind can and must keep the condemned in place by force of arms. In the elect societies there is a high coincidence between social justice and individual "human rights," which are anchored in private property. The poorer societies are struggling with the seemingly intractable problems of a scarcity of capital and natural resources and of cultural poverty; these problems have impeded the development of better economic organization to deal with the pressures of proliferating marginal populations. Under these conditions, individual liberties are less prized, private property is coveted by the disenfranchised, and "Western" traditions of liberty and property tend to conflict with collective pressures for social justice. The "Western" response, understandably, is that what we have must be preserved in good condition and, for the rest, there just isn't enough to go around.

Recent developments in Latin America, indeed, have led many to believe that "revolutionary" pressures of the type generated in poor societies can be easily contained. It is probable, for instance, that the guerrilla forces in several countries, despite their own weaknesses, would have scored a much wider success if the Latin American regular armies opposing them had not been back-stopped by large amounts of U.S. military aid and advice. Since 1950, the U.S. has provided roughly $1.5 billion in military aid to Latin American armies, mostly in arms donations; in one place alone—Fort Gulick, Panama—the U.S. has trained more than eighteen thousand Latin American military men in counter-insurgency techniques. On April 6, 1966, General Robert W. Porter, chief of the U.S. Army Southern Command in Panama, explained the value of the military aid program before the Foreign Affairs Committee of the House of Representatives. He said the program was "austere in the light of U.S. objectives, Latin American military needs, and the total U.S. effort in Latin America. The cost is only 3.9 per cent of the total U.S. effort, and I believe that 3.9 per cent is a low premium rate for the insurance received."

In Guatemala, to take but one example, the presence of U.S. military advisers in the guerrilla zone has been reported by foreign missionary priests and by guerrillas themselves. U.S. officers, some of Cuban and Puerto Rican descent, were reported accompanying Guatemalan army patrols. General Porter revealed in his testimony that U.S. army engineers were engaged in the guerrilla zone in a "civic-action" program of public works, and were being helped in their work by U.S. army Special Forces officers with Vietnam experience. "In [neighboring] Honduras the [U.S.] engineer battalion is also working up in the high country along the Guatemalan border," Porter said. "This is a part where you don't know where the border is." Earlier this year, a correspondent for the *Economist* described how the Guatemalan counter-insurgency drive subsequently developed: [15]

The clean-up of the guerrilla zone has been carried out in military style by a proliferating number of right-wing terrorist groups. Some of these are phantom organizations under whose name soldiers in civilian dress carry out their more grisly operations. The principal terrorist organization, the "White Hand," is a creature of the *Movimiento de Liberacion Nacional*. In 1954, the MLN spearheaded the CIA-organized invasion from Honduras which, with the connivance of the Guatemalan military high command, overthrew the pro-Communist regime of Col. Jacobo Arbenz. Since last July the MLN leaders in the Oriente and many of their followers have been disappearing into Honduras. A new low-range radio station, Radio America, based in Honduras, has been warning peasants of a new invasion with massive American support. The Americans have made no visible move, but the White Hand's anti-Communist vigilantes in the Oriente have received roughly two-thousand rifles and machine guns which were given to the Guatemalan army under the American military aid program. These weapons have been used in the slaughter of guerrilla collaborators and sympathizers in the towns and villages along the Atlantic Highway, where guerrillas used to harass trucking and troop movements with near impunity. Since the army began its offensive, between forty and fifty of the estimated two hundred to three hundred hard-core guerrilla fighters have been killed. Army sources have put the death toll at roughly two thousand in the eastern departments of Zacapa and Isabal, the central area of rebel activity. The surviving rebels have withdrawn into a deeper portion of the thicket, or into Guatemala City. Captured guerrillas in black hoods are now accompanying army patrols in order to point out those who have collaborated with the insurgents, as well as guerrilla campsites and buried arms deposits. As a result, rebel activity has dropped to almost nothing in recent weeks, and the leaders of the MLN have begun to talk of a "definitive solution." . . . The violence of recent months is believed to have claimed more lives than all the insurgent activity of the past five years.[16]

V

Most revolutions are born of war, and others of foreign intervention. "When the enemy comes we fight, when he goes we plough," wrote the great North Vietnamese strategist Truong Chinh in 1947 at the beginning of the Vietminh war with the French.[17] The fusion of nationalism and social vindication in the scramble of global war produced the wave of revolutions issuing from World War II (China, Vietnam, Egypt, India, Burma, Indonesia, Malaya, the Philippines, Algeria, Greece, Yugoslavia, and Kenya), nearly all in countries that were hosts to the greater conflict, with foreign troops fighting on their soil and the "democratic" propaganda of the Allies vying for the support of colonial and semicolonial populations. The Bolshevik revolution in Russia and the Nazi revolution in Germany issued from national defeats in World War I, with Lenin and

[15] "Guatemala: Death in the Hills," June 10, 1967.

[16] On May 9, Guatemala's Catholic Bishops' Council issued a statement which said: "We cannot remain indifferent, while entire populations are decimated, while each day leaves new widows and orphans who are victims of mysterious struggles and vendettas, while men are seized in their houses by unknown kidnappers and are detained in unknown places or are vilely assassinated, their bodies appearing later horribly mutilated." *Grafica* (Guatemala) May 10, 1967.

[17] "The Resistance Will Win," in Truong Chinh, *Primer for Revolt*, Praeger, 1963.

Hitler both using returning war veterans and "treason" propaganda in what have become classic techniques of agitation. Similarly in Bolivia, it was returning veterans from the disastrous Chaco War (1932–35) with Paraguay who started the major events in motion. Like the Russians at the front in World War I, the Bolivian veterans included intellectuals as well as illiterate peasants (mostly Indians who had left Andean villages and haciendas for the first time to fight a dimly understood war, in an inhospitable lowland desert, under a military leadership whose corruption and incompetence dissipated the Bolivian advantage in numbers). The mobilization of 250,000 Bolivians for war (56,000 died, 10,000 deserted, and 17,000 were taken prisoner) gave many their first sense of nationhood; Bolivia's humiliating territorial loss to Paraguay provoked widespread reflections on national destiny and sent thousands of veterans home to organize peasant and miners' *sindicatos* as well as radical political movements that were the engines of the social revolutions of 1946 and 1952.

The rural slaughter this year in Guatemala is somewhat reminiscent of the World War II anti-Communist "extermination" campaigns carried out in China and Yugoslavia by the Japanese and Nazi armies, which drove thousands of peasants to seek refuge in the ranks of Mao's and Tito's partisans.[18] It also recalls the incredible campaign in Colombia—led by Conservative President Laureano Gomez, a starchy oligarch impressed by the Fascist success in Spain—to eliminate the Liberal party by sending the police to kill, burn, and destroy crops (especially coffee trees) in rural Liberal areas. This in turn led to what has become known as the *violencia,* the savage tribal warfare between Liberals and Conservatives which in ten years (1948–58) cost some two hundred thousand lives and sent many more peasants for refuge in the proliferating slums of Colombia's cities, the five largest of which doubled in population between 1950 and 1965.

Not long ago, in a wildly-vegetated ravine of the Cordillera de los Cobardes in the mountains of eastern Colombia, I met a peasant named Juan Prada, a lean man in his late fifties with narrow, ironic eyes, taut lips, and a hairless face. Prada had been a Liberal "soldier" in the *violencia,* and had followed a former Liberal police chief named Rafael Rangel Gomez who was subsequently elected to Congress. Since 1958, he had been organizing peasant "self-defense committees" in collaboration with some Communist labor leaders from nearby oilfields. He still walked with the exaggerated swagger common in those mountains. Above a boxwood table in his unfinished straw hut was an old photo of a group of armed men, including himself, in khaki peasant clothes and cheap Panama hats, with ammunition belts and blankets draped over one shoulder and old rifles of many kinds posed in their hands for the photographer. "I saw the police carry their dead in burlap bags down from the hills to the town of San Vicente de Chucuri," Juan Prada told me. "They came into the hills—uniformed policemen, detectives, revenue agents, and peasant bands from Conservative villages—to take Liberal peasants from their houses in the middle of the night. They were marched to the edge of a ravine and either beheaded or shot. On many farms the cattle were led away by these bands. Entire harvests were stolen and entire plots of coffee trees, which take so many years to bring into cultivation, were burned. Many peasants were frightened

[18] An excellent comparative account of these wartime movements is given in Chalmers A. Johnson, *Peasant Nationalism and Communist Power,* Stanford, 1962.

of such a death. They had no way to live but to go to the hills. I had a small piece of land in Rio Sucio when the *violencia* began in Santander. My woman had gone away and my two little boys had died before, but I took my little girl called Yolanda—who was seven years old—into the mountains with me when the *violencia* began. I carried my little girl with me through the forests with the Liberal guerrillas for two years. All that we took with us was rifles and cartridges, and we slept on the ground. Very little food was grown in the country."

It is hard under these circumstances to talk of a "definitive solution." But we should, for a start, consider the spontaneous character of most revolutionary developments in Latin America, where "Marxism" evidently has come with too little, too late, and has extended itself far beyond its bases of intellectual and material supply. Throughout the world, these major social conflicts are activated, if not by war itself, then by some other jolt. In this connection it might also be opportune to cite Lin Piao's prophecy [19] that "U.S. imperialism, like a mad bull dashing from place to place, will finally be burned to ashes in the blazing fires of the people's wars it has provoked by its own actions."

If we were to take this remark seriously, and adjust our sights accordingly to the "spontaneous" rather than to the "ideological" aspects of social revolution, we would, I believe, be in a better position to reap the advantages of revolutionary aspirations in underdeveloped societies. Let me offer but one example. All Castroite guerrilla insurgencies in Latin America, including Castro's own rising in Cuba's Sierra Maestra, have occurred in or very near coffee-growing areas [20] with dispersed hillbilly populations living on *minifundia* (tiny subsistence plots) where endemic conflicts between landlord and peasant have been aggravated by declining world coffee prices. Colombia President Carlos Lleras Restrepo said last year in an interview: "I believe *minifundia* are far more dangerous politically than *latifundia* [great estates]. These increasingly smaller properties cannot maintain a family, and the *minifundia* problem is constantly aggravated by the divisions imposed by inheritance laws and by the powerful demographic explosion [doubling Colombia's population every twenty-five years], creating a class of 'proletarian proprietors' with even lower incomes than the miserable sugar cane cutters." Lleras claimed that the fall in world coffee prices has cut Colombia's per capita export income from $53 in 1964 to $32 in 1966. A 1965 survey of Latin America by the *Economist* said the region has never recovered from the world depression of the late 1920's: between 1928 and 1932, Latin America's exports dropped by nearly 60 per cent, and the real per capita value of its exports (excluding those of oil-rich Venezuela) are now only 32 per cent of what they were in 1928. Food production, moreover, has been declining in relation to population growth. Under these circumstances, it may be wiser to devote more energy toward developing a substitute for this moribund coffee economy than to try to convert "counter-insurgency" into a viable political doctrine.

In the meantime, while guerrilla movements in Latin America so far have failed to demonstrate, in Lin Piao's words, that "the countryside, and the countryside alone, can provide the revolutionary bases from which the revolutionaries can go forward to final vic-

[19] "Long Live the Victory of the People's War!" *Peking Review,* September 3, 1965.
[20] The only exception was Che's Bolivia experiment.

tory," the region's cities are developing a revolutionary profile strikingly similar to that of the European urban concentrations at the time of the popular revolts of 1848 and 1871. Professor William L. Langer has written on the subject: [21]

> In the years from 1800 to 1850 the growth of the European capitals was stupendous, with the result that at the end of the period a large proportion of the population was not native-born. It consisted largely of immigrants, permanent or temporary, coming either from nearby areas or abroad. In the 1840's alone about 250,000 persons came into London, 46,000 of whom were Irishmen, who were particularly disliked and feared by the English workers because of their incredibly low standard of living. As for Paris, the number of inhabitants just about doubled between 1800 and 1850, due very largely to immigration. . . . Most of the newcomers were from the neighboring departments, but there were many foreigners as well. . . . The situation in Vienna and Berlin was much the same. Overall conditions in the crowded cities of the early or mid-19th century were such as to create chronic social tension. . . .

Following the 1848 revolutions, Marx wrote that "Europe has taken on a form that makes every fresh proletarian upheaval in France directly coincide with a world war." [22] In Latin America, the two world wars have generated or coincided with major upheavals in Mexico, Guatemala, Venezuela, Colombia, Peru, Bolivia, and Argentina. The effect of the great agrarian revolutions (and land reform programs) has been a proliferation of tiny and (eventually) desiccated peasant subsistence plots which, even in their uneconomic form, have failed to keep pace with the growth of the rural population. Studies by Mexicans predict a rural population including five million landless peasants in the not-too-distant future; [23] 27 million Mexicans of a total population of 45 million have a monthly family income of less than $10—this at a time of spectacular economic growth with per capita income having doubled since 1940 (despite a doubling of the population during the same period). The great Mexican land reform of the 1930's and 1940's drew the peasant back into primeval village life (the basic unit of land distribution was the communal *ejido*) while industrialization with depressed wages permitted large capital accumulations in the postwar years, after Mexico had served as an international money haven in World War II. Yet Mexico seems to be approaching a Malthusian bottleneck, not so much because of population growth as because of a lack of sufficient land and water to keep the proliferating peasant population in agriculture. Thus the complex and expensive land reclamation projects in Mexico's northwest desert-states of Sonora and Sinaloa have been imperiled in recent years by a decline in the underground water table as a consequence of the use of deep-draft mechanical pumps for agriculture. The scarcity of arable land, and the rising urban living standards, have sent the peasants scurrying for the cities—which now double in population roughly every seventeen years—and for the border towns along the U.S. frontier, which have increased fivefold in population over the past generation. If Mexico is an indicator, within a relatively few years Latin America will have developed such heavy urban slum concentrations, and

[21] William L. Langer, "The Pattern of Urban Revolution in 1848," in *French Society and Culture Since the Old Regime,* Holt, Rinehart & Winston, 1966.

[22] Marx, "The Class Struggles in France," 1850.

[23] "Mexico: South of the Border," by Mary Goldring. The *Economist,* May 13, 1967.

disposable land for agrarian reform will have become so scarce, that for the first time in our century land reform will cease to be a meaningful revolutionary banner.

The long march of Latin America's rural population is one of the great social epics of the postwar years, and one to which both "Marxist" and "Western" political thought have given very scant attention. According to the Inter-American Economic and Social Council, 37 per cent of the region's urban population (130 million) live in squatter slums, and this figure will rise to 43 per cent (216 million) by 1980. The population of Santo Domingo doubled during the 1950's alone, and is expected to have doubled again by 1968; a full-scale inundation has occurred since the 1961 assassination of Rafael Trujillo. In the crowded warrens of wood-and-cardboard shacks beneath the Duarte Bridge, where the slumdwellers of Santo Domingo defeated crack tank and infantry units of the Dominican armed forces in the April 1965 revolution, unemployment has reached 90 per cent among adult males in some *barrios,* and the people talk constantly of resuming their revolution as if the fight against the Americans had been their finest hour. The American "anti-Communist" intervention in 1965 to save the Dominican army attempted to stop the revolutionary effervescence uncorked when the CIA supplied the arms for the Trujillo assassination four years before.[24] The whole episode recalled the words of Ho Chi Minh when he was an obscure Indochinese exile in Moscow in 1923: "They began hunting down Communists among the Annamese peasantry at a time when there wasn't a trace of a Communist. And that way they spread the propaganda." [25]

Other capitals in the hemisphere offer the same perspective. Lima has tripled in population since 1940, with hordes of *cholos* (Indians converting to Hispanic culture) subverting the old Viceregal social structure which had stayed intact for four centuries. Since 1936, Venezuela's demographic pattern has shifted from 70 per cent rural to more than 70 per cent urban (Caracas having doubled in population since 1950), and virtually every major city in the region is growing by at least 5 per cent yearly. In rural areas, feudalism has been abolished and for the first time peasants are acquiring radios,[26] schools, roads, store-bought clothes, bicycles, shoes, trucks, and buses; after acquiring these things they move even faster into the cities. In Latin America one must distinguish between informal and formal revolution; that is, between spectacular social change and the seizure of political power by a "Marxist" revolutionary organization. In view of this distinction, the legacy of Ernesto Guevara may turn out to be other than it at first appears. While the guerrillas have so far failed, the revolution is in full career; what is lacking today is the leadership of a revolutionary party.

[24] See my "How Trujillo Died," the *New Republic,* April 13, 1961.

[25] "An Interview with Ho Chi Minh—1923," by Osip Mandelstam. *Commentary,* August 1967.

[26] The USIA has estimated that there are 38.6 million radio sets in Latin America—a ratio of almost one to a family.

Robert L. Heilbroner teaches economics at the New School for Social Research in New York and is well known for his books *The Great Ascent*, *The Limits of American Capitalism*, and *The Future As History*, among many others. He turns in this essay to the question of why the United States, in this age of revolution, is generally allied everywhere with conservative forces and powers.

Counterrevolutionary America

ROBERT L. HEILBRONER

Is the United States fundamentally opposed to economic development? The question is outrageous. Did we not coin the phrase, "the revolution of rising expectations"? Have we not supported the cause of development more generously than any nation on earth, spent our intellectual energy on the problems of development, offered our expertise freely to the backward nations of the world? How can it possibly be suggested that the United States might be opposed to economic development?

The answer is that we are not at all opposed to what we conceive economic development to be. The process depicted by the "revolution of rising expectations" is a deeply attractive one. It conjures up the image of a peasant in some primitive land, leaning on his crude plow and looking to the horizon, where he sees dimly, but for the *first time* (and that is what is so revolutionary about it), the vision of a better life. From this electrifying vision comes the necessary catalysis to change an old and stagnant way of life. The pace of work quickens. Innovations, formerly feared and resisted, are now eagerly accepted. The obstacles are admittedly very great —whence the need for foreign assistance —but under the impetus of new hopes the economic mechanism begins to turn faster, to gain traction against the environment. Slowly, but surely, the Great Ascent begins.

There is much that is admirable about this well-intentioned popular view of "the revolution of rising expectations." Unfortunately, there is more that is delusive about it. For the buoyant appeal of its rhetoric conceals or passes in silence over by far the larger part of the spectrum of realities of the development process. One of these is the certainty that the revolutionary aspect of development will not be limited to the realm of ideas, but will vent its fury on institutions, social classes, and innocent men and women. Another is the great likelihood that the ideas needed to guide the revolution will not only be affirmative and reasonable, but also destructive and fanatic. A third is the realization that revolutionary efforts cannot be made, and certainly cannot be sustained, by voluntary effort alone, but require an iron hand, in the spheres both of economic direction and political control. And the fourth and most difficult of these realities to face is the probability that the political force most likely to succeed in carrying through the gigantic historical transformation of development is some form of extreme national collectivism or Communism.

In a word, what our rhetoric fails to bring to our attention is the likelihood that development will require policies and programs repugnant to our "way of life," that it will bring to the fore governments hostile to our international objectives, and that its regnant ideology will bitterly oppose capitalism as a system of world economic power. If that is the case, we would have to think twice before denying that the United States was fundamentally opposed to economic development.

But is it the case? Must development lead in directions that go counter to the present American political philosophy? Let me try to indicate, albeit much too briefly and summarily, the reasons that lead me to answer that question as I do.

I begin with the cardinal point, often noted but still insufficiently appreciated, that the process called "economic development" is not primarily economic at all. We think of development as a campaign of production to be fought with budgets and monetary policies and measured with indices of output and income. But the development process is much wider and deeper than can be indicated by such statistics. To be sure, in the end what is hoped for is a tremendous rise in output. But this will not come to pass until a series of tasks, at once cruder and more delicate, simpler and infinitely more difficult, has been commenced and carried along a certain distance.

In most of the new nations of Africa, these tasks consist in establishing the very underpinnings of nationhood itself—in determining national borders, establishing national languages, arousing a basic national (as distinguished from tribal) self-consciousness. Before these steps have been taken, the African states will remain no more than names insecurely affixed to the map, not social entities capable of undertaking an enormous collective venture in economic change. In Asia, nationhood is generally much further advanced than in Africa, but here the main impediment to development is the miasma of apathy and fatalism, superstition and distrust that vitiates every attempt to improve hopelessly inefficient modes of work and patterns of resource use: while India starves, a quarter of the world's cow population devours Indian crops, exempt either from effective employment or slaughter because of sacred taboos. In still other areas, mainly Latin America, the principal handicap to development is not an absence of national identity or the presence of suffocating cultures (although the latter certainly plays its part), but the cramping and crippling inhibitions of obsolete social institutions and reactionary social classes. Where landholding rather than industrial activity is still the basis for social and economic power, and where land is held essentially in fiefdoms rather than as productive real estate, it is not surprising that so much of society retains a medieval cast.

Thus, development is much more than a matter of encouraging economic growth within a given social structure. It is rather the *modernization* of that structure, a process of ideational, social, economic, and political change that requires the remaking of society in its most intimate as well as its most public attributes.[1] When we speak of the revolutionary nature of economic development, it is this kind of deeply penetrative change that we mean—change that reorganizes "normal" ways of thought, established patterns of family life, and structures of village authority as well as class and caste privilege.

What is so egregiously lacking in the great majority of the societies that are

[1] See C. E. Black, *The Dynamics of Modernization.*

now attempting to make the Great Ascent is precisely this pervasive modernization. The trouble with India and Pakistan, with Brazil and Ecuador, with the Philippines and Ethiopia, is not merely that economic growth lags, or proceeds at some pitiable pace. This is only a symptom of deeper-lying ills. The trouble is that the social physiology of these nations remains so depressingly unchanged despite the flurry of economic planning on top. The all-encompassing ignorance and poverty of the rural regions, the unbridgeable gulf between the peasant and the urban elites, the resistive conservatism of the village elders, the unyielding traditionalism of family life—all these remain obdurately, maddeningly, disastrously unchanged. In the cities, a few modern buildings, sometimes brilliantly executed, give a deceptive patina of modernity, but once one journeys into the immense countryside, the terrible stasis overwhelms all.

To this vast landscape of apathy and ignorance one must now make an exception of the very greatest importance. It is the fact that a very few nations, all of them Communist, have succeeded in reaching into the lives and stirring the minds of precisely that body of the peasantry which constitutes the insuperable problem elsewhere. In our concentration on the politics, the betrayals, the successes and failures of the Russian, Chinese, and Cuban revolutions, we forget that their central motivation has been just such a war *à l'outrance* against the arch-enemy of backwardness—not alone the backwardness of outmoded social superstructures but even more critically that of private inertia and traditionalism.

That the present is irreversibly and unqualifiedly freed from the dead hand of the past is, I think, beyond argument in the case of Russia. By this I do not only mean that Russia has made enormous economic strides. I refer rather to the gradual emancipation of its people from the "idiocy of rural life," their gradual entrance upon the stage of contemporary existence. This is not to hide in the smallest degree the continuing backwardness of the Russian countryside where now almost fifty—*and formerly perhaps eighty*—per cent of the population lives. But even at its worst I do not think that life could now be described in the despairing terms that run through the Russian literature of our grandfathers' time. Here is Chekhov:

> During the summer and the winter there had been hours and days when it seemed as if these people [the peasants] lived worse than cattle, and it was terrible to be with them. They were coarse, dishonest, dirty, and drunken; they did not live at peace with one another but quarreled continually, because they feared, suspected, and despised one another. . . . Crushing labor that made the whole body ache at night, cruel winters, scanty crops, overcrowding, and no help, and nowhere to look for help.

It is less certain that the vise of the past has been loosened in China or Cuba. It may well be that Cuba has suffered a considerable economic decline, in part due to absurd planning, in part to our refusal to buy her main crop. The economic record of China is nearly as inscrutable as its political turmoil, and we may not know for many years whether the Chinese peasant is today better or worse off than before the revolution. Yet what strikes me as significant in both countries is something else. In Cuba it is the educational effort that, according to the New York *Times,* has constituted a major effort of the Castro regime. In China it is the unmistakable evidence—and here I lean not alone on the sympathetic account of Edgar Snow but on the most horrified descriptions of the rampages of the Red Guards—that the younger generation is no longer fettered by the traditional view of things. The very fact that the Red Guards now revile their elders, an unthinkable defiance of age-old Chinese custom, is testimony of how deeply change has penetrated into the texture of Chinese life.

It is this herculean effort to reach and rally the great anonymous mass of the population that is *the* great accomplishment of Communism—even though it is an accomplishment that is still only partially accomplished. For if the areas of the world afflicted with the self-perpetuating disease of backwardness are ever to rid themselves of its debilitating effects, I think it is likely to be not merely because antiquated social structures have been dismantled (although this is an essential precondition), but because some shock treatment like that of Communism has been administered to them.

By way of contrast to this all-out effort, however short it may have fallen of its goal, we must place the timidity of the effort to bring modernization to the peoples of the non-Communist world. Here again I do not merely speak of lagging rates of growth. I refer to the fact that illiteracy in the non-Communist countries of Asia and Central America is increasing (by some 200 million in the last decade) because it has been "impossible" to mount an educational effort that will keep pace with population growth. I refer to the absence of substantial land reform in Latin America, despite how many years of promises. I refer to the indifference or incompetence or corruption of governing elites: the incredible sheiks with their oildoms; the vague, well-meaning leaders of India unable to break the caste system, kill the cows, control the birthrate, reach the villages, house or employ the labor rotting on the streets; the cynical governments of South America, not one of which, according to Lleras Camargo, former president of Colombia, has ever prosecuted a single politician or industrialist for evasion of taxes. And not least, I refer to the fact that every movement that arises to correct these conditions is instantly identified as "Communist" and put down with every means at hand, while the United States clucks or nods approval.

To be sure, even in the most petrified societies, the modernization process is at work. If there were time, the solvent acids of the 20th century would work their way on the ideas and institutions of the most inert or resistant countries. But what lacks in the 20th century is time. The multitudes of the underdeveloped world have only in the past two decades been summoned to their reveille. The one thing that is certain about the revolution of rising expectations is that it is only in its inception, and that its pressures for justice and action will steadily mount as the voice of the 20th century penetrates to villages and slums where it is still almost inaudible. It is not surprising that Princeton historian C. E. Black, surveying this labile world, estimates that we must anticipate "ten to fifteen revolutions a year for the foreseeable future in the less developed societies."

In itself, this prospect of mounting political restiveness enjoins the speediest possible time schedule for development. But this political urgency is many times compounded by that of the population problem. Like an immense river in flood, the number of human beings rises each year to wash away the levees of the preceding year's labors and to pose future requirements of monstrous proportions. To provide shelter for the three billion human beings who will arrive on earth in the next forty years will require as many dwellings as have been constructed since recorded history began. To feed them will take double the world's present output of food. To cope with the mass exodus from the overcrowded countryside will necessitate cities of grotesque size—Calcutta, now a cesspool of three to five millions, threatens us by the year 2000 with a prospective population of from thirty to sixty millions.

These horrific figures spell one importunate message: haste. That is the *mene mene, tekel upharsin* written on the walls of government planning offices around the world. Even if the miracle of the loop is realized—the new contraceptive device that promises the first real breakthrough in population control—we must set ourselves for at least another generation of rampant increase.

But how to achieve haste? How to convince the silent and disbelieving men, how to break through the distrustful glances of women in black shawls, how to overcome the overt hostility of landlords, the opposition of the Church, the petty bickerings of military cliques, the black-marketeering of commercial dealers? I suspect there is only one way. The conditions of backwardness must be attacked with the passion, the ruthlessness, and the messianic fury of a jehad, a Holy War. Only a campaign of an intensity and single-mindedness that must approach the ludicrous and the unbearable offers the chance to ride roughshod over the resistance of the rich and the poor alike and to open the way for the forcible implantation of those modern attitudes and techniques without which there will be no escape from the misery of underdevelopment.

I need hardly add that the cost of this modernization process has been and will be horrendous. If Communism is the great modernizer, it is certainly not a benign agent of change. Stalin may well have exceeded Hitler as a mass executioner. Free inquiry in China has been supplanted by dogma and catechism; even in Russia nothing like freedom of criticism or of personal expression is allowed. Furthermore, the economic cost of industrialization in both countries has been at least as severe as that imposed by primitive capitalism.

Yet one must count the gains as well as the losses. Hundreds of millions who would have been confined to the narrow cells of changeless lives have been liberated from prisons they did not even know existed. Class structures that elevated the flighty or irresponsible have been supplanted by others that have promoted the ambitious and the dedicated. Economic systems that gave rise to luxury and poverty have given way to systems that provide a rough distributional justice. Above all, the prospect of a new future has been opened. It is this that lifts the current ordeal in China above the level of pure horror. The number of human beings in that country who have perished over the past centuries from hunger or neglect, is beyond computation. The present revolution may add its dreadful increment to this number. But it also holds out the hope that China may finally have been galvanized into social, political, and economic attitudes that for the first time make its modernization a possibility.

Two questions must be answered when we dare to risk so favorable a verdict on Communism as a modernizing agency. The first is whether the result is worth the cost, whether the possible—by no means assured—escape from underdevelopment is worth the lives that will be squandered to achieve it.

I do not know how one measures the moral price of historical victories or how one can ever decide that a diffuse gain is worth a sharp and particular loss. I only know that the way in which we ordinarily keep the books of history is wrong. No one is now toting up the balance of the wretches who starve in India, or the peasants of Northeastern Brazil who live in the swamps on crabs, or the undernourished and permanently stunted children of Hong Kong or Honduras. Their sufferings go unrecorded, and are not present to counterbalance the scales when the furies of revolution strike down their victims. Barrington

Moore has made a nice calculation that bears on this problem. Taking as the weight in one pan the 35,000 to 40,000 persons who lost their lives—mainly for no fault of theirs—as a result of the Terror during the French Revolution, he asks what would have been the death rate from preventable starvation and injustice under the *ancien regime* to balance the scales. "Offhand," he writes, "it seems unlikely that this would be very much below the proportion of .0010 which [the] figure of 40,000 yields when set against an estimated population of 24 million." [2]

Is it unjust to charge the *ancien regime* in Russia with ten million preventable deaths? I think it not unreasonable. To charge the authorities in pre-revolutionary China with equally vast and preventable degradations? Theodore White, writing in 1946, had this to say: ". . . some scholars think that China is perhaps the only country in the world where the people eat less, live more bitterly, and are clothed worse than they were five hundred years ago." [3]

I do not recommend such a calculus of corpses—indeed, I am aware of the license it gives to the unscrupulous—but I raise it to show the onesidedness of our protestations against the brutality and violence of revolutions. In this regard, it is chastening to recall the multitudes who have been killed or mutilated by the Church which is now the first to protest against the excesses of Communism.

But there is an even more terrible second question to be asked. It is clear beyond doubt, however awkward it may be for our moralizing propensities, that historians excuse horror that succeeds; and that we write our comfortable books of moral philosophy, seated atop a mound of victims—slaves, serfs, laboring men and women, heretics, dissenters—who were crushed in the course of preparing the way for our triumphal entry into existence. But at least we are here to vindicate the carnage. What if we were not? What if the revolutions grind flesh and blood and produce nothing, if the end of the convulsion is not exhilaration but exhaustion, not triumph but defeat?

Before this possibility—which has been realized more than once in history—one stands mute. Mute, but not paralyzed. For there is the necessity of calculating what is likely to happen in the absence of the revolution whose prospective excesses hold us back. Here one must weigh what has been done to remedy underdevelopment—and what has not been done—in the past twenty years; how much time there remains before the population flood enforces its own ultimate solution; what is the likelihood of bringing modernization without the frenzied assault that Communism seems most capable of mounting. As I make this mental calculation I arrive at an answer which is even more painful than that of revolution. I see the alternative as the continuation, without substantial relief—and indeed with a substantial chance of deterioration—of the misery and meanness of life as it is now lived in the sinkhole of the world's backward regions.

I have put the case for the necessity of revolution as strongly as possible, but I must now widen the options beyond the stark alternatives I have posed. To begin with, there are areas of the world where the immediate tasks are so far-reaching that little more can be expected for some decades than the primary missions of national identification and unification. Most of the new African states fall into this category. These states may suffer capitalist, Communist,

[2] *Social Origins of Dictatorship and Democracy,* p. 104.
[3] *Thunder Out of China,* p. 32.

Fascist, or other kinds of regimes during the remainder of this century, but whatever the nominal ideology in the saddle, the job at hand will be that of military and political nation-making.

There is another group of nations, less easy to identify, but much more important in the scale of events, where my analysis also does not apply. These are countries where the pressures of population growth seem sufficiently mild, or the existing political and social framework sufficiently adaptable, to allow for the hope of considerable progress without resort to violence. Greece, Turkey, Chile, Argentina, Mexico may be representatives of nations in this precarious but enviable situation. Some of them, incidentally, have already had revolutions of modernizing intent—fortunately for them in a day when the United States was not so frightened or so powerful as to be able to repress them.

In other words, the great arena of desperation to which the revolutionizing impetus of Communism seems most applicable is primarily the crowded land masses and archipelagoes of Southeast Asia and the impoverished areas of Central and South America. But even here, there is the possibility that the task of modernization may be undertaken by non-Communist elites. There is always the example of indigenous, independent leaders who rise up out of nowhere to overturn the established framework and to galvanize the masses—a Gandhi, a Marti, a pre-1958 Castro. Or there is that fertile ground for the breeding of national leaders—the army, as witness Ataturk or Nasser, among many.[4]

Thus there is certainly no inherent necessity that the revolutions of modernization be led by Communists. But it is well to bear two thoughts in mind when we consider the likely course of non-Communist revolutionary sweeps. The first is the nature of the mobilizing appeal of any successful revolutionary elite. Is it the austere banner of saving and investment that waves over the heads of the shouting marchers in Jakarta and Bombay, Cairo and Havana? It most certainly is not. The banner of economic development is that of nationalism, with its promise of personal immortality and collective majesty. It seems beyond question that a feverish nationalism will charge the atmosphere of any nation, Communist or not, that tries to make the Great Ascent—and as a result we must expect the symptoms of nationalism along with the disease: exaggerated xenophobia, a thin-skinned national sensitivity, a search for enemies as well as a glorification of the state.

These symptoms, which we have already seen in every quarter of the globe, make it impossible to expect easy and amicable relations between the developing states and the colossi of the developed world. No conceivable response on the part of America or Europe or, for that matter, Russia, will be able to play up to the vanities or salve the irritations of the emerging nations, much less satisfy their demands for help. Thus, we must anticipate an anti-American, or anti-Western, possibly even anti-white animus from any nation in the throes of modernization, even if it is not parroting Communist dogma.

Then there is a second caution as to the prospects for non-Communist revolutions. This is the question of what ideas and policies will guide their revo-

[4] What are the chances for modernizing revolutions of the Right, such as those of the Meiji Restoration or of Germany under Bismarck? I think they are small. The changes to be wrought in the areas of greatest backwardness are much more socially subversive than those of the 19th century, and the timespan allotted to the revolutionists is much smaller. Bourgeois revolutions are not apt to go far enough, particularly in changing property ownership. Still, one could imagine such revolutions with armed support and no doubt Fascistic ideologies. I doubt that they would be any less of a threat than revolutions of the Left.

lutionary efforts. Revolutions, especially if their whole orientation is to the future, require philosophy equally as much as force. It is here, of course, that Communism finds its special strength. The vocabulary in which it speaks—a vocabulary of class domination, of domestic and international exploitation—is rich in meaning to the backward nations. The view of history it espouses provides the support of historical inevitability to the fallible efforts of struggling leaders. Not least, the very dogmatic certitude and ritualistic repetition that stick in the craw of the Western observer offer the psychological assurances on which an unquestioning faith can be maintained.

If a non-Communist elite is to persevere in tasks that will prove Sisyphean in difficulty, it will also have to offer a philosophical interpretation of its role as convincing and elevating, and a diagnosis of social and economic requirements as sharp and simplistic, as that of Communism. Further, its will to succeed at whatever cost must be as firm as that of the Marxists. It is not impossible that such a philosophy can be developed, more or less independent of formal Marxian conceptions. It is likely, however, to resemble the creed of Communism far more than that of the West. Political liberty, economic freedom, and constitutional law may be the great achievements and the great issues of the most advanced nations, but to the least developed lands they are only dim abstractions, or worse, rationalizations behind which the great powers play their imperialist tricks or protect the privileges of their monied classes.

Thus, even if for many reasons we should prefer the advent of non-Communist modernizing elites, we must realize that they too will present the United States with programs and policies antipathetic to much that America "believes in" and hostile to America as a world power. The leadership needed to mount a jehad against backwardness—and it is my main premise that only a Holy War will begin modernization in our time—will be forced to expound a philosophy that approves authoritarian and collectivist measures at home and that utilizes as the target for its national resentment abroad the towering villains of the world, of which the United States is now Number One.

All this confronts American policymakers and public opinion with a dilemma of a totally unforeseen kind. On the one hand we are eager to assist in the rescue of the great majority of mankind from conditions that we recognize as dreadful and ultimately dangerous. On the other hand, we seem to be committed, especially in the underdeveloped areas, to a policy of defeating Communism wherever it is within our military capacity to do so, and of repressing movements that might become Communist if they were allowed to follow their internal dynamics. Thus, we have on the one side the record of Point Four, the Peace Corps, and foreign aid generally; and on the other, Guatemala, Cuba, the Dominican Republic, and now Vietnam.

That these two policies might be in any way mutually incompatible, that economic development might contain revolutionary implications infinitely more far-reaching than those we have so blandly endorsed in the name of rising expectations, that Communism or a radical national collectivism might be the only vehicles for modernization in many key areas of the world—these are dilemmas we have never faced. Now I suggest that we do face them, and that we begin to examine in a serious way ideas that have hitherto been considered blasphemous, if not near-traitorous.

Suppose that most of Southeast Asia and much of Latin America were to go Communist, or to become controlled by revolutionary governments that espoused collectivist ideologies and vented extreme anti-American sentiments. Would this constitute a mortal threat to the United States?

I think it fair to claim that the purely *military* danger posed by such an eventuality would be slight. Given the present and prospective capabilities of the backward world, the addition of hundreds of millions of citizens to the potential armies of Communism would mean nothing when there was no way of deploying them against us. The prospect of an invasion by Communist hordes—the specter that frightened Europe after World War II with some (although retrospectively, not too much) realism—would be no more than a phantasm when applied to Asia or South America or Africa.

More important, the nuclear or conventional military power of Communism would not be materially increased by the armaments capacities of these areas for many years. By way of indication, the total consumption of energy of all kinds (in terms of coal equivalent) for Afghanistan, Bolivia, Brazil, Burma, Ceylon, Colombia, Costa Rica, Dominican Republic, Ecuador, El Salvador, Ethiopia, Guatemala, Haiti, Honduras, India, Indonesia, Iran, Iraq, Korea, Lebanon, Nicaragua, Pakistan, Paraguay, Peru, Philippines, U.A.R., Uruguay, and Venezuela is less than that annually consumed by West Germany alone. The total steel output of these countries is one-tenth of U.S. annual production. Thus, even the total communization of the backward world would not effectively alter the present balance of military strength in the world.

However small the military threat, it is undeniably true that a Communist or radical collectivist engulfment of these countries would cost us the loss of billions of dollars of capital invested there. Of our roughly $50 billions in overseas investment, some $10 billions are in mining, oil, utility, and manufacturing facilities in Latin America, some $4 billions in Asia including the Near East, and about $2 billions in Africa. To lose these assets would deal a heavy blow to a number of large corporations, particularly in oil, and would cost the nation as a whole the loss of some $3 to $4 billions a year in earnings from those areas.

A Marxist might conclude that the economic interests of a capitalist nation would find such a prospective loss insupportable, and that it would be "forced" to go to war. I do not think this is a warranted assumption, although it is undoubtedly a risk. Against a Gross National Product that is approaching ¾ of a trillion dollars and with total corporate assets over $1.3 trillions, the loss of even the whole $16 billions in the vulnerable areas should be manageable economically. Whether such a takeover could be resisted politically—that is, whether the red flag of Communism could be successfully waved by the corporate interests—is another question. I do not myself believe that the corporate elite is particularly war-minded—not nearly so much so as the military or the congressional—or that corporate seizures would be a suitable issue for purposes of drumming up interventionist sentiment.

By these remarks I do not wish airily to dismiss the dangers of a Communist avalanche in the backward nations. There would be dangers, not least those of an American hysteria. Rather, I want only to assert that the threats of a military or economic kind would not be insuperable, as they might well be if Europe were to succumb to a hostile regime.

But is that not the very point?, it will be asked. Would not a Communist success in a few backward nations lead to successes in others, and thus by degrees engulf the entire world, until the United States and perhaps Europe were fortresses besieged on a hostile planet?

I think the answer to this fear is twofold. First, as many beside myself have argued, it is now clear that Communism, far from constituting a single unified movement with a common aim and dovetailing interests, is a movement in which similarities of economic and political structure and ideology are more than outweighed by divergencies of national interest and character. Two bloody wars have demonstrated that in the case of capitalism, structural similarities between nations do not prevent mortal combat. As with capitalism, so with Communism. Russian Communists have already been engaged in skirmishes with Polish and Hungarian Communists, have nearly come to blows with Yugoslavia, and now stand poised at the threshold of open fighting with China. Only in the mind of the *Daily News* (and perhaps still the State Department) does it seem possible, in the face of this spectacle, to refer to the unified machinations of "international Communism" or the "Sino-Soviet bloc."

The realities, I believe, point in a very different direction. A world in which Communist governments were engaged in the enormous task of trying to modernize the worst areas of Asia, Latin America, and Africa would be a world in which sharp differences of national interest were certain to arise within these continental areas. The outlook would be for frictions and conflicts to develop among Communist nations with equal frequency as they developed between those nations and their non-Communist neighbors. A long period of jockeying for power and command over resources, rather than anything like a unified sharing of power and resources, seems unavoidable in the developing continents. This would not preclude a continuous barrage of anti-American propaganda, but it would certainly impede a movement to exert a coordinated Communist influence over these areas.

Second, it seems essential to distinguish among the causes of dangerous national and international behavior those that can be traced to the tenets of Communism and those that must be located elsewhere. "Do not talk to me about Communism and capitalism," said a Hungarian economist with whom I had lunch this winter. "Talk to me about rich nations and poor ones."

I think it *is* wealth and poverty, and not Communism or capitalism, that establishes much of the tone and tension of international relations. For that reason I would expect Communism in the backward nations (or national collectivism, if that emerges in the place of Communism) to be strident, belligerent, and insecure. If these regimes fail—as they may—their rhetoric may become hysterical and their behavior uncontrolled, although of small consequence. But if they succeed, which I believe they can, many of these traits should recede. Russia, Yugoslavia, or Poland are simply not to be compared, either by way of internal pronouncement or external behavior, with China, or, on a smaller scale, Cuba. Modernization brings, among other things, a waning of the stereotypes, commandments, and flagellations so characteristic of (and so necessary to) a nation engaged in the effort to alter itself from top to bottom. The idiom of ceaseless revolution becomes less relevant—even faintly embarrassing—to a nation that begins to be pleased with itself. Then, too, it seems reasonable to suppose that the vituperative quality of Communist invective would show some signs of abating were the United States to modify its own dogmatic attitude and to forego its own wearisome clichés about the nature of Communism.

I doubt there are many who will find these arguments wholly reassuring.

They are not. It would be folly to imagine that the next generation or two, when Communism or national collectivism in the underdeveloped areas passes through its jehad stage, will be a time of international safety. But as always in these matters, it is only by a comparison with the alternatives that one can choose the preferable course. The prospect that I have offered as a plausible scenario of the future must be placed against that which results from a pursuit of our present course. And here I see two dangers of even greater magnitude: (1) the prospect of many more Vietnams, as radical movements assert themselves in other areas of the world; and (2) a continuation of the present inability of the most impoverished areas to modernize, with the prospect of an eventual human catastrophe on an unimaginable scale.

Nevertheless, there *is* a threat in the specter of a Communist or near-Communist supremacy in the underdeveloped world. It is that the rise of Communism would signal the end of capitalism as the dominant world order, and would force the acknowledgement that America no longer constituted the model on which the future of world civilization would be mainly based. In this way, as I have written before, the existence of Communism frightens American capitalism as the rise of Protestantism frightened the Catholic Church, or the French Revolution the English aristocracy.

It is, I think, the fear of losing our place in the sun, of finding ourselves at bay, that motivates a great deal of the anti-Communism on which so much of American foreign policy seems to be founded. In this regard I note that the nations of Europe, most of them profoundly more conservative than America in their social and economic dispositions, have made their peace with Communism far more intelligently and easily than we, and I conclude that this is in no small part due to their admission that they are no longer the leaders of the world.

The great question in our own nation is whether we can accept a similar scaling-down of our position in history. This would entail many profound changes in outlook and policy. It would mean the recognition that Communism, which may indeed represent a retrogressive movement in the West, where it should continue to be resisted with full energies, may nonetheless represent a progressive movement in the backward areas, where its advent may be the only chance these areas have of escaping misery. Collaterally, it means the recognition that "our side" has neither the political will, nor the ideological wish, nor the stomach for directing those changes that the backward world must make if it is ever to cease being backward. It would undoubtedly entail a more isolationist policy for the United States *vis-à-vis* the developing continents, and a greater willingness to permit revolutions there to work their way without our interference. It would mean in our daily political life the admission that the ideological battle of capitalism and Communism had passed its point of usefulness or relevance, and that religious diatribe must give way to the pragmatic dialogue of the age of science and technology.

I do not know how to estimate the chances of affecting such deepseated changes in the American outlook. It may be that the pull of vested interests, the inertia of bureaucracy, plus a certain lurking fundamentalism that regards Communism as an evil which admits of no discussion—the anti-christ—will maintain America on its present course, with consequences that I find frightening to contemplate. But I believe that our attitudes are not hopelessly frozen. I detect, both above and below, signs that our present view of Communism is no longer wholly tenable and that it must be replaced with a new assessment if we are to remain maneuverable in action and cogent in discourse.

Two actions may help speed along this long overdue modernization of our own thought. The first is a continuation of the gradual thawing and convergence of American and Russian views and interests—a rapprochement that is proceeding slowly and hesitantly, but with a discernible momentum. Here the initiative must come from Russia as well as from ourselves.

The other action is for us alone to take. It is the public airing of the consequences of our blind anti-Communism for the underdeveloped world. It must be said aloud that our present policy prefers the absence of development to the chance for Communism—which is to say, that we prefer hunger and want and the existing inadequate assaults against the causes of hunger and want to any regime that declares its hostility to capitalism. There are strong American currents of humanitarianism that can be directed as a counterforce to this profoundly anti-humanitarian view. But for this counterforce to become mobilized it will be necessary to put fearlessly the outrageous question with which I began: is the United States fundamentally opposed to economic development?

PART V

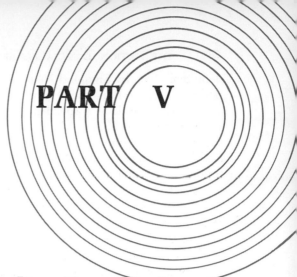

The National Socialist Revolution

Whether National Socialism was really a revolutionary movement is a matter for debate. Certainly, Adolf Hitler and his followers never hesitated to call themselves revolutionaries, although what they meant by the term is not exactly clear. The Nazis came to power legally in January 1933, according to the provisions of the constitution of the Weimar Republic, but they did not hide the fact that they intended to make far-reaching changes in German society. (That they might have similar intentions toward the rest of Europe was something about which they were less explicit.) In pursuit of this goal, they were to embark upon a policy of ever-increasing violence, culminating, finally, in a war of unprecedented scale and intensity.

Before Germany was defeated and the National Socialist movement stopped, much of Europe was in ruins and some forty million of her people, including at least twenty million Russians, four or five million Germans, and over five million Jews, had been slaughtered. Within Germany itself, most of the great cities had been leveled, millions of inhabitants uprooted and turned into homeless refugees, the territory divided and subjected to total military occupation, and political and administrative matters placed completely in the hands of the victors. Did these consequences, intended or unintended, of National Socialism constitute a revolution? One's point of view here depends on what one conceives revolution in the modern world to be.

Few would dispute that Hitler was acting in a revolutionary manner when he abrogated the constitution of the Weimar Republic and destroyed the existing forms and procedures of political life. But revolution, as the term has come to be understood in the twentieth century, involves something more than simply a change of government or regime. In the almost classic definition given by Sigmund Neumann, revolution is "a sweeping change in political organization, social structure, economic property control and the predominant myth of a social order, thus indicating a major break in the continuity of development." As Neumann further points out, revolution in the twentieth century is also by its all-embracing quality and the magnitude of the task it must accomplish, totalitarian. National Socialism was certainly totalitarian, but it must be admitted that it corresponds only imperfectly to the other elements in this particular definition. The structure of German society was not radically different after 1945 from what it had been before 1933, nor had there been any widespread redistribution of property.

Since the days of Karl Marx, students of revolution have tended to analyze the dynamics of the revolutionary process in terms of the legitimate discontents of a given social class. This class has generally been defined by its economic interests and has been assumed to be the most vital and progressive one in society at that time. The revolution, if it is successful, is then understood as having alleviated the discontents of this class. Such would be the case of the bourgeoisie in the French Revolution, the proletariat and possibly the peasantry in Russia, and the peasantry in China. If, before 1933, the National Socialist movement spoke for the discontents of any one class, it was the *petite bourgeoisie*—the small, independent shopkeeper, losing out in competition with the great chain or department stores, or the proprietor of the small, no longer economically viable farm, or perhaps the alienated young intellectual unable to find a job worthy of his education or his talents (see Schoenbaum).

But once the Nazis had achieved power, their economic policies tended to favor the large-scale enterprises, with a legal limit being placed on the minimum size of a business. The "little man" benefited from the Nazi regime only to the same degree that every German gained from the economic upswing of the years after 1933. Any other benefits were likely to be in the nature of psychological compensation, as his national pride swelled at the spectacle of Hitler systematically dismantling the restrictive clauses of the Versailles *diktat.* The evident bias of Nazi economic policy in favor of big business, plus the financial support given to the Nazis by certain of the Ruhr and Rhineland industrialists, has led some scholars to place Nazism within an essentially Marxian framework and to see it as the logical outgrowth of the capitalist system. It was thus in no way revolutionary, but rather a counterrevolutionary movement underwritten by the capitalists to defeat the legitimate goals of the working class in Germany. This view may well be too simplistic. Although it may explain why some of the big business interests supported Hitler before 1933, it does not take into account the basically irrational, uneconomic, even anti-economic policies of the German state after the Nazi take-over of power. Nor does it explain the way in which the state, rather than allowing the industrialists a free rein, severely limited them in the free disposal of their profits, requiring that most of them be reinvested. The Nazi state undoubtedly restricted the liberty of the working classes, but the big business interests found that they were by no means absolute masters in their own house, let alone the manipulators of state policy.

The goal of the protagonists of the great revolutions of the past has been either to rearrange the political life of society to correspond with the facts of economic power, as in 1789, or to go one step further, and to rearrange the property relations within society, as in Russia in 1917. These aims, however, were only incidental to the avowed intentions of National Socialism, which were to effect a "racial" revolution. Germany and Europe would first be purged of their racially "impure" elements and then reorganized in accordance with the principles of racial hierarchy as they were first set forth in tentative fashion in *Mein Kampf.* This book, written some nine years before Hitler came to power, is too diffuse and unsystematic a work to provide more than the vaguest indications about the eventual shape of what he would come to call his "New Order." Still, it remains the official bible of the movement, the closest Hitler ever came to an extended and authoritative statement of the Nazi ideology. In *Mein Kampf*, social and economic questions per se are of no great significance, and are treated only in so far as they pertain to the larger political theme of the book, the necessity for the state to preserve and promote the welfare of the Aryan race.

There is no general agreement as to how seriously Hitler and other leading Nazis took the official ideology of the party or felt themselves bound by it (see Holborn), but the ideology was nonetheless promulgated as part of the school curriculum and enshrined in law. Nazi policy towards the Jews and other "inferior" peoples ended by being far more extreme than anything advocated in *Mein Kampf.*

Whether Hitler contemplated anything so monstrously grandiose as the extermination of European Jewry when he came to power, or whether he simply allowed himself to be propelled towards such a goal by the logic of increasing violence, cannot be known, but having by the end of 1941 subjugated the European continent and conquered a large part of the Soviet Union, he gave the order for the "Final Solution." Three and a half years later, on the eve of their final defeat, the Nazis were within sight of having carried it out. They had also made great strides in their program of destroying the social structure of such despised peoples as the Poles and reducing them to the status of enslaved beasts of burden in the service of their German overlords. All of this, plus the absence of any coherent intellectual or social program and accomplishments, has led one observer, Hermann Rauschning, himself a former Nazi who early broke with Hitler, to see the essence of National Socialism as violence pure and simple, with no aim but domination and destruction for their own sake (see Rauschning). Such a movement may well be revolutionary, but not in the accepted sense of the word.

If something called "modernization" is to be understood as either the primary goal or the eventual consequence of the archetypical revolutionary movements of the twentieth century, Germany would hardly appear to be a likely setting for this phenomenon. Germany was not a traditional society, seeking to create a modern industrial order by forced draft means. Rather, by almost any criterion—the number and size of its cities, its level of industrialization and economic development, the extent and effectiveness of its governmental services—Germany was the embodiment of a modern society. What is striking in this regard is that Nazism in its official rhetoric and its political imagery appeared to reject the modern world and to appeal to a deep longing for some lost sense of community that was supposed to have existed before the advent of industrial society. At this level then, it was less a revolution of modernization than a revolt against modern society, although the rhetoric of the Nazis may have hidden their real intentions.

When measured by the conventional standards of what constitutes a truly revolutionary and/or modernizing movement, National Socialism evidently falls short. Yet the fact remains that Germany was profoundly affected by the experience of National Socialism. Germany is today a far more liberal and resilient, not to mention prosperous, society than it was before Hitler took power, and it is something of a grim paradox that a phenomenon as illiberal and immoral as National Socialism made a crucial contribution to this state of affairs, although this was hardly what it intended.

By limiting our definition of revolution to large-scale, objectively measurable changes in the political, social, and economic order, we may be ignoring one vital component of human reality, namely what a person perceives society to be and how he conceives of his role within it. Germany in 1933 was a modern society in that it was urbanized and industrialized, but in terms of the attitudes of its elites and its subordinate elements, it was not peopled by modern men. The remarkably rapid industrialization of Germany in the imperial epoch had been carried out under the aegis of a traditional ascriptive ruling class whose authority was rooted in a rural, decentralized social order. They were fearful of the new emerging economic forces transforming the shape of Germany, and, unlike their counterparts in England, lacked confidence as to how to come to terms with them. As a result, their reaction was to try by all possible means to maintain the political *status quo*. The new, supposedly dynamic classes, whether captains of industry or workers, when faced by the uncertain and overly rigid attitudes of the ruling elite, either remained in an unnatural state of tutelage or assumed a too assertive posture in defense of their position in society. This unhealthy equilibrium of social forces survived the defeat of 1918 and persisted through the Weimar Republic. Indeed, it contributed greatly to the downfall of that regime. Under Nazism, the last vestiges of the effective prestige and power of the traditional ruling elite disappeared, thus clearing the way for the emergence of a potentially liberal and even democratic society. As the German sociologist, Ralf Dahrendorf, has postulated, the Nazi experience destroyed the bases of a system that made the Germans either subjects or anxiety-ridden rulers and opened at least the possibility of their behaving as citizens (see Dahrendorf). By having cleared the way for a transformation in that area where transformations are most difficult to effect, that is, in man's perception of the social order he inhabits and in his moral attitude toward it, may Nazism not also have been a revolutionary force?

The growing impotence of the Weimar Republic reflected and had its origins in certain weaknesses in the structure of German society. What some of these weaknesses were and how they were exploited by the National Socialists is described in this selection by David Schoenbaum, taken from his book *Hitler's Social Revolution.*

The Third Reich and Its Social Promises

DAVID SCHOENBAUM

The concept of a sick society causes problems if only because no one knows exactly what constitutes social health.[1] But to the extent that the concept has meaning, Germany after 1918 was an appropriate place for its application. The most spectacular symptoms—the propensity to physical violence, the hyperbolic inflation of 1923, and the near-overnight disintegration of the economy in 1929–30—had their equivalents elsewhere. But elsewhere they led to crises and convalescence recognizably within the limits of previous historical experience and the status quo. In Germany, however, the permanent disaffection of major social groups, the alienation of those groups who presumably support a liberal republic, was reflected in the progressive and total collapse of all liberal parties, and in the discrepancy between social reality and its political interpretation. They testify to a latent malaise whose consequences, even without Adolf Hitler, would have led to major social and political transformation. This need not have led to war and Auschwitz. But with high probability, it would have been fatal to the Weimar Republic in the form envisaged by the authors of its constitution.

National Socialism was not the cause of the malaise, nor was its ultimate totalitarian, imperialist form the inevitable consequence. Its programmatic demands were neither original nor peculiar to Hitler's Party. The Nazis came to power by miscalculation rather than by some exclusive popular demand focusing on the person of Hitler or his Party. The mandate with which Hitler took office was a conglomerate of disparities and contradictions long apparent to anyone interested in politics, both outside the party and in it. The common denominator of Nazi appeal was as remote as the smile of the Cheshire cat. In its negative form, it was a promise to make things different, in its positive form, a promise to make things better. But as far removed as it was from the unitary political will Hitler claimed to see in the uniform columns of the SA (Sturmabteilung—Storm Troopers, "brown shirts") or the ecstatic acclamation of a mass audience, there was in it nonetheless a homogeneity great enough to cover the yawning cracks in the Party program with ballot papers. This was the homogeneity of common disaffection.

The disaffection was structural, endemic in all Western industrial societies, but intensified in Germany by special historical factors: a non-competitive,

From *Hitler's Social Revolution: Class and Status in Nazi Germany* by David Schoenbaum, copyright © 1966 by the author. Reprinted by permission of Doubleday and Company, Inc., Garden City, N.Y. Pp. 1–15 and 36–45.

[1] Cf. Harry Pross, *Vor und Nach Hitler,* Freiburg im Breisgau, 1962, pp. 9 f.

highly concentrated, high-priced industrial economy, the disproportionate influence of a small class of large landowners, a high birthrate until World War I, too many rural smallholders, an inflated urban petite bourgeoisie. All of these had been built into Bismarck's Reich. Carried along on the winds of economic expansion, they formed a fair-weather constellation whose stability was virtually identical with the success of its political leadership in balancing the conflicting demands and requirements of industry and agriculture, labor and capital, West and East, centralism and particularism, Catholic and Protestant, rich and poor. Success created a clientele that included even the nominal enemies of the established order. Their own vested interest in this order was certainly an important factor in the SPD (Social Democrat) decision to vote war credits in 1914.[2] But the compromises of the old order failed to solve, even precluded solving, the problems of an industrial society. The collapse of the monarchy in 1918 with its chaotic "return to normalcy" only reintroduced the problems of the prewar era after four uneasy years of civil truce. But they were now complicated by the by-products of defeat: a "lost generation" of demobilized soldiers; a floating population of eastern refugees, many of them aristocrats; the liquidation of millions of war loans floated with middle-class savings; and a large disproportion in the demographic relationship of women to men. Finally, there were the economic consequences of the war: reparations, loss of export markets, exhaustion of both plant and raw materials, and inflation. The latent social problems of the prewar era were further complicated by a crisis of legitimacy in the political order coinciding with economic disintegration. The results were paradoxical; on the one hand, consistent and uninterrupted extension of the social tendencies of the prewar era, on the other, an ideologized misinterpretation of these tendencies that effectively prevented the solution of the maladjustments they caused.

A statistical résumé leaves no doubt about the unambiguous course of social development (see Table 1).

TABLE 1
GERMAN OCCUPATIONAL DISTRIBUTION IN % OF POPULATION[3]

Year	*Agriculture*	*Industry & Handicrafts*	*Services*
1882	42	36	22
1895	36	39	25
1907	34	40	26
1925	30	42	28
1933	29	41	30

This was the classical pattern of industrialization, urban growth, industrial rationalization, and the development of distribution and service industries. While only 5 per cent of the German population had lived in cities of over 100,000 in 1871, the proportion had grown by 1925 to 27 per cent.[4] Equally striking was the relative redistribution of ownership and economic status (see Table 2).[5]

While the figures were neutral as economic indicators—pointing only to advancing industrialization and relative only to success in feeding, housing, and clothing an industrial population—they were full of implications as a reflection of social and political tendencies. The

[2] Cf. Julius Leber, *Ein Mann geht seinen Weg,* Berlin-Schöneberg, 1952, pp. 196–201.
[3] Quoted in Fritz Croner, *Soziologie der Angestellten,* Cologne and Berlin, 1962, p. 196.
[4] Joseph A. Schumpeter, "Das soziale Antlitz des deutschen Reiches" (1929), *Aufsätze zur Soziologie,* Tübingen, 1953, p. 217.
[5] Quoted in Croner, op. cit., p. 196.

TABLE 2
GERMAN OCCUPATIONAL STATUS IN %
OF POPULATION

In %	*1882*	*1895*	*1907*	*1925*	*1933*
Independent	38	35	27	21	20
Their employed dependents	4	4	8	10	11
White collar including civil service	8	11	14	19	18
Workers	50	50	51	50	52

loss of economic independence, the employment of family members, the ballooning white collar population characteristic both of the big city and the bureaucratic state and economy all affected the self-respect of the people they touched—or at least were capable of doing so as soon as they seemed to coincide with a decline in the standard of living. If the processes themselves were characteristic of capitalism, it stood to reason that those affected by them would come to consider themselves anti-capitalistic, without, however, accepting the theoretical Marxian implications of their misery and disappearing in the traditional proletariat. Theodor Geiger estimated, on the basis of the 1925 census, that 25,000,000 Germans could be classed, socially, as proletarians. But 45,000,000, roughly three quarters of the population, were living—during a period of increasing prosperity nearly five years before the depression—on proletarian incomes.[6]

Particularly characteristic of this tendency were the retail traders, a bumper crop sown by the imperial order and in constant fear of being mowed down by the economics of the Republic. Between 1882 and 1907, the number of small retail traders had grown faster than both population and the national product as people sought to exploit urban growth and a rising living standard in tobacco shops, groceries, drugstores (Drogerien), and delicatessens (Feinkostgeschäfte). Even before the war, existing statistics pointed to a decline in professional quality. A survey of Brunswick grocers (Kolonialwarenhändler) in 1901 established that only 34 per cent had had any vocational training compared with 67 per cent in 1887. Even before the depression, the economic consequences of the peace had revealed the weaknesses of the small shopkeeper, exposed to the business cycle, unresponsive to shifting population, and inadequately trained for either successful competition or other employment.[7] Added to his problem on the one hand were the price-sinking creations of advancing technology and concentrated capital, the chain and department stores, and on the other, the vast overaccumulation of non-competitive manpower in retail trade. Between 1907 and 1925, the number of retail outlets rose from 695,800 to 847,900, an increase of about 21 per cent. Between 1924 and 1929 it increased another 3 per cent. Geiger estimated that in 1925 nearly 45 per cent of those engaged in retail trade were already living on proletarian incomes.[8]

Meanwhile the number of department store subsidiaries rose from 101 in 1925 to 176 in 1929. While their absolute share of retail turnover was still small enough, their relative share by 1928 was growing 22 per cent faster than the total volume of retail trade.[9]

[6] Theodor Geiger, *Die soziale Schichtung des deutschen Volkes*, Stuttgart, 1932, pp. 72 f.
[7] L. D. Pesl, "Mittelstandsfragen," *Grundriss der Sozialökonomik*, Vol. IX, Tübingen, 1926, pp. 104 ff.
[8] Geiger, op. cit., p. 73.
[9] Heinrich Uhlig, *Die Warenhäuser im Dritten Reich*, Cologne-Opladen, 1956, p. 25.

Between 1925 and 1931 so-called "specialty" shops lost 5 per cent of their share of retail volume, a relatively small figure but one magnified by higher operating costs, lively imaginations, and then by the depression. A 1929 tax study showed that the department stores had, in fact, taken over only 4 per cent, the chain stores at most 1.1 per cent of retail trade.[10] This included, however, up to 6 per cent of the turnover in clothing and 20 per cent in household goods and furniture. By 1928 retail pressure groups were pressing for increased taxes on department stores, a goal achieved by 1929 in Munich and Frankfurt, Main.[11] In 1932, the Brüning government declared a limit on further department store expansion, followed before the year was out by a similar ban on chain stores. Whether his misery was caused by his own inefficiency, his aversion to co-operatives, to the methods, economics, or good advertising of larger units within his own line, or by the department stores was a matter of indifference to the retail merchant whose effective desire was a self-contradiction: free enterprise minus its attendant risks.

But while the economic implications of retail trade seemed to point in the direction of the Marxist prognosis, toward concentration, intensified competition, and the strangulation of the small, independent proprietor, another development pointed in the opposite direction. This was the rapid growth of the white-collar population, "sociologically perhaps the most significant development of the last decades," as Ferdinand Fried called it in 1931.[12] It was indeed characteristic of the period that the white-collar workers formed one of the best-observed of all social groups, their origins, attitudes, and habits becoming a subject of considerable public interest. Siegfried Kracauer's Marxist phenomenology of the white-collar worker ran for weeks in a daily newspaper [13] in 1929 while the white-collar "little man" became in 1932 the hero of a fictional best seller, Hans Fallada's *Little Man, What Now?*

Coming as they did both from the ranks of the traditional bourgeoisie and from the proletariat, it was nonetheless clear that the white-collar workers were neither workers nor middle class in the traditional sense. Contemporary social science begged the problem of categorization rather than solved it by calling the entire group, from shop clerks to graduate engineers, "the new middle class." [14] But this was hardly a guide to their behavior, which was, from the Marxist point of view from which they were most often observed, a collection of anomalies.

The white-collar worker was usually employed in a big city and by a big employer. He—or still more likely, she—was often of working-class origins, even before the war. Hans Speier quoted a number of surveys (see Table 3).[15]

White-collar workers showed a progressive tendency to organize, and in a relatively militant organization from which employers were excluded. But both the form and the objectives differed

[10] Ibid., pp. 47 f.

[11] Ibid., p. 39. Uhlig thought, however, that this had more to do with considerations of local finance than with effective pressure by the shop owners.

[12] Ferdinand Fried, *Das Ende des Kapitalismus*, Jena, 1931, p. 12.

[13] Reprinted as *Die Angestellten, Eine Schrift vom Ende der Weimarer Republik*, Allensbach and Bonn, 1959.

[14] Cf. Emil Lederer and Jakob Marschak, "Der neue Mittelstand," *Grundriss der Sozialökonomik*, Vol. IX, Tübingen, 1926, pp. 122 ff.

[15] Hans Speier, "The Salaried Employees in German Society," mimeographed, Columbia University Department of Social Sciences and WPA, New York, 1939, pp. 97–99.

TABLE 3

Year	*Job classification*	*Working class origins*
1906	Berlin saleswomen	33.6%
1909–11	Young Munich saleswomen	66.9
1932	Cologne saleswomen	51.5
1929	Apprentices of Gewerkschaft der Angestellten (clerical union):	
	Male	33.6
	Female	42.9

from the traditional union pattern, corresponding in part to the different social origins of the membership, in part to the nature of their employment. While Geiger estimated that less than 4 per cent of the working-class population was skilled (qualifiziert), he estimated that 70 per cent of the white-collar population had some professional qualifications.[16] This alone might have led them away from the traditional union demands. While 80 per cent of the workers were organized in the so-called "free" socialist unions in 1931, only 25 per cent of the white-collar workers were organized in the socialist Gewerkschaft der Angestellten (clerical union), while 22.6 per cent were in the national-liberal Hirsch-Duncker unions and 34.1 per cent in the so-called "Christian-National" organizations like the Deutschnationaler-Handlungsgehilfenverband (German National Sales Clerks Association) (DHGV), perhaps the only economic-interest organization in Weimar Germany that combined a racist-nationalist (völkisch) program with mass membership.[17] It is also of interest that 39 per cent of the DHGV membership came from working-class origins.[18]

While the white-collar union was a tough negotiator and the pressure of economic circumstances could bring about a professional solidarity great enough to overcome the ideological divisions separating the white-collar groups, white-collar consciousness made itself felt in a preoccupation with salaries instead of wages, long-term contracts, and pensions; [19] reflections of a concern with security—including the security of social status—that distinguished it from the blue-collar unions. Weimar legislation continued to distinguish white collar (Angestellter) from blue collar (Arbeiter), granting the former special job security, separate status in wage contracts, and a separate insurance fund.[20]

Both Schumpeter and Lederer-Marschak claimed to see the line between blue collar and white collar fading, Schumpeter because the workers were coming to live like petits bourgeois,[21] Lederer and Marschak because the white-collar workers were coming to behave like other workers.[22] The depression proved the contrary. Unemployment hit blue collar and white collar alike, but psychologically it hit the white-collar worker harder. Speier quotes an unemployed white-collar worker: ". . . one is immediately ostracized, one is déclassé, without means of support, unemployed—that's equal to being a Communist." [23] Déclassé is clearly the important word, reflecting a

[16] Geiger, op. cit., pp. 74 f.
[17] Speier, op. cit., p. 76.
[18] Ibid., p. 87.
[19] Lederer and Marschak, op. cit., p. 131.
[20] Cf. Kunibert Piper, "Das Wesen des Angestellten," Greifswald dissertation, 1939, pp. 31 ff.
[21] Schumpeter, op. cit., p. 225.
[22] Lederer and Marschak, op. cit., p. 141.
[23] Speier, op. cit., p. 20.

sensitivity of self-esteem different from that of the traditional working class. The increased employment of women —between 1913 and 1921 the proportion of women in the white-collar organizations had grown from 7.7 to 23.8 per cent [24]—tended to increase the tension by making higher paid male jobs more vulnerable and compounding class war with sex war.

A key group in the white-collar population was an academically trained class, multiplied by postwar circumstances beyond its prewar numbers and increasingly absorbed in salaried employment in an economy that placed growing demands on technically trained manpower. The economic crises of the first Weimar years fell with particular weight on them, a group already sensitive to its exclusion, in part real, in part apparent, from traditional careers in the Army and civil service. While the social structure of Germany's political leadership changed significantly, the structure of the university population changed little except to the extent to which it grew and suffered. The 1922 Who's Who revealed that 20.3 per cent of the political entries came from the working class and 30.8 per cent from lower-income groups while only 40.8 per cent came from the old upper classes (Oberschicht).[25] But the universities were peopled by the sons of the groups most conscious of the loss this revolution had caused them. The relative frequency of sons from the families of professional men went up in proportion to the restrictions imposed on business and the military.[26] But while the sons of lawyers cautiously chose to make their ways in other areas, considerable numbers in medicine, pharmacy, and the natural sciences, the law faculties were filled with the sons of the petite bourgeoisie seeking the traditional prewar way to the top.[27] In 1929, 23.4 per cent of all students were from the families of university graduates, 11.5 per cent from the homes of the rich—big landowners, company directors, etc. But 64.2 per cent came from the middle class [28] intent on making their way in a world whose political direction was increasingly dominated, as they would tend to see it, either by the discredited representatives of the old order or by their social and cultural inferiors.

"The age of the self-made man is past," Robert Michels claimed.[29] The only career open to the talented working-class boy was political. At the same time there was every evidence of dissatisfaction in a university graduate population of 840,000 while the student population tended to grow by 10 per cent a year. Since the routes to the top narrowed, and the traffic increased, the result appeared to be fewer and fewer rewards for higher and higher qualifications. Fried, who clearly felt himself a victim of the process, was eloquent in his description of its consequences: four to six years of university study, costing from five to nine thousand marks, rewarded with starting salaries ranging from two to four hundred marks monthly and advancing to a level commensurate with family obligations and social status only when its recipient reached the age of forty or fifty.[30] The university graduate, Fried declared, felt as he had once felt during his first weeks

[24] Lederer and Marschak, op. cit., p. 131.

[25] Quoted in Robert Michels, *Umschichtungen in den herrschenden Klassen nach dem Krieg*, Stuttgart, 1934, p. 79.

[26] Ibid., p. 60.

[27] Ibid., p. 59.

[28] Ibid., p. 62.

[29] Ibid., p. 64.

[30] Fried, op. cit., pp. 105–8.

of military service: spiritually and physically exploited. But while he might once have become a reserve officer for his pains, his civilian occupation under present circumstances offered him the chance of one day becoming—with the best of luck—a prokurist, a kind of economic sergeant. "The way to the top is blocked off," [31] he concluded, including among the obstacles the oligarchy of age. Reichstag deputies were, on the average, fifty-six years old, the two hundred leading economic figures, sixty-one years old—"rigid, dead, outdated and reactionary like the SPD." [32]

One other major social group, the farmers, shared the general disaffection. Geiger estimated that nearly 60 per cent of them were living on proletarian incomes.[33] The intensity and quality of their disaffection varied according to region and market conditions but was ultimately reducible to the classic problem of agriculture in an industrial society: the farmer's inability to control prices and production in an otherwise manipulable economy. The result was a curious dilemma. Massive economic disintegration might bring him short-term advantages, as it did during the 1923 inflation which liquidated his debts and brought him the short-term benefits of a barter economy and a sellers' market. But in the long run, the farmer suffered as the general economy suffered. On the other hand, prosperity, even as it brought him higher prices, tended to increase the lag between farm and industrial income on one side and farm and industrial prices on the other. His efforts to overcome this gap resulted in overproduction with a consequent decline in prices.

The basic problem of German agriculture was not really a problem of water, climate, or soil chemistry. Nor was it necessarily a problem of education or administration. German farm administration was respected, its research stations admired, its statistics exemplary. A growing number of farmers were aware of scientific breeding, crop rotation, soil chemistry, and mechanical rationalization. The chronic problem was relative—too much rural population to guarantee all of it an acceptable income. While grain constituted up to 40 per cent of German agricultural production, German conditions all but precluded competitive operation against overseas imports, and milk, butter, meat, eggs, which could be produced more economically, were vulnerable to the wide fluctuations in purchasing power in the Weimar economy. The solution, as in any other industrial country, was inevitably the creation of alternative forms of employment. But it was this that the Republic, for various reasons, avoided. On the contrary, among its earliest economic measures was a homestead act intended in the short run to drain off demobilized military manpower by redistribution of defaulted eastern estates, but, in the long run, intended to reverse the prewar trend toward urban concentration. It was characteristic of Weimar economic policy that subsidized industrial development of East Germany through exploitation of its plentiful waterpower sources was never seriously considered.[34] But while Prussia's eastern provinces stagnated in industrial underdevelopment, the farm problem west of the Elbe was one of rural overpopulation. In 1925 30 per cent of the German population was engaged in agriculture. To be sure, as Schumpeter observed, one and a half million had left the land

[31] Ibid., p. 100.
[32] Ibid., p. 127.
[33] Geiger, op. cit., pp. 72 f.
[34] Henning von Borcke-Stargordt, *Der ostdeutsche Landbau zwischen Fortschritt, Krise und Politik*, Würzburg, 1957, p. 46.

between 1882 and 1925 while the number of farm owners had remained constant.[35] During the same period there had also been a relative decline in the number of large holdings and consequent increase in "healthy" middle-sized units. But a survey of land ownership in a relatively average, prosperous West Elbian landkreis (county) indicates the narrowness of the productive base. Nearly 40 per cent of the farms around Kassel were under 12½ acres,[36] only 4.7 per cent of all holdings had any sort of power-driven machine, only 25 per cent machines of any sort.[37] A labor shortage that required the importation of Polish help, alternating with spasmodic phases of severe rural unemployment, reflected the general instability.[38]

The farmer reacted to all this as he always had, in two ways, by intensification that often transgressed the law of diminishing returns, and by expanded production. During the years 1919–30 German and Prussian wheat yields per hectare (abbr. ha., equal to 2.471 acres) exceeded comparable American yields by 100 to 150 per cent.[39] Given 1880=100 as a base, general productivity per hectare, 186 in 1913, had reached 188 by 1927 and 212 by 1933.[40] The milk output of a farm in Lower Saxony nearly doubled between 1925/26 and 1932/33 while the price fell by nearly half.[41] By 1933 when the price of wheat had fallen by nearly 50 per cent, of swine by nearly 65 per cent, of cattle by 55 per cent of their 1929 level[42] and the farm debts that had financed both the intensification and the surpluses had reached unprecedented heights, the Weimar Republic had fully lost the confidence of its farmers. The state of emergency declared in East Prussia in May 1929 had, by July 1932, extended to all of East and Central Germany, Lower Bavaria and the Upper Palatinate, and by 1933 to all of Germany.[43]

None of these problems was new or unique to Germany. In one form or another they had been, since the middle of the nineteenth century, not only the raw material of German politics but in varying degrees of the politics of all industrial and industrializing countries. In America similar phenomena had fueled political controversy since at least the election of Jackson in 1828 and formed the bases of the mass Populist and Progressive movements before World War I and later the basis of the New Deal.[44]

What complicated solution in Germany was not a failure to recognize the structural inadequacies of industrial society, but rather a failure to find an alternative social model adequate to correct them. Advancing literacy, urbanization, industrialization, and the development of overseas agriculture all pointed to the liberal society envisaged

[35] Schumpeter, op. cit., p. 218.

[36] Walter Schreiner, "Agrarpolitische Untersuchungen im Landkreis Kassel," Giessen dissertation, 1929, p. 35.

[37] Ibid., p. 80.

[38] Ibid., pp. 50–52. In April 1926 unemployment was estimated at 3320, in October 1927 at 209, during the winter of 1927/28 at 1400.

[39] H. W. Graf Finck von Finckenstein, *Die Entwicklung der Landwirtschaft in Preussen und Deutschland, 1800–1930,* Würzburg, 1960, p. 68.

[40] Elisabeth Steiner, Agrarwirtschaft und Agrarpolitik, Munich dissertation, 1939, p. 18.

[41] Ludwig Preiss, *"Die Wirkung von Preisen und Preisveränderungen auf die Produktion in der Landwirtschaft,* Berichte über Landwirtschaft, Vol. XXIII, No. 4, Berlin, 1938, p. 639.

[42] Ibid., pp. 637 f.

[43] Cf. Leo Drescher, *Entschuldung der ostdeutschen Landwirtschaft,* Berlin, 1938, pp. 7 f.

[44] Cf. Arthur Schlesinger, Jr., *The Age of Jackson,* Boston, 1945; Richard Hofstadter, *The Age of Reform,* New York, 1955.

by the Weimar Convention. But the main currents of social thought since at least the constitution of the Reich pointed away from it. They aimed instead at what René König calls "the two revolutions that didn't occur."[45] One of these was Marxist. The other was what Fritz Stern has called "the politics of cultural despair,"[46] a kind of Peter Pan ideology for a society that didn't want to grow up. As aware as the Marxists of the evils of industrialization, the cultural pessimists saw their correction not so much in a redistribution of ownership as in the elimination of industrial society itself. They waged war against the city, turned rural emigration into the pejorative "Landflucht" as though it were a form of desertion, created a distinction between Gemeinschaft, the Arcadian community of the rural village, and Gesellschaft, the soulless rat race of urban society, and turned the sociological discussion of the period into an exhaustive analysis of "class" and "estate." The homestead act of 1919 and the economic parliament foreseen by the Weimar Constitution were testimony to their influence even during the brief honeymoon of popular support for the liberal Republic. In the form of land reform and conventions of estates (Ständekammern) and supplemented with demands for industrial profit sharing, nationalization of trusts, and redistribution of department store properties to small business, both measures found their echo only a few months later in the "inalterable" Nazi program of 24 February 1920.

This was less evidence of Nazi originality than of the Zeitgeist. The infant Party was obliged to climb on the bandwagon to remain in the race. What subsequently turned the NSDAP into a mass organization with a voter potential of fourteen million, and finally into Germany's governing Party, was at no point its programmatic command of the issues or pseudo-issues, but its manipulation of them. It was the mobilization of disaffection.

. . . .

Hitler's first major electoral breakthrough came in underdeveloped Thuringia, a land of high unemployment, home labor, and latent Protestant radicalism, where Frick was carried into a coalition in 1929. Carrying out his mandate against the twentieth century, Frick purged what remained in Weimar of the Bauhaus, the symbol of a hopeful symbiosis of craftsmanship and industrial technology.[151] In September 1930 another major electoral victory, combined with traditional bourgeois animosity toward the SPD and Hugenberg's determination to bring Hitler into the "Harzburg Front" with his own conservative German Nationalists, brought the Nazis into the government in equally underdeveloped Brunswick. While the SPD lost votes to the KPD, all other parties showed major defections to the Nazis, despite a Volkspartei campaign against the socialist wolf in nationalist sheep's clothing.[152] The base broadened as the rest of Germany turned, in effect, into a larger Thuringia, though the tendency was complicated by other, regional conditions. The conservative parties sustained their highest losses in the districts adjacent to the Polish border, where nationalism was an important issue. Where it was less important, in districts like Schleswig-

[45] René König, "Die Soziologie der zwanziger Jahre," *Die Zeit ohne Eigenschaften,* ed. Leonhard Reinisch, Stuttgart, 1961, pp. 82–118.

[46] Fritz Stern, *The Politics of Cultural Despair,* Berkeley, 1961; Anchor Books, 1965.

[151] Brenner, op. cit., pp. 24 f., 30 f.

[152] Ernst-August Roloff, *Bürgertum und Nationalsozialismus,* Hanover, 1961, pp. 115, 27, 65–76. The Nazis elected in Brunswick included a tax official, a farmer, a worker, a mechanic, two merchants, a baker, a bank employee, a teacher, and a lawyer.

Holstein, conservative voters continued to vote conservative while small holders, who in other western and northern districts voted liberal, switched to the Nazis. But from 1930 on, the Nazi gain was effectively proportional to the liberal loss, particularly to the loss of regional and special-interest parties. Marburg on the Lahn, where support for anti-Semitism in the '90s, for the radical liberalism of Friedrich Naumann in the years before the war, and for the bourgeois triad of DDP, DVP, and DNVP in the early '20s turned into Nazi support well above the Reich average from 1930 on, is an ideal case of the social-political continuity the Nazis drew on. Between 1928 and 1932 the Wirtschaftspartei lost 93 per cent of its voters. In 1932, as Lipset writes, the ideal type of the Nazi voter was an economically independent Protestant of the middle class who lived either in the country or in a small town, and had previously voted for a party of the center or a regional party that had campaigned against both big industry and trade unions.[153] This was reinforced, particularly in 1930, by the advent of new voters in a number of districts and of previous non-voters, particularly women, who in 1932 comprised up to half of the Nazis' electoral support though only 3 per cent of the Party membership.[154] Electoral support also included demonstrable defections from the KPD.[155]

The basic elements of Nazi support were again reflected in the 230-man Reichstag delegation of October 1932, which included 55 blue- and white-collar employees, 50 farmers, 43 independent representatives of trade, handicrafts, and industry, 29 full-time Party functionaries including editors, 20 career civil servants, 12 teachers, and 9 former officers. Compared with 1930, this showed a significant increase in the representation of farmers, a slight increase in the representation of the commercially independent, and a very slight increase in the representation of employees.[156] All other major groups declined. As before, the majority were under 40, 21 between 20 and 30, 121 between 30 and 40, 64 between 40 and 50. This was a 5 per cent decline in the proportion of deputies under 40, but still impressive and again comparable only to the KPD where the relationship was 62 of 75. The SPD ratio, by further comparison, was 19 of 133.[157]

Between the September election of 1930 and the Machtergreifung, Party membership rose to 850,000, an increase of over 650 per cent. Broken down into occupational groups, the Party was made up as shown in Table 4.[158]

[153] S. M. Lipset, "Faschismus," *Kölner Zeitschrift für Soziologie und Sozialpsychologie*, 1959, pp. 417 ff.; Rudolf Heberle, *From Democracy to Nazism*, Baton Rouge, 1945, pp. 111 ff.; Irmgard Neusüss-Hunkel, "Parteien und Wahlen in Marburg nach 1945," Marburg dissertation, pp. 33–36.

[154] Kirkpatrick, op. cit., p. 57; Reinhard Bendix, "Social Stratification and Political Power," *American Political Science Review*, June 1952, pp. 369 ff.

[155] Geiger, op. cit., p. 110.

[156] A letter from the general director of the Edeka grocery chain of 22 July 1932, complaining about apparent Nazi reluctance to present Mittelstand candidates, throws an interesting light on the constitution of the Party list. Edeka had made an effort to get party members in its employ accepted on the list but with no success. The director had then gone to see Otto Wagener, the Party's economic spokesman, who again turned him down, assuring him that economic representation would be dealt with in the future outside the Reichstag, in an economic parliament to be created for that purpose. Quoted in Uhlig, op. cit., p. 195. The continued heavy representation of Mittelstand deputies reveals no change of heart, of course, but testifies to the Party's effective independence of the interests it sought to exploit.

[157] Reichstags-Handbuch, *VI. Wahlperiode*, Berlin, 1932, pp. 270 f.

[158] *Partei-Statistik*, Vol. I, 1935, p. 85.

TABLE 4

Workers	31.5%
White collar	21.1
Independent	17.6
Civil servants including teachers	6.7
Farmers	12.6
Miscellaneous	10.5

This, compared with 1930, meant a relative increase in the number of workers, clearly an effect of unemployment. From the end of 1928 to the beginning of 1931, growth in Party membership was parallel to growing unemployment, although from 1931 on unemployment tended to level off while Party growth continued to rise.[159] All other groups, excepting the miscellaneous, showed a relative decline. Compared, however, with the total population, there was still a striking underrepresentation of workers and farmers. The latter was a testimonial to the loyalty of rural Catholics to the Center, particularly in west and south Germany. White-collar workers, on the other hand, were represented up to 90 per cent, the economically independent up to 100 per cent, the civil servants and teachers about 25 per cent,[160] beyond their representation in the general population.

The age structure of the new membership was as shown in Table 5.[161]

In Halle-Merseburg, Koblenz-Trier, Kurhessen, the Palatinate, Weser-Ems, and Württemberg-Hohenzollern, over 45 per cent of the membership was under 30. In Catholic Koblenz-Trier and Württemberg-Hohenzollern, the high proportion of youthful members coincided with absolute membership well below the Reich average, perhaps a reflection of the relative effectiveness of clerical opposition to National Socialism on different generations. An indigenous liberal tradition in Württemberg-Hohenzollern might also have been a factor. In Halle-Merseburg, the high proportion of youthful members coincided with absolute membership above the Reich average, pointing probably to the effects of industrial unemployment in a Protestant area. Common to all except Halle-Merseburg was the crisis of the small farmer.

TABLE 5

18–20	1.8%
21–30	40.4
31–40	27.8
41–50	17.1
51–60	9.3
61–	3.6

At the same time, a survey of Oschatz-Grimma, a light-industrial county in Saxony, showed:[162]

TABLE 6

	Population (1933)	*SPD (1931)*	*NSDAP (1931)*
18–30	31.1%	19.3%	61.3%
31–40	22.0	27.4	22.4
41–50	17.1	26.5	8.0
51–	29.8	26.8	8.3

Regionally, the relative influx of new members increased most spectacularly in the Palatinate, Danzig, and Schleswig-Holstein; fell behind in Franconia and Lower Bavaria, which had set the pace before September 1930; and was at its lowest level, as before, in the predominantly Catholic districts of Main-Franconia and Cologne-Aachen.[163] While difficult to derive from statistics, this trend would seem to point to both ideo-

[159] Ibid., p. 18.
[160] Ibid., p. 53.
[161] Ibid., pp. 202-6.
[162] Ibid., p. 157.
[163] Ibid., pp. 28–30.

logical and geographical diffusion, a transition in the direction Hitler desired, from völkisch provincialism to Volkspartei (a popular mass party). If this is so, the relative decline in Franconia and Lower Bavaria reflects the relative saturation of Nazi support in those areas by 1930; those attracted to Hitler were already in the Party. The gain in Danzig, the Palatinate, and Schleswig-Holstein, on the other hand, was obviously a consequence of economic misery and the apparent failure of all other alternatives.

Possible confirmation of this hypothesis is the influx of women members who, by their limited number—barely 6 per cent of total membership in January 1933—might be assumed to have been proportionally more "idealistic" than men and thereby a more sensitive index to the effectiveness of the Nazi appeal. Before 1930, while male enrollment in the fastest growing Gaue (party districts), Franconia and Lower Bavaria, ran only 3 to 3½ per cent ahead of the Reich average,[164] the enrollment of women in Franconia exceeded the Reich average by 23½ per cent, in Lower Bavaria by nearly 10 per cent, and in Munich and Upper Bavaria by roughly the same rate. But between September 1930 and January 1933, while the Reich average increase was over 700 per cent, women's enrollment in Franconia rose only about 30 per cent and scarcely doubled in Upper and Lower Bavaria. At the same time, women's enrollment in Danzig rose by 2100 per cent, in East Prussia by 1900 per cent, and in Westphalia-North by 1700 per cent. Unlike male enrollment, which showed considerable regional variation, there was relatively little deviation from the general Reich average in the growth of women's enrollment, save in Catholic areas like Cologne-Aachen, where membership grew by nearly 1000 per cent but, relative to the total female population, was still only about 50 per cent of the Reich average.[165]

One last aspect of interest was the constitution of political leadership in the Party relative to the general membership. Including honorary as well as salaried Party leaders, it comprised: [166]

TABLE 7

	To 14 September 1930	*To 1 January 1933*
Workers	18.5%	22.0%
White collar	25.2	23.4
Independent	20.3	19.7
Handicraftsmen	9.9	9.9
Trade	8.1	7.6
Professions	2.3	2.2
Civil servants	11.4	10.4
Public officials	8.7	7.6
Teachers	2.7	2.8
Farmers	18.4	18.4
Miscellaneous	3.8	3.1
Unemployed family members	1.2	1.6
Housewives	0.9	1.3
School, college students	0.3	0.3
Pensioners	1.2	1.4

Compared with Party membership, worker representation in Party leadership lagged visibly, the gap growing between 1930 and 1933, while farmers, civil servants, white-collar workers, and the economically independent were strikingly overrepresented. Considering that particularly in the white-collar and worker groups large, if statistically nondemonstrable, numbers had been exclusively employed by the Party for long periods, the discrepancy, particu-

[164] Ibid., pp. 28–30.
[165] Ibid., pp. 28–30.
[166] *Partei-Statistik,* Vol. II, 1935, p. 164. Since both columns far exceed 100%, it is safe to assume many functionaries filed double answers.

larly in worker leadership, was probably still greater than it appeared.

Age distribution ran roughly parallel to that of the general membership though, as might be expected, there was a tendency toward reinforcement of the middle-aged groups.[167]

TABLE 8

	To 14 September 1930	*To 1 January 1933*
18–20	0.2%	0.7%
21–30	26.0	28.2
31–40	39.1	36.3
41–50	21.9	23.1
51–60	9.8	9.0
over 60	3.0	2.1

In both cases, 65 per cent of the Party leadership was under forty years old.

Seen against its social background, National Socialism is far too complicated a phenomenon to be derived from any single source or reduced to any single common denominator, whether it be the depression or the course of German history. Its very dynamism precluded easy generalizations. If, before 1930, the NSDAP tended to be a Party of völkisch true believers, like the Göttingen Nazis who saw their mission in the compilation of a directory of Jews in German academic life,[168] it tended after 1930 to be an organization of the economically desperate with a considerable admixture of opportunism. "When I joined the NSDAP," Fritzsch testified at Nuremberg, "I did not have the impression of joining a Party in the conventional sense since this was a Party without a theory. . . . All the Party theoreticians were under fire. . . . There were already whole groups of former DNVP members in the NSDAP or of former Communists. . . ."[169]

"The formula, 'National Socialism is exclusively that which So-and-so says or does,' whereby the particular proponent was referring to himself, replaced the Party program . . . ," Hans Frank declared in his memoirs. "Any number of names filled the formula at the start: Hitler, Goering, Strasser, Röhm, Goebbels, Hess, Rosenberg, and more. There were as many National Socialisms as there were leaders."[170]

The most general theory—that National Socialism was a revolution of the lower middle class—is defensible but inadequate.[171] National Socialism had a striking appeal for the Auslandsdeutsche, Germans who had spent the impressionable years of their lives in a German community abroad.[172] Whether at the microcosmic level of the Göttingen Party or in important positions in Munich, like Rosenberg or Darré, there was an impressive number of them. National Socialism was no less a revolt of the young against the old. While a theory of National Socialism as a lower middle-class phenomenon applies very well to voter behavior, it fails to account for important sectors of Party leadership with their violent animosity toward the social forms for which their voters yearned. Himmler's contempt for the bourgeois self-indulgence of railway dining cars[173] was no more a lower

[167] Ibid., p. 167.

[168] Haase, op. cit., pp. 692 ff.

[169] International Military Tribunal, Vol. XVII (German edition), p. 154.

[170] Hans Frank, *Im Angesicht des Galgens,* Munich, 1953, p. 184.

[171] Cf. Harold Lasswell, "The Psychology of Hitlerism," in his *Analysis of Political Behaviour,* London, 1949, p. 236; Helmuth Plessner, *Die verspätete Nation,* Stuttgart, 1959, pp. 157 f.

[172] Cf. Karl Mannheim, *Mensch und Gesellschaft im Zeitalter des Umbaues,* Darmstadt, 1958, p. 111, footnote.

[173] Krebs, op. cit., p. 210.

middle-class attitude than the longing for action, power, nights of the long knives, or a radical reorganization of society, shared by the Party's leaders. National Socialism drew unmistakably on the historical reserves of liberal support, but its leaders were unequivocally sworn to the destruction of liberal values and liberal society.

This hard core of revolutionary destructiveness existed before the depression in quantities too great to be dismissed as simple personal idiosyncracy. The longing for security that it exploited existed before the depression as well, but sought its objectives elsewhere in unrevolutionary places. What brought them together, leaders and followers, was a common hostility to the status quo at a moment of unique desperation, a desperation only two parties, the KPD and the NSDAP were fully prepared to exploit. In promising everything to everybody, the Nazis promised nothing to anybody. The tactical pursuit of power obviated any immediate urgency in the discussion of what was to be done once it was attained. As it was to Frank and Fritzsch, this was clear to the farmer who told Heberle ". . . we believe that in the Third Reich, we, the farmers, will be so strong a power that we can shape it as we desire." [174] From a contemporary standpoint, National Socialism was wide open, its disparity not a handicap but a positive advantage. What united it ultimately was not a mandate for war and Auschwitz, but a universal desire for change.

[174] Heberle, op. cit., p. 120.

Hitler's own account of what National Socialism had attempted and accomplished in Germany in its first years of power can be found in the selection below. It is taken from a speech delivered on the fourth anniversary of the Nazis' coming to power. Among other things, Hitler here deals with the question of what, in his estimation, really constituted the Nazi Revolution.

The National Socialist Revolution

ADOLF HITLER

Gentlemen, Members of the German Reichstag:

This session of the Reichstag takes place on a date which is full of significance for the German people. Four years have passed since the beginning of that great internal revolution which in the meantime has been giving a new aspect to German life. This is the period of four years which I asked the German people to grant me for the purpose of putting my work to the test and submitting it to their judgement. Hence at

From the Reichstag Speech of January 30, 1937. Published as *On National Socialism and World Relations,* by M. Müller und Sohn, Berlin.

the present moment nothing could be more opportune than for me to render you an account of all the successes that have been achieved and the progress that has been made during these four years, for the welfare of the German people. But within the limits of the short statement I have to make it would be entirely impossible to enumerate all the remarkable results that have been reached during a time which may be looked upon as probably the most astounding epoch in the life of our people. That task belongs rather to the press and the propaganda. Moreover, during the course of the present year there will be an Exposition here in Berlin which is being organised for the purpose of giving a more comprehensive and detailed picture of the works that have been completed, the results that have been obtained and the projects on which work has been begun, all of which can be explained better in this way than I could do it within the limits of an address that is to last for two hours. Therefore I shall utilize the opportunity afforded me by this historic meeting of the Reichstag to cast a glance back over the past four years and call attention to some of the new knowledge that we have gained, some of the experiences which we have been through, and the consequences that have resulted therefrom—in so far as these have a general validity. It is important that we should understand them clearly, not only for our own sake but also for that of the generations to come.

Having done this, I shall pass on to explain our attitude towards those problems and tasks whose importance for us and for the world around us must be appreciated before it will be possible to live in better relations with one another. Finally I should like to describe as briefly as possible the projects which I have before my mind for our work in the near future and indeed in the distant future also.

At the time when I used to go here and there throughout the country, simply as a public speaker, people from the bourgeois classes used to ask me why we believed that a revolution would be necessary, instead of working within the framework of the established political order and with the collaboration of the parties already in existence, for the purpose of improving those conditions which we considered unsound and injurious. Why must we have a new party, and especially why a new revolution?

The answer which I then gave may be stated under the following headings:—

(1) The elements of confusion and dissolution which are making themselves felt in German life, in the concept of life itself and the will to national self-preservation, cannot be eradicated by a mere change of government. More than enough of those changes have already taken place without bringing about any essential betterment of the distress that exists in Germany. All these Cabinet reconstructions brought some positive advantage only to the actors who took part in the play; but the results were almost always quite negative as far as the interests of the people were concerned. As time has gone on the thought and practical life of our people have been led astray into ways that are unnatural to them and injurious. One of the causes which brought about this condition of affairs must be attributed to the fact that the structure of our State and our methods of government were foreign to our own national character, our historical development and our national needs.

The parliamentary-democratic system is inseparable from the other symptoms of the time. A critical situation cannot be remedied by collaborating with the causes of it but by a radical extermination of these causes. Hence under such conditions the political struggle must necessarily take the form of a revolution.

(2) It is out of the question to think that such a revolutionary reconstruction could be carried out by those who are the custodians and the more or less responsible representatives of the old regime, or by the political organisations founded under the old form of the Constitution. Nor would it be possible to bring this about by collaborating with these institutions, but only by establishing a new movement which will fight against them for the purpose of carrying through a radical reformation in political, cultural and economic life. And this fight will have to be undertaken even at the sacrifice of life and blood, if that should be necessary.

In this connection it is worthy of remark that when the average political party wins a parliamentary victory no essential change takes place in the historical course which the people are following or in the outer aspect of public life; whereas a genuine revolution that arises from a profound ideological insight will always lead to a transformation which is strikingly impressive and is manifest to the outside world.

Surely nobody will doubt the fact that during the last four years a revolution of the most momentous character has passed like a storm over Germany. Who could compare this new Germany with that which existed on the 30th. of January four years ago, when I took my oath of loyalty before the venerable President of the Reich?

I am speaking of a National Socialist Revolution; but this revolutionary process in Germany had a particular character of its own, which may have been the reason why the outside world and so many of our fellow-countrymen failed to understand the profound nature of the transformation that took place. I do not deny that this peculiar feature, which has been for us the most outstanding characteristic of the lines along which the National Socialist Revolution took place—a feature which we can be specially proud of—has hindered rather than helped to make this unique historic event understood abroad and among some of our own people. For the National Socialist Revolution was in itself a revolution in the revolutionary tradition.

What I mean is this: Throughout thousands of years the conviction grew up and prevailed, not so much in the German mind as in the minds of the contemporary world, that bloodshed and the extermination of those hitherto in power—together with the destruction of public and private institutions and property—were essential characteristics of every true revolution. Mankind in general has grown accustomed to accept revolutions with all these consequences somehow or other as if they were legal happenings. I do not mean that people endorse all this tumultuous destruction of life and property; but they certainly accept it as the necessary accompaniment of events which, because of this very reason, are called revolutions.

Herein lies the difference between the National Socialist Revolution and other revolutions, with the exception of the Fascist Revolution in Italy. The National Socialist Revolution was almost entirely a bloodless proceeding. When the party took over power in Germany, after overthrowing the very formidable obstacles that had stood in its way, it did so without causing any damage whatsoever to property. I can say with a certain amount of pride that this was the first revolution in which not even a window-pane was broken.

Don't misunderstand me however. If this revolution was bloodless that was not because we were not manly enough to look at blood.

I was a soldier for more than four years in a war where more blood was shed than ever before throughout human history. I never lost my nerve, no matter what the situation was and no matter what sights I had to face. The same holds good for my party colleagues. But we did not consider it as part of the programme of the National Socialist Revolution to destroy human life or material goods, but rather to build up a new and better life. And it is the greatest source of pride to us that we have been able to carry through this revolution, which is certainly the greatest revolution ever experienced in the history of our people, with a minimum of loss and sacrifice. Only in those cases where the murderous lust of the Bolshevics, even after the 30th. of January, 1933, led them to think that by the use of brute force they could prevent the success and realisation of the National Socialist ideal—only then did we answer violence with violence, and naturally we did it promptly. Certain other individuals of a naturally undisciplined temperament, and who had no political consciousness whatsoever, had to be taken into protective custody; but, generally speaking, these individuals were given their freedom after a short period. Beyond this there was a small number who took part in politics only for the purpose of establishing an alibi for their criminal activities, which were proved by the numerous sentences to prison and penal servitude that had been passed upon them previously. We prevented such individuals from pursuing their destructive careers, inasmuch as we set them to do some useful work, probably for the first time in their lives.

I do not know if there ever has been a revolution which was of such a profound character as the National Socialist Revolution and which at the same time allowed innumerable persons who had been prominent in political circles under the former regime to follow their respective callings in private life peacefully and without causing them any worry. Not only that, but even many among our bitterest enemies, some of whom had occupied the highest positions in the government, were allowed to enjoy their regular emoluments and pensions.

That is what we did. But this policy did not always help our reputation abroad. Just a few months ago we had an experience with some very honourable British world-citizens who considered themselves obliged to address a protest to me because I had some criminal protégés of the Moscow regime interned in a German concentration camp. Perhaps it is because I am not very well informed on current affairs that I have not heard whether those honourable gentlemen have ever expressed their indignation at the various acts of sanguinary violence which these Moscow criminals committed in Germany, or whether they ever expressed themselves against the slogan: "Strike down and kill the Fascist wherever you meet him", or whether, for example, they have taken the occasion of recent happenings in Spain to express their indignation against slaughtering and violating and burning to death thousands upon thousands of men, women and children. If the revolution in Germany had taken place according to the democratic model in Spain these strange apostles of non-intervention abroad would probably find that there was nothing which they need to worry about. People closely acquainted with the state of affairs in Spain have assured us that if we place the number of persons who have been slaughtered in this bestial way at 170.000, the figure will probably be too low rather than too high. Measured by the achievements of the noble democratic revolutionaries in Spain, the quota of human beings allotted for slaughter to the National Socialist Revolution would have been about 400.000 or 500.000; because our population is about three times larger than that of Spain. That we did not carry out this mass-slaughter is apparently looked upon as a piece of negligence on our part. We see that the democratic world-citizens are by no means gracious in their criticism of this leniency.

We certainly had the power in our hands to do what has been done in Spain. And probably we had better nerves than the murderer who steals upon his victim unawares, shunning the open fight, and who is capable only of murdering defenceless hostages. We have been soldiers and we never flinched in the face of battle throughout that most gruesome war of all times. Our hearts and, I may also add, our sound common sense saved us from committing any acts like those which have been done in Spain.

Taking it all in all, fewer lives were sacrificed in the National Socialist Revolution than the number of National Socialist followers who were murdered in Germany by our Bolshevic opponents in the year 1932 alone, when there was no revolution.

This absence of bloodshed and destruction was made possible solely because we had adopted a principle which not only guided our conduct in the past but which we shall also never forget in the future. This principle was that the purpose of a revolution, or of any general change in the condition of public affairs, cannot be to produce chaos but only to replace what is bad by substituting something better. In such cases, however, something better must be ready at hand. On the 30th. of January four years ago, when the venerable President of the Reich sent for me and entrusted me with the task of forming a new Cabinet, we had already come through a strenuous struggle in our efforts to obtain supreme political control over the State. All the means employed in carrying on that struggle were strictly within the law as it then stood and the protagonists in the fight were the National Socialists. Before the new State could be actually established and promulgated, the idea of it and the model for its organisation had already existed within the framework of our party. All the fundamental principles on which the new Reich was to be constructed were the principles and ideas already embodied in the National Socialist Party.

As a result of the constitutional struggle to win over our German fellow-countrymen to our side the party had established its predominance in the Reichstag and for a whole year before it actually assumed power it already had the right to demand this power for itself, even according to the principles of the parliamentary-democratic system. But it was essential for the National Socialist Revolution that this party should put forward demands which of themselves would involve a real revolutionary change in the principles and institutions of government hitherto in force.

When certain individuals who were blind to the actual state of affairs thought that they could refuse to submit to the practical application of the principles of the movement which had been entrusted with the government of the Reich, then, but not until then, the party used an iron hand to make these illegal disturbers of the peace bend their stubborn necks before the laws of the new National Socialist Reich and Government.

With this act the National Socialist Revolution came to an end. For as soon as the party had taken over power, and this new condition of affairs was consolidated, I looked upon it as a matter of course that the Revolution should be transformed into an evolution.

The new development which now set in, however, meant that there had to be a new orientation not merely of our ideas but also in regard to the practical policy which we had to carry out. Even today certain individuals who have fallen behind in the march of events refuse to adapt themselves to this change. They cannot understand it because it is beyond their mental horizon or outside the sphere of their egotistic interests. Our National Socialist teaching has undoubtedly a revolutionizing effect in many spheres of life and has interfered and acted under the revolutionary impulse.

The main plank in the National Socialist programme is to abolish the liberalistic concept of the individual and the Marxist concept of humanity and to substitute therefor the folk community, rooted in the soil and bound together by the bond of its common blood. A very simple statement; but it involves a principle that has tremendous consequences.

This is probably the first time and this is the first country in which people are being taught to realize that, of all the tasks which we have to face, the noblest and most sacred for mankind is that each racial species must preserve the purity of the blood which God has given it.

And thus it happens that for the first time it is now possible for men to use their God-given faculties of perception and insight in the understanding of those problems which are of more momentous importance for the preservation of human existence than all the victories that may be won on the battlefield or the successes that may be obtained through economic efforts. The greatest revolution which National Socialism has brought about is that it has rent asunder the veil which hid from us the knowledge that all human failures and mistakes are due to the conditions of the time and therefore can be remedied, but that there is one error which cannot be remedied once men have made it, namely the failure to recognize the importance of conserving the blood and the race free from intermixture and thereby the racial aspect and character which are God's gift and God's handiwork. It is not for men to discuss the question of why Providence created different races, but rather to recognise the fact that it punishes those who disregard its work of creation.

Unspeakable suffering and misery have come upon mankind because they lost this instinct which was grounded in a profound intuition; and this loss was caused by a wrong and lopsided education of the intellect. Among our people there are millions and millions of persons living today for whom this law has become clear and intelligible. What individual seers and the still unspoiled natures of our forefathers saw by direct perception has now become a subject of scientific research in Germany. And I can prophesy here that, just as the knowledge that the earth moves around the sun led to a revolutionary alteration in the general world-picture, so the blood-and-race doctrine of the National Socialist Movement will bring about a revolutionary change in our knowledge and therewith a radical reconstruction of the picture which human history gives us of the past and will also change the course of that history in the future.

And this will not lead to an estrangement between the nations; but, on the contrary, it will bring about for the first time a real understanding of one another. At the same time, however, it will prevent the Jewish people from intruding themselves among all the other nations as elements of internal disruption, under the mask of honest world-citizens, and thus gaining power over these nations.

We feel convinced that the consequences of this really revolutionising vision of truth will bring about a radical transformation in German life. For the first time in our history, the German people have found the way to a higher unity than they ever had before; and that is due to the compelling attraction of this inner feeling. Innumerable prejudices have been broken down, many barriers have been overthrown as unreasonable, evil traditions have been wiped out and antiquated symbols shown to be meaningless. From that chaos of disunion which had been caused by tribal, dynastic, philosophical, religious and political strife, the German nation has arisen and has unfurled the banner of a reunion which symbolically announces, not a political triumph, but the triumph of the racial principle. For the past four-and-a-half years German legislation has upheld and enforced this idea. Just as on January 30th, 1933, a state of affairs already in existence was legalized by the fact that I was entrusted with the chancellorship, whereby the party whose supremacy in Germany had then become unquestionable was now authorized to take over the government of the Reich and mould the future destiny of Germany; so this German legislation that has been in force for the past four years was only the legal sanction which gave jurisdiction and binding force to an idea that had already been clearly formulated and promulgated by the party.

When the German community, based on the racial blood-bond, became realised in the German State we all felt that this would remain one of the finest moments to be remembered during our lives. Like a blast of springtime it passed over Germany four years ago. The fighting forces of our movement who for many years had defended the banner of the Hooked Cross against the superior forces of the enemy, and had carried it steadily forward for a long fourteen years, now planted it firmly in the soil of the new Reich.

Within a few weeks the political debris and the social prejudices which had been accumulating through a thousand years of German history were removed and cleared away.

May we not speak of a revolution when the chaotic conditions brought about by parliamentary-democracy disappear in less than three months and a regime of order and discipline takes their place, and a new energy springs forth from a firmly welded unity and a comprehensive authoritative power such as Germany never before had?

So great was the Revolution that its intellectual foundations are not even yet understood but are superficially criticized by our contemporaries. They talk of democracies and dictatorships; but they fail to grasp the fact that in this country a radical transformation has taken place and has produced results which are democratic in the highest sense of the word, if democracy has any meaning at all.

With infallible certainty we are steering towards an order of things in which a process of selection will become active in the political leadership of the nation, as it exists throughout the whole of life in general. By this process of selection, which will follow the laws of Nature and the dictates of human reason, those among our people who show the greatest natural ability will be appointed to positions in the political leadership of the nation. In making this selection no consideration will be given to birth or ancestry, name or wealth, but only to the question of whether or not the candidate has a natural vocation for those higher positions of leadership. That was a fine principle which the great Corsican enunciated when he said that each one of his soldiers carried a marshal's baton in the haversack. In this country that principle will have its political counterpart. Is there a nobler or more excellent kind of Socialism and is there a truer form of Democracy than this National Socialism which is so organized that through it each one among the millions of German boys is given the possibility of finding his way to the highest office in the nation, should it please Providence to come to his aid.

And that is no theory. In the present

National Socialist Germany it is a reality that is considered by us all as a matter of course. I myself, to whom the people have given their trust and who have been called to be their leader, come from the people. All the millions of German workers know that it is not a foreign dilettante or an international revolutionary apostle who is at the head of the Reich, but a German who has come from their own ranks.

And numerous people whose families belong to the peasantry and working classes are now filling prominent positions in this National Socialist State. Some of them actually hold the highest offices in the leadership of the nation, as Cabinet Ministers, *Reichsstatthalter* and *Gauleiter*. But National Socialism always bears in mind the interests of the people as a whole and not the interests of one class or another.

The National Socialist Revolution has not aimed at turning a privileged class into a class which will have no rights in the future. Its aim has been to grant equal rights to those social strata that hitherto were denied such rights. We have not ruined millions of citizens by degrading them to the level of enslaved workers. Our aim has been to educate slaves to be German citizens. One thing will certainly be quite clear to every German; and this is that revolutions as acts of terror can only be of short duration. If revolutions are not able to produce something new they will end up by devouring the whole of the national patrimony which existed before them. From the assumption of power as an act of force the beneficial work of peace must be promptly developed. But those who abolish classes for the purpose of putting new classes in their place sow the seeds of new revolutions. The bourgeois citizen who has the ruling power in his hands today will become a proletarian if he is banished to Siberia tomorrow and condemned to enforced labour there. He will then yearn for *his* day of deliverance, just as did the proletarian of former times, who now thinks that his turn has come to play the despot. Therefore the National Socialist Revolution never aimed at bringing in one class of the German people and turning out another. On the contrary, our objective has been to make it possible for the whole German people to work, not only in the economic but also in the political field, and to guarantee this possibility by organising the various classes into one national unit.

The National Socialist Movement, however, limits its sphere of internal activity to those individuals who belong to one people and it refuses to allow the members of a foreign race to wield an influence over our political, intellectual, or cultural life. And we refuse to accord to the members of a foreign race any predominant position in our national economic system.

In this folk-community, which is based on the bond of blood, and in the results which National Socialism has obtained by making the idea of this community understood among the public, lies the most profound reason for the marvellous success of our Revolution.

Confronted with this new and vigorous ideal, all idols and relics of the past which had been upheld by dynastic interests, tribal affiliations and even party interests, now began to lose their glamour. That is why the whole party system of former times completely collapsed in a few weeks, without giving rise to the feeling that something had been lost. They were superseded by a better ideal. A new movement took their place. A re-organisation of our people into a national unit that includes all those whose labour is productive simply pushed aside the old organisations of employers and employees. The symbolic emblems of the recent past, which was a period of disintegration and disability, were banished, not—as in 1918 or 1919 —through a resolution voted by a committee appointed to invent a new symbol for the Reich, as if the choice were to depend on the results of a prize competition. But all these old emblems were now displaced by that flag which symbolised the militant period of the National Socialist Movement and which was borne by us on the day of Germany's resurgence. Since that day it has become the consecrated symbol of this national resurgence on land and sea and in the air.

There could be no more eloquent proof of how profoundly the German people have understood the significance of this change and new development than the manner in which the nation sanctioned our regime at the polls on so many occasions during the years that followed. So, of all those who like to point again and again to the democratic form of government as the institution which is based on the universal will of the people, in contrast to dictatorships, nobody has a better right to speak in the name of the people than I have.

Among the results of this phase of the German Revolution I may enumerate the following:—

(1) Since that time there is only one trustee of supreme power among the German people and that trustee is the whole people itself.

(2) The will of the people finds its expression in the Party, which is the political organisation of the people.

(3) Therefore there is only one legislative body.

(4) There is only one executive authority.

Anybody who compares this state of affairs with the condition of Germany before January 1933 will realise what a tremendous transformation is indicated by these few short statements.

But this transformation is only a result that has followed from carrying a fundamental axiom of the National Socialist doctrine into practical effect. This axiom is that the only reasonable meaning and purpose of all human thought and conduct cannot be to create or to maintain structures, organisations or functions made by men, but only to preserve and develop the innate character of the people itself; for Providence has given us this character as the groundwork of all our constructive efforts. Through the successful issue of the National Socialist Movement the people as such was placed above any organisation, construction or function, as the sole element that is always there and will permanently abide.

The meaning and purpose which Providence had in mind when it created the different races cannot be investigated by us, human beings, and no theory about it can be laid down. But the meaning and purpose of human organisations and of all human activities can be measured by asking what value they are for the maintenance of the race or people, which is the one existing element that must abide. The people—the race—is the primary thing. Party, State, Army, the national economic structure, Justice etc, all these are only secondary and accidental. They are only the means to the end and the end is the preservation of this nation. These public institutions are right and useful according to the measure in which their energies are directed towards this task. If they are incapable of fulfilling it, then their existence is harmful and they must either be reformed or removed and replaced by something better.

It is absolutely necessary that this principle should be practically recognised; for that is the only way in which men can be saved from becoming the victims of a devitalized set of dogmas in a matter where dogmas are entirely out of place, and from drawing dogmatic conclusions from the consideration of ways and means, when the final purpose itself is the only valid dogma.

All of you, gentlemen and members of the German Reichstag, understand the meaning of what I have just said. But on this occasion I am speaking to the whole German people and therefore I should like to bring forward a few examples which show how important these principles were proved to be when they were put into practice.

There are many people for whom this is the only way of explaining why we talk of a National Socialist Revolution, though no blood was shed and no property wrecked.

For a long time our ideas of law and justice had been developing in a way that led to a state of general confusion. This was partly due to the fact that we adopted ideas which were foreign to our national character and also partly because the German mind itself did not have any clear notion of what public justice meant. This confusion was evidenced most strikingly by the lack of inner clarity as to the function of law and justice.

There are two extreme poles which are characteristic of this mental lack:—

(1) The opinion that the law as such is its own justification and hence cannot be made the subject of any critical analysis as to its utility, either in regard to its general principles or its relation to particular problems. According to this notion, the law would remain even though the world should disappear.

(2) The opinion that it is the main function of law to protect and safeguard the life and property of the individual.

Between these two extreme poles the idea of defending the larger interests of the community was introduced very timidly and under the cloak of an appeal to reasons of state.

In contradistinction to all this, the National Socialist Revolution has laid down a definite and unambiguous principle on which the whole system of legislation, jurisprudence and administration of justice must be founded.

It is the task of justice to collaborate in supporting and protecting the people as a whole against those individuals who, because they lack a social conscience, try to shirk the obligations to which all the members of the community are subject, or directly act against the interests of the community itself.

In the new German legal system which will be in force from now onwards the nation is placed above persons and property.

The principle expressed in that brief statement and everything it implies has led to the greatest reform ever introduced in our German legal structure. The first decisive action taken in accordance with the fundamental principle I have spoken of was the setting up not only of one legislator but also of one executive. The second measure is not yet ready but will be announced to the nation within a few weeks.

In the German penal code, which has been drawn up with this wide general perspective in view, German justice will be placed for the first time on a basis which ensures that for all time to come its duty will be to serve in maintaining the German race.

Although the chaos which we found before us in the various branches of public life was very great indeed, the state of dissolution into which German economic life had fallen was still greater. And this was the feature of the German collapse that impressed itself most strikingly on the minds of the broad masses of the people. The conditions that then actually existed have still remained in their memories and in the memory of the German people as a whole. As outstanding examples of this catastrophe we found these two phenomena:—

(1) More than six millions of unemployed.

(2) An agricultural population that was manifestly doomed to dissolution.

The area covered by the German agricultural farms that were on the point of being sold up by forced auction was as large as the whole of Thuringia (more than 8.000 square miles).

In the natural course of events the falling off in production on the one side and the decrease in purchasing power, on the other, must necessarily bring about the disruption and annihilation of the great mass of the middle class also. How seriously this side of the German distress was then felt might subsequently be measured by the fact that I had to ask for full powers for the period of four years especially for the purpose of reducing unemployment and putting a stop to the dissolution of the German agricultural population.

I may further state that in 1933 the National Socialists did not interfere with any activities which were being carried out by others and which at the same time promised success. The Party was called to take over the government of the country at a moment when the possibilities of redeeming the situation in any other way had been exhausted and particularly when repeated attempts to overcome the economic crisis had failed.

After four years from that date I now face the German people and you, gentlemen and members of the Reichstag, to give an account of what has been accomplished. On this occasion I do not think you will withhold your sanction from what the National Socialist Government has done and you will agree that I have fulfilled the promises I made four years ago.

It was not an easy undertaking. I am not giving away any secrets when I tell you that at that time the so-called economic experts were convinced that the economic crisis could not be overcome. In the face of this staggering situation which, as I have said, appeared hopeless to the minds of the experts, I still believed in the possibility of a German revival and particularly in the possibility of an economic recovery. My belief was grounded on two considerations:—

(1) I have always had sympathy for those excited people who invariably talk of the collapse of the nation whenever they find themselves confronted with a difficult situation. What do they mean by a collapse? The German people were already in existence before they made any definite appearance in history as it is known to us. Now, leaving out entirely what their pre-historic experiences may have been, it is certain that during the past two thousand years of history, through which that portion of mankind which we call the German People has passed, unspeakable miseries and catastrophies must have befallen them more than once. Famines, wars and pestilences have overwhelmed our people and wreaked terrible havoc among them. It must give rise to unlimited faith in the vital resources of a nation when we recall the fact that only a few centuries ago our German people, with a population of more than eighteen millions, were reduced by the Thirty Years War to less than four millions. Let us also remember that this once flourishing land was pillaged, dismembered and devastated, that its cities were burned down, its hamlets and villages laid waste, that its fields were left uncultivated and barren. Some ten years afterwards our people began again to increase in number. The cities were rebuilt and began to be filled with a new life. The fields were ploughed once more. Songs were heard along the countryside, in concord with the rhythm of that work which brought new life and livelihood to the people.

Let us look back over the development, or at least that part of it known to us, through which our people have passed since those dim historic ages down to the present time. We shall then recognise how puny is all the fuss that these weakling footlers make who immediately begin to talk about the collapse of the economic structure—and hence of human existence—the first moment a piece of printed paper loses its face value somewhere in the world. Germany and the German people have mastered many a grave catastrophe. Of course, we must admit that the right men were always needed to formulate the necessary measures and enforce them without paying any attention to those negative persons who always think that they know more than others. A bevy of parliamentarian weaklings are certainly not the kind of men to lead a nation out of the slough of distress and despair. I firmly believed and was solemnly convinced that the economic catastrophe would be mastered in Germany as soon as the people could be got to believe in their own immortality as a people and as soon as they realised that the aim and purpose of all economic effort is to save and maintain the life of the nation.

(2) I was not an economist, which means that I have never been a theorist during my whole life.

But unfortunately I have observed that the worst theorists are always busy in those quarters where theory has no place at all and where practical life counts for everything. It goes without saying that in the economic sphere and with the passing of time experience has given rise to the employment of certain definite principles and also definite methods of work which have been proved to be productive of good results. But all methods and principles are subject to the time element. To make hard-and-fast dogmas out of practical methods would deprive the human faculties and working power of that elasticity which alone enables them to face changing demands by changing the means of meeting them accordingly and thus mastering them. There were many persons among us who busied themselves, with that perseverance which is characteristic of the Germans, in an effort to formulate dogmas from economic methods and then raise that dogmatic system to a branch of our university curriculum, under the title of national economy. According to the pronouncements issued by these national economists, Germany was irrevocably lost. It is a characteristic of all dogmatists that they vigorously reject any new dogma. In other words, they criticise any new piece of knowledge that may be put forward and reject it as mere theory. For the last eighteen years we have been witnessing a rare spectacle. Our economic dogmatists have been proved wrong in almost every branch of practical life and yet they repudiate those who have actually overcome the economic crisis, as propagators of false theories and damn them accordingly.

You all know the story of the doctor who told a patient that he could live only for another six months. Ten years afterwards the patient met the physician; but the only surprise which the latter expressed at the recovery of the patient was to state that the treatment which the second doctor gave the patient was entirely wrong.

The German economic policy which National Socialism introduced in 1933 is based on some fundamental considerations. In the relations between economics and the people, the people alone is the only unchangeable element. Economic activity in itself is no dogma and never can be such.

There is no economic theory or opinion which can claim to be considered as sacrosanct. The will to place the economic system at the service of the people, and capital at the service of economics, is the only thing that is of decisive importance here.

We know that National Socialism vigorously combats the opinion which holds that the economic structure exists for the benefit of capital and that the people are to be looked upon as subject to the economic system. We were therefore determined from the very beginning to exterminate the false notion that the economic system could exist and operate entirely freely and entirely outside of any control or supervision on the part of the State. Today there can no longer be such a thing as an independent economic system. That is to say, the economic system can no longer be left to itself exclusively. And this is so, not only because it is unallowable from the political point of view but also because, in the purely economic sphere itself, the consequences would be disastrous.

It is out of the question that millions of individuals should be allowed to work just as they like and merely to meet their own needs; but it is just as impossible to allow the entire system of economics to function according to the notions held exclusively in economic circles and thus made to serve egotistic interests. Then there is the further consideration that these economic circles are not in a position to bear the responsibility for their own failures. In its modern phase of development, the economic system concentrates enormous masses of workers in certain special branches and in definite local areas. New inventions or a slump in the market may destroy whole branches of industry at one blow.

The industrialist may close his factory gates. He may even try to find a new field for his personal activities. In most cases he will not be ruined so easily. Moreover, the industrialists who have to suffer in such contingencies are only a small number of individuals. But on the other side there are hundreds of thousands of workers, with their wives and children. Who is to defend their interests and care for them? The whole community of the people? Indeed, it is its duty to do so. Therefore the whole community cannot be made to bear the burden of economic disasters without according it the right of influencing and controlling economic life and thus avoiding catastrophes.

In the years 1932/33, when the German economic system seemed definitely ruined, I recognised even more clearly than ever before that the salvation of our people was not a financial problem. It was exclusively a problem of how industrial labour could best be employed on the one side and, on the other, how our agricultural resources could be utilized.

This is first and foremost a problem of organisation. Phrases, such as the freedom of the economic system, for example, are no help. What we have to do is to use all available means at hand to make production possible and open up fields of activity for our working energies. If this can be successfully done by the economic leaders themselves, that is to say by the industrialists, then we are content.

But if they fail, the folk-community, which in this case means the State, is obliged to step in for the purpose of seeing that the working energies of the nation are employed in such a way that what they produce will be of use to the nation, and the State will have to devise the necessary measures to assure this. In this respect the State may do everything; but one thing it cannot do—and this was the actual state of affairs we had to face—is to allow 12.000 million working hours to be lost year after year.

For the folk-community does not exist on the fictitious value of money but on the results of productive labour, which is what gives money its value.

This production, and not a bank or gold reserve, is the first cover for a currency. And if I increase production I increase the real income of my fellow-citizens. And if I reduce production I reduce that income, no matter what wages are paid out.

Members of the Reichstag: Within the past four years we have increased German production to an extraordinary degree in all branches. And the whole German nation benefits by this increase. For if there is a demand today for very many million tons of coal more than formerly, this is not for the purpose of superheating the houses of a few millionaires to a couple of thousand degrees, but rather because millions of our German countrymen are thus enabled to purchase more coal for themselves with their increased income.

By giving employment to millions of German workers who had hitherto been idle, the National Socialist Revolution has brought about such a gigantic increase in German production. That rise in our total national income guarantees the market value of the goods produced. And only in such cases where we could not increase this production, owing to certain conditions that were beyond our control, there have been shortages from time to time; but these bear no proportion whatsoever to the general success of the National Socialist struggle.

The four-year plan is the most striking manifestation of the systematic way in which our economic life is being conducted. In particular this plan will provide permanent employment in the internal circulation of our economic life for those masses of German labour that are now being released from the armament industry.

One sign of the gigantic economic development which has taken place is that in many industries today it is quite difficult to find sufficient skilled workmen. I am thankful that this is so; because it will help to place the importance of the worker as a man and as a working force in its proper light; and also because in doing so—though there are other motives also—we have a chance of making the activities of the party and its unions better understood and thus securing stronger and more willing support.

Seeing that we insist on the national importance of the function which our economic system fulfils, it naturally follows that the former disunion between employer and employee can no longer exist. But the new State will not and does not wish to assume the role of entrepreneur. It will regulate the working strength of the nation only in so far as such regulation is necessary for the common good. And it will supervise conditions and methods of working only in so far as this is in the interests of all those engaged in work. Under no circumstances will the State attempt to bureaucratize economic life. The economic effects that follow from every real and practical initiative benefit the people as a whole. At the present moment an inventor or an economic organiser is of inestimable value to the folk community. For the future the first task of National Socialist education will be to make clear to all our fellow-citizens how their reciprocal worth must be appreciated. We must point out to the one side how there can be no substitute for the German worker and we must teach the German worker how indispensable are the inventor and the genuine business leader. It is quite clear that under the aegis of such an outlook on economic life, strikes and lock-outs can no longer be tolerated. The National Socialist State repudiates the right of economic coercion. Above all contracting parties stand the economic interests of the nation, which are the interests of the people.

The practical results of this economic policy of ours are already known to you. Throughout the whole nation there is a tremendous urge towards productive activity. Enormous works are arising everywhere for the expansion of industry and traffic. While in other countries strikes or lock-outs shatter the stability of national production, our millions of productive workers obey the highest of all laws that we have in this world, namely the law of common sense.

Within these four years which have passed we have succeeded in bringing about the economic redemption of our people; but we realise at the same time that the results of this economic work in town and city must be safeguarded. The first danger that threatens us here is in the sphere of cultural creativeness. And that danger comes from those who are themselves active in that sphere. For our fellow-countrymen who are engaged in artistic and cultural productivity today, or are acting as custodians and trustees of cultural works, have not the necessary intuitive faculties to value and appreciate the ideal products of human genius in this sphere.

The National Socialist Movement has laid down the directive lines along which the State must conduct the education of the people. This education does not begin at a certain year and end at another. The development of the human being makes it necessary to take the child from the control of that small cell of social life which is the family and entrust his further training to the community itself.

The National Socialist Revolution has clearly outlined the duties which this social education must fulfil and, above all, it has made this education independent of the question of age. In other words, the education of the individual can never end. Therefore it is the duty of the folk-community to see that this education and higher training must always be along lines that help the community to fulfil its own task, which is the maintenance of the race and nation.

For that reason we must insist that all organs of education which may be useful for the instruction and training of the people have to fulfil their duty towards the community. Such organs or organisations are: Education of the Youth, Young Peoples Organisation, Hitler Youth, Labour Front, Party and Army—all these are institutions for the education and higher training of our people. The book press and the newspaper press, lectures and art, the theatre and the cinema, they are all organs of popular education.

What the National Socialist Revolution has accomplished in this sphere is astounding. Think only of the following:—

The whole body of our German education, including the press, the theatre, the cinema and literature, is being controlled and shaped today by men and women of our own race. Some time ago one often heard it said that if Jewry were expelled from these institutions they would collapse or become deserted. And now what has happened? In all those branches cultural and artistic activities are flourishing. Our films are better than ever before and our theatrical productions today in our leading theatres stand supreme and alone in comparison with the rest of the world. Our press has become a powerful instrument to help our people in bringing their innate faculties to self-expression and assertion, and by so doing it strengthens the nation. German science is active and is producing results which will one day bear testimony to the creative and constructive will of this epoch.

It is very remarkable how the German people have become immune from those destructive tendencies under which another world is suffering. Many of our organisations which were not understood at all a few years ago are now accepted as a matter of course: the Young People, the Hitler Youth, BDM., Womanhood, Labour Service, SA, SS, NSKK, but above all the Labour Front in its magnificent departments—they are all building stones in that proud edifice which we call The Third Reich. . . .

The basic components of the National Socialist ideology were ideas and prejudices that had been current in the intellectual life of Europe for a century or more. What gave the ideology its novelty and its peculiar force was the virulent synthesis of these elements made by Hitler. That synthesis is here described by Professor Hajo Holborn, probably the foremost German historian of his generation.

The Origins and Political Character of Nazi Ideology*

HAJO HOLBORN

I

"The ideology is intolerant and cannot be content with the rôle of 'a party among other parties.' It imperiously demands its own, exclusive, and unqualified recognition as well as the complete transformation of the whole public life according to its views." [1] With these words Hitler in 1926 proclaimed his determination not to tolerate any ideology other than the National Socialist one. Only pure ideology can engender the "fanatic" faith that will build the "movement" and the "racial community" (*Volksgemeinschaft*). In the last weeks before his death, in what he called "the last quarter-hour" of the Third Empire, Hitler said that the Allies would now erase the German people as well as the National Socialist ideology.[2]

But in spite of the emphasis laid not only on ideology but also on pure and correct ideology, there existed few canonic National Socialist writings. The party program of 1920, written by the engineer Gottfried Feder, contained among its twenty-five points more economic than political demands, some of which soon became meaningless, since they were geared to the peculiar conditions of Germany in the first years after World War I. In 1925 after Hitler had returned from prison, discussions on a new party program were held, for which apparently Gregor Strasser had prepared a draft. But Hitler, anxious to restore his leadership of the party, opposed a new program and insisted that the program of 1920 should be publicly pronounced "unalterable." Just the same, it was changed later by the dubious reinterpretation of certain points, while others were simply shelved after 1933.

Hitler's *Mein Kampf* is by far the most important source for Nazi ideology. He opened the second volume, written in 1925 with the subtitle "the National Socialist movement," with a chapter on "ideology and party." It is noteworthy that Hitler never mentions

* Presented at the Annual Meeting of the American Political Science Association in New York City on September 6, 1963.

Reprinted with permission from *The Political Science Quarterly,* Vol. 79 (December 1964), pp. 542–54.

[1] Adolf Hitler, *Mein Kampf* (3rd ed.; Munich, 1928), 506.

[2] February 6, 1945, see F. Genoud (ed.), *Le Testament Politique de Hitler, Notes Récueilliés par Martin Bormann,* préface de H. R. Trevor-Roper (Paris, 1959), 65.

any of Feder's points specifically, although he starts the chapter with a glowing reference to the first National Socialist mass meeting, at which Feder's program was adopted by acclamation, and goes on to explain that a program to a party is what dogma is to a church. Hitler obviously was cautious not to commit himself to very specific objectives which were likely to limit the appeal of National Socialism with groups that he hoped to win over. His bombastic and rambling book remains fragmentary in many respects and does not offer a systematic presentation of Nazi ideology. This again is partly due to political considerations. To give only one example, although Hitler's radical anti-Christian attitude was well established and a careful reader could sense it most distinctly, the issue of National Socialism versus the Christian churches is covered up in the book.[3] Other political calculations are revealed in the changes made in the text after 1933. Whereas the first and early editions said: "the movement stands . . . for the principle of a Germanic democracy: election of the leader, but absolute authority for him . . ." the passage later reads: "the movement stands . . . for the principle of the absolute authority of the leader, coupled with the highest responsibility. . . . The leader is always appointed from above and at the same time endowed with unlimited power and authority. . . ." [4]

But although political and propagandistic reasons of the moment explain many omissions as well as the obliqueness of many references, the unsystematic character of *Mein Kampf* is essentially the true expression of Hitler's peculiar mind. His was an unkempt and primitive mind that lacked the power of discrimination but excelled in reducing simple ideas to even simpler terms while believing thereby to have achieved a higher wisdom. On this account he considered himself an original thinker and never cared to give credit to any person from whom he had borrowed his ideas. Moreover he was interested only in those ideas that through propaganda would build organizations. The growth of the Nazi movement became to him a criterion of the truth of the Nazi ideology.[5] He did not pay any attention to the subsequent systematic expositions of National Socialist ideology. Thus he did not read Alfred Rosenberg's *The Myth of the Twentieth Century* (1930), taken by most people as the official treatise on Nazi philosophy,[6] nor any other of the theoretical writings of the Nazis and Nazi fellow travelers.

The quality of Hitler's mind and the tactical nature of all of his statements make it necessary even for the study of ideology to analyze his actions and the political reality created by them, as Franz L. Neumann was the first to do in his *Behemoth*. Yet at the time Neumann wrote his still important book only two canonic writings were known to Hitler's followers and the world at large, the

[3] This largely continued after 1933. A shocking preview of what Nazi policy with regard to the Christian churches would have been after a victorious war can be gleaned from the church policies of the Nazis in the conquered and annexed Polish territories. See Martin Broszat, *Nationalsozialistische Polenpolitik, 1939–45* (Stuttgart, 1961), 167 ff.

[4] See Hermann Hammer, "Die Deutschen Ausgaben von Hitlers 'Mein Kampf,'" *Vierteljahrshefte für Zeitgeschichte,* IV (1956), 161–78.

[5] When in 1932 a group of economists, among them Alfred Weber and Wilhelm Roepke, challenged him to a debate on problems of economic policy, he replied that the professors should first prove their ability to build up something like the NSDAP or SA before he would debate with them.

[6] See Hitler's statement in Henry Picker, *Hitlers Tischgespräche im Führerhauptquartier 1941–42,* edited by G. Ritter (Bonn, 1951), 275.

party program, which is of only limited value, and *Mein Kampf,* while by now we have a wealth of authentic Hitler material, spread over the years down to April 1945, which allows us to describe the Nazi ideology as well as the motivation of Nazi action rather exactly.[7]

II

What stands out most clearly today is the consistency and continuity of Nazi ideology. Hitler was a great opportunist and tactician, but it would be quite wrong to think that ideology was for him a mere instrumentality for gaining power. On the contrary, Hitler was a doctrinaire of the first order. Throughout his political career he was guided by an ideology, parts of which were played down or even publicly denied occasionally or even for a considerable length of time because they seemed to frighten people whom he intended to subject to his will. But step by step he realized his basic ideas, which from 1926 onward do not show any change whatsoever.

Fundamental in his thinking was the conception of life as an eternal struggle for survival and domination. Hunger and love he called the elemental forces behind this process.[8] Struggle rules supreme within peoples and among peoples. This crude social Darwinism is then linked up with an equally primitive racialism; not peoples but races are the primordial forces of history. Hitler admitted that there are no pure races and that, for example, the Germans mixed with peoples whom they conquered and with invaders they later absorbed.[9] But as a rule that did not keep him from asserting the superiority of pure races.[10] The strength of the Germanic race may be sapped by the admixture of other races, and Hitler ascribed the individualistic party spirit of the Germans to this fact. Once the true Germanic elements will have gained full power over the people, it will be possible to eliminate racially inferior groups and to enhance the breeding of the superior racial stock.

Among the races the Nordic or Aryan race is the highest and its chief representative is the German people. It deserves the satisfaction of all its needs for life and growth. Since agriculture cannot raise production beyond the present level, Germany needs a greater *Lebensraum,* which can only be gained by war and the expulsion, if necessary even annihilation, of other peoples. Already

[7] A bibliography is now readily available in the monumental work of Karl Dietrich Bracher, Wolfgang Sauer, and Gerhard Schulz, *Die Nationalsozialistische Machtergreifung* (Cologne, 1960). Hugh R. Trevor-Roper ("Hitlers Kriegsziele" in B. Freudenfeld [ed.], *Stationen der Deutschen Geschichte* [Stuttgart, 1962]) likes to give preference to the "four windows through which light falls into the most recondite thoughts of Hitler at the four turning points of his political career." These are the hours "of his political defeats" (*Mein Kampf*); "of his political triumphs" (Rauschning conversations 1932–34. H. Rauschning, *The Voice of Destruction,* [New York, 1940]); "of his military triumphs" (*Table-Talks* 1941–42, see footnote 6 above); and "of his military defeat" (Bormann dictations, 1945, see footnote 2 above). To these Trevor-Roper would probably be willing to add G. Weinberg (ed.), *Hitlers Zweites Buch* (Stuttgart, 1961), written in 1928 on the eve of the big expansion of the Nazi party. But there are many other documents, particularly between 1933 and 1945, which though not as extensive as the aforementioned sources are of primary importance.

[8] *Hitlers Zeites Buch,* 46.

[9] Picker, 444.

[10] Usually he declared the American people to be inferior for this reason. But occasionally he argued that if it had been possible to create in two hundred years an American nation it was because the immigrants had been the best people, and that meant mostly the Nordic elements of Europe! *Hitlers Zweites Buch,* 131.

in *Mein Kampf* racialist nationalism looks to the East for the conquest of *Lebensraum,* and Hitler never modified these ideas which led to his ultimate doom.[11]

Hitler's biological materialism tolerated no ethics. In the pursuit of its struggle for power, which is the dictate of the blood, the racial people may use any means. Any restraint is *Gefühlsduselei,* silly sentimentality. Hitler gloated that his conception of race was the true revolutionary principle of the twentieth century, as the idea of nation had revolutionized the preceding century.[12] In this connection he used almost Marxist terminology in deriding the stupidity of the bourgeoisie and the old upper classes for being hampered by humanitarian scruples and for their inability to conceive of better programs than the restoration of the German frontiers of 1914. Only "dynamic" or "fanatic" people fully believing in "race" would be able to fight without being bothered by humanitarian and traditionalist inhibitions. Hitler readily admitted that this fact called for barbarians.[13]

Anti-Semitism was the major instrument in this policy of barbarization.[14] Through the vilification, torture, and mass murder of the Jews the ruthlessness was produced that Hitler wanted to inculcate in his followers. He described quite often the practical political value of anti-Semitism, particularly in the sense that in order to arouse hatred among people it was essential to personify the enemy.[15] But it cannot be stressed enough that Hitler himself was a passionate believer in extreme anti-Semitism. The anti-Jewish demonstrations and pogroms of April 1, 1933, and of November 8–9, 1938 (*Reichskristallnacht*) were carried on in public, but when in 1942 Hitler ordered the physical extermination of all the European Jews, he knew that this "final solution"[16] of the Jewish problem would frighten most Germans and it was therefore secretly executed. It was a personal act of Hitler. But anti-Semitism was only part of Hitler's racism. While the Jews were to him subhuman, there were also low human races, such as the Slavs, whom he did not propose to destroy but to deprive of further growth and of their national education. The Nazi occupation policies in eastern Europe provide indications of these intentions.[17]

The use of terror against enemies of the party and regime was another means of barbarization, but not even terror and violence were mere instruments of power. Hitler believed in their permanent value. People do not have a natural herd instinct, he said;[18] if left alone they will rather fight among themselves. Only the fear of an authority commanding and using force can create a community.

The National Socialist ideology, which Hitler did not wish to be called "the myth of the 20th century" but "the science of the 20th century,"[19] included the self-esteem and worship of its prophet. In him the Germanic race has

[11] See Wolfgang Sauer in *Nationalsozialistische Machtergreifung,* 744 ff.

[12] Rauschning, 231 ff.

[13] Rauschning, 80.

[14] See Hannah Arendt, *The Origins of Totalitarianism* (New York, 1951) and Eva G. Reichmann, *Hostages of Civilization* (Boston, 1951).

[15] Rauschning, 235–38.

[16] G. Reitlinger, *The Final Solution* (New York, 1955).

[17] See Alexander Dallin, *German Rule in Russia, 1941–45* (New York, 1957).

[18] Picker, 71.

[19] *Ibid.,* 275.

come to full consciousness of its inner self and of its mission in the world. With the deepest insight he combines the greatest will-power, hallmarks of the born leader. Therefore he must demand complete obedience from the whole people.

The Nazi ideology was quite rigid. Its activist racialism and totalitarian authoritarianism contained distinct and immutable principles for a political theory and even for specific policies. We must assume that Hitler had acquired a faith in the main body of these ideas before he left Austria and a good many years before he decided to enter politics. These crude ideas were originally his personal revenge on the old society of property and education, in which he, in his own eyes a budding genius, had been a misfit. In all his intimate conversations one can sense a profound contempt of generals, of the bourgeoisie, and especially of professors, which changed to outbursts of fiery hatred when the underlying feeling that these gentlemen considered him an upstart welled up in him. This social resentment made him embrace the basic ideas from which the Nazi ideology developed. Its conception of "people" or "race" leveled down all social classes and attached no significance to educational differentiation.

Essentially, this was all that Hitler's "socialism" meant. Equality was his idea only in the abstract sense that everybody was a racial tribesman, for each person was placed immediately into a hierarchical system of military subordination that makes equality a sham. The rise to higher rank was made less dependent on class than before and more on service and loyalty to the party and leader. Equality was not linked to any specific economic system. Hitler was quite ignorant of economic affairs. He was originally concerned only with agriculture as the source not only for the physical survival of the people but also as the ideal breeding ground for pure race and the right ideology that goes with it. There is little in Hitler's statements about the artisan and craftsman, but obviously they were considered creative producers. This attitude carried over to industry, whereas big commerce and finance smelled of profiteering and exploitation.

Such general sentiments were inadequate foundations for a principled economic policy. Hitler's vacillations in this respect reflected his lack of knowledge as well as interest. Prior to 1933 he subordinated economics to propaganda, as shown by his reinterpretation of Gottfried Feder's program. After he had come to power he followed an economic policy that seemed to promise him the maximum of war production. He quickly stopped the activities of the party in favor of artisans, small businessmen, and the like, and before very long gave up the attempt at building a corporative state. What came into being is probably best called a "command economy," a term coined by Franz L. Neumann.[20] It was not corporatism, nor socialism, nor state socialism or state capitalism, but an economy more and more directed by the state. The process of integrating the economy into the totalitarian state was in the beginning slower than the imposition of totalitarian controls on other activities, but it was accelerated by the approaching war and in the end equally far-reaching. But Nazi economic policies were less directly affected by Nazi ideology, except insofar as the latter was bent on war.

[20] Franz I. Neumann, *Behemoth* (New York, 1942), 293 ff. See also his *The Democratic and the Authoritarian State. Essays in Political and Legal Theory,* edited by Herbert Marcuse (Glencoe, Ill., 1957).

III

The discussions of the origins of Nazi ideology have often negelected to reduce the pattern of ideas to those that served the double function of a political ideology, namely, to win through propaganda a people as well as to set up a model of ultimate political action. I have tried to confine my definition of Nazi ideology largely to those elements of Hitler's political thinking that constantly and decisively determined his general course of action. It also is a common mistake to describe Nazi ideology as the summary of all the ideas that came to the fore in Germany in the period before 1933. There can be no doubt that some of the ideas of the so-called conservative revolution, in the first place Moeller van den Bruck's "Third Empire," were taken over by Hitler and made part of the official ideology. But actually van den Bruck's conception assumed an entirely different meaning in the context of genuine Nazi ideology. Other "conservative" ideas were left uncensored, because Hitler or Goebbels thought they would gain for National Socialism the support of groups not otherwise easily accessible to Nazi ideology or because they thought it useful to throw sand into the eyes of their opponents.[21] Although naturally all these ideas are of the highest importance for the study of the acceptance of National Socialism by the German people and particularly by a large section of the German intelligentsia in 1933, they are of secondary importance for the understanding of the origins of the genuine Nazi ideology. Italian fascism, too, was of no significance for the growth of Nazi ideology. Mussolini's actions, particularly the March on Rome, made a profound impression on Hitler, but fascist ideology was too nebulous and volatile to change Hitler's ideas. The adoption of corporatism by Italian fascism found some imitation among the National Socialists, but it did not become official policy after 1933.

We still do not know enough about the reading Hitler did in his formative years and down to 1926. It is clear, however, that it was neither very extensive nor critically selective nor systematic. Some books obviously were only read in part, others were misunderstood or not understood at all. There is no indication that books helped him to improve his abominable style, which remained to the last turgid and full of clichés, and aimed at impressing his readers or listeners by stuffing an unbearable number of overworked metaphors into a single sentence.[22] One of the signs of a half-educated person, the preference for words borrowed from foreign languages and their occasional use in the wrong place and with the wrong meaning, is characteristic of Hitler.[23] With this evidence we are well advised not to look for any original philosophical or literary works as the immediate sources of Hitler's first ideas. As a matter of fact, he received them from the political marketplace and even lowlier sources.

The Pan-Germanism of Georg von Schönerer and the Christian Social movement under Vienna's Mayor Karl Lueger gave Hitler his first notions about anti-Semitism and its potential power to move the masses. His theoret-

[21] See Hitler's curious statement on Rosenberg's *Myth,* "It gives me considerable pleasure to realize that the book has been closely studied only by our opponents," in Picker, 275.

[22] On Hitler's metaphors see the recent article by Hermann Glaser, "Adolf Hitler's 'Mein Kampf' als Spiesserspiegel," *Aus Politik und Zeitgeschichte,* Bonn, July 24, 1963.

[23] Privately Hitler disapproved of the public agitation of purist Nazi linguists. Picker, 382 f.

ical enlargement on anti-Semitism in this period derived from the cheap little *Ostara* pamphlets, issued by a former monk who called himself Lanz von Liebenfels[24] (alias Adolf Lanz) and who peddled a racialist "theozoology" of his own concoction. These tracts, sold at tobacco stands, and probably similar sheets, together with certain newspapers,[25] provided his chief literary fare. He no doubt read Richard Wagner's political and anti-Semitic writings and found in them the confirmation of the racialist and anti-Semitic faith that he had adopted in his Vienna years. Richard Wagner was to Hitler the conclusive proof that the right ideology would produce the highest art. Hitler was familiar with the book by Richard Wagner's English-born son-in-law, Houston Stewart Chamberlain, *Foundations of the Twentieth Century,* the widely read racialist interpretation of world history. He knew, of course, about Count Arthur de Gobineau's *Inequality of the Human Races,* although it is doubtful whether he ever did more than dip into it. Passing on to original thinkers, I have been unable to discover any specific reference to Nietzsche.[26] Whether, if he ever read him, he was repelled by the philosopher's contempt of anti-Semitism and Germanism no one can say. We have, however, a statement by Hitler on the deep impression that Schopenhauer had made on him. Yet he was quite incapable of indicating what was the special fascination of Schopenhauer's philosophy or what concretely he had learned from it. Even Wagner had misunderstood Schopenhauer in many respects, but Hitler's whole thinking did not show the slightest impress of Schopenhauer; it was indeed a world apart from a philosophy strongly opposed to man's being submerged in the state and looking for salvation from the ills and sufferings in the negation of the will for life.

It was on the basis of his limited reading in popular and often cranky and murky writings that Hitler formed his original racialist and anti-Semitic ideas. In this respect he did not add any new ideas during his years in Germany.[27] But Hitler experienced the full impact of German militarism and imperialistic nationalism. The Austrian Pan-Germanists prior to World War I were chiefly concerned with the merger of the German parts of the Habsburg Empire with the German Empire. There are some signs that Hitler's dreams were already in these prewar years going beyond the mere realization of a Greater Germany; his migration to Germany in 1912, his obvious reluctance to report for obligatory military service in Austria prior to 1914 and, by contrast, his enthusiastic welcome of the outbreak of World War I as well as his immediate volunteering in a Bavarian regiment point in this direction. But irrespective of what conclusions Hitler may have drawn from the Pan-German propaganda before 1914, only the outbreak of the war made it possible to think of an early realization of the Pan-German demands for world power. Hitler undoubtedly came into close contact with these ideas which since August 1914 not only constituted the war aims program of the German rightist parties but

[24] Wilfried Daim, *Der Mann, der Hitler die Ideen gab* (Munich, 1958).

[25] On the Vienna newspapers at this time see William A. Jenks, *The Young Hitler* (New York, 1960), 126 ff.

[26] There is a brief reference to Nietzsche's superman in one of the conversations with Rauschning, but it is the latter who introduces Nietzsche. Rauschning, 246 f.

[27] Except that the acquaintance with *The Wise Men of Zion* after World War I may have given his anti-Semitism an even more poisonous character. Rauschning, 238 ff.

colored the policies of the parties further to the Left. Within the German army, particularly after Ludendorff had become its leading spirit in the fall of 1916, intensive indoctrination of the troops was carried on in which the alleged superiority of the German people over the degenerate French, the mercenary English, the brute and servile Russians served as the justification for German conquests sufficient to make any future aggression against Germany impossible and to establish her as a world power.[28]

There was already talk in public and in government councils about removing foreign populations in lands adjacent to Germany for the settlement of Germans. Hindenburg promised the soldiers land for settlement after the war. The peace treaties of Brest-Litovsk with the Ukraine and Soviet Russia as well as subsequent military and political actions created a vast orbit of German satellites and colonies that reached from the White to the Black and Caspian Seas. These experiences of World War I emboldened Hitler to draw the most extreme consequences from his racialist nationalism. Besides, we may surmise that four years of participation in the slaughter of that war stirred up the ferocity that was in his nature. The loss of World War I by Germany confirmed his belief in his own political mission.

While Hitler adopted some of the major objectives and methods of the imperialistic German nationalism of World War I, he also firmly rejected others. Although his great scheme of eastern expansion was clearly a continuation of the Pan-German aspirations of World War I, he sharply criticized the German government and the German nationalists for simultaneously aiming at the acquisition of colonies overseas, thus antagonizing England. Yet he was even more critical of the methods by which the imperial German government had expected to achieve its ends. He radically disapproved of its mismanagement of internal affairs, particularly by its toleration of opposition parties and a critical press. In this situation a mass movement such as the Fatherland party with its four million members was doomed to failure. The Fatherland party, founded by Admiral von Tirpitz and Wolfgang Kapp in order to mobilize popular support for the Pan-German war-aims program, by claiming to be a national movement above the existing political parties, was a direct forerunner of the Nazi party. Hitler must have watched it with great interest and found it wanting. The Fatherland party, though heightening the patriotic sentiment of its bourgeois membership, did not produce determined fighters against the double enemy at home and abroad. When the revolution came, they surrendered to the internal enemy and broke off the war.

Although Hitler in his propaganda against the Weimar Republic made the utmost use of the "stab-in-the-back" legend and of the "November crimes," he was always convinced that the old regime was responsible for its own downfall. Its national ideology was weakened by liberalism and by lack of knowledge about the vital needs of the nation. Moreover, the Pan-German ideology, even if adequately propagated—and this should have begun years before the war—was not likely to integrate all classes. Something more elementary and robust was needed. Hitler believed that in his own ideology he possessed

[28] A full view of the war aims of the German government, army, and political parties is presented by a recent historical work that exploits for the first time all the relevant German archives, Fritz Fischer, *Griff nach der Weltmacht* (Düsseldorf, 1962).

the right principles for building a powerful Germany that would resume the battle for German supremacy. Before this war could be won abroad, it first had to be won at home by the destruction of liberalism, socialism, and communism as well as by the implementation of a common ideology that would make the German people immune to foreign propaganda and ready to fight with unmatched determination for *Lebensraum* and race superiority. Hitler made another correction in the World War I ideas of Pan-Germanism. To be sure, anti-Semitism had been a strong ingredient of the movement from the beginning, but, as everywhere else in Central Europe, this anti-Semitism aimed at taking full citizenship away from the Jews and inflicting other humiliating conditions on them. Its intention was to harry the Jews, not to exterminate them. Only National Socialism proceeded to that level of crime. It is impossible to say exactly at what particular moment Hitler set his mind on the physical destruction of the Jews. But the racialist nationalism developed by him during World War I to feverish pitch was bound to give his anti-Semitism the highest radical note.

Hitler derived his ideology from few sources, all of them of a rather low type. Many German writers during the Nazi period endeavored to relate Hitler to the great classic tradition of German philosophy—Leibniz, Kant, Fichte, and Hegel—or even linked him with Luther. National Socialism then appeared as the crowning achievement of the German spirit. Outside Germany this view has often been expressed, though usually in polemics against Germany. But all the evidence that we possess forbids this interpretation. Not even the fact that a large segment of the German intelli gentsia fell for Hitler's ideas in 1933 can be explained in such manner. Actually, this event cannot be traced back ideologically beyond the eighteen-forties and must be explained largely in political and social terms. The phenomenon of Hitler himself also calls chiefly for a political and social interpretation, since he was satisfied with the mere rudiments of an ideology that allowed him to act as the charismatic leader of the German people.

Few observers were better placed to assess the true nature of the National Socialist movement than the author of the following selection, Hermann Rauschning. Head of the Nazis in the Free City of Danzig, he was an intimate of most of the leading members of the party. Rauschning left the party soon after 1933, once he saw that its goals, in his opinion essentially nihilistic, differed from his own conservative vision of Germany's future.

The Nature of the Nazi Revolution

HERMANN RAUSCHNING

The Aims of National Socialism

"Our aims are perfectly clear. The world is only surprised at our attitude because it does not know us." The German propaganda leader wrote this, with his characteristic pregnancy, on the occasion of Lord Halifax's visit to Germany in 1937. "The aims of National Socialism are being achieved, one after another. . . . It will come. It is coming, bit by bit. We have time!" he continued. It is true enough that the world still does not know National Socialism, but it is not correct to say that the aims of the party were clear. We have to combat two views, one that the course followed in the Reich was carefully planned and thought out and directed toward definite objectives fixed once for all, and the other that National Socialism is guided on the whole by doctrinaire program points. There are many who will contend that National Socialism reveals a broadly conceived, dogmatically defined philosophy, possessing absolutely definite doctrines in regard to all human relations which must be unreservedly accepted by every loyal citizen. Nevertheless, we must ask: is National Socialism doctrinaire? It is, of course, beyond question that it is the product of doctrinaire ideas and that doctrinaire personages play a part in it to this day. Of much greater importance is the question of the connection of what was regarded as National Socialist doctrine with the two elements that characterize the movement, the irrational passions that undoubtedly play an important part, and its leading personalities. A sharp distinction must be drawn in National Socialism between this genuinely irrational revolutionary passion, affecting not only the mass of followers but the leaders themselves, and the very deliberate, utterly cold and calculating pursuit of power and dominance by the controlling group. We may generalize: The doctrine is meant for the masses. It is *not* a part of the real motive forces of the revolution. It is an instrument for the control of the masses. The élite, the leaders, stand above the doctrine. They make use of it in furtherance of their purposes.

What, then, are the aims of National Socialism which are being achieved one after another? Certainly not the various points of its program; even if some of these are carried out, this is not the thing that matters. The aim of National Socialism is the complete revolutionizing of the technique of government, and

From *The Revolution of Nihilism,* by Hermann Rauschning, pp. 18–28, 32–34, 45–49. New York, Alliance, 1939.

complete dominance over the country by the leaders of the movement. The two things are inseparably connected: the revolution cannot be carried out without an élite ruling with absolute power, and this élite can maintain itself in power only through a process of continual intensification of the process of revolutionary disintegration. National Socialism is an unquestionably genuine revolutionary movement in the sense of a final achievement on a vaster scale of the "mass rising" dreamed of by Anarchists and Communists. But modern revolutions do not take place through fighting across improvised barricades, but in disciplined acts of destruction. They follow irrational impulses, but they remain under rational guidance and command. Their perilousness lies in their ordered destructiveness—it is a misuse on a vast scale of the human desire for order—and in the irrationality and incalculability of their pressure for the "victory of the revolutionary new order." This pressure is completely uncalculated, unconsidered, the pressure of men with no program but action, instinctive in the case of the best troops of the movement; but the part played in it by its controlling élite is most carefully and coolly considered down to the smallest detail. There was and is no aim that National Socialism has not been ready for the sake of the movement to abandon or to proclaim at any time.

The National Socialist revolution, at the outset a nationalist seizure of power, is viewed much too much in the light of historic precedents. There are no criteria and no precedents for the new revolutions of the twentieth century. The revolutionary dictatorship is a new type, in its cynical, unprincipled policy of violence. The outsider overlooks above all the essential distinction between the mass and the élite in the new revolutions. This distinction is vital in every field. That which is intended for the mass is not applicable to the élite. Program and official philosophy, allegiance and faith, are for the mass. Nothing commits the élite—no philosophy, no ethical standard. It has but one obligation, that of absolute loyalty to comrades, to fellow-members of the initiated élite. This fundamental distinction between élite and mass does not seem to have been sufficiently clearly realized, but it is just this that explains many inconsistencies, many things done, that leave the outsider dumbfounded.

There has scarcely been a single old National Socialist who attached any importance to the program and program-literature of the party. If any section of the party was in it for action and nothing else, and completely uninterested in programs and ideologies, and strong for that very reason as the real backbone of a brotherhood, it was the section of the party that was its vital element, the Storm Troops. Their repugnance to programs was well known, there was no success in training them in "theories." And the National Socialist "Bible," that remarkable book which is now accorded the sanctity of verbal inspiration, was far from playing its present part among old "Pg's" (*Parteigenossen*), old members of the party; they paid no particular attention to it. Nobody took it seriously; nobody could, for nobody could make head or tail of it. The mass understood and understands nothing and does not want to understand. Each individual holds to whatever he can comprehend in it, to any particular bit that concerns him personally The things that stir most men and fire their enthusiasm are the rhythm, the new tempo, the activity, that take them out of the humdrum daily life: with these things much can be done, the masses can be inflamed. They are matters of emotion, with much the same appeal as the call of the first *Wandervogel* movement, which brought men away from the security of their homes and sent them on a roving life: an emotion compounded of romance and boredom. The initiated member, the old Pg, knew that the whole tableau of philosophical outlook and party doctrine was only of symbolic value, something to stir men's imagination, to divert their thoughts from other things, to discipline them. It was a cover for realities which must not be "given away" to the masses. He himself, the old Pg, was a Catilinarian, a mere *condottiere;* or, if he was an idealist, in his progressive liberation from the crude ikon-worship of the National Socialist masses he felt a pride of partnership in the reality behind it, the heroic nihilism of the party, inculcated in the young men as soon as they were old enough for the senior groups of the Hitler Youth. If we try to understand what it is that tempts Hitler again and again to dwell on Freemasonry, on the Jesuits, or on the Teutonic Order, we come close to the essential secret of the National Socialist élite, the "mystery," as the Teutonic Order called it, the esoteric doctrine confined to the brethren who were called to initiation. It was the piecemeal character of their initiation into secret aims, the aims and methods of a ruling class, by stages of discipline, enlightenment, liberation, that set the eyes of National Socialism in envious rivalry on such organizations as Freemasonry.

The movement has no fixed aims, either economic or political, either in home or foreign affairs. Hitler was out even in 1932 to liberate himself from all party doctrines in economic policy, and he did the same in all other fields; and this "realist" attitude was adopted, and still is, not only by the leader but by every member holding any official position in the party, or admitted at all into its confidence. The only objective was the victory of the party, and even favorite doctrines were abandoned for the sake of this. The rise of National Socialism compelled the élite of the movement to become realists, and when they came into power they made this acquired pragmatism the foundation of the fanatical activity of the movement in the new, national field. It is no doctrinaire commitment of the movement that drives National Socialism into lines of action which from a realist and rationalist standpoint are incomprehensible, but its revolutionary, irrational character, which continually prompts it to any possible revolutionary destruction of existing institutions.

The fight against Christianity is not a matter of doctrine or program; this is clear to any reader of *Mein Kampf* or of the party program; yet it has come, simply because it lies more than anything else precisely in that direction of the destruction of existing institutions. For all practical purposes it should suffice for the racial State and for independence from all alien, supernational, superstate powers, if a German National Church were started. But the revolutionary destruction of the Christian basis goes much farther than this. A schismatic separation of German Catholicism from Rome, inevitable as it seems to-day, has already been put out of date by the developments in Germany. It will be a brief episode on the way to the comprehensive aim of destroying the Christian faith as the most deep-seated root of Western civilization and of the social order. It will be a stage that will assist the revolutionizing of the soul of the masses, not the actual final aim. Similarly the fight against Judaism, while it is beyond question a central element not only in material considerations but in those of cultural policy, is part of the party doctrine; but, for all that, it is now an element in the revolutionary unsettling of the nation, a means of destruction of past categories of thinking and valuation, of destroying the liberalist economic system based on private initiative and enterprise; it is also a sop to the destructive revolution-ism of the masses, a first lesson in cynicism.

This irrational element in National Socialism is the actual source of its strength. It is the reliance on it that accounts for its "sleepwalker's immunity" in face of one practical problem after another. It explains why it was possible for National Socialism to attain power almost without the slightest tangible ideas of what it was going to do. The movement was without even vague general ideas on the subject; all it had was boundless confidence: things would smooth themselves out one way or another. Give rein to the revolutionary impulse, and the problems would find their own solution. An open mind and no program at all—that is what enabled National Socialism to win through in its own way with its practical problems. Its strength lay in incessant activity and in embarking on anything so long as it kept things moving. Conversely, it abandoned anything that could hinder it, such as the construction of the Corporative State and the reform of the Reich. What it needed and intuitively took up were the opportunities of revolutionary dislocation.

Nothing is more idle than to engage in heated discussions of the capitalistic and monopolistic character of National Socialist economic policy, or of the question whether Socialism or Reaction has been the driving force in its schemes of social reconstruction. National Socialist "anti-capitalism" is similarly just a bargain-counter, like almost everything else. If there is one thing that does not and cannot exist among the National Socialist élite, it is a genuine sense of social solidarity with the propertyless classes of the nation. One may count on finding just the opposite, and it is easily discernible in Hitler himself—an unconcealed contempt of the crowd, the common people, the mob: they are there not to be served but to be used.

National Socialism is action pure and simple, dynamics *in vacuo,* revolution at a variable tempo, ready to be changed at any moment. One thing it is not—doctrine or philosophy. Yet it has a philosophy. It does not base its policy on a doctrine, but pursues it with the aid of a philosophy. It makes use of its philosophy as it makes use of all things men have, and all they want, as fuel for its energy. Its policy is exactly what a critic of the era of William II said of the policy of that time: it is "opportunist policy," though in quite a different, a much more "realist", sense. It is opportunist policy in the sense of making use of every opportunity of doing anything to increase the movement's own power, and to add to the elements under its domination.

National Socialist policy is in the highest degree subtle and sly, aimed at keeping to the front a system of "inflammatory ideas," in order the more effectively and the more startlingly to seize each opportunity. People used to say that any policy of important scope always needs justification by a great idea. But that was intellectual, ideological generalizing. It assumed that there are still ideas in which men believe. To the conscious nihilist there are no ideas. But there are substitutes for ideas which can be foisted on the masses by suggestion, and he has little hesitation in imposing on them whatever they can swallow.

The National Socialist "philosophy" is not the outcome of any lofty intuition; it is deliberately and carefully manufactured. Originally it developed out of much the same doctrines as those which Sorel formulated in his gospel of violence: a myth must be created to give the masses the energy for action. Thus the ruling consideration in the production of the National Socialist philosophy is its power of influencing the masses by suggestion, of instilling into them the sense of the duty of obedience. The great paradox of this revolution is that its lack of principle is one of the main secrets of its effectiveness. It is its strength; it is precisely in this characteristic that the actual revolutionary power of the movement lies, and its character of a "permanent revolution," impossible to bring to a close. The naïve element among its mercenaries has largely been removed by the decimation of the Storm Troops, but the subtler and far more effectual element, the élite under the leader's protection, has remained. This élite keeps alive the revolutionary spirit, in spite of all announcements of the ending of the revolution. National Socialism cannot abandon this dynamic element; in doing so it would be abandoning itself. And the question becomes more and more insistent, how long can a State, a nation, a society, endure a governing élite devoid of all principle, without disintegrating?

Error and Deception

Error or deliberate deception? Which was it? Was the National Socialist party in doubt as to its own real character; did it genuinely regard itself as a movement of national rebirth, or did it cleverly and deliberately adopt that disguise in order to attain power? Undoubtedly both the one and the other. There was an honest belief among a great number of the members of the party, and among its followers, that they were laboring in the service of national recovery. Even among the élite the consciousness of the actual part they were to play came only with the first great successes. But there were some among them who knew how matters stood, probably long before the arrival in power. Hitler himself pursued carefully calculated tactics: he damped down the Socialist tendencies in the movement and brought the Nationalist ones into the foreground. He was out to gain powerful patrons and friends who could help the movement into power. The temporary veto on the anti-capitalist propaganda desired by Gregor Strasser was due to his insistence. And this was not because Hitler was himself a reactionary, but because at that moment the Socialist note would have interfered with the political developments envisaged. It was precisely at this point that Hitler showed his real superiority over his élite: at the right moment he took a course which was extremely awkward for him and an extremely unpopular one, but which alone led along the road to power—the camouflage of the "dynamic" revolution as a movement of national renewal. He put up with the dissatisfaction and disgust of his élite, and allowed them to abuse him for his "inadequacy" as an "advocate," and for his supposed idea that he could attain power by means of speeches and parades, threats and extortion, and secret deals with bankers and soldiers, industrialists and agrarians. Yet from the point of view of the movement and of its aims his course was the only possible one. He was justified in the outcome, and encouraged to continue in that course. He brazenly joined forces with the monarchists; brazenly denied his own views and affected to be a reactionary. With a technique of camouflage unprecedented in Germany, he arranged the deal that associated his party with the national rising which ended in the National Socialist revolution. He succeeded in a concealment of the true facts on a scale never before known. The deception continues to this day—a presentation of the revolution as an innocent affair, middle class and moderate. Deliberately concealing the true nature of the National Socialist revolution, the new élite successfully occupied Germany. Under its disguise it succeeded in foisting on the country, in place of an authoritarian State, an instrument of dominance that serves simply and purely for the maintenance of its own absolute power. Under the mask of a movement of national liberation, it achieved the despotic repression of the nation, with the voluntary assistance of the middle classes and large sections of the working class.

Only these facts provide the standpoint for a judgment of what National Socialism regards as its creative achievements, its work in the field of constitutional, social, and economic affairs. The outstanding feature to-day in these fields is beyond question their universal subjection to despotic control. A machinery of absolute and universal dominion is being erected in an entirely disorganized State. Nothing is more mistaken than to talk of a "totalitarian State" or a "classless society" within the realm of a nihilist revolution. In the place of these there is the machinery of absolute dominion, recognizing independence in no sphere at all, not even in the private life of the individual; and the totalitarian collectivity of the *Volksgemeinschaft,* the "national community," a euphemism for an atomized, structureless nation.

The retrogression from the conception of the State to that of the party in what a German sociologist has defined as its primitive sense, that of an organization for rule by violent means, is paralleled by the retrogression from the sphere of legality and constitutionalism to the primeval conception of Leader and Followers and the principle of absolute power and blind obedience. Within this organization of dominance which has replaced the State, there has developed as the indispensable means of rule the segregation of a privileged élite from the totally unprotected and disfranchised mass. The control of the remnants of the State by a party ("the Party commands the State") may be regarded as a phase in the process of the dissolution of the old forces of order by the revolution. This process ends with the absorption of the State and its functions by the "organization for rule by violent means." To-day the State is nothing but an administrative machine. There is no true sphere of the State in the Third Reich.

The Doctrine of Violence

National Socialism does not mean the crushing of the "mass revolt" but the carrying of it to completion. The astonishing thing is not that this could have happened, but that it could be done under the mask of a movement in the opposite direction, without those affected realizing the reversal of the course. To-day, after six years, there are, to say the least, still many respectable people associated with German "dynamism" who have not yet realized that their imagined national and racial rebirth amounts to nothing more than the adoption of the revolutionary system of "direct action" as the fundamental principle of the carrying of the "mass revolt" to completion.

Direct action is defined as "direct integration by means of corporativism, militarism, and myth"; this is to replace democracy and parliamentarism. But the true significance of direct action lies in its assignment of the central place in its policy to violence, which it then surrounds with a special philosophical interpretation of reality. Briefly this philosophical system amounts to the belief that the use of violence in a supreme effort liberates creative moral forces in human society which lead to social and national renewal. "Civilization is the endeavor to reduce violence to the *ultima ratio,*" writes Ortega y Gasset. "This is now becoming all too clear to us, for direct action reverses the order and proclaims violence as the *prima ratio,* or rather the *unica ratio.* It is the standard that dispenses with all others." Violence, says Sorel, is the basic force in life. When all other standards have been unmasked by scepticism of all doctrines, reason itself is robbed of all force. The anti-intellectual attitude of "dynamism" is not mere chance but the necessary outcome of an entire absence of standards. Man, it holds, is not a logical being, not a creature guided by reason or intelligence, but a creature following his instincts and impulses, like any other animal. Consequently reason cannot provide a basis for a social order or a political system. The barbaric element of violence, which reformist Socialism and moderate Marxism would place in safe custody under lock and key, is the one element that can change a social order. That is why revolutionary direct action has won the day against the responsible, non-revolutionary Socialism of the working class, just as it has violently eliminated the middle class itself as the ruling class. Hostility to the things of the spirit, indifference to truth, indifference to the ethical conceptions of morality, honor, and equity—all the things that arouse the indignation of the ordinary citizen in Germany and abroad against certain National Socialist measures—are not excrescences but the logical and inevitable outcome of the National Socialist philosophy, of the doctrine of violence. This hostility to the intellect, to individualism and personality, to pure science and art, is not the arbitrary invention of a particularly vicious system of racial philosophy, but the logical outcome of the political system of revolutionary direct action with violence as its one and only historic motor. . . .

The New Elite

. . . The revolutionary élite can maintain itself in power in its permanently critical situation only by continually pushing on with the revolutionary process. In its effort to hold on to power it is compelled to destroy the old social and political institutions, since it is in these that the strength of the old ruling class lies. When the political structure of the country has been razed to the ground, the élite will march over the frontier, to upset the existing international order.

The right men in the right place—that is a typical rule in civil life in peaceful times. In revolutionary times, and then only, there is no need for the "right" man. Any man will do who will exercise power with ruthless brutality. Only in a revolutionary period can the difficult problem of selection of personnel be treated with the negligence, indeed the criminal negligence, shown by National Socialism. But this can continue only so long as there is little or no effort at genuinely constructive work, little being done beyond the using up of accumulated reserves, and revolutionary destruction. For such work, the less education the leaders have the better.

The new élite of National Socialism is an affront to all historic and traditional standards. It is a deliberate breach with the past and the seal of a new order. The "ruling element with a historic mission" is formed by the National Socialist élite, and by them alone. This is due to their determined struggle for power after the coup-by-arrangement of January 30th, while the élite of the capitalist parties rested content with the externals of leadership, with posts from which they were driven out one by one as opportunity offered.

After all this it will surprise nobody that the National Socialist revolutionary élite are entirely without moral inhibitions, and that individually they reveal so strange a mixture of extreme nihilism with an unashamed adoption of the ways of the half-educated lower middle class. The cool and calculating resolution that marks the political dealings of this élite has hitherto been associated in people's minds with outstanding intelligence or at least versatility—at all events, when not dealing simply with criminals. In these people we find, however, a mixture of qualities, a naïve mixture of qualities always regarded up to now as irreconcilable with one another. But the unusualness of the mixture must not blind us to the fact that the operative part in the duality of these natures is a hard, resolute, ruthless will, even if their German is ungrammatical and their intellectual equipment manifestly of the lowest. It is characteristic, too, of National Socialism that it is only in exceptional cases that its leaders are removed on account of incorrect dealings—to put it euphemistically—under the civil code. Lack of morals in civil life is not frowned on: it is no ground for suspicion of a member's National Socialist orthodoxy. National Socialism demands, indeed, of its sworn élite that all personal moral scruples shall be overridden by the needs of the party. Anyone who reveals that he is allowing himself the luxury of guidance by his own conscience has no place in the élite and will be expelled. It is not surprising to find that absence of moral scruples in the private life of a member of the élite is dealt with very gently by the party authorities. It is impossible to demand scrupulous correctness in a member's private life when any crime may be required of him in the interest of the party. . . .

At the back of all National Socialist activities is a thoroughly marked preference for immoral methods. The immoral course is always more effective, because it is more violent. The immoral course also gives the illusion of strength and daring in persons who are merely underhand by choice. It is a fundamental principle of National Socialist tactics to strike fear by deliberate and pronounced incivility and violence, and by making a show of readiness to go to any length, where the same purpose could be achieved without difficulty by milder means. But National Socialism is never single-mindedly in pursuit of anything; it always has the additional aim of further shaking the existing order with every success it gains. Its robust methods are deliberately calculated. And most of the roughness of manners and habits and of the barbaric style of government aims at producing the illusion of an elemental strength which the system does not in reality possess, an illusion for which there is no need where a certain reserve of strength is always in hand.

This preference for violence as the typical revolutionary method is not inconsistent with the crafty and very successful appeal of National Socialism to the lower middle class self-righteousness. Its violent character is only superficially inconsistent with its practice of posing always as the champion of justice, denouncing wrongs that cry aloud to heaven. Everything it does is represented as done simply in the defence of a sacred right and a moral mission. It could beat its breast, for instance, over the detention camp in which National Socialists were placed in Austria, as though there were no atrocities in the German concentration camps, and could denounce the intention it alleged of falsifying the Austrian plebiscite with an assumption of supreme unconsciousness of its own terrorist methods. Every lie is adorned with a show of virtue. Always National Socialism is defending a right, always pursuing honor and faith. Moral indignation comes next after brutality in the National Socialist armory of effective propaganda. It takes the place of reasoned argument. The revolution is true to type in its eternal moralizing, in its defence of "virtue" like the great French Revolution, in its sentimentality and emotionality. Its "Leader" always has sobs and tears at his command, exciting wrathful derision in the old militants of the party. This assumption of virtue and morality falls short, it is true, of the primitive naïveté of a genuine revolution. In its insincerity it is entirely in character with the brutality and the cynical amorality revealed in the everyday activities of the National Socialists.

Should terrorism produce discontent, there is always a public enemy to be discovered. Public indignation is poured over him from time to time, so that collective outbursts of rage may provide a diversion for accumulating private resentment. To provide continual diversions, and never to leave the citizen to himself with nothing to do, is another tactical rule of general application. It is an effectual method of treatment not only for the masses but for all opponents, including opponents abroad of German foreign policy. Keep people busy, give them something to think about, startle them, never allow them time for reflection; always lie in wait, ready to pounce; always take the initiative and so maintain the lead.

Hitler's very realistic estimation of the masses was revealed in *Mein Kampf*. It may be said in general that at the back of the whole tactics and method of propaganda of National Socialism there is a complete contempt of humanity: the whole system is based on taking men as they are and pandering to their weakness and their bestiality. Such is its universal recipe. National Socialism banks on human sloth and timidity—just as much in the case of the intellectuals, the middle classes, and the old ruling classes, as with the masses. It does so especially with foreign countries. In Germany it yields a much more effective means of domination than would the exclusive dependence on terrorism. The exploitation of envy and ill-will, of the lowest human instincts, the sowing of dissension between opponents, and the appeal to their ignoble qualities and notorious weaknesses have thus far unfailingly helped National Socialism to success, incidentally destroying the basis of a general sense of morality which was weak enough to begin with.

The system owes its internal strength to the general voluntary co-operation in the work of the secret police, the general acceptance of denunciation as a patriotic duty. But the completely amoral regime of National Socialism steadily ignores the fact that this resort to the worst of human motives, and to the extreme of brutality and violence, to hatred, vengeance, envy, ill-will, to licentiousness, to robbery, to lying on principle, its resort to all these motives and methods has set in motion a ruin of the national character on a scale hitherto unimaginable, which must inevitably recoil in the end on the ruling élite themselves. The élite are clearly untroubled by the dangers of this whole course, because in spite of their bombastic declamations about the thousand years of their "Third Reich" they have a very strong subconscious sense that their furious, hysterical onward drive has not a very long course ahead of it. In any case, the greatest statesmanship could not set up a "revolutionary new order of this world" on a nihilistic moral foundation of this sort.

The Reichstag fire, organised for political purposes by party members on the instructions of German Ministers, is a thoroughly illuminating example of the method universally adopted by the party. It is the party's special device, applicable universally. Crimes are arranged and attributed to opponents. The people are kept in a state of fear, utterly intimidated. At the same time they are stirred up into a blaze of indignation, given the sense that they have been saved from destruction, and made to feel thankful to a strong regime that gives them security. Hundreds of times this plan is carried out on varying scales. National Socialism is always ready to make play with its Bolshevist propaganda-bogey on a vast scale. The nation is kept in a state of alarm, and meanwhile, in the same breath, the regime takes credit for the maintenance of peace and order. Few things are more characteristic of the regime than its unscrupulous, lying glorification of an existing law and order which it destroys or publicly insults by whatever it does.

One word, finally, on the simplest and most elementary, but perhaps most effective and most characteristic method of domination employed by National Socialism—the marching. At first this marching seemed to be a curious whim of the National Socialists. These eternal night marches, this keeping of the whole population on the march, seemed to be a senseless waste of time and energy. Only much later was there revealed in it a subtle intention based on a well-judged adjustment of ends and means. Marching diverts men's thoughts. Marching kills thought. Marching makes an end of individuality. Marching is the indispensable magic stroke performed in order to accustom the people to a mechanical, quasi-ritualistic activity until it becomes second nature. No less an authority than the pseudo-German Rosenberg, in his *Gestaltung der Idee*, has given the classic explanation of this occupation with marching: "The German nation is simply out to discover at last its own style of living, a style of living that is fundamentally distinguished from what is called British Liberalism. . . . It is the style of a marching column, no matter where or to what end this marching column may be directed." At the back of all these night marches, marches out, marches back, these mass demonstrations and parades, was the consideration that the sense of primitive community through functional integration is created and fostered by marching in columns, military drill, military evolutions, the rhythm of a host in step. Nothing could show more shockingly, more grimly and indeed spectrally, the utter emptiness of a political movement and its concentration on mere externals than this elevation of marching to be its motto and essential principle. We have it here admitted that the nation is marching aimlessly, just for the sake of marching. It is a confession of the lack of any sort of doctrine in this revolution for revolution's sake, this hustling activity just to distract men's minds.

That the German people could not help but be affected by the experience of Nazism would appear to be self-evident, but how profoundly and in what particulars it is extremely difficult to assess. In the following piece, taken from his book *Society and Democracy in Germany*, the noted German sociologist Ralf Dahrendorf attempts to provide some indications in this regard. It is his conclusion that Nazism had consequences for German society that were revolutionary in their implications.

National Socialist Germany and the Social Revolution

RALF DAHRENDORF

The social history of National Socialist Germany has not yet been written. Understandably, German historians have devoted their interest first of all to the dramatic events of the years from 1932 to 1934. But once the history of the subsequent period is written from a social rather than a national point of view, it will reveal many a surprise. Even in respect to the National Socialist seizure of power in 1933, historians speak of a revolution, a "revolutionizing process" (Helmut Krausnick), a "legal revolution" (Karl Friedrich Bracher). What they mean is the rapid and firm transformation of the political constitution of the country. But the concept might prove adequate even if one considers the changes in German society that followed the political revolution. Here—to use Theodor Geiger's terms—not only the "style" of an epoch, but the "epoch" itself was transformed. National Socialism completed for Germany the social revolution that was lost in the faultings of Imperial Germany and again held up by the contradictions of the Weimar Republic.

The substance of this revolution is modernity. Autonomous equality of opportunity for all men, which epitomizes modernity, does not, as we have seen, come about by itself. It is not a necessary consequence, or a condition, of industrialization. Moreover, wherever it did come about, at least the beginning of the process was violent. Entering the modern world proved painful for those involved everywhere. It required revolution and insecurity, uprooting and human sacrifice. The conclusion is hard to avoid that the road to modernity was not taken spontaneously and happily by men anywhere, that force was always required to make people embark on it. Only afterwards, if at all, did it find the agreement of men freed of the chains of minority. Breaking with the closed society hits people the harder, the later it occurs—harder in Germany than in England, harder in the new nations of our own time than in Germany. However, brutal as it was, the break with tradition and thus a strong push toward modernity was the substantive characteristic of the social revolution of National Socialism.

Even the intimation of a comparison between the National Socialist leadership clique and the Jacobins, or even the Bolsheviks, is bound to raise doubts and objections. While this will not allay such doubts, it should be added that the social revolution effected by National Socialism was an unintended, if inevitable result of its rule. It would clearly be wrong to say that Hitler set out to complete the revolution of modernity. On the contrary, his writings and speeches, indeed the entire cloudy National Socialist ideology seem to demand the recovery of the values of the past; the Nazis liked to appear Catonic where they were in fact radical innovators. For whatever their ideology, they were compelled to revolutionize society in order to stay in power.

The contradiction between the ideology and practice of National Socialism is as astonishing as it is understandable. It means, however, that the veil of ideology must not deceive us. As such, it was little more than an episode and in its substance a horrible mixture of all the half-truths of the time; but its social effects make the Nazi regime—quite apart from the consequences of the war it started—far more than an episode in German history. It gave German society an irreversible push, which exposed it to totalitarian dangers and opened it to liberal chances at the same time. The starting point of this development may be found in the political constellation of the year 1933. Hitler came to power on January 30, 1933, by virtue of the historical error of the alliance between an anti-democratic right and an anti-democratic center, which was concluded before the background of a general mood of hostility toward the constitution of liberty. If we add that Hitler and his followers had no intention of giving up their power again, much else follows almost by necessity. The short road of the conservatives from allies to bystanders and then to opponents of the Nazis is a symptom of this course of events, if one that can tell a story worth recounting. But to stick to the actors for the time being, for them maintaining power meant extending it into total power and stabilizing it as such. Hitler could find a foundation and anchor for his rule only by demolishing parliamentary democracy. But he was well aware that this process of destruction required more than an enabling law or the outlawing of political parties; he had to remove what social realities there were behind these methods as well, but above all he had to attack the much more pronounced patterns that, while they did not support democracy, worked even more strongly against claims to total power. Total power presupposes the destruction of the power of all partial institutions, of all even faintly autonomous secondary centers. The revolution took its course along these lines.

The social basis of German authoritarianism, thus of the resistance of German society to modernity and liberalism, consisted in a structural syndrome that held people to the social ties in which they had found themselves without their doing and that prevented them from full participation. In Germany, the constitution of liberty was jeopardized by the institutionalized minority of its people. But—and this is not always seen—the claim to total power advanced by a political clique was necessarily jeopardized by such structures too. Authoritarian leaders find the chances and outlets for their peculiar mixture of benevolence and suppression in secondary centers without a claim to comprehensive influence. But for claims to total power even private virtues, and certainly the institutions springing from them, become a source of resistance. Just as the rulers of the new nations of our time have to break the tribal loyalties of their peoples in order to establish their power, the National Socialists had to break the traditional, and in effect anti-liberal, loyalties for region and religion, family and corporation, in order to realize their claim to total power. Hitler needed modernity, little as he liked it.

Hitler's speech of February 1, 1933, was an apparent praise of tradition:

> Beginning with the family, by way of all notions of honor and faith, people and fatherland, culture and economy up to the eternal foundation of our morals and our beliefs, nothing is spared by this purely negative, universally destructive idea. Fourteen years of Marxism have ruined Germany. . . . [The national government] is going to conserve and defend the foundations on which the strength of our nation is based. It will take Christianity as the basis of our entire morality, and the family as the seed cell of the entire body of our people and state, into its safe protection.

On this very day, however, Hitler's deeds were in fact directed to the goal he imputed to the parties of the Weimar Republic: the destruction of the traditional basis of German society in family and religion and all other spheres.

The beginning of this process was the deliberately pursued *Gleichschaltung*, co-ordination; to this extent we can agree with Krausnick when he says, " 'Co-ordination' *is* the revolution." The process of co-ordination soon and effectively put the Weimar Constitution de facto out of force and abolished the rights of parliament. This was not by itself a process of very great social consequence; but other measures were to follow in the first year of Nazi rule. The restriction and eventually abolition of the rights of the *Länder,* for example, attacked one of the characteristic traditions—and faultings—of German social structure. The blend of regional loyalty and national unity that characterized Imperial Germany and the Weimar Republic may not have been very effective politically, but it symbolized a mixture of modern requirements and binding traditions that nobody had dared touch before, while it took Hitler only three months to dissolve the mixture at the expense of traditional loyalties.

Public bureaucracy and the courts had certainly not been sources of modernity or liberalism in the Weimar Republic; we have seen how their effects were—partly unintentionally, but often quite deliberately—authoritarian throughout. This was due to some considerable extent to the traditional character of these institutions, which the Weimar parties again had not dared touch. Hitler was less hesitant. In the first months of his rule he enacted the laws and created the institutions that were needed to "co-ordinate" the bureaucracy and the legal system. This meant that he wanted to subject them to his rule; and the interventions in traditional autonomies and customs and habits required by this intention were so profound that they had to change these institutions almost out of recognition.

Co-ordination soon reached the other institutions too. It neutralized the Reich President until his office disappeared after the death of Hindenburg. It broke into the army as it had revolutionized public bureaucracy and the legal system before. It led to the abolition of the autonomous economic institutions that had amounted to a system of industrial relations however incomplete, and that were replaced by state-controlled organizational patterns. It robbed the press of its independence and subordinated it to the total purposes of the state. Later on, co-ordination began to approach those institutions that were further removed from the state, the churches and private organizations, universities and traditional associations, in order to subject all sectors of society to rigid control.

The notion of "co-ordination," which —like that of the "total state"—is not an invention of interpreting scholarship, but was introduced by the National Socialists themselves in the early years of their rule, was meant politically. But inevitably it had a social dimension as well. "Co-ordination" always means the abolition of uncontrolled autonomy. Wherever relatively self-sufficient institutions or organizations exist, they have to yield to organizations directed to the one purpose of the state and its personification in the Leader. In this process people are removed from traditional, personal, often especially close and intimate ties, and made equal in kind, if not in rank.

One can put this more metaphorically and thereby indicate once again the contradiction between the ideology and practice of National Socialism by saying that the Nazi regime tried everywhere to replace organic social structures by mechanical formations. Instead of an interdependence of a diversity of institutions with a degree of autonomy, and often with their own historical dimension, National Socialism needed the uniform orientation of all institutions to one purpose. In the place of many partial elites of limited but independent significance stepped a monopolistic clique; in the place of a multitude of binding partial roles stepped the diffuse role of the *Volksgenosse,* the compatriot, or comrade of the (same) people, with its numerous expectations.

The contrast to an ideology dominated by organic notions—if in a primitive or vulgar version—could hardly be more acute. But then a view of state and society as an organic system of interdependent elements could not be in the interest of the claim to total power. The organic theory of the state is an authoritarian notion. It concedes to the constituent elements a life of their own, so long as this does not affect the claim to certainty advanced by the leading stratum. Since the leading stratum claims merely the ultimate, and not the permanent right to decide, since its legitimacy is founded on the non-participation, and not on the permanent organization and control of the subjects, the area of autonomy remains quite large. What happens in family and school, church and community, indeed to some extent in the army and the courts, the bureaucracy and voluntary organizations, does not worry the authoritarian political class so long as its position is not threatened by it. But a totalitarian leadership group is threatened by any autonomy of institutions. It cannot afford that generosity that allowed even cartoonists and satirical writers their cat-and-mouse games with censorship in Imperial Germany. It needs that mechanical co-ordination that involves the destruction of all loyalties that support the autonomous life of the individual.

The contrast between the National Socialist ideology of the organic and the mechanical practice of co-ordination remains so striking that one is almost tempted to believe that the ideology was not simply an instrument to mislead people deliberately. Possibly the National Socialist leaders themselves believed in some of their sentimental traditionalisms, that is, they sought authoritarian rule. But even if this was so, their wishes had to remain unfulfilled. The return of Imperial Germany in any version, including modified forms, was probably impossible even in 1933; it was certainly impossible for Hitler and his adherents to bring about such a return. As a traditionless clique that could hardly be described as conservative in outlook, the Nazi leaders were inescapably doomed to the path of totalitarianism to find a basis for their power. This in turn presupposed the co-ordination of all institutions with any degree of autonomy, the destruction of all loyalties of men not devoted to the state, the unbounded extension of the social role of the *Volksgenosse*. The National Socialist leaders had the choice of either disappearing as such or setting in motion a social revolution in Germany with all brutality.

"Co-ordination" in the strict sense of the early years was only the beginning of this process. In the years before the war it was supplemented by a number of consequential measures of which only the most significant need be mentioned here. Two basic structures of social differentiation in all societies are those of regional differentiation and of social stratification. These may assume very different forms. They can both produce somewhat artificial, passing roles, which may be acquired and also shed; or they may be burdened with a long history and surrounded by far-reaching expectations. One of the aspects of German traditionalism before 1933 was that regional differentiation and social stratification were, for many, far more than systems of achievable positions. They bound the individual in a way that resounds with notions of the closed society. These were ties that introduced an element of immobilization and thus an obstacle to the development of democracy in the country.

But—this is the tragic figure of modernity at the basis of our argument—obstacles to democracy are also obstacles to totalitarianism. The National Socialist leaders had to try to weaken the binding force of ties of region and class, and they did so. Moving people away from their inherited (or even chosen) places of residence is not a Russian or Polish invention; it was a principle in National Socialist Germany as well. Even where no "resettlement" of larger groups took place, there were plenty of well-planned occasions for alienating people at least temporarily from their accustomed environment and thereby casting doubt on custom and heritage for those concerned. The mass organizations of the party and its affiliations, and later on the army, offered many an occasion of this kind. These institutions served at the same time to level social strata, the differentiation of which was ideologically reinterpreted, following the Soviet pattern, as one of "workers of the forehead" and "workers of the fist." Clearly, this would not make the differentiation itself disappear; but its halo of customs and expectations shrank in view of the expansive claim of the "comrade of the people"—a role that, not unlike the role of "citizen" in this respect, makes the unequal equal and the ascribed achievable, and in that sense has specifically modern traits.

The struggle against the loyalties of memberships, which, while they may be achievable, were often sanctified by long tradition, assumed many more pronounced forms from the early years of the Nazi regime. To many it seems contradictory today that among the victims of this struggle we find the traditional organizations of socialist trade unions as well as of student clubs. But in terms of totalitarian rule there is no contradiction here; both types of organization and others of similar kinds allocate roles to their members, the substance of which is taken away from the general, equal role of the *Volksgenosse* and thus the disposable general public. They withdraw a part of the public activity of the individual from general access and control by the state and have to abide, therefore, by the verdict of co-ordination, which is inescapable for the establishment of totalitarian power.

This is true for church membership as well. Discussion of the question of whether the Catholic church lacked moral fiber in its attitude toward the crude and eventually murderous anti-Semitism of the Nazis has obscured our vision to the fact that the churches had to be entirely unacceptable islands of autonomy for the Nazi leaders. The struggle for the social realization of total power had therefore to be directed from the outset against the churches. This was all the more necessary since the churches were powerful in Germany and represented, at least in the case of the Catholic church—as shown by the development of the vote for the Center Party in the Weimar Republic—stable political counterweights. In the case of the Evangelical church, this struggle soon led to more than superficial successes for the regime, although decidedly anti-Nazi groups emerged almost equally soon from the midst of the coordinated Protestants. The adaptation of the "German Christians" was followed by the resistance of the "Professing Church." So far as the Catholic church is concerned, Nazi successes were certainly more limited. But one development affected both churches and is therefore of particular interest in our context: National Socialism made disinterest in, and even hostility to the churches socially acceptable in Germany. Before 1933, the "dissident" was recognized only in the subculture of the labor movement; but the "God believer" (a secularized non-Christian type promoted by the Nazis) became a creature clearly approved by the state. In this way more than by direct influence on the churches, that is, by inroads on religious traditionalism rather than the politicization of religious institutions, the Nazis won their successes in their struggle against the churches.

The most striking and consequential testimony to the National Socialist's struggle against traditional loyalties—and to the contradiction of ideology and practice—can probably be found in terms of the position of the family. There is no shortage of Nazi declarations in praise of the family and its crucial social significance. But in reality, the Nazis' family policies all amounted to the systematic reduction of the functions of the family to the one overwhelming task of reproduction. Where the family could not fulfill this task, or not fulfill it sufficiently by ruling standards, the masters of the regime quite consistently did not care about the institution; whether the "spring of life" (*Lebensborn*) and state-supported promiscuity for demographic purposes existed or not, there can be little doubt that the rights of the family ended where it failed to meet its alleged obligations, and this meant a reduction of its right to nearly nothing.

These obligations were conceived entirely in terms of a public aspect totally alien to the family itself. They had little to do with promoting cohesion within the family, to say nothing of the happiness of men, but were derived from goals like the military strength of the nation, which are far removed from the individual and his rights. For that reason also the rulers of National Socialist Germany took from the family the task that above all documents the prevalence of private virtues: the education of children.

National Socialist school policies, and even more strongly the significance of obligatory membership in the Hitler Youth for all children from ten years of age, involved an increasing and deliberate restriction of familial rights and tasks. The Hitler Youth emphasized even among the ten-year-olds independence from, and indeed—exploiting the age-old antagonism of generations—hostility toward their parents. Total power involves at least the intention of permanent control of every person by the rulers and their organizations. Such control presupposes the extrication of people from all social spheres that are removed from the grasp of public agencies. In this sense, the family was an obstacle on the path to the establishment of total power. In this sense, the educational policies of the Nazis promoted public values—if in the form of the public vices of uniformed demonstrations, the denunciation of friends, and unquestioned activities of other kinds.

Thus the role of the *Volksgenosse* grew in substance all the time. Many other memberships and loyalties were swallowed by this equal and public role. The *Volksgenosse* participated in public affairs without influencing them; the effect of his appearance was at best a demonstration of somebody else's power; yet he had to participate because this alone enabled the powerful to control his activity as they had to. This meant, of course, that the fellow and the friend, the Christian, and the son or father, and many others had to yield their claims to the *Volksgenosse*. In addition to their immediate purposes, policies of this kind satisfied the wishes of youth; its universal aversion to ascribed loyalties appeared sanctioned by the state, and in this way the leaders of the future were tied to the leaders of the present. The *Volksgenosse* was the figurehead of the National Socialist revolution.

But we have to stop here in our account of the social history of this role; for its victory was by no means absolute. Like every revolution in history, the National Socialist revolution of modernity did not remain undisputed. This is evident in the fact that, for example, many a corner of society was never reached by the process of "co-ordination." The attitude of "inner emigration," which many German intellectuals displayed, would have been as impossible in a perfect totalitarian state as in a perfect modern society. Nevertheless not only intellectuals succeeded in the "inner emigration." Many a highly regarded and declaredly anti-Nazi politician of the Weimar Republic survived nearly unmolested until July 20, 1944, and occasionally even to the end of the war. The hold of state and party on the family did not extend into every family by any means. The churches managed in many places to avoid "co-ordination" altogether. Despite government-sponsored mobility, regional ties frequently remained as intact as patterns of social stratification. Schools and universities, courts and prisons, large sectors of the army and of the economy, and many private organizations maintained a certain autonomy. Even in 1938, National Socialist Germany bore not only the features of totalitarianism, but equally pronouncedly authoritarian traits, among which the unprotesting non-participation of many must also be counted. While "co-ordination" was the dominant tendency, it was clearly not generally realized before the beginning of the wars of conquest.

To the unplanned resistance against the social concomitants of the totalitarian seizure of power, more or less open active opposition against the regime was soon added. This opposition is generally described as "resistance." In terms of our thesis, the German resistance must indeed be understood as largely a reaction; in this we encounter one of the most difficult and tragic chapters of recent German history. If it is true that, in order to establish its total rule, the Nazi regime had to bring about a social revolution, then resistance against the regime may be described as counterrevolutionary. Given the premise, the substance of resistance is the attempt to resurrect the prerevolutionary state. Where the National Socialist revolution promoted, however reluctantly, modernity, the counterrevolution aimed at the conservation of traditional ties to family and class, region and religion. While the social revolution of National Socialism was an instrument in the establishment of totalitarian forms, by the same token it had to create the basis of liberal modernity; the counterrevolution on the other hand can be understood only as a revolt of tradition, and thus of illiberalism and of the authoritarianism of a surviving past.

Whoever, as a German, considers this phase of German history, cannot but envy a people that can despise its ancien régime and praise its revolution. For the perversions of German history are such that even the liberal has to praise the ancien régime because revolution fell upon it in such a devilish form, and the counterrevolution was so humane. German resistance against Hitler is a leaf of fame in German history; but it is not a step on the path of German society toward the constitution of liberty. Worse still, it was Hitler who effected those transformations of German society that make the constitution of liberty possible, while the resistance against his regime acted in the name of a social tradition that could provide a basis only for authoritarian rule. Nowhere did morality and liberalism part company as visibly as in Germany; nowhere is it therefore as difficult to desire the free and the good society at the same time.

It soon became evident that the alliance of National Socialists and conservatives, which destroyed the Weimar Republic, was plainly a mistake. Much as Freisler would praise the National Socialist state as a rule of a new type, the adherents of the traditional rule of law were not pacified by such transparent sophistry. Among the supporters of the institutions subjected to "co-ordination," the universal interest in maintaining the status quo was added to moral indignation. Both, however, moral indignation and resistance to all threats to vested interests, were first aroused among those conservatively inclined groups that had originally joined forces with the Nazis to destroy the Weimar Republic. From the point of view of the new rulers, these conservative groups clearly had to appear as a major threat even after the alliance was concluded. Nobility and higher bureaucracy, military leaders and some lawyers, as well as several other groups were, after all, the survivals of the society of Imperial Germany. They embodied the very traditionalism in German society that the Nazis had to destroy if they wanted to generalize their power. It was a rather late insight therefore if Ulrich von Hassell noted in his diary in 1944 that the Nazis intended to push from their position, and indeed exterminate physically "nobility and the educated classes." In fact, this was the necessary policy of the party from the first day of its rule, because its hope of survival lay in the total and brutal modernization of German society.

The German resistance movement comprised many groups; but with the one exception of the Communists—remarkably weak as they were as a force of resistance—they can all be described as deliberate or unintentional defenders of the ancien régime. This claim is not refuted by the alliance of the military with the Social Democrats in preparing July 20, 1944. The explicit goals of this alliance were largely negative; understandably, they consisted in the abolition of the Nazi regime and the end of the war. In their generally vague positive conceptions, resistance groups differed greatly; even within the military, and equally within the Social Democratic Party, there were considerable disagreements. But at least by implication, if not by explicit declaration, the intention was common to all to reestablish many of the values and institutions that had shaped the Weimar period and that provide a basis for an authoritarian rather than a liberal society. The question must even be raised whether the resistance groups of July 20 did not deliberately envisage an authoritarian form of government at least for the period immediately after the success of their revolt. In view of our earlier analyses, notably that of the widespread aversion to social conflict, the union of the military with the Social Democrats appears indeed neither surprising nor accidental in this context. It is the open continuation of a tacit coalition that had its origin in Imperial Germany.

July 20, 1944, described the tragic conclusion of the social revolution brought about by the National Socialist regime in Germany. It was clear after this that German society could never return to the structures of Imperial times. So far as their human agents are concerned, it is relevant to note that after many young members of the nobility had been killed in action during the early years of the war, German nobility lost its best representatives after July 20. Much the same may be said, at least with respect to the effects of July 20, for leading Social Democrats, and for bourgeois politicians as well. July 20 and the persecutions resulting from its failure mark the end of German political elite. Along with its human basis, the reality of an idea passed away—an idea that is symbolized for many by the name of Prussia. Prussian discipline, lawfulness, morality, but Prussian illiberalism as well, the honest directness but also the authoritarianism of Prussian tradition, the humanity but also the deliberate minority of the many in the political landscape of the Prussian tradition—all this found its last triumph on July 20, 1944. Moral values, and frequently their reality in the German past, were held up against the arbitrariness of the Nazis; the old regime was indeed a morally better world, but its revolt failed and the brutal path to modernity took its further course.

There are, to be sure, many causes of the failure of the revolt of July 20. Furthermore, nothing is further from my intention than to justify, even by innuendo, this failure. Even the liberal was forced to long for the pleasure of an authoritarian rule of law in the face of the terrors of National Socialism. But it cannot be denied that the direction of the social development the Nazis set in motion told against the politics of German resistance. This may also well be a major reason why the conclusion is unavoidable that National Socialist rule in Germany was legitimate, at least in the sense of factually recognized validity. In so far as the absence of widespread protest is by itself a testimony to legitimacy, this was clearly the case; the invisible and ineffectual forms of private protest that many claimed for themselves after the war were, in fact, subservient ways of agreement. Further than that, there was in all phases of National Socialist rule the more or less silent agreement among the large majority of men that is expressed in emergency situations as readiness to defend the regime.

We have tried earlier to answer the first of three questions about National Socialism: How was January 30, 1933, possible? Now the second of our questions becomes relevant: How was the nearly complete absence of resistance, thus the evident acceptance of the National Socialist regime by the population possible? This question, too, we can now answer, although in doing so it seems proper to differentiate between the prewar period and the war period.

In respect to the structure of society, the Weimar Republic marked a phase of hardly bearable stagnation. Moving to and fro between old regime and modernity, people found no point of orientation for their behavior; the parties with whom they sought such points of orientation usually disappointed them. In that sense the mere fact that something happened under the new rulers seemed a relief. That this involved rigid forms of organization, strengthened the new feeling of security, although it was precisely this basis of security that was precarious and would hardly have withstood a longer period of peace. If the push into modernity meant a painful loss for many, others saw primarily the gain; Karl Mannheim has pointed out the special relevance of youth for the legitimacy of National Socialist rule, which we have discussed before. If one adds that the unambiguous departure from the uncertainties of the past was combined with a period of economic prosperity, the legitimacy of the Nazi regime can hardly come as a surprise. Indeed, it is almost surprising that the leaders of the regime met with any resistance at all.

Ernst Nolte suggests that the absence of resistance to the National Socialists must be explained above all by their policy of "war in peace." The permanent invocation of a national state of emergency may indeed lead to suspending all internal divisions, so that even personal enemies find solidarity together. There can be little doubt that their noisy nationalism rendered a useful service to the Nazis in this respect. But the social psychological motive that emerges here dominated the period of the war itself much more clearly. It was only then that absolute "co-ordination" turned from program to reality; during the war, even the islands of inner emigration were threatened. If resistance nevertheless did not grow beyond all limits, this was clearly due to the handicap of legitimacy enjoyed by every wartime government. On the other hand, the fact that even in wartime resistance grew to a revolt documents the precarious power position of totalitarian leaders.

All this amounts to the conclusion that National Socialism was not merely an episode. It was not a work of seduction by a small clique, but, by its toleration, a German phenomenon. We have to remember, of course, that factual legitimacy does not establish moral legitimacy; what works, does not have to be good. Our third question, how the National Socialist crimes were possible, remains unanswered, unless our observations about humanitarianism and inhumanity in Germany are taken for an answer. Morally, the road to modernity could hardly assume more brutal and inhuman traits than it did in Germany.

What remains of the social revolution of National Socialism? If our thesis is correct, that is, if National Socialism was not an historical episode but the German revolution, it must have left its traces in the subsequent phase. This is indeed the case, although these traces are obscured by that other heritage of Nazi rule, which results from total defeat. The starting points of German social development after the war consisted first of all in a number of simple, if consequential facts. By war damage and war consequences Germany's economy was thrown back to an almost preindustrial state. By the expulsion of millions of people from the eastern territories, economy and society in Germany were faced with extraordinary additional tasks. The disappearance of the entire National Socialist leadership elite made it necessary to form a new political class. The subdivision of the country into zones of occupation and the enmity of the occupation powers, which soon became apparent, imposed many additional limitations on the situation from which Germany took off. Even a sociologically informed account of German postwar development has to start with these initial conditions, and we shall do so. But by way of summarizing this chapter, there is the more general and possibly more important question: Which was the path prescribed to German society after the war in respect to the task of mastering the problems mentioned? Which path was precluded for it? In answering these questions, the lasting result of the social revolution of National Socialist Germany becomes evident.

German society remained illiberal in

its structure and authoritarian in its constitution throughout the decades of industrialization. Although many of the bases of the absurd yet effective mixtures of old and new in the politics and society of Imperial Germany had gone in 1918, the Weimar Republic departed only very partially and anxiously from the old patterns. In times of crisis the nostalgia for past experiences grew. The mistaken alliance of conservative and National Socialist opponents of parliamentary democracy in 1933 was founded on this nostalgia; but soon after the seizure of power its false assumptions became clear. In order to maintain their power, the National Socialists had to turn against all traces of the social order that provided the basis for authoritarian rule. They destroyed inherited loyalties wherever they could; they coordinated all traditional institutions equipped with a life of their own; they generalized the social role of the *Volksgenosse* as far as they could.

Despite the indescribable ruthlessness with which the process took place, they did not succeed wholly. There remained corners of tradition, sources of resistance and counterrevolution. But the push into modernity succeeded sufficiently to remove the social basis for future authoritarian governments along traditional German lines. National Socialism has finally abolished the German past as it was embodied in Imperial Germany. What came after it was free of the mortgage that burdened the Weimar Republic at its beginning, thanks to the suspended revolution. There could be no return from the revolution of National Socialist times.

For the direction of postwar development itself, this by no means tells the whole story. The National Socialists demonstrated the ambiguity of modernity. Where the *Volksgenosse* prevails, the subject cannot return; this is his specifically modern face. But he may be followed by the citizen as well as the comrade, and perhaps there are other, still unknown social figures of modernity with similar problems. This is why the pathology of democracy in Germany is not completed even with the brutal revolution of the Nazi *Reich*.

In the end, National Socialism despite the violence it engendered, did not effect a radical transformation in the structure of German society or in the way Germany's economy functioned. For this reason many students of the subject doubt whether it was truly a revolutionary movement. Professor Alexander Groth, of the University of California at Davis, who is the author of the following selection, would concur with this view. He also questions to what degree National Socialism, or indeed any Fascist movement, may even be considered effectively totalitarian, especially when compared to such phenomena as Russian and Chinese Communism.

The "Isms" in Totalitarianism

ALEXANDER J. GROTH

A major theme in political literature since the nineteen fifties has been a "unitotalitarian" approach to the study of modern dictatorships. The principal totalitarian "isms"—Fascism, Nazism and Communism—have been viewed as examples of one common species, containing no doubt some variations and differences; but practically, or operationally, the divergencies have been thought considerably less important than the similarities.[1] The emphasis has been heavily on the structure and methods underlying the exercise of political control by the "Leader" and the "Party." In what is undoubtedly the outstanding modern study of the subject, Friedrich and Brzezinski have attempted to extrapolate predictive hypotheses from the common pattern of totalitarian dictatorship expressed in a familiar syndrome of six interrelated characteristics. In 1956 they wrote: [2]

> "The Fascist and Communist systems . . . have shown a continuous, though intermittent, tendency to become more 'totalitarian' . . . . If one extrapolates from the past course of evolution, it seems most likely that the totalitarian dictatorships will continue to become more total, even though the rate of intensification may slow down."

If the prophecy has remained visibly unfulfilled in the case of Soviet Russia, may we not attribute its failure to the method underlying the prediction?

I

The unitotalitarian approach has undoubtedly served a valuable purpose. It has focused attention upon a common range of means employed by modern dictatorships with justified emphasis

Reprinted from *American Political Science Review*, vol. 58, December 1964, with the permission of the author and the American Political Science Association.

[1] Carl J. Friedrich and Zbigniew Brzezinski, *Totalitarian Dictatorship and Autocracy* (Harvard University Press, Cambridge, 1959), p. 7: " . . . it is very important to explain [that] the totalitarian dictatorships, Communist and Fascist, are *basically alike*." *Cf.* William Ebenstein, "The Study of Totalitarianism," *World Politics*, Vol. 10, No. 2 (January 1958), pp. 274–288, and Daniel Bell, "Ten Theories in Search of Reality: The Prediction of Soviet Behavior in the Social Sciences," *ibid.*, No. 3 (April 1958), pp. 327–356.

[2] Friedrich and Brzezinski, *op. cit.*, p. 6 and *ibid.*, p. 300.

upon what totalitarians do rather than what they ideologically or propagandistically profess. It has shifted the inquiry from a deceptive point of maximum apparent divergence to one of closest apparent identity.[3] On the other hand, "unitotalitarianism" has had some serious disadvantages.

Preoccupied with structural and outward uniformities it has been less sensitive to the differences, particularly among the respective socio-economic contents of the "isms." It is argued here that a common theoretical framework of totalitarianism for the analysis of systems widely divergent in other respects (social, economic and cultural) is likely to be misleading if the uniformities are construed too broadly and their significance is over-emphasized. The problem is in a sense analogous to the development of a political model for such widely differing entities as for example Great Britain, Ceylon, United States, India, and Venezuela on the basis of shared political traits: absence of official ideologies; economies combining private enterprise with government controls; popularly elected legislatures and elective executives; freedom of the press, religion, petition and assembly; the existence of law courts, theoretically and constitutionally independent of the executive; multiplicity of political parties, trade unions and interest groups, etc. It is clear that, though having much in common, the political process in each of these societies is sufficiently distinct and molded by such diverse traditional, cultural, social, economic and religious influences as to render reliance on a single common denominator very dubious. That is, the reliance is dubious if one expects to be able to predict the future course of these entities from the common model, or to understand each through the traits common to all. Such insight would naturally require at least equivalent attention to the underlying differences.

The problem of "totalitarianism" is analogous in this sense. The common traits attributed to Italy and Germany on the one hand and Soviet Russia on the other have been in varying degrees and at various times characteristic of all three: official ideology, mass party and leader, terror, monopolistic propaganda, centralized control of the armed forces and the economy, etc. If these regimes —and any others—have in fact shared such characteristics one may certainly be justified in giving them a common classification and in assuming that comparable "inputs," other things being equal, have produced comparable "outputs"—that terror, *e.g.*, has produced widespread fear and thus rendered the given societies in some respects the "same" or "similar."

On the other hand, it goes beyond mere logical deduction or plain reading of the evidence to conclude that what is similar in some respects is similar in all, or that the "similarities" rather than the "differences" offer the best key to the understanding of the working of all these regimes.

While alike in many ways, the regimes of Fascist Italy and Nazi Germany may actually offer us few, if any, clues to the future development of Communist states. This will certainly be the case if the "differences" between these regimes are more important operationally than the similarities, particularly with respect to that admittedly very elusive term: "change."

The purpose of this essay is not to explore all the characteristics which differentiate the several "totalitarian" systems. It is rather to focus attention

[3] Though that is not to say that the discounting of ideologies as "mere words" or "ritualistic formulas" is helpful or useful. *Cf.* Z. Brzezinski, *The Soviet Bloc* (Harvard University Press, Cambridge, 1960), pp. 386–395 for an excellent account.

on the socio-economic aspect of the subject, an aspect which is particularly neglected in the "unitotalitarian" interpretation, and one which is certainly crucial to an understanding of the Fascist, Nazi and Soviet states.

Even if one assumes that the political scientist is interested in a very narrowly defined conception of the political process—with a bare minimum of concern for the impact of "politics" for such areas as culture, religion and the economy, and assumes also that political phenomena are "significant" only to the degree that they are manifested in outward behavior, he must nevertheless concern himself not merely with *what* is being done, and *how,* but also with the problem of "*who* does it to *whom.*" If we grant that actions have consequences, political techniques must be viewed as inevitably reacting upon their users, and upon the entire political process of which both the "techniques" and the "technicians" are a part. Political techniques, after all, may be used to produce changes which alter the whole group basis of politics. Such changes may ultimately affect the identity of the "rulers" themselves and thereby (if not for other reasons) also the nature of the methods employed as well as a host of other factors. In different contexts similar, even identical, political techniques could very well produce divergent results—and *vice versa.* Hence, the question of context, certainly the problem of the identity of the power holders and the particular distribution of rewards and punishments by them, are no less important than the techniques.

It is not argued here in Marxist fashion that the political structure is either solely or predominantly determined by the socio-economic "substructure." An important reciprocal influence, nevertheless, seems obvious. Friedrich and Brzezinski say, however: [4]

> Such questions as who holds formal title to property, how 'profits,' that is to say, rewards, are determined, and whether former owners and decision makers continue to hold positions, provided they conform to the regime's commands are of relatively minor significance. What is decisive is the overpowering reality of totalitarian control by the dictator and his party.

One might be justified in asking of "minor significance" to whom? The business elite, for example? If the matter is not, after all, of "minor significance" to business, might it not have consequences which the political scientist should find "significant?" The question of *what* is being done is no doubt important but so is the matter of *who* does it. To illustrate, business communities anywhere could not be indifferent to the matter of whether they are to be "in" or "out." There is some evidence that in the past this has influenced their behavior and might under some conditions do so again. On the other hand, was it not of importance to Hitler that the leaders of the armed forces who were similarly under the "overpowering reality of totalitarian control by the dictator and his party" were not, by and large, party men themselves? (Even if allegedly he alone decided whom the armed forces would fiight, when they would fight and under what conditions.)

We need to know the group physiognomy of the regime, its impact upon the group structure of the society it rules, and what sorts of changes capable of influencing the social structure the regime sponsors or fosters.[5] Nothing less can give us an understanding of the

[4] Friedrich and Brzezinski, *op. cit.,* p. 211. *Cf.* Peter F. Drucker, *The End of Economic Man* (New York, 1938), p. 149.

[5] *Cf.* David Apter, "A Comparative Method for the Study of Politics," *American Journal of Sociology,* Vol. 64, No. 3 (November 1958), pp. 221–237, for a general model concerned with "mobility opportunities."

potentialities for change inherent in any system, notwithstanding the difficulties in gathering evidence.

The drawback of the unitotalitarian approach is that it is implicitly indifferent to empirical research on the nature of the "isms" from the standpoint of their differential socio-economic consequences.

The studies of the 'thirties and 'forties, by scholars like Franz Neumann, Gaetano Salvemini, R. A. Brady, C. T. Schmidt, Welk, Sweezy and others (even if sometimes marred by a Marxist bias) could undoubtedly be augmented, enriched and modified from available postwar sources on the Nazi and Fascist dictatorships.[6] They could also be significantly correlated with continually accumulating data on the Soviet and Communist states. Pending further research, however, there is considerable evidence already available for the view that in important respects the Fascist, Nazi and Communist regimes are basically different and that these differences are likely to result in divergent paths of development for Communist as compared with the defunct Fascist and Nazi states.

II

The Communists, wherever they have succeeded in capturing power, have generally undertaken measures directly and indirectly uprooting existing socio-economic elites: the landed nobility, business, large sections of the middle class and the peasantry, as well as the bureaucratic elites, the military, the civil service, the judiciary and the diplomatic corps. They have done this through mass expropriation, expulsion, persecution and, as in the case of Soviet Russia, even through mass slaughter. In the case of the forty-six year old Russian dictatorship it would not be an exaggeration to say that the bureaucratic elites of pre-1917 society had been virtually exterminated by the mid-1930s.[7] In the places of political, economic, administrative and military managers of Russian society before the October Revolution, new personnel had appeared: new both in terms of their physical as well as largely their social identity.[8]

Second, in every instance of Communist seizure of power there has been a significant ideological-propagandistic commitment toward a proletarian or workers' state, particularly to the worker-peasant concept of the ruling Party.[9] This commitment, however tarnished and compromised in everyday practice, has been accompanied by opportunities for upward social mobility for the economically lowest classes, in terms of education and employment, which invariably have considerably exceeded the opportunities available under previous regimes. Finally, in every case the Communists have attempted to change basically the character of the economic

[6] See Arthur Schweitzer, *Big Business in the Third Reich* (Indiana University Press, Bloomington, 1964), for an excellent postwar reappraisal.

[7] See, *e.g.*, C. E. Black (ed.), *The Transformation of Russian Society* (Harvard University Press, Cambridge, 1960), pp. 235–350.

[8] Although these changes have almost never been accompanied by an increased standard of living for the "stationary" members of the working class, and in many cases have involved a decline. *Cf.* Alex Inkeles and R. A. Bauer, *The Soviet Citizen* (Harvard University Press, Cambridge, 1961), pp. 33–34, 81–82, 83–84, *e.g.*, see also Alex Inkeles, "Social Stratification and Mobility in the Soviet Union: 1940–1950," *American Sociological Review*, Vol. 15 (August 1950), pp. 465–479. *Cf.* Milovan Djilas, *The New Class* (New York, 1957), p. 61.

[9] *Cf.* Leonard Schapiro, *The Communist Party of the Soviet Union* (New York, 1960), pp. 435–7, 522–6.

systems which fell under their sway, typically from an agrarian to an industrial economy.[10]

In this threefold sense, Communist regimes, particularly that of Russia, have been revolutionary. They have been revolutionary not merely to the extent of the changes they effected upon seizure of power but revolutionary also in terms of their long-term social goals and consequences. The "New Soviet Man" emerged from a society rendered, by any standard, vastly more industrialized, urbanized and literate.

Fascism (both in the German and Italian versions) to the extent that it can be judged by its performance in power, was socio-economically a counter-revolutionary movement. Assuming control in periods of social crisis it certainly did not dispossess or annihilate existent socio-economic elites,[11] however thoroughly it tamed them. Quite the contrary.[12] Fascism did not arrest the trend toward monopolistic private concentrations in business but instead augmented this tendency.[13] Fascism did not secure a radical change in the division of na-

[10] See, *e.g.*, Nicolas Spulber, *The Economics of Communist Europe* (New York, 1957), particularly pp. 340, 343. East European increases in industrial output and in the ratio of producers' to consumers' goods, by 1955, even in the case of the already substantially industrialized Czechoslovakia, far exceeded comparable Italian or German efforts prior to 1939.

[11] *Cf.* U. S. Senate Committee on Military Affairs, *Hearings on the Elimination of German Resources for War* (hereafter cited as the Kilgore Hearings), Washington, June–July 1945.

[12] A large body of literature testifying to this point appeared during the 1930s and the Second World War. Outstanding examples were Gaetano Salvemini, *Under the Axe of Fascism* (Victor Gollancz, London, 1936); Franz Neumann, *Behemoth* (Oxford University Press, New York, 1942); R. A. Brady, *The Spirit and Structure of German Fascism* (New York, 1937); Maxine Y. Sweezy, *The Structure of the Nazi Economy* (Harvard University Press, Cambridge, 1941); and Carl T. Schmidt, *The Plough and the Sword* (Columbia University Press, New York, 1938). Whatever their Marxist biases and predilections, these works presented a considerable body of factual evidence showing that the social and economic consequences of Fascism were advantageous to the affluent and either relatively or absolutely disadvantageous to workers, small business, and other lower income groups. Before and after the War much, if not all, of this evidence was ignored and discounted despite the fact that corroborating postwar data on the Fascist economic systems had become available. Thus, in rebutting Neumann's 1942 assertion that the Nazi economy was essentially "capitalist," Friedrich and Brzezinski relied on the rather inconclusive evidence of Gunther Reimann's *Vampire Economy* of 1939 but not on the Kilgore Committee Hearings of July 1945, which in some 1600 pages presented evidence gathered directly by U. S. Government research teams after the Nazi defeat. *Cf.* Friedrich and Brzezinski, *op. cit.*, p. 210.

[13] In view of amply documented Fascist policies with respect to land reform, reprivatization of nationalized properties, restrictions on small business, subsidies, taxation, education and many other matters, it is difficult to accept the Friedrich-Brzezinski position (*op. cit.*, p. 8): "It is indeed true that more of the institutions of the preceding liberal and constitutional society survived in the Italian Fascist than in the Russian Communist society. But this is due in part [?] to the fact that no liberal constitutional society preceded Soviet Communism. . . . In Czechoslovakia and in the Soviet Zone in Germany . . . we find precisely such institutions as universities, churches and schools surviving. . . . " Naturally, however, the authors could not extend the parallel to expropriation of landed property or confiscation of industry. *Cf.* Legislative Reference Service of the Library of Congress, *Fascism in Action* (Washington, G.P.O., 1947). On the subject of Fascist subsidies to business, Gaetano Salvemini wrote: "In actual fact, it is the State, *i.e.*, the taxpayer who has become responsible to private enterprise. In Fascist Italy the State pays for the blunders of private enterprise. . . . Profit is private and individual. Loss is public and social." Salvemini, *op. cit.*, p. 416. Undoubtedly, the Fascist economic system was not a free market economy and hence not "capitalist" if one wishes to restrict the use of this term to a *laissez-faire* system. But did it not operate in such a fashion as to preserve in being, and maintain the material rewards of, the existing socio-economic elites?

tional income.[14] On the whole, the status and relative affluence of the small business man, the worker and the poorer farmer *vis à vis* the more privileged social groups could only be described as either stationary or declining.[15]

The Fascists did not undertake the wholesale destruction of the existing bureaucracies controlling the apparatus of the state. They required submission and outward conformity to their policies. Undoubtedly, they treated the civil service as a "spoils plum" and, while disposing of "unreliable elements," they added to the existent structures from among their Party supporters. But Conservative and "quietist" elements in the civil service were frequently absorbed into the New Order, both in Italy and in Germany, sometimes by merely formal acceptance of party status.[16] Hence, much of the pre-Fascist apparatus survived Fascist rule.

Persistently, and not surprisingly, the Fascists have been regarded as the militant allies and defenders of besieged reactionary and capitalist interests.[17] In power, the Nazis and the Fascists did not preach egalitarianism nor did they undertake large scale programs which might increase the mobility prospects and opportunities of the lower social strata. On the whole, they followed *status quo* and even retrogressive social policies.[18] The Fascists did not attempt a basic reorientation of the national

[14] See Max Ascoli and Arthur Feiler, *Fascism for Whom?* (New York, 1938), p. 255. *Cf.* Kilgore Hearings, *op. cit.*, p. 439. See Donald R. Matthews, *The Social Background of Political Decision Makers* (New York, 1954), pp. 48–52, 53–4.

[15] *Cf.*, *e.g.*, Salvemini, *op. cit.*, pp. 182–9; Neumann, *op. cit.*, pp. 434–436; Schmidt, *op. cit.*, pp. 159–175.

[16] See, *e.g.*, Karl W. Deutsch and L. J. Edinger, *Germany Rejoins the Powers* (Stanford University Press, Stanford, California, 1959), particularly pp. 80–86. *Cf.* Herman Finer, *Mussolini's Italy* (New York, 1935), pp. 270–271; Max Ascoli (ed.), *The Fall of Mussolini* (New York, 1948), pp. 22–23.

[17] The orthodox Marxist view is a caricature. *Cf.* R. Palme-Dutt, *Fascism and the Social Revolution* (International Publishers, New York, 1935), p. 100: "Fascism . . . is from the onset fostered, nourished, maintained and subsidized by the big bourgeoisie, by the big landlords, financiers and industrialists." See also John Strachey, *The Menace of Fascism* (Covici Friede, New York, 1933), p. 128.

[18] Thus, *e.g.*, under Fascist rule in Italy university tuition exemptions were abolished in 1933. The number of university students declined from 43,865 in 1920–21 to 27,013 in 1928–29, then increased to an average of about 38,000 for the years 1933–35—thus falling short of totals which had already been reached in 1918–19 and failing to keep up with the expansion of the population. H. R. Marraro, *The New Education in Italy* (S. F. Vanni, New York, 1936), pp. 249, 255, 432. In Germany, the decline under the Nazis was even more precipitous. Mussolini at least strengthened primary and secondary education, though his pace of progress did not match in many respects the 19th Century growth of elementary education in Italy. *Cf.* L. Minio-Paluello, *Education in Fascist Italy* (Oxford University Press, London, 1946), pp. 15, 29, *e.g.* Under Hitler's rule the number of elementary schools declined from 52,959 in 1931 to 49,720 in 1940; the number of full-time teachers from 190,371 to 171,340; enrolment declined from 7,590,466 to 7,327,556. Highly significant from a mobility point of view, the number of university students fell from 95,807 in 1931 to but 39,236 in 1939. The number in higher technical institutes declined from 23,749 to a mere 10,307. By a decree of 1933 only ten per cent of students admitted to universities could be women. R. H. Samuel and R. H. Thomas, *Education and Society in Modern Germany* (Routledge and Kegan Paul, London, 1949), pp. 38, 50, 112, 132–33. On the other hand, the Soviets expanded regular secondary and primary school enrolment from 7.9 million before 1917 to 34.6 million in 1939, and from 1940 to 1959 total university enrolment increased from 75,682 to 213,000. Nicholas deWitt, *Education and Professional Employment in the U.S.S.R.* (G.P.O., Washington, 1961), pp. 133, 210.

economy in Italy,[19] and in Germany they did so only when, and insofar as, it promoted rearmament, mainly from 1935 onwards.[20]

Fascism preserved the economic basis of traditional elites in business and agriculture by maintaining both private profit and the right of inheritance. Whatever the nature of the regimentation and controls which the Fascist regimes imposed upon property and property owners, these controls did not spell confiscation and class extinction. Postwar evidence does not indicate, as some thought during and before the Second World War, that the Fascists "cancelled" real profits through such devices as forced loans, bribes and blackmail.[21]

Fascism also preserved an important political role for the old elite groups, in both official and socio-economic senses of the word. The representatives of the "established interests" participated both in the shaping and the implementation of political and military policies of the Fascist and Nazi regimes—a far cry from mere regimented subservience and the simple one-way "order-taking" sometimes alleged.

In Germany, Hitler clearly was not anybody's "mere puppet" before or during World War II; but obviously he did not make or implement all of the decisions of the Third Reich either. Nor must we assume that if non-Party influences were subordinated to the Party and the Leader, they were therefore nil.

Despite voluminous evidence to the contrary, a persistent myth, and one of

[19] Considerable evidence on this is supplied by Colin Clark, *The Conditions of Economic Progress* (3d ed., Macmillan, London, 1957), and Vera Lutz, *Italy: A Study in Economic Development* (Oxford University Press, London, 1962).

[20] *Cf.* Kilgore Hearings, *op. cit.*, pp. 218–421. Only at the end of 1935 did the ratio of capital goods investment to national income in Germany exceed the boom year of 1928.

[21] On this question a vast amount of evidence remains to be gathered but the actual, tangible consequences of Fascist rule certainly *can* be empirically analyzed. Whether Fascism destroyed or preserved the existing socio-economic order inherited in 1922 and 1933, respectively, can be deduced from comparisons of data on land distribution, occupational structure, the fate of private fortunes and a host of other factors. If some changes could always be expected, anywhere and under any circumstances, and if these changes must, in part, be attributed to causes other than the policies of the Fascist regimes, the results must nevertheless be considered highly significant. See Morris Janowitz, "Social Stratification and Mobility in West Germany," *American Journal of Sociology*, Vol. 64 (July 1958), pp. 6–24; *cf.* Deutsch and Edinger, *op. cit.*, pp. 35–37, 260–265; F. Edding, *The Refugees as a Burden and Stimulus to the West German Economy* (Hague, Martinus Nijhoff, 1951), p. 56 (Diagram 3). Though data presented in these sources were gathered some years after the War and were complicated by the influx of refugees from East to West Germany, remarkable structural stability between 1939 and 1955 emerges. This stability and the survival of pre-Fascist socio-economic elites are corroborated in a variety of other sources. *Cf., e.g.*, Heinz Abosch, *The Menace of the Miracle* (Collet's, London, 1962), pp. 82–87; Alfred Grosser, *Western Germany* (George Allen and Unwin, London, 1955), pp. 95–97. An interesting example of research having potential sample significance is Norbert Muhlen, *The Incredible Krupps* (New York, 1959). Pp. 164–65 are particularly revealing. The author affirms that a "high extent" of both profit and competition was maintained in the Nazi economy but the regime drastically minimized the entrepreneurial share in economic management. See also Samuel and Thomas, *op. cit.*, p. 177, on the remarkably stable upper class predominance in German universities from Weimar to the postwar period. On Italy, among other sources, comparisons of land-holding patterns from 1930 to 1947 are highly interesting and consonant with the interpretation offered here. *Cf. Fascism In Action*, *op. cit.*, p. 132 and Lutz, *op. cit.*, pp. 155–156. Also S. M. Lipset and R. Bendix, *Social Mobility in Industrial Society* (University of California Press, Berkeley, 1960), pp. 22–3. In its impact on socio-economic elites Fascism was apparently a system of totalitarian controls without totalitarian consequences.

the underlying assumptions of unitotalitarianism has been the notion of overwhelming, one-sided direction and control of the Fascist, and particularly the Nazi, system by the Leader and his Party. The fact that pre-Fascist elites both *could* and *did* play highly important political roles in the Fascist and Nazi regimes is often either denied or completely minimized. The question is certainly one of crucial significance and it cannot be simplified to the query: (a) was Hitler a puppet of the industrialists and the military, or (b) was he an "absolute ruler"? Political processes are not so simple. Friedrich and Brzezinski assert that:

> While the dictatorships of Mussolini and Hitler as well as that of Stalin were intact, there existed no scientifically reliable way of resolving this question, since the testimony of one observer stood flatly opposed to that of another. We are now in a more fortunate position. The documentary evidence clearly shows that Mussolini and Hitler were the actual rulers of their respective countries. Their views were decisive and the power they wielded was "absolute" in a degree perhaps more complete than ever before (*op. cit.*, p. 17).

It would not be inconsistent with any of the postwar accounts of the Fascist systems to argue that Hitler and Mussolini were by far the most important individual decision makers in their respective regimes, but the absolute, all-embracing power of the leaders, whether exercised directly or through their party followers, is mythical. The July 20, 1944 conspiracy in Germany would have been unthinkable and the successful removal of Mussolini in July 1943 likewise impossible, had totalitarian control been monolithic. In 1940 Mussolini did not bother to consult his Fascist Grand Council on Italy's entry into the War but he did consult the King, and the King seriously considered stopping him.[22] Ultimately, as Charles F. Delzell has written: [23]

> The Duce fell chiefly because of his own disastrous foreign policy, for when it became clear that Italy had lost the war, he forfeited the support of the powerful forces (Crown, capital, clergy, army and bureaucracy) which in the past had generally welcomed and benefited from his dictatorship.

Writing of the political role of the German Army, John W. Wheeler-Bennett has said: [24]

> Up to 1938 the Army had been the final arbiter of the political destinies of the Reich. They had first supported, and then condoned the overthrow of, the Republic and had made a major contribution to Hitler's coming to power. They had entered into a pact with the Party in order to preserve their privileged status and influence and had, as a result, been guilty of complicity in the Blood Purge of June 20, 1934. Well knowing what they did, they had accepted Hitler as Chief of State and had pledged their loyalty to him personally as their Supreme Commander, always with the reservation that at their own good pleasure they could unmake the Caesar they had made.

Whatever the specific merits of each of these assessments, it is clear that the German Army was not a cipher and that its influence after 1933 in Germany finds no parallel in Soviet experience after 1917, or for that matter in *any* of the Communist states. If the armed forces have been a factor in Soviet politics, they certainly were not the Tsarist

[22] Charles F. Delzell, *Mussolini's Enemies* (Princeton University Press, Princeton, New Jersey, 1961), p. 182. *Cf.* L. Villari, *The Liberation of Italy* (C. C. Nelson, Appleton, Wisconsin, 1959), p. 14.,

[23] Delzell, *op. cit.*, p. 223.

[24] *The Nemesis of Power* (Macmillan, London, 1953), p. 694.

armed forces.[25] Such illustrations could be multiplied. Postwar Allied inquiry into German economic organization confirmed at least a co-partnership role for leaders of large business firms in the planning and policy-making functions of the German economy.[26] Discussing the pre-war record of Nazism, Arthur Schweitzer writes: [27]

> The party dominated the political and ideological—the main informational and educational—lines of action but was forced to stay out of the military and most of the economic ministries of the state and had to tolerate the military and economic ideals and policies of its allies. The SS controlled the regular and secret police and the instruments of terror but had to abstain from military intelligence and refrain from acting within the spheres of power belonging to the military and to big business. Whereas in fundamental conflicts there prevailed a close partnership between the party and the SS, or between the generals and big business, in daily policy decisions and administrative matters the lines of authority and influence were clearly drawn.

However subordinated to the dictators, the old elites were neither extinguished nor impotent. A significant decision-making role involving a considerable measure of influence, discretion, or delegated authority, and in some instances blunt bargaining power, rested with representatives of elites which were not creatures of the Nazi regime and whose status, influence and outlook owed nothing to the Nazis. The same was true of Italy. The old elites, both bureaucratic and socio-economic, typically looked down upon the Fascist politicians as crude upstarts who may have been useful, or perhaps even indispensable once, but who were certainly not directly identified with the old elites themselves—their "pedigree," their traditions, their values, etc. To these elites, the Fascists were part of a passing scene.

III

In this "coexistence" between the Fascist and pre-Fascist elites lay at once the strength and the weakness of the Hitler and Mussolini brands of totalitarianism. If the Fascist and Nazi managers, party chieftains and administrators represented a new stratum, it was nevertheless a stratum superimposed upon and commingled with the upper layers of an established socio-economic order. The "revolutions" of 1922 and 1933 were as easy as any in history. But the price of power shared with the "pre-revolutionary" elements spelled drastic vulnerability to the Fascists. The displeasure and opposition of some of the old elites endangered the very existence of the Fascist regimes—and the lives of their leaders—when subjected to the ordeal of defeat in war. Certainly the "plots" against Hitler and Mussolini are highly revealing on this point. It was not simply that some of the well established pre-Fascist elements became the sources of anti-Fascist conspiracy. Above all, they had both the *access* to the leaders and the *capability* of wielding the apparatus of the state wherewith to dispose of their dictators. Where the German military narrowly failed (and

[25] In Russia 71.9 per cent of the divisional commanders and 100 per cent of the corps commanders were Communists in 1928. Merle Fainsod, *How Russia is Ruled* (Harvard University Press, Cambridge, 1958), p. 401. *Cf.* I. deSola Pool *et al.*, *Satellite Generals* (Stanford University Press, Stanford, California, 1955), p. 4.

[26] Kilgore Hearings, *op. cit.*, pp. 1047, 1064, 1560.

[27] Schweitzer, *op. cit.*, p. 505. *Cf.* also pp. 5–6 and 506–7 for the author's conclusions on these points. Summarizing the experience of the thirties, the author says: "Whether in terms of power or functions, the top Nazi leaders were only occasionally able to influence, and could not lay down, the economic and military policies of the regime", p. 507.

most accounts agree that their ultimate failure was due not to the simple preponderance of Nazi power confronting them but to lack of group resolution within)[28] the Italian King and his coterie of military and royal supporters succeeded.

In the history of the Soviet regime, despite many well-nigh staggering strains and defeats, no genuine attempt at Stalin's power was ever launched "from the inside."[29] Could it be that the Communist revolution in Russia, more difficult to achieve, had acquired some characteristics of greater durability? In the long run, the answer is probably yes, on grounds analogous to those once advanced by Machiavelli: he who would rule absolutely must remould the society over which he rules. Absolute claims to power cannot be made good without correspondingly absolute sources at one's command. Veto-groups cannot be long tolerated:[30]

> . . . he who proposes to set up a despotism, or what writers call a tyranny, must renovate everything. . . . organize everything in that state afresh; *e.g.*, in its cities to appoint new governors, with new titles and a new authority, the governors themselves being new men; to make the rich poor and the poor rich.

In the upshot of Fascist rule for twelve years in Germany and 22 in Italy the group structures of their respective societies endured remarkably stable and relatively unchanged. None of the traditional economic elite groups had been eliminated or significantly diminished. The have-nots made very few inroads upon the haves.[31]

IV

These facts have great political significance: they provide some elements for a rational understanding of group behavior as well as predictive implications for the respective "isms."

Both internally and externally, Fascism, Nazism and Communism have addressed themselves to, and relied upon, different "clienteles."[32] If we wish to understand what groups and social strata are both potentially and

[28] *Cf.* Gerhart Ritter, *The German Resistance* (New York, 1958), pp. 152–155; Constantine Fitzgibbon, *20 July* (New York, 1956), pp. 186–194; see also George K. Romoser, "The Politics of Uncertainty: The German Resistance Movement." *Social Research,* Vol. 31, no. 1 (Spring, 1964) pp. 73–93.

[29] It is assumed here that the "Doctors' Plot" of 1948 was a figment of Stalin's—and MVD's —imagination.

[30] *The Discourses of Niccolo Machiavelli,* trans. L. J. Walker (New Haven, Yale University Press, 1950), vol. I, p. 233. Hitler apparently perceived the problem of "unassimilated" and politically significant groups as being a "brake" on his dictatorship. What, if anything, he might have done about this "after the war" is another matter. *Cf. The Goebbels Diaries,* ed. and trans. Louis P. Lochner, (Garden City, New York, 1948), p. 287. Goebbels recalls, *e.g.:* "With a certain bitterness [Hitler] observes he must conduct [the war] with the present corps of generals. But once the war is over he wants to withdraw more than ever from military affairs and again devote himself to things which suit him much more personally. He is deeply shocked at the infidelity of the generals. They are ungrateful. . . . " (March 1943.) And Goebbels himself wrote on November 17, 1943: "I regard it as a cardinal error in the relationship between Party and Wehrmacht that the Party has not had the opportunity and possibility [!] of injecting its ideas into the Army. As a result the Army today is not so dependable as it really ought to be in times of severe strain." p. 515.

[31] *Cf., e.g.,* Leonard Krieger, "The Interregnum in Germany: March–August 1945," *Political Science Quarterly,* Vol. 64, No. 1 (March 1949), pp. 507–532; and Arthur Schweitzer, "On Depression and War," *ibid.,* Vol. 62, No. 3, (September 1947), pp. 321–353.

[32] *Cf.* Daniel Lerner *et al., The Nazi Elite* (Stanford University Press, Stanford, California, 1951), pp. 69–72, 84; Finer, *op. cit.,* pp. 364–376.

actually providing support for these movements, we must understand something of their image: a compendium of their policies, their ideologies and their propaganda themes. If these movements are "basically alike"[33] why do they appeal to different, rather than to similar or even identical, clienteles?[34] Is it politically "significant" that Communism has actively courted non-white races while Fascism rejected and attacked them? Is it "significant" that Communism has found widespread following among urban workers in several Western European countries, whereas Nazism and Fascism have appealed heavily to the middle and lower-middle classes?

On the other hand, the reciprocal relationships are important also. If the nature of the clientele is largely determined by the nature (or image) of the "ism," it is reasonable to assume that the clientele, in turn, exerts an influence upon the whole framework of institutional, ideological and policy expressions of a given "ism." Clearly the roles of totalitarian leaders cannot be understood apart from the claims and expectations of their followers and the flexibility of leadership, however authoritarian, must always be discounted to some extent by this factor.[35]

Both internal and external constituencies must be taken into account in appraising the nature of a particular "ism." Thus, the "isms" differ not merely in the "facts" which give rise to their being differently perceived. They also differ because of these divergent perceptions themselves, which in turn give rise to different kinds of expectations and claims upon the behavior of the particular regimes. The role of the external constituency may vary widely but it would not be unjustifiable to apply Neustadt's concept of the President's external constituency in an ever greater degree to Khrushchev or Mao than to the President of the United States.[36]

A movement's reputation for being "rightist" may in itself alienate traditionally "leftist" sources of support and *vice versa.* Under certain conditions some groups may be more likely than others to support or oppose the movement; an ordinarily unwelcome choice between "two great evils" may nevertheless be made far more coherently than the possibilities of random selection would indicate. Similarly, the difficult decision to oppose an entrenched regime is also likely to reflect the impact of the regime's policy upon diverse groups and social strata. Before the totalitarian seizure of power in Germany and Italy business and landed interests

[33] Ascoli and Feiler, *op. cit.*, p. 269: "National Socialism must be understood as truly being the present-day German version of present-day Russian Bolshevism." *Cf.* R. C. Tucker, "Towards a Comparative Politics of Movement Regimes," this REVIEW, Vol. 55 (June 1961), pp. 281–282: "Though the political symbolisms differed in all essentials, the two types of systems were identical." (Before Stalin's death, *i.e.*)

[34] *Cf.* Seymour Martin Lipset, *Political Man* (Garden City, New York, 1960), pp. 131–176.

[35] David B. Truman, *The Governmental Process* (New York, 1962), ch. 7, pp. 188–210: " . . . the occupant of a leadership position is the object of expectations on the part of other members of the group—expectations that become stronger as the leadership position becomes more inclusive." (p. 191) and . . . "a leader who changes his norm sharply after the group norm has been established may not be followed by others." (p. 192).

[36] Richard E. Neustadt, *Presidential Power* (New York, 1960), p. 7. The Soviet policy of support of Cuba, carried on despite considerable risks of Soviet-United States involvement, appears to have been much influenced by a Sino-Soviet competition for the following of the external Communist constituency. The Stalin-Trotsky power struggle was undoubtedly affected by the "revolutionary fizzle" of the external constituency. The adoption of the Soviet 1936 "democratic" constitution and Italian Fascist adaptations of racism even before World War II also have their "external constituency" aspects, in the sense of efforts made to conform with expectations or claims or kindred groups abroad.

were on the whole much more favorable to the Nazis and Fascists than toward the Communists.[37] After 1938 in Germany, the military elites provided more anti-Nazi resistance than did the business interests.[38] According to evidence which can be similarly related to regime policies, Soviet peasants oppose the Communist system more strongly than do industrial workers, who in turn are less attached to the system than the new Soviet intelligentsia.

Political loyalties, elite recruitment, group demands on the decision makers and, indeed, the choice and shape of political policies themselves are bound to be seriously influenced by the social and economic characteristics of a society and the socio-economic policies pursued by its rulers. The reorganization of the whole social structure—or its absence—is likely to have far-reaching political consequences for the development of a regime. Stated in terms of an ideal, rather than actual, polarity, the implications of socio-economic development for the totalitarian regimes might be stated as follows:

If "Fascism" or "Nazism" does not basically change the social structure over which it rules, if it does not remake it in a common image, then indeed it has no alternative to the cycle: serious crisis—unrest—insecurity of the regime—increased use of violence and repression—or capitulation.

If "Communism" does change the underlying social structure in the direction of a desired homogeneity, it may in time dispense with the political tool of mass violence, and, even in periods of crisis, rule with the use of subtler methods, closer to persuasion than to physical compulsion.

It is not argued here that the actual, historical differences between Fascism and Nazism on the one hand and Communism on the other have been quite so great. The Russian Communists did not change everything in sight nor did the Fascists and Nazis leave all things as they found them. But, so far as the record of history serves us, the gap or divergence in the socio-economic characteristics of these regimes has been very considerable. Such divergence, even if it be in many respects one of degree (in the area of social mobility, *e.g.*) suggests not "similar" but "different" tendencies of development and therefore, also, "different" rather than "similar" political implications.

If political attitudes and behavior are the resultants of a variety of factors of which propaganda, education, coercion, status, religion and income are examples, then a regime which effectively manipulates the greater number of such factors is more "totalitarian" than one which manipulates fewer, and the difference of degree may be ultimately as significant as one between "medicine" and "poison." All other things being equal, the regime with the greater range of means at its command should be able to exercise more effective control and enjoy more flexibility in policy.

If Fascism and Nazism do not basically restructure the societies over which they rule, and if, because of clientele

[37] This relative and contingent (crisis-born) preference does not seem to be subject to any serious dispute although the question of precisely how effective and important was the support of business interests, in bringing the Fascist regimes to power, continues controversial and unresolved. Works often cited on both sides of the issue are far from conclusive: L. P. Lochner, *Tycoons and Tyrant* (Chicago, 1954), p. 115–117; Fritz Thyssen, *I Paid Hitler* (New York, 1941), p. xv. *Cf.* Lipset, *op. cit.*, pp. 148–149.

[38] *Cf.* Deutsch and Edinger, *op. cit.*, p. 100–103 for some comparisons of the anti-Nazi resistance records of business, trade union, and S.P.D. and C.D.U. elites. *Cf.* Gabriel A. Almond and W. H. Kraus, "The Social Composition of the German Resistance," *The Struggle for Democracy in Germany*, ed. G. A. Almond (University of North Carolina Press, Chapel Hill, 1949), pp. 64–107.

considerations they are really unable to do so, then despite the framework of terror, propaganda and indoctrination of the Hitler-Jugend and Balilla variety, the "isms" can operate effectively *only* by not making demands which would outrage the class and caste interests, and attitudes, of elites inherited from previous regimes. Where demands for total obedience are pressed upon a highly heterogenous political clientele, violence may indeed prove a frequent and indispensable tool of enforcement for the totalitarian regimes. Where vital interests of the old elites and the new regimes clash, a relapse into a conservative neo-constitutionalism of the Franco variety is highly likely. This could occur either through the more or less voluntary accommodation by the dictator, as in Franco's case after 1940, or through a *coup d'état* as in Italy in 1943.

Understandably, mass violence and social upheaval were far less characteristic of Fascism and Nazism at the outset of their existence than of Communism, since these regimes did not attempt to modify seriously the socio-economic *status quo;* they were more characteristic of Russian Communism precisely because it sought to change so much. Conversely, however, Fascism never rid itself of the resort to crude violence because it did not sufficiently mold its political clientele. To the end of their existence, both Fascism and Nazism relied heavily on the personnel of the prerevolutionary elites whose identification with the totalitarian regimes was always conditional. These elites served Hitler and Mussolini only because and insofar as the Nazi or Fascist policies appeared to them useful and unavoidable for the realization of particular objectives: defeat of Communism, maintenance of their own perquisites, the realization of a "Greater Germany," and so on.

It is widely agreed, and there is certainly substantial evidence, that the great majority of these elites in Germany continued to adhere to Hitler's cause, out of conviction or despair, until his defeat. But so long as they shared the political, military and economic apparatus of the German state and remained a pillar of the Nazi movement, they constituted a potentially dangerous element for the dictatorship, a threat requiring constant maintenance of surveillance, terror and repression.

V

Time and war cut short the existence of the totalitarian regimes of Italy and Germany, so that today we could not compare some forty-odd years of development for all three "isms." Would the Nazi and Fascist States have grown more or less "total" had they survived? Would they have tended to approximate more closely or diverge more widely from the older, more "mature" Soviet totalitarianism?

The unitotalitarian approach necessarily suggests that, driven by the common pursuit of power, all three dictatorships were, in fact, proceeding in the same direction.

The unitotalitarian scheme interprets the divergent socio-economic policies of the totalitarian regimes as derivative from one pattern, permeated by the same purposes and different mainly, if not exclusively, in terms of their timetable. In comparing the policies of the Communists and Fascists, we find Brzezinski asserting somewhat cryptically that: "Very specific circumstantial factors prevented the Fascist and Nazi regimes from launching similarly large-scale schemes of social reconstruction." [39] An analogy is implied between,

[39] Z. Brzezinski, "Totalitarianism and Rationality," this REVIEW, Vol. 50 (Sept. 1956), p. 757. *Cf.* Inkeles and Bauer, *op. cit.*, p. 235.

on the one hand, the entire period of Fascist rule in Italy from 1922 to 1944, and in Germany from 1933 to 1945, and the 1921–1928 NEP period in Russia on the other. The implication of the analogy is that all totalitarians wish to "change everything" but the revolutionary process requires some tactical pauses for a "consolidation of forces."

The evidence for this proposition rests most heavily, and most plausibly, on the experience of the Second World War. Few authorities would maintain that up to 1939, for example, Soviet Russia and Fascist Italy were equally "totalitarian" even in terms of merely the six specific criteria employed in the Friedrich and Brzezinski study. Yet, as of 1939 only about five years separated the Communist from the Fascist tenure of office. At most, twenty-two years of "Communism" confronted seventeen years of "Fascism"; if, with greater realism, the periods of power are considered from the assumption of effective control over the whole of the respective countries, they are about equal. In terms of displacement of the traditional, pre-revolutionary elites, the comparison of Italy and Russia in the 1930s shows far greater divergences. During all these years it is quite impossible to discover the evidence of Fascism's "dangerous designs on the bastions of wealth and privilege" from its actual accomplishments. And it would require extraordinary artfulness to deduce a menacing attitude toward the socio-economic *status quo* from the official, publicly disseminated Fascist pronouncements during this period. Mussolini's *The Doctrine of Fascism* could hardly be confused with Lenin's *State and Revolution* on this score.

In the case of Germany, the period of prewar Nazi control, 1933–1939, is somewhat more plausible in comparison with Russian Communist rule for several reasons. First, the Nazi record in terror and brutality quickly appeared to outdo Mussolini's "best efforts." Second, capitalizing on German military traditions and the more sophisticated manipulative apparatus of a highly industrialized state, the Nazi regime presented to the world a much more plausible image of totalitarian unity, cohesion and might. Third, and foremost, the entire period was sufficiently short so that Hitler could always be credited, by the credulous, with not having had enough time to carry through even "further reforms."

In this interpretation, the Roehm Purge was a tactical maneuver analogous to Lenin's tactical repudiation of the Left extremists in the Communist Party of 1921. The Roehm Purge, however, was not preceded by mass expropriation of landlords and *entrepreneurs* in Germany as was NEP in Russia. Nor was it ever followed by such expropriation. And what of Hitler's actual policies with respect to the established elites and elite recruitment? Up until 1938 the Army Generals enjoyed a position of relative autonomy and privilege within the Nazi regime. And the 1938 shift in command was a far cry from the "proletarization," "communization" and "politicization" which the Soviet regime was intensively applying to the Red Army from its inception. Nor was the treatment of the Army Generals an isolated case. The pre-1933 leaders of industry, commerce and agriculture were no closer to either personal or financial liquidation in 1939 than in 1933.

Was the Nazi social revolution to be planned and implemented by the aristocratic, and middle class elites which had patronized the Nationalist Party and other conservative causes? Clearly, these elements would not have favored, let alone spurred, such a revolution. Did Hitler himself advocate a social upheaval? In *Mein Kampf* he was vague and cynical about the Party's "unalterable" 1920 program; but on the other hand, he specifically courted and praised such established interests as the Army and the bureaucracy, and even had some kind words for the Monarchy. If anything, Hitler's own pronouncements after 1925 on such subjects as property and class warfare tended toward increasing socio-economic conservatism, not radicalism. The last major remnants of the Nazi nucleus of social radicalism had, in fact, been purged with Ernst Roehm in 1934. The extirpation of the Jews was genocide, not class warfare.

Admittedly, the Second World War brought about a great intensification of totalitarian controls and terror within the Fascist and Nazi systems, particularly after the July 1944 conspiracy against Hitler. Yet, the conclusion that somehow this increase in totalitarian activity was equivalent to, or even a forerunner of, a social and economic revolution falls far short of available evidence. Unlike the Soviet precedent, Hitler's terror at home was aimed not at whole social classes but at suspected individuals.

The intensification of Party control in the apparatus of the State—political, economic, military—did not have any really new social and economic orientation. The criterion of Nazi attitudes toward actual and potential opposition was loyalty to the Party and to the Fuehrer. But the concept of Party in Nazi Germany, unlike Russia, had no specific class content and orientation. Hence, for all the punitive and "radical" measures taken by the Hitler regime during the war and particularly after 1944, none—except as against Jews—included significant expropriation of landed or major industrial properties, wholesale expulsion of the members of the old nobility or the Junker class from government service, nor even large scale expulsion of non-Party members from important positions in the armed services, provided their loyalties to Hitler were not in any doubt. On the "positive side" there was no attempt during the war to attract the following of the lower class strata by the kind of Party recruitment drives which periodically recur in the Communist movement. There were no tangible, widely publicized legislative and fiscal concessions to the social and economic interests of these classes at the expense of, or even to the apparent disadvantage of, the upper strata.

Until the very last days of his regime, Hitler did not undertake any measures changing the hitherto existing balance between the "haves" and "have-nots" of Germany. In this sense, his totalitarianism did not deeply plough the ground of German society. The record does not support an easily accomplishable "bolshevik about-face" by either of the Axis chiefs; Mussolini's belated, personal attempt at "social radicalism" was one of utter failure and frustration.[40]

Both Hitler and Mussolini obviously attempted to make themselves thoroughly invulnerable and durable through such devices as terror, propaganda and educational indoctrination of the youth. But, hampered by the very constellation of forces which helped them to seize and maintain power, they, unlike the Communists, did not supplement these totalitarian devices with socio-economic measures of equal radicalism

[40] *Cf.* Z. Brzezinski, "Totalitarianism and Rationality," *loc. cit.*, p. 757: "Nonetheless it is sufficient to read Starace's plans to change the Italian national character or Mussolini's remarks on the need to eradicate the Italian 'softness,' as well as some of the party regulations on daily behavior of the citizen issued in 1938 to realize that such a revolution was being seriously contemplated in Italy. In the case of the Nazis, there is even more ample evidence that the New Order in Europe would have resulted in revolutionary changes in Germany proper, changes highly inimical to the established order. Hitler's war-time conversations and Himmler's plans for the S.S. are full of projects that would have involved radical changes in German society and economy."

(or "totalitarianism"). Hitler effectively outlawed the political organizations of the non-Nazi Right but he did not destroy its social and economic base. Until the very last he was served and surrounded by the Right's former supporters and sympathizers in the General Staff, the bureaucracy, the diplomatic corps and the economy. To move with them involved little risk. To move against them could have been literally fatal as the events of July 1944 very nearly proved.

When the fortunes of war turned against the Fuehrer, neither the Hitler Jugend nor the Gestapo could undo the consequences of Nazism's compromising affiliations—the ominous presence of Colonel Claus von Stauffenberg and others like him in high places. This presence was no accident. Such vulnerability was an intrinsic part of the basic socio-economic design of Fascism and Nazism.

Both regimes failed to carry through the social and economic revolutions which alone could have given them a monopoly on the production of new elites and the suppression of the old. The outward appearance of mastery was compromised by the reality of interdependence and partnership between an old and a new order. Fascism and Nazism alike failed to deal with the economic bases of class antagonism and class differentiation inherited from previous regimes. Each regime imposed the gloss of political and police controls upon societies which, from the standpoint of the distribution of wealth, with all its implications, reflected an inherited old order, not a new one. Without a socio-economic revolution, the Fascist and Nazi dictators could never free themselves of their Rightist associations with all the implicit vulnerability; without it they could not meet most of the traditional demands of the working class and of the clientele of the political Left. In consequence of this failure to revolutionize, the Fascist and Nazi regimes were rendered "brittle," precarious and vulnerable from many quarters. Above all, however, the disaffection of the inherited Rightist elements always represented the most immediate danger to the dictators since these elements were in the best positions of access in the bureaucratic-military apparatus of the two regimes.

VI

It is frequently asserted and implied that the Nazi and Fascist dictatorships could somehow escape the perils of their domestic vulnerability by means of externally directed violence. Might not conquest, and the preparation for conquest abroad, stabilize these regimes internally? Could the pursuit of warfare silence and eliminate domestic conflicts, thus making it unnecessary for the dictators to employ violence at home? Undoubtedly, the policies of the Fascist and Nazi regimes were oriented in this direction. War could produce beneficial, however shortlived, economic consequences at home in terms of increasing employment, wages and profits. It could also mobilize considerable loyalties of national patriotism toward the support of the respective regimes. It likewise provided a more or less "natural" opportunity for these regimes to extend and tighten administrative and police controls. Yet war-making, no less than other enterprises, was bound to involve problems and consequences peculiar to itself. If the war effort were to be accompanied by widespread material and moral deprivations at home, and if it appeared to be doomed to failure, the stresses and strains in the social fabric which the war sought to prevent would be likely to reappear. The elites which were convinced of Hitler's genius in 1940 were unlikely to display equal fervor and conviction in 1943 or 1944. The "monolith" was doomed to show its hidden fissures just as it did in the case of Mussolini's Italy where the war, ironically mocking the dictator's design, proved to be his undoing, not his salvation. The resort to violence became actually more, not less, necessary. Only a very successful and unlikely "Orwellian war of indefinite duration" could have averted such consequences for Fascism and Nazism.

On the other hand, the conclusion that the successful termination of war (which in 1940 certainly seemed plausible for the Axis) would have enabled Fascism and Nazism to expand indefinitely war trends and war policies is highly suspect. It does not make allowance for the actual disappearance of the war stimulus, and it assumes (but does not prove) the complete passivity, docility and unimportance of Fascism's, and Nazism's, elite allies. Considerable evidence is to be found for the opposite point of view.[41]

Granted that both dictators realized the difficulty of their position, it is not enough to show that they personally, from time to time, wished for changes. Like all politicians, they faced environmental limitations which circumscribed their ability to act, and these limitations were, in turn, characteristic of the very nature of the movements they both led. If they had won, it would have been far easier for Hitler and Mussolini to maintain, like Franco, an impeccable, albeit authoritarian conservatism than to embark on schemes of radical social upheaval, even if they personally desired such an upheaval. Postwar efforts by either dictator to carry out policies fundamentally hostile to the basic values of the bureaucratic and socio-economic elites upon which both regimes had always depended might well have dislodged the Fascist and Nazi Parties from power. It is not without significance that by Hitler's own choice the last chieftain of the Third Reich was Grand Admiral Doenitz, a representative of the pre-1933 bureaucratic military establishment. The "establishment" proved more durable than the Party and survived the Party.[42]

The assumption that ultimately Italy and Germany would have proved as "reformist" as Russia is based on scant evidence such as face-value acceptance of private remarks made by the embittered Fascist leaders on the verge of defeat and in part on acts and decrees which they issued when both victory and effective control were being irretrievably lost. Given their past performance, their ideological-propagandistic commitments and the constellation of forces supporting them, within and without the Fascist parties, it is difficult to believe that military victory could have made successful social reformers out of Hitler and Mussolini.

On the other hand, the "social engineering" of the Russian communist regime has conferred a remarkable degree of invulnerability upon it. Probably since the 1920s, and certainly since the 1930s, Stalin was beyond the physical reach of any but his own party creatures. In all the later succession conflicts, including the grim Beria episode, the issue has never been "Communism, yes or no;" instead it has been a question of the identity of the leadership and of the nuances of policy. The issues in Germany in 1944 and Italy in 1943 were much more critical than that. In one case, after a rule of 21 years, the Party was ousted from power by the *coup* against the dictator; in the other case it

[41] F. W. Deakin explores, very instructively, the problem of what *did* happen to Mussolini when he attempted some "social radicalism" in 1944. *The Brutal Friendship* (New York, 1963). See esp. pp. 670–671.

[42] *Cf.* Arthur Schweitzer's conclusion, p. 555.

would have been ousted, had the *coup* succeeded.

Thus it would appear that in response to external or internal pressures, the Fascist and Nazi systems were likely to revert through a *coup d'état* to a more traditional, or *status quo ante* order of society.

Using Soviet Russia as a model of Communism it is obvious, however, that reversion to a *status quo ante* is, and for a very long time has been, precluded: unless the dead be, virtually, recalled. The physical liquidation of one leadership group by another remains a constant, though today probably greatly diminished, possibility; the Communist facade of the regime is far less vulnerable. The key decision makers—military, economic and political—are overwhelmingly Communist themselves, reared in a single political tradition over a span of two generations and on the whole far more homogenous than the Fascists or Nazis in their social background. Formal renunciation of "Communism" would be tantamount to a gratuitous self-repudiation for the members of these elites; [43] this was Khrushchev's difficulty in renouncing Stalinism. It is not suggested here that the development of Russian Communism must necessarily be one toward "more and more freedom" or something akin to a parliamentary democracy on a western model as is sometimes believed.[44] On the contrary, elements indigenous to Russian history, tradition and culture could very well impede such tendencies. What is implied is a transition from overt violence to conditioned, voluntary compliance. Communism, having largely uprooted the old order of society and substituted new elite groups may in time pass on to less overt methods of pressure and manipulation. The Khrushchev regime in Russia was fosterer of this transition.

A note of caution, however, is in order. The socio-economic variable, though highly important, is obviously not the only one and its time-table is problematical. Communism in Russia, and internationally, may well fail in the solution of tasks other than the creation of new socio-economically homogeneous elites. It may prove unable, for instance, to establish a homogeneity of national interests and attitudes; national conflicts, as in the Sino-Soviet case, may impede and thwart the processes of socio-economic transformation within the various Communist states, perhaps ultimately even defeating the grand design of Communist "social engineering." Such contingencies, however, should not invalidate or preclude the identification of any important trends evident so far.

On socio-economic grounds alone, the future development of the other Communist states is not really accounted for by the Soviet experience. Important differences must be recognized. Most of the Eastern European nations in 1944 possessed larger upper and middle classes in relation to the rest of their populations than did Russia in 1917. And in no case were the former elite groups subjected to such an intensive process of physical liquidation as happened in the U.S.S.R. in its Revolution, Civil War and collectivization drives. Nor was the process of material expropriation as drastic and swift in all cases as it had been in Russia. Thus Poland today retains a far greater measure of private ownership in both land and industry, 19 years after 1945, than did Russia at the corresponding period in

[43] *Cf.* Fainsod, *op. cit.*, p. 484: "The members of the elite in the final analysis have a vested interest in the perpetuation of the Soviet System."

[44] In 1953 Isaac Deutscher saw three alternatives for future Soviet developments: relapse into Stalinism; military dictatorship, and the most likely: "socialist democracy." ***Russia: What Next?*** (Oxford University Press, New York), p. 208.

1936. The Communist parties of all the satellite nations are still largely "pre-revolutionary" in their derivation and have "coopted" many members from the old middle classes and from other political movements.[45] All these factors combine to give them a vulnerability which is still comparable to that of the Fascist regimes, and which could only be removed or minimized by the successful implementation of radical Communist policies over a prolonged period of time. Yet, the stimulus and support for such policies could well depend on the Soviet attitude which has been undergoing profound changes of erosion and relaxation from the Stalinist demand for conformity and militancy among the satellites.

In any event, the "totalitarian" similarities among Fascist Italy, Nazi Germany and Soviet Russia have not been such as to warrant predictions of the future development of each from a pattern common to all. The characteristics of totalitarianism commonly emphasized during the 1950s are certainly valid and important descriptions so far as they go, at least of Nazi Germany and of Soviet Russia. But the entire construct is too static, narrow and substructurally insensitive to support significant predictions on the future of the presently surviving totalitarian regimes.

[45] Brzezinski, *op. cit.*, p. 374. *Cf.* Richard F. Staar, *The Communist Party Leadership in Poland* (Georgetown University, Washington, 1961).